Praise for *Dam Buster*

'A comprehensive, deeply researched and insightful portrait of one of Britain's greatest engineers'   Saul David, *Daily Telegraph*

'A stunningly good and surely definitive biography of one of the most fascinating British engineers ever to have lived'
James Holland, author of *Brothers in Arms*

'Fascinating ... Wallis was in the unenviable position of being one of Britain's most talented engineers who was nevertheless under-appreciated in his lifetime ... Morris does a sterling job of re-establishing his reputation as an innovator in countless fields, in highly readable fashion'   Alexander Larman, *Observer*

'A genuinely gripping narrative ... this is a biography that anyone with an interest in Britain's military engineering past will read with profit'   *The Past*

'A thorough and dutiful account of the designer's journey from airship to spaceship. Morris puts emotional clothes on the man himself ... the book fleshes out Wallis, revealing his vulnerability'
The Times

'Characterises Wallis as a flawed yet indomitable genius ... a probing yet thoughtful account of [a] brilliant mind'
BBC History Magazine

'A superb book ... for an account of a major name in British aviation history this is, I would suggest, as good as it can get'
Tony Buttler, *Aerospace*

RICHARD MORRIS (b. 1947) is an archaeologist and historian. He grew up in north Worcestershire and began his career working on excavations under York Minster. Among the themes in his writing are: buildings and belief; place, identity and cultural memory; and aviation and its people. *Dam Buster* joins two earlier biographies – *Guy Gibson* (1994) and *Cheshire: The Biography of Leonard Cheshire VC* (2000) – which connect in the world of flight and the deeds of No. 617 Squadron RAF.

Also by Richard Morris

Guy Gibson
Churches in the Landscape
Cheshire: The Biography of Leonard Cheshire
Time's Anvil
Yorkshire
Evensong

Dam Buster

Barnes Wallis, the Lost Visionary of British Aviation

RICHARD MORRIS

WEIDENFELD & NICOLSON

First published in Great Britain in 2023 by Weidenfeld & Nicolson
This paperback edition first published in 2024 by
Weidenfeld & Nicolson,
an imprint of The Orion Publishing Group Ltd
Carmelite House, 50 Victoria Embankment
London EC4Y 0DZ

An Hachette UK Company

3 5 7 9 10 8 6 4 2

A CIP catalogue record for this book is
available from the British Library.

ISBN (Mass Market Paperback) 978 1 4746 2343 8
ISBN (eBook) 978 1 4746 2344 5
ISBN (Audio) 978 1 4746 2345 2

Typeset by Input Data Services Ltd, Bridgwater, Somerset

Printed in Great Britain by Clays Ltd, Elcograf S.p.A.

MIX
Paper | Supporting
responsible forestry
FSC
www.fsc.org   FSC® C104740

www.weidenfeldandnicolson.co.uk
www.orionbooks.co.uk

For Elisabeth, and to the memory of Mary

Contents

PROLOGUE

Sometime in the 1950s the aeronautical engineer Barnes Wallis took a sheet of foolscap paper and in his clear, firm, hand wrote 'Autobiography' in blue ink at the top. He began:

> How I wonder does one write an autobiography? For as one looks back on one's life, so many trivial incidents stand out assuming an importance that they may or may not possess that to give them their appropriate value requires an accurate description of all the conditions under which, and the surroundings in which they occurred.[1]

The influence of 'trivial incidents' led Wallis to think that the only person who could write with authority about his life was someone who knew what they were – himself. He accordingly opened a file marked 'Autobiography' and into it began to put jottings of names, dates, places and fragments of memoir. Intriguingly, for a man who valued craftsmanship, he never acknowledged that history-writing calls for historical skills, or that the position of an observer affects what is observed. But then again, perhaps he knew that deep down, for as far as we know, the lines above were all he ever wrote. His ambitions to tell his own story nonetheless became a handy way to fend off journalists and publishers who wanted to do it for him. When the BBC screened a documentary about him in his eightieth year, such propositions rose to a flood. The programme told of his designs – airships, the structural system of the Wellington bomber, weapons that had breached dams and smashed V-weapon sites, aircraft that could change shape in flight – and asked why none of his post-war innovations had been taken forward. A few days after it broadcast, Wallis agreed that the writer and scholar Jack Morpurgo should be his biographer.

Morpurgo had been badgering Wallis for years to do the job. Wallis now acquiesced for several reasons. One was his acceptance that the time left to do it himself was limited. Another was his confidence in Morpurgo, whom he had got to know through membership of the governing body of their old school, Christ's Hospital, and upon whom he had come to rely for advice in dealings with publishers and the media. The clincher was Morpurgo's warning: if he did not have it done 'more or less as you want it done, others will do it as you do not want it done.'[2] Morpurgo's biography was published in 1972, and until now it has been the only full-length account of Wallis's life.[3]

Why another? Large questions still await answers. Wallis is but one of three civilians – Alan Turing and Winston Churchill are the others – who have found a place in Britain's pantheon of the Second World War.[4] Collective memory is said to be 'one of the most – if not the most – powerful affective social forces';[5] what is it in its working that has singled him out?[6] What formed him? In what ways and contexts did his gifts operate? Why did none of his later projects come to fruition? And if he was Britain's greatest engineer of the twentieth century, where is his legacy?

As time passed Wallis came to inhabit his own legend, gradually rearranging facts and events to suit a particular narrative.[7] This tendency continually to amend his own story is met in his minor correspondence, in reminiscences he put into replies to contacts from old colleagues, and recollections for members of his family. Here he is, for instance, on Saturday, 11 August 1945. The afternoon was warm, and Wallis spent it working in the garden of their home at White Hill House, Effingham, on the dip-slope of the North Downs in Surrey. The garden covered about three quarters of an acre and everything in it – trees, shrubs, lawns, beds – had been put there by him and his wife Molly since their arrival fifteen years before. On this day Wallis sieved earth for a new croquet lawn (the old one having been dug up in 1940 to grow vegetables), picked plums and selected apples for stewing. He relished physical activity, although since 1939 there had not been much time for it. For five years he had worked long hours for at least six, and often seven days a week, and had taken no holidays. The end of the war in Europe allowed a little more time to himself, but the war in Asia continued and he was gripped by new ideas.

Molly and their eldest daughter Mary were away in Broadstairs visiting the family of one of Mary's friends. Around teatime Wallis went indoors to wash and fetch his fountain pen. Returning to the garden he settled in a deck chair and did what he always did when he and Molly were apart: write to tell her about his day. Mary's friend, Wallis realised, lived close to a place he remembered from his own childhood: a grand house in grounds with double gates, called Charingbold. Charingbold's chatelaine had been Adeline Bell, 'Aunt Bell', a school friend of his mother. Wallis drew a map to show where the house stood and recalled happy days in the 1890s when he, his elder brother John and younger sister Annie had stayed there. To understand that kind of pleasure, he told Molly:

> you must have lived all your little life in a poor dirty and noisy house, in the days of horse traffic & iron shod wheels on the great cobbled surface of the New Cross Road; in unconcealed anxiety as to where the money to pay all the bills was to come from next; with a stricken Father, fighting an unending battle with infirmity and illness; with one skittish and filthy maid in a basement; in a world that knew not yet even a phonograph, in which wireless was undreamed of; when music for the masses was provided by the tinkle of the barrel organ and the songs of the music hall; and the streets at night echoed to the drunken shouts and fights as the mobs were turned out of the pubs at midnight.[8]

'Poor' ... 'dirty' ... 'unending battle' ... 'anxiety' ... Was it really that bad? Take, for instance, the account of Aunt Bell's household that Wallis went on to give. Wallis asked Molly to imagine him as a

3

small, romantic-minded boy who had been transported from the ill-omened surroundings of New Cross to 'a sort of fairyland', a place 'where they dressed for dinner every night, and the women wore beautiful clothes.' The boy sometimes sat under a grand piano upon which Aunt Bell played 'soul-shattering music'. Barnes, Annie, and John loved to slither on the polished floor between the piano's legs and pedals. In the household were friendly grooms, gardeners, ostlers, an under nurse, more maids than you could shake a stick at, and a head nurse who read them thrilling adventures at bedtime. There was a dairy, wherein a five-year-old Barnes (already showing a mechanical turn of mind) withdrew a bolt and accidentally released a flood of buttermilk.[9] Wallis recalled glowing primroses and daffodils, and luscious meals with 'long, succulent pork sausages.' Also in his mind was 'one early and awful morning' when the brake drew up to take them to the station. In 'a smother of smuts, smoke and sulphur (fitting for gates of hell) the old South-Eastern Chatham & Dover Railway bore us slowly and sadly back to the drabness, dirt, worry and anxiety of the London streets.' Was all this detached recollection, or was Wallis's recall coloured by self-pity – a kind of imagined victimhood? Either way, at this point he paused and looked at his watch. 'Seven o'clock', he wrote. 'I must go in and set about some supper.'

Next morning, Sunday, Wallis walked down the hill to matins in Effingham's parish church of St Lawrence. Afterwards he resumed his letter. 'By the way, did you look out for the church with the two towers – if your train came through Herne Bay you will have passed quite close?' The church stands on a bump of ground overlooking the beach at Reculver on the north Kent coast. In spring 1943 Wallis had spent anxious days there watching trial drops of a weapon remembered today as 'the bouncing bomb'. It was being tested in variant forms, one (UPKEEP) for use against dams, another (HIGHBALL) for warships. Locals had befriended him during the trials. He urged Molly to look them up.

. . . walk down to the sea, and have a meal at the tea-hut, run by my old friend Sergeant Major Shepherd – don't forget to thank him for all the choc. biscuits, the rabbit etc etc and see his white parrot, and all his other birds – he is an authority on birds. Ask after his daughter and grandson, and give him my very kindest remembrances. Also walk boldly up to the coastguard's lookout room, and tell them who you are, and give them the same messages from me.[10]

If part of a biographer's job is to disentangle Wallis from his own narratives, another duty is to extricate him from the narratives of others. In 1955 the public marvelled at glimpses of UPKEEP and HIGHBALL in Michael Anderson's film *The Dam Busters*.[11] They took to the softly spoken, slightly abstracted genius portrayed by Michael Redgrave, who spoke lines written by R. C. Sherriff. Sherriff's screenplay depicted Wallis as meek yet determined, neither downcast by snags and disappointments nor resentful of others' scepticism, socially awkward yet warm. The souvenir programme for the film's premiere said that experts had 'scoffed' at his ideas, but his faith had 'never wavered' as he tramped from one ministry to another seeking support for his 'impossible' brainchild. This is, indeed, how Wallis himself described it. Yet while Wallis's projects often met opposition, and UPKEEP was no exception, it has long been realised that neither the weapon nor the squadron formed to use it could have emerged without sustained support. It is also clear that far from being 'unwavering', Wallis was racked with worry. Moreover, the film looks past the failure to break the Sorpe dam, and with it the nub of what the raid was meant to achieve. The film's version of events nonetheless endures, and with it the idea of a contest between daring imagination and timid officialdom that has since been extrapolated to other enterprises in his long working life.[12]

Aback of the Wallis created by repetition and trope run competing histories in which he has come to stand for different views of post-war Britain. For traditionalists he represents originality and intellectual uprightness in the presence of a British establishment devitalised by indecisiveness, political interference and rivalries. For those suspicious of nationalism, he signifies what has been called 'reactionary modernism' in the face of imperial retreat and alleged technological decline. In what follows, he emerges instead as a twentieth-century Victorian. This is no surprise: Lord Salisbury was prime minister in the year he was born, and he was well into his teens when Queen Victoria died. We shall find him steeped in late-nineteenth-century cultural conservatism, with which came interests in religion and philanthropy, faith in technology, and the idea of an organic Anglo-British nation which it was the duty of privileged sons to help give shape and take forward.[13]

Connections between Wallis's achievements, his legacy and place in public and national memory form one of the themes that this book sets out to explore. Many of those who lived through the Second World War or grew up in its shadow still think of him as a patriotic genius. Opinions among their children and grandchildren are more diffuse. Some have never heard of him, or when prompted think only of the film, or of Guy Gibson's dog. Others see his cult as a sickly symptom of continuing nostalgia for the Second World War. Several historians invite us to reflect on the apparently paradoxical relationship between Wallis's scientific vision and his attachment to tradition. Wallis himself would have been puzzled by this, as he did not see custom and innovation as opposites, holding rather that age-long traditions make good nurseries for the kinds of mind that produce 'bold and original thought'.[14] As for the vision, although his conceptions were often original, the theoretics upon which they rested were usually conservative; his heroes were figures like Christopher Wren and Isaac Newton; to the end, his physics remained 'firmly pre-Einstein'.[15]

This book has been written in the belief that an individual's actions should first be judged by the standards of the time in which they took place. It gives an account of Wallis's upbringing, considers what he did and the surroundings in which he did it, seeks the inner man, and asks how the idea of a gifted maverick struggling to pitch original ideas to an overcautious establishment took hold when contemporary sources place him in a richly networked community.

By the time of his death how had he come to be regarded, at the same time, as Britain's most famous yet most neglected twentieth-century engineer? Later chapters investigate not only the seeming inconsistency whereby Wallis became simultaneously revered while being professionally sidelined, but also whether he was sidelined. For years this was the given story, but since the turn of the century some historians have suggested that it exemplifies a trope fostered by Britain's technocratic elite, who by repeatedly saying they were marginalised nurtured a general belief that this is what happened.[16] Wallis epitomises the question.

With all said, there is a further question, whether Wallis's relegation might be because his work was less significant than many claimed at the time. Airships and geodetics were dead ends; UPKEEP in the end was a one-trick pony; HIGHBALL was never used; none of the late visions materialised; even the thinking behind apparent wartime successes like his deep penetration bomb has been called into question.[17] Given that science is a global enterprise, what is his international standing? We are led to an uncomfortable question: does his reputation as a national figure stem primarily from his engineering or from the harmonics of 'national'?

SKITTEN

WEYBRIDGE

BURHILL

To
LONDON

BROOKLANDS

FESHIEBRIDGE

R. WEY

FOXWARREN

ST LAWRENCE
PARISH CHURCH

GREAT BOOKHAM

LOCH STRIVEN

To
GUILDFORD

EFFINGHAM

WHITE HILL
HOUSE

NORBURY
PARK

HELENSBURGH

EDINBURGH

N O R T H   D O W N S

ELSWICK

✷ BROOKLANDS & EFFINGHAM

GREAT LANGDALE

KENTS BANK

SOME PLACES
ASSOCIATED WITH
BARNES WALLIS'S
LIFE AND WORK

BARROW-IN
-FURNESS

HOWDEN

SHEFFIELD

SCAMPTON

TRUSTHORPE

RIPLEY

WOODHALL SPA

BROUGHTON

GRANTHAM

BECCLES

N

CASTLE
BROMWICH

THURLEIGH

PULHAM

BORTH

MARTLESHAM
HEATH

NANT-Y-GRO

CARDINGTON

MAENCLOCHOG

PRINCES RISBOROUGH

HIGH
BEECH

CRAYFORD

HIGH WYCOMBE

LON
DON

KINGSNORTH

HARMONDSWORTH

✷

FARNBOROUGH

BOSCOMBE
DOWN

WOOLSTON

HORSHAM

RECULVER

THE FLEET

COWES

WORTHING

ASHLEY WALK

PORTLAND
BILL

ISLE OF PURBECK

PREDANNACK

LULWORTH

I

Childhood and Empire, 1887–1904

Barnes

Edith Eyre Ashby and Charles Wallis, both twenty-six, married in the church of St John, Woolwich, on 9 September 1885.

Edie was from an affectionate family that had pioneered progressive education. Charles was a medical student, one year short of qualification. His mother had died twelve days after his birth, whereafter his father George, a clergyman, delegated his upbringing, first to his dead wife's grandparents and then to the rector of a remote parish in Lincolnshire. His education was supported by £2000 left in trust by a grandfather, Joseph Robinson. The costs of a new household and wife made inroads into what was left of these funds. Edie was uneasy, the more so when in November she realised she was pregnant. Next June, unease turned to panic. Some of the remaining trust money had been invested in India; ten days after the birth of their son, John, Charles told her that the company had gone into liquidation.[1]

Charles achieved membership of the Royal College of Surgeons in the same month. In the autumn he sat for the diploma of Licentiate of the Royal College of Physicians and passed. He was now qualified but lacked the means and connections to join a practice in London. Charles accordingly accepted a post as assistant to Dr Josiah Allen, district Medical Officer and Public Vaccinator in the industrial town of Ripley, east Derbyshire.

As 1886 neared its end an unexpected Christmas card arrived: 'To Edith and Charlie from Uncle Barnes and Aunt, with love and best wishes.' 'Uncle Barnes' was Lt Col. Barnes Slyfield Robinson,

Charles's mother's brother. Until then they had heard little from him, mainly because he had usually been somewhere else enforcing Britain's colonial will. Barnes's regiment, the 89th Regiment of Foot, had fought in the Crimean War where he had served during the siege and fall of Sevastopol in 1855. The regiment then moved to Cape Colony (in what is now South Africa), there countering a rising by the Xhosa, followed by eight years in India that included service during the Indian Mutiny. Since then there had been another tour in India and Burma. By 1886 Barnes was living in Dover.

Early in the New Year Edie recorded that she was again in an 'interesting condition'. The second child was born soon after 3 a.m. on Monday, 26 September. It was a quick labour, and the baby slept later in the morning. Edie's mother was there to assist and described the newcomer to her eldest daughter: 'a nice plump little man – weighs 8lbs – at present is very red and has a lot of darkish hair with a largish nose somewhat like the Father's. In fact, I think it will resemble Charlie very much'.[2]

Names were aired. One was Victor (Queen Victoria's Golden Jubilee had just been celebrated). Another was Edward Neville Wallis, after Edward Ashby, Edie's favourite uncle, and Neville Frewer, a medical friend of Charles, both of whom were to be godfathers. Edie, however, was superstitious about Edwards: two relatives with that name had died young, and her sister Maria – to be godmother, but then away in India – knew of two more. Then came news that Uncle Barnes was poorly. Barnes was Charles's last living link to the mother he had never known; on 25 October a telegram told that he was dying. Edie wrote at once to her sister Lily:

> Charlie is much cut up. Col. Robinson was the last left of his mother's family, and though Charlie saw so little of him, from that link to the past, I know he was sincerely attached to the little gentleman. I am so glad I wrote and told him Neville was also to be 'Barnes'.[3]

Tuesday, 15 November was chilly, with a north-east wind, bright intervals, and flurries of snow. Early in the afternoon Edie held her new son and stepped up to the font in the church of All Saints, Ripley. George Wallis had received permission from the vicar to take the service. He dipped his hand in the water and said, 'Barnes Neville, I baptise thee in the Name of the Father, and of the Son, and of the Holy Ghost.'

Ashbys and Wallises

Edie was the third daughter of John Eyre Ashby (son of a City grocer, an astronomer and dissenting minister) and Maria Smith (daughter of a coal and corn merchant). Her elder sisters were Maria Eyre Ashby (b.1849), known as Minna inside the family, and Elizabeth Eyre Ashby (b.1852), known as Lily.

In 1855 John and Maria bought a school. Its premises were a large Georgian house in Enfield called Gothic Hall, where young gentlemen were prepared for the Civil Service of the East India Company, military colleges and universities.[4] Gothic Hall was a good place for young people. It had attics for hide and seek, roofs down which to slide, and a summer house roof on which to climb. In the grounds were forks of apple trees in which to perch, a walnut tree canopy, and beeches yielding nuts for which you could forage in autumn. Around the house were pet rabbits, guinea pigs, cats and dogs. There were hay parties (in which you were buried in hay), Christmas tree parties, expeditions into Epping Forest, and fireworks. John Ashby had a telescope through which the boys could study the moon, stars and the Great Comet that appeared in 1860. A natural science table bore a spectroscope, magnetic boxes, a skull, a Roman intaglio, and prehistoric flint tools.

Edith Eyre Ashby was born into this blooming environment on 17 March 1859. She was coddled by the boys, who admired her blue eyes and golden hair and noted her enthusiasm for animals in preference to dolls. As the sisters grew, differences of temperament emerged. Minna was calm and affectionate. Lily, energetic and generous, could also be explosive – bitten pillows, thumped walls. Edie was precocious and excitable.

The happy times ended in late 1863 when John Ashby succumbed to Bright's disease and died. Maria sold up and moved to Brighton to start a school of her own. They called it Enfield House, in memory of John, and it opened with six pupils in the autumn of 1864. Enfield House did well enough as a school but was borderline as a business, and as years passed Maria became careworn. Minna worked as her assistant until 1870, when she married. Lily likewise taught until she too married. Both husbands were former Gothic Hall boys with whom the Ashbys had kept in touch. Minna's young man was Tom Francis, now a solicitor. Lily's marriage was to Theo Maxwell, who had studied medicine, and after qualification served as an ambulance officer in the Franco-Prussian war. Both couples moved to India, Tom to be legal adviser to the Maharaja of Dabhanga in Bihar, Theo as a medical missionary.

Minna, Lily and Edie were ardent letter writers. Lily told of long treks in the mountains of Kashmir, of poverty and beauty. Minna described moments of imperial grandeur, like the launch of *Victoria*, the Maharaja's lake steamer, and of tragedy, like the death of her third child.

Edie took singing lessons, worked hard at the piano, and played chamber music. She loved her animals, which included rats ('I think of giving them away, and am looking for an eligible person'), birds and hens. In that enthusiasm, however, was a kind of acquisitive carelessness which saw creatures of any kind as existing for her pleasure. She took creatures into captivity regardless of what they were or how, even whether, they could be kept. Her letters are full of chatter about their anthropomorphised personalities.

In 1877, Maria Ashby decided to close Enfield House. Edie was now eighteen, the age at which young women put their hair up. Her journal suggests someone assured, talkative, given to adolescent high spirits and flirtatious fun, but also to self-reproach over her lack of devotion. Before they left she went into the garden to look at old nooks where 'I used to build fairy palaces of mud' with spent matchsticks as little men. The garden was now overgrown with briar and meadowsweet; she recalled places where sunshine had fallen, or where the wall would be in shade: 'At such points I would hang my bird's cage, that poor old Dick might be happy as long as possible.' 'Ah well! I suppose now begins my real woman life. My old associations are all to be broken up, everything will be new.'

Lily and Theo, back from India, were setting up a practice to serve the middle classes around Woolwich Common and staff of the Royal Military Academy. They bought a large house on the edge of the Common, and in April 1878 Maria Ashby and Edie joined them. The following month, Minna arrived with her three children and a fourth in her womb, for whose birth she had returned. Lily herself was in the last weeks of pregnancy and gave birth to a daughter a fortnight later.

For a few months, then, most members of the family were back under one roof, Theo's prospects looked good, and Maria was surrounded by her grandchildren. But there were shadows. Lily's child died the following January, and when Minna returned to India in November 1879, it was in the knowledge that her husband Tom had begun to drink, and without her eldest sons. It was the British custom in India to send boys home for schooling when they reached seven or eight. Thomas (known as Taf) and John (known as Jef) were now left behind and sent to boarding school.[5] When Minna said goodbye to Jef, he 'did not know I was looking my last on him for long years.'

Thus did things stand when seven months later a young medical student called Charles Wallis was shown into Theo Maxwell's drawing room. Charles was born in January 1859 at Paglesham, a fishing community in eastern Essex, where his father was curate. At his baptism he was given the names Charles (after a maternal uncle), George (after his father) and Robinson, the maiden name of his mother, Anne Georgina, who had died of a postnatal infection three days before.

Both grandparents came from military families. George's father was a purser in the Royal Navy, Anne the daughter of Major Joseph Robinson of The King's Royal Rifle Corps and Anne Bowles, of Dublin and Chester. The Robinsons were in their sixties, and it was to them that George turned for the care of his motherless son. Charles lived with them until he was six, whereupon he was put into the care of the Rev Henry Owen and his wife Catherine at Tru-thorpe, an agricultural parish of some 300 souls on the Lincoln-shire coast, where Henry was rector.[6] It was here, rimmed by wide skies, among fields of beans and turnips, overlooked by brick windmills, lapped by the sea along the long ribbon of Trusthorpe's beach, that he spent the next six years.

The Owens had children of their own, and there was another boarder. Amid the bustle, Catherine did what she could to mother the outsider. Charles's memories of himself as a solitary boy skating along frozen dykes on winter afternoons, pole-vaulting over ditches or wandering among the stumps of prehistoric trees revealed by neap tides were all of a piece with a conviction that he had been banished. This is possible: when George Wallis married Caroline Millett, the daughter of the rector of Lyng, Norfolk, in 1863, Charles was not at first invited to join them.

George Wallis was short and stubby, hot-tempered, with a squarish face framed by mutton-chop whiskers. He was a man of id-iosyncrasies which included an insistence on bristly Jaeger woollen underwear, nightshirts, and pillowslips; a personal egg-boiler fuelled by a charge of methylated spirit sufficient to boil one egg; reliance upon fermented goats' milk as a remedy for all ailments; and a system of ropes and pulleys of his own devising for hoisting the trunks and hatboxes of visitors to upper floors. His fiercely evangelical outlook was reflected in long sermons wherein torture loomed large, and daily family prayers in which the sins of those present were closely examined. George disliked anything that smacked of ritualism, such as flowers on an altar, insisted that the word 'God' be spoken softly as 'Gawd', and that each time it was written it had to be with a new pen nib. He was obsessive about words. A mispronunciation by a young relative was likely to trigger an on-the-spot lecture about its articulation and etymology. As he grew older and his hearing failed, such harangues became ever louder, and on occasion attracted be-wildered crowds.[7]

His new wife Caroline led a gentle but persistent campaign to reunite her husband with his first-born son, in result of which Charles was eventually admitted to his father's household. On the rare occasions when Charles later talked about his father it was with respect rather than affection. Charles was nonetheless imbued by George's religiosity. He recoiled from risqué chat, and if he found himself in the presence of students using swear words or telling dirty jokes, he tried to summon 'the courage to rise and go'. The young man who went up to Merton College Oxford in October 1877 was reserved, sometimes morose and given to sighs, with a latent expressive side which awaited someone to waken.

Mixed feelings

On the first anniversary of their meeting Edie wrote: 'This time last year I saw Charlie first. He thought me prim, severe, frigid and one who would "district visit". I thought him compact, and rather fast – with a very powerful face that I didn't understand.'[8] First impressions had since been revised. By November Charles had produced a hand-made book of sonnets, each page wreathed in leafy garlands and faced by a pen-and-ink drawing. Next May they became engaged.

Charles was now a medical student at Guy's Hospital, and marriage was some way off. However, the wedding, when it came, came in a hurry. In August 1885 Minna was home from India; perhaps on impulse it was agreed that the marriage should take place before she returned. Since Minna's passage was booked in mid-September, this meant a special licence for the ceremony. When the day arrived, Edie was led in on the arm of her father's brother, Uncle Edward (coiner of 'EdiePuss'), followed by two bridesmaids, Charles's half-sister Ethel, and Minna's nine-year-old daughter Elf. The ceremony was conducted by the vicar and Charles's father, with whom, interestingly, Edie had formed a good relationship.

It is worth summarising characteristics of the two families that were now connected. Common to both were strong evangelical convictions, commitment to education, forebears in the military and holy orders, and careers spread across the British Empire. The Bible, learning through inquiry, and empire formed the ground on which their children would stand. In the background was recurrent giftedness in mathematics on Edie's side, and a sense of victimhood on Charles's.

Back at Woolwich in the autumn, Charles was Assistant Physician Clerk to his tutor, studying for final exams, and Edie was pregnant. In May the next year, just before the birth and the exams, they took a short holiday in Eastbourne. While they were there Edie wrote her only journal entry that year.

> Now my Charlie has gone to church, I will just scribble a few lines. This is our second honeymoon, – I think it will be our last . . . For always after this I hope there will be someone else with us. It does seem strange! To think that next month I expect to have a baby in my arms, that little baby I feel stirring within me as I write. Oh! God, make us wise parents, and bless the little one . . .[9]

Looking back three years later, it had not turned out quite like that.

> We married rashly, before he was qualified, and thus hampered ourselves. My John, my ever dear John, began to come too soon, and all those months of anxiety and terror, while Charlie worked for his exams, and every month was eating up our money, I carried with me – my John. The walks, the roads of Woolwich must be paved with my prayers, I prayed so much.[10]

'I shall gobble you all up'

Ripley was the company town of the Butterley Iron and Coal Co Ltd. Edie remembered it as 'crowning a lonely, windswept hill – you could see it high up against the horizon for miles round – its tall square Church tower, oversized Town Hall, Factory chimney and Waterworks being landmarks that stood out against the cold grey sky.'[11] The closest she and Charles had so far come to such places was from the windows of trains, and their first impressions in September

1886 were unnerving. Charles's southern accent, Oxford education and dislike of profanity did not stand him in good stead with colliers. When Edie saw miners emerging from the pit she asked Charles 'if they ever washed and he says yes they do.'[12]

At the start, Charles fell into 'a miserable condition of mind'.[13] He had few patients, so 'just now meals, smoking and walking are the principal occupations.' There were compensations. Dr Allen was a good mentor. Edie was impressed by the cost of living: laundry, bread, freshly churned butter and service were all cheaper than in Woolwich. Edie was determined to live as a gentlewoman and delegate duties to servants. There was thus a live-in maid who worked six and a half days a week (and 'spoke Derbyshire'), and a nurse (who spoke English) who cared for baby John.

Gradually, life began to look better. Charles's list of patients grew; John began to sleep at night; Edie amassed animals; invitations arrived to play readings in the vicarage, organ recitals, and dinner with new friends. In December, Lily and Theo brought books and a Christmas hamper. But Edie felt marooned. Christmas, and the re-alisation that she was again pregnant, heightened her longings: 'Oh! I really must come South in May. I hunger for a look at you all'. She would come for several months, visit Charlie's parents on the Isle of Wight and her friend Adeline Bell, and above all, Woolwich: 'I shall fly into the arms of Dockyard Station Master with the big nose, and the first uniform [of Woolwich Academy] I see I shall kiss. But lunacy will commence at Derby. I shall stand on my head as the train steams out. I shall gobble you all up . . .'[14]

In August 1887, the Wallises moved into No. 4 Butterley Hill, a detached brick house picturesquely clad in ivy and pyracantha which they took on a four-year lease.[15] It was here that Barnes was born the following month. At the age of one, he was 'sturdy and jolly, and so self-willed.' For a year or more he was known by his second name, Neville. At two, he was Edie's 'Derbyshire man', and by three he had become 'Toby Tubbs' – a nickname that stuck long enough for at least one family friend to forget what his real name was. There were favourite toys – a clockwork train from Minna, a telescope from Edie's close friend Adeline Bell. Out on walks, the boys were fascinated by the flickering light and irregular clangs from the iron-works; the bell in the pit engine house that signalled the readiness of a cage to come up; the clatter-bang of its gates; calls of lapwings that jinked across fields near slag heaps; and the slow, pulsing exhalations of an engine that hauled trucks of coal from the canal. Barnes and John loved to watch the trucks and were sometimes invited into the engine house to see the machinery turning.

Edie took an observant interest in Ripley, even accepting an invitation to go down the pit, about which she wrote a vivid description. But cares lay beneath. She was convinced that her sons should have a sister, but worried lest the third child be another boy; she remained financially anxious; she was worried about Minna, whose husband's alcoholism had worsened; in July 1889 she was desolated by the death of their mother; and she began to suffer from asthma. Beyond all this, and after a pause of several years, she resumed her journal. Charles now had

> many interests, and his patients, and I, save for my two babes, have nothing more than I had at first. He has grown even colder, if that is possible, and reserved – I never get a kiss, or loving touch, a smile of welcome. He never cares that I should show any solicitude about him, – a very iceberg. And my affection is withering, blighted. No wife would have come to him more loving, and more prepared to love – but this killing coldness which allows no display of affection on either side is enough to destroy the most ardent passion.

She wondered if the marriage had been a mistake, but told herself 'I *did* love him, oh! I *did* love him.' Edie saw a new path:

> my children open up a new tenderness in me, and new capacities of loving, daily; and so it is that a thawing and a freezing go on in me side by side. Their little lives teach me to love, and his life kills my love to him. So all the wealth that should be his, is slowly, slowly going to them . . .[16]

What about New Cross?

Family life now centred on the household of Lily and Theo. Edie yearned to be near them. After five years at Ripley Charles felt sufficiently experienced for a practice of his own, and in 1891 he consulted with Theo Maxwell about moving back to London. Maxwell knew of a young, recently married doctor who was planning to move and wished to sell his practice in New Cross; what about that? Edie and Charles hesitated, then scraped together what funds they could, and in 1892, with help from Lily, said farewell to Ripley and took over the departing doctor's lease on No. 241 New Cross Road.

New Cross was favoured among families of City clerks and office workers because it was the only area south of the Thames from which you could reach London's City, West and East Ends without changing trains. During the later nineteenth century, Georgian mansions along the London–Dover road were demolished to release their parks for housing. By the time the Wallises arrived most of the area was built up, with terraced houses towards the Thames and larger houses of the middle classes on the slopes of its terrace to the south. New Cross Road was still bordered by lofty elm trees, beneath which plied horse buses driven by coachmen in shiny waterproof top hats.

No. 241 itself stood on a corner. It was tall and thin, three floors and cellars below, with landings connected by over a hundred stairs down which the boys liked to toboggan on trays. The landing walls were hung with engravings of famous buildings and events, and their floors were dappled by colours thrown through stained glass in the over-lights. Running water was not available above the ground floor, which meant upstairs treks with ewers and pails. There was a gas lamp in the kitchen, but the rest of the house was lit by candles and paraffin lamps which left films of soot that had to be wiped down. The children were bathed in a hip bath by the nursery fire. In the cellar were the usual shallow sink, large copper, and a mangle.

Opposite the house was the park of an abandoned mansion, Fairlawn, which gave the immediate outlook a rural feel. Beyond lay fields on Telegraph Hill, where a succession of nurses took the boys on walks. To the east was Greenwich Park, Blackheath where golfers wore red coats to warn passers-by of flying balls, and Woolwich. Edie was back in her home ground, and by late autumn of 1892 she was carrying her third child.

The following June, John and Barnes were sent to their grand-parents George and Caroline, who were now at Ryde on the Isle of Wight. A nurse went with them; the plan was for them to stay for about a month and return after the birth. Barnes and John had no idea that a new member of the family was in the offing. The hoped-for daughter arrived at breakfast time on Wednesday, 28 June. She was christened Annie in memory of Charles's mother Anne Robinson, 'Theodora', the gift of God, in commemoration of the love between Edie's parents, and 'Janet', a name which appears nowhere else in the family.

On 1 August Charles retired to bed with poliomyelitis, a viral disease which in severe cases can infect the spinal cord and cause paralysis. The disease kept him bed-bound for fourteen weeks and left his left leg useless. Edie, meanwhile, was unable to feed Annie, and difficulties in sterilising her bottles led to a series of stomach infections. Edie was at her wit's end. The practice was in crisis, and the boys were stranded on the Isle of Wight with their sixty-eight-year-old evangelical grandfather and the kindly Caroline.

Gradually, things settled. Charles was transferred to Woolwich. Lily gave financial help. Theo Maxwell helped to organise locums to hold the practice together. By September Edie had resumed her letters to the boys. Barnes was delighted with the clockwork engine he received on his sixth birthday, and the box of Scottish soldiers sent by Aunt Lily to join forces with John's regiment to 'fight the Zulus'.

Just before Christmas 1893 Edie sent greetings to her boys, saying how pretty the shops looked. On Boxing Day she wrote again to 'her own pet Barnes' to thank them for the 'useful box'. Daddy was pleased with his paper rack. He was up and about on crutches, but still in pain. If all went well, they could come home in January. But on return, 'remember you must be the sunshine and sunbeam of your Daddy's grey life.'

We do not know how the boys were affected by their six-month exile, or reacted to the changed circumstances – a new sister, a crippled father, a determined but increasingly neurotic mother. Charles gradually resumed his practice. He wore a leg-iron, and periodically fell headlong when it skidded. On several occasions the leg brace snapped, leaving him stranded. A pony and trap enabled him to visit patients, he bought a tricycle, and the house was reorganised to limit the need for stair climbing. Nonetheless, a year later Edie told her sons that their father's 'irreparable' illness was the greatest sorrow of her life. Her financial anxieties deepened. Asthma attacks increased.

Edie and Charles took several holidays on their own, apparently to rekindle some of the warmth that had been lost. One of them was to Weeley in Essex, where in July 1896 George Wallis was standing in for an absent rector, and the large rectory was available free of charge. Edie was impressed by the rector's fox terrier, a ferret, Tom and Prince (horses), and poultry. While Charles roamed on his tricycle, she laid waste to local wildlife, wishing to catch butterflies for John, but without a net or knowledge of how to kill them. 'Last night I picked up a dear little toad that was hopping on the path. He was quite young. I will bring some toadies and froggies home with me.' When Wallis started a family of his own, there were no pets.

Back at New Cross, Edie obtained permission from Fairlawn's caretaker for the children to play in the grounds. Here was a realm that combined gothic frisson with nature and liberty: deserted stables, a lovers' walk of stately elms, the stone tomb of someone's favourite horse, a pets' graveyard, a colossal copper beech, and the remains of a fountain and pool filled with dry leaves that crunched when you jumped into them. Large frogs congregated in the shady damp of a dripping water-butt in the kitchen garden. They lit bonfires and baked potatoes in the ashes. Among the horseboxes and hay John, Barnes and Annie took turns at being horse and driver, with reins of string, authentically attached so that they 'made our mouths sore'. The house was out of bounds, although from time to time they penetrated a thick curtain of wisteria to step across its threshold and listen to mysterious sounds.

John was intellectually able and artistic. Annie saw in him Edie's traits of vivacity and wit, given to flippancy and a tendency to see the funny side of anything. When he reached his teens, John was playful with young Annie, tempting her to hysterics during meals and practical jokes. He saw life itself as a kind of joke, and hoped for a career in history, perhaps as a museum curator.

The two brothers 'did everything together'. They played cricket in the garden, eventually causing Edie to reorganise the space, with the hens in one part and the scullery window wired 'so that your cricket balls may no longer break the glass'. They shot with an air rifle, aiming at tin cans, or with home-made bows and arrows, at one point using Annie for target practice, which nearly ended in tragedy. Each August there was an annual holiday in a cottage near Bognor, where they raced through country lanes on bicycles and visited ancient churches in remote Sussex countryside.

Barnes was dexterous as well as physical. He learned to make things with paper, delighting Annie by bringing her 'lovely paper houses' with roofs that could be lifted off, 'with talc windows and painted red talc for fires', chairs from chestnut bark, paper tables, and always a witch 'with a head of candle fat, hair of black darning wool, matchstick arms and legs.' Barnes and John used the big front bedroom as a workroom. Here they co-operated in crafts that included carpentry, making string, and – in Barnes's case – ornamental metalwork. Barnes accumulated a large collection of specialised tools. Relatives knew to save pieces of rosewood, cedar and mahogany from cigar boxes for the boys' use. Annie often stood by to watch them, and learned to use the tools. She liked to accompany the brothers to choose timber at a nearby carpenter's yard, where the owner wore an old tricorn hat and 'a delicious smell of pine' hung in the air.

There was music in the house. When the brothers' voices broke they joined with Annie to sing part-songs, with Edie at the piano. A favourite pursuit of Charles and Edie was to read aloud to each other. Charles enjoyed Tennyson and Browning (who had lived locally); Edie liked novels, especially the writings of Robert Louis Stevenson and Dickens.

John and Barnes were schooled at nearby Haberdasher Aske's. Reports spoke of Barnes's 'exemplary conduct', attentiveness in class, and work that was never less than good and often 'highly satisfactory'. In only one area did his teachers voice concern: he was too often absent. At Christmas 1894 the headmaster described him pointedly as 'very good, when present'.[17] Edie was the usual cause of his non-attendance. He did indeed suffer from chronic coughs and colds, and London's carbon-laden air, not to mention the sooty atmosphere inside No. 241, was not a good environment for anyone. However, Edie's concern went further. Any symptom set her a-flutter; she worried that Barnes might have contracted TB; when he told her that his heart thumped after exercise, she feared heart disease.

In March 1898 the family grew with the birth of another boy, named after his father. John was now twelve, Barnes eleven, and it was time to plan their next steps. A public school combining scholarly excellence with gentlemanly tradition was unaffordable, but Edie's City connections suggested another path: to Christ's Hospital, in Newgate Street, where able boys from families of 'reduced means' were schooled with support from charitable endowments. Bluecoat boys, so-called for their uniform of knee-length dark blue coat and bright yellow stockings, substantially unchanged since the school's foundation in 1552, were a familiar sight in the City. To qualify, the applicant's family had to provide evidence of its circumstances, the boy must be 'presented' by a recognised nominator, and there was a competitive exam. John's application was successful, and in 1899 he became a Bluecoat boy.

Early in 1900, Barnes, too, was presented, and came seventh out of one hundred in the examination for the ten available places. At the start of summer term Barnes was to be brought to the school 'clean, free from ringworm', with hair 'newly cut' and 'free from grease'. He should bring with him a Bible, the Book of Common Prayer, a hairbrush and comb, toothbrush, and a pair of stout slippers.

On 11 May Barnes made the journey to Newgate with John: past the tanning yards at Bermondsey, the warehouses at Little Britain, past the long, high brick wall to the three-arched gateway, and under the eye of Ozzy the Beadle, in he walked.

Lamplight and tradition

Christ's Hospital is a religious, royal, and ancient foundation. For Wallis these formed an undivided trinity, and it is through them that his life-long devotion to the school, his faith and Anglocentrism are best explained.

The affection with which Wallis looked back on his life at Christ's Hospital is interesting to compare with his anxiety at its start. A fortnight after his arrival the twelve-year-old 'scrub' sent a postcard to his mother saying that some of the work he had been given was beyond him and that he was accordingly being threatened with a Saturday detention. Both things troubled him. His parents were due to visit on the Saturday, so he would miss them, and he was completely unused to criticism for lack of effort. Diligence was woven through his soul, yet here he was being accused of slacking. His father replied consolingly, telling him that it was 'no disgrace if you have done your best. You see the master cannot know much of you as yet and he may set down to idleness what is due to your being slow or new to the work.' Charles added: 'If you do get kept in on Saturday either I or mother will come up to see you on Sunday, so cheer up'.[18]

Students moved through Christ's Hospital not by year or cohort but according to individual ability. Wallis later explained: 'I won a scholarship, principally I think on my mathematics, and on the strength of that examination I was placed directly in the Upper School on the Modern Side.'[19] However, since Christ's Hospital did not prepare pupils who lacked classics for entrance to Oxford or Cambridge, Wallis's father put his foot down.

> My Father . . . insisted that I should continue to learn Latin, in spite of the fact that the headmaster told him that that would involve my entering on the *bottom* form of the Lower School on the Classical Side. That is, I must become a 'narrowie' instead of a 'broadie',[20] a sad blow to my boyish pride . . . I absolutely rebelled – I hated Latin and was perfectly stupid at it. So my Father at last gave way and wrote to the Headmaster – the Rev

Richard Lee – to say that he would agree to my transfer to the Modern side.[21] The Head retaliated by placing me on the bottom form but one in the *Lower* School of the Modern Side,[21] among a despised race of rather stupid boys, instead of restoring me to my rightful place as a 'broadie' where I really belonged on my mathematical and scientific ability, and where I would have *started* my school career, had not my Father, with the best intentions in the world, flouted the Headmaster's advice. I thus lost a whole year's seniority . . . a discouraging, disappointing and frankly an infuriating start to my school life, and in a way a psychological disaster for a child of 12.[22]

John Wallis recalled Richard Lee's round face, black whiskers, stout profile, and little feet. In 1900 he was nearing the end of his reign. Small, at once comical and riveting, when teaching he drew rapid breaths 'as if in pain' and spoke Wallis's name as 'Wallidge'.[23] The Minor Wallidge now reacted to his relegation by embarking on subversion. Looking back, he believed his motive had been to try to recover his self-esteem by drawing attention to himself.[24] The aim of this brinkmanship, he said, was to discover how far he could go 'before the thunderbolt fell on one's defenceless head.'[25]

The reference to an unprotected head was literal. Until 1902, Christ Hospital's monitors – junior prefects – were free to administer physical punishment for minor misdemeanours. There were different kinds of penalty. One, a heavy blow to the cheek and side of the head administered with the flat of the hand, was known as a 'fotch'. Another was the 'owl', in which a monitor rapped the top of his victim's head with the knuckles of his clenched fist. The recipient of a fotch was expected meekly to tilt his head sideways, openly presenting his ear and the side of his face; a boy about to be owled was required to lean forward and await the blow.

A single owl was so severe that at the instant of the blow one literally 'saw stars' dancing before one's eyes, and a lump the size of half a small walnut would rise and stay on one's skull for two or three days.[26]

It could be worse:

> In cases when a monitor was exasperated beyond bearing, he
> would pull his victim's head downwards by the hair, and then
> assault him with both hands, giving 'fotches' and 'owls' with
> either hand, as an opening presented itself.

Some monitors offered a victim the choice of fotch or owl. Since a
mis-aimed owl could hurt the knuckles of the monitor who delivered
it, Wallis always chose to be owled. He later reckoned that rarely a
day passed during his time at Newgate Street without him receiving
'one or two or more owls or fotches, and on occasion a prolonged
beating'.[27] Forty-five years afterwards, in the course of treatment for
polyps in his nasal cavities, doctors found that one of his cheekbones
had been 'pretty badly broken' at some time in the past.

Wallis rode out the brutality. In letters home he described routine
incidents of mob justice:

> There has been a row about Snell, he refused to play cricket for
> the ward match & so has practically lost us the match. He has
> no reason for not doing so, so the chaps held a trial over him
> this morning, he is to receive a fotch from every chap & to be
> sent to Cov[entry] for the rest of the term.[28]

Being quite strong, very determined, and (with an elder brother)
well briefed, he escaped many of the casual torments that attended
many new boys, some of whom would be mugged within seconds
if they brought cake or sweets through the gate on return from an
exeat.[29]

At first, Charles or Edie came to take their sons out on most
Saturday afternoons, returning them to Newgate at 8 p.m. Later,
the boys took themselves home for exeats. During the week, Edie
filled her letters with news of the hens and cats, Annie's doings,
parish duties, family events, her singing birds, Jim (the latest dog,
who bit patients), the roars and screams of infant Charles and the
strategies of Nurse Lena to subdue him. Edie had a low opinion of

Nurse Lena, and mimicked her pretensions: 'My highly superior pusson (person) the Nurse, is out for the day; wherefore we all sing and rejoice'.[30]

Edie gave vivid descriptions of public reaction at times of national and imperial celebration or sorrow. The death of Queen Victoria:

> . . . she is now at rest after a long life spent for her subjects, & we may thank God that she had such a peaceful end, & was surrounded by her loving family. Did you notice the big Bell? We have kept the blinds down all day, & when I went out, I noticed most houses had theirs drawn; black crepe was on the whips of many drivers.[31]

The funeral procession:

> Cousin Arnold saw the procession from the roof of a house in a side street. He travelled with 26 in an ordinary single compartment meant to seat 10. After the procession passed & he left his perch, & got into the road . . . some troops came along, & the crowd was pressed out of the centre of the road. He says he was lifted quite off his feet & borne along with the stream of people.[32]

The end of the Boer War:

> Peace! Oh! Isn't it just beautiful! I can't tell you how glad I am. Last night [Sunday] I went too early to bed . . . when I reached the landing window, according to my wont I looked out across London – And Lo! I saw a rocket go up, & then another . . . About 11 Jim barked, & I again went to the window, & opened it . . . & again I saw rockets . . . then in about half an hour, I heard hurrahs in the street. I bounced up, saying, 'It's Peace, it's peace', & I saw rockets . . . & then I saw *lots* of rockets, – & Father came to look and we opened the window. Then we heard the big Bell, either Paul's or Westminster, and its sound was most wonderful, a sort of ululation filling the midnight air . . .[33]

In September 1900 Wallis was transferred to the 'Modern Side', albeit at a lower level than his scholarship had merited. However, even in the Latin School (where his place for Classics had been 29 out of 29) his ratings for diligence were never less than fair, and for conduct were uniformly good.[34] He was teased in the new class, apparently by boys of less ability who regarded him as a swot. This was another new experience, to which Wallis reacted with surges of fierce temper that added to the pleasure of his tormentors.

At the end of the first year Wallis achieved first place in class for mathematics and German, second in French, and third in English; conduct and diligence were consistently described as good; his performance in the mathematics examination won a prize – a calf-bound copy of Walter Jerrold's biography of Lord Roberts of Kandahar. In the autumn of 1901 he was finally promoted to the Upper School, and thereafter he flourished.

Flourishing at CH called for more than scholastic effort. There was a vocabulary to learn – titch, swob, kiff, flab, gag and all the rest[35] – customs to observe, and a spartan lifestyle with which to come to terms. There were no dayrooms at Newgate and the wards (dormitories) were out of bounds during the day. Most of the day was thus spent either in class or outdoors. During longer periods of leisure perhaps a dozen games of 'Housey rugger' were played simultaneously in the area known as 'Hall Play', between the great gates that bounded Newgate Street and the frontage of the vast medieval-revival dining hall. Hall Play was surfaced with asphalt and creased by shallow gutters of cobble stones, so any kind of contact game was dangerous, and tackling low was forbidden. Even so, there were accidents when heavy tackles led to concussions or broken limbs.[36] During shorter breaks boys tended to walk to and fro in small groups, a habit known as spadging. If it was wet, you spadged in the cloisters.

Seven hundred boys on one site with limited facilities and primitive sanitation posed a challenge for public health. There were frequent minor epidemics, and some that were serious. CH's infirmary (known as 'the Sicker') was well used. For most of his life Wallis was fit and physically robust, but there were episodes of ill-health. At various times he suffered from scarlet fever, mastoiditis (not helped by the fotches rained on the side of his head), and migraine. When Wallis first experienced migraine he staggered to the infirmary, to be met by an unsympathetic nurse who ascribed the abrupt onset of a blinding headache, bleached-out vision and vomiting to too much cake. Wallis endured attacks for the rest of his life, sometimes at the rate of several a month.

All boys below the level of monitor performed a service for the community, known as a 'trade'. Menial trades like washing dirty plates or serving bread went to junior boys; more dignified tasks, like the supervision of other trades, were performed by trades-monitors who were one step below the rank of monitor.[37]

The masters at Newgate lived out, and when teaching was over at 4.15, off they went. Discipline out of school hours was accordingly overseen by a warden. In Wallis's day the warden was a retired colonel, who kept watch on boys' conduct through the eyes of patrolling beadles, mostly former policemen, whose duties included breaking up fights and keeping boys from going out in the rain or kicking footballs in the cloisters. They belonged to a rich supporting cast of CH characters who included top-hatted Mr Horn, a little man with a square-cut beard who kept the gate; Ginger Stocks, the porter and superintendent; Sgt Major Thompson, the drill instructor; 'Shoey' the cordwainer, and the dames who were responsible for discipline and behaviour in the wards. Wallis's ward, Number 7, was overseen by Dame Clarissa Smith who was rumoured to be the widow of a doctor.

Between forty and fifty boys slept in each ward, which was a cross-section of the age structure of the school. The ward itself was a rectangle with a low axial partition against which eight or nine numbered beds stood at right angles to either side, arranged like the bones of a kipper. More beds stood against the outer walls. Dame Smith occupied a small chamber in one corner, while the head of ward, a classical Grecian, was provided with a curtained cubicle. (Grecians were senior boys preparing for university; they enjoyed a common room in the headmaster's house, ate at high table, and were allowed into the city.) Bedsteads were iron-framed with wooden boards, hair mattresses and hard pillows. On rising at 6 a.m. (6.15 in winter) to the blast of a bugle from the foot of each staircase the beds were stripped. Daily washing was at a lead-lined trough fed by cold taps, wherein half the ward's members washed together while the other half cleaned their shoes with liquid blacking. Breakfast on weekdays was a cob of brown bread with salt butter or dripping, and a bowl of hot milk and coffee; on Sundays there were sausages. Before eating, the boys knelt on bare boards to say a prayer which had been written by Henry Compton, a former bishop of London (1675–1713). Bed-making after breakfast was undertaken with the exactness demanded of military recruits – hospital corners, squared-off edges, bolsters ordered with the help of a pole – and inspected by a monitor. The school lavatories – 'bogs' – were too few for 700 boys, so there was always a crowd waiting to use them after breakfast.[38] Boys carried, and closely guarded, their own lavatory paper ('bodge'). In the 1840s a room containing twenty-eight bathtubs had been established, enabling every boy to have a warm bath once a fortnight.[39]

At the foot of each bed was a tall, narrow rectangular box with sides of iron sheet and a wooden lid. The box was called a settle; in it, boys kept their books, hairbrush and other possessions. A penalty for small contraventions was 'standing on', where a boy would stand on his box, hands behind back, for up to forty minutes. Another punishment was early-morning drill. The whole school practised drill each week, with marching and counter-marching. At lunchtime all boys formed up like a medieval army behind their ward banners to march into Hall to the accompaniment of the school band.

A variety of dishes were served for lunch – beans, beef, mutton pork – with boiled potatoes. For the evening meal there was bread again, tea, and perhaps jam or sardines. When boys returned to their Wards in the evening there was the option of milk or bread and cheese at 8 p.m. Wards were lit by fish-tail gas lamps. The nearest lamp to Wallis's bed was about forty feet away, so reading was difficult. Lights out was preceded by a prayer which compared going to sleep with the hour of death.[40]

Newgate's walled-in world hummed with echoes. The Great Hall evoked late-medieval ceremonial spaces like guildhalls and royal chapels. Its materials – Portland stone, granite, brick, oak – symbolised England's foundations. In the Middle Ages the Greyfriars had been supposed safe from incubi and flying demons and had thus been attractive as a peaceful burying place; nobles, ladies and queens lay there. Small wonder that when boys like Wallis or his contemporary John Middleton Murry looked down at a tablet in the cloister: 'Here lyes a Benefactor: let no one move Hys Bones', there was a stir in their souls.[41] At Christ's Hospital they joined a family which endowed them with ancestors.

Newgate's interiority was balanced by what you could see out of it if you tried. In the older buildings there were forgotten rooms and blocked-up staircases. When Barnes and his brother explored them they found a vantage point from which they could see the spires and towers of City churches; Westminster Abbey and the Houses of Parliament outlined against red winter sunsets; and Hampstead Heath under snow. For Wallis, two of the most transfixing sights were closer: the steeple of Christ Church just outside the walls, and the dome of St Paul's. Both had been designed by Christopher Wren. Wren was Wallis's hero: an artist who was also a practical engineer. Christ Church could also be seen from the nursery window of 241 New Cross Road. On summer evenings Edie sometimes looked out, surveying the Monument, Tower Bridge, and Christ Church; by looking at Christ Church she 'felt I could almost see my two dear sons'.[42]

For the best part of half a century it had been agreed that Newgate Street was not a good site for a boarding school. There had been argument between progressives who wished to see a purpose-built campus on a green-field site, and traditionalists who protested that such removal would cut ties to donors, punish working-class parents by distancing them from their children, and extinguish ancient memories. The case for removal was periodically strengthened by incidents such as an outbreak of scarlet fever that closed CH for nine months in 1893.[43] By then the decision to relocate had been taken, and a thousand-acre site had been selected in Sussex near Horsham. Nine more years were to pass, however, before Christ's Hospital moved to its promised land. On the last evening, Grecians bearing candles processed in single file to beat the bounds of the old site, kicking the walls of well-known spots as they passed.[44]

During the Easter holiday that followed, John Wallis went back to look. Through the railings he could see piles of housebreakers' planks and scaffold-poles. He walked back along Newgate Street and through the Lodge.

> It was empty. No Beadle! No boys! The place was forlorn and deserted . . . I walked along the Giffs and on to the further end of the Hall Play. As I returned, a short figure dressed in black issued from the Hall Cloi and confronted me, his hands clasped behind his back.
>
> 'Well, Wallidge, did you think term had begun?' Richard Lee grinned up at me.
>
> 'No, Sir,' said I, 'I came to see whether life had ended.'
>
> 'Life never ends', said he, 'it may, it must – (and he slowly waved his hand towards the contractors' materials lying around us), it must change its environments and its expressions, but it does not end.'[45]

The London, Brighton and South Coast Railway built a station to serve the new campus at Horsham. When the boys alighted on Thursday, 9 May 1902, they found that nearly half the teaching staff had been replaced by younger men, and a new headmaster the Rev Dr Arthur William Upcott.[46]

Heights and blue horizons

After a few weeks Charles Wallis reproached Barnes for being 'rather neglectful of your Mother in letter writing since you went to Horsham'. At Newgate Barnes had written once a week, and there had been visits. Now that he and John were further away Edie yearned for the old weekly contact. 'Mother misses you both very much and thinks constantly of you . . . we seem to know little or nothing of your new life'.[47]

The new life was good. Cricket and rugby could be played on

grass. The houses of orange-red brick had lockers, dayrooms, studies for senior boys and warm water. And whereas Newgate's Wards had simply been numbered, Horsham's houses bore the names of distinguished Old Blues. Ward 7 was now Peele A – the Peele in question being the Tudor poet and playwright George Peele (1556–96).[48] In place of the Dames each house was under the charge of a housemaster; in Peele A's case this was the Rev D. F. Heywood, one of the school's grammar masters and head of the Modern Side. A few architectural features, and some traditional items had been carried from the old site to the new, but Wallis was less taken by these tokens of continuity than by the place itself. At Newgate they had been shut in behind walls of yellowish London stock brick among buildings of different ages; here the buildings were new and generously spaced, and around them were places to discover, distances to be travelled, flowers and butterflies to identify. Edmund Blunden, who joined CH five years after Wallis left, celebrated its 'prospects of heights and blue horizons'.[49]

Science at Newgate had been taught in an improvised laboratory converted from an old Ward; here there was a well-equipped science block. More than this, there was an Art School and a Manual School in which things could be designed and made. By the time he reached Horsham, Wallis had already set his heart on a career in engineering. Charles's half-brother, 'Uncle' Wwyn, was an electrical engineer.[50] He gave advice to Edie, who passed it to Barnes:

> . . . he says that above & before *everything* in your equipment for successful engineering, must come drawing – mechanical drawing, so father will write to Mr Heywood about it, – also *languages*, especially German. So do put your back into your work for the sake of our future welfare, – now's the time for you to learn.[51]

Spurred by Wwyn's advice, Wallis's academic career began to prosper. At the end of the 1902 summer term he was promoted to a higher form. Edie was thrilled.

I cannot tell you dear, how thankful we are about your move. You must have worked splendidly; it is very good indeed. Your good work makes all the difference to Father's life; he is so proud and pleased, & shakes out his feathers, as if to say 'I myself did it'.[52]

Wallis's Christmas present list at the end of the year shows his direction of travel:

One thing I know is an enlarger for Brownie filums 6/6[53] . . . I should like a moulding plane of this pattern [sketch] . . . Also a 1 inch lathe chisel, 1 or 2½ plate developing dishes (xylonite or celluloid) about 6d each . . . Some pencils (ordinary lead). A plank of oak about 6 ft long (to make frames) & 1 inch thick (it's about 1/-).[54]

Edie's last letter before the 1902 Christmas holiday congratulated Barnes on winning prizes for book-keeping and science: 'I nearly skipped out of bed'.[55]

The new science facilities were the result of campaigning by the chemist and educationalist Professor Henry Edward Armstrong (1848–1937) who in 1897 was the Royal Society's nominee to Christ's Hospital's Council. Armstrong duly persuaded the school to adopt his investigative method of science teaching and recruited a fellow-chemist, Charles E. Browne, to lead it.[56] Armstrong's method involved supporting students to discover things for themselves through experiment. It was the opposite of the rote-learning epitomised in the CH geography exam question which asked Wallis to 'Name the principal headlands on the west coast of England (including Wales), and say which town is nearest to each.'

Terms passed. Wallis turned out regularly to train for Peele A's rugby team. He joined CH's debating society, practised small-bore rifle shooting, ran across Sussex countryside, played inter-house cricket, immersed himself in photographic processing, and enjoyed winter entertainments (with 'Mr Arthur Berridge at the piano, and Fred Frampton, humourist'). He picked primroses and posted them to his mother. He joined the geology section of the Natural History

Society, travelled on field trips led by Charles Browne, and made a contour survey of CH's surroundings. Browne's wife took to him, invited him for tea on half holidays and called him 'Barnes'.

A visit by Eric Bruce, secretary of the Aeronautical Society of Great Britain, made an impression. Bruce arrived with a cylinder of compressed hydrogen, which Wallis and a friend (both of whom were just then recovering from a visit to the school dentist) helped to carry to the lecture hall. (This was perhaps no mean feat. The dentist (who looked like 'a bumptious old cock, white spats, Norfolk suit & a very red face') took no more than two or three minutes over each boy. As Wallis went in, he was shouting at the previous patient, who had not yet come round from anaesthetic. 'They kick you out of the chair half asleep'.[57]) Bruce lectured on the use of balloons in war. He had brought a working model of an airship, 'wound up the propeller & sent it sailing down the Hall. He steered it round one of the electric light chandeliers.'[58]

Wallis's delight in making things drew him closer to Charles Brown: 'I asked the Science Master if I could go and carpenter . . . at the science schools & he said yes he'd be glad of someone to come & help the men make stands and things & I could do in there any time out of school.'[59] A few days later:

> I go carpentering every day now, except half holidays. The man there who is making all the wooden things for the science school is a tremendous dab. He took me into the lathe room the other day. It is quite like a factory in a small room. There is a huge lathe, a circular saw, drills & other things driven by electricity. They are turned from overhead shafts . . .[60]

By the end of the 1903 spring term Wallis was top in his form. Edie was delighted:

> You literally couldn't have done better, oh dear Barnes, how *joyful* . . . You *have* worked, I know. Father & I are awfully proud of you, for we consider you are really forwarder in proportion than John was at your age.[61]

Wallis took aim at the Willcox Prize for science, which began with an exam to sift out the ten worthiest candidates. The real test followed: a challenge to devise an experiment and apparatus to determine the volume of gas released by the dissolution of two grams of metal in sulphuric acid.

> That lasted all Wed morning and all Thurs afternoon. Dr Moody who I imagine is some great man came down on Wed to inspect the way we put up our apparatus . . . I doubt if I shall get it . . . Wouldn't it be a grand thing though?[62]

On July 20th, a postcard: 'Dear Mother, I've got the German prize on U7B.' In reply:

> I could have danced for joy when your simple little card came. You *have* given us pleasure, I felt as if I could eat two breakfasts, it did me so much good . . . Oh! I am pleased. You are a credit to your family . . . I know you have worked for love, & your success is the more honourable and brilliant.[63]

On the 22nd, a telegram: 'Got Willcox Prize love Barnes.' And on the 23rd:

> Words quite fail me . . . you have done splendidly . . . warmest congratulations . . . I feel quite overwhelmed . . . simply marvellous . . . How you must have worked . . . You are like a meteor, quite brilliant in your career . . .[64]

The prize was a medal, and £6.10s to be spent 'on whatever is most useful to you when you leave.' He used the money to buy a lathe, and thereby taught himself to cut, drill, smooth and turn materials.

Edie bathed her son in a continuous stream of encouragement and praise. By telling him of her own heartfelt responses to his achievements she stirred him to strive even more. Her sharing of frank opinions about CH staff and other adults fostered an uncompromising directness. And behind it all – 'do put your back into your work for the sake of our future welfare' – she had implanted the idea that he was to live his life as much for them as for himself.

Barnes's letters reveal wide-ranging curiosity, an eye for surroundings and for grace in structures, verbal playfulness, pithy expression, and a wry wit. In a long letter about a field trip he caught both the fun and sense of the day, describing the veal and ham pies they had for lunch, dedication crosses on the walls of a church, lime kilns, fossils, the ecology of snails, a comical scene on the platform of CH station, and the smell of a room in the Bridge Hotel.[65] By the end of his third year contemporaries and masters alike saw him as industrious, intelligent, conscientious, and capable.

It was an iron rule that the only boys who were permitted to remain at Christ's Hospital beyond the term in which they turned sixteen were those whom the school considered should be given the opportunity to compete for open scholarships to university. These were young men of outstanding ability – the Grecians – and university meant Oxford or Cambridge. The career path of a Mathematical Grecian typically led to business, commerce or the City, while that for a Classical Grecian ran to the Civil Service, medicine or the Church. At this date no boy on the Modern side could be a Grecian, and since Wallis had elected to stay on the Modern side to pursue science, that was that: when he returned to Horsham in the autumn of 1903, he expected this to be his last term.

There are several accounts of what followed. One says that Wallis was selected for the honour of being the school's first Science Grecian, but refused it.[66] Another says that Browne hoped to persuade the school to retain Wallis as a Science Grecian and send him to London or Manchester, but that 'battle with the authorities' about the idea was never joined because Wallis was 'restless' and determined to leave to make his way in the world.[67]

What actually happened is best introduced by Edie, who paid a visit to CH in mid-October.

> Mr Heywood was *most* kind; he said of course I knew you were due to leave at Xmas, but he had said you were to stay till Easter,

& any way he intended you to remain till Midsummer.[68]

Wallis had risen in Heywood's estimation. He appointed Wallis as a monitor and talked to Browne about his future. Browne regarded Wallis as destined for a distinguished scientific career; he supported the arrangement for him to stay on at least until Easter 1904, and asked Upcott to allow him to remain beyond that to sit for university entrance. Wallis knew this, telling his father that the idea was 'to get a few fellows with an aptitude for science and to try and send them to the university'.[69] Moreover, in Browne's own account the plan was to enable Wallis to sit for a scholarship to 'one of the older universities'.

Battle was indeed then joined. Browne's proposal was opposed by CH's senior mathematical master and several conservative classics masters.[70] Upcott sided with the traditionalists. However, there was a compromise: Wallis could stay on for the summer term, effectively as an independent student studying for the London Matriculation examination which he would sit after leaving.[71]

The end of a CH term was marked by a light-hearted concert. On the last evening of the 1904 summer term the boys filed into the hall to hear the choir sing 'Land of Hope and Glory', a part-song and 'a humorous song'. Four boys and a master in drag performed a one-act farce. Upcott, remembered by one pupil as a 'pious sadist', amused the boys with 'a turn'. There followed Mendelssohn duets, improbably arranged for four cornets. At the end, everyone stood to sing 'God Save the King'.

The last day. Wallis had seen it before. Now he was one of the leavers who lined up in Chapel in order of seniority. One by one they were called forward. A Bible, stamped with the school crest and inscribed with the words *The Gift of the Governors of Christ's Hospital*, was put into the hands of each, and Upcott read to him the solemn Charge:

I charge you never to forget the great benefits that you have received in this place, and, in time to come, according to your means, to do all that you can to enable others to enjoy the same advantage; and remember that you carry with you, wherever you go, the good name of Christ's Hospital. May God Almighty bless you in your ways and keep you in the knowledge of His love.

In time to come and according to his means, Wallis acted on this.

2

The Wand of Youth, 1905–13

Into the shops

> The young professional engineer does not simply learn in the
> works how to file and chip. He learns the time required for all
> manner of jobs, the finish required in each class of work, the way
> the various parts are handled, the forms which are convenient,
> the routine of the shop, the character of the men – the system
> of storage, the materials and sizes to be bought in the market,
> and hundreds of other facts, which can only be made his own
> after contact with manufacture on a full scale. We cannot imitate
> this in college.[1]

Wallis agreed. He was on all fours, too, with Le Corbusier's view
that 'invention originates only in the workshop'.[2] In old age Wallis
argued that creation was not possible without handling and mas-
tery of the materials with which the maker works. Achieving that
kind of control, he said, meant 'spending something like five years
in the workshops.' Unsurprisingly, five years was the length of his
apprenticeship, and he embarked on it because he failed the London
matriculation.

The failure is a puzzle. Wallis was well versed in mathematics and
science, competent in French and German, and his skills in English
were good. Anyway, there it was: when the list of those who had
passed was issued in October 1904, his name was not on it.

Four years before Charles Wallis had attempted to influence his son's direction and had come close to wrecking his schooling by doing so. More recently he had insisted that Barnes be prepared for the London matriculation, and no good had come of that either. He now stood back. What did Barnes want to do? The family could not support him for long. Uncle Wwyn recommended apprenticeship as the route into engineering. Charles and Barnes looked for a firm willing to accept an apprentice, and found the Thames Ironworks Ship Building and Engineering Company.

Thames's activities were spread across several sites in east London. The main campus was a shipyard and ironworks beside the mouth of Bow Creek, the tidal estuary of the River Lea which wound across Bromley Marsh and joined the Thames near Blackwall. Across the river in Greenwich was a works on Blackheath Road, inherited from the marine engine makers John Penn and Sons, with whom Thames had recently amalgamated. Thames had been busy in the late nineteenth century but by the 1900s business was falling away. This was partly because the Blackwall yard was cramped, but the main reason was that they were being outcompeted by shipbuilders in north-east England and Scotland. Between 1901 and 1905 only two Admiralty contracts were awarded to Thames, and after that only one, for the cruiser *Black Prince*. In 1912, the main company went out of business.

Thames made efforts to diversify. The firm's departments already included civil engineering and manufacture of drills and cranes; to these they added motor vehicles. Under the brand name 'Thames' a motor department began to build petrol-driven 'motor carriages' (cars), vans, lorries, taxicabs, charabancs and omnibuses. This department was co-located with the marine engine division at the old John Penn site, and having promised his new employers faithfully their secrets to keep and lawful commands obey, it was here that the seventeen-year-old Barnes reported on the first Monday in 1905.

Industrial apprenticeship began with a probationary period when the newcomer was given lowly chores such as cleaning equipment and running errands. Pay in the first year was five shillings a week – about £45 at today's values – with another shilling for each year completed. In due course, different types of task were introduced, initially – but not always – under the eye of a seasoned worker or foreman. Shifts of ten or twelve hours were normal, although Thames had recently reduced its shifts to eight. Indentures were a way of providing methodical training in which the expectations of both parties were laid out. Apprentices looked for skills training and suitable mentoring. For their part, employers expected their apprentices to play a full part in whatever they were asked to do. Tasks like taking messages to the shipyard where the *Black Prince* was a-building were thus par for the course. Wallis loved the shipyard at night when jets of sparks sprayed into the dark and crucibles of candescent molten iron were poured.

The Greenwich works lay scarcely a mile from 241 New Cross Road, so he lived at home and for the next year and three quarters, six days a week (the Saturday shift was shorter) cycled to and fro. His route coincided with what had become a class boundary. The low-lying area towards the river was predominantly poor and densely populated, whereas on the steep slopes of the river terrace to the south there were semi-detached three-storeyed houses occupied by middle-class families. New Cross Gate itself was a kind of elongated island between the two, raised, paved, and thronged by news vendors and costermongers. Further on, manufacturing and processing crowded around Deptford Creek. From Deptford Bridge Wallis could see or smell a distillery, a brewery, tannery, linseed, tar and chemical works. Roperies, mast ponds, flour mills, coal wharfs, the foreign cattle market, and the river itself were daily reminders of sea-borne trade and empire. For all its clamour and muck his route to the works also evoked an older England: it was the way to Kent, Rochester and Canterbury, with echoes of Dickens, Falstaff, and the setting forth of Chaucer's pilgrims. As if in keeping with that, Thames Engineering had customs which echoed the ceremonies of Christ's Hospital. The senior manager walked the shop floor in a shiny black top hat and frock coat. The foremen of the Machine and Fitting Shops wore bowler hats.

Wallis's seemingly serious countenance led fellow apprentices to nickname him 'the Dr'. Coincidentally, a number were amateur musicians. Alf Cansdale sang and played the violin; Billy Lloyd

wrote arrangements; Percy Tibbs and Wallis were enthusiastic vo-
calists. During summer lunch breaks the four took their sandwiches
to a nearby park and gave *sotto voce* performances. Lloyd's setting
of Byron's 'Hills of Annesley' became a favourite which Wallis liked
to pick out on the piano. Lloyd introduced him to music of the
Irish composer Michael Balfe (1802–70); extracts from the overture
to Balfe's opera *The Bondman* joined their repertoire; one of Edie's
friends introduced Wallis to a singing teacher on the Old Kent Road.

Employers accustomed to apprentices who haunted music halls
and pubs would have been bemused by Wallis, who in addition to
his lunchtime singing became a choirman at the parish church. In
the course of a week he drank perhaps one glass of cider or lager.
Weekends were given to reading (nineteenth-century novels, poetry
(Tennyson a favourite)), church, or occasional visits to relatives or
friends. His only concession to works culture was smoking – he took
up a pipe, and, occasionally, cigarettes.

He taught himself to drive. His father had already acquired a
motor car, a two-seater Panhard with tiller steering, but Charles was
not mechanically minded and for some time drove it in convoy with
the pony and trap, lest the vehicle fail. Barnes was the only one in
the family who could be relied on to make it go; his account of a
journey from the south coast to New Cross in April 1906 reveals
growing accomplishment. On leaving Worthing the car did not pull
properly and eventually stopped. Wallis 'got down' and diagnosed
an ignition fault, which he fixed by the roadside. However, he continued drily, the car's pull was so poor that 'the terrific head-wind
took off more power than we could well spare'. Three miles from
Horsham he stopped again 'to do up a loose bolt on the bad tyre'.
Twelve miles out of Dorking 'I again had to tie up the bad tyre in
two places.' A mile or two later the problem recurred. He jacked up
the wheel and changed tyres. After all this, he said, the remaining
ten miles 'were quite uneventful'. Near the end, indeed, they had
overtaken a large four-seater car.[3]

At Thames things were less satisfactory. Early in August 1907
Edie, Charles and members of the family holidayed at Milford on
Sea on the Hampshire coast. Wallis came home early to return to

work and regretted having done so. 'Everything is very slack there' he wrote to Edie. 'I might just as well have had an extra week, for I have done little but stand about idle since my return.'[4] In that week the sun blazed. The heat intensified his ennui. Wallis decided to look for another employer.

Wallis's work on marine engines and visits to the shipyard had reinforced his interest in ships and seagoing. Word of mouth and study of *The Engineer* magazine identified progressive shipbuilding firms. One of them was J. Samuel White at Cowes on the Isle of Wight. Whites built launches for rivers in Africa and South America; paddle steamers for the West Indies; torpedo boats and destroyers for the Royal Navy; and steam yachts for the wealthy. They were active in marine engine design, making steam, petrol and paraffin engines for launches, and turbines, water tube boilers and diesels for larger vessels. Uncle Wwyn had a house on the island and knew some of White's staff. A further reason for Wallis's interest in the company may be that back in the late 1850s the man at its head, John Samuel White (1838–1915), had been a pupil of his grandfather John Ashby at Gothic Hall.

The transfer was negotiated with Uncle Wwyn's help, which included a loan of £40. J. Samuel White undertook to 'use their best means to teach and instruct' B. N. Wallis for the next three years. Thus it was that at the end of October 1907, just over a month after his twentieth birthday, he went out into the world.

'I woke . . . and thought so much of you'

Edie was keen to picture Barnes in her mind's eye. She accordingly travelled down with him and stayed in Mrs Cox's boarding house on Castle Road for several days.

Edie liked Cowes and admired the view across the Solent from Castle Road. Her impression of Mrs Cox, which turned out to be wrong, was that she would be 'very anxious' to take care of her son. Wallis was allocated a sitting room on the first floor and an unheated attic bedroom which was separated from the Coxes by a matchboard partition and lit by a candle. For the rooms and an evening meal Mrs Cox charged twenty-three shillings a week.

Wallis unpacked his clothes, a heavy works overcoat, books, kettle, saucepan, two small stoves that ran on methylated spirits, a chessboard and box of chessmen. Promising as it all seemed, however, when the moment of parting came Edie found it difficult. She wrote her first letter to Barnes even before she had left.

My darling Son

There seem to be so many things to say to you still, but they all resolve themselves into this – my dear love to you, & may God bless you in your new life & work. You know it all, & how dear I hold you & how close to my heart.

Also I would say, if you find this too noisy you must move, but of course you will find something of drawbacks everywhere . . .

In your 'work box' darling, you will find a red silk scarf, to wear when the cream one is dirty, also your old comb! & some more lint, & another candle. I will send your bike clips, so that if you desire, you can ride on Saturday. I will also send you some more 'baccy, as I see your pouch is nearly MT!!

I think, – nay I feel sure, you will like Cowes as a place. The end of the Parade is so pretty . . .

When you read this, I shall just be steaming into dirty, noisy London, to resume my work which lies so largely in keeping warm for my precious children, the home to which you can always turn.

Edie told him she had been 'rested' by seeing landmarks of their recent holiday across the Solent. 'To me, it was almost like looking out for home.' When he saw them, she and he would be re-connected. In any case:

It will not be long . . . before you come & see home again, so cheer up. You know you are always in the thoughts &

prayers & love of
   Your devoted mother
   God be with you till we meet again[5]

Mrs Cox propped the letter on a sideboard, where Wallis did not find it until the following evening. 'I got your note at dinner time. It seemed so empty coming back and not finding you there & I did not notice your note till I started dinner when I chanced to look round.' He had had dinner with another apprentice who had just joined White's ('quite a rarity, a gentleman's son I should think'), been for a walk in half a gale, and was about to go down for 'a smoke and a talk' with Mr Ruddle. Mr Ruddle was the curate at Holy Trinity church (where Mr Cox was verger) and another of Mrs Cox's lodgers. One of his hobbies was playing bells strung on a pole, and since his room was directly below Wallis's Edie began to worry lest the noise should keep her son awake.

For the rest of her life Edie wrote almost daily. She and Charles sent a weekly allowance to cover the cost of Barnes's lodgings. Alongside family news, advice, parish gossip and comments about the vicar's health and sermons came presents of food, cigarettes, and extra shillings scraped together between herself, Aunt Lily and others. For his part, Barnes told of long walks, strumming on Mrs Cox's piano, the backgrounds of new acquaintances, his patent method for using a hip bath in his sitting room, and churchgoing at Holy Trinity where the choir was a 'hotbed of pique and jealousy'. Holy Trinity's vicar was a chaplain to the Royal Yacht Squadron, 'wherefore he always dressed as a yachtsman – brass buttons, yachting cap and all complete!'

Edie tried to manipulate Barnes's social life from afar. At the start, she used the family's clerical connections to identify curates on the Isle of Wight who might befriend him. This soon led to a gentle protest:

I received a card from Grannie today, saying that Mr Storrs of Sandown has written to the Chaplain at Osborne who has written to a Mr Lemon, curate of St James', E. Cowes, who says he will try to call on me. Let's hope he doesn't, for it is really getting a bit too strong. Awful thought! Suppose all my numerous clerical 'lookers-up' all 'looked-up' on the same evening![6]

Relations with Mrs Cox worsened. Edie became concerned by Barnes's reports of her cooking, and worried lest she come snooping and read one of the letters: 'It would be fuel to the fire if she picked one up & saw any of it.'[7] Did his Gladstone bag have a lock? Early in 1908 Wallis left for cheaper lodgings with better food. During his last week at Castle Road Edie vented her feelings:

> My darling Barnie
> I have been thinking so much of you, – travelling with you, arriving with you, – feeling (mentally) the discomforts, and wishing oh! So much, that my love could take, & could bear all the burdens. But alas! It cannot. I can only keep on loving you . . . [Mrs Cox] is one of those scatterbrain, hysterical women that one cannot be too careful with . . . She is a Vixen – But try & pretend she is not, just for the week.[8]

Meanwhile, Wallis had settled into White's routine. From Monday to Saturday he rose at five to ready himself for the day shift which began at six. White's whistle blew at a quarter to six, the gates were closed at six sharp and stragglers let in at 6.15. Anyone arriving after this had to wait for three hours, thereby losing a quarter of a day's wages. A faulty alarm clock led to some close calls. Edie accompanied him in her imagination.

> I woke at 5 AM & prayed for you, & stayed awake thinking of you till past 6. So you had company you knew not of.[9]

Again:

> I woke at 4.50 this morning, & thought so much of you, & I slept in snatches till past 6 – & had you in mind throughout.

I fear you had a horrid cold wind, – it blew strong here from the N.[10]

And again:

. . . it did so pour here about 6 o'cl. I thought so of you, & did so hope we had the rain and you had the dry. Minna tells me she is always awake between 5 & 6 AM & always praying then for you. You are so constantly in the thoughts of the family, to say nothing of your parents. You ought to feel a sort of warm envelope, it is an atmosphere of love.[11]

Wallis took to working through his lunch break, munching bread and cheese as he did so. The day shift finished at five thirty in the afternoon, except on Saturdays when the yard closed at one. Safety was hit and miss, and mostly left to the individual. In one letter Wallis told of a gas explosion.[12] In another he described a near-fatal incident involving the swinging jib of a crane and a visiting photographer.[13] He thrived on the activity, enjoyed the rhythm of the week, and relished the training.

Getting on

During the next three and a half years Wallis worked hard, formed friendships, kept fit through sport, obtained qualifications, and achieved some independence from his mother without weakening their relationship. 'He had purpose and ambition . . . he was young, strong, basically healthy, active and sociable. In so far as his mother would let him, he disregarded his ailments, and though he revered and loved his parents deeply, especially his mother . . . his life was too full of plans, hopes, interests and activities to pine and languish.'[14] The period is minutely documented: well over a thousand letters passed between Wallis and his parents between 1907 and 1911, nearly all of them survive, and while most of them went from New Cross to Cowes, Wallis's weekly letters home paint bright pictures. For example:

3 April 1910

[. . .] Soper is back from College for the Easter vac so
Cooper I and he arranged to have supper in my room.
We played cards & had six bottles of soda water, & six
pennyworth of oranges & a shillingsworth of cigars & made
merry . . . After supper we felt inclined for a spree, so they
decided not to go home for the night. We played bridge
to see who should sleep in the bed and after an hour & a
half play, Cooper was declared winner with 7 points. Soper
had 64 & I had 20. I seemed fated to lose my bed from
the very first game. Fortunately there are two mattresses
on the bed so Soper & I shared one mattress on the floor.
We also dragged the sheets & a pillow each & a blanket
leaving Cooper two blankets a bolster & the coverlet. We
laid a table & my trousers presser on edge to keep off the
draught & with my rug & overcoats we spent a comfortable
night. We turned in about halfpast two but we couldn't
sleep for laughing ever so long. Mrs B was awfully decent.
We thought she didn't know as she went to bed early, &
they were just going home for breakfast, when she poked
her head round the back door & said 'Won't you stop to
breakfast, you may as well make a week of it now you are
here.' So they all came in again. [. . .][15]

In contrast:

10 January 1909

[. . .] today I walked with [Cooper] from 2 till 6. We
went all along the Osborne Estate . . . It's awfully pretty
along the shore, all wooded right down to the sea wall.
We saw the old Queen's bathing place, now in ruins, & a
highly ornamental bathing machine, drawn up under a big
roof which also housed a large frame . . . which had rails
running into the sea, I should imagine for launching a boat.
The bathing machine was on a long stone causeway with
grooves for the wheels running right out to sea to enable a

bather to get a good dip at any state of the tide. Everything was more or less in ruins . . . I am told that in the Queen's time everything was most beautifully kept & that one can drive 12 miles on the estate without traversing any road twice.[16]

Or again:

15 January 1911

[. . .] I got on very well on Friday when the boat went out on trial.[17] I was down in the engine room about five hours altogether & was not at all sea sick. We went out about 9.30 & ran three trials of one hour each, out in the Channel at the outside of the island. During the three hours I took just on 350 records of pumps, gauges etc. It was pretty rough & a strong north wind was blowing. We did about 28 knots on the full power run.

The firm look after the draughtsmen very well, even providing one with great leather gauntlets in case you should hold of a red hot pipe. One has to do a great deal of climbing about & should one in a dreadful lurch catch hold of something hot, one is faced with the fearful alternative shall I let go & break my neck or shall I hold on & burn my hand. They gave us an awfully good dinner, tho' we didn't get it till nearly three. I had soup (not tomato) chicken & ham, apple tart & cream & a whisky & soda followed by free cigarettes. I don't think I've eaten so big a dinner since I was in camp at August & didn't have indigestion either. We got back about 4.30.

[. . .] I am going to tea and supper at Fishers tonight to meet a brilliant pianist.[18]

Wallis's head was full of melody. 'I never knew how much I loved good music till I came down here, where one never hears any.'[19] On night shifts he sometimes sang with Harold and Archie Paskins, sons of a fish merchant in Cowes High Street who farmed oyster beds in the Newtown estuary. Harold had a fine tenor voice. During night shifts Harold sang popular songs with which others joined in improvised harmony. Their performances became so exuberant that nearby residents complained. Wallis's letters hummed with references to performances by the local operatic society, organ recitals after evensong, visiting musicians, brass bands, songs, recitals. The 'brilliant pianist' seems to have been Daisy Jones, who spent most weeks in London where she was an assistant professor at the Royal Academy of Music and came down to Cowes at weekends. Wallis was struck by the Chopin nocturne she played that evening; he had assumed that a nocturne would be restful and was startled by the drama of its middle part. Daisy was four years older than Wallis, and had already appeared in another letter:

> On Friday the Tennis Club gave a small dance, about 60 being present. The hall was very prettily decorated & and the floor was in splendid condition . . . I had an introduction to & a set of Lancers with a Miss Jones . . . She's quite young & jolly & not a bit professor-like.[20]

Wallis joined the tennis club in 1908, calculating that by doing so he could combine fitness, new friendships (mixed doubles, croquet alongside the courts), and off-duty opportunities to mix with senior staff from J. Samuel White. In winter the club fielded a football team in which Wallis played as a back.

Club social events included dances, and Barnes began to take dancing lessons. Edie was aghast. 'Be careful about the dancing!' she told him. 'So afraid of this mixed company.'[21] Edie feared that Barnes would fall in love and turn away from her – an eventuality that gained in likelihood from January 1909 when romance bloomed between John and Violet Clara Kington Statham, daughter of the vicar of All Saints, Hatcham Park.[22] Edie implored Barnes: 'I do ask you just to be a little careful not to lose your heart to any of the girls you meet'.[23] Wallis's reaction to news of his brother's engagement was muted. Edie piled on the pressure:

I feel I have lost something, dearest Barnes, before I gained it. It is quite impossible for John & you to realize how Father and I have looked forward to the young manhood of you two, & to leaning on you both for counsel & strength. We denied ourselves all the advantages we should have reaped had we put you both at 16 to office or business work, – & now just when we looked for reward & return, John hies him away most definitely, upon another quest. He is now beyond my influence altogether, – he belongs to someone else, so I turn more than ever to you, dear son – & much as I desire your happiness, I do hope it will not just yet take the form of an engagement – else indeed I shall feel deserted . . . Remember how I lean upon you.[24]

Several following letters are missing, perhaps because they were destroyed. To judge from the next of Wallis's that survives, Edie's emotional blackmail became unacceptable and he put his foot down.[25] There were more episodes like this, although whether it was loyalty to his mother or simply chance that averted romantic entanglement at Cowes we do not know.[26] At any rate, there are no signs of a lost heart in following letters, although his Christmas list for 1909 suggests preoccupation with appearance:

I want a good razor strop, some soft shirts John will tell you what sort if you don't know, a tie from Annie whole colour. No pipes, or tobacco. I could do with some fancy socks, tho' I don't think any of you would make a decent choice, except perhaps Auntie May.[27]

Earlier that year the lease on 241 New Cross Road had expired and the Wallises moved to 12 Pepys Road, a larger residence in a more prosperous area on the slope of Telegraph Hill. The house had a basement and a small terrace at the back with steps down into a long narrow sooty garden, at the end of which was a tram shed 'with attendant squealing and clanking of trams going in and out'.[28]

Wallis's friends in Cowes were predominantly male and around his own age. They included Archie Watts and John Cooper, fellow apprentices at White's. Also in the circle were Douglas Civil, a student, and his elder brother Henry (known as Vic) who worked as a schoolmaster in Ramsgate. Archie Watts and John Cooper had sisters with whom Wallis became friendly. 'Arch', Wallis and the Civils often operated as a foursome, liking to sail on the Solent in summer and camp among the creeks, meadows and ancient woodlands around Newtown in August. For Wallis, this district became an enchanted landscape: a secret realm of pools, glades, lancing sunlight and stag-headed oaks to which, years later, he went back.

John Cooper was a frequent companion on long walks and cycle rides. Cooper's father was a former coastguard, 'a nice old chap' who told yarns about shipwrecks on the Cornish coast. Wallis was touched when the family invited him to visit whenever he liked, even though 'they are not gentlefolk'.[29] Not central to this circle, but overlapping with it, were Herbert and Aileen Fisher, who were married and older. Wallis got to know them in September 1909. Herbert was a GP in East Cowes whose father's career as a naval surgeon had taken the family across the world and culminated in his appointment as Inspector-General of Hospitals and Fleets. 'He has a very nice wife & they asked me to go in whenever I wished & to tea on Sundays.'[30]

The Fishers' link with Daisy Jones was the piano: piano playing was Herbert Fisher's chief pastime. In the spring of 1910, he exchanged his upright for an Ibach concert grand, the structural properties of which Wallis wasted no time in getting to know: 'Two of the notes were just a shade hard, so we took the action out and softened the felts a little.' Wallis explained that it was only necessary to undo one bar in front of the keyboard '& all the action slides out onto your knees'.[31] Wallis often mentioned the piece which Fisher was currently practising – the Grieg sonata 'sounded magnificent'. Edie sent Fisher a copy of Chopin's B flat minor sonata in thanks for his generosity to her son. For a time, Wallis toyed with the idea of learning to play himself.

Wallis became as close to the Fishers as with anyone around this time. He often stayed with them at weekends, sat up with them on New Year's Eve, and campaigned for Herbert's election as chairman of the Tennis Club. Aileen was a trained nurse and when Wallis was ill she mothered him. Affinity was helped by similarities of background – a GP household, lots of music – and Wallis may have valued confidantes who were emotionally calmer than his own mother.

Wallis certainly needed to protect his objectivity in the face of Edie's excitable daily reports about health, injured pets, malfunctioning gas fires, young Charles falling behind at school and upsets blamed on unreliable servants. In addition, she encumbered him with lists of looming financial commitments and possessions to be sold to meet them. Such letters were a source of deep distress to Wallis. In May 1910 Edie itemised forthcoming costs of intensified tuition for young Charles, whose entrance exam to CH was approaching. Wallis replied:

> [. . .] I am so very very sorry to think of your having to sell those two plaques. I feel such a useless log. I've only got £2 in the Arsenal and 7/6 in the PO but you are very welcome to that if you want it, tho' I know it's perfectly useless being such a drop in the ocean [. . .][32]

Wallis resolved to sell the lathe he had bought with the Willcox prize money, and a month later wrote to say that a money order for £12 – over £1000 at today's prices – was on its way. The next day he added good news: his weekly salary was to be raised. 'The Chief saw me today & is giving me 35/-. I only really hoped for 30/- wh[ich] is what the others in my p[o]s[itio]n have always got so I was very pleased.'[33]

Initially, Edie accepted the lathe money with good grace.[34] But this was not the end of it. John was living at home, and three weeks later Edie's cook gave notice.

> This makes everything very awkward, I am puzzling what to do. But, in any case, my dearest Barnie, Father & I, (as John has nothing in prospect, & may be at home in the Autumn) feel we really ought *not* to spend to go away, – not even your

loving present, which is really needed to help in the necessities, Father is getting no bills paid to him, – & we have exhausted our credit overdraft, – so that what we are going on now, is his salary paid last June, & £20 Auntie has advanced for the trap. I have to meet, Father's insurance, (£7.12), Charlie's School fees (£7) the servants' wages, & our keep, & all incidental, small expenses, – as well as eventually to pay the trap in Sept but then I shall have £16.13.4 from Ben towards it that month – that is why we can use the £20 Auntie advanced.

This says nothing about Father's drug bills. Of course, if we could depend on the money coming in that is due to him, it would be different. For instance, Mr Adams owes him £17, a Mr Warren £8, and Mrs Boughton £3.10 those *three alone* make £28.10 – but there it is . . . we must face the fact that we may have John at home for some time. It is a year now since he took his degree & during that time till now, he has been principally not merely at home. But, poor darling, quite dependent on us for pocket money, minor clothes (such as shirts, collars, repairs etc – I paid 30/- for this the 1st week in June) . . .

Not for anything would I have him think we grudged it, *because we don't*, nor should I even talk to him as I am doing to you, but I think I owe it to you, to tell you freely else you might think I *ought* to use your gift otherwise. Annie's travelling to the Sch. of Art comes to 2/6 a week, & I have just had to pay £3 fees, for her, (last week) and last week too £4.4 for rates. So much did I hate giving poor dear John money, for *his* sake, that I used – but you must not breathe a word please . . .[35]

And so on. Edie's periodic dumping of cares at her son's feet some-times recalls the lamentations of Mrs Bennet in *Pride and Prejudice*. In this instance, the immediate crisis soon passed: 'Aunty Lily is very kindly paying Father's insurance & Chaggles' fees, which will leave us free to use your £12 you so generously gave us for a holiday, & we hope to come down to Cowes on, or about, Aug 17, if that suits you.'[36] However, this was a lot less than the two months out of London that Barnes had urged and for which he had sold his lathe. Nor does Edie seem to have thought through the implications of depicting John as part of the problem over which Barnes was agonising.

Edie's letters told much of the doings of John and Violet – who was usually known by her nickname 'Ba' (pronounced 'Bay', short for 'baby') – often in ways that added to the emotional burdens that Barnes was being expected to carry. John had completed his degree at Oxford, set his heart on a post at the British Museum, but failed to obtain it.

> John has said very little about his failure. How did he take the news? It was awful sending it. And how *could* you go off without telling him, & yet leave the empty envelope about! Father and I spent nearly an hour discussing that telegram, & how best to save John a moment of unnecessary pain . . .[37]

Two months later John was invited to interview for a teaching post at Uppingham School. Edie was thrilled: if he succeeded their financial pressures would be much reduced.

> The screw is £230 to start, & after a year, probably an increase of £30, & private pupils, & – in 10 or 15 years, a housemastership, £1000 a year – and you retire at 60 with a pension.[38]

But the school chose someone else. 'I am so sorry for poor old John' wrote Wallis; 'I am afraid you must have rather built on his getting it tho' nobody liked to say so.'[39] In due course John was appointed as an assistant master at CH.

Ba was the 'treasured only child' of Hatcham's vicar, the Rev Dr Sherrard Montagu Statham, and his wife Clara. Annie described her as at once quiet yet gently outgoing, sociable yet contained. Annie was impressed by her dexterity in technical things, like repairing clocks, woodwork, or working a stocking knitting machine. She had received no training in such skills, and since the Rev Statham had schooled her at home, teaching her Latin and Greek 'as though she were a boy', it was not clear how they had been acquired. Similar mystery attended Ba's prowess as a pianist. She was capable of playing almost anything at sight, and the Wallis's house in Pepys Road rang to her performances. Edie and her sisters periodically urged that she be given formal training, but Dr Statham declined.

The Stathams had arrived in Hatcham in 1907. Since then, Wallis's father had been elected a churchwarden. Parochial quarrels, church fundraising and Statham's sermons (his handbook *One Hundred Brief Aids to Extempore Preaching* was published in 1937) became regular topics in Edie's letters. The engagement naturally led to greater closeness between the two families and introductions to relatives. Wallis's life at Cowes kept him clear of most of this, for which he was glad. He did not have much time for Sherrard Statham, and even less for Statham's younger brother, Samuel Percy Hammond Statham, who was also ordained, and who to Wallis's dismay arrived on the Isle of Wight in 1909 as chaplain at Parkhurst prison. Ba and her parents thus gained reason to visit the island, and periodically did so. On these occasions Edie wrote in advance to encourage the coming together of Stathams and Wallises. A trial of wills ensued in which Edie's fixation with the need to show correct behaviour towards the Stathams was parried by Wallis's equal and opposite determination to avoid them.

Wallis's principal interest in Parkhurst at this time was boxing.

I am glad to say I have been able to arrange to get some boxing with Arch up at Parkhurst for 5/- each fortnight on Saturday afternoon. We went up yesterday & had a fine time. The instructor is Corporal Hemmings who is an ex lightweight champion of India. He's been home six months & his weight has gone from 9 to 11 stone so there's not much light weight about him now. We have the whole gym to ourselves. He seems a very good man.[40]

Wallis took up competitive rifle shooting (which drew from Edie the comment that 'it is a sort of *duty* for an Englishman to learn to shoot'), while his enthusiasm for tennis had a lot to do with the location of the club's courts. He loved their seclusion in the wooded grounds of East Cowes Castle and spent contented hours there re-aligning the courts to optimise their orientation in relation to sun and shadow, cutting grass, and wiring fairy lights in trees for evening soirees. His election as club secretary went hand in hand with his quest for fitness, for it was his job to wheel the heavy tea urn and stove up to the courts in a barrow.

The head of White's drawing office, Herbert Harper (known as 'the Chief'), was the tennis club's treasurer. Wallis thus had opportunity to meet him out of hours. However, Wallis's promotion to the drawing office in September 1909 (at twenty-five shillings a week) was entirely a result of his ability and industriousness. Even when suffering from migraine he would try to do essential work, sometimes vomiting in the street on the way to or from the works (an act he disliked because he thought it ungentlemanly). Assiduous timekeeping had sometimes prevented visits home; on one occasion he sent his mother a parcel of primroses he had picked to compensate for his absence.[41] Earlier in the year he told her: 'the Chief seems to view me favourably tho' I'm not counting on anything & think Carnt [White's managing director] might stand in my way. I hope if he does, to fall back on Wwyn's persuasive powers.'[42]

Wallis's apprenticeship had been combined with technical school and private coursework. During winter, there were classes on two evenings a week with others given to study. Wednesdays were for dancing, and there was Whist Club on Fridays. Wallis sometimes varied the routine, joining Watts and the Civils for supper (usually followed by card games and singing into the small hours), or a trip to the 'animated pictures' at Poole's Picture Theatre.

Wallis often went to Archie Watts's house to study; the two worked on opposite sides of the table. The evening classes led to a Mechanics Exam in May 1909 and an Applied Mechanics Exam in April 1910, both of which he passed. In September 1910 Wallis regis-tered for further study of applied mechanics through the University Correspondence College in London. In spare moments he taught himself Morse code, and the Greek alphabet.

Whites were at the mercy of irregular government procurement.

Five warships were laid down for the Royal Navy in 1907, and five in 1908, but in 1909 only two contracts were awarded. In some periods there was business from foreign governments, but at the start of 1911:

> Things are very slack in the office.
>
> Two fellows have left within the week & another has just had notice bringing the staff down to 15, whereas the full strength is about 25. I expect I shall have to look for another job soon as there is not a scrap of work nor any in prospect for months.[43]

White's were nonetheless keen to keep him.

Wallis lived his industrious early twenties against a background of daily reports of his mother's asthma, bronchitis and consequential heart trouble, and his father's ailments. In addition to his disability, Charles was often laid out by excruciating headaches which impeded his work, and thus his income. Both parents suffered from a high frequency of dental problems. It was Edie's asthma, however, that dominated. Its cruelty became a kind of continuum: few of her letters fail to mention attacks, and her son opened most of his by being sorry to hear of them. By later 1908 the condition had worsened to a point at which nursing was needed. By 1910 Edie was more or less resigned to the life of a semi-invalid. At times she was unable even to dress herself and prone to attacks that became life-or-death crises. There were times of remission ('My asthma has been better since Monday, I feel a different creature . . . & I am sleeping better') but overall, the path was downhill.

Insight into the extremity of Edie's condition is provided by an hour by hour record she kept in August 1910. She believed that attacks were linked to weather, and recorded both. Her emergence from a 'very prolonged attack' that began in the early hours of 19 August prompted her to write 'The Lord stood by me'. Still awake at a quarter to five that morning she watched a thrush and blackbird searching for worms as the dawn came up. Here was another terrible feature: for days at a time Edie was getting very little sleep.

Edie believed that attacks were activated by the approach of rain. She also thought they could be triggered by geography, a person being more at risk in some places than in others (she regarded the Isle of Wight with extreme suspicion in this respect), and by celestial events. When Halley's comet appeared in May 1910 she became extremely wary. Side effects of treatment involving adrenaline, sometimes by injection,[44] included vasoconstriction that increased blood pressure and heart rate, and incidentally caused her to feel nervy and fretful – characteristics of her letters after acute attacks. However, adrenaline provided only short-term relief. At various times Edie was taken to specialists, whose prescribed treatments – an operation on her jaw, for example, or a special diet – did nothing to ameliorate the asthma and increased her distress.

It seems that no one, save possibly Barnes, considered environmental factors like smog, smoke in the household, or the fluff from her canaries (now named after famous musicians) as possible aggravating influences. In 1910 she acquired a puppy, Tinker, who grew large and boisterous, ruled her affections, and shed hair and dander around the house. As for air pollution, Edie's descriptions of winter smogs stand beside those of Dickens, as when Charles visited a patient in the Lewisham workhouse and found so much vapour drifting in a large ward that the inmates were mere shadows.

Edie's distress was accompanied by widening swings of mood. At some times she presented herself as cheerful, still able to see the funny side of a situation and eager for her children. At others she was depressed, fearful, even accusatory. 'I am still very weak & ill, but must try and get a letter to you, for I feel anxious about you – partly because although you knew I had been so ill, I have had no letter, or PC . . .' In previous days Edie had been dangerously ill, but Aunt Lily's reports had downplayed the seriousness of her condition. Wallis was accordingly mortified by the charge of indifference, the more so for the fact that he was just then working twelve-hour days for Whites and flat out for Matriculation. 'I must complain very strongly against the carefully edited accounts which I am permitted to receive when you are ill . . . As if life weren't wretched enough already without having a letter like that.'[45] His distress was increased by Edie introducing wishes in the event of her death: 'I should wish John and Ba to marry, & Father to make his *home* there'; Charles would be at school '& I should like you to take Annie. I think it could be arranged, about her support, with help perhaps from her Aunts, & a little from Father'.[46] To which Barnes responded: 'I do not wish to discuss the breaking up of our home by letter, & will only remark that I should be of the opinion that I am a quite unsuitable person for a young girl of Annie's nature to come & live with.'[47]

Edie explained. '*If* at any time whilst living at Cowes, it should seem best for Annie to come and live with you, I should want her to have as many friends of her own position as possible, – it is so much easier to fall unconsciously to a lower standard of friendly inferiors . . .'[48] 'Friendly inferiors' meant people like Cooper and the Civils (whose father was a house-painter). Moreover, since the only consistent mark of a gentleman was formal education we have a context for Charles's reaction to the telegram in late July 1911 that reported Barnes's Matriculation result:

> Hearty congratulations on your success! It is indeed capital. You have the reward of all your hard work. Mother is so pleased and no doubt has written to say so. She is so much better.[49]

As the summer of 1911 drew on, things did indeed seem to be looking up. There was more work in the yard so overtime restarted, which meant greater security and opportunity to send extra money home. After the exams Wallis was free of migraine. The weather was dry and warm for weeks, which meant light clothes in the drawing office and swimming before breakfast. He remembered Annie's eighteenth birthday without being prompted and looked forward to the start of his week's camping with Archie and the Civils at the end of July. After that he suggested that Charlie and Annie should come down to Cowes for three weeks. They could even bring Tinker. Their holiday would give Edie a break.

On 12 August, he met them as they stepped off the ferry. Charlie was unwell for a few days, and Wallis found the dog a nuisance but Aileen Fisher helped to look after both, prompting Edie to offer one of her canaries in recompense. Edie's health had again been giving concern. On 25 August Charles Wallis took her to see a specialist for an opinion on her heart problems. His reaction encouraged her. She told Barnes: 'I don't gather anything is serious'.[50]

'Everything in the world to me'

Four days later, identical telegrams were delivered at breakfast time to Southwick Villa and Whites: 'Mother dangerously ill – all come at once – wire time of arrival – Father'.[51]

Wallis gathered Annie and Charles, took them to the ferry and caught the train to London. In fact, Edie was already dead. She had gone in the night. Charles had worded the telegram to prepare them for the worst.

It is not clear how far Barnes was aware that his mother had been emptied. She had been debilitated for four years and he had received daily reports. Maybe that was why he was unprepared; there had been intermittent improvements, and on these he had pinned his hopes, whereas the episodes of remission had been against a background of underlying decline. At any rate, the death took him unawares and left him in a kind of melancholic shock. To the end of his life, he carried a small, framed photograph of Edie and himself, taken that June, the last to show them together.

The loss changed him. Hitherto he had been buoyed by hopes and optimism; now, he said, the future seemed 'dark and unpromising'. Much later, when he had fallen in love, he was unable to mention Edie without breaking down.

You may think it silly for a man, but although it's nearly twelve years since she died, I simply cannot talk about it without making an idiot of myself. You see, she was everything in the world to me . . . I simply worshipped her.[52]

A month on:

> I've never talked to a soul about her and she filled so large a
> part of my life. During the latter years I used to have a letter
> from her every day of the week. I've got them all still treasured,
> hundreds and hundreds. You see I went away to school when
> I was 12, then was at home just for 2 years from 16 to 18, and
> have never been at home since, except for an odd time or two
> . . . and never during her lifetime.[53]

John registered the death. Letters of condolence arrived from
those who lived too far away to give them in person. Herbert Harper,
his supervisor in the drawing office, wrote: 'I lost my mother under
similar circumstances so know how you must be feeling . . . Make
your own arrangements about returning to business & do not
hurry.'[54] Letters from friends reveal the extent of his circle. It was
not large. Nine wrote from Cowes, and a tenth (an old acquaintance
from Thames Engineering) from Lewisham. Archie and Teresa Watts
each sent a letter; so did Herbert and Aileen Fisher, who had taken
charge of the dog. Aileen wrote twice, the first on the same day as
the telegram in the belief that Edie was still alive and holding on.
Vic Civil wrote on behalf of his mother and Doug. Mrs Bloomfield,
his landlady at Gordon Road, sent a 'wee tribute of Lilly's' (lilies),
and forwarded his best black boots.[55] On Friday 1 September he
polished and wore them for the funeral at All Saints. Some of those
on Charles's GP list stood in silence as they passed on the way to
Brockley Cemetery.

Wallis stayed on at Pepys Road with John, Annie, and his father
until the middle of the following week. Back at Cowes a letter awaited him. It was from his father, who told him it would be 'a very
inadequate substitute for the loving greeting that your dear Mother
used to send to your rooms on your return to Cowes. And yet it
is a greeting from her – for it is her influence that induced me to
think of writing to you.' Charles continued: 'It is perhaps given to
our beloved dead to influence our minds and wills in ways we are
not conscious of.'[56] He would never be carefree or merry again, 'but

please God I shall try to be cheerful, because I know that would please her best.'

During Wallis's absence Archie Watts and a Civil brother had bought a small sailing boat; on the following Saturday they determined to take Wallis out in it to distract him. There was wind and the Solent was rough. After the stifling heat and funereal formality Wallis enjoyed the energy and force, telling his father that they had returned soaked through and that he was 'thinking of going shares' in the boat 'with Arch and one of the Civils'. He hoped Annie was better.

In fact, Annie was traumatised. The following week Charles asked Wallis to send the dog back to comfort her. This caused minor embarrassment as Tinker had now settled in with the Fishers, who were expecting to keep him. In due course Wallis took the dog to Southampton, bought a chain and handed him into the keeping of the guard of a London-bound train.[57] From that day until the end of his life Wallis had nothing to do with pet animals. He moved out of his lodgings. Herbert and Aileen Fisher offered him a room which he accepted. He told his father: 'Have come over here to live as lodgings were unbearable.'[58]

Wallis tried to stifle grief by being busy. In free time he ran across the island's chalk hills and designed a cross for Edie's grave. But he was in a daze. In place of Edie's daily chatty letters that told of her canaries, hens, sisters, who had been to tea or which Rachmaninov prelude Ba was practising, there was nothing. Headaches returned. He wondered if long hours of drawing were affecting his eyesight. On Sunday 24 September he wrote to his father: 'Have had to stop working overtime for a bit. The chief was very kind.'

Earlier that same day naval men at the other end of the country were guiding His Majesty's Airship No. 1 out of the shed where she had been under construction since mid-1910. The ship was nicknamed 'Mayfly', and her builders were the firm of Vickers in Barrow-in-Furness. The Admiralty had commissioned No. 1 because airships looked likely to alter the balance of power. They enabled naval commanders to see their adversaries long before they became visible at the surface. From the deck of a destroyer, the horizon was about nine sea miles away. From an airship at three thousand feet, it was over sixty. Nine military airships had already flown in Germany; in Britain, none. It was hoped that the experience of building and flying No. 1 would begin to redress that. Vickers had tried to launch her before, but problems forced her return for modification. Within twenty minutes of her re-emergence *Mayfly* folded at the centre. The court of inquiry concluded the wreck was the result of a sudden squall; others said this was a canard to avert embarrassment.

The debacle was well publicised, but given Wallis's other preoccupations it is a question whether he took much notice. Edwin Carnt, White's managing director, was setting up an aviation department,[59] but when Wallis wrote to him six months later it was about something else.

> Dear Sir
>
> Since the adoption of the Diesel Engine by Messrs White, and as their output increases, it may be possible that the firm will require some trained men to send out to run each engine for a start . . . judging by the engineers sent out with the M.A.N. engines,[60] I gather that a man of some theoretical as well as practical training is required.
>
> If you are thinking of training anyone for this purpose, I should be glad to offer myself for the post.[61]

Wallis was willing to gain necessary experience by working 'in the shops at the usual men's hours . . . and to work at the test bench as a fitter'. He reminded Carnt of his motor engine experience at Thames, his good timekeeping and his recent qualification as a student of the Institution of Civil Engineers. Beyond this, he had 'some knowledge of French and German'.[62] In a nutshell, with Edie gone he was making himself available to represent the firm overseas. Whites agreed and raised his salary to thirty-five shillings a week.

That month, another diesel specialist joined the company. He was twenty-four years old, tall, with dark hair and a lean face. Looking at photographs it is easy to imagine him as serious-minded, perhaps even dour, but his letters reveal a sunny temperament. He was also clear-minded, always striking through to the point. His name was Hartley Blyth Pratt.

Pratt

Pratt came to Cowes in March 1912 from Barrow-in-Furness where his father, Robert Pratt, was head of the town's School of Science and Art. Robert and his wife Jeannie came from Scotland. Barrow had been their home since 1882 and all but two of their seven surviving children were born there. Among them were two elder brothers, Alexander, an engineer draughtsman, and Robert, a marine engineer, both of whom worked for Vickers.

Pratt had followed them into the company and by 1909 was working in the submarine diesel engine department. In May that year the Admiralty contract to design and build Airship No. 1 was awarded to Vickers, who placed the project in the hands of Charles Roberton, a Glaswegian in his mid-fifties who managed their marine engine department. Roberton was a good engineer, but like everyone else in Britain at that time he had no experience of building rigid airships. He did not realise how much theoretical work was needed to enter the new field, and it has been said that even if he had, he did not possess the mathematical training to put it into effect.[63] One who did was Hartley Pratt, who was duly seconded to the airship design team.

Roberton produced his initial design before the Admiralty had given proper thought as to what it wanted their airship to do. When the full specification did arrive efforts to meet it were dogged by a flow of ever-changing demands which added weight.[64] Roberton became anxious and decided to lighten the ship by removing parts of her structure. Pratt calculated that in this altered condition the structure would fail, which it duly did. Roberton took Pratt's advice as a challenge to his own judgement and sent him back to the engine drawing office. When shortly afterwards Vickers asked all the drawing office staff to sign five-year contracts, Pratt refused. Vickers responded by giving him one week's notice.

Pratt looked around for work. He applied to Whites, who just then were taking up marine diesel design. Harper noted that Pratt and Wallis had mutual interests and sat them side by side. Wallis introduced Pratt to the works and to his friends. Pratt, like Wallis, was a committed runner and as evenings lengthened they ran together or went out in the boat.[65] When summer came there was an early-morning swim. Close in age, with like interests and at similar stages in their careers, they became good friends.

In May Uncle Wwyn instigated discussion about whether Wallis should move to broaden his experience. Wallis discussed the idea with Carnt, who persuaded him to stay. In November Wwyn tried again, telling Wallis of a meeting he had had with the superintendent of Southern Nigeria. 'The pay is good, & the leave (every year) is long, 3 or 4 months I believe'.[66] Wallis replied, still writing on black-edged paper: 'I hope some of the trade the *Daily Mail* is raving about has come your way – it hasn't struck poor old John Samuel.' White's order book was again low. 'I expect they will make up for it by sacking about 2 clerks.'[67]

A few weeks before Pratt's arrival *The Engineer* magazine had published an article about airships which warned that their 'bulky mass' and 'unwieldy habits' predestined them to 'failure and disaster'. The future, it said, lay with heavier-than-air aeroplanes. The proper place for the airship was 'the lumber room of the inventor', but there were still many who clung to their faith in it.[68]

It was not only optimists who were thinking about airships. In mid-1912 the Admiralty considered a report from a sub-committee of the Committee on Imperial Defence which said that it was 'difficult to exaggerate' the advantage to Germany of vessels that could reconnoitre large areas of the North Sea and thereby 'accomplish the work of a large number of scouting cruisers'. Next to a cruiser, moreover, an airship was cheap.[69] Towards the end of 1912 there came a national psychosis in which members of the public began to report sightings of airships all over Britain. Such stories multiplied, and since Britain herself possessed no airships it was widely assumed that the supposed visitors must be Zeppelins, which in turn fed fear of German ill-intention. 'Scareship' fever was intensified by the press and given spurious authority by the attention it received in Parliament. By March 1913 hysteria had reached a point at which Britain's inability to counter the imagined intrusions had become evidence of her ill-preparedness.[70]

On 29 March *Flight* published an international table of government-owned airships in which Britain barely featured. Two days later the first of three articles about future warfare by H. G. Wells appeared in the *Daily Mail*.[71] In the second, entitled 'Put not your trust in Dreadnoughts', Wells warned that things like torpedo boats, sea planes and aeroplanes were cheap to make and expendable to use; they could readily be set against battleships that were being built at vast public expense. He continued: 'On the cloudy and foggy nights so frequent about these islands he will have extraordinary chances, and sooner or later, unless we beat him thoroughly in the air above and in the waters beneath, for neither of which proceedings we are prepared, some of these chances will come off, *and we shall lose a Dreadnought*.'[72]

The third Wells article coincided with a Parliamentary debate about air defence.[73] Rowland Hunt, the member for Ludlow, had asked the prime minister if he was aware of a claim that any German airship could fly to Ireland non-stop, overfly Portsmouth and Plymouth on the way and return by way of the Orkneys and Edinburgh. Since night-flying airships might go undetected until after they had engaged in acts of war, what steps did the Government propose to guard against this danger?[74] The Member for Dulwich asked if there were armed German rigids with a range of more than 500 miles, capable of 40 miles an hour or over. If so, how many, and 'how many airships of equal value are in the possession of, or have been laid down for, the British Navy?' Churchill replied that the British navy had none but would be acquiring two in the next month. He did not say that they were being bought from Germany. When pressed on whether Britain would build airships Churchill said that the matter was 'under consideration'.[75]

Churchill's oblique reply was given in the knowledge that Vickers had just been put on notice that airship building would resume. But it would do so from scratch. Sir Trevor Dawson, Vickers' managing director, faced the same problem as had existed in 1909: no one in his company had any experience of how airships were built. This is one reason why British intelligence had shown much interest in events of the previous week when a new Zeppelin, the LZ 16, had inadvertently landed on French soil.[76]

Dawson thought back to the *Mayfly*. He remembered Pratt and asked after him, only to be told that he had gone. Dawson ordered him found, and several days later invited him to Vickers House in Westminster. Dawson asked him to head the new airship department. To ensure progress and minimise resentment at Barrow, Dawson ruled that the new airship unit should be based in London and report directly to him.

So it was that a concatenation of public hysteria, media flimflam and political frenzy led Pratt to give his notice to J. Samuel White and re-join Vickers. A week later Wallis walked with him to the ferry. As the paddles began to thrash Wallis called out: if Pratt ever needed an assistant, he would be glad to join him.

'This amazing adventure'

It took the government another three months to confirm its intention to commission airships. Pratt used the hiatus to travel to France and Germany to glean what he could about airship construction. His companion on this reconnaissance was a naval officer, Edward Masterman.

Wallis, meanwhile, continued with experimental diesel work, and fettled his sailing dinghy. Friday, 1 August 1913 dawned dull and a little cool. The works holiday fortnight had begun; he was looking forward to a day's sailing. As he stepped out he met the postman.

Private and Confidential
Vickers House
Broadway
Westminster

July 31st /13

Dear Wallis

I expect this letter may find you away on your holidays but I trust may be forwarded to you in good time.

I have at last got things settled down to working order in the Airship Dept.

I am, as you know, Chief Draughtsman. The D.O. is to remain in London as my headquarters, where all the designing and technical work is to be done.

There is also at Barrow a D.O. to be devoted solely to the getting out of detail drawings and working drawings for the shops from the designs supplied from London.

I have sent the man I had with me here to Barrow as leading hand there and started a number of detail men there.

I have now to get several first-class men for the London office who will be engaged on design work only.

I have not yet definitely engaged any men and none are available from Barrow.

I have a free hand to engage the men I require; the one condition being that I know sufficient about them to be responsible for their secrecy on the work.

If you care to consider taking the position of Chief Assistant I could assure you of good salary and prospects.

As I would occasionally be away in Barrow and elsewhere the position would involve frequently having charge of the office and so coming into contact with Sir Trevor Dawson the head of the firm to whom I am directly responsible for the design.

I may tell you in strict confidence that we now have

orders for 3 Parseval Ships and one Zeppellin [sic] larger than any yet made, for the design of which I am responsible.[77] The Admiralty have promised orders for a large number of Zepellins [sic] as soon as we produce the goods.

If you are in town for the holidays I would be pleased to see you and discuss the matter.

Kindly let me know as soon as possible if you care to consider the offer.

Kindest regards

Yours sincerely

H. B. Pratt[78]

Wallis replied by telegram. The following weekend Pratt returned to Cowes. The two went out in the boat. Pratt was full of enthusiasm. Wallis agreed to join him. Vickers moved fast: three days later a confirmatory letter arrived inviting Wallis to start in their Airship Drawing Office on 1 September. The weekly salary would be £3.5s.0d – more than twice what he was earning at White's.[79]

So it was that on the fourth Saturday of August 1913 Wallis paced the long deck of the old steam paddle ferry that plied between Cowes and Southampton. His years at Samuel White had been good, and the firm's reference reflected that: it said that Wallis had 'given complete satisfaction in every respect', that his dealings had been 'gentlemanly and correct', and that his work was 'accurate and reliable'.[80] Wallis had been happy but left without regret.[81] His state, rather, was a kind of elated bewilderment.

> . . . there lay before me all the mystery of a life of almost unimaginable technical adventure – to design a great Rigid Airship – Pratt and I, just we two . . . a great future was believed to lie before the Airship both for Naval and Civil purposes, and here was I, chosen by Pratt from all the men he knew . . . Me, poor, struggling, *ill*-educated by any standard, having left C.H. when I was only 16; and starkly ignorant by standards of today. Whatever made him do it?[82]

Wallis could hardly believe his luck, although aside from the circumstances that had brought him and Pratt together, luck had nothing to do with it. Pratt knew that Wallis was able, in good health, toughened by five years of manual work and sport, intellectually alert. He also saw an imagination awaiting its opportunity. Wallis recalled the thrill when he realised what was being offered.

> Joy, joy and joy! All the intellectual rapture – pleasure is far too weak a word – of continuous creation . . . And I, I, I had been chosen from a ruck of junior draughtsmen . . . to share with him this amazing adventure![83]

The ferry docked. Wallis boarded a train for Waterloo. Two hours later he was back at Pepys Road. At nine o'clock on the following Monday morning he walked into the airship department's office in Victoria Street. The adventure had begun.

3

Before Marching and After, 1913–23

'Pleasure is far too weak a word'

Pratt's department was in a room on the fourth floor of a building on the south side of Victoria Street, nearly opposite Broadway where Vickers was headquartered. The room was L-shaped in plan. Pratt had a cubicle to himself screened off at the end of the upstroke; as other staff joined the rest of the space filled up with drawing boards resting on wooden benches. Wallis's place was between Pratt and the others.

The office looked down into a central atrium faced with white-glazed bricks which amplified sound from other parts of the building, notably the duralumin department, where the director's use of the telephone was so loud as to suggest that he doubted whether it was working. Duralumin was an aluminium-copper alloy which combined lightness and strength; the material had been developed in Germany and licensed by Vickers; over the next fifteen years it became the main medium in Wallis's working life.

Their task was to design a new class of rigid airship. Zeppelin had been developing airship technology since the end of the nineteenth century, and it has been said that the Admiralty never had a policy for airships, 'merely a series of reactions to German successes'.[1] Pratt's brief was to assimilate as much as was already known on the subject.[2] The first vessel was designated No. 9r, the 'r' standing for 'rigid'.[3] Pratt produced designs and sketches which he passed to Wallis to work up into complete design drawings. The drawings were then sent to Barrow, where the Works had been instructed to organise a subsidiary drawing office in which detailed and working drawings could be got out for the shops. However, Barrow was still under the charge of Charles Roberton, who was irked by the news that Pratt had been re-engaged. He warned Pratt to expect no favours.

They worked by themselves, seven days a week, carrying on until eight or nine in the evening on weekdays and stopping a little sooner on Saturdays. Once or twice a week they kept themselves fit with late-evening visits to Stempel's School of Arms for fencing, and on Sundays they finished at four and went to the new Lyon's Corner House where a five- or six-course meal could be had for 7/6d and an orchestra played. Half a century later Wallis said that he had 'never worked with such joy and enthusiasm before or since.'[4]

Edie continued to rule from beyond the grave. Until 1911 John had resisted her efforts to coax him into holy orders. Four months after her death he changed his mind. John was ordained on Trinity Sunday 1913. Charles told him that it was what she would have wished.[5]

As for Annie, she recalled: 'No one knew what to do with me.'[6] Annie knew: after all those years hanging around her brothers' workshop she was dexterous, creative, had recently enrolled at Blackheath College of Art and determined to specialise in enamelled jewellery. However, Barnes doubted that this would be a viable occupation, and even if it was he assumed she would be a drain on family finances until she could support herself. Barnes and Charles accordingly proposed to remove her from Blackheath and put her in Edie's place to run the household and help administer the practice.

Annie was horror-struck. Aside from the cancellation of her career, she was neither trained nor prepared to greet private patients, organise servants, make social calls, run a kitchen, or keep household finances. She was still traumatised by her mother's death and reacted by becoming a recluse. Luckily, one of Charles Wallis's doctor friends had recently married a lively journalist called Beatrice Kendall who swooped in one evening and took Annie off to dinner. 'From that day' Annie recalled, 'my life . . . was changed'. Beatrice became a surrogate aunt, throwing her house open to Annie and young Charles in the evenings, introducing them to friends, taking them to shows and plays, and on long walks with their dogs.

At Victoria Street, enough progress had been made by the year's end to warrant the appointment of more staff. Among them were John Edwin Temple, a gifted mathematician who specialised in stress work, and George Bower, whose real calling was rock climbing. With them came two draughtsmen, Thomas Sharratt and Arthur Forrest.

At Barrow, meanwhile, work had begun on a new shed in which to build the airship.[7] It was prefabricated (with parts from Germany) and stood on Walney, a narrow island some ten miles long that lies parallel to mainland Barrow. The shed's dimensions were Gothic – longer than York Minster, loftier than the vaults of Lincoln Cathedral.[8]

Wallis kept in touch with his friends. In April Aileen Fisher wrote about the glorious weather. Archie Watts's sister Teresa wrote from Cowes on the last day of July 1914. Was he coming down for a holiday? These were fateful days: Teresa told that two steam packets had just been commandeered by the Navy, there were territorials at Parkhurst, and regulars at Freshwater. 'Quite warlike!'

'Budmouth Dears'

Churchill's telegram instructing the Fleet to 'commence hostilities against Germany' was sent at two minutes past eleven on the evening of Tuesday, 4 August. Next day, Wallis went to the drill hall of the Royal Naval Volunteer Reserve's London Division in Lambeth, where he asked to enlist as an engineer. A naval doctor noted his height (five foot eleven), brown hair, grey eyes, and pronounced his physique 'very good'. Wallis returned to the office and told Pratt, who promptly wrote to the London Division's CO to say that Wallis was unavailable because he was 'engaged on very urgent and important Admiralty work'. To soften the blow Pratt added that he hoped to be able to release Wallis 'immediately his services can be spared'. In fact, Pratt was no less eager to enlist than Wallis.

No. 9 was nearly ready for erection, and since both men had been working flat out for months, leave was due. They took it in succession. While Pratt left for a walking holiday in the West Country, Wallis described life to his old friend Herbert Fisher. He alluded to the strains with Barrow ('It's a most extraordinary firm') and went on:

> There are six men now & will be 7 tomorrow . . . They include one BSc, one Whitworth Scholar, & all the rest are engineering college men of one sort or another & most of them are fearful bloods at mathematics. So you can imagine that I have a pretty anxious time trying to hide my ignorance. It's not that I have not the necessary ability, but simply that I have not had the time to go ahead with the higher maths part of engineering, & also I am rather slow. I suppose Pratt knows.[9]

Was this real uncertainty or false modesty? Whichever, Wallis went on to liken his colleagues to musicians who know all there is to know about harmony and counterpoint but cannot write a tune. 'I do not think there is one of them who can equal me as a designer.'[10]

Down in Devon, Pratt was tramping across Exmoor and exploring the Doone valley. He wrote to tell Wallis of juicy blackberries, swimming, buying cider for girls and smoking his pipe on the rocks at Lynmouth. Then:

> To enlist or not to enlist that is the question
> For who would bear the cares of office
> The Barrow muddling the Admiralty demands
> Whether 'tis nobler in the office to endure the trials and
>   troubles of our vocations
> Or to take arms against the German nation.[11]

And the answer:

> Once more to the set square dear Wallis, once more
> And fill the waste baskets with your designs.
> In peace there's nought so befits a draughtsman
> As modest effort and peaceful overtime.

But when the blast of war blows in your ears
Then must our sore task not divide the Sunday from the
    week and
Our sweaty haste make the night labour with the day.
Then sharpen up the pencils and get good T-square set,
Cover tracing paper with lines both good and true
While round the compasses and long trammels[12] too.
Then off to those fair ladies who on cloth with ink do ply[13]
Next to the men who blue prints and true-to-scale who
    make
Then stamp with a bang and sign them if you can
With a nice H.B.P. and your day's work is done.[14]

Young man's stuff, but the irony is telling.

Pratt suggested they meet for the Saturday evening Prom: 'We could talk matters over.' Between Brahms's *Hungarian Rhapsodies* and a Vivaldi concerto they mulled over prospects for discharge from Vickers. The concert ended with Elgar's *Pomp and Circumstance No. 1* and a rousing rendition of the French national anthem. Despite the patriotism the two men glumly recognised that their chances of release were remote at least until No. 9 was complete.

Wallis took his leave in September. He had hoped to follow Pratt and go walking in Devon but dropped this when he found that John and Ba were unable to look after his father. Ever dutiful, he volunteered to take Charles with him, and looked for somewhere suitable. Places east of Bournemouth were out because they reminded him of holidays with Edie. They went instead to Weymouth, which Wallis imagined as somewhere small and quiet, but turned out to be swarming with soldiers, sailors, and 'dashing officers in full naval uniform'. The USS *Tennessee*, a four-funnelled cruiser, was in harbour, on her way to protect American interests in Europe, and there were British warships at anchor.

Weymouth was Thomas Hardy's model for Budmouth, the seaside town in *The Dynasts* where off-duty hussars strolled in their sling-jackets and jangling spurs hoping to catch the notice of local girls.

Wallis thought the town 'pretty', but his experience of it was 'utterly miserable'. An attempt to sunbathe on a remote cliff ledge was disrupted by a company of route-marching territorials who assumed him to be a shirker, jeered and showered him with clods of earth. Shaken, he told Pratt that if it had not been for the need to look after his father, he would have gone 'straight back to town'.[15]

Charles returned to London by train a few days later. Wallis was now free and spent the remaining days of his leave walking towards London across country. Nine years later he recalled:

> There is no holiday in all the world – away with Switzerland, France, Germany – to compare with packing your rucsac [sic] and your little tent and going off on your own to tramp and camp when and where you please, in ENGLAND.[16]

For the next five days he lived the life of a wanderer. Setting off on Thursday, he paused after ten miles to swim at Lulworth Cove, reached Corfe Castle after dark and spent the night at an inn. Next day he walked to Swanage, then on to Bournemouth where he pawned his gold shirt links for 8/6 because he had no money.

> The next night I slept somewhere near New Milton, and the next day or evening rather, got lost in the New Forest, only getting to Hythe about 10 at night. (I hate sticking to roads and without a really good map I tried to cut my own way across the Forest.)[17]

After 'green days in forests' and 'the broad road that stretches' he arrived in Southampton,[18] looked up a friend from Samuel White days, cadged the train fare back to London, and returned to work next day.

Interlude

Early in February 1915 the Admiralty instructed Vickers to stop work on Airship No. 9. The decision was taken partly because aircraft were cheap in comparison with airships,[19] and because whereas aircraft were quick to build and evolving rapidly, No. 9 was taking years and would be obsolete before she flew. The new plan was to boost aircraft production and rely on makeshift non-rigid patrols in the meantime.[20] The decision was ratified on Friday, 12 March.

Wallis and Pratt were now free to do what they had been aching to do since the outbreak of war: enlist. No more white feathers, company turf wars or political vacillation. Pratt and Temple joined the Royal Naval Volunteer Reserve and were commissioned as lieutenants in May. Wallis wrote off to the Royal Engineers, the London Rifle Brigade, the Honourable Artillery Company, and the Artists' Rifles. The Engineers turned him down. The London Rifle Brigade was still largely drawn from members of the Stock Exchange, the Baltic, large banks and insurance offices. Wallis turned to the Artists' Rifles, who said they would be glad to see him for interview at their depot near Euston station. The Artists attracted alumni of public schools and universities; they ran a recruits' course for potential officers, which began with several months' basic training followed by an advanced course of field training. After toying with the Army Service Corps for a position in mechanical transport Wallis chose the Artists. He passed his medical examination, which included a balance test in which he hopped around the room on one foot, and on the following Monday stepped through the terracotta entrance of the Duke Road drill hall to be declared Private 3582 B. N. Wallis in the 3/28 Battalion, the London Regiment, and swear by Almighty God to be faithful and bear true allegiance to King George the Fifth, His Heirs and Successors. At first, he lived at home, rising early each day to polish his buttons, belt, boots, and badge, before crossing London to report for six hours of drill and physical training. In due course the battalion moved into camp in Richmond Park, and in July to High Beech in Epping Forest.

At Richmond, Wallis made the first in a succession of lasting friendships. Alfred Egerton Cooper was an artist in his early thirties who had worked as John Singer Sargent's assistant. Generous, spontaneous, a raconteur, it is not clear how or why he hit it off with Wallis, but they kept in touch following Cooper's departure for officer training. Later in the war Cooper spent some of his leaves with Wallis, and took opportunities to fly and paint airships and aerial perspectives.[21]

Wallis's conscientiousness enabled him to immerse himself in any kind of task. He enjoyed the anonymity and removal of need to make choices; he relished the scratchy rag-wool uniform because, like guard duty in the rain, it seemed to epitomise the essence of soldiering. His ability indefinitely to defer gratification enabled him to endure all kinds of discomfort because in his imagination he could always look beyond it.

Private Wallis was at ease with himself, too, because he was good at things expected of him. Physical exercise, route marches, running and washing in cold water all suited him. He had had experience of boxing and musketry back in Samuel White days. In the classroom he was introduced to new things in some lectures and found himself already accomplished in others. Night exercises were an adventure; fieldcraft, map-making and map-reading were already part of his life. Instructors noted his aptitude. By August he had been promoted to lance corporal, in charge of a small group of recruits and instructing men in the use of compass and protractor to make accurate field sketches while on exercise. It was noted, too, that he was an engineer. Since sanitary drainage at High Beech had been overwhelmed by the battalion's arrival, he was deputed to design a new system.

High Beech had been a pleasure resort before the war; the new temporary camp centred on the King's Oak Hotel, and Riggs Retreat, an enormous pavilion café on Wellington Hill that had catered for day trippers. In the Forest were stag-headed oaks, secret ponds and fallow deer that reminded him of the late-summer days he had passed with Archie Watts and the Civils. The camp itself was less agreeable. The hutting was cramped and leaky and the food was poor.[22] Ill-cooked the food may have been, but for no apparent reason – a bet? a set-up by other soldiers? – a serving girl from the Royal Oak stepped up to Wallis one day and kissed him smack on the lips. He was approaching his twenty-eighth birthday. It was his first kiss.

Turf wars and hostilities

Epping Forest's ridge gave a grandstand view of a Zeppelin raid during the night of 17/18 August. It was not the first thereabouts; a few bombs had fallen on Stoke Newington and Hackney at the end of May, and as on that occasion mistaken navigation meant that bombs intended for inner London fell elsewhere – in this instance on Walthamstow and Leytonstone. From a purely military point of view, indeed, the Zeppelins did not do very well; of the four that set out for London on that evening, two turned back because of mechanical troubles and a third bombed Ashford in Kent because its navigator mistook it for Woolwich. This was par for the course. The truth was that while Zeppelins were useful for shadowing at sea and keeping vigil for U-boats, as a direct raiding threat they hardly ever found what they were looking for, and even when they did the damage was of little consequence. However, that side of the balance sheet took no account of their political and economic effect, of public anxiety, nor of the frustration that stemmed from initial inability either to fight them off or retaliate. In result, and since it was the navy that guarded Britain's shores, large resources of RNAS aircraft and personnel were held back that could otherwise have been somewhere else.

These points were not lost on the coalition government that came to office in May in the wake of discontent over reports of munition shortages, discord in the Admiralty, and the failure of the Dardanelles operation. In June a new regime at the Admiralty resolved to reform the RNAS, to seek closer alignment between air assets and operations at sea, and to resume work on No. 9. Beyond that was a plan to build more rigids. Doing any of this, however, meant moving staff around, redeployment of workforces, and reassembling the team that had been scattered in March. Vickers was not formally told to restart work on No. 9 until the end of August, and it was not until 7 September that Wallis was released from the Artists' Rifles.[23]

A new and fundamental question was who now owned the project. Was it still a Vickers venture or did the Admiralty lead it? A sign it was the Admiralty was Wallis's transfer into the RNAS, in which he was granted a temporary commission.[24] However, this did not answer the question of what he and Pratt were supposed to do, where they should do it, or how they would interact with their old employers. Pratt and Wallis were posted to the RNAS air stations at Kingsnorth and Barrow, respectively, while they waited to find out.

Two sets of events lay behind the hiatus. One was the future of the RNAS, which had just come under new leadership. The other was an emerging plan to form a central naval design department for rigids. Such a step would displace Vickers, but no one knew when it might happen. Up at Barrow, Wallis felt isolated

The airship station was on Walney Island, where Vickers had sited their first airship shed, close to a thicket of smoky chimneys. The RNAS had commandeered the shed for assembly of its own SS airships which were put together from shipped-in components. The space alongside emerging No. 9 was thus cluttered with envelopes, fuselages, wire, pots of rubber solution, and the two workforces got in each other's way. Wallis had no authority over the Vickers team, whose workmanship he found substandard, and which to his alarm had been making unauthorised alterations to their design. Pratt told him to 'fight with the Vickers people' over the changes and pointed out that since he had not been given any executive power, he could not be held responsible for any resulting delay if he did so.

The underlying problem at Barrow was partly generational: the general manager, Sir James McKechnie, their old adversary Charles Roberton, and the head of the fabric shop (a man called Ryan) had formed a coalition to freeze Pratt out. Pratt told Wallis that Roberton had given him 'an ultimatum and said if I come it will be war to the knife'.[25] McKechnie enjoyed a lavish lifestyle, wielded 'absolute power', and was 'dreaded for what he could do to people'.[26] The hostility towards Pratt was symptomatic of deeper disarray. McKechnie had allowed rivalries to breed between the shipyard and the engineers, each group blaming the other when delays or difficulties arose.[27]

In mid-October Pratt told Sir Trevor Dawson that he was unable to take charge at Barrow because he could not guarantee any results. He proposed to go and see Masterman; if the Admiralty could take control of works at Barrow, or remove the diehards, then there might be hope. 'Don't be down-hearted old chap' he told Wallis, 'we may get a chance yet. Our education in the diplomacy business is proceeding at any rate.' With such spleen at Barrow, 'One does not need to go to the trenches for a fight.' Pending a resolution, he urged Wallis to take soundings among potential allies in the drawing office, and to 'take every opportunity of giving trouble up there'.[28] Wallis duly produced a statement about weaknesses in management of the airship department,[29] and an excoriating report on the work it had undertaken.[30]

On Tuesday, 17 October Pratt was taken to lunch by Commander Charles Craven. Craven was a former submariner, more recently Dawson's assistant for Admiralty liaison, and a man of 'incendiary charm'. Pratt surmised that he was being sounded about the reasons behind his unwillingness to return to Barrow. Pratt did some sounding of his own, forming the impression that McKechnie was being left in place until he had made such a mess of things that Dawson could make a clean sweep.[31] But by early November Pratt had had enough. On Thursday, 11 November he handed his resignation to his squadron commander, Thomas Cave-Brown-Cave, with a request that he be allowed to accept the promise of a commission in the Royal Artillery. Cave passed the letter to Kingsnorth's Wing Commander, Neville Usborne, who forwarded it to the Admiralty, where it arrived on Masterman's desk the following Monday. Masterman immediately summoned Pratt and told him that a fortnight before, the Sea Lords had concluded that responsibility for the design and construction of rigid airships should be transferred to the Director of Naval Construction, within the Admiralty. The decision had taken explicit account of Pratt and Wallis, both of whom would to be invited to join the staff of the DNC.[32] They could take up post immediately, either in civilian or RNVR capacity. Would they accept?

Before they had time to answer, Commander C. I. R. Campbell, an Admiralty structures specialist, returned from Barrow to report on the bungled erection of No. 9 and discord. In its light, the Admiralty issued an ultimatum to Vickers: no new airship orders would be forthcoming unless or until the company dealt with its problems. Dawson called McKechnie to London and told him that he intended to give Pratt a free hand. McKechnie and Roberton resigned, Dawson invited them to reconsider, which they did, now conceding that Pratt would be sovereign in airship matters and report directly to Vickers's directors through Dawson. In the light of these events, Masterman invited Pratt to return to Barrow and Vickers.

Pratt was on a roll. He made his acceptance conditional on an absolute guarantee from Dawson that Roberton would be sidelined, that Ryan would be confined to the fabric shop, and Admiralty agreement that Wallis, Sharratt, Temple and other former colleagues would be released from the RNAS to re-join him. Pratt would be their general manager; Wallis would become chief draughtsman.

The Admiralty agreed. They ruled that Pratt and Wallis should work in a civilian capacity, and on 8 December the Admiralty accepted Wallis's resignation of his commission 'in pursuit of his acceptance of an appointment with Vickers, Barrow'.[33] Pratt was cock-a-hoop: 'I think we have the nucleus of a very efficient organisation.' The Admiralty was talking about a fleet of new airships, some of which would be built by Beardmore and Armstrong Whitworth to their designs, 'so we shall practically run the entire Rigid Airship industry!'[34]

Barrow

Wallis's sixty-one days as a naval officer had coloured his views on airship development. The Submarine Scouts being put together in the Walney shed were fair-weather craft. Barrow's seaside weather meant that on most days the SS ships could not fly. Watching them on the days when they did, and occasionally flying in them, was not reassuring.

When conditions for flight were suitable, the first step was for Barrow's eighty-odd naval ratings, petty officers and warrant officers to stop whatever they were doing in the shed and turn themselves into a ground-handling party. Next, they would walk the SS out onto the airfield. There would then be a balance test, easing up the guys to see if she was free to lift; if she lifted too readily the party would hold her while more water ballast was put aboard. This could be awkward. If it was sunny the hydrogen heated up and buoyancy increased; if there were sunny intervals, buoyancy lessened when the sun went in and increased when it came out again.

When the ship was in balance the order was given to let her go. The pilot aimed for a gradual increase in speed and height; for a training circuit this meant rising to about a thousand feet. As pressure in the envelope rose, he would relieve it by valving air from ballonets inside the envelope to keep the vessel in trim. On return the goal was to approach the landing party head to wind, to arrive overhead at about twenty feet, and drop the trail rope into their hands. The need to keep the engine running to maintain relative pressure in the gasbags made overshoot likely; experience was needed to time the descent; there was a risk of the ship becoming flabby, with consequent falling away of control; and if she arrived over the ground party at, say, 20 miles an hour, the stalwarts who were needed to catch hold of the trailing ropes would be dragged along until the rest caught up. Contrariwise, if the sun went in and the descent accelerated, the ground party might be drenched by a sudden release of water ballast. Last but not least, if anyone in the landing party grasped the landing rope before it had been earthed he was likely to be knocked over by an electric shock from the static charge. As a way of going to war, this was not very efficient.

Wallis formed a circle of friends and professional relationships at Walney. He met three within days: Victor Goddard, George Scott, and Philip Teed. Goddard and Scott were flight lieutenant pilots. Goddard, ten years younger, had been a naval cadet at the Royal Naval Colleges at Osborne and Dartmouth, served as a midshipman aboard the battleship *Britannia*, and entered the RNAS earlier in 1915 via its madcap balloon course at Hurlingham. (Since most of England was then in the hands of landed families, Hurlingham trainees carried a copy of *Burke's Landed Gentry* on balloon cross-country training flights: out-landings gave opportunities for tea with their daughters, while servants helped to pack the balloon and carry it to the nearest railway station.) Goddard combined a sunny manner with wholeheartedness in action.[35] Like Scott, his combination of approachability and skill in the air made him well-liked by flight crews.

Scott was a phenomenon. Pre-war, he had been an engineer and had practised in Spain. In 1914 he joined the RNAS, where his gift for the esoteric skills of lighter-than-air flight soon brought him to notice.[36] At Barrow, he commanded No. 4, the largest and most sophisticated airship then in British naval service.[37] No. 4 was a Parseval, an airship of German design which had been bought by the Navy in 1913.[38] Essentially a non-rigid, with a system of rigging that bore an underslung car, she was powered by two Maybach engines, carried weapons, radio, and a crew of two officers and seven men. Remembered as looking 'rather like a shark with a pointed tail',[39] No. 4 was the nearest thing to a large airship that the navy then possessed, and for that reason it was the platform for establishing methods of operation and for training future captains and crews of the rigids that were on Wallis's drawing board. 'Scotty' was affable, funny, musical, and given to chewing on a large pipe held between crooked teeth. Ladies liked him, and when not airborne his ideal habitat was a party. Wallis flew with him once on a night patrol in No. 4, narrowly escaping collision with Walney's chimneys. Scott captained or test-flew two of Wallis's airships.

The third person who entered Wallis's life in September 1915 was a twenty-six-year-old polymath, Philip Litherland Teed, who before the war had pursued parallel careers in law, materials science, and metallurgy, and excelled at all of them. He joined the RNAS in 1914, and by the time he arrived in Barrow had added hydrogen to his scientific interests. His skills were soon noticed, and in the following year he was co-opted to assist in the inflation of No. 9 – a process beset by problems which he helped to solve.[40] Thereafter, like a character in a Hardy novel who keeps reappearing, Teed was Wallis's right-hand man at later stages in his professional life.[41]

Others who joined the circle were Pratt's erstwhile ally Edward Masterman, who took over as Barrow's CO in March 1916, and Ralph Cochrane, a young flight lieutenant who arrived in November to observe the launch of No. 9. Masterman commanded No. 9 on her maiden flight. He was effective, a cool leader, and behind the calm was an original wit; he could conjure a joke out of almost anything, and in his letters often did so. At Walney, he joined forces with Wallis to think through the challenge of how to secure unwieldy airships when they were at rest, arriving at the concept of a new kind of mast to which airships could be moored, head to wind from any direction. They became staunch friends.

Cochrane's itinerary thus far had been akin to Goddard's: Osborne, Dartmouth, midshipman aboard a battleship, transfer to the RNAS, Hurlingham, Kingsnorth, and Barrow. The battleship was HMS *Colossus*, aboard which he had spent the winter of 1914/15 with the Grand Fleet in Scapa Flow, punctuated by sweeps into the North Sea. The midshipmen's quarters in *Colossus* were so far forward that Cochrane's hammock was slung from a hook on the stem post, which meant that when she was bucking into a head sea he had to endure a rise and fall of 80 feet. Water washing over the fo'c's'le invariably found its way down and clothes were never really dry. During a sweep in March 1915, when *Colossus* was making for the Norwegian coast in a full gale 'rolling as only a top-heavy Dreadnought could', Cochrane was on the bridge 'feeling far from well' when a signal came in from the Admiralty asking for 'volunteers for special duty in the south'. He entered his transfer request at the same time as he handed the signal to the captain.[42] Twenty-six years later, Cochrane would be the officer in charge of the Dams Raid.

Linked to this circle through Masterman was Alfred Pippard, a young mathematician and civil engineer who had been hired as a technical adviser to the Admiralty's Air Department. Pippard's speciality was the mathematics of how the skeletons of aircraft and airships twist, bend, shear, compress or tense.[43] Like Teed, he became another of Wallis's gurus,[44] but of a different kind; whereas Teed was usually nearby doing something resourceful, over the next forty years Pippard became a sounding board, making introductions and providing mathematical help on airship structure,[45] geodetics, explosions, wing controlled aerodynes, and dams. Remarkably, his thesis had been on the structure of dams.[46]

The warmest of Wallis's new friendships was with the air station's medical officer, Edgar Boyd, who had grown up on the outskirts of Manchester where his father ran a calico printing firm. Boyd had studied medicine at Cambridge and St Thomas's Hospital in London, and at the outbreak of war turned from paediatrics to join the navy as a Surgeon Lieutenant. After service at sea, newly married, he arrived at Walney in April 1917. Boyd exemplified a type of Englishman Wallis admired: industrious, fit, at once academic and sporting, gutsy (a capable boxer),[47] open-hearted, Godfearing. The two had other things in common. Boyd, like Wallis, had a brother in holy orders, and they were both devotees of music. The relationship pulls us back to Wallis's friendship with the Fishers, and just as Aileen Fisher had mothered Wallis at Cowes, so Boyd's wife Marion developed a soft spot for Barnes. She called him Woggins. In what little spare time he had, it was Wallis's delight to explore the Lake District. He bought a motorcycle (a Zenith) on which to ride into the hills, and then walk.[48] Boyd was a likeminded companion, and when at the war's end Boyd settled in nearby Ulverston as a GP, his home became Wallis's base for walking and climbing.

While Wallis was making new friends in the north, he was gaining a stepmother in the south. Frances Bloxam, known as Fanny, was the eldest surviving daughter of Charles Loudon Bloxam (1831–87), who for seventeen years had been professor of chemistry at King's College London,[49] and Frieda Abel, daughter of a musical German family.[50] Fanny and Edie had been teenage friends, and when Charles first appeared on the scene his affections might have gone in either direction. Edie and Fanny remained close, and after Edie's death Charles came to rely on Fanny's support. Now in her late fifties, Fanny looked striking, slender, with long silver hair wound in a bun, and the brightest of smiles. She eased Charles's melancholy and encouraged his work; Charles took renewed interest in his medical practice and began to prosper. Fanny and Charles were married at a quiet ceremony on 24 April 1916. Fanny had always been popular among the children, who now welcomed both the marriage and the reduction it brought in Charles's dependency on themselves.

Rigids

Airships, meanwhile, had been taking shape. In old age Wallis wrote that following the reorganisation No. 9 'was soon flying'. In fact, nearly a year passed before she flew. As No. 9 approached completion, a bewildering succession of other types was in development. Three rigids (Nos. 23–25r) had been ordered as far back as October 1915. These were styled the 23 Class, essentially a stretched and improved version of No. 9. Wallis designed it, albeit with frustration in the face of ever-changing Admiralty demands which added weight and slowed progress. Vickers had capacity for only one other new ship, so construction of No. 23's sisters was assigned to William Beardmore and Armstrong Whitworth.[51] Five more 23 Class ships were ordered in January but only one of these was actually built,[52] the other four quickly being converted to orders for an improved design that became known as the 23X Class.[53] The 23X Class in its turn was superseded by yet another form of ship that was in design in the Admiralty by mid-1916.

All this was then overtaken following events on the evening of Saturday, 23 September, when twelve Zeppelins of the Imperial German Navy left Nordholz in Lower Saxony to attack England. Eight were bound for targets in the Midlands, while four newer ships headed for London. Annie Wallis watched as three of them approached. She had retrained as a nurse, and by 1916 was working at the Infants Hospital in Vincent Square. The hospital had a flat roof onto which during air raids Annie and other nurses went out '. . . in our nighties to watch the Zepps and collect shrapnel'. On this night there was plenty to see. Amid searchlight glare and the ragged yellow-red stars of exploding anti-aircraft shells, one airship approached from the south and dropped bombs from Streatham through to Kennington. A second, L32, was deterred by the fierce barrage and released its bombs over eastern outer suburbs. The third, L33, passed over east London, bombing at intervals between Bromley and Wanstead.

L32 was caught by a fighter, witnessed by a flash that first flared pink then turned into a red-orange downward plume as the bits and crew fell thirteen thousand feet.

Shortly after midnight L33 was hit by a shell and later engaged by fighters. Shell splinters pierced several gas cells. Gear and guns were jettisoned to compensate for the loss of lift, but as they neared the Essex coast it was clear to her commander, Lois Bocker, that she would not be airworthy for much longer. Bocker accordingly turned inland and made a soft forced landing at Little Wigborough. All the crew survived. Bocker spoke good English and considerately rapped on the doors of nearby residents to warn them that he was about to fire the ship. This he then did, but when the flames died down much of its frame remained intact; indeed, one of the Maybach engines was still in working order and later fitted to No. 9. The Allies had been gifted with the latest example of Zeppelin technology.

Souvenir hunters, tourists and refreshment sellers flocked to the crash site, while specialists from Barrow and the Admiralty's Air Department began to study L33's structure. They found that Germany's lead in rigid building was greater than anyone had imagined.[54] They already knew that the 23r and 23Xr Classes were outdated, but the Admiralty's emerging new design was itself far behind. Orders were thus placed for yet another type (later known as the R33 Class) to incorporate what was now being learned.[55] The initial order for the Zeppelin clones was five,[56] one of which was allocated to Vickers.

No. 9, meanwhile, had flown.[57] She had been largely complete since August, but insufficient lift had required nine of her fifteen gasbags to be changed, which in turn called for the partial deflation and reinflation of adjoining bags to avoid imposing undue strain on parts of the frame. Even so, her disposable lift was one ton less than expected, and during the inaugural flight over Morecambe Bay she did not at first properly answer her helm. After further trials she was laid up for alteration, re-emerging in March 1917 with lighter bags, L33's engine in place of two of the originals, single plane control services and other alterations. Lift and handling were much improved, and early in April she was flown to the Yorkshire airship station at Howden, where for the next six months, commanded by George Scott, she provided officers and crew members with experience in mooring and handling.

No. 9 served her purpose, just: she was an experimental ship; part of the experiment had been to learn things that only building her could teach.

Moving on

Five weeks after No. 9 left Walney, Wallis was best man at Pratt's wedding. The announcement in *The Times* was both telegraphic – 'Hartley Blyth Pratt to Kathleen Mary Linton, both of Barrow'[58] – and potentially deceptive, for while Kathleen was a Barrovian she and her siblings had wide horizons. She was youngest of four. One of her brothers worked as a teacher in north Wales; another was travelling the world as a ship's mate; and her elder sister had recently become an American citizen. Kathleen herself had read modern literature at Trinity College Dublin, where in 1914 her studies culminated in prize-winning work on the languages of medieval France. She might have been set for an academic career, but while in many ways Barrow felt closer to Dublin than the rest of England, the war and growing nationalism in Ireland had kept her at home. (One of the reasons why the completion of No. 9 was delayed was the Easter Rising in 1916, which disrupted the supply of flax needed for nets to secure her gasbags.)

Kathleen's parents personified the cross-currents. Her mother, Caroline, grew up in Dublin and converted to Catholicism early in her twenties. George, her father, left school at fourteen and went straight to work for the Furness Railway, which with its red locomotives and dark blue-and-white coaches was a world in itself. The company had been formed in the 1840s to carry minerals, then expanded for freight and passengers, and later – making the most of a line that wound around the shores of Morecambe Bay with connection to Windermere – developed for tourism. George was a part of this, first as a junior accounts clerk, later as the company secretary's chief clerk, and from 1918 as the company secretary.

Pratt and Kathleen set up home on the outskirts of the market town of Ulverston, whence Pratt usually took a train to Barrow each weekday morning. Inevitably the marriage introduced a degree of distance between Wallis and Pratt; however, late in 1917, Wallis exchanged his lodgings in Barrow for an apartment in a large stone-built house across the Leven estuary at Kents Bank. The house overlooked Morecambe Bay, with wide views of saltmarsh and changing weather. Wallis liked to commute on his motor-bike, but Kents Bank station was nearby, just two stops from Ulverston, and when the Barrow-bound train pulled into Ulverston each morning at 7.25, Wallis was sometimes aboard. This was their chance to gossip or share thoughts outside the office. Things to talk about just then were the approaching completion of R26 (last in the Class 23 quartet),[59] and an entirely new venture which had been authorised by the Admiralty a few days before Wallis moved to Kents Bank: R80.[60]

R80's design had existed in outline for over a year; it was put in hand now because government muddle had left Vickers with a gap in its construction schedule. We recall that following the capture of L33, Vickers had been put on notice to build one of the ships based on her design. The order was placed early in January 1917, but Walney's shed was too small to accommodate her and a larger shed and associated workers' housing were begun near Flookburgh on the Cartmel peninsula. However, work in the new shed had scarcely started when shortage of steel led the government to cancel it. The R37 contract was passed to Short Brothers, while Vickers were given permission to use the space at Walney to build a smaller ship of their own design.

The R80 was the first of Wallis's fully original creations, and in her we can see characteristics that attended many of those that followed. Thus, she was conceived in a contrarian spirit (her sleek, streamlined form departing from conventional opinion about shape and resistance), and Wallis used his initial freedom from Admiralty direction to do things which hitherto had not been possible, notably to design a hull giving utmost economy in weight while being at least as strong as larger types of vessel. However, progress was fitful. There was a skills shortage, and lack of lighting in the shed meant that the shed doors had to be kept open; later, the Admiralty demanded a succession of adjustments;[61] in mid-1919 the Cabinet decided that the ship was of no foreseeable value and work was temporarily suspended; latterly, Vickers supported Pratt and Wallis to produce a scheme to refit her for commercial use.

All experience of rigids and non-rigids showed that they were unwieldy, and particularly so when they were being handled on the ground. Whereas a fixed-wing aircraft could taxi under its own power or be hangered like a car, hundreds of men were needed simply to walk a rigid in or out of its shed; the manoeuvre could only be undertaken in the calmest conditions, and large damage could result from the smallest errors. Wallis accordingly collaborated with Masterman in the design of a mast to which non-rigids could be moored, the ship then floating like a weathervane, head to wind from any direction. Wallis ceded his patent interest in this to Masterman, but in parallel devised an associated ball-and-socket system for the actual attachment. At the same time he designed a full-scale high mast (complete with interior electric lift and associated terminal building) for mooring, replenishing and providing crew and passenger access to large rigids.[62] Such mooring of course brought with it further needs: an airship at mast had to be maintained in equilibrium – in effect, flown – which called for a resident service crew to make constant adjustments to trim through ballast and gas in response to changes in temperature and barometric pressure. Even when it was doing nothing, an airship was a bundle of unceasing demands.

Wallis hoped to centralise mooring experiments at Barrow, and doubtless thereby extend Vickers's hegemony over all matters to do with airships. He was thus frustrated when in spring 1918 the RNAS shifted mooring trials to Pulham in Norfolk. This was partly because Masterman had recently left Barrow and was no longer available to supervise, but also because Vickers itself had recently objected to a proposal that No. 24r should be stationed at Barrow, and thereby undercut Wallis's case for mooring experiments involving a large rigid. As Masterman told him, different techniques needed to be compared under identical conditions, which meant putting them in one place.

The annoyance over mooring is one of several signs that in 1918

Wallis was coming under growing pressure. Another was the care that Vickers took to retain him. Following the power struggle between McKechnie and Dawson in autumn 1915, Charles Craven had been sent to Barrow as Dawson's emissary and as McKechnie's heir apparent. Craven's winning ways made a big difference to company atmosphere and processes. In February he sent Wallis a handwritten letter of thanks in appreciation of 'all you have done for the Company since you came to Barrow'. Craven told him: 'I know personally that you have had many difficulties to overcome'.[63] At the beginning of May his salary was raised from £500 to £600.

A third sign is that he was worrying about his health. In April he went to see a consultant, fearful that feelings of faintness when he was working at height (apart from flying) might indicate a heart disorder. Nothing amiss was found beyond signs that 'he has drunk too much tea and coffee (5 cups daily) and probably smoked too many cigarettes.' The consultant noted that since the sensations of faintness never led to loss of consciousness, they probably stemmed from anxiety rather than anything physiological: 'I think it is best to let him take his chance and avoid making him apprehensive'.[64]

The Armistice was followed by the cancellation of unfulfilled existing orders for new airships and the decommissioning of most of those that existed. A few part-built ships were carried through to completion,[65] but military demand for new ships was ended. Having invested heavily in the genre during the war, Vickers found itself stranded. What was Pratt's department now to do? Pratt and Wallis worked flat out through 1919 looking for answers. They produced brochures and sales literature which emphasised Vickers's unique expertise in providing landing and mooring gear for airships; special tools for airship construction; and the only staff in Britain capable of producing 'airship liners' that could travel the world. In due course they could build vessels that could carry 100 passengers non-stop for 5000 miles, or 50 tons of freight for 10,000 miles. Pratt wrote a book entitled *Commercial Airships* (1920).

At the heart of their case was the axiom that airships must be the future of long-distance civil aviation because no one could visualise how fixed-wing aircraft might compete with them. As if to bear them out, Zeppelin's passenger-carrying LZ120 began a scheduled service between Berlin and Friedrichshafen, while in July the new-built R34 with George Scott in command flew the Atlantic in both directions. In October Pratt and Wallis produced a business case for a civilianised R80 to fly a twice-weekly service between London, Paris and Rome. They modelled air transport services, pointed to destinations further afield – Nairobi, Cape Town, Australia – and explained how a £2.6 million capital investment would provide a service between London and New York.

In mid-November Pratt addressed a meeting of the Barrow and District Association of Engineers on 'The case for the commercial airship'. He regretted the government's unwillingness to invest in new designs. But virtually no one was listening, and when a few days later *The Sphere* magazine published Egerton Cooper's striking painting of London seen from an airship, it might have come from another world. At the end of that month Wallis was Cooper's best man at his wedding to Irene Clements. Egerton and Irene had met back in 1915 when he and Wallis were training together in Epping Forest, and the girl had walked up out of nowhere and kissed him. In the eyes of Wallis's friends, being a best man now seemed likely to be the closest he would ever get to a wedding.

Shadows

Meanwhile, something terrible had happened to Wallis. Its cause, he said,[66] was a cumulative build-up of strains. He was unable to sleep; he became depressed, delusional, emotionally unstable, and erratic. The inability to work conflicted with his sense of duty, which made it worse. Late in November 1919, Pratt ordered him home to rest.

Craven told him to take a month off. Charles stepped in, called his son back to Pepys Road and used his medical connections to obtain specialist advice.[67] Wallis was admitted to a nursing home in Bayswater where there were to be no visits and no incoming letters.[68] News of Vickers's attempt to boost his morale with another salary increase thus did not reach him until mid-February 1920.[69]

Shortly before Christmas he sent a postcard to Pratt, which gave Pratt the impression that he was feeling a little better. Pratt replied on Christmas Eve, enclosing post and cards, passing on office chit-chat, greetings from colleagues, and news of John Edwin Temple's leaving party the day before.[70] However, it is not clear when this letter reached him; on Boxing Day Charles wrote to Pratt to explain that the doctors had found no 'organic trouble' but his son was to receive neither post nor visitors for at least the next three weeks, and then only on condition that there should be no mention of 'affairs of business'. Pratt replied on New Year's Eve, asking to be told when visitors would be allowed.[71]

Pratt and Wallis met for the first time in nearly three months on Tuesday, 24 February 1920. Their talk was genial,[72] and Pratt left feeling optimistic that his friend had turned a corner. One of the topics on which they touched (in defiance of Wallis's consultant) was the way in which the Airship Department at Barrow was structured. Soon after Pratt left Wallis sat down to write to him about this.[73] The letter addressed what seems to have been a deep-seated, gnawing anxiety that centred on the way in which different parts of the department interrelated. To illustrate, he drew an organogram which showed Pratt (the general manager and chief engineer) in charge of an organisation that consisted of 'practically three separate departments': the works and its staff, the expert calculator, and the drawing office. The drawing office was run by the chief designer, Wallis, who was also assistant general manager and in overall charge when Pratt was away. Until his departure just before Christmas the expert calculator had been John Edwin Temple, and it was upon Temple's role, or more precisely the interplay between the role and Temple himself, that Wallis's worries centred.[74]

The seven pages it took to get this off his chest partly reflected the extent to which the matter had tormented him, and partly his need for absolute clarity. In the last he succeeded, for when Pratt replied three days later it was to say, in almost a throwaway manner, that Wallis's second organisational diagram was exactly what he had in mind all along and into which, but for 'personal idiosyncrasies', Temple had been meant to fit.[75] If it was that simple, we might wonder, why had this not been straightened out in one of those talks on the 7.25 from Ulverston? The answer, perhaps, was Wallis's respect for hierarchy.

Wallis was discharged in mid-March to a convalescent holiday with his friend Egerton Cooper. They went to Shanklin on the Isle of Wight, where Cooper taught him the rudiments of golf. Pratt asked to be told when he would next be in London, 'so that I can have a yarn with you'. However, when he did next hear, anxiety had returned; Wallis felt guilt at leaving Pratt in the lurch and he was wondering whether to leave Vickers. Pratt replied with a gentle scolding and encouragement: 'For God's sake do not worry about me or about returning prematurely. Take another two months if necessary rather than come back without a complete cure & as for talking about resignation that must be the result of want of sleep. We may not have seen eye to eye on everything in the past but anyhow I do appreciate good solid work & loyal assistance & the way in which you have driven yourself to breakdown.'[76]

Victor Goddard, perhaps at Pratt's prompting, wrote cajolingly: 'where are all those letters you were going to send me?' He wondered cheerily whether he was 'too busy trying to defeat Colonel Bogey at the Royal and Ancient to worry about an old stiff like me. Or have you found the girl at last?' Then the nub: 'What seems to me though, to be rather unpleasantly probable, is that your poor old head has been worrying too much for you to think of writing'. Goddard tried to coax ('Up socks old man! No more morbid depression') and to reassure: many were asking after him; he had 'the guts of ten'; one day he would be 'the very deuce of a man'.[77] The cycle of upturn and relapse continued, but the recovery phases grew longer and those of anxiety lessened. Late in May Wallis returned to Barrow.

R80 had been inflated in his absence; George Scott was waiting to take her skyward. Other key members of R80's crew – the coxwains, navigator and several engineers – were also at hand, having been posted to the ship during the latter stages of her erection. Among them were Victor Goddard and Scott's deputy, Ivor Little. However, although the ship was ready by the end of June the weather was not. July was wet, cold, and windy and it was not until the 18th that conditions improved. Next morning R80 was walked out of her shed before several thousand onlookers and many pressmen.

Goddard's recollection of the flight was that it began well enough; the Maybach compression-ignition engines ran sweetly; following departure they sailed head to wind out over the Irish sea, performed a series of turning manoeuvres, and turned back towards Barrow at 1500 feet. Goddard climbed up to look at the gas valves, moving from forward to aft to inspect each in turn. However, as he neared the stern, he was shocked to find that the walkway on which he stood had sagged by about 18 inches. Looking about, he found the top girder broken, guys to the elevator plane and controls slack, and the tail loose. Goddard quickly made his way down through the hull to the control car, wherein (as he later put it) there was 'considerable consternation'.[78] Wallis was alarmed – the ship's behaviour seemed inexplicable; the helm was jammed hard over; she was moving in circles, downwind away from Walney. Little had handed over to Scott, who was flummoxed. Goddard had once had experience of a jammed rudder and offered a suggestion: if they put the engines full ahead at the moments when R80 was pointing towards Walney, and then shut the throttles during periods between, she could be gradually manoeuvred back in a series of loops until she was above the airfield. And so she was, arriving head to wind to be taken in hand by the landing party so smoothly that spectators and the press noticed nothing amiss.

Investigation traced the near disaster to events around the start of the flight. It had been a hot day, the service crew had been slow in leaving the ship, and gas pressure built up while awaiting cast-off. The gas valves responded automatically, but with no through ventilation the vented gas filled the keel corridor, and when the ship was released her ascent was so rapid that excessive strain had been imposed on rear girders and parts of the frame.[79] On the upside, R80's ratio of lift to weight bettered any other British airship of the day.[80]

The R80 was returned to the shed for repair and improvement. She re-emerged early 1921, just in time for the Controller of Civil Aviation to announce that she was no longer needed. Before being decommissioned she was flown across to Howden where for several months she was used to train a crew from the US Navy that had arrived to take the new R38 to America.

The R38 had originated as the Admiralty's final attempt to build a long-range maritime patrol airship that would improve on Zeppelin technology. Designed late in the war, in many respects she was a Zeppelin clone, but scaled up from examples with neither full understanding of their structural rationale nor calculation from first principles. A purchase offer from the United States had saved her from cancellation. On 24 August R38 broke up over the Humber while undergoing trials. All but four of the forty-nine people on board perished. Among the dead were Ivor Little; veterans of airship development like Edward Maitland; the head of her design team, Commander C. I. R. Campbell;[81] and sixteen American airshipmen.[82] Pratt and Wallis sent a wreath to the mass funeral which brought Hull to a standstill. The tragedy reinforced the government's decision to abandon airships. Eighteen days later R80 was flown to Pulham and laid up. She never flew again. In the unsentimental world of aviation, where, in Le Corbusier's words, 'everything is scrapped in a year', Britain's first original airship had been airborne for just 73 hours.[83]

'Things are very distressing here'

R80's decommissioning was a bellwether for the Airship Department itself. Efforts to drum up business had drawn a blank, and Lloyd George's coalition government showed no interest in providing the meteorological, navigational and mooring infrastructure that would be needed for long-distance routes. Pratt's book title *Commercial Airships* looked like an oxymoron.

Wallis had known for some time that his future with Vickers was uncertain; in January 1921 he offered his services to the United States Navy's Bureau of Construction, only to be told that American opinion was no more sympathetic to public investment in airships than it was in Britain.[84] Vickers as a whole was hurting. The steelworks had been awarded an 'involuntary holiday' late in 1920; orders for new merchant ships had fallen. By the end of 1921 even men in supposedly safe positions were on short time. It was said that birds had begun to nest in the dockside cranes.

At the end of September 1921 Wallis was stood down by Vickers. The company offered him an annual retainer of £250, the idea being that he would return if economic conditions improved and interest in airships revived. In fact, economic conditions deteriorated further, and Craven wrote to warn him that even the retainer was no longer affordable. On 4 December the letter of severance duly arrived, with thanks 'for your loyal and efficient service to the Company' and notice that the second stage payment would be made on 31 December. Wallis replied to the informal letter, saying that he understood the difficult position in which Craven found himself. Craven wrote again on the 7th to reiterate his thanks. 'Things are very distressing here, and I do most cordially dislike dispensing with people . . .'[85]

Wallis left his lodgings at Dalton on 13 October 1921, returned to Pepys Road, enlisted with the University of London's Tutorial College, sat its external examinations for a BSc, and sailed through.[86] The academic promise seen by Charles Browne seventeen years before was at last fulfilled.

In April 1922 Masterman wrote from Cologne, where he was now a member of the Allied Control Commission which had been set up to oversee the dismantling of Germany's aeronautical industry and reallocate its assets. He had received a royalty payment on a mooring mast that Vickers had supplied to the Japanese government and enclosed a cheque for a third of its value.[87] 'Let me have the pleasure of doing this, which is only fair to you, who did all the work, I beg you.' He was curious about Wallis's plans: 'Will you be a professor?' Wallis did not know. Neither did Masterman. 'I hope to get a three months' holiday, if possible, but have not the faintest idea of what I shall do next.'[88]

'No question of "choice"'

The following Saturday Fanny welcomed her nieces Molly and Barbara – 'Baba' – Bloxam to Pepys Road. Her brother Arthur had just moved his family from Berkshire to a house in Hampstead, and Fanny was keen that its members should become better acquainted with the Wallises. Coincidentally, Arthur Bloxam and Wallis already knew each other: Arthur managed the firm of patent and trademark attorneys which had handled Wallis's mooring mast patent applications. Arthur was an avid reader of Victorian novels, a keen walker, an evangelical Anglican, stern and retiring in the eyes of outsiders, and doted on his daughters.[89]

Molly was seventeen, Baba a year older. Both girls were due to enter University College London in the autumn. When Wallis heard they were due to visit Pepys Road, he found an excuse to stay out late and arrived home at a time when he hoped they would have gone to bed. Molly, too, was apprehensive. She told him later: 'I was dreadfully afraid you'd be horrid and superior, and altogether lazy and fashionable.' Instead, Molly noticed his handwriting, which struck her as 'nice and strong and firm'.[90]

A few days later, Sunday, 23 April, both families attended a service in Southwark Cathedral. They travelled by bus. A passenger making small talk asked Molly if she had plans for her life. Molly replied that she would like a career in medicine. The questioner scoffed, saying that the idea of a woman doctor was absurd. Wallis flared and rebuked him. On the instant, Wallis realised that he was in love. Afterwards he told her: 'Molly, it just *happened* – there was no question of "choice" or deliberate seeking. From that first moment, I simply loved you'.[91]

Wallis was thirty-five. His closest relationship with a woman hitherto had been with his mother. Now, in a flash, he was transfixed by a girl less than half his age. His first reaction was panic, and an effort to subdue his feelings in the hope that they would wane. He made no attempt to develop the acquaintance, and when the Bloxams invited him to visit he found reasons to stay away. He threw himself into other things. But the fire was ablaze, and nothing would put it out.

All this was obvious to Fanny, who encouraged her stepson to talk. To his relief, Wallis found that Fanny and Charles were not only aware of what had befallen him but also welcomed it. It may even be that Fanny had engineered the visit by Molly and Baba in the hope of promoting it. They also realised, as did he, that Molly had been brought up in a highly protected household, with no experience of male company or indeed of anything much outside her family.[92] A hesitant, sporadic correspondence began.

Wallis was still out of work. Years later he said that having twice been made redundant because of the chanciness of airship building, he resolved to turn to technical salesmanship and to that end took a temporary teaching post in Switzerland to polish his French and German. This is possible, but all the signs are that school-mastering was initially a stopgap.[93] At all events, he applied to an agency for a teaching job, and early in September was invited to teach mathematics and physics at Chillon College, a private boarding school in Villeneuve, Switzerland where sons of wealthy British and American families were prepared for university entrance. Wallis accepted, and since term began in early October it became necessary to ask Arthur Bloxam for permission to continue to write to his daughter. Both men had been brought up in religious families, steeped in Victorian manners, and it would not have occurred to Wallis to do otherwise. Fanny arranged for them to visit the day before his departure, to say his farewells and talk to Molly's father. In the event, Fanny dropped out.

On the evening of the last Monday in September Barnes arrived at Kidderpore Avenue in Hampstead. The Bloxams' house bore no number. Edgy, he walked back and forth to make sure he had found the right doorstep. He knocked; there was no response. He found the bell pull; no one answered.

. . . so I simply bolted, and I didn't stop till I got to Charing Cross, where I treated myself to a lonely and miserable cup of tea. I'm awfully sorry Molly. I did want to see you all so much, but having to wait gave me complete cold feet. I don't suppose you will understand, but that is really and truly what happened.[94]

He wrote this in the train to Dover next morning. It was his birthday, and he was leaving England for the first time in his life.

Fanny visited her brother to tell him how things stood. Arthur Bloxam agreed that Wallis could continue to write to his daughter, but there was to be no 'nonsense'. They must confine themselves to such subjects as might safely be 'exchanged between two pen-friends'. Wallis was to write 'nothing that might pose a threat to Molly's life at College and her open-minded contact with men her own age'.[95]

So began a correspondence that was to last for 712 days. It opened with Molly describing her first week at university, and Wallis telling her about Chillon. On arrival he was exhausted and sorry for himself. 'I've never been homesick since I first went away to school . . . I thought I was beyond such weakness, but I *have* been so wretched . . .' But after three days: 'This is a most gorgeous place. There are no words.' The school occupied a former hotel on the shore of Lake Geneva. Wallis wrote from a balcony in blazing sunshine, looking up at snowy peaks under 'the most priceless blue sky'. His bedroom faced Chillon Castle across a small bay. The lower slopes behind were clad with vineyards. The air rang to pieces of tin plate hung in the wind to scare crows, and the chime of cowbells.[96]

Chillon was known as the 'Eton of Switzerland'. Wallis hit it off with the headmaster, the Rev Franklyn de Winton Lushington, whose career thus far had taken in several headships, parish ministry, the Archdeaconry of Malta, authorship of *Sermons to Young Boys*, chaplaincy to the Guards during the Great War, and a lot of golf and tennis. Wallis was less impressed by the pupils:

I've been getting so cross with some of my people – I thumped a desk today. People seem so *stupid* over maths. I don't mind how much explaining I do, or what pains I take to make them understand, but inattention and wilful stupidity I cannot tolerate.[97]

And Molly? Barnes was in her thoughts. While writing to a friend about her family's new house, the kidnap of UCL's college mascot, and a talk by Edith Sitwell, she alluded to 'that Barnes person' who she had earlier described as 'most awfully brainy'.[98] In her letters she told him about the freshers' social, dancing fox-trots with young men, and a lecturer who gabbled. One of the young men was Hurley McCormick, a dental student at University College Hospital who was 'very attentive'. Hurley lived in Hampstead, so they often travelled together on the tube. He captained the college Fives team and took her to matches.[99] She described her course, which took in botany, chemistry, zoology and physics. She was comfortable with the first three, but the physics was hard going. 'I've never done any before, and when I read it by myself, it's dreadfully muddling'.[100]

Wallis swooped. 'If you would only send a *card* to say what you have difficulty on, I should so love to help.'[101] Molly told him of her problems with mechanics – she had never heard of fundamental or derived units, or of dimensional equations. 'I'm afraid you'd thump the desk pretty hard if I were in your class.' Wallis replied: 'If only you knew the elements of Calculus, all these things become so simple.' There and then he launched into an example: $s = ut + \frac{1}{2}at^2$, where s = displacement or distance, u = initial velocity, a = acceleration and t = time. Since all other formulae concerning velocities, acceleration and time could be derived from this, he said, it was the only one she needed to memorise.

Then, after two pages of equations, he broke off to answer a question. In her previous letter Molly had reminded him of her first visit to New Cross and asked, 'What did you think we'd be like?'

What did I expect you to be like? Honestly I hadn't formed any mental picture at all. The mere fact that you were a girl was enough to frighten me when I heard you were coming. And how could I ever dream you could be as you are?[102]

Molly replied that she had found him not 'horrid' or 'superior' but 'as decent as possible'.

Barnes (25 October): I love your expression 'as decent as possible'. Poor fellow, he has no doubt made the best of a bad job!

Molly (29 October): Barnes, you know really what I meant by 'as decent as possible'. I didn't mean anything about making the best of a bad job. I meant as decent as it was possible for any human being to be.

Barnes (6 November):

Yes, I did know, or at least guessed, which meaning was to be attached to your phrase 'as decent as possible'. I don't know what to answer Molly – I've been stuck here for over a quarter of an hour, from which you will conclude that there isn't any answer. [Next Day]. The only answer I can give, Molly, is this, that what you say is very far from being the truth, but if you chose to believe it of a man, he would make the most tremendous efforts to live up to your ideal, for your sake.

And that, perhaps, was as much as might be safely exchanged between two penfriends.

For several months Wallis strove to abide by Arthur Bloxam's conditions. He said nothing more about his feelings, applied himself to explaining calculus, described skiing lessons ('awfully difficult, but the most tremendous sport') and life at school ('I function as engineer in chief to this place . . . with only one carpenter to run the chauffage, lift etc. Also I am the stage electrician – they are mad on acting; and I've got to produce a 10 minute sunset at the end of term'). Lushington noted his versatility and asked him to become a permanent member of staff. Wallis agreed to 'stay for a bit' but said that his heart was in engineering. Earlier in the year there had been reports of a plan to build six airships to provide services between the UK, India, and eventually to Hong Kong and Australia.[103] If this came good, he must go back. He wanted to go back in any case. During the autumn he had become ever more certain about Molly and determined to gain her love. He reasoned that university would have widened her horizons. Eight days before Christmas he set out for New Cross. It was time to talk.

Winter journeys

Wallis arrived home dog-tired after a two-day journey involving four trains, no sleep, and a stormy Channel crossing. His first act was to talk things through with Fanny, who said she had spoken to her brother, and gave the impression that it would be acceptable for Wallis to talk openly to Molly about his feelings. Within minutes he fired off a letter to her, asking if they could speak alone before the two families met on Christmas Day.

The Thursday before Christmas found Wallis back on the doorstep from which he had fled at the end of September. Molly's mother made him welcome, and he was soon being cross-examined by Molly's sisters. To escape the family, Wallis asked Molly to walk with him to the station. It was pelting with rain and every time he turned to talk to her a spout of water drained from the rim of his new bowler hat onto her face. Standing in the downpour, Wallis described his feelings, his hope that one day Molly would marry him, and his intention to explain matters to her father on Christmas Day. He had no wish to put her under any pressure – he was not looking for a reply until she was ready to give one. Having reached the station, he walked Molly back to Kidderpore Avenue. Molly was encouraging but also puzzled, imagining that Wallis had singled her out and wondering why he had done so in preference to her elder sister. A year would pass before he could give her the answer.

That evening Molly told her parents what had happened. Arthur Bloxam's first words were: 'Oh, my *poor* child.' Molly responded that she was 'the proudest, richest person in all the world'.[104] 'I told them', she explained later, 'simply because it was so lovely and I was so glad, that I had to tell someone; and you have to tell your father and mother when anything great and exciting happens to you.'[105] Arthur Bloxam did not take this well. Fanny's belief that she had prepared the way turned out to be 'some awful misunderstanding' and Bloxam assumed that Wallis had broken his word about what he was putting into his letters. He told Molly not to see him again. Wallis, meanwhile, felt that he had made a mess of what he had meant to say, and on Christmas Eve he wrote a letter of explanation which he planned to put in Molly's hand next day.

When Bloxam and Wallis met on Christmas morning, Bloxam accused him of bad faith, ignored his explanations, and imposed new boundaries: one letter a fortnight, no visiting, and absolutely no expression of sentiment. Wallis realised that argument would be counterproductive. Inwardly, he was nettled by the suggestion of discreditable behaviour and frustrated that his aim to proceed honourably had been defeated in a way that suggested the opposite. Worst of all, the new embargo meant that he could not give his letter of clarification to Molly.

Despondent but unbowed, on Boxing Day he packed a rucksack with old clothes, took a train to Horsham, and set forth on foot. Walking like Schubert's haunted traveller he tramped into the Sussex Weald and on into Hampshire – a winter journey in reverse of his great walk in September 1914. A fortnight after the debacle at Kidderpore Avenue he told Molly 'I've been wandering about all over the place'. By then he was with the Boyds in Ulverston. He called on Charles Craven for advice about a job managing a car factory. Craven counselled against this, saying that Vickers might offer him a post in their commercial department in London.

In mid-January he was at Victoria station waiting to shepherd boys back to Chillon for the spring term. Wallis had cannily reasoned that Arthur Bloxam's ban on visiting Molly could not be extended to his entire family, so the previous Sunday he had called at Hampstead to say goodbye to them all. While there he mentioned the hoped-for Vickers job: it looked likely that they would engage him to liaise with overseas clients. And if Vickers re-joined the airship business, he would be in the right place to return to his calling.[106]

During February and March Wallis recorded the arrival of Molly's letters in his diary and marked the days, sometimes even the hours, when he posted letters to her. Later, they called these 'weathery letters', since apart from calculus they were restricted to subjects such as daily events or weather that would pass Arthur Bloxam's prohibition on anything to do with feelings. It rained a lot in the late winter. Wallis told of playing fives, refereeing hockey matches, exploring Chillon Castle, a failed attempt to give up smoking, and an ascent of the 1300-metre Mount Sonchaux. Somewhere during this trek Wallis plucked a gentian, which he enclosed with his next letter. Molly kept the flower and sent a hellebore in return. Names of more flowers and plants appeared in following letters, wherein wild thyme, lavender, meadowsweet, and lilac became proxies for frames of mind.

In mid-March the job offer from Vickers was confirmed. 'I feel jolly sad at leaving' he wrote in his last letter from Switzerland, but on Good Friday he stepped onto the train for Paris, and by mid-evening on Saturday he was home. On Easter Sunday, 1 April 1923, he visited the Bloxams. Eight days later his new job with Vickers began. He told Molly that the post was 'an exceptionally good one', with 'very good prospects of advancement.' But he reflected: 'Some funny fate pursues me. I never seem to be able to settle down, and think I'm safe for life, but something else crops up, and off I go again. I've had 14 different sets of rooms in 16 years. When shall I have a home of my own? What a book I could write on landladies!'[107] Fate was about to knock on his door again.

4
Woggins in Love, 1923–25

Commander Burney makes a call

> Oh Molly, such exciting times. Yesterday, at a moment's notice
> I had to attend a conference on Commander Burney's financial
> scheme for starting a great Imperial Air Transport Company. He
> didn't know who I was but during the night he must have found
> out, for first thing this morning he rang me up, and asked me
> to go and talk to him. And then and there he asked me to join
> in with him in the new company.[1]

Charles Dennistoun Burney was a bustling, charismatic figure. On
early acquaintance Molly found him at once mannerless and charming. Dapper, stocky, cigar often in hand and his glamorous American
wife Gladys often on his elbow, he was a year younger than Wallis
and his career so far had included active service in the Royal Navy,
design work for the Bristol Aeroplane Company, and co-invention
of a wartime minesweeping device that had earned him a fortune.
Since 1920 he had been in discussion with the government about an
air service to connect Britain, India, and Australia. Lloyd George's
administration was lobbied on this subject from several directions,
and ignored all of them.[2] Burney, however, was persistent, and by
1922 his scheme was the main one left in the field.

On 30 March 1922 Burney, Alfred Ashbolt (Tasmania's Agent-
General in London)[3] and Wallis's old comrade George Scott outlined
their thinking to a meeting in Caxton Hall.[4] Opinion then held that
the main air routes of the British Empire would be flown by airships,

with aeroplane connections branching off over shorter distances.[5] Burney and Scott proposed an initial fleet of six airships to provide a bi-weekly service connecting London, Bombay and Rangoon. In due course this could be followed by services to India on alternate days with extensions to Hong Kong and Australia. At times of international tension the airships would be available to the navy.

Burney envisaged a mix of funding, from Vickers, Shell, and other investors, with contributions from the governments of India, Australia, and the UK. Britain was expected to provide facilities such as mooring masts and meteorological services along the routes. Burney and Scott believed that initial experience would swiftly lead to improvements and hence the rapid obsolescence of the first airships and early emergence of a second generation of more efficient vessels. Since initial running expenses and depreciation could not be recovered until this later stage, it was recognised that interest on debentures and shares would need to be underwritten by the taxpayer until the scheme became sustainable. Burney called for tax incentives, and the free transfer to the provider of existing airship bases at Cardington and Pulham.

Winston Churchill, Secretary of State for the Colonies, was underwhelmed.[6] Sir Robert Horne, Chancellor of the Exchequer, gave his advice against a background of record unemployment, the shrinkage of staple industries and cuts to hold off inflation. He observed that 'the Government is never invited to intervene except where the chances of success are so remote as to render it impossible to raise funds in the market'. When airships could pay their way, he said, they would arrive without Government help. Until then, he advised the Cabinet to avoid speculative plans which involved additional expenditure.[7]

The Cabinet invited the view of the Committee of Imperial Defence.[8] The Committee's advice, relayed by Lloyd George to the House of Commons five days later, endorsed the Chancellor's view that taxpayers' money should not be used to develop an airship service. However, this apparently clear verdict was coupled with a further and inconsistent recommendation, namely that a special sub-committee should be formed 'to study in detail the technical aspects of Commander Burney's scheme' to ascertain if his claims were well founded.[9]

The special sub-committee was chaired by the Conservative MP Leo Amery, with members drawn from the Admiralty, Air Ministry, Colonial Office, and Treasury. This looked like more stalling, but when the sub-committee reported on 1 August it found firmly in favour of developing an airship service. By now, however, the Conservative-Liberal coalition was in its last days. A general election was held in November, at which the Conservatives led by Bonar Law won an overall majority and Burney was returned as MP for Uxbridge, the better to promote his scheme. But as 1922 ended, *The Times* described the year as one in which Burney's proposals had been 'passed from one committee to another' without tangible result.[10]

Law's government had other things on its mind, like ratification of the Irish Treaty, unemployment and the state of agriculture. It seemed that a decision on Burney's scheme was fated to be put off indefinitely. Coincidentally, when Wallis re-joined Vickers in April 1923 ('It's absolutely ripping being back in engineering again'[11]) one of his first assignments was to make yet another review of Burney's figures.[12] He told Molly they were unrealistic. 'Until the Government feel rich enough to start experimenting in a relatively small way, I fear nothing will happen.'[13] Yet a few days later, here he was, about to throw in his lot with Burney. What had happened?

The answer is that several things had been happening at once. One was that the sub-committee set up the year before had shed its old skin and lived on in a new guise with changed terms of reference. Samuel Hoare (Secretary of State for Air) was now its chairman.[14] During the spring of 1923 the tone and direction of its questions encouraged Burney to think that its eventual recommendations would be positive.[15] Another stimulus was the Board of Trade, which had begun to argue for a subsidised air mail service as far as Egypt to accelerate postal links between the UK and Australia.[16]

A third factor was Bonar Law's health. In Cabinet he was reticent because he was finding it difficult to speak. On 1 May he left for what was hoped would be a restorative holiday in Mediterranean sunshine. However, within days his son and close friends saw that he was seriously ill. Throat cancer was diagnosed on 17 May; he was advised to step down. On the same day, sensing change in the offing, Burney convened a meeting at Vickers House to look afresh at the costs of his scheme.[17]

Over the Whitsun holiday Whitehall hummed with rumours about Law's successor.[18] Burney hoped that the new premier and Cabinet would be more receptive; he accordingly stepped up his planning and networking. He had hopes of Lord Curzon, who as a former Viceroy of India, took a keen interest in Imperial communications, but in the event it was Stanley Baldwin who was summoned by the King on 22 May, and who brought the Secretary of State for Air into the Cabinet as a full member. Next morning Wallis wrote to tell Molly that he was leaving for Germany 'at a moment's notice'. 'I am going with Commander Burney to Friedrichshafen to advise him on the purchase of the Zeppelin Airship Works. Fearfully secret!!'[19]

Wallis's unexpected journey was the climax of a week which had swung between extremes of hope and regret. Burney's first summons had put him into an ecstasy of indecision. On Tuesday, 15 May:

. . . suppose I join Burney, and in another few years Airships once more break down? I shall never get another opening in Vickers such as they offered me last Christmas . . . It's a big decision. Which will it be, Molly, adventure again, or safety?[20]

By Wednesday it looked like safety, not because he wanted it, but because his director had said that Vickers was unlikely to loan him to Burney for more than a few months.

Then on Thursday: 'I'm feeling rather heartbroken Molly.' Wallis had just emerged from an all-day conference attended by Pratt (who had shaken the meeting by pointing out that hitherto only 43 per cent of the weight of Duralumin purchased for an airship actually went into its structure, the rest being wastage),[21] and Pratt's arrival had raised a question of loyalties. It was Pratt who had drawn Wallis into the airship industry, Pratt who had stood firm during the turf wars at Barrow, Pratt who had led his department, Pratt who had campaigned for commercial airships, and Pratt who had looked out for him during his breakdown.[22] If there was to be a new post of chief engineer in Burney's new company, in justice should it not go to Pratt?

That evening he told Molly he was 'out of airships' because 'the only decent thing I could do was to stand aside and let Pratt, who has been my colleague for many years, step into the place that Burney offered me.' The decision revealed his real feelings. 'When the thing was undecided, I could see many arguments against joining Burney . . . now that it is all over, I feel perfectly miserable!'[23]

Despondency deepened. On Friday, Fanny and Charles left for a Whitsun break. Alone at Pepys Road, Wallis asked the Bloxams if he could visit on the coming Bank Holiday. Recently, Arthur Bloxam seemed to have become more tolerant: during April Wallis had twice been invited to Hampstead, Molly and Baba had been allowed to visit Pepys Road and the three of them had been for a walk in Greenwich Park. But this time the answer was no (or as Molly put it, 'Daddy is absolutely unpersuadable'), and Wallis was mistaken about Arthur Bloxam's tolerance: he sent a note requesting that Wallis visit less often. Wallis duly spent the Bank Holiday writing to Molly about Cartesian geometry and put 'Black Monday' in his diary.[24]

It is not clear what happened on the Tuesday, but events give the gist. Burney was preparing to head for Friedrichshafen to negotiate an agreement with Zeppelin. To do this he needed the best possible technical expertise. Following Wallis's decision on the previous Thursday to cede his place to Pratt, he assumed this would be Pratt. Pratt, however, had been thinking things over. He already had a job, and he had a settled home and family in Ulverston. Did he wish to exchange them for the vagaries of a project that would uproot his family and might threaten his career?[25] More than this, after months of hardship there were hints of better times ahead for the Barrow yard. Charles Craven was taking over from their old foe McKechnie, while Pratt had a new role in the submarine mines department, and with that had come new loyalties. We can assume that he talked this through with Kathleen, and that either they decided against joining

Burney or that Pratt knew in his bones that it was Wallis's design skills that Burney really needed. Whichever, on Tuesday or very early on Wednesday Burney turned back to Wallis. This time Wallis accepted, and just before noon the two met at Victoria station and boarded the train for Paris.

Friedrichshafen

Dinner at the Café de Paris and the night train to Basel gave Burney an opportunity to explain what they were doing. He envisaged two new entities: a state-subsidised airline, and an airship construction company with which the airline would work in tandem. Neither yet existed. The aim of their trip was to boost the credibility of the concept in the eyes of Baldwin's new government by forming a partnership-in-waiting with Zeppelin. There were several reasons for doing so. One was reputational: Luftschiffbau Zeppelin (LZ) was the world leader in airship making; if its directors took Burney seriously then Britain's air minister and his advisers would surely do so too. A second factor was money: most of the costs in Burney's scheme would be incurred long before it attracted any income, so it made sense to spread them. A third and important aspect was access to LZ's patents and accumulated knowledge.[26] As to what might be in it for LZ, the answer was survival. The Treaty of Versailles had imposed an interdict on Germany's airship industry; an international partnership could be a way to keep it in being.

Friedrichshafen is on the Bodensee's north shore, and the last stage of the journey was aboard a ferry from Romanshorn across the lake. The town had a reputation as Swabia's Nice, and as the ferry docked late in the afternoon Wallis admired its classical planning and domed baroque towers. LZ had been quartered there since the end of the nineteenth century.[27] Other aviation interests had taken root nearby, and LZ had acquired the lakefront Kurgarten Hotel to accommodate business visitors. Wallis had barely had time to admire his luxurious bathroom or wonder at the Alpine view from his balcony before he and Burney were swept into their first meeting.

Across the table were LZ's managing director, Dr Hugo Eckener, and Ernst Lehmann. Eckener was becoming one of the best-known and most popular people in Weimar Germany. In airship matters he was the most respected figure in the world. During the war he had been responsible for training most of his country's airship captains (including Lehmann), while since its end, now as LZ's head, he had fended off Allied demands for the demolition of remaining airship works by building ZR-3, ostensibly a passenger airship, destined for the United States Navy as a war reparation. Lehman, too, cut an impressive figure. He had trained as an engineer, served as a Zeppelin captain during the war, was now a member of LZ's board, and had recently spent months in Stockholm and Chicago studying the economics of airship passenger and freight transport. Burney was aware that Lehmann and Eckener were already in discussion with the US Goodyear Tyre and Rubber Company about a joint subsidiary to manufacture airships in America.

Burney and Wallis emerged late in the evening and took stock. Zeppelin's structure was akin to a pyramid made of modules; part of their task was to work out how to connect with it. At the apex was the Zeppelin Trust, which was the exclusive shareholder in the holding company, Luftschiffbau Zeppelin. LZ in its turn controlled subsidiary companies that included Zeppelin Werft (the actual airship-building firm), Maybach (which made engines for Zeppelin), and other entities concerned with fabric, airship sheds, gas production, gear cutting, and Dornier flying boats. Since the Treaty of Versailles, the companies had sought to keep themselves busy through diversification, using Duralumin stocks to make kitchenware, and engineering expertise to build cars and engines for boats. Amid all this, Eckener had succeeded in retaining the capacity to resume airship building when opportunity arose.

Eckener and Lehmann had stamina as well as expertise. The Friday meeting ran until 11 p.m., and Saturday's conference continued until midnight. The long days were partly to accommodate Burney, who wished to leave for London on the Sunday, but also because there was a lot to discuss. By Saturday evening they had roughed out an agreement that provided for operating and holding companies on each side, exchanges of shares, and protocols for placing technical knowledge at each other's disposal. In parallel, they discussed a new passenger airship, twice the size of the ship then being built for the United States. Eckener and Lehmann shared lessons they had learned through services operated by DELAG: for an airship of the size they were contemplating, no more than 150 passengers, one class only, and a strict limit on baggage weight. Wallis was intrigued by their realisation that since fuel was cheaper than cargo space, fuel rather than water could be used as ballast.

Wallis had been expecting to leave with Burney, but at the last minute, Burney asked him to stay on to finalise the draft agreement and glean more technical data. Wallis was flattered. 'As the whole affair involves capital to the extent of over eight million pounds (English) it is no small affair, and the interrelated companies are very complex. I hope to goodness I don't make a mess of it, but do not feel much worried.' Did he know that Eckener's doctorate was in psychology?

On Sunday afternoon, Burney gone, Wallis walked for an hour by the lake, then went back to the Kurgarten to continue a letter to Molly. 'I cannot resist writing a line to send you *one penny*, in the form of a thousand-mark note.' While Germany's hyperinflation was mind-boggling, he was fizzing from his discussions with Lehmann and Eckener:

> There is now, in my mind not the least doubt that in 2 or 3 years from now, we shall have the most wonderful series of air lines running from England to India, twice a week and back, in 2½ days! Carrying 200 passengers each, and mails and parcels. I don't care if I die after that. It will only be the start of course, and the line will subsequently be extended to Australia and New Zealand . . .[28]

And the food! 'Molly I'm not a pig, really I'm not, but I have consistently eaten too much ever since I came. We all have. It's the most delicious, most tastefully served, food I have ever eaten.' Yet he was lonely. The Kurgarten was full of couples and families. 'Everyone else seems to have a particularly charming and jolly companion, and you sit alone and glum at your little corner.'[29]

Monday: more meetings. The draft agreement was ready for typing by Tuesday evening; Wallis posted it to London on Wednesday. Thursday was a national holiday. Eckener and Lehmann invited Wallis to join them and their wives for an afternoon sailing on the Bodensee. The yacht was a 52-foot cutter which had formerly been owned by King Wilhelm II. 'We had the most topping time, and I got as brown as anything.'[30] Wallis had been anxious about etiquette and asked the Kurgarten's head waiter ('a most important person') whether he should contribute food; the head waiter said this would be advisable and provided a basket of sandwiches, hard-boiled eggs, wine and mineral water. Wallis arrived at the yacht as bidden, at 11 a.m. There was no one there. 'Presently in the distance I saw the Lehmanns (I always want to say the Lehmen!) plus servant, carrying 2 large baskets. We stood and looked at each other.' In due course, Eckener and his wife Johanna appeared, with an even larger basket. 'At this we all burst out laughing!'

Lehmann brought a large accordion on which he played folk-songs, while another guest, a former banker, walked back and forth along the deck humming the words. 'Somehow I felt absolutely at home among them.' Eckener and Lehmann produced an elaborate cooked lunch; coffee and cakes were served in mid-afternoon; Wallis's sandwiches and eggs were eaten at six; 'about nine I got back to my hotel and had dinner!'[31]

After final discussions, Wallis was taken to see ZR-3 a-building in the Luftschiffhalle at Löwenthal.[32] On the last evening, Lehmann drove him to the mountaintop village of Heiligenberg for a farewell dinner. Looking out past the castle, across the shimmering Bodensee to the Alps, here he was, guest of the greatest airshipman in the world and feeling as if he was on top of it. 'I got quite heart-achy when it was time to leave. I wish one didn't get so fond of places.'[33] But he left in hope, and sure enough, after the early boat, train after train – to Zurich, Basel, Paris, Victoria, New Cross – and the late-evening walk up Pepys Road, there it was: 'Found letter from Molly.'[34]

The passing of the year: Burney

Burney's revised scheme was put to the government in the same week. It was divided into three stages and called for public subsidy over seven years. Stage one would be the formation of a construction and guarantee company with a capital of £0.6 million, of which half would be allotted to Zeppelin, £0.1 million kept in hand for general purposes and contingencies, and the remainder put towards the formation of an airship company. The government's contributions at this point would be £0.4 million, and the transfer of its remaining airships and bases at Pulham and Cardington. Stage one deliverables would include infrastructure, like mooring masts, and a 5 million-cubic-foot capacity airship to provide a pilot service between England and Egypt.

Stage two would require a subsidy of £0.4 million for three years, at the end of which a weekly service would be running between England and India. In the third phase a fleet of six airships would provide a bi-weekly service to India. In the latter stages the company's capital would be increased partly by discounting the government subsidies and partly by the injection of new capital from the company's resources. Since progression to each stage would require successful completion of the one before, it was argued that the government's exposure to risk was limited.[35]

At noon on Friday, 20 July Stanley Baldwin's Cabinet met to consider these proposals.[36] After discussion they agreed to adopt the scheme 'in its general lines'.[37] Their decision was hedged with riders,[38] but it was brave: at this date there were no certainties about any aspect of air travel, and there was no precedent for spending public money to support civil aviation.[39]

The Cabinet wished the news to be withheld until the end of the parliamentary session. This suited Hoare, who had a mass of further negotiations to complete, and it may have suited Burney, who now had a company to form and capital to find. Equally, the Imperial Conference was due in October, and both national representatives and the public wished to know where things stood. Hoare told the Conference that a final decision would be taken 'as soon as possible'.[40]

Early in November he advised the Cabinet that negotiations with Burney were 'practically settled', and that a 'cardinal factor' in them being so was Burney's undertaking to provide £0.5 million of private capital during the life of the project. Ministers were told that the agreement was virtually ready for signature.[41]

Other things supervened. On 2 November Zeppelin accepted Goodyear's offer to buy the patents and manufacturing rights for its airships and accessories.[42] This meant that the partnership negotiated back in May fell through. Discussions with the Treasury had been so protracted that the opportunity was lost.

Worse followed. Stanley Baldwin's majority was comfortable, but he wanted an explicit mandate for his policies of protectionism and Empire preference and decided on a snap election. Parliament was prorogued on 16 November. Hoare pleaded for parliamentary time to see through the enabling legislation to conclude the agreement – but Burney's new Airship Guarantee Company was not incorporated until 29 November,[43] and by then all unfinished parliamentary business had fallen. Burney and his company secretary signed the agreement with the Treasury and waited in the hope that the Conservatives would be returned to ratify it.[44] But when votes were counted a week later, Parliament was hung. In the new year Labour and the Liberals voted down Baldwin's King's Speech. By 24 January 1924 Ramsay MacDonald was in Downing Street, and there was a new Secretary of State for Air: Christopher Birdwood Thomson.

The passing of the year: Wallis

After Friedrichshafen Wallis went back to his job at Vickers House.[45] The position Burney had offered awaited the formation of the new company, and the new company awaited the completion of negotiations with the Treasury that awaited the decision of the Cabinet. Wallis used the summer to renew friendships, produce more calculus and trigonometry tutorials, and say more about himself in his fortnightly letters to Molly. He told her about Victor Goddard, who just then was lovelorn, and Edward Masterman, who had side-stepped another of Wallis's refusals to accept a royalty by presenting him with a handsome grandmother clock.

He joined the Territorial Army: 'Oh, for lots of reasons Molly,'[46] one of them being his wish to work off the effects of the Kurgarten's cuisine. He was now a gunner, in a mobile anti-aircraft unit.[47]

> I had to enlist for 4 years and am not taking a commission, just going in the ranks – it's much more fun. It doesn't really take much time, one has to do 40 drills a year and go into camp for 15 days a year . . . it helps to keep one fit and hard, and what weighed with quite a lot – the best way to learn how to make airships invulnerable is to find out all about the methods available for shooting them down![48]

In July, 'tired of being lonely',[49] he holidayed with the Boyds at Borth in mid-Wales. While he was there, Molly went to stay at Pepys Road. Fanny organised this in cahoots with Barnes, to give Molly a fuller picture of the family and its history. Molly was given Barnes's bedroom ('I love this room of yours, and this delightfully comfy bed'), and the red and white roses that awaited her were 'topping'. Fanny produced some family photographs.

> You were a funny, solemn, fat little boy. Poor Barnes, I know you hate seeing and hearing things about you when you were small, so I'll stop. But one thing Auntie Fanny told me, and that is that you can knit. And you have knitted a sock on two needles. I have yet to discover the thing you are incapable of doing.[50]

On the day that Wallis returned from Borth the Bloxams were aboard a train bound for north Wales. Wallis worked out where their trains would cross and waited for the momentary blur as he and Molly passed a few feet from each other.

His return coincided with Hoare's announcement in the Commons that the government had decided to support Burney's scheme.[51] 'Molly, I do believe I'm going back to airships again.' He went to see Burney's secretary, who confirmed that Burney was 'very anxious' that Wallis should join him. This was doubly good news, as Vickers had just offered him a new post he did not want.[52]

> Airships are the only thing I really care about. I've given up all my time and energy to them for the last ten years nearly, staked my future on them as it were. I don't think anyone knows quite how hard I've worked . . . The year before the war I hardly ever had even a Sunday off . . . I felt in a way that that was my special work, and it became a way of worshipping one's Creator to work to the utmost limit of one's strength and ability. Do you think you could see it that way?[53]

Burney's formal summons did not come for some weeks. This suited Wallis; in mid-August his anti-aircraft battery went into camp at Holme-next-the-Sea.

Holme is a remote place in the angle between Norfolk's north coast and the eastern shore of the Wash. On arrival at Hunstanton there was a five-mile march to the site. The men slept in bell tents, six in each, feet to the pole, on narrow straw-stuffed palliasses, three blankets apiece. A day began at 06:00, followed by forty-five minutes of physical training, with drill and gunnery parades for the rest of the day. When the sun shone, necks and arms were burned; when they fired, nails and knuckles were torn as they caught on breech blocks. At any hint of an unoccupied moment, a kit inspection, equipment cleaning, or extra drill was ordered to fill it. For washing, one out-of-doors tap was shared by 180 men.

Wallis loved it. At night, he delighted in the flap and motion of the tent, the wind on his neck, and the smell of damp straw. By day, his one complaint was that his wish to be in the ranks had been thwarted by promotion to lance bombardier. The end of the second Tuesday in August thus found him in charge of the guard which protected the guns and ammunition, some way off from the main camp, practically on the seashore.

> I am writing to you by an inch of guttering candle stuck on my upturned enamel plate. The door of the tent is open, it's ten to

> twelve, and pouring with rain, simply beating on to the tent . . .
> We've just had our supper, dry bread and cheese – and a mug
> of beer, thousands of moths are in the candle and the beer, and
> as I drained my mug – there was a large earwig drowned in the
> bottom.

Around him, stretched out, were off-duty guards, while the man
on duty periodically appeared in the tent doorway to shelter from
the downpour. Their rifles, stacked tripod-fashion, cast a flickering
shadow high up inside the tent. 'We are doing Molly something that
men have done from time immemorial I suppose.'[54]

Live firing was exhilarating. He relished the intricate rhythm of
twelve men working one gun, each performing different tasks a split
second apart from the others to achieve a firing rate close on 20
rounds a minute. At the end, he was put in charge of the guard for
the convoy of lorries that towed their guns back to London. During
an overnight stop in Cambridge, he lay on his back in one of the
trucks, listening to the notes of bells from different parts of the town
that mingled in the damp night as they told the hours and quarters.[55]
Molly replied: 'I can just picture you lying in that lorry, listening to
the chimes . . . I do think men are lucky being able to do things like
that.'[56] He sent photographs of himself. So did Molly, her hair now
put up – a sign of adulthood.

The long-awaited call came on 13 September. 'Molly, Commander Burney has asked me to join him in the new Air Ship Company
this afternoon.'[57] He was to go to the airship station at Pulham in
Norfolk 'to survey two old airships and report to him as to whether
we can re-commission them to start a training service'.

There came a time when Wallis could scarcely bear to be in the
same room as Burney, but just then: 'I like Burney very much and
shall love working for him.' The salary (£650) would be higher than
his present level, which was a relief, 'in case anything happens to the
Pater'. Everything was right.

> Besides, Molly, it's the most wonderful work in the world. Some
> day I shall be able to take you all over a ship, and then you will

see for yourself. You see it's all new, and one is thinking out new things all the time.[58]

Pulham was where the R33 and R36 were mothballed under the eye of George Scott, Wallis's old comrade from Barrow who had commanded the R34 on her Atlantic crossing. 'Scottie and his wife are the most delightful people.' Pointedly, maybe sighingly, he added: 'They've been married nearly 5 years, but seem just as much in love as ever – I felt quite in the way sometimes. He's the same age as me, and she was married when she was nineteen or twenty and they have two ripping children.'[59]

As the expected sign-off with the Government neared, he 'started work on the new airship in earnest', working late every night to satisfy Burney, who 'wanted to see what my proposals were, so I've had a rush'.[60] Burney gave him the go-ahead to recruit. Straight away he wrote to colleagues from Barrow days. Entries in his diary show him tracking down John Edwin Temple and George Bower, founder members of the original team in Victoria Street ten years before. Pratt helped him to trace Philip Teed, his right-hand man during the inflation of No. 9 and No. 23r. Like Richmond, he had been working for the IAACC in Germany. Teed agreed to join when the time came. In answer to questions about where the new airship would be built, the working assumption was that it would be at Cardington.

Two other diary entries in November told of matters ahead: 'Harley Street' and 'Design Committee'. In Harley Street he saw a specialist about the more or less permanent head cold from which he suffered. The specialist found an old boxing injury which had closed off part of a nasal cavity and recommended an operation to open it up again. Wallis arranged for the procedure to be done over the Christmas holiday – an arrangement he regretted when he found that it clashed with the first dance to which Molly had invited him.

As for the Design Committee, Burney reasoned that following the run-down of Britain's airship industry it would make sense to bring together the very few people left who possessed any relevant experience. This was logical, but it was not to Wallis's liking. For one thing, at first his position on the committee was as chief draughtsman and secretary – he was to be in attendance and be advised. For another, none of the experts whom Burney had collected were people whose advice he respected. Among them were Reginald Colmore and Vincent Richmond, whose experience had been with non-rigids. Colmore by this stage was essentially an administrator.[61] Richmond was a structural engineer, but his work in the RNAS had centred on dopes and the treatment of non-rigid fabric covers (whence his nickname, 'Dopey'). In the eyes of his friends, Richmond was modest, a good listener, collaborative, well-read. Like Wallis, he had an out-and-out faith in the future of rigids for long-distance transport. In other circumstances the two might have come together; as it was, the AGC's Design Committee was an environment in which they fell out. Wallis believed that Richmond had asked Burney for the post of Chief Designer and having been refused now 'rather tries to prove that anything I do is wrong'.[62] Whether this was true or sprang from Wallis's intermittent sense of persecution, we do not know, but Wallis had developed a tendency that became more pronounced as time passed: if he found someone unqualified for a task – as he believed Richmond to be – this would take precedence over other characteristics, such as friendship or tolerance, or loyalty; the effect in others' eyes being perceived as pitiless.

Preparations for the new airship were all-consuming ('Do you realise that I have not seen you since September 8th?' he asked Molly in mid-November), while Baldwin's decision to call the snap election set a new cat among existing pigeons:

> This wretched election is upsetting all our Airship plans, because the Bill . . . was to have been passed this session; and now, of course, it can scarcely get thro' the new Parliament until say March. And if the Liberals come back that awful man Winston Churchill is a bitter opponent of Rigid Airships and very likely he may try to stop it altogether. It puts me in a very difficult position as I had started engaging a new staff . . . and it is awkward if a man is already in a good post, and perhaps married, to ask him to give it up to join me, and then perhaps have to wait for ages.[63]

Wallis entered the Park Lodge nursing home for his operation five days before Christmas. The operation was not straightforward. The surgeon discovered a split septum which he had to dissect and then reconstruct. 'It's quite an uncanny feeling being able to breathe thro' the right side of my nose – a thing I haven't done for years.'[64]

Rules of engagement

Wallis's week in bed gave him time to think. The result was a carefully crafted letter to Arthur Bloxam in which he asked him to reconsider the rules imposed the year before. Wallis said that by keeping to these rules he did not know the current state of Molly's feelings, because feelings had not been discussed. He pointed out that when the time came for Molly to make up her mind, 'the present restrictions will do nothing to make her change it'. He was now well paid, well insured, and enjoyed the brightest prospects. He would not press Molly for an engagement or commitment and promised 'not to attempt to urge her or hurry her into a decision in any way, without your further approval.' All he asked for was unrestricted friendship.[65]

Bloxam agreed to relax his rules. Wallis could now write as often as he wanted and, within reason, be open about his feelings. Molly, on the other hand, was not to mention feelings.

Wallis reported all this in a long letter three days later. He explained that she was 'entirely free', and that when the time came it would be for her to decide whether to accept or reject him. But he was now free to write from the heart. He looked back over the past eighteen months – his going to Switzerland, his despondency the previous Whitsun when Arthur had asked him not to visit so often – and reminisced about her encouragement at difficult times. On the 19th they met for lunch at the Waldorf, shy and excited, then on to the Empire Theatre to see *Treasure Island*. At the end of the afternoon Wallis put into her hand the letter he had written on Christmas Eve 1922 and then withheld after the row with Arthur. Molly read the letters side by side. 'I love them both and have read and re-read them until I almost know them by heart. But how could you write such a beautiful, wonderful letter as the one you sent me last week, I can't think. Oh Barnes, I don't want you to go out of my life; I want you to be in it for ever and ever.'[66]

The 'weathery letters' of 1922 and 1923 explored opinions, because feelings were banned. The 1924 letters, in contrast, thrum with a new energy as the couple returned to discover and compare what their real feelings had been. And, at last, they were allowed to be in each other's company, albeit usually still lightly chaperoned. On 2 February they went to a dance in Hampstead. Wallis wrote in his diary: 'My first dance with Molly.' Molly told a friend: 'He dances absolutely rippingly.'

Thomson and the two ships plan

Ramsay MacDonald described his friend Christopher Thomson as ambitious, bookish, a connoisseur of good food and wine, lover of music, a linguist, and inclined to hot temper. He came from an Indian Army family and had set out as a career soldier. During the Great War he had seen service in the Royal Engineers and politically in Bucharest, where he came under the enduring spell of an already-married Romanian princess. At the war's end he served as a staff officer at Versailles. Unimpressed by what followed, he left the army and joined the Fabian Society, nursed a parliamentary constituency, lost two elections, and finally entered Parliament in 1923. MacDonald moved him to the Lords with a barony and made him Air Minister with a seat in Cabinet.

Thomson refused to endorse the agreement that Samuel Hoare had negotiated. He was wary of Burney, but smitten by airships, and when Labour came to office he embarked on a rethink. On 14 May 1924, Burney was in the Commons chamber when Ramsay MacDonald rose to speak. He dismissed the scheme negotiated by his predecessors on the grounds that it would have created a virtual monopoly, and that it was open to financial and technical objections,[67] but went on to agree with them that airship development was necessary. His government would therefore instruct the Air

Ministry to embark on new research and experiment in lighter-than-air transport. The work would be based at Cardington. It would include experiments with an existing ship, to be reconditioned for the purpose, and a new airship with capacity of 5 million cubic feet. The Air Ministry would build an air terminal and an intermediate base overseas, with facilities to enable the two ships to be operated between England and India.

In parallel, 'the Air Ministry would give the Airship Guarantee Company the first offer of a contract for the construction of a second ship for commercial purposes.' The contract would accordingly provide for the ship's repurchase by the AGC, at a reduced figure, on the successful completion of flying trials. 'By these means' said MacDonald, 'private initiative will be linked with lighter-than-air development from the start, and, in the event of success, the early inauguration of commercial airship services open to all firms likely to be interested will be facilitated.'

MacDonald pointed out that the second vessel would 'provide the nucleus of a reserve of personnel and material', and that since the Government and commercial ships would be laid down concurrently, they should go into service sooner than under the original scheme. A further advantage would be the presence of two separate airship manufacturing plants and other ground facilities on a scale which would allow subsequent rapid expansion.

During ensuing exchanges, Samuel Hoare tersely challenged MacDonald's comparative figures, while Burney gave a blustering and convoluted reply to several MPs who asked how the main outline of the scheme had already appeared in that morning's *Times*.[68]

MacDonald's criticisms of the Burney scheme were fair. Burney's timetable and financial arrangements rested on optimism, there was insufficient contingency, and if any of it had worked the result would have been a state-subsidised operating company in which the state had no voice and Vickers enjoyed control of airship construction. Beyond this, Burney soon realised that the airship he was setting out to build was too small to be commercially viable.

History's opinion of Thomson's replacement scheme has since been coloured by the calamity in which it ended, and by its supposed capitalist-socialist binary. In fact, it had positive aspects, and if it did not go far enough to breathe new life into a forsaken sector, it went a good deal further than did Burney as whittled down by Baldwin. Thomson and his Air Ministry advisers saw the need for overseas infrastructure, for underpinning services like meteorology and radio, for materials research, for adequate bases, and for an airworthy ship in which to recover flying skills that had been all but lost. With this said, concentrating untried features in one machine would not make for safety, and the idea that the RAW airship should be a laboratory for innovation was unwise. Thomson further overlooked the fact that Britain just then contained only three people with experience of designing a rigid airship, that one of them (Pratt) had left the field, and that the other two (Wallis and Temple) were working for Burney. Instead of bringing scarce expertise together, his scheme separated what little of it there was. It also introduced another risk: Thomson's plan cast the Air Ministry both as a protagonist in the new scheme and as its regulator. These were not roles that could be safely combined.

Wallis did not react to Ramsey MacDonald's two-ship announcement in letters at the time. The government had been discussing the scheme almost from the moment it took office,[69] and the AGC had known about it since March. Moreover, since Colmore and Richmond now had an airship of their own to build, they would be leaving the AGC's Design Committee – which pleased him. Another reason for his indifference was that his mind was elsewhere. Molly's exams were approaching, and on the day of the statement he was in Swan's pen shop on Oxford Street, taking advice about the gold Eternal nib of the pen he was buying for Molly. She thanked him for it with a mathematical proof:

Data	Pen
To prove that	The pen belongs to Molly
Proof	Barnes bought the pen

∴ The pen belongs to Barnes
but Barnes belongs to Molly
∴ The pen belongs to Molly
Q.E.D.[70]

Wallis replied that it was 'a nice sensation' to feel that he belonged to her, but it would be 'a thousand times nicer' if she were to treat him as her servant.[71] Writing this reminded him of Thackeray's novel *The Newcomes*, in which Clive Newcome, in love with his cousin (who has an unpleasant father called Barnes), says: 'Make a slave of me. Let me get a silver collar and mark "Ethel" on it, and go through the world with my badge.'[72] Wallis mused: 'Which rather reads as if I would wear it, if you were to send a collar to me. I wonder if you would?' He imagined himself coming down in the morning and finding a parcel containing a collar, 'complete with a little padlock and key and a note saying that you ordered me to wear it day and night during your pleasure'. Imagination now in flight, a silver collar would be cold, hard, expensive; 'a leather dog collar would be much more comfortable'. He went on: 'I don't believe you've got the courage to risk my disobedience, so I jolly well dare you! I say, what a sell for me, if you do and I have to obey!'[73]

In reply Molly sent him a length of velvet ribbon, and with it, a note.

To: Barnes Wallis

It is my pleasure that you wear this collar with my name on it round your neck as a sign that you are my really truly servant and will do whatever I wish – from taking me to the theatre, to eating chocolate blancmange . . . You will wear it always, except when you are bathing and when you are wearing tennis flannels with a shirt which is open at the neck, until next September 12th when I will tell you if you are to keep it or throw it away. And whenever you see or feel the collar you will remember that I am your mistress and you will do what I order you to do for ever and ever world without end.

(signed) Molly[74]

Then came a crunch.

I will tell you what happened last night. I lost my temper, Barnes, really truly and completely lost it. Ever since I was the merest kid I've had a dreadful temper, and I've been trying to squash it . . .[75]

Molly had asked her father if Wallis could visit on the following Sunday. Arthur said no. An argument followed in which Molly asked why he disliked Wallis; he replied that he had not – he thought well of him. Molly then asked why he did not apply similar rules to the courtship of Baba, her elder sister. Arthur replied that since Baba's admirer was far younger, the possibility of marriage was years away, giving Baba 'plenty of opportunity for changing her mind'. The argument ran on calmly until Arthur said that Molly was at her most troublesome after meetings with Wallis. At this, she 'rushed up into the spare room and sat in the dark getting angrier and angrier'. Arthur Bloxam followed and apologised. 'Then he asked me to do what he wanted because it hurt him when I didn't.'

I simply can't understand why it should, but Barnes he is old and pathetic – at least he was then – and we are young and strong, so I said I'd do what he wanted till next September.

September was the month of Molly's twentieth birthday.

After that I can't help it, if it hurts him, it will have to. Barnes, I'm not cruel, but after all it is our life – yours and mine – and we've got to live it . . .[76]

Wallis told her that it was partly because she was 'stout hearted, great souled' that he had fallen in love with her.[77] Clouds lifted in the following days. 'We can manage to hang on till September.'[78]

'You would have laughed at me'

Molly's exams began early in June. Letters went back and forth about Chemistry ('a horrible subject'); she was glum about the

Physics papers. Wallis spent the second weekend with his aunt May at Rudgwick in Sussex.

> You would have laughed at me yesterday afternoon. Just as I finished your letter, I saw the postman flash past the cottage on his bicycle. I simply tore out, letter in one hand, envie in the other, and shouted and whistled. But he was already too far down the road to hear.

Wallis set off in pursuit. 'Alas, he went downhill on free wheel' and was soon out of sight. Wallis pressed on to Bucks Green, where there was another post office, but no sign of the postman and no ticket on the box to say whether its letters had yet been collected. Returning in heavy rain, Wallis was overtaken by the postman, who explained that he did not collect from Rudgwick until 4 p.m. 'I was too happy to be annoyed.'[79] He was in a cloudy state. The day before he had gone to Horsham by train, walked three miles to Christ's Hospital, then set off to catch a train home. Finding there was no train for nearly an hour, he set out to walk to the next station, but was still a quarter of a mile short when the train left. This left him with 'nothing for it but to walk on to Rudgwick about another 4 miles.' Merely thinking about Molly gave him seven-league boots.

In mid-June he provided 'four ripping seats' in the front row of the Regent Theatre's dress circle for *Romeo and Juliet*, and on the month's last Friday they went to see Sybil Thorndike in the London premiere of George Bernard Shaw's *Saint Joan*. Eighty-one years later, the remains of a red rose lay enfolded in each programme.[80]

Saint Joan was their last meeting for nearly three months. Arthur Bloxam knew that little time was left in which to distance his daughter from Barnes in a way which might bring her into the vicinity of other men. His last throw of the dice was to send her and Barbara to Switzerland. An old friend of their mother, Miss Erskine Scott, would go with them. Miss Scott was 'a seasoned traveller and one full of propriety', but since Molly provided Barnes with full details of their itinerary his letters were waiting wherever they went. Miss Scott quickly became attuned to the situation.

On 3 July, not long before they left, Wallis wrote '71' in his diary – the number of days left before Molly gave him her decision. If in hindsight the result looks obvious, in foresight maybe it was less so. Hurley McCormick had been a determined suitor and was still in touch – eventually he married Molly's sister. Molly had set out to be a doctor, done well in the sciences, and was of independent mind. With all that ahead, in an age when marriage convention was assumed to be like the law of gravity, why turn aside towards a crash course in cookery, deference to men, and child-rearing?

> 58 I am I know the luckiest man in the world; that is if Molly *does* accept me, and I know only too well how very very unworthy of her I really am. But I simply worship the very ground the Child treads on.[81]

> 55 I had a private letter from the secretary of the Airship Company a few days ago, saying that the Directors had voted me a salary of £1500 a year, to date from June 1st last . . . So your Father cannot possibly object to me on financial grounds, which is a great relief as this salary is really a big one, for a man of my age.[82]

Masterman, now in charge of the RAF's Central Flying School at Upavon, took Wallis to Stonehenge.

> 46 You feel as if there is only one person in the world who you wish to be with, when you see a thing like that for the first time. I console myself by storing up in my mind all the beautiful places to which some day we shall go together, if you so decree.[83]

> 40 . . . I've ceased to note in my business diary 'Wrote to Molly' as I have done for 2 years now. It looks simply absurd when one has to put it down every day and sometimes twice.

Molly, writing at quarter to five in the morning, looking out on an Alpine sunrise: 'Barnes, I cannot tell you now what I should have done if Daddy had succeeded in keeping you from me – not because

I don't know; I am quite certain . . .' Wallis had never kissed her. She reminded him of a dance after which he had asked if she knew how much he had wanted to. Her reply at the time had been guarded. 'Well, I did know . . . I hadn't realised that there had been another me. I don't s'pose you'd understand, but one part of me – the hot eager part, I think all the pulses I have in my body – wrist and temples and fingers and everywhere in me – kept on saying "Barnes, kiss me . . ."'[84]

Back at camp, Holme-next-the Sea, among the natterjack toads and dragonflies near the dunes, now promoted sergeant:

> 24 We arrived here yesterday Sunday – very very wet after the 5 mile march from Hunstanton, as our overcoats were packed in the kitbags, and it simply poured, most of the way . . . *Later* I never dreamt that you were the very one woman who does not want to be mastered, but to master. And yet for us to be happy I am sure you must master me – a real fight and victory of your deep force of character against mine.[85]

Molly, in the train from Paris to Calais: 'I'm so excited. The train is saying "I'm going home, I'm going home."'[86]

> 10 Tomorrow night I am dining with Burney, and may not have time to write, and on Wednesday I will send my letter to Hampstead to welcome you home. I will not write after that, until I write for your birthday.[87]

But he did write again. The day before Molly's birthday, Burney demanded Wallis's attendance next morning at Crayford to make arrangements about AGC accommodation.

> o Year, month, day and hour – you can imagine my feelings – anyhow I told him that I had a most important private appointment of long standing, and arranged for Teed to go instead . . . I will call on you as near 11 o'clock as I can get . . . You *can* arrange for me to see you alone straight away, can't you? Because I simply cannot face the family until I know. (I'm all shaky now.)[88]

Next day, Friday, nearly two years since the September evening when he had wavered on the doorstep, and nineteen months since he had asked Molly to marry him, Molly agreed. No one in either family was surprised, 'and all, with the exception of Molly's father, were delighted.'[89]

On Saturday Wallis put 'Write Boyd' in his diary. Edgar Boyd replied:

> If ever there existed a real dirty dog in this world I think its name was Wog. Just fancy you sly old devil, keeping this so infernally quiet and here have I been working my fingers to the bone in order to find you a wife and all the time – really Wog it's too bad and I shall not forgive you until I've made 'Mollies' [sic] acquaintance. Anyway I think I can safely claim that amongst all your old pals there is not one more glad than I am.[90]

Marion Boyd:

> You have absolutely taken our breaths away!! Just fancy putting all your voluminous correspondence down to business! Probably the book you were writing last year at Borth was 'business' too! I am most awfully glad to hear about it, Woggins, and from the bottom of my heart wish you both every happiness.[91]

In the last hours, Molly had talked to her father about things he had done in his own youth. 'It's a queer business, of two people living together. Let's not make a mess of it.'

Structures

On 22 October the Airship Guarantee Company and the Air Council signed the indenture for the construction of the airship that would become known as R100.[92] The ink was scarcely dry when a week later the Conservatives won a landslide victory in the third general election in two years. Baldwin was back in Downing Street,

Thomson was gone, and Samuel Hoare was reinstated to the Air Ministry. However, if Hoare gave thought to revoking Thomson's two-ship scheme, he did not think for long. The scheme was in process, and best left to run.

Early in November, Sir Trevor Dawson accordingly announced the order for a great new airship. When ships like her came into service, he said, people would be able 'to visit the United States for a week-end'.[93] Details of R101 were announced by the Air Ministry a fortnight later. She would be the world's biggest airship, able to carry twenty tons of goods or a hundred passengers for 2500 miles non-stop. Built from stainless steel, diesel powered, using a new kind of fabric for her gas cells, she would be ready to fly by the end of 1926.[94] Thus began a publicity contest in which size mattered, and optimism was to the fore: in the event, neither ship flew until 1929.

Specifications for the two ships had been issued under the direction of Air Marshal Geoffrey Salmond, the Air Member for Supply and Research. They came through Air Commodore Peregrine Fellowes, the Director of Airship Development (inevitably known as 'Dad'), but in reality they were drawn up by his deputies Vincent Richmond and Reginald Colmore, with contributions from Thomas Cave-Brown-Cave (who had been Pratt's CO at Kingsnorth back in 1915). Richmond, in other words, played a central part in specifying the ship that he went on to design. Explicitly, his team's task was to produce an innovative design, while the AGC vessel was intended as an insurance against failure and would thus optimise existing practice.[95]

Existing practice meant Zeppelin, which by now had built 117 rigid airships – more than all other builders put together – for which Wallis had much respect. He knew that the hull of their latest vessel consisted of thirteen main longitudinal members bolted to the apices of thirteen-sided trusses. The trusses were braced with radial wires, rather like a bicycle wheel, and each of the thirteen sides was a low triangle with its apex facing inwards. Every triangle was braced by a kingpost which projected beyond its base to carry a light, secondary lengthwise member. The result was a hull with twenty-six sides. Two lesser transverse frames were located between each pair of trusses;

these were unbraced because of the presence of gas cells within them; their purpose was to help stiffen the end-to-end members.[96]

Earlier in October, Wallis and Burney went back to Friedrichshafen. ZR-3, the ship they had seen a-building in May 1923, was about to fly to the United States, and at Eckener's invitation they returned to witness her departure. The journey stirred keen interest on both sides of the Atlantic, and the visit gave Wallis an opportunity to study the completed vessel. ZR-3's hull was state-of-the-art. However, he saw that while the intermediate frames did not add much to her strength, they and their subsidiary longitudinals did add weight. He also considered that the gas cells should occupy as much of the volume enclosed by the outer cover as possible. For R100 he accordingly decided upon trusses of sixteen sides carrying sixteen longitudinals: that is, a hull frame with more principal end-to-end members than a Zeppelin, but fewer overall. This left greater areas of unsupported cover, but these could be supported by tapes and wires which would pull the fabric inwards.[97]

Zeppelin girders were formed of channel sections linked by diagonal strips of stiffened duralumin. Wallis saw that tubes would have greater intrinsic strength. Such tubes were unavailable, so he decided to make them by designing a machine to wind duralumin strip helically, then close-rivet the spiral overlap. Trios of such tubes could be formed into triangular-section girders by linking them diagonally with duralumin box sections. In places where end-to-end members and transverse frames met, the joints were articulated by a spider wherein forces converged at its arithmetic centre. The beauty of the spider (achieved in the face of initial scepticism from colleagues such as Temple) was that identical units could be used for every joint in the hull.[98] The result of these systematising inventions was a structure which made use of only fifty-one individual components; indeed, Wallis pointed out that if you ignored variables like thickness of material or diameters, the number of distinct components was just eleven.[99]

Thicknesses, dimensions and forces were the business of stress engineers, and one of the key appointments left for Wallis to make was that of the AGC's chief calculator.[100] In mid-September he contacted

Alfred Pippard, the Admiralty's stress analyst back in Walney days, who now held the chair of engineering at Cardiff and advised the Aeronautical Research Committee on analysis of airship frames. Pippard recommended Nevil Shute Norway, a twenty-five-year-old engineering science graduate, who at the time was working for de Havilland.[101] Wallis met him on 1 October and took up references next day. Norway was invited to join the AGC for a three-month trial, and accepted.[102]

Mooring safely

1925 saw the first London buses with roofed top decks, publication of Adolf Hitler's *Mein Kampf,* and Molly Bloxam's introduction to her fiancé's hero, Christopher Wren. In January they visited St Paul's, walking hand in hand as Wallis explained how Wren had configured the dome. In the Whispering Gallery, he pointed out that the new airship would be twenty feet wider than the space across which they looked, and around twice the height of the dome if you stood it on its end. Docking and mooring a vessel this size would be a challenge in good conditions, yet here they were talking of scheduled intercontinental services year round, in foul weather as well as fair. Mooring and docking raised other questions. Should mooring towers be in the hands of private owners or public institutions like the Port of London? In either case, would it not make sense to agree international standards, to enable airships of different nations to moor at each other's towers?

Burney and Wallis explored these things with Hugo Eckener and Ernst Lehmann, who following ZR-3's triumphant Atlantic crossing were in London to share thinking about transatlantic services. Over dinner, they discussed a universal mooring system. Burney and Wallis had been scoping a standard mooring mast with revolving platform and horizontal docking arms to embrace the nose and give a two-point fixing. Burney was ever prone to telling the press about distant plans in a way that suggested they were already accomplished fact, and when news about a new type of Burney-Wallis mast duly appeared in *The Times*,[103] Wallis's old friend Edward Masterman wondered if it drew on the system which he had patented through Vickers. He accordingly wrote to Wallis:

> As you appear to have got this adopted provisionally by the German and American commercial airship firms, I began in anticipation to see visions of wealth . . . Can you let me know whether I should order the new car now or must I be content with the old one for a bit longer?[104]

The episode did not go down well in the Air Ministry, where Burney's démarche was seen as an impertinent intrusion into government business.[105]

The long-running trial of wills between Wallis and Arthur Bloxam, meanwhile, was coming to an end. During February Arthur agreed that his daughter could be married before her twenty-first birthday. After so much delay Wallis was eager for an early date but agreed to 23 April – the third anniversary of their meeting – because (as Molly told Mary Turner) 'that will be more obliging to Daddy'.

Where to live? Finding an answer was complicated by new uncertainty over where R100 would be built, and how long it would take. Early in March they found a flat in Blackheath, but Burney advised against it on the ground that they would not be there long enough to justify its five-year lease. He then offered them an apartment adjoining his own in Carlton House Terrace. Apart from rates it would be free, but Molly was daunted both by its size (she thought it would need two maids) and the prospect of Burney as a neighbour before whom one would need to be 'everlastingly properly dressed.' Later in the month they were told of a vacant flat in Macartney House, a brick mansion in Greenwich Park. The location was ideal, the surroundings agreeable, and their offer to rent it for a year was accepted.

It was during these house-hunting weeks that Wallis solved one of the multifaceted challenges of R100's design: how to incorporate her gas cells in a way that would avoid shortcomings in existing systems, maximise gas volume within the outer envelope, transmit lift to the surrounding structure under all conditions of flight,[106] and meet the Airworthiness Panel's requirement that the cells should not exert any force upon the ship's longitudinal members. Deflation of a gas cell could cause adjacent cells to bulge into the vacated space, so distorting radial wiring and leading to structural damage, rubbing against girder-work or nipping between wiring. His elegant solution was a helical mesh of opposingly-wound cables in which each cable traces a great circle – the shortest distance between two points on the surface of a sphere. In this way, each cell could both be kept clear of the longitudinal girders and prevented from heaving fore, aft or sideways while the ship was in motion.[107]

Six years later, this concept would reappear as the basis for one of Wallis's greatest achievements. At the time of its birth, Wallis realised that his mathematics were not good enough to work out the co-ordinates for the mesh of wires where no single gas cell would be a cylinder with parallel sides. John Edwin Temple, his former colleague from early Vickers days, now back in touch as the project's mathematical adviser, said that the scheme was unworkable. Wallis turned for advice to a former colleague, who directed him to Louis Filon, Professor of Applied Mathematics and Mechanics at the University of London.[108] Filon's field was mechanics, elasticity theory and the mechanics of continuous media. He told Wallis that the scheme was feasible, that the wires in the non-parallel-sided hull would be geodesics on the surface of the cells, and provided the maths that Wallis needed to work out their co-ordinates to achieve equality of loading per foot run of each wire.[109] It was Filon who introduced Wallis to the mathematics of geodesics in surfaces of double curvature that eventually would lead to the Wellington.

Three weeks before the wedding, the *Daily Mail* reported that R33 had been brought out of storage, re-inflated and reconditioned. She was to be a testbed for experiments to inform design of 'the great airship for India service to be built by the Air Ministry'.[110] Londoners were told that she could be expected overhead any day. Molly was awake and thrilled in the small hours of 6 April as she whirred over Hampstead, lights aglow, Scottie in the control car.[111] Ten days later R33 was torn from her mooring at Pulham in a gale.

The small watch-keeping crew led by Flt Lt Ralph Booth and Chief Coxswain George Hunt started the engines, gained limited control, lashed down the flapping cover, and made holding repairs to prevent further damage.[112] However, since the westerly gale was blowing at nearly three times the speed of which R33 was safely capable, she was borne across the North Sea to the Netherlands. By mid-evening the wind had dropped enough for Booth and his exhausted crew to return to Pulham. The British knack of passing disaster off as victory came to the fore: newspapers told of R33's safe return and paid tribute to the airmanship of Booth and his colleagues. Not everyone was reassured.

> It was blown off its perch. It was blown 130 miles down wind, although its engines were going. It crawled back at ten miles per hour. It was pushed into its shed by 300 men. Do something if you can – words fail me![113]

But press opinion, broadly, was that since Britain had an Empire to run, she must persevere with airship development.[114]

Heart in heart

The day came. The ceremony was to be in St Luke's, Hampstead, an Arts and Crafts-cum-Perpendicular building of red brick which stood a minute's walk from the Bloxams' home. Wallis had no say in this: Arthur and Winifred Bloxam were parishioners of St Luke's, and since Arthur was giving his daughter away, albeit reluctantly, he was going to do it in his own church. Thereafter, the initiative passed to Wallis. The honeymoon was to be in the Lake District; he wanted to be there within the day; hence, the service would begin at 10.30. A large party held two evenings before removed the need for a long reception on the day itself.

The service was taken by Wallis's brother John,[115] before close family. Thursday's weather was cool and cloudy, but good enough for photographs in the garden which show the bouquets of tulips, the conservatism of Wallis's spats, and the ladies in fashionable drop-waist, loose, straight-fit, below-knee dresses and Mary Jane shoes. Then to Euston, and the train north. By evening they were in Great Langdale.

The New Hotel at Dungeon Ghyll was overlooked by the Langdale Pikes and hemmed in by fells with names like Crinkle Crags and Pike o' Blisco. Apart from a couple of farms there was nothing else there. Wallis knew the place from his Barrow days; Victor Goddard's mother lived nearby; they walked over to see her on the first evening. She gave them a copy of E. F. Benson's *Miss Mapp*.

For the rest of her life, when the anniversary of the honeymoon arrived, Molly reminisced. In her memories are glimpses: sheltering from hail behind a wall during their walk from Ambleside to Coniston; gazing across the fells from the Old Man of Coniston; the taste of ice-cold draught cider after a hot climb over Kirkstone Pass ('The whole point is the walking from one lake to another via the passes'); lying on the bed in her petticoats after a hot bath while Barnes read *Miss Mapp* to her before dinner. As she put it to Jack Morpurgo: 'How clever I, to "fall in love" with him half a century ago, not to worry about his Mother, to make of us a pair of happy uninhibited lovers.'[116]

To Cardington and Howden

Molly's youth, silk dresses and high heels boosted Wallis's reputation at company social events. At one of these, a garden party hosted by Sir Trevor Dawson, he introduced her to Masterman. They had not met for two years, and Molly likened them to 'two babies, bouncing and prancing about, so pleased were they to see each other again.'[117] Soon afterwards she confided to Mary Turner that she was herself carrying a child.

The undying question of where R100 would be built was partly settled in July. Although Vickers had bought the derelict RNAS station at Howden, Burney had continued to hanker after Pulham or Cardington – Pulham because it was near one of his houses, and

Cardington because it would be handy for London and the AGC's interactions with the Air Ministry and Royal Airship Works. However, interaction with Burney was the last thing the Air Ministry wanted. Pulham and Cardington were refused; he had to settle for Howden.

Howden's airship station dated from 1915 and was where No. 9 had seen most of its service.[118] Everything about its great shed was mind-boggling. When finished in 1919 it was the largest structure of its kind in the world. Seven and a half acres – about five football pitches – were sheltered under its roof. Each door weighed 190 tons. The doors ran on railway tracks and took nearly a quarter of an hour to open.[119] Six years on, the shed was why the Airship Guarantee Company had acquired the site. A small team overseen by Burney's personal assistant was sent to fettle the site. At this point, however, it was still imagined that the airship's parts would be made at Vickers's Crayford works in Kent, then taken to Howden for erection.

At Cardington, meanwhile, work had begun on R101. Whereas the AGC's design process ran through one mind – Wallis's – the Royal Airship Works was more like a college. Its dean was Peregrine Fellowes, who disliked Burney and snubbed the AGC's requests for sharing structural test data and results of aerodynamic trials.[120] Beneath Fellowes were assistant directors with responsibilities in different fields. His own deputy was Colmore, another member of the clique of former RNAS airshipmen that lived on inside the RAF. Alongside him were Scott, whose title would now be Assistant Director of Airship development (Flying and Training), and the Assistant Director of Airship Development (Technical) – Richmond.

Richmond was in overall charge of design, but its processes were distributed. The gas cell wiring was overseen by his assistant Michael Rope; mechanical installations were the responsibility of Cave-Brown-Cave;[121] details of the stainless-steel hull structure were in the hands of John North of the Norwich firm of Boulton and Paul. In Wallis's eyes R101 was created more by a working party than a designer. In mid-September Ralph Cochrane, now a squadron leader, took a day off and travelled to Cardington for lunch with old RNAS friends. He found the R101 team 'very optimistic' but confided to his diary 'on the whole I think Vickers will turn out the better ship'.[122]

Wallis now spent much of his time at Crayford, where Norway and his calculators were working out the loads, bending moments and deflections that the airship's structure might undergo under different conditions, and translating these into dimensions needed for the drawing up of individual components.[123] The work took on heightened meaning when news came that the American naval airship USS *Shenandoah* had broken up in mid-air.[124]

The AGC was now nearly halfway through its intended three-year programme to design, build and successfully fly an airship. Pressure to move from design to construction was mounting, not least because the first-stage payment to the AGC was being withheld until the Air Ministry considered progress to be sufficient. A prerequisite for progress was the machine to wind strip metal into long lengths of tube. Wallis's design for the machine had been passed to a firm of machine tool makers in Tottenham. It epitomised his resourcefulness, but teething troubles in its realisation meant that he often worked late into the evening to solve them.

The tube-making machine influenced what followed not only because it spun the yarn with which they would weave the ship, but because its portability removed the need to prefabricate R100's structure in one place and erect it in another. Everything could be done at Howden. Over Christmas, spent in turn at Hampstead, New Cross, and Greenwich there was thus much to talk about: a new baby, a new airship, a new home.

In January, Molly and Barnes re-enacted their first afternoon together:

> On Saturday Barnes and I went to see *Henry VIII*. It was the same day we went to see *Treasure Island* two years ago. We had lunch at the same place – the Waldorf Hotel in the Strand – and then went on to the Empire. It was such fun comparing ourselves with the shy, rather embarrassed, frightfully excited Barnes and Molly of two years ago. We sat at practically the same table, only this time we did the thing in style & had the table d'hôte lunch

& some delectable Chianti, and last time we were so agitated that we can only remember we had something fishy, & water to drink. Oh I am happy nowadays.[125]

Just over a fortnight later, Wallis wrote to his father and Fanny: 'A little son was born to us at 2.30 p.m. today.'[126] They called him Barnes Winstanley. By the time of his christening the Airworthiness Panel had agreed that construction of R100 could proceed. Amid a regime of four-hourly feeds and intermittent alarm when Burney arrived to talk about airships, they prepared to move. With them would go Norway and his calculators, and Philip Teed. In early April they returned the keys of 6 Macartney House and boarded a train for Selby. Before them were a night in a hotel in the shadow of Selby's abbey, another ten miles to Howden, and a new chapter in their strange eventful history.

5

Prince of Clouds, 1926–30

Shed music

> Next day we came on here. It is such a queer place. There are
> many little red brick bungalows and one white one – ours. We
> have rabbits running about in the grass outside our back and
> front doors, and cows can come and poke their heads in at your
> bedroom windows![1]

The station's neighbours were three or four farmhouses, the brick
hamlet of Spaldington, and clumps of isolated dwellings with names
like Brind, Willitoft and Gribthorpe. Howden town lay three miles
to the south. Much of the area had once been common land. Enclo-
sure hedges and trees in their turn had been grubbed out to make the
vast clear space that airships needed to come and go in safety. From
above, the airfield looked as if it had been created by a giant who
had splashed some caustic chemical across Yorkshire's landscape.

On the first evening Molly and Barnes went to look at the shed.
They marvelled at the space, looked up at the staircases that rose
at intervals through the steel frame to walkways 145 feet above.
Aside from pigeons and loose corrugated iron panels grating in
the wind, there was silence. Wallis found an abandoned trolley, sat
Molly on it and for several minutes giddily rushed her around the
floor. Then they subsided in laughter, and shouted, and sang, and
marvelled at the echoes. 'When Barnes shouted there were fifteen
echoes, and more because you couldn't count after that; they ran

into each other.'[2] Nearly forty years later he wrote to her: 'Do you remember the joy of singing in the great shed at Howden, when we first came, and it was empty? . . . Long live resonance!'[3] The station had been closed for five years and mothballed for three. In 1924 the government sold the site to a firm that had been formed to salvage its materials. By the time the AGC acquired it most of it had been picked clean. The shed still stood only because the cost of taking it down exceeded its scrap value.

Equipment, presses, lathes, tools, and the tube-making machine arrived. The station's locomotives had been sold, so materials were mostly brought in waggons drawn by horses plodding along the old rail spur. A drawing office and machine shop were opened. Riveters, riggers, labourers and tracers were hired. Some came from the old Vickers airship team at Barrow, others were recruited locally; some of the riggers were trawlermen from Hull. Progress was disrupted by the General Strike in early May, but not by much: designs for the first four transverse frames were advanced by the middle of the month. Wallis and Teed travelled hither and yon – Edinburgh, London, Birmingham, Berlin – to talk to specialist suppliers and assess results of structural tests.

The tube-machine went into production. Sub-assemblies took shape. Problems were solved.[4] One of them was the time and cost of reconfiguring six Beardmore Typhoon diesel engines. In September this was answered by switching to reconditioned Rolls-Royce Condors. The Condor ran on petrol. It weighed less than the Typhoon, which suited Wallis, and it suited Burney because the Air Ministry was wary of petrol in the tropics – which meant that R100 would be sent across the Atlantic rather than to India.

A challenge was how to produce hydrogen. The original water gas plant and gasholders had been sold by the salvage company. Teed dealt with this by installing equipment for the Silicol process that would give high output of near-pure hydrogen.[5] Around the same time, Teed's fluency in German assisted the signature of a contract for gasbags with the Zeppelin subsidiary BG Textilwerke.

A new building was erected to house the process for heat-treatment of duralumin. By October the production of duralumin parts had begun. The components hardened well but were vulnerable to corrosion, especially so in the damp, unheated shed. A team of workers, mainly women, was accordingly employed to seal the airship's duralumin structure with protective coats of varnish. Since there were eleven miles of framework, the varnish added a ton to R100's weight.

Most of the workforce lived in the town or lodged in nearby farms and villages. Some walked or cycled, others used a daily bus service provided by an enterprising Howden family who owned an elderly single-decker coach. R100 attracted visitors – officials from the Air Ministry, contractors, politicians, mathematicians and physicists who came to provide expert help – and a former station building was reconditioned as a hostel to accommodate them.

A Howden day began at 7 a.m. when the donkey engine that pumped water and generated power clanked into life. No other alarm was needed. Wallis liked to rise at half past six, put porridge on the stove and boil the kettle for cups of tea. His cold bath followed, then breakfast. At five to eight he climbed the stile over the boundary fence and walked to the shed. As Young Barnes grew, he walked with his father to the stile to wave him off. The official working day ran from 8 a.m. to 6 p.m., with a break for lunch between 1 and 2 p.m. At lunchtime Wallis usually walked back to the bungalow for bread and cheese, but there was a station canteen where he sometimes went when his need to talk to colleagues overrode his aversion to its food. At busy times he took sandwiches and a flask of tea and worked on into the evening.

Burney and Wallis had estimated that a year and a half would be needed to build R100. It was soon obvious that it was going to take much longer. Assembly of the sixteen polygonal transverse rings at the core of her frame ran behind schedule from the start, while Wallis's perfectionist attention to the smallest details was soon in tension with Burney, who repeatedly gave over-optimistic forecasts to the press.

Barnes didn't get home to his supper till 9.45 last Thursday – things kept going wrong . . . if we – or he – doesn't get a holiday soon, I fear he will break down. It's the responsibility that's so awful . . . if anything does happen, ever, it's all his fault; so that every last detail has to be seen to with the utmost care and meticulous attention by himself . . . And – I suppose it's the same in every big works – there are internal strife and unfaithful workers – all of which Barnes has to see to.[6]

The rings and the longitudinal girders that linked them were all formed in the same way. Each was made up of three parallel duralumin tubes joined by lattice work to give a triangular section. A girder could be made to any length up to 70 feet, and by early 1927 rows of them were being laid out on the shed floor, ready for assembly. By March the first of the transverse rings had been constructed, tested and readied for hoisting into position.

R100 was built hanging from the shed roof. The raising of the rings into their positions was a performance involving methods not very different from those used to hoist roof timbers by builders of medieval cathedrals five centuries before. The rings were fabricated in the flat and braced by radial wires. Since the airship's framework was to be assembled in suspension, it was necessary to manoeuvre each ring to a point on the shed floor corresponding to its eventual position. This was done by hand, around sixty men being needed to carry each ring. Slings were attached and the ring, still level, was hoisted upwards. Power for the lift came from the men, now organised in single file on the axis of the shed, each man grasping a cable that was attached to the slings and passed over special beams in the roof. On command, the men walked as a body away from the ring, and thereby drew it upwards. When the ring reached a height of 140 feet the slings were gradually relaxed until it hung vertically, suspended in the positions of ten o'clock and two o'clock by bridles from a pair of parallel beams in the roof. The beams were configured to enable the bridle anchorages to be slid back or forth along tracking, allowing each ring to be moved to its precise position in relation to the ship as a whole.

It took five months to erect the transverse frames, and some months more to attach the longitudinal girders via a system of spider joints. The joints were another Wallis achievement, each being a point at which the ends of transverse and longitudinal members connected and a node at which wire cables were swaged into one permanent junction. As the ship grew it became a self-scaffolding structure, but since it was suspended it was of course prone to movement, and since the upper girders were over 100 feet above the floor the work of aligning and coupling them with the joints called for agility and courage. Riggers ascended wheeled fire escape ladders to build the lower parts of the framework. The ladders extended to 90 feet, but with nothing steady against which to rest them, they wafted back and forth as the riggers climbed.

In the same week that the first ring was hoisted into position, a story about R100 appeared in the press:

> I am told that the great airship which the Vickers-Burney Syndicate is building at Howden will probably fly to Canada this autumn, going out by the Azores and returning direct by Newfoundland. The Syndicate considers that its first object should be to establish a regular airship service over the Atlantic for mails, gold, and passengers, as this route would yield the most certain profit.[7]

The article ended with Burney's prophecy that Howden would soon be building airships capable of carrying more than four times R100's payload for 3000 miles in just over a day.[8]

Such talk might be attributed to Burney's quixotic optimism. In fact, it reflected his new business model. Burney already knew that R100 would be too small to be commercially cost-effective; essentially, she was an experiment, almost a doodle. The AGC's contract contained a clause that enabled the AGC to buy her back from the government after the trials. Burney's plan was to use R100 as a bellwether for transatlantic carriage of high-value goods and passengers, and thereby demonstrate to potential investors that larger intercontinental airships would be commercially viable. But for this plan to work, he would need a bigger shed, and he needed R100 to fly. In March 1927 neither he nor Wallis foresaw that she would be hanging from the shed roof for another two years.

'Noah's ark in the mist'

Fifteen families lived on the station. The Wallis bungalow was converted from a former office. Its limewashed walls were one brick thick; in winter, a bedside glass of water often froze. The bungalow stood in waste ground; Molly wanted a garden; Wallis duly enclosed an area in an attempt to exclude the sheep, goats and brown hares that periodically laid waste to vegetables and perennials. He built a veranda where they could eat al fresco. Some of the other bungalows still had the faded names of the original RNAS occupants on their doors.

'It is fun living in this place; you just pass the word that you want summat done, and men flock forth.'[9] Molly was ten years younger than any other wife on the station and enjoyed the attention this brought her. These particular helpers were drinking beer in her kitchen in reward for helping Wallis to erect an aerial for the wireless he was installing in the bungalow. They left mud and snow on the floor. 'However, Barnes'll clear that up after dinner.' The wireless was 'most perfect'. 'Of course, I simply can't tear Barnes away from it. He is clever.'[10]

The station residents between them had twenty-two children, for whom the aerodrome's ruins, nearby streams and woodlands were a paradise for finding plovers' nests and den-building. Out of hours, the shed was used for badminton and occasional social events. The workforce formed a football team.

The nearest settlement, Howden, was a small market town of brick houses and inns. The bricks were red, orange and brown and gave the place a warm feel. Many of the houses had been built in a Georgian-Regency heyday when the town had been a centre for coaching traffic and its September horse fair was the largest in England. Originally an inland port, the town was formed by two streets, Bridge Gate and Hailgate, which bracketed a market street and the parish church of St Peter. St Peter's looked like a small cathedral, which in effect it was, its splendour deriving from the prince bishops of Durham, to whom the area was gifted shortly after the Norman Conquest. For Wallis and Molly, Howden epitomised True England.

They took delight in their surroundings. Wallis, lover of mountains and downs, also rejoiced in the extremes of flatness. With Molly, he came to love the wide horizons and vast sky. One blustery autumn evening he worked late, then went for a walk to clear his head. After a mile or so, beside a line of poplars soughing in the gale, he turned back, to be faced by Orion the hunter rising over the shed.[11] Molly became a fearless climber, liking to sit on the shed roof whence on clear evenings she could look across to the Lincoln Edge, west to the Pennines, north to the Wolds, and east to the Humber's gleam.

In spring cowslips and primroses dotted the sites of former buildings and the airfield sounded to larks and the lamenting calls of curlews. Molly kept of a copy of Bentham and Hooker's *Handbook of the British Flora*, and when unknown plants were found leaves or flowers were taken back to the white bungalow for identification. There were frogs in soggy places; moorhens and their chicks swam on pools; snipe probed wetlands for worms and insects. One spring day during a walk on the Wolds they rested beside a small wood, wearing new green and white May blossom. 'In front of us was our great plain with the shed just discernible looking exactly like Noah's ark in the mist.'

On summer evenings they walked round the shed and listened to nightingales. If it was warm, they slept on the veranda, waking early to watch the dawn. In late summer the garden of the white bungalow was wreathed in heady scents of nicotianas, roses and phlox. Molly made sloe gin, pickled beetroot, and bottled blackberries. When ground mist formed, there were times when just the horns and backs of grazing cattle could be seen, as if floating.

In the first months Molly set about cultivating her garden, and walked or cycled into Howden once or twice a week for meat and groceries. When a resident left the site, he or she would go round the bungalows to ask what could be brought back. 'We have someone from York bringing us lettuces and tomatoes, from Leeds bringing us greens, and from Howden bringing us apples and rhubarb.'[12] On some days she made the six-mile round trip on foot; a short cut to North Howden along the rail spur became a favourite walk, along which, as he grew, young Barnes liked to jump from sleeper to sleeper, counting them as he went. There were about nine hundred.[13] On other days she cycled or took the elderly De Dion-Bouton which was the airship station's car. After some months a grocery van began to call at the station and they bought a car of their own, an open Peugeot which everyone knew as Mr Wallis's Pug. Molly baked her own bread and walked to Spaldington every Thursday to fetch the week's butter and a jar of cream. The butter was made by the farmer's wife in a wooden churn. In hot weather, if it did not 'come' she wrapped it in a rhubarb leaf before putting it into greaseproof paper. Milk came from Mrs Faulkner in North Howden, where they dipped their jugs into a milk pail and brought them out 'creamy and frothing'. On Saturday afternoons Barnes and Molly took to walking into Howden, where they had discovered Mrs Kellington and her teas – cakes, buns, whipped cream – in a high kitchen behind her shop.

For racier entertainment there was York, nineteen miles away, where they encountered the first talkies at the Picture House Coney Street, and savoured Terry's 'heavenly ices'. Now and then they ventured further afield, as when Philip Teed drove them to Hull for dinner and *Rose-Marie* at the theatre to celebrate their second wedding anniversary. Molly was more taken with the meal than the show, afterwards regaling Mary Turner with its details (hors d'oeuvres, soup, sole, duck, ices, champagne, coffee), the cocktails beforehand ('I love wine and cocktails and liqueurs, don't you?') and the puncture on the way home. Revelling in the minutiae of meals might seem to be at odds with the Wallises' later reputation for abstemiousness, but the reality was more nuanced. There was a place for good or sufficient food, and even a glass of something on a special occasion, but not for over-eating or insobriety. Works social events, like the September sports day followed by a dance in the shed, were noted for drunkenness. Wallis's contribution to the sports was organising heats for the riggers' tug of war. Molly feared the dance would be 'an extremely rowdy and rather tight affair'; Wallis went on his own, made a short speech, and left. Molly said Barnes loathed dancing 'with scenty powdery women'.

Mr Wallis's Pug enabled them to explore Yorkshire. 'It's the most beautiful country in the world' wrote Molly after a walk across Goathland Moor.[14] The white bungalow, with its garden and rural freedom was a good place to bring up children, and by early spring 1927 Molly was again pregnant. Molly was convinced that the second child would be a girl and told Mary Turner that she would be named Mary. Mary Eyre Wallis was duly born at 12.25 on Friday, 7 October. The contractions began before breakfast; Wallis drove Molly to the nursing home in York and walked the two-mile circuit of the city's medieval walls during the birth. By late afternoon he was back at Howden.

At first there was a maid, Maud. Then Nan arrived. Nan's real name was Jessie Valentine Ley, the daughter of an east London shipwright. A beauty in her youth, she had worked as a dressmaker for fifteen years before joining the Bloxams to look after their children.[15] Nan now took over most of the cleaning, fire-lighting, nappy-changing, cooking and mending. 'Nan's awful' wrote Molly; 'she won't let me do anything – goes careering around doing all my jobs. My hands are becoming almost clean.'[16] Yet Nan's care for the children allowed Molly to retain the kind of spontancity that in the 1920s was often stifled by marriage and child-rearing. Nan was an ardent monarchist – an unannounced visit by Queen Mary's nephew 'thrilled Nan to the marrow' – and had views on politesse that she quietly enforced. Among them was her belief that tea should be drunk from small, dainty cups; Barnes and Molly liked to drink from big ones but felt able to do so only when Nan was away. During meals, Wallis resigned himself to the creaking of Nan's dentures. Nan's support would continue for another seventeen years.

Young Barnes and Mary were introduced to the sea at Filey and Bridlington. Picnic places were discovered at Patrington in Holderness and on Skipwith Common; there were walks into Nidderdale's limestone country from Pateley Bridge, where there were Bloxam relatives. They did impulsive things, like walking five miles across country with compass and map, over streams, bogs and barbed wire, to visit the Dixons, or leaving Howden for a weekend with the Boyds at Ulverston. On one trip to the Lake District they walked over Sty Head Pass to Wastwater, bathed in Piers Gill, and climbed Great Gable, where Molly watched rock climbers: 'That is the one sport I have any sympathy with.'

Winter flooding of the washlands of the lower Derwent attracted migrant swans and widgeon. In mid-December 1927, daytime temperatures stayed below freezing for five consecutive days; on two nights the thermometer outside their back door registered sixteen degrees of frost. The deep cold lasted into January: 'We've bought me a pair of skates and Barnes has been teaching me. Of course this is the country for skating – fields and fields flooded and frozen – and it's perfectly lovely.'[17] Skating reminded Barnes of his father, when young Charles spent hours on end gliding over frozen ditches and grazing marsh. After work, Molly and Barnes sometimes skated under the stars. 'At Bubwith where the river has overflowed there are miles and miles of ice – they say 15, I don't know – and it's perfectly lovely.' In February 1929 the temperature fell to 15°F (-9°C) and for four days did not rise above freezing during the day. 'Everything is frozen from the beer to the water in the glass by your bed. Still, we are so used to it we hardly mind it now . . . And the skating's lovely.'[18]

Skating weather was not good for progress on R100. The unheated shed meant everyone working in it had to wear thick clothing when it froze. Such garb was cumbersome for fitters and for seamstresses in the fabric shop, where 10,000 yards of cotton fabric were being cut into panels for the outer cover and industrial sewing machines were used to attach tapes, loops, and fixings.[19] For riggers who worked at height, heavy winter coats were very awkward indeed. The shed leaked. On wet days rain blew in and soaked parts of the structure. When damp on the girders turned to ice the riggers were grounded. The shed's clammy atmosphere caused water to condense on the cold duralumin and mould to grow on panels of the outer cover. The chronic wet also raised new concerns about corrosion, which was eventually countered by wire-brushing the entire frame and re-covering it with varnish. Re-varnishing added to construction time, another ton in weight, and friction with Burney.

Spanners in the works

Towards the end of their life at Howden Molly reflected: 'I shall be sorry to leave this darling place; it is a most romantic existence. We have been extraordinarily fortunate to have had four such happy years.'[20]

Wallis was to all intents and purposes his own boss at Howden, responsible both for design and construction, and for direction of the specialised team he had gathered. Like Howden's prince bishops five centuries before, for most of the time he ruled what amounted to a rural principality. However, responsibility brought strain as well as fulfilment. His insistence on keeping all aspects of the project directly under his own eye meant long days and short holidays; in some periods he took no breaks at all. Wallis's greatest difficulties came from a deteriorating relationship with Dennistoun Burney. At first, he had supposed Burney to be straight-talking, but as time passed faith in his integrity dwindled. This was partly a clash of temperament, whereby Burney's brash manner became ever more irksome not just in itself but because in Wallis's eyes it came to symbolise poor judgement and empty promises. But there was more to it than this. While Wallis focused on building one airship – and was doing so far too slowly for Burney's liking – Burney was laying plans for the next generation of Atlantic class vessels. Building such a fleet would call for succession planning, and it meant finding a deputy for Wallis who would minimise the AGC's exposure to risk in the event of illness or accident. It would also mean keeping Howden's works organisation in being. Burney accordingly needed to find investors so that work on the new airships could be put in hand without hiatus. Early in 1928 he travelled to the United States in search of American backers, sending Wallis a succession of cables and long letters from expensive hotels. However, since his sales pitch needed completion of R100 as proof that the AGC could build viable airships, his impatience mounted. May 1928 found him stumping about Howden issuing unrealistic directions for her immediate completion to enable an Atlantic crossing in October.[21]

Burney visited Howden irregularly, sometimes calling on the way to his grouse moor in Scotland. His tendency to gather information randomly by walking around the site, cross-examining anyone in his path, and to cut across established chains of command, created problems and ill-feeling. Such behaviours influenced Howden's already fragile industrial relations. There were strikes, and tensions over union recognition. Towards the end morale flagged; when it became clear that R100 was to be the only vessel that AGC employees were likely to build, the incentive to finish her waned.[22]

Burney attracted admirers as well as critics. Norway thought him 'outstanding', and unlike Wallis (who on several occasions said that Burney could not tell one end of an airship from another) credited him with 'the keenest engineering imagination' of anyone he had ever met. Norway admired Burney's 'ability to stand back and take a bird's eye view of an entire industry'. He regarded Burney, like Wallis, as a genius, and reflected: 'Perhaps two geniuses in one company would always find it difficult to work together.'[23] Norway's warmth towards Burney, and Wallis's confidence in Norway, stood all three in good stead in 1929 when Norway was appointed Deputy Chief Engineer.

Burney's habit of turning up without warning challenged Molly and Nan, when Wallis rang up at half an hour's notice to ask if they could provide him with lunch. Burney's American wife Gladys took to dropping in at the white bungalow, where Molly smiled through clenched teeth as she smoked in her kitchen and told her how to bring up children while her young son, Cecil (described by Molly as 'a horror') climbed on the furniture. 'I am having another visitation from Mrs Burney today. She always seems to come on my letter day.'[24] Burney regarded his social visits as opportunities to debrief on progress, discuss his plans, and obtain free advice about ideas he was putting into a forthcoming book on the future of air travel.

For a time, Burney used the station's resources and staff to assist development of another of his ventures, a streamline car. He was puzzled by the conservatism of manufacturers who ignored the effects of drag and 'continued to turn out boxes with a bonnet where the horse had been'.[25] His response was to harness airship design principles and materials to car design, arriving at a teardrop-shaped vehicle with a long wheelbase, rear-wheel drive, luxurious interior, and a cornucopia of ingenious features. The company he formed for the purpose was based in Maidenhead, but some of the initial technical development was done at Howden. In April 1928, for instance, Molly wrote that while Burney had 'invented' a new car, 'Mr Palmer and others have done the work'. Burney came up to Howden to test drive it, but since he was 'too scared to do it himself' the driving had been done by the works manager, Jimmy Watson, who had been kept up late to do it. 'He is a little beast.'[26] The following month Molly reported that Wallis had not been to supper all week because he had been working until 9 p.m., once to 11 p.m., on 'the Burney Rolls Royce'.

Wallis developed strategies to counter Burney's unannounced visits. One of them was to immobilise the electric doorbell ('I did at first intend to stand outside and press until the bell ran down' but then thought 'don't waste energy . . . so stuck a pencil in the wheels'[27]). Another precaution was to turn out the lights and lock the front door, to give impression that no one was at home. This sometimes backfired, as on the occasion when Nan and Molly each thought the other had locked the door and Burney walked in on a conversation about himself.

For most of the time Wallis was resilient, even thriving under the pressures. He was becoming known nationally. He received invitations to lecture and publish on airship design. When *The Times*'s Aeronautical Correspondent visited Howden in November 1927 he noted that duralumin was being used in a 'radically different way from Zeppelin.'[28] In September 1928 the Royal Aeronautical Society honoured him with its silver medal.[29] Molly rejoiced in the recognition but remained wary. When Cecil Dixon's new bridge connecting Goole and Howden was opened in 1929, she was 'disgusted' that no one at the ceremony mentioned his name: 'he who has built the whole thing, who has gone early and stayed late, who has missed his meals and weekends for it. I bet that's exactly what will happen when the ship comes out; there'll be no such thing as B. N. Wallis, merely Sir Dennis Burney.'[30]

Despite Wallis's general well-being there were periods when the struggles with Burney and long hours touched his health. At the end of March 1927, amid a dispute over Burney's plan to bring in a new senior executive, he was smitten by recurrent migraines. Edgar Boyd pronounced him fit but warned that his 'brain was in need of a holiday'. The need for a break became a refrain. On one occasion Molly's determination 'to get the man off this beastly station' was thwarted when Burney invited eighty MPs to visit. A planned trip to the Cairngorms was cancelled, leaving Molly 'cross and fed up as two sticks.' A few months before, Wallis had found himself coughing up blood and spent an anxious Christmas awaiting the result of tests for TB. The tests came back clear, together with advice to stop smoking, which he now did, for good. At different times he suffered from heavy colds, bronchitis, and dental pain. In some periods worry led to insomnia, which added to exhaustion. Burney was given to writing peremptory letters and memos that demanded information, looked ahead to new projects, or gave directions on points of detail; the directions were often days or weeks in arrears of what was happening, but nonetheless called for carefully worded replies, the crafting of which added to Wallis's workload.[31] Towards the end, there were very tense exchanges.[32]

Burney was not the only source of pressure. Criticisms of the airship programme in the press and at Westminster were accompanied by demands from the Air Ministry for technical information to use in rebuttal. In 1927 Wallis was called in reply to *The Great Delusion*, a book written under the pseudonym 'Neon' which argued that airships would be unreliable.[33] A few days after he gave up smoking he was drawn in to rebut another book, *This Airship Business* by Edward Frank Spanner, a former naval architect who in later life had answered callings to write science fiction and attack the airship industry. Molly was annoyed that her husband should have to give up his time to write 'squashing replies' to a book by an eccentric who twisted his words, quoted him out of context and made 'heaps of technical mistakes'.[34] In the following year R100 and R101 were derided in the *English Review* as 'aerial Mastodons'.[35]

Wallis's annoyance at being side-tracked reflected more general frustrations. Whereas at Cardington there were 'five men to one

Barnes', 'no end of works managers', clerical staff, and 'men to see to progress and propaganda', at Howden there was one works manager and a solitary secretary. The contrast was in some respects reflected in the airships. When Norway first saw R101 at close quarters the quality of her finish struck him as 'extraordinarily good, far better than that of our own ship.' On the other hand: 'The design seemed to us to be extraordinarily complicated; she seemed to be a ship in which imagination had run riot regardless of the virtue of simplicity and utterly regardless of expense.'[36]

Molly eventually prised Barnes away for a long break. 'We really are going!' she wrote on 10 November 1928. The children were left with Nan and the Bloxams for Christmas while they went to a 'ripping' hilltop hotel in Menton, a town of huddled red-tiled roofs on the French-Italian border. Wallis was unwell on arrival but reassured by a local doctor, who put his symptoms down to overwork. For five weeks they walked, swam, climbed into the mountains, sunbathed, and 'slept like tops'. Around them were lemons, figs, oranges, mimosa, olives the size of damsons, bushes of lavender, sage and thyme – lizards, butterflies, and fireflies at night. On Christmas Day they braved the company of elderly maiden ladies and retired colonels for an eleven-course dinner, drank the health of the king and danced until 11.30 p.m. On 29 December they were back in foggy London.

'This huge, wonderful thing'

Five days before they left for France, Molly had told Mary Turner:

> I say, please be pleased. We have got a new and settled job with Vickers Aeroplane Works. Isn't it simply ripping. You can't think what a relief it is to us to have something certain at last. Of course, it will be sad leaving Howden and airships; but anyway, there will be nothing doing with the latter for a year or two, and we shall be in Vickers' firm. And Weybridge is a ripping place everybody (including Barnes who went to see it) says. It's only 25 minutes train from London.[37]

Wallis's recruitment to Vickers Aviation was the result of several influences, the most significant of which was the arrival on the scene of Sir Robert McLean (1883–1964). McLean was an austere, independent-minded engineer who had recently retired from managing India's railways and in 1928 became responsible for Vickers Aviation. He found an aero industry made up of private firms with one main domestic customer – the government. This was entirely so in the case of military aircraft, and effectively so in the commercial sector because Imperial Airways was state-subsidised. McLean further discovered that economic depression coupled with the government's practice of spreading orders to keep the industry in being meant small production runs, which in turn fostered conservative construction practices. McLean reasoned that the surest way for Vickers to obtain new business was to produce progressive designs which out-performed their competitors. He shared his thinking with Vickers's chief designer, Reginald 'Rex' Pierson. McLean's aim was to augment Pierson's talents and network in two particular new directions: civil aviation and metal construction.[38] Wallis's experience of metal construction, originality and commitment to intercontinental aviation made him a candidate, and in June 1928 Pierson was sent to Howden to sound him out.

Pierson brought his young son, with whom Wallis struck an immediate rapport. After a tour of the airship Wallis took them to the white bungalow for lunch. Molly's references to 'getting down china' and 'polishing silver' in the midst of wiping up young Barnes's sick show that the visit was at short notice, and when Wallis rang ahead he emphasised its importance. The encounter went well. Wallis was invited to Brooklands to meet McLean and visit the works. At the end of October, the Vickers board gave its approval for McLean's new business model and the move was agreed.

Molly did a lot of entertaining. 'Somebody to lunch, then four of them came, then another tea for Mrs Burney, then another couple turned up (Christ's Hospital old boys), then another odd man, then Burney.'[39] The station hostel, run by a large lady called Mrs Jones, was for duty visitors like government inspectors and members of the Airship Directorate; special visitors were often accommodated at the white bungalow. When Molly looked back at the end of 1928, she reckoned that thirty-five people had slept in her spare room on 91 out of the previous 156 nights. Among them were relatives, old friends like the Boyds, the Lushingtons from Chillon days, Hartley Pratt, and Chas Browne, and senior officials like Fellowes and Colmore from Cardington. Molly found some of the visits challenging. The Lushingtons alarmed her by appearing for supper in dinner jacket and evening dress. Sir William Sefton Brancker – short, dapper, monocled, and Britain's Director of Civil Aviation – struck her as a 'horrid beast'.

As completion neared, visits by members of R100's future crew and the Airship Directorate became increasingly frequent. Among them were Sqn Ldr Ralph Booth, hero of the R33's mooring adventure and the ship's captain-to-be, and her first officer, Captain George Meager. With them often came George Scott, now the Airship Directorate's director of flying, who sometimes brought his wife Jessie.

> Periodically 100's of officers come up from Cardington to see how she's progressing. We have two here at the moment feeding with us. I think they jolly well ought to give us a maintenance allowance for all the food and drink we provide for H.M. officers. Scott had brought up his Mrs, and to get away from Burney . . . we all went to York. Well, she and he drank 2 whiskeys and soda and 3 cocktails before the meal, a stiff whiskey at the meal, a liqueur after it, and another whiskey after the pictures. She drank all that as well as he.[40]

Five years before Wallis had written of his long-standing friendship with George Scott and admiration for the romantic warmth of his marriage. The Scotts now seemed rather too convivial. Molly looked forward to 'living at Weybridge when we shall have an only occasional settled lunch or dinner party'. But for that to happen, R100 had to fly.

By early 1929 all design work for R100 was complete. Norway increasingly took over for day-to-day purposes, allowing Wallis to give time to work for Vickers, and outside engagements such as lectures. The remaining tasks were practical – the electrical system; installation of fuel tanks along the length of the keel; water storage tanks, each holding a ton; bags of rubberised canvas for water ballast; the control car and controls. In the control car there were separate control wheels for pitch and yaw, with a Wallis-designed reduction gear to enable the elevators and rudders to be moved by only small actions of the controls. When word from Cardington said that R101 was being provided with power-assisted control surfaces, Wallis and Norway were puzzled and a little unnerved, revisiting their calculations to see if they had missed something in the course of designing their simpler and much lighter system.

Molly was enchanted by R100's passenger quarters. The balcony, dining room and cabins were 'too wonderful for words'. Before they were enclosed the structure reminded her of a Meccano set[41] – a comparison of which Wallis disapproved, on the grounds that Meccano gave young people a misleading introduction to the behaviour and properties of materials. Towards the end the ship became a visitor attraction, with conducted weekend tours to the public at a shilling a time. William Temple, the newly appointed Archbishop of York, was among the tourists. He visited the white bungalow for lunch and bounced young Mary on his knee. Afterwards young Barnes helped him over the stile and escorted him into the airship's passenger accommodation. Temple was described by Molly as 'rather stout' and when they inspected a cabin the boy said politely 'I think you should sleep in the bottom bunk.'[42] In Molly's eyes R100 had become 'this huge, wonderful thing'; when she flew, she would be the prince of clouds.

In preparation for inflation, new fire precautions were introduced, with immediate dismissal for anyone who ignored them.[43] Inflation began on 30 July.

We have actually started inflating! And mighty little do I see of Barnes. Up at the shed at 8 after I have given him his breakfast at 7.15; 40 minutes for lunch, home at 8.30 or 9 dead tired. Thank goodness it doesn't go on for long. Poor Barnes. They started on

Tuesday and have partially inflated four bags without any serious mishap, which I gather is rather good. They ought . . . to finish the first partial inflation in a fortnight. It's a great strain on all parties concerned.[44]

Everything about R100's gas cells seemed to involve strain. There were fifteen of them, the largest weighing half a ton. They were expensive and delicate, and together could hold 1.156 million cubic feet of hydrogen. Since autumn 1928 they had been kept carefully wrapped around the airship's axial girder. Now came the moment of truth as one by one they were unfolded, valves fitted, and gas flowed in. The flow was not steady but came in a succession of pulses from individual chemical reactions, each from a charge of caustic soda, water, and ferro-silicon. The quantities were prodigious: a single charge required one ton of soda alone, and 249 charges were needed to gas the ship. A by-product of the process was a sludge, of which nearly 1000 tons were produced in the course of inflating the ship.

As each bag expanded care was needed to prevent it creeping along the axial girder and to steer it into the covering mesh of wires. The hydrogen was supplied from the generating plant which Teed had established next door. It was costly – £800 for one large bag – so mistakes were expensive. Moreover, since the gas was produced by a chemical reaction that could not be halted once it started there was need for careful budgeting of volumes. Furthermore, the reaction was not constant and called for judgement. The early stages produced little rise in pressure, so tempting an unskilled operator to add more ferro-silicon; however, as the reaction proceeded the temperature rose gradually until it reached the neighbourhood of 82°C, whereupon it became practically instantaneous, releasing its pulse of hydrogen in a rush.[45]

The aim was to inflate to 75 per cent capacity at the first stage. Booth and Meager oversaw inflation of the first two bags, to demonstrate the method to AGC design staff who then took over. The team in the generating house and the riggers in the shed were widely dispersed, threatening mix-up if messages were shouted at the same time. A system was accordingly devised whereby Wallis oversaw each inflation and used a megaphone to issue directions. Each evening he returned to the shed to check that all was well. Molly sometimes went with him; she liked to climb up to the roof and was struck by the glimmer of Wallis's safety lamp moving inside the ship like some will-o'-the-wisp.[46]

After a cautious start, and an accident that made a fifteen-foot gash in No. 4 bag, the tempo picked up. By early August they were inflating two bags a day. A gasbag specialist from Luftschiffbau Zeppelin who was there to advise was impressed by the versatility and willingness of the team. By 18 August fourteen of R100's fifteen gasbags were correctly positioned, and the first stage was complete. R100 was now buoyant but still earthbound; the fifteenth bag was left uninflated until they were ready for airborne trials.

Second stage inflation came in mid-September. The hundred-ton airship was now floating in the shed, tethered by crates full of weights and steadied by earth-filled oil drums slung through blocks in the roof that acted as balance weights.[47] It was a tight fit: at the point of R100's maximum girth only a yard separated the top of her cover from the roof, while the propeller tips cleared the shed's concrete floor by fifteen inches. Although the ship was airborne, the bridles to the roof from which she had been suspended during construction were not yet cast off, lest they should again be needed.[48]

Engine trials began on 25 September. Each pair of engines was run at cruising power for ninety minutes, half an hour astern, and five minutes at full throttle. The noise from engines with open exhausts in the reverberant shed was ear-splitting. While the Condors ran it was essential for the ship to be held absolutely steady. At the stern end the shed doors were opened to allow for dispersal of the propwash. Despite all precautions the hull moved up and down in the turbulence, and for the rest of his life Norway recalled the engine cars straining at their drag wires, 'suspended from a hull that was completely full of hydrogen'.[49] Shed testing the engines was hazardous, and Norway was mystified as to why the Air Ministry insisted on it. He or Wallis stood by each power car during its trial, eyes fixed on registration pointers that had been put in place to indicate the ship's motion and propeller clearance. The propeller tips whirled so close to the ground that they generated a blueish halo of static electricity. Water sprayed to quench the static was whisked by the propwash into roiling spouts and vortices that danced across the floor.

At the beginning of October Molly wrote to Mary Turner: 'We have now got to the final inflation of R100. So we can't be long now. Barnes is due for three weeks holiday – where goodness knows.'[50] The following Thursday Burney's book was published.[51] He called it *The World, the Air and the Future*, and in it he argued that existing airships were too slow and short of lifting capacity to operate commercially. He alleged that the R101 would have nil available payload, and that his own R100 would not be much better. Airships were so unwieldy that scheduled services would not be possible until ways were found to dock and hangar them without reliance on specialised infrastructure and in different weathers. Further, since the lift of an airship varies with temperature and height the idea of 'standard conditions' was a subjective estimate – the benchmark for a commercial service must be the ability of an airship to operate in poor rather than ideal conditions. A chapter by Norway concluded that commercially viable long-distance air travel using heavier-than-air aircraft would not be possible for many years. The conceptual case for airships thus still stood – but only if they were of much enhanced performance and if existing limitations of docking and ground handling could be overcome. Burney outlined several new and characteristically gargantuan ideas about how this could be done.[52]

Advance copies of the book were sent to the press, and on publication day the newspapers were ready. The *Daily Mail* led the charge, crying 'New British Airships a Failure' and headlining its report OUT-OF-DATE BEFORE BEING LAUNCHED, TWO SLOW AND NOT BIG ENOUGH. *The Times* was less strident but said much the same thing: 'Statements that the two new state airships, R100 and R101, are commercial failures, and that the airship built by the State at the Royal Airship Works, Cardington, and now about to start its flight trials, is incapable of carrying any useful load at all on a flight to Egypt, are made by Sir Dennis Burney in a book published today . . .' Or as the *Manchester Guardian* put it in a paragraph headed

'The Burney Bombshell':

> It is very startling to find that at this moment when the two airships are about to be tested, Sir Dennistoun Burney has published a book in which he not only criticises the commercial qualities of the two airships, but also says that unless certain novel devices or their equivalent are developed successfully 'I do not see much future for the airship.'[53]

Burney replied in the *Observer* a few days later. The experience of building the R100 and R101 had taught important lessons, he said, and it was 'arrant nonsense' to claim they were obsolete even before their trials were over. Burney also stated, with what in hindsight was tragic irony, that the two vessels were safer than any yet built.[54]

Burney's book caused deep resentment at Cardington and Howden, tempered with wonder at his feat in managing to claim credit for something he simultaneously seemed to belittle. Burney's acknowledgement of Wallis in the Preface as someone who had 'assisted' him in the construction of the R100 appeared to bear out Molly's prophecy that in due course he would present himself as the airship's architect.[55]

The media uproar distracted attention from what most of his book was about. At its heart were two ideas about empire development. One was a deterministic claim that the secret of England's 'commercial supremacy' and 'world-wide dominion' lay in her position on the planet. Such ideas of geographical determinism were widely held in the later nineteenth and earlier twentieth centuries; Burney took this particular variant from a book by his friend George Bowles, a lawyer and Conservative politician who held that England 'lies wholly in the sea and yet at the precise centre of all the land of the earth'.[56] In result, England possessed global 'sea centrality'. Now that air was becoming a medium for travel and transport, and in the face of 'trade centrality now passing into the hands of the United States', it was necessary to secure air centrality as well.

The other idea centred on the future of the nation state. Burney noted that economic activity was increasingly trans-national; the

doings of oil companies, volume manufacturers and mineral combines were no longer contained by national borders. Nations needed
to adapt to these new realities. One way to do so would be through
merger – for instance, to form an entity like a United States of
Europe. Another would be to transform the British Empire into a
consolidated cultural community and economic union. In either
case, fast, efficient air communication would be needed. We shall
see that a quarter of a century later Wallis drew upon this thesis in
a series of essays and lectures about the need for air centrality to
counter political and economic decline and to reinvigorate the Commonwealth. The lecture became his signature, and he took its title
from George Bowles's book: *The Strength of England*.[57]

By coincidence, Burney's book appeared just four days before
R101's maiden flight. Controversy about Burney's allegations was
thus concurrent with R101's trials. Every trial was news, and in the
press the news was always good. It was as if each press statement
had been crafted to rebut one of Burney's criticisms. *The Times* recorded her 'successful launch'.[58] Far from being short of lift, record
passenger-carrying ability was claimed; she was like a 'flying hotel'.[59]
During her endurance flight she 'behaved splendidly', covering a
thousand miles 'without showing the slightest symptom of possible
weaknesses likely to cause trouble in her engines or installation'.[60]
On the night of 11/12 November there was a public relations gift
when she rode out hurricane-force winds while moored at the Cardington mast.[61]

The Air Ministry's public affairs department presented R101 as
a national vision. Like Gloriana on progress, the routes of her test
flights were calculated to present her to key viewers. Thus, her launch
was a 'glittering spectacle', and her return to mast at the end of the
maiden flight was before a great and cheering crowd. During the
flight Londoners contracted 'airship neck' while the Prince of Wales
watched from his private aeroplane. In the course of a subsequent
flight George V and Queen Mary saw her pass over Sandringham.
She over-flew Norwich in salute to the makers of her frame. Lord
Thomson, begetter of the two-ship scheme in 1924, was now back in
office following the election of May 1929. R101 accordingly toured

the skies over industrial cities with Thomson aboard, the flight being so smooth that he ostentatiously undertook his ministerial day's work while airborne.[62] Bedford's mayor was taken aloft. A flight for a hundred MPs and peers was arranged but postponed because of high winds. The excursion was rescheduled, but again cancelled because of blustery weather. On the second occasion MPs and peers were taken aboard for lunch while R101 floated at Cardington's tower. To keep them aloft the ship had to be lightened by offloading fuel and stores. A story circulated afterwards that some MPs were so drunk 'that they thought they actually *had* been flying'.[63] Noël Atherstone, R101's first officer, confided to his diary:

> The Air Ministry were terribly bucked at having pulled off this stunt, but I fail to see that it can have served any useful purpose. The whole show was merely stupid, a lot of illegal things were done in order to gain enough lift to carry this load, amongst others . . . we heard that the Speaker and a few friends would be coming tomorrow at 1130 to have a look . . .[64]

In such ways was R101 passed off to legislators and the public as a triumph. When her trials finished at the end of November their real results were downplayed. On the strength of what had been published, few would have guessed that one of the modest 'adjustments' now needed would involve cutting her in two to insert an extra bay to accommodate another gas cell. Atherstone wondered if the Air Ministry realised 'how *damned* lucky we are to have got away with it so far?'

> We have never had any confidence in the machinery and we have not made a single flight on that [sic] something or other has not broken down. The way the engines were nursed through their tests before they were passed as airworthy was a bare-faced wrangle . . . The ship has no lift worth talking about, she is very tail-heavy, ballasting arrangements are inadequate in their rates of discharge and filling, gassing is too slow, interior communication for voice pipes is rotten and there are no telephones. The

speed of the ship is nothing wonderful being slightly below the theoretical speed, but the arrangement for getting stern thrust is a joke. Fancy carrying a whole complete power unit weighing 4 tons so as to be able to go astern![65]

In Atherstone's eyes R101 was an accident waiting to happen. To 'a very large extent', he said, this was due to inept design that came from lack of experience.[66]

Wallis, meanwhile, had been dividing his time between overseeing completion of R100 and development of new forms of wing and fuselage structure for Vickers.[67] In mid-October he received a summons from McLean, who wanted to revisit plans for Wallis's forthcoming role. The original understanding was that when his duties at Howden were done he would join Vickers Aviation at Weybridge. McLean had since had second thoughts; would Wallis go to Supermarine instead?

Vickers had bought the Southampton-based firm of Supermarine Aviation eleven months before. The company was small but had expertise in flying boats which fitted the part of McLean's new business model that was tailored to long-distance civil aviation. McLean was particularly keen to secure the services of the company's chief designer, Reginald Joseph Mitchell. A condition of the purchase was that Mitchell should be bound to the company for at least five years.[68]

McLean's admiration for Mitchell did not extend to Supermarine's working practices. He saw scope for improvements on the manufacturing and organisational side and had brought in a young and forceful works manager called Trevor Westbrook to apply them. McLean also looked for change in Supermarine's technical department, and it was for this that he called on Wallis. During their talk McLean promised Wallis a free hand, with authority to restructure the department, hire and fire. McLean thought that the shake-up would take about a year, during which Wallis's creative contribution would be towards the design of large flying boats.[69] An early task would be to rectify the undue flexibility of the wings of a luxury flying yacht that was being built to the order of the brewing tycoon Ernest Guinness. After that he would join the design team at Weybridge.

Wallis seems to have accepted this new brief on the spot, for later the same day – now at Cardington to watch R101 return from a test flight – he rang Molly to ask her to join him. Early on the following Monday they were both on a train to Southampton 'where we hope to find something in the shape of a house, though I fear we shan't do much in a day'.[70] In fact, they did find what Molly called 'a darling gem of a house' midway between Winchester and Southampton. It was called Deerhurst, and Molly was already furnishing it in her mind's eye. She was particularly smitten by its garden. 'It's got lavender bushes, and jasmine, and honeysuckle and roses, and it's just such a dear place for a family to grow in.' 'The trouble is that we may be shunted off to Weybridge after a year or so, so we ought to rent a house for a year, and I don't know if they'd let Deerhurst for such a short time.'[71]

Back at Howden, on 5 November, it was announced that the launch of R100 had been set ten days hence, 'if the weather is favourable and the mooring mast at Cardington is not in use by the sister ship'.[72] However, when the time came the weather was not favourable, and the sister ship was still at mast.

While R100's crew waited, lawmakers asked more questions about the cost of the airship programme.[73] When members of both Houses of Parliament visited Cardington, they discovered that only one airship could be at the mast at a time. The penny dropped that for R100 to fly, R101 must go back into her shed, where she would stay for months. In private, as we have seen, this suited R101's builders, who needed time to tackle her problems. For the public and politicians, however, it was an anticlimax. Why stop now? Lord Newton voiced his frustration to the Secretary of State for Air: 'I cannot understand why the noble Lord and his friends set to work to build two of these airships simultaneously.' Lord Thomson explained that the two vessels were structurally different, and added: 'The contract was given to the Airship Guarantee Company in order that the company might be rewarded, and its chairman in particular, Sir Dennistoun Burney, for having kept airships alive during the period of neglect and depression which they suffered for several years sub-sequent to 1921.'[74] Burney himself parried scepticism with his usual braggadocio, telling journalists of his plan to build a fleet of seven giant airships at Howden, that airships would soon provide 48-hour Atlantic crossings, of regular links to Germany and the Netherlands, and his latest idea for a new airport near Hull.[75]

R100 was handed over to Booth and his crew on 22 November. Three days later came checks on her disposable lift and trim. Norway described the moment:

> It seemed almost incredible to us who had worked on her for five years that there should really be nothing more to do to her before she flew, but the day came when we ballasted her up in the shed . . . determining accurately for the first time the loads that she would carry. It was a simple procedure; we mobilised a hundred men to hold her by the power cars and the control car so that she neither floated up into the roof nor sank on to the floor. After each readjustment of the weights the men let go of her altogether on the blast of a whistle; we watched to see if she would rise or fall. After a few trials she hung motionless, poised in the air above the floor of the shed.[76]

The trim test found R100 to be well balanced about her centre of buoyancy. However, the lift test found her 7.4 tons short of the expected 60 tons. While this was smaller than the discrepancy afflicting R101, it still came as an unwelcome surprise. Wallis and Norway re-ran their calculations. What had changed? Part of the answer lay in the environment in which R100 had been built. The gasbags had been absorbing moisture since their installation back in 1928, while the outer cover had been periodically wetted by leaks in the shed roof. In theory the cover was protected by dope but tensioning of the cover had caused the dope film to crack and in places the cover was sopping. Vulnerable areas had been re-doped, but protection had been piecemeal and was variably effective. New doping would be needed.

On Monday 25 November the Directorate of Civil Aviation

assessed the problems. They issued R100 with a temporary permit to fly, valid for two months.

A press conference was held later that week. The day was gloomy and wet. Journalists and photographers who stepped off the train in sheeting rain were glad to get into the shelter of the shed, where *Flight* magazine's writer Major F. A. de V. Robertson nonetheless noted rainwater 'pouring freely through one section of the roof'. The pressmen were divided into groups, to each of which an AGC staff member was assigned to guide them round the ship. Lunch was served on board. Then Burney made a speech.

> He told us, to begin with, that the ship was lifting 30 tons of fuel and ballast, and that there were nearly 100 people on board. Yet she had to be held down to the floor by weights. He went on to express his thanks to all who had taken part in the building of R100, and said that the completion of a piece of work like that always had its sad side. He recalled that someone had dubbed R100 'the Cupid airship' because some twenty of the workers had married local girls while the work was going on, and he drew a sad picture of these twenty homes, only recently set up, now to be dismantled because there was no more work at Howden. He hinted at the need for more airship research, evidently having in his mind the scheme for an elliptical airship which he has advocated in his book. But he stated definitely that the firm of Vickers would not spend any more money on airship development on terms similar to the contract just completed.[77]

Burney continued to bang the drum for larger airships, realistic investment, and long-distance air travel to foster imperial cohesion. Towards the end he pointed out that R100 had cost less to build than a single naval cruiser, that she would be far faster than a cruiser, and that her smaller crew made her cheaper to run. Yet Howden would soon close and the special skills of its workforce would be lost while Britain continued to build cruisers. Robertson thought he seemed 'rather downcast'.

Two days later, 30 November, R101 was eased back into her shed.

Cardington's mast was clear. All R100 now needed was fair weather. During early December one deep low after another blew in from the Atlantic and secondary depressions whirled high winds and heavy rain across the north-east. 'It seems as if there will never be a calm day again and that we shall go on sitting here for years' wrote Molly. Wallis had run out of things to do with R100, and the waiting left him taut. For some weeks he had been writing letters to thank and compliment contractors and suppliers who had provided materials and services.[78] Since late summer he had also been seeking advice on metallurgical questions to inform the structural ideas he was taking to Vickers. By the end of November, however, he was at a standstill. For a time, he hoped to visit Friedrichshafen to inspect the new Dornier Do X flying boat – a huge twelve-engine machine with a duralumin hull – but dropped the idea when Vickers declined to cover his expenses.[79] For relief he took the family to the Cairn Hydro, a hotel they had discovered in Harrogate back in 1926. They liked its grand rooms, the winter garden, the coloured glass, the Grimms' fairy tale turrets and friendly staff. In early December 1929, however, Wallis was listless, ate little and complained of back pain. Molly wrote on the 13th: 'B. on edge with migraines, headaches etc etc. I don't know what to do.'[80]

Next day the wind dropped and the barometer rose. Howden's meteorologist forecast settled weather. On Sunday the 15th the programme's senior figures and remaining crew members arrived from Cardington.[81] Complete calm was predicted for the following day. Ralph Booth telephoned the Cairn. Wallis was out walking, but the message was relayed on return. Suddenly feeling hungry, he sat down to dinner with Molly and then drove back to Howden.

In the shed, Booth, Meager, the coxswains and a number of riggers were disconnecting the bridle suspensions and bringing stores aboard. Water ballast was adjusted to provide slight buoyancy, leaving the floating ship to swing from balance weights upon the ground.[82]

Burney beckoned the media. Reporters and newsreel cameramen were already waiting. With them came spectators. By the early hours of Monday thousands were heading for Howden, by car, bicycle, horse and cart. Coach owners had hired their vehicles to visitors from afar who now arrived to see the launch. Long before dawn the surrounding roads were crammed, and crowds had formed at vantage points. Truck drivers bringing the 400-strong handling party of soldiers struggled to find a path through the jams.[83] People camped on verges, lit fires to cook early breakfasts and bought coffee from mobile stalls. Some visitors brought wind-up gramophones, whence music sounded through the frosty dark.

Around four thirty Wallis joined Norway in the shed. Outside it was still and moonlit. The ground-handling soldiers had arrived. The crew were in position at five. Within the shed, R100 swayed gently. At half past six her engines were started and run slowly to warm them. Shortly before seven the engines were stopped, the shed doors were opened and Burney, Teed, Wallis and Norway went aboard. Molly stood nearby keeping up 'a foolish conversation' with Barnes through the control car's sliding window. Booth called for quiet and addressed the handling party: the walk-out was to be in silence, so that commands could be heard and promptly acted on. Booth pointed to a white line that had been painted on the axis of the shed floor and out onto the aerodrome. Plumb bobs hanging from the bow and stern of the ship were to be kept over the line. On command, the soldiers were to form two lines along either side of the ship and take hold of the handling cables that had been attached to weights, or rails on the control and power cars.[84]

The soldiers formed up. Scott took charge at the tail, Johnston at the bow;[85] at 07.20 walk-out began. Over the next eight minutes, like the emergence of some great moth from its pupa, R100 was moved into the open. Molly walked beside the control car, save for a minute or two when she dashed out onto the aerodrome to see what the scene looked like: 'perfectly beautiful, the moon turning her silver as she emerged, tail first'.[86] When the bow cleared the shed onlookers cheered. The walk continued, then slowly the ship was turned and eased into the lee of the shed. From some angles she eclipsed the dawn, while panicked hares rushed hither and yon. Towards eight o'clock the soldiers were told to shorten their cables until the men were immediately below the ship. Scott and Johnston went aboard. At 07.53 Booth gave the order 'Let go!' Water ballast fell like powder.[87] R100 rose gently for about a minute to cheers and the blare of car horns. The engines were started. At five hundred feet Booth called for two of the engines to be rung slow ahead. Wallis and Norway watched anxiously in the control car as the ship gathered way and began to answer to her controls. Would she behave as intended?

Molly watched as she circled Howden and turned pale pink in the sunrise. They looked back into the empty shed: 'I feel so frightfully sad; it is terrible to go to the shed and see no beautiful thing there.'

Booth directed R100 up to York, where they circled for fifteen minutes, then set course for Cardington. The coxswains who governed height and steering found her easy to handle. Wallis's automatic clutch and free-wheel gear worked as intended.[88] Relieved and elated, Wallis and Norway went to the saloon to join other passengers for breakfast. One of the engines developed a fault and was shut down, but this notwithstanding they were over Bedford in less than two hours. They cruised in the area for an hour, rehearsed the mooring approach procedure several times and were locked home to the mooring tower by half past one.

A conference about small defects followed.[89] It was agreed to make another trial flight on the following day. Wallis left liaison about this to Norway. Molly arrived. She had been driven down in the station car and came to take him home to Hampstead. It was nearly Christmas. It was done.

6

Landfall, 1930–31

False moves

The 'darling gem of a house' upon which Molly had set her heart back in October was no longer available, so January's first days were spent searching. 'I am so down hearted & miserable. We cannot find anything to let. I'd be content with anything with 4 bedrooms and 2 sitting rooms, but Barnes is so jolly particular and keeps saying wait.'[1] Molly pined for the white bungalow. 'I don't suppose we shall ever know another such an adorably, romantic, lovely, happy time'.[2]

Wallis presented himself at Supermarine's works at Woolston on Monday, 13 January. McLean knew he was taking a risk by introducing him into Mitchell's settled team and tried to minimise it with these instructions:

> With immediate effect, Mr Wallis is appointed Deputy Chief Designer to the Supermarine Aviation Works, to be in charge, in the first instance, of the detail Drawing Office and all detail design.
>
> He will be responsible generally to Mr Mitchell, whose general ideas are not to be departed from without his concurrence.[3]

McLean's terms of reference gave each man room to accommodate the other, if they wanted to. But neither of them did. Mitchell ran a cohesive team, which he rightly suspected Wallis was being sent to examine and reorganise. Mitchell also knew he was indispensable to McLean's plans. For his part, after four years of sovereignty at

Howden and supposing himself to be McLean's angel of reform, Wallis took being 'in charge' of the Drawing Office literally. Sensing trouble, he bought a large hard-backed notebook in which to keep a record. At the end of the first day, he wrote:

Arrived works 11.15 a.m. Saw Mitchell & discussed general topics
. . . After lunch M. briefly referred to my duties, & announced intention of forming new D[drawing] O[ffice] for design work taking Holroyd etc etc out of D.O.[4]

In other words, even before Wallis arrived Mitchell had decided to marginalise him by setting up a parallel structure. And since McLean had not said where the boundary between 'general' and 'detail' should lie, Mitchell would decide it for him.

Mitchell did not appear next day. Supermarine colleagues knew such absences to be a sign of his displeasure. However, nobody explained this to Wallis, who drew a diagram of the staff structure and proceeded to interview its members one by one. There is an officious tone in his notes. Over the next two days, still with no sign of Mitchell, Wallis busied himself over details of two current projects, the troubled Guinness Air Yacht, and the prototype Mark X Southampton.

Late on the Friday afternoon he caught a train for London. The full power trial of R100 had disclosed standing ripples along her outer cover. A further trial was arranged for the following Monday, when R100 flew over London and on to Farnborough with Burney and Wallis aboard. A RAE aircraft flew alongside to film the cover,[5] while Norway crawled about inside the hull with the riggers. At cruising speed, 'about seventy miles an hour, they found that the cover was quite normal'.[6] Norway and Wallis concluded that the ripple effect was some sort of harmonic deflection resulting from eddies of air passing over the hull, and that it was of no basic importance.[7]

Next day Wallis took the train back to Southampton and Supermarine's Drawing Office. Mitchell reappeared. After lunch they talked frankly – or as Wallis portentously put it, he 'interviewed Mitchell'.

Mitchell wants entire control & exclude me from control of Plans Office. I do not think this will work and say so. Decide to go to town to place position before Sir R[obert].[8]

Wallis told McLean and John Chamier (Vickers's Technical Director) that Woolston's drawing office was inadequately led, that Mitchell's timekeeping was poor, and that Mitchell's grasp of structural design was imperfect.[9] McLean noted Wallis's comments about Mitchell's unwillingness to compromise, but since his giftedness had been one of the main reasons why Vickers acquired Supermarine in the first place, it made no sense to lose him by ruling in favour of Wallis.[10] In any case, there was another option. Wallis concluded his day-book entry for Thursday, 30 January: 'Started Weybridge.'

To Brooklands and Effingham

Vickers Aviation's design office was tucked alongside the motor racing circuit at Brooklands. Here, scores of draughtsmen worked at rows of drawing boards in an atmosphere akin to that of an examination hall, invigilated from a dais by the chief draughtsman and his assistant. Leading off the main area were the offices of Pierson and now Wallis.

Pierson was broad-shouldered, generous and painstaking. Known as 'Rex', he amused colleagues by the nimble way in which he manoeuvred his hefty frame in and out of a baby Fiat that he drove nippily along Surrey's lanes. Pierson was glad to share original ideas with competitors in whom he had faith. When deep in thought he had a habit of slipping off a gold ring and spinning it on the desktop until a decision was reached. A good listener, his calm persistence and unselfishness enabled Wallis's creative individuality to flourish.

Wallis and Molly lived apart while they looked for a house. During the week Wallis took a room in the Hand and Spear pub next to Weybridge station, whence he walked to work, while Molly and the children stayed at Pepys Road or with friends. The Piersons occasionally invited Wallis for an evening meal and a game of cards. At the beginning of March Molly rented rooms as a base for what she called the 'miserable house hunt'. Homesick for Howden, she reckoned to have slept in twenty-three different beds in twelve weeks. 'If only we can *settle*.'[11] Wallis, meanwhile, normally a connoisseur of hardship, complained about the 'awful bed' at the Hand and Spear.

On weekdays Wallis wrote to Molly during the lunch hour, filling in the blanks of pre-printed Vickers notepaper with romantic quips ('*When replying refer to* SLAVE; *Enclosures* KISSES') and peppering the letters with gossip ('Mitchell's flying yacht is suffering torsional weakness of the wings. I cd. have told them so'). To cheer her – or perhaps himself – he drew jokey cartoons recalling their 1924 servant-slave exchanges, such as his design for a slave's harness (made from 'a simple rug strap which one can buy anywhere for a few shillings').

The work went well. Within a week he told Molly that the company had offered to raise his salary to £3000 in three years by yearly increments. He added, perhaps with a touch of bravado, that he had not yet accepted: 'I hope to do better.'[12] In the same letter: 'They have decided to build one complete 12-seater monoplane to my designs!'

Several things were going on here. McLean, Pierson, and Wallis all realised that the future of aircraft architecture lay with metal, which offered structural possibilities entirely different from the wooden trusses that until then had formed the basis of airframes. Wallis had been brought to Weybridge to explore such possibilities and find ways to put them into practice. The first of them was a new kind of wing based on the stainless-steel spar drawn from high-tensile steel strip upon which he had been working since the middle of 1929.[13] In Wallis's first week he was introduced to Robert Mayo, consulting engineer to Imperial Airways, and from this encounter came the proposal for a 12-seat 'Imperial Airways fuselage'.[14] This quickly became blurred with (if it was ever entirely distinct from) another 12-seater project that was already in development: the Vickers Viastra, a tri-motor all-metal monoplane intended for use from rough airstrips overseas.[15] By the end of February it was agreed that a Viastra should be used to test an experimental wing of Wallis's design.[16] Experiment is the theme. Five months after the Wall Street crash, McLean wished his designers to excel so that 'we get at least our fair share of the available business'.[17]

Negotiations about Wallis's terms of employment ran on until late March. Discussions with Chamier led him to think that Vickers would accept his entitlement to 'special remuneration' for use of his inventions and that patents would remain his own negotiable property.[18] He was soon set straight by McLean who told him that he was being paid for his full-time services, 'inclusive of your accumulated knowledge and any new ideas that may come forward'. Moreover, since the terms being offered were identical to those that already applied to Mitchell and Pierson, it was not possible to consider bespoke clauses that would operate in his favour alone. McLean sweetened his firmness by lifting the initial basic salary offer from £2000 to £2500, plus an annual commission on sales.[19] The contract would run for five years in the first instance.[20] Wallis accepted, and on 1 May he signed the contract whereby he became Chief Designer (Structures) to Vickers (Aviation) and its subsidiaries.

The contractual discussions coincided with anxieties about young Barnes. In January he had complained of ear pain. Mastoiditis was diagnosed; the condition worsened; in mid-February he underwent surgery; recovery was slow. The specialist overseeing it held that the boy's health would be helped by living in a high, dry environment. Out came the map. Places along the dip-slope of the north Downs looked promising. Three weeks before signing the contract Barnes and Molly had driven out in the pug to explore them. Clandon, West Horsley, East Horsley, Effingham . . .

> Mary, I *think* we've got a house! I'm so frightfully excited. We keep saying to each other we mustn't set our hearts on it; don't get excited; etc. But I can't help being a little bit. It's at a place called Effingham about 7 miles from Weybridge.[21]

The site was 400 feet up on chalk and thus '*very* good for [young] Barnes'. Beech Avenue was narrow, 'not very traffic-y', and there really was an avenue of beeches. 'It's brand new – not yet finished, and garden there is none; at least it stands in about ¾ acre of field. It faces south and looks over Effingham golf links . . . It's on the side of a hill and the garden's on a slope. There were two reception rooms, five bedrooms – "Oh Molly, *do* shut up. It may not come off."'

Beech Avenue was a road leading from the village up to the scarp of the North Downs and the house was one of several being erected beside it by a speculative builder. It might have been designed with Wallis in mind: although it was fitted with progressive features like central heating, its leaded panes, tall chimneys, faux timber-framing and hints of jettying implied an idealised, traditional England, a kind of cultural Venn diagram in which the worlds of Elizabeth, Charles I and the 1930s overlapped.

Molly was suspicious of central heating ('I fear it inclines you to be soft and feeble')[22] but Arthur Bloxam steadied their nerves about the cost ('Daddy thinks the house might be thought of as an investment').[23] The contract with Vickers promised security for the next few years. The fact that the building was not quite complete allowed the possibility of minor bespoke alterations, which following his own measured survey jotted into a spare diary Wallis duly requested. Molly feared that Barnes's finnicky demands might irritate the builder and cause him to sell to someone else, but they moved in at the end of May, called it White Hill House, sank their souls into the place and lived there until the end of their lives.

Funeral music

Parents, friends, and relatives visited White Hill House over the summer. The Wallises became friendly with Aubrey and May Dibdin, neighbours on the downhill side of Beech Avenue. By September Aubrey was 'Dibby', and by then, R100 had crossed the Atlantic.[24]

Wallis was not aboard. 'Sir Robert was v. nice today but absolutely refuses to let me fly to Canada.'[25] McLean wished to protect his investment. Wallis thus missed the huge crowds that greeted R100's arrival and her subsequent flights over Toronto and Niagara. In his absence Burney proclaimed himself as the ship's designer.[26] Molly complained that the achievement was largely ignored in Britain, but the record shows keen press interest and newsreel coverage. The voyage even inspired two popular songs.[27] Problems met during the journeys (covers torn from the empennage and a violent dive during a squall above the St Lawrence; loss of cooking facilities due to ingress of water) were talked down on return. Indeed, the widely held idea that R100's voyage was an unqualified success underestimates the hazards that attended all airships – their unwieldiness, susceptibility to small defects that became dangerous if they were compounded, and vulnerability in poor weather. The real position was well put by Norway: 'Considered purely from the technical aspect, it was not very prudent for either airship to attempt a long flight at that stage of development. We did it, and got away with it.'[28] Nonetheless, on return from Canada Colmore told Sir John Salmond, now Chief of the Air Staff, that with 'a new and stronger cover and new gasbags, an extra bay and dieselised Condors, R100 will be a very good ship'.[29]

Booth wrote to Norway on 28 August listing repairs and modifications that were in the offing. The need for many of them, he said, was obvious.[30] However: 'what defeats me entirely is that the main cover system and the plane cover system is being scrapped and reefing booms or intermediate girders fitted in her.' This would add at least four tons of weight. He continued: 'I cannot find out why this is being done except to make a bastard R101 out of R100!' Booth said he had told the 'heads' (as Colmore, Scott and Richmond were known at Cardington) 'that they were giving up a system which had not been proved wrong for a system which definitely had not been proved right.'[31]

The proposed change to the cover was to push its fabric panels outwards, thereby giving the ship a more rounded shape, in contrast to the hollow-cheeked appearance of the original design. This presumably reflected Colmore's opinion that R100 needed a stronger cover, but Booth could get no explanation for it. Forty years later Wallis told his biographer that the insistence of Richmond and others upon it implied either their misunderstanding or ignorance of the mathematical argument which had led him to it in the first place.[32]

Meanwhile, the time had come for R101 to embark on her own

voyage. Since late June she had been modified and refurbished. These works were completed on Friday, 26 September. Lord Thomson, begetter of the two-ship scheme back in 1924, wished to fly in her to India. Thomson originally hoped to start for India the following weekend, thus enabling his return for the Imperial Conference that was due to start in London in early October. However, this schedule had since been put back. The latest plan was to depart early in October, returning to enable Thomson to join the conference on the 20th of the month.[33] Decisions on further funding for airship development were in abeyance pending his return. At the end of August, Cardington had submitted proposals for a five-year development programme that included two new and larger airships – the R102 and R103. The Treasury had made an earmark for these, subject to endorsement by the Imperial Conference, but it was Colmore's understanding that such funding would not be forthcoming if Thomson was not borne to India and back in time for the Conference's discussion.

R101 was supposed to undergo a trial endurance flight and full speed test before she departed. However, the calm weather needed to bring her forth and put her to the tower did not arrive until 1 October. This left no time for the full trial programme if Thomson's deadline was to be met. Thomson in his turn was under political pressure to produce results for the investment of public money.

The 'heads' conferred. Anxious to please, they agreed to curtail the trials.[34] The ultimate decision rested with AVM Hugh Dowding, who was now the member of the Air Force board with responsibility for supply and research. But Dowding had only been in post for a month, and he knew little about airships. He accordingly deferred to Colmore, who thereby became judge in his own cause. Earlier cautionary advice was set aside, and a certificate of airworthiness was issued.[35] Thus it was that on Friday, 3 October the decision was taken for R101 to leave for India at 1800 hours on the following day. Noël Atherstone described the mood:

> Everybody is rather keyed up now, as well feel that the future of airships very largely depends on what sort of a show we put up.

There are very many unknown factors and I feel that that thing called 'Luck' will figure rather conspicuously in our flight. Let's hope for good luck and do our best![36]

R101 slipped the mast in drizzle just after half past six. Aboard her were forty-two officers and crew and twelve passengers. Apart from Thomson, the passengers included Sefton Brancker (UK Director of Civil Aviation), Colmore (Director of Airship Development), Scott, and the ship's chief architect, Vincent Richmond. An hour later, a small boy in north London watched agog as she passed over, lights a-glitter, the bass growl of her engines fading as she crossed Hackney Marshes and away into the gloom.[37]

The weather worsened. A little after two next morning, Sunday, R101 grounded near Beauvais in northern France. She slid a few tens of yards and settled. The impact was gentle, and it is likely that everyone aboard survived it. In seconds, however, she was aflame. Even the ground burned. Fire took the lives of forty-eight souls.[38]

The duty officer at Cardington telephoned the news to Vickers Aviation, whence it was passed to Wallis around 7 a.m. Wallis listened in such stillness that the caller 'thought he had not heard and started to tell the story all over again'.[39]

Word spread during the day. Some heard it from announcements at church services. Others read about it in late special editions of newspapers. The BBC gave a solemn report at 6 p.m. Next day, Monday, *The Times* devoted seven pages to 'The work of rescue', 'Scenes at Beauvais', 'Scene at the wreck', 'Prime Minister's Tribute', 'Great Airship Disaster'. In the *Daily Mail*: 'Great Dirigible Crashes in Flames', 'Village of Sorrow', 'Died like heroes', 'The officers and passengers.' On the Tuesday Wallis travelled up to Howden, where AGC's design team was still in being, at work on recently agreed modifications to R100 and clinging on in the hope for a contract for one of the new ships. He found the team in shock. Several former AGC riggers had been in R101's crew, and two of her officers had served in R100. Scott, once Wallis's close friend, since disparaged, was gone.

While Wallis was in Yorkshire, R101's dead were being taken from Beauvais to Boulogne, where two naval vessels waited to carry them

Barnes at Ripley, 1889

The Rev George Wallis with his second wife Caroline (back centre) and sister (upper left), their children Leslie (lower left), Tacy, 'Uncle Wyn' (upper right), and Ethel (lower right), with Charles and Edie Wallis (centre front) and their sons John and Barnes, respectively. Isle of Wight, c.1892

Dinner parade on 'Hall Play', Christ's Hospital, Newgate, 1902

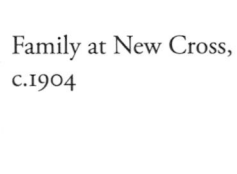

Family at New Cross,
c.1904

J. Samuel White works outing to Beaulieu, August 1911

Wallis with Archie Watts (right), Vic and Doug Civil, August 1911

Hartley Pratt c.1909

With the Artists' Rifles,
Epping Forest, summer 1915

No. 9 at Barrow, November 1916

Wallis on his
motorcycle, 1917

Launch of R80 at Walney, 19 July 1920

Molly and Barbara Bloxam with Charles and Fanny, 1924

Clowning with Norman and Edgar Boyd (second from left)
and friend, at Borth, July 1923

The wedding,
23 April 1925

The White Bungalow
at Howden

Off duty at Howden,
the shed beyond

R100 under construction hanging in the Howden shed, 1928

to England. The surge of public grief and state-organised lamentation that followed was on a scale not seen since the return of the Unknown Soldier in 1919. The journey began in a long column of carts, preceded by a company of troops and muffled drums. The King was represented by Lord Tyrell, the UK's ambassador. With him were Sir John Salmond, Chief of the Air Staff, and André Tardieu, France's Prime Minister. France declared Tuesday a day of national mourning. Thousands stood in silence at rural railway stations as the train bearing forty-eight coffins passed. At Boulogne the coffins were placed on the destroyers *Tempest* and *Tribune*. With ominous symbolism, *Tribune* then broke a propeller, leaving *Tempest* to carry them all to Dover. A funeral train bore the coffins to London. Victoria Station was virtually empty as the train drew in in the small hours of Wednesday morning. Waiting in silence were Air Ministry officials, the reserve watch of R101, R100's crew, and Ramsay MacDonald. The coffins were transferred to a line of RAF tenders to the accompaniment of the distant rumble and desolate hoot of a shunting engine.

Analogy with the Unknown Soldier goes further: over half the victims were so charred that they could not be identified. This being so, a common funeral in a single grave in Cardington's churchyard was decided upon, to take place on Saturday, 11 October. A memorial service in St Paul's Cathedral would be held the day before. And on the day before that, Thursday, 9 October, the victims' coffins lay in state in Westminster Hall. From 8 a.m. members of the public filed past the coffins, each on a purple-draped bier and covered by a Union Jack, aligned in pairs down the centre of the Hall. At one stage the queue stretched for half a mile. When the doors in St Stephen's Porch were finally closed after midnight, ninety thousand people had walked through.

Next day Molly wrote to Mary Turner: 'Barnes has gone to the service at St Paul's today and goes to Cardington tomorrow. He is so upset.'

Of course, the terrible part about it all is that it needn't and shouldn't have happened. I mean she wasn't fit to fly . . . if they'd asked Barnes's advice it wouldn't have happened because she wouldn't have flown. The truth is that they had little more idea how to build an airship than you or I have.[40]

The memorial service was attended by ambassadors and envoys from over fifty nations, and broadcast to the Empire. For an hour St Paul's became 'the Empire's parish church'. In the congregation were the Prime Minister, his Cabinet and two former prime ministers. A large Indian delegation was there; so too were delegates to the Imperial Conference that Thomson had expected to attend; heads of government departments; the Board of the Admiralty, the Army Council, leaders of industry. With them were office-bearers familiar to Wallis from his days at Newgate Street: the Lord Mayor, sheriffs, aldermen and Corporation of London. The King and Queen were represented by the Prince of Wales, who had watched R101 from his personal aircraft on her maiden flight and now arrived to the sound of a tolling bell. A double-decker bus chartered in Bedford drew up at the foot of the steps; from it, veiled and dressed in black, emerged the widows and close family of R101's crew. Among them was Jessie Scott, before whom Wallis had felt 'quite in the way' when he had stayed with the Scotts at Pulham seven years before. Within, R100's crew was seated in the gallery under the dome.

The next morning a two-mile-long procession set out from Westminster at 10 a.m. bound for Euston Station. The column passed through Whitehall, The Strand, Aldwych, Kingsway and Southampton Row before half a million onlookers. The head of the procession reached Euston at noon. The coffins were transferred to a special train drawn by two locomotives, *Arabia* and *Persia*, the first of them bearing a large wreath of white chrysanthemums, red carnations and blue forget-me-nots. The train carrying the dead proceeded along cleared tracks, past silent crowds on railway stations, embankments, at level crossings. When it reached Bedford, wrote a spectator, 'it seemed to have come a much longer journey'.[41]

The sun was shining as the final procession set out for the five-mile journey to Cardington. Bystanders watched the dark tops of twenty-four RAF tenders, each bearing two coffins, as they slowly wound across the countryside. Tens of thousands lined the verges. In the churchyard, waiting mourners heard snatches of Chopin's funeral march from across the fields, mingled with a bell that tolled from the church tower. The churchyard wall was covered by cards and wreaths from well-wishers. Beyond, across the fields, stood Cardington's two great airship sheds.

The grave was a large rectangular pit with battered sides draped in turf, gladioli and carnations. It took over half an hour for the coffins, each borne by six servicemen, to be carried down a sloping ramp to the pit floor. Members of the crew of R100 lined the grave edge. With them stood the Bishop of St Albans, a Roman Catholic bishop, Methodist and Presbyterian ministers. Alongside were relatives, official mourners, Hugo Eckener and Dennistoun Burney, and a crowd that had followed the procession.

The sun was low when the last flag-draped coffin was placed in the grave. The Vicar of Cardington spoke the opening sentences of the Anglican burial service.

> I am the resurrection and the life, saith the Lord: he that believeth in me, though he were dead, yet shall he live . . .

Michael Furse, the Bishop of St Albans, led the rest of the service. Prayers said by the two Nonconformist ministers followed. After the benediction, the Roman Catholic bishop prayed for the souls of four crew members who had been Roman Catholics.

For all this time a firing party had been waiting, motionless, heads bowed. When the rites were done, on command they raised their rifles and fired a volley. Twenty seconds' silence followed as they lowered their weapons, reloaded, and re-raised their rifles. A second volley. Another pause for reloading. The third volley. Six buglers played the last post. 'Hardly anybody moved.'

The ceremonies in Boulogne, Westminster, St Paul's and Cardington, and the journeys that linked them, formed a continuous drama that lasted for five days. Millions watched on the streets and beside railways and millions more saw the newsreels.[42] The depth of national shock was in equal and opposite reaction to the euphoria which had attended R101's launch and trials almost exactly one year before.

Wallis was at once close to and distanced from what followed. He was peripheral because it was not his airship, and he was not consulted about what had happened to it; close, because many of the dead were his friends and colleagues, and because as time passed his views on the causes of the disaster – essentially that R101 was doomed from the start – came to outweigh those of the inquiry.[43]

The inquiry opened on 28 October. It was chaired by the veteran politician Sir John Simon and sat for thirteen days.[44] The inquiry was told that R101 had flown into the worst weather ever encountered by a rigid airship at night and found that the immediate cause of her crash had been a loss of forward buoyancy due to weather-induced damage. The aviation pioneer John Moore-Brabazon and the engineer Professor Charles Inglis sat with Simon as expert assessors. Brabazon made notes summarising his own conclusions. Under the heading 'Blame' he wrote that technical problems had been subordinated to political pressure, and that setting forth in bad weather was 'a contributory cause to the accident'. Another factor was 'the introduction of many new devices'. The innovations 'necessitated extensive trials to try them out', but such trials had either been curtailed or skipped.[45] And finally:

> The organisation of the Air Ministry shows no over-riding power of veto on the airship colony at Cardington. Higgins and Dowding, no doubt distinguished officers, were quite unable to take a strong line on airship policy, the whole of Cardington found themselves practically forced to take the bidding of the Secretary of State.[46]

The Airship Guarantee Company's remaining staff at Howden were disbanded a month later.[47] Wallis had planned to attend the Paris Aero Show, where Vickers were exhibiting examples of his new wing structures, but instead returned to Howden to make his farewells. In December, as Cardington was shrouded in a succession of thick fogs, R100's gas cells were deflated and the ship was left suspended in her shed pending the outcome of the inquiry.

The inquiry report was published in March 1931. Two months later, Ramsay MacDonald made a statement to the House of Commons in which he outlined three options: retention and refurbishment of R100 and continuation of the programme; mothballing or experimental use of R100 pending a change of circumstances; or axing of the programme.[48] MacDonald ruled out the first while making his statement. Discussion about possible refitting and modification of R100 continued for several months more, but everyone knew it was finished.[49]

The prince of clouds was scrapped over the winter of 1931/32.[50] A visitor 'found the sight too brutal' and turned away. 'Talk about breaking a butterfly on the wheel!'[51] Molly was more philosophical. 'Yes, we are feeling a bit sad about R100. It does seem a fearful waste. We keep remembering this and that about her – times when she was worrying and difficult, times when she was beautiful and proud, anxious times and jolly times. Oh well, it's all over.'[52]

Even before one chapter ended, another began. Three months before, Wallis had registered a patent for a new concept in aircraft frameworks: geodetics.[53]

7

Earth to Love, 1931–40

Aircraft in the making

'Barnes is frightfully in love with the Downs and Sussex.' On August Bank Holiday 1931 they walked in heat on Black Patch Down. Thyme-scented air, the ring of sheep bells, mysterious dewponds, the softness of turf: 'Have you read Kipling's "Sussex"?[1] Because it's all that exactly.'[2]

A fortnight later, the 1931 Schneider Trophy contest was held before half a million spectators who crammed the shores of Southsea, Hayling Island and Gosport to see the aircraft trace a triangular course over the Solent. A select group watched from the White Star liner *Homeric* which had been chartered by the Royal Aero Club as a floating hotel and viewing platform. White Star was glad of the business: demand for the *Homeric*'s normal transatlantic service had been cut by the Depression.

Molly and Barnes went aboard early on the Friday evening, having travelled down with the rest of the Vickers party in Pullman luxury. At dinner there were oysters ('never had such food in my life') and there was dancing into the early hours.

The competition was scheduled for the next day, but poor weather caused its postponement, while the withdrawal of entries from France, Germany and Italy meant that the British flew unopposed. Wallis and Molly explored the ship, and when the weather lifted, they played deck tennis. Others repaired to the open bars. Free drink was a 'ghastly mistake' wrote Molly, who was agog at how much was being put away: 'the beasts just sat there getting redder & redder

& tighter & tighter . . . I'm glad then that Barnes drinks naught. It's frightfully difficult I gather when you're entertaining people like that not to drink too much.'

McLean asked Wallis to socialise with specified diplomats and industrialists from whom Vickers hoped to secure orders. At dinner, their task was to entertain the Greek and Yugoslavian air attachés and their wives, and a French air marshal. When the guests discovered it was Molly's birthday they ordered champagne, which Barnes declined. In discussion they decided that the English drank more than other nations. After dinner, Molly found herself dancing with 'strange men' in the cause of promoting Vickers Aviation's business.

Sunday's weather was glorious. Soon after 1 p.m. Flt Lt John Boothman took to the air in a specially prepared Supermarine S6B and retained the trophy for Britain by flying seven laps of the course at an average speed of 340.08 miles per hour. Later in the afternoon Flt Lt George Stainforth made four high-speed runs. The flying required a dive before the start to gain speed, and to be perfectly level 500 metres before the course threshold. The laps were recorded by cinecameras. Analysis of the film showed that Stainforth had averaged 386.1 mph. Molly was unimpressed by many of the ladies aboard ('What an awful existence – to have nothing more to worry about than whether your face tones with your frock') and not much interested in the flying. It was fine, she said, 'but honestly I wouldn't walk an inch to see such a thing'. During the afternoon, she started to knit.

Mitchell was ashore for most of the weekend, attending to the aircraft. In following days, encouraged by McLean, he oversaw the fine-tuning of an S6B for a further record attempt, which was made early in the evening of 29 September, using an exotic fuel mix – 30 per cent benzole, 60 per cent methanol, 10 per cent acetone, tetra ethyl lead additive – for the Rolls-Royce R engine. Stainforth was again at the controls and on return told colleagues he believed he had exceeded 400 mph. He was right. The news was passed to the King; a jubilant *Daily Mail* noted that Britain now held the world speed records for aircraft, motor cars, motorcycles, and motorboats. In the 1930s, speed and national status went together. The S6B was taken to London in triumph and put on public display at the International Motor Show. Britain was told that it all redounded to the credit of the 'Supermarine works of Vickers Aviation'.[3]

Something else that would soon redound to the credit of Vickers Aviation was an entirely new system of aircraft construction. It would be logical to imagine Wallis arriving at this through a series of steps. The reality was that he was experimenting with at least six forms of original construction in parallel, and that each of them was at a different stage and progressing along different lines. Among them was a monospar monoplane wing; a tubular spar fuselage;[4] monospar control surfaces for a prototype bomber;[5] a monocoque construction for a prototype interceptor fighter;[6] and the structure of an alternative wing for Supermarine's projected Giant flying boat.[7] The focus on experiment reflected McLean's view that progressive design offered Vickers a surer path out of the Great Depression than hack work such as reconditioning obsolescent Virginias and Victorias or making spare parts. Amid all this, paragraph thirteen of a half-yearly note on Vickers Aviation's technical position in December 1931 reads almost as an afterthought:

> Another development at present in its early stages, is the construction of a fuselage with convolute diagonals which, while taking the stresses in the structure, are also the formers of the fairings; in other words, except for the longitudinal strips of little weight, all fairing structure is eliminated. It is hoped to save as much as 200 out of 500 lbs in the case of the after end of the 19/27 fuselage if this method of construction proves satisfactory. The mathematical investigation has been completed and a short section is now under construction for static test.[8]

Afterthought or not, these words put us on the threshold of one of Wallis's greatest achievements.

Rex Pierson's earlier aircraft designs were essentially boxes tapered off at their ends, with high drag taken for granted. Wallis suggested streamlining, and noticed that Pierson's response was to streamline an existing fuselage by introducing members that rendered the interior unusable abaft the wings. Pondering this, Wallis realised that geodesic lines could be drawn on the streamline surface, that such lines need not be of constant curvature, and that if opposite-handed geodesics were to be rigidly joined at the points where they crossed, they would bear equal and opposite forces.[9] Back in 1925, when searching for a way to secure R100's gas cells, Louis Filon had coached him in the mathematics of geodesics on surfaces of double curvature; in July 1931 an invitation from the Air Ministry to submit a design for a general-purpose aircraft (specification G.4/31) provided an opportunity to put such a structure to the test.[10] Its promised merits of lightness and strength would extend range, increase carrying capacity and free aircraft interiors for passengers, cargo, or weapons. Vickers entered two airframe designs for the competition: a biplane with a wing of standard construction and a geodetic fuselage (this became the Vickers Type 253), and a fully geodetic monoplane (the Vickers Type 246, which became the Wellesley).

A year and a half later, Wallis told Molly: 'My geodetic fuselage gave most astonishingly good results on test today – really wonderful, and shows that my new method of calculation is on the right lines.'[11] In due course the Air Ministry issued a prototype contract for the biplane, which in 1935 went on to win a production order for 150 machines. Meanwhile, however, McLean had persuaded the Vickers board to build a prototype of the monoplane at the company's own expense.[12] This posed design challenges that took over eighteen months to solve,[13] but when the monoplane eventually flew in June 1935 its performance was so far ahead of the biplane that McLean was emboldened to urge the Air Staff to change their order, which in September they did. By this time the prototype all-geodetic bomber that would become the Wellington was also taking shape. This was in response to yet another call (Air Ministry specification, B.9/32), while a month later Vickers was awarded a contract to build a prototype heavy bomber that would eventually become known as the Warwick. The aerodynamics of these designs came from Pierson, but it was Wallis who provided the structure for an entire family of machines that would span a decade.

McLean's enterprise and faith in backing geodetic construction has often been remarked. Less has been said about the circumstances in which he exercised his judgement. Britain was in depression. Business was fragile. In March 1932 a cut of 5 per cent was imposed on the salaries of Vickers's staff.[14] McLean's success a month later in persuading his board to commit over £30,000 (about £2 million at today's prices) to realise the monoplane design was thus an extraordinary gamble, the more so (shareholders were warned) because phasing out old methods would mean a drop in income during the transition to new ones.

Yet more extraordinary was the way in which he went about it. In 1930 Wallis had been struck by the pally way in which McLean hobnobbed with senior officers at the Air Ministry. By 1932 his style had become more forthright. Aero engineers in this period were not expected to have views about air power theory or tactical requirements, merely to provide designs in response to Air Staff requirements, yet here were McLean, Pierson and Wallis bringing into being a bomber with range and carrying capacity for which at that point the Air Staff had not asked. Far from being appreciative, some senior figures saw this as impertinent. McLean faced internal as well as external hostility. The workforce hankered after the old simplicities of manufacturing wooden aircraft in small numbers, and resented the difficulties associated with metallisation and streamlining. Wallis said later that opposition within the works had been so great that without McLean's backing the system could not have been introduced.

The name 'Wellesley' was approved for the new bomber in November 1935. News of the 'Wallis-Vickers system' was formally released early in January 1936. Annie wrote: 'John and I have searched the papers for many years, expecting to see what I see today . . . you have at last got your reward'. She added: 'But do try and last a few years longer. My paper yesterday said you were a silver-haired gentle-voiced vegetarian', but today's announces that you are "*frail*".' Here began the later-flowering legend of Wallis as elderly and mild-mannered. Burney wrote a generous letter, reminiscing about old times, and telling how plans to produce his car in the United States had been scuppered by the slump.[15] Masterman was quick off the mark:

Dear Wally
Had I the wings of a Turtle Dove
Far, far away would I fly,
But had I Wally Geodetic wings, I would fly a d[amned]
    sight further.

Then:

White wings that never grow weary, could these foreshadow
the Wally geodetic wing? All our best congratulations on
your arrival at the Temple of Fame . . . I can see reporters
besieging the house and foreign emissaries arriving hat in
hand, invitations to broadcast . . . You are a made and marked
man from now on.[16]

And he was. Reporters doorstepped relatives to ask for personal
details. *The People* proclaimed him 'Britain's Mystery Inventor
No. 1', so 'naturally modest' that colleagues who had worked with
him for years did not know if he was married. Journalists on the
lookout for analogies to explain geodetics came up with 'Spider
Web' 'Planes' and 'Egg Shell Aeroplanes'.[17] Philip Sassoon, Under-
Secretary of State for Air, told MPs that the system epitomised 'the
vitality and the ingenuity of our designers'.[18] The Royal Aeronautical Society awarded Wallis its silver medal. *Flight*'s correspondent
dwelt on the Wellesley's speed, agility and 'grim aspect', reflecting
on how its independently retracting wheels added to the 'bizarre
fascination of the big bomber' as it climbed. King George VI
toured the Wellesley production line and sat in a Wellesley cockpit.[19] *Aviation* magazine said that geodetic construction increased
bomber range by a factor of two and a half. As if to prove it, in
July 1938 four specially modified Wellesleys of the RAF's Long-
Range Development Unit flew direct from Cranwell to Ismaila in
Egypt and Shaibah in Iraq. A greater journey followed, when on
5 November, three Wellesleys set out from Ismailia for Australia.
Over 48 hours later, having flown 7000 miles non-stop, two of
them reached Darwin. Masterman's telegram 'Per ardua ad Astralia'

[sic] was among scores of congratulatory messages that poured into White Hill House.

Vickers-Wallis construction thus seemed vindicated. Wallis nonetheless continued to complain that it had caused offence among 'ignorant people in high places'.[20] One of its critics, he said, was Air Marshal Sir Wilfrid Freeman, who in 1936 was appointed the Air Member for Research and Development, a role which brought with it responsibility for selecting aeroplanes with which to equip the RAF. Wallis believed Freeman to be prejudiced against geodetics, and to favour Handley Page because of its lavish hospitality and smoother way of doing business. Freeman was one of the RAF's most capable and effective leaders, and his original view of geodetic construction was much more nuanced than either Wallis or McLean later allowed.[21] While McLean believed the Air Staff to be a stick-in-the-mud, the fact is that they were quick to concede the Wellesley's superiority and the Wellington's potential and commit to their production.[22] From Freeman's perspective, the basic issue was not a dislike of geodetic structure, but the need to weigh up its ramifications.[23] In 1936 it was reckoned that eight years would pass between the specification for a heavy bomber and its entry into service. Committing to geodetics would thus tie Vickers to what looked like a complex and labour-intensive system for at least a decade and might stymie future Vickers production if it turned out to be a dead end. With RAF expansion in progress, the system was also at odds with the government's wish for standardisation of components across the aero industry. For their part, Vickers Aviation's managers, hitherto accustomed to selling small numbers of expensive aircraft during a depression, were unpractised in mass production, while the expertise of their workforce was being diluted by its rapid expansion.[24]

The Wellington's geodetic structure embodied some 1650 differently curving members, each of which was unique.[25] The prototype was 'virtually hand built' – an exacting process which posed a challenge for the works engineers who were charged with putting it into production. Matters came to a head one evening in 1936 when the first geodetic fuselage was inadvertently dropped while being readied for carriage to Farnborough for testing. Coincidentally, McLean was nearby when Archie Knight (the works manager, regarded by Wallis as 'a foul-mouthed bully') shouted, 'That's right! Drop the bloody thing – it's cost £1 million already' and fired him on the spot. When Muller, the works superintendent, heard of the incident next day, he too resigned.[26] McLean reacted by bringing Trevor West-brook, Supermarine's works manager, to Weybridge and putting him in charge of Wellington production. Westbrook was described by the *Daily Mail* as an 'aviation genius' who had the 'rare knack of getting every ounce out of his workers', and by most of those who worked for him as a hyperactive tyrant. Westbrook was energetic, fearless, sometimes impetuous, and often rude. One colleague said that photographs of him were rare because he was seldom able to stand still long enough to stay in focus.[27] At Southampton he had been reorganising production procedures for the Spitfire. On arrival at Brooklands, he agreed to take on the challenge of Wellington production provided Wallis stayed out of it. His success in doing so rested in large measure on the contribution of Jack East, a tool designer, and Charles Smith who with Westbrook's encouragement produced a power-operated forming machine that could roll flat strip into members of correct section and any curvature. George Edwards later said that without Westbrook and East 'nobody would ever have built a Wellington'.[28]

Geodetic aircraft raised other tensions too. To hasten rearmament, from 1936 it was government policy to spread technical knowledge and subcontract production. McLean resisted both, saying that the Wellington was unsuited to shadow production.[29] AM Sir Cyril Newall, the Air Member for Supply, took this for obstruction. In spring 1938, revised plans for a Wellington production group comprising Austin, Armstrong Whitworth and Gloster foundered when Vickers failed to issue the necessary drawings.[30] Misreporting of McLean's statement that the Warwick was originally intended to share 80 per cent of its components with the Wellington but had become 'one hundred per cent dissimilar' because of changes demanded by the Air Ministry led the Air Staff to think that Vickers was blaming production difficulties on them.[31]

Cumulatively, these frictions threatened a breakdown. Early in

August 1938 Wallis broke his family holiday to return to Weybridge: 'just in time for a long conference with Sir R. I knew things were going to blow up . . .'[32] The impasse was broken the following month when Freeman proposed that the whole technical and commercial management of Vickers-Armstrongs be applied to a comprehensive scheme to increase production. The year before, the board of Vickers Ltd had put the operations of Vickers Aviation and Supermarine into the hands of Vickers-Armstrongs, and appointed Sir Charles Craven to chair the two companies. At this point McLean was still a board member, but Freeman's proposal in September 1938 was intended to break McLean's dominion. In mid-October, Alex Dunbar, the general manager of the English Steel Corporation (another Vickers subsidiary) accepted an invitation to take control of Vickers-Armstrongs' aviation interests. Marginalised, McLean resigned. In November Vickers Aviation and Supermarine were subsumed by the parent company. An assembly plant for Wellingtons, to be operated by Vickers-Armstrongs, was then built at state expense just outside Chester at Broughton.[33]

These changes were in several ways positive for Wallis, who was given a new position, as Assistant Chief Designer of Aircraft, which extended his responsibilities to aerodynamics as well as structures.[34] However, he was dismayed by McLean's downfall. McLean had been his backer, as he had been Mitchell's, and because of him Britain would enter the Second World War with two aircraft, the Spitfire and the Wellington, which the Air Staff did not originally know it needed.

At work

George Edwards joined Vickers Aviation in February 1935. He was then twenty-seven years old, a design draughtsman who considered himself 'proper working class'. He had grown up in a suburb of Walthamstow, where his father ran a tobacconist; his secondary schooling had been at the local technical institute, and his degree had been earned by rising at 5 a.m. for part-time study while working as a junior engineer at Hay's Wharf in London docks. At Hay's Wharf he had designed cranes and elevators, laid out cold stores and organised the engine rooms of tugs. One of his colleagues there was Archie Watts – Wallis's bosom pal during their apprentice days at Cowes. With another war being talked of, and the RAF on the threshold of re-equipment and expansion, Vickers was recruiting. Watts suggested that a job with Vickers might give Edwards more scope to exercise his abilities than he was getting at Hay's Wharf.

This is how it turned out: within ten years Edwards was chief designer, and by 1953 he was managing director. But on that first day, knowing nothing about aircraft, he was put under the charge of 'a plain straight-arsed engineer' called George Stannard who showed him round the works. During the tour they came upon an 'enormous bully-looking man', stripped to the waist, leading a gang of men with sledgehammers who were breaking up what looked like a brand-new aeroplane. The large man turned out to be Wallis's *bête noire* Archie Knight, and the wrecking party was Edwards's first indication that 'selling aeroplanes was pretty difficult'.[35]

Edwards and Wallis each had an instinctive gift for mathematics; they had learned their craft on the shop floor; and they had studied hard in their own time for their professional qualifications. There were also differences. Edwards was outgoing, had outside interests (notably cricket, at which he excelled), was considerate towards colleagues, and brought a blokeish humour to his work. Wallis, in contrast, was socially reserved. While he was dutiful in attending Works social events such as the Fitters' Dinner or judging at the Sports Day, he never went to the pub, did not mingle with colleagues out of hours, and rarely invited any of them to his home. According to Edwards he was not popular among junior staff, who saw him as aloof and having 'the ability to drive chaps mad.'[36]

> Having told a lad how he wanted something done a week or two before, the lad would do his best and burst his boiler to make it look decent. Then Wallis would turn up and say a few words like: 'I've never seen such rubbish.'[37]

During the lunch hour he occasionally toured the drawing office, tearing off sheets he did not like, or writing 'Not this – BNW' alongside someone's drawing.[38] Was this how things had been at J. Samuel White, or was it a habit he had developed himself? Edwards put it down to his perfectionism. Wherever it came from it brought him into conflict with his own creed, for whereas beyond the Works he preached the gospel of learning through doing and experiment, inside it he expected staff to do as they were told. Perfectionism made him an unwilling delegator, and insofar as he did allocate tasks it was to a small circle of people in whose abilities and judgement he had confidence. In due course this came to limit the size of his projects and the rates at which they could progress.

Trevor Westbrook's arrival at Weybridge in 1937 left Supermarine facing an emergency. Nine months previously, the firm had accepted an order for 310 Spitfires, the first of which were due for delivery in autumn that year. However, the company lacked the experience or capacity to produce so many aircraft in the promised time. In due course this led to a political crisis. To tackle the problem, Craven turned to Wallis's old friend and mentor, Hartley Pratt.

Under Pratt's leadership Supermarine enlarged its works at Woolston, built a new factory nearby, expanded the workforce and reorganised systems. The pace of Spitfire output quickened. By mid-1939 deliveries were exceeding 100 a quarter and by the end of that year the first contract for 310 machines had been fulfilled. Many of the measures to achieve this had been identified or put in hand before Pratt's arrival, but it was he who co-ordinated their implementation, overcame delays caused by others and put Spitfire production onto an ever-improving footing.

Pratt came to tea at White Hill House on the day of his appointment, and Wallis showed him round the Weybridge works the following day.[39] However, there is a sense that the friendship had cooled. Nine months earlier, we are told, Pratt had pleaded for help in returning to the aero industry, which Wallis refused on the grounds that he had been out of it for too long.[40] This has been taken as an example of Wallis putting professional currency before friendship, which it probably was; however, the further suggestion that for Wallis 'intimacy was impossible and that, being impossible, it was also undesirable',[41] is contradicted by possibly the most intimate friendship of his life which was blossoming at the same time – with the merchant banker and promoter of air transport, Leo d'Erlanger (1898–1978).

D'Erlanger's father, half-American, half-German, was a painter and authority on Arabic music; his Italian mother was the daughter of Pope Leo XIII's chamberlain. The Pope, indeed, was Leo's godfather. D'Erlanger was at once retiring and determined, a man of charm who combined munificence with personal frugality and multi-cultural tastes with devotion to England. His American wife Edwina, a society beauty, was pictured or mentioned in newspapers and magazines almost every week. Leo, in contrast, kept the lowest of profiles. Through newspapers we catch occasional glimpses of him at memorial services, exhibition openings, or company general meetings, but references to him are otherwise rare. He and Wallis appear to have met first in 1936; they were certainly well acquainted by 1937, when Wallis's diary often shows them together. Whatever the first occasion, its context was a series of mergers of UK non-subsidised airlines which late in 1935 led to the formation of British Airways. D'Erlanger was already a backer of one of the constituent companies,[42] he had shares in another, and it was his merchant bank that provided the new airline with working capital. He stayed in the background but kept in close touch through his younger cousin Gerard d'Erlanger, himself a flier, who joined its board.

British Airways aimed to run well-organised fast passenger and mail services across Europe.[43] However, there was a dearth of up-to-date British-built civil aircraft with which to do so.[44] Civil aviation in 1930s Britain had fallen behind France, the Netherlands, Germany, and the United States. (When Molly went to Croydon airport to see Barnes off on a trip to Paris in December 1938, she was astonished to see him board an 'ancient, ancient, ancient machine. I can't think why Imperial Airways has such awful old things.') British Airways accordingly looked to aircraft bought from overseas firms such as Lockheed and Junkers. It was a British Airways Lockheed 14, indeed, whence Neville Chamberlain emerged on his return from Munich with news of 'peace in our time'. D'Erlanger and his colleagues were thus on the lookout for British machines which could match aircraft like the new DC-3s being flown by KLM. Range, speed, and capacity were merits offered by geodetic airframes, so it was natural that d'Erlanger should turn to Vickers and Wallis to discuss them. This led to a comparative study of the Lockheed 14 and Wellington, proposals for a civilianised Wellington,[45] and conversations between d'Erlanger, Wallis and Nigel Norman about airport layout and design.[46] A further result was that when Wallis framed ensuing proposals for bombers, he did so with their civil potential in mind. And aback of that was a deepening friendship.

We have seen that Wallis socialised little and seldom grew close to a colleague. D'Erlanger was an exception for several reasons. For one, he was encouraging. Time and again he stroked Wallis's ego ('Rejoice over magnificent demonstration of the excellence of your wares' he telegrammed following the Wellesleys' flight to Australia[47]). Wallis was prone to mope when he was under pressure but would brighten if praise came from the right quarter. Leo d'Erlanger became his muse. In 1944 Wallis reflected: 'None of the things we have ever done together has been a certainty, although they look so obvious and easy after the event; and it is during the nerve-racking anticipatory period that your support is an essential stimulus to face the anxiety and risk of a damaging failure.'[48]

Wallis's reference to things 'done together' points to his use of d'Erlanger's network. He was formidably well connected, and from now on, if Wallis needed an ally or a source it was usually through d'Erlanger that one was found. It was d'Erlanger who in 1939 introduced Wallis to Fred Winterbotham, a retired RAF officer, sometime lawyer, and farmer, who in 1930 became a member of the air intelligence branch of SIS.[49] Winterbotham was soon an admirer of Wallis's work, and during the war became a flagbearer for his causes. D'Erlanger was one of the few people whom Wallis would address by his Christian name when writing, and whom he enjoyed having under his roof. In Molly's eyes he was her husband's 'millionaire admirer', who sent asparagus, roses, and peaches when Barnes was ill. To the elder children he was Uncle Leo, always interested in what they were doing, and the bearer of gifts like a Ridgmount portable gramophone.

While the affection that flowered between d'Erlanger and Wallis was exceptional, other companionships thrived. Despite the rocky start with R. J. Mitchell, the two saw a fair amount of each other, and met regularly to compare notes on their respective projects until Mitchell was taken by cancer. Wallis made several technical contributions to Supermarine designs, and when in 1936 Mitchell's design for a heavy bomber prototype was chosen in preference to his own, he applauded it.

Other valued colleagues who enter the picture were Harold Roxbee Cox (1902–95) and Norbert Rowe (1898–1995). Cox (later Lord Kings Norton) was a lively, genial aerodynamicist who had worked on R101 and then moved to RAE Farnborough where his focus in the early 1930s was upon the torsional and flexural stiffness of aeroplane wings. Wallis was a frequent visitor to Farnborough and came to rely on Cox's advice during development of the Wellesley. Norbert Edward Rowe, 'Nero' to his circle, worked at the Aeroplane and Armament Experimental Establishment at Martlesham Heath until 1938, when he moved to the Air Ministry. He too became a valued adviser, and one of the few with whom Wallis would socialise. Tall, with a lopsided smile, large ears, and horn-rimmed spectacles, he became a steadying influence at times of strain.

In parallel with work on airframe structures, Wallis embarked on research into different aspects of airpower theory. In 1938, following the submission of tenders to a succession of Air Ministry specifications for future bombers, he set out to determine what the most economical size of a bomber might be. In doing so he concluded that a bomber's optimal size would be one that gave the maximum offensive power for the minimum outlay of personnel, material, time, and money. These headings were in their turn broken down into constituent things. Under personnel, for instance, he factored in aspects such as numbers, efficiency, safety, and maintenance. Money included initial cost and maintenance cost. Time included man hours and skills. 'Offensive power' was defined as the weight of bombs carried, in relation to range and speed of delivery. Likening the progress of aircraft to evolution in the natural world, he defined a series of evolutionary laws which suggested that both civil and military aircraft showed increasing efficiency with increase in size, and that the limit of economical size was not yet in sight. The resulting curve showing the relationship between offensive power and gross weight demonstrated that a large fleet of smaller aircraft would call for roughly twice the numbers of people to fly and maintain, and twice the quantities of material and time to build.[50]

In November 1938 Wallis circulated his paper to officials in the Air Ministry, where the prevailing wisdom said that a force made up of smaller bombers of diverse type was a precaution against risks that might arise if all eggs were put in one basket. In correspondence with Walter Runciman (Lord President of the Council), Wallis pointed out that the eggs-in-several-baskets model had been arrived at 'without perhaps having considered the mathematical chances operating against five bombers in place of one of superior speed and armament.'[51]

In another piece of research, he used the Works wind tunnel to discover how the carry of a golf ball might be affected by its surface finish.[52] The study was made at the prompting of McLean, a keen golfer, who duly shared its results with the golf correspondent of *The Times*. Readers were told that balls with differently patterned surfaces each had different resistance coefficients, and that balls with dimpled surfaces carried furthest.[53]

These projects set Wallis thinking. The size of bombers begged questions about what was expected of the bombs they carried, while golf balls heralded other kinds of sphere.

At home

Christmas Eve 1930 saw the start of a family tradition. When the children went to bed the house was its usual self. Next morning, the living room and hall were agleam with intricate paper ornaments, holly, and a tree with electric lights. After church and lunch, there was a race uphill for the young in the last hour of daylight. In following years, there might be a family concert on Boxing Day, with a written-out programme, instrumental performances of increasing variety and ambition, part-songs, and a solo of 'Where'er You Walk' by Barnes. If it was cold, between Christmas and New Year the family would cycle five miles to skate on the mere by Wisley Common.

Charles, Fanny and Wallis's sister Annie were among the guests that year. Charles was now known as 'Thickun', in contradistinction to Molly's father who was 'Thin Daddy'. Collectively the parents were 'the Olds'. In spring 1932 Charles and Fanny retired to Worthing. New Cross had been the family base since Wallis's childhood and their departure left him with a sense of emptiness. The feeling of a divide being crossed was reinforced by the deaths in 1934 of Edie's elder sister Lily, who had done so much to help them in the 1890s and 1900s, and Edie's bosom friend Adeline Bell. Minna died in the following year.

The passing of a generation was paralleled by Wallis's emergence as paterfamilias. Ordinarily that role would rest with Charles, or if not him with John. However, Barnes still bore the sense of duty that had been stirred by the precarious finances of his parents in the early 1900s. Now that he was well paid he began to use his means and experience for the benefit of his siblings and father. Charles's retirement prompted him to pen eleven pages of financial advice,[54] and from June 1932 he began to make quarterly contributions to supplement his father's pension.[55] Annie was financially stretched and in due course he supported her family too,[56] initially with a quarterly allowance and then with help to buy a house in Leicester.[57] Clergy stipends are small, and in 1936 he offered to guarantee the college fees of John's eldest daughter.[58] John himself had begun to show signs of stress; spring 1936 found him depressed and miserable. Barnes urged him to take time off and pressed him: 'Are you financially *unable* to take a holiday, or merely too busy?'[59] There were times when Wallis's interventions appeared condescending or officious. On one occasion Annie returned a cheque, and in 1938 he intervened heavy-handedly in a romance between Molly's younger sister Pamela and a Swiss Olympic rower.[60]

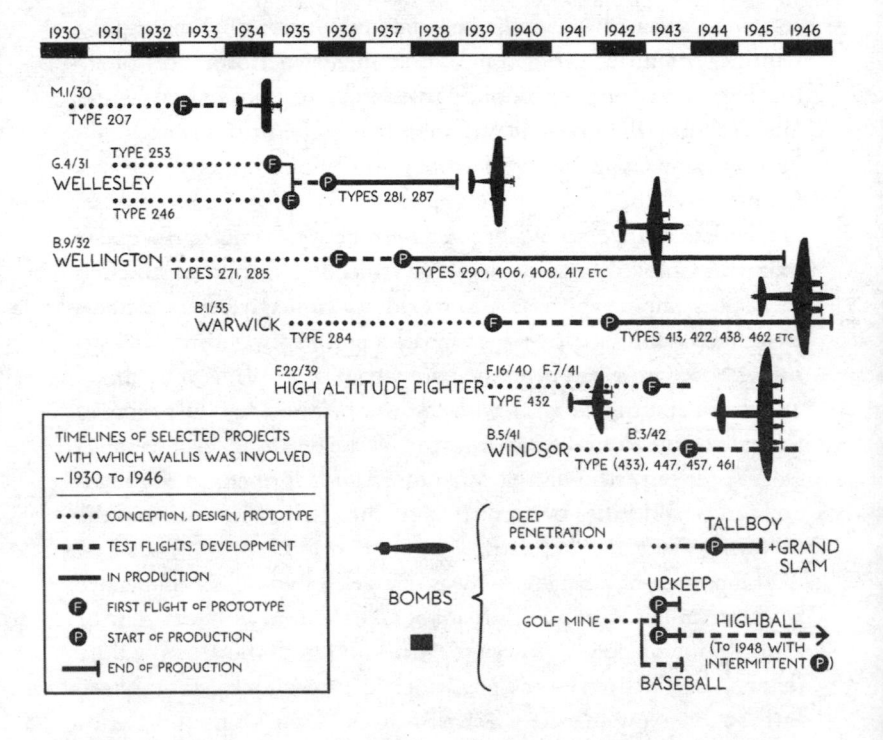

1930 1931 1932 1933 1934 1935 1936 1937 1938 1939 1940 1941 1942 1943 1944 1945 1946

M.1/30
TYPE 207

G.4/31   TYPE 253
WELLESLEY
TYPE 246   TYPES 281, 287

B.9/32
WELLINGTON   TYPES 271, 285   TYPES 290, 406, 408, 417 ETC

B.1/35
WARWICK   TYPE 284   TYPES 413, 422, 438, 462 ETC

F.22/39   F.16/40 F.7/41
HIGH ALTITUDE FIGHTER   TYPE 432

B.5/41   B.3/42
WINDSOR   TYPE (433), 447, 457, 461

TIMELINES OF SELECTED PROJECTS
WITH WHICH WALLIS WAS INVOLVED
– 1930 TO 1946

•••• CONCEPTION, DESIGN, PROTOTYPE
– – – TEST FLIGHTS, DEVELOPMENT
——— IN PRODUCTION
Ⓕ FIRST FLIGHT OF PROTOTYPE
Ⓟ START OF PRODUCTION
⊢ END OF PRODUCTION

BOMBS {

DEEP PENETRATION   TALLBOY   +GRAND SLAM

UPKEEP
GOLF MINE   HIGHBALL
(TO 1948 WITH INTERMITTENT Ⓟ)
BASEBALL

More children were born: Elisabeth in 1933, Christopher in 1935. Their upbringing, as of young Barnes and Mary, was largely left to Molly. 'He leaves me to decide everything about them, & doesn't play with them very often & never interferes unless the child is being disobedient or rude; tho' I must say he shows endless patience in mending things for them & showing barnes [sic] how to hold tools.' For most of the time Wallis left the children to their own devices provided they were polite, punctual, well-mannered at mealtimes, and played a full and willing part in household duties. The willingness was important: a half-hearted or sullen response to a request might elicit a rebuke, or even a walloping.

Handling tools and the correct performance of tasks became sources of tension. Young Barnes bore the brunt of this, partly because he was the eldest and liked to imitate his father doing practical things. In Wallis's eyes, using a tool in the wrong way was a grave fault, and he came to compare his son's performance in a job to the standard he himself claimed to have attained at the same age. Molly became increasingly sceptical about these comparisons but was at a loss to know whether or how to intervene when trouble arose. As the boy grew and began to stand up for himself flare-ups became explosive. Molly reflected: 'When he is in a bad mood big Barnes can be utterly beastly to his young.'[61] However, there were also moments of joy: from time to time Wallis would take his children on at chess, tennis, or golf, and on Sunday evenings Elisabeth and Christopher watched spellbound as he folded scraps of paper into figures, animals, and mythological creatures.

Beyond this sporadically participatory Wallis, there was indeed a more remote one. There were several reasons for his detachment. For one, he was often distracted by his job; it was only during longer holidays that he became more of a father. For another, he kept visitors at bay because they took up time that he could otherwise be spending with Molly. Trivial chatter irritated him. When Baba and her husband bought a house nearby, he feared a procession of relatives who would call uninvited and talk loudly about unimportant things. Since he had been brought up to treat guests with courtesy and generosity, being politely attentive to them was itself a source of strain. In autumn 1931 he dealt with this by designing an extra room on the roof called 'The Refuge', and 'nobody is to be allowed in it but Barnes & me, & he will go there when our friends and relations come and stay, and when they & I talk! It's going to be perfectly adorable & it has a little balcony on which two camp beds will go side by side – a balcony all up high, with a wonderful view . . .'[62] When Molly was away one of Wallis's greatest pleasures was to write to her from The Refuge. There was a ritual to this: late evening, soft light from the desk lamp set at just the right angle, warm toes, solitude. Words then flowed through his fountain pen.

The young reacted to Wallis's absence by finding their own pathways. All four spent long hours outside, where they climbed trees, cooked sausages on fires, and learned to ride. From 1933 there was a baby grand piano in the house on which to practise; Mary took up the violin; young Barnes became an accomplished cellist. As he grew, Christopher escaped to 'Beetle Lodge', a substantial den he built in the garden. For a time, Elisabeth became a 'holy terror' who 'shouts and is rude', one of whose pastimes was to frustrate golfers on the adjoining golf course by hiding their balls.

As the children entered their 'teens they were sent to boarding schools: Barnes and Charles to Dauntsey's in Wiltshire (where at the start of young Barnes's first term Molly was cheered to be mistaken for his sister), Mary and Elisabeth to Godolphin, near Salisbury. Molly was an active, protective mum, an encourager of interests, concerned about Christopher's stammer or young Barnes's eyesight, and careful to shield her children from her neurotic mother ('I wouldn't let a cat go and stay there'). She it was who organised the music and riding lessons, arranged special tuition, and organised trips to plays and concerts. Molly was also competitive, prone to rank her children against those of her friends. She described a daughter of their neighbours the Dibdins as 'such a mess to look at – hair awful, no buttons, terrible shoes, safety pins, undone hems', violin 'hopelessly out of tune'. Another girl (with whom young Barnes was 'very taken') was 'perfect to look at, hair neat and pretty, complexion nice (tho' she has yellow teeth, but not as foul as Dibdin teeth)' and had 'a lovely figure instead of a sack tied round the middle like poor Jill and Judy [Dibdin].'

The children remembered these years variously. Young Barnes recalled his father's obstinacy: 'In my experience he never admitted to being wrong – about anything . . . And you didn't dare argue.'[63] Mary seems to have found ways to avoid the kinds of incident that led to friction and recalled a sunny childhood. For Elisabeth, the family was an emotional mess – materially well provided for but starved of close affection because Wallis's craving for Molly left little to spare for the children.[64] For warmth Elisabeth looked to Nan, whose threat when pushed too far to 'Put on my bonnet and run' alarmed her. Elisabeth's unruliness came to a head at the age of eleven when she was expelled from her local prep school. Thereafter she began to flourish; at Godolphin she felt valued and secure; her relationship with her father warmed.

There was emphasis on general health, which among other things

meant being outdoors as much as possible. If you want a good complexion, said Molly, 'bathe your face in the May dew on Mayday'. If
it was warm enough the family often ate outside. Wallis had a reputation for asceticism; George Edwards remarked that 'If Wally had
been home and had a good steak and kidney pie like I had instead
of his carrot juice in the office, he would be a lot happier bloke.'[65] In
fact, when Molly was away, Wallis's lengthy descriptions of what he
ate and how economically he prepared it suggest he was fixated by
food. Shopping lists included prunes, oats, salad, potatoes, apples,
and honey. He liked fish and considered red meat dangerous. He
drank tea, water, and glucose each day, alcohol seldom, although
beer, cider, and sherry were kept in the house for visitors, and a
tablespoonful of rum with orange squash, honey, water and ice
was a treat on birthdays and anniversaries. The general ethos of the
household was the 'cheapest of everything possible . . . consistent
with lastingness'.

Molly and Barnes spent long hours working in the garden, which
they planted with trees chosen for their seasonal colours,[66] and an
orchard with different English varieties of apple. In due course Wallis
took to keeping bees and marvelled at their skills. He subscribed to the
quarterly journal of the Sunlight League, and joined the Men's Dress
Reform Party, which believed in freeing the neck from constricting
collars and ties, preferred sandals to shoes, advised loose underwear,
and shorts rather than trousers. He kept himself very fit. Holiday
photographs show him lean, and firm muscled long into middle age.
Beyond the garden, their leading pastime was music. They joined
the Bookham Choral Society, sang in a madrigal group, and became
friendly with their near neighbour Ralph Vaughan Williams, in whose
Leith Hill Music Festival performances they often took part. Wallis
was wary of contemporary composers, but Vaughan Williams was an
exception, perhaps because like himself he strove to say new things
without straying off the highway of tradition. Elisabeth recalls family
visits to Vaughan Williams's home, where the composer played piano
duets with Ruth Dyson, and they were introduced to his new muse,
Ursula Wood.

In 1937 a new figure entered their lives: Marie Stopes, playwright, poet, palaeobotanist, traveller, pioneer female academic, eugenicist, campaigner for women's rights and contraception. Molly and Barnes had read *Married Love* (1918). They were candid with their children about how babies are conceived, open about bodies and sex, accepted that divorce could be right, and (in Molly's case at least) saw birth control as a means for ridding society of inherited diseases and improving its mental health. In 1935, Molly attended a Stopes lecture, wrote in congratulation, and received a warm reply. Stopes lived nearby at Norbury Park (an 'absolute mansion') with her husband, Humphrey Verdon Roe,[67] and their son Harry. Stopes wished Harry to have suitable companions, young Barnes was about the same age, and during 1937 he was invited to Norbury Park. Molly and Barnes attended Stopes's lectures on 'Constructive Birth Control', met 'twinkling' Humphrey ('a lovely man who helps her in every way'), and ferried Mary and young Barnes to a Stopes firework party. In spring 1938 the day came when Marie Stopes and Harry were invited to White Hill House for tea.

Molly found Stopes unsentimental and 'inclined to be dictatorial', while Harry's 'appalling' table manners 'nearly caused Barnes to pass out'. On the other hand, Harry was 'a very healthy young animal', and she appreciated his friendly dealings with Elisabeth and Christopher. After tea, Harry, young Barnes, and Mary cleared away and played table tennis. Games of chess ensued. Wallis was victorious against Stopes; Harry beat young Barnes, who responded with a short cello recital.

An invitation and a suggestion ensued. The invitation was for young Barnes and Mary to spend a week in September at Old Higher Lighthouse on Portland Bill, which Stopes had bought as a summer residence. The suggestion was prompted by Molly's refusal to join the Mothers' Union ('I can't take its smugness') and annoyance with an MU lecturer who said that parents should not tell their children anything about the sexual aspects of marriage ('Gosh, I nearly blew up . . . I do think the MU is a serious retarding force today'). Stopes recommended that Molly should instead apply for training as a marriage guidance counsellor, which she did.

Church, friends and neighbours

It did not take Harold Floud, Effingham's rector, long to notice the Wallises' talents. Young Barnes was in due course recruited to the choir, and within months of Floud's arrival Wallis was elected to the Parochial Church Council. The church was 'dirty, disrepaired, gas, no hassocks but a few strawey motheaten things, no prayer or hymn books but a few battered copies . . . The one really old beautiful bit – St Nicholas's chapel – was a sort of rubbish place'.[68] Wallis did much to help its restoration,[69] and made a remarkable discovery in doing so. St Lawrence's had been substantially rebuilt in the nineteenth century, but engineering logic led Wallis to forecast the survival of an earlier timber roof above the plaster ceiling that covered St Nicholas's chapel. Removal of the plaster in 1933 duly exposed a fine oaken crown-post roof which had been framed up in the early fourteenth century. If the roof went back that far, Wallis pointed out, it followed that the walls upon which it rested must be at least as old.

St Lawrence was restored, said Molly, 'with all Barnes's heart & soul & work.'[70] The work included putting in an electric clock mechanism which retained the face and bells of a chiming tower clock that had been installed in 1890. Wallis had a fondness for clocks,[71] and developed a special affection for this one. In December, often between Boxing Day and New Year, it became his custom to climb the ladder to the clock chamber to service its machinery. Nowhere was he more content than here, in the solitude and fading light of a midwinter afternoon.

In 1932 Molly was disconcerted when her brother George became 'frantically High Church'. Molly had been brought up 'so Protestantly' that Anglo-Catholic ritual struck her as play acting. Barnes, on the other hand, 'would be a good Roman Catholic; he must always have something beautiful to worship'. Molly's descriptions of her husband's faith suggest he had a mystic's sense of truths that are accessible only through contemplation. He took delight in the state of awestruck enchantment which can result from *not* knowing something through reason. With that ran an attachment to rules.

If there were right and wrong ways to hold a chisel, then surely there were correct ways in which to pray, receive forgiveness or make confession – and Roman Catholicism had clear rules. A decade later we shall find him exploring such questions with a spiritual adviser. Meanwhile, a crisis arose.

In mid-March 1938, Wallis was admitted to the Mount Alvernia nursing home in Guildford for an operation to remove a painful growth on his neck.[72] The home had been built by Franciscan Sisters who in parallel with their devotional lives were trained in medical professions such as radiography, pharmacy, and theatre management. The operation left him in great pain. He was given morphia, and after fifteen days the surgeon operated again.[73] A third operation was on the cards. On several occasions when Molly took the children to visit, he was too groggy to talk. Leo d'Erlanger, himself a devout Catholic, sent delicacies to lift his spirits. By early April Wallis was thinking about converting to Roman Catholicism.

The Sisters impressed him. He admired their professionalism, and as the days passed there were conversations about faith. They lent him literature about penance and the Eucharist. On 13 April he confided this to Molly, who, on return to White Hill House, wrote: 'Barnes, I'm very glad you told me such things this afternoon. Don't be different. I can't bear another Barnes. I wish you were here.' At the end: 'I do love you so much. Please don't be different.'

Several worries lay behind the fear that her husband was turning into someone else. One sprang from her evangelical upbringing and aversion to Catholic practices. Doctrine on birth control was another, and a third was the fear that if the spiritual laws of Catholicism, like the laws of flight, were non-negotiable, then a corollary of not belonging to the Roman Catholic Church was that in its eyes their marriage was not authentic. Next morning, she wrote another card: 'It is perfectly hateful you not being here. I feel very much like I did that first Christmas when Daddy said we couldn't, & I told him I might live to be 58 & how could I bear it without you. And now how can I. Oh can't you come home?'[74]

She telephoned Wallis's father. Charles Wallis was unsurprised to hear that his son was attracted by the Roman Church and duly wrote to him to say so. He had once been so tempted himself – it was all very appealing, the ritual, the devotional system. But, he continued, God had caused himself and Barnes to be baptised into the Church of England. Then the nub: 'It is not a matter of taste, it is a matter of duty.'[75] Charles wrote separately to Molly, saying that the crisis fitted into a pattern: there had been an earlier flirtation with an American revivalist sect. 'It is all rubbish.' Charles added that it all went to show that Barnes was not properly acquainted with Anglo-Catholicism. 'Get him out of that home as soon as you can.'

They went to Lyme Regis for Barnes to convalesce. Other guests at the Hotel Alexandra mistook them for a honeymoon couple,[76] which suggests the crisis had passed. However, when not walking the cliffs with Edmund Sanders's *A bird book for the pocket* Molly read books about theology borrowed from a nearby chapel, trying to clear her mind.[77] For the time being Wallis accepted his father's opinion that being an Anglican was non-negotiable but did so by acceding to his argument that 'for us English folk' the Church of England '*is* the Catholic Church'. Back in Effingham, he invited Alvernia's Franciscan sisters to tea at White Hill House and put a statue of St Francis in the garden.

King, country, Wosses and Dibs

Wallis had been raised to view social class as ordained by nature. Nan and the maid were accordingly expected to use the outdoor lavatory, the children were forbidden to read Nan's *Daily Mirror*,[78] and the way to get things done in a hotel was to tip heavily, because money 'paves all paths where the lower classes are concerned'.[79] Behind the stereotyping, Wallis was not much interested in political theory. According to Molly he was a conservative more by default than conviction. He was, however, an ardent monarchist. This was in contrast to Molly herself, who was wary of patriotism and its symbols. She told friends that she had no sense of loyalty to England. Not for her the king-and-country nationalism that lay aback of the Great War.

The thought of her family being 'broken and hurt' by another war left her 'terrified'. She wanted 'peace at *any* price'. A relative who gave a toy gun to young Barnes was reprimanded.[80] It is not clear how Molly reconciled such feelings with a husband who designed bombers. What is clear is that neither she nor her husband shared the kind of pro-Nazi sympathies that were held by deep Englanders like Arthur Bryant and Henry Williamson.[81] Nor were they attracted to the meld of technology, nationalism and anti-Semitism that drew aeronauts like John Chamier and Humphrey Roe's brother towards the British Union of Fascists. Indeed, the marriage in 1937 of Molly's younger sister Bettina to an orthodox Jew, Jacob Henry Lazarus, put opposition to German expansionism and the radicalisation of Nazi Jewish policy ('this terrible madness against the Jews' as Molly put it) into the family's foreground. It is important to establish this, since during the war to come we shall find Wallis under suspicion in some quarters as a potential collaborator with the Germans.

Beech Avenue in the 1930s reverberated with echoes of King, country and Empire. Col. Leopold Lenfestey, late of the Indian Army, lived a few doors away, while five years' war service in India had primed their next-door neighbour Aubrey Dibdin for a career first in the India Office, then from 1936 as Assistant Permanent Secretary at the Burma Office.[82] Chirpy, five years younger than Wallis, Dibdin lived his work by carrying a Tiffin basket to Whitehall each day, and brought news about parts of the British Empire with which Wallis hoped his aircraft would one day connect. It was the Dibdins who led the Wallises to the Isle of Purbeck, which for the next twenty-five years became the garden for their souls.[83]

Purbeck is not an island, but it feels like one. Water laps on three sides: sea to the south and east, the drowned valley of the River Frome that makes Poole Harbour to the north. Tracts of empty furzy heath, now mostly gone but memorialised by Thomas Hardy in *The Return of the Native* (1878), divide it from inland Dorset to the west. In 1932, Dibdin suggested that the two families join in a camping holiday near Swanage. This was so successful that for the rest of the decade they returned each August to live under canvas. They called it Camp. It was the high point of the year.

Swanage is Hardy's 'Knollsea', 'lying snug within two headlands as between a finger and thumb. Everybody in the parish who was not a boatman was a quarrier, unless he were the gentleman who owned half the property and had been a quarryman, or the other gentleman who owned the other half, and had been to sea.'[84] For centuries Purbeck had been quarried for the dark limestone that takes a polish like marble, and for the Portland Stone that is bedded below. Old workings left an underworld of voids and caves which could be entered through window- and door-like openings in sea cliffs at places like Dancing Ledge and Winspit. Purbeck's contrasts, her hollows, heaths, hazel-hedged lanes, pinewoods, the lofty chalk ridge of Nine Barrow Down, and little inland seas epitomised the kind of outermost corner of England that appealed to neo-romantic imagination.[85]

The families rented a farmer's field fringed with trees and erected their tents, Wosses at one end,[86] Dibs at the other. Camp took Wallis back to his days in the TA, and the happy times with Archie Watts and the Civils. Once again, he could align bell tents with precision and dig latrines. Water drawn from a faraway tap was carried in metal pails, balanced to either side, with a hoop of his own invention to keep them from knocking against his knees. He lodged a barrel of cider in the fork of a tree for ease of pouring and flung plates while drying up to see if anyone was alert enough to catch them. For the children, Camp was the time when their father returned to something like his old self – up for adventures, a scruff ready for a joke, teaching them to splice ropes or explore a quarrier's tunnel. They revelled in the glow worms at dusk, adders, the great green Emperor Moth caterpillars that forged across heathery sand dunes, above all, the sea. On most mornings they piled into family cars (and from 1938, a Jowett van) for the twenty-minute journey to Studland Bay where they rented a beach hut and kept a dinghy, the Molly May (the May from May Dibdin, Aubrey's 'sweet and authoritarian' wife). Here they swam, voyaged, and dammed streams. As years passed and the children grew, young friends joined them.

As is often the way when people go to the same place year after year, there were rituals. Ceremonies began before they left when the ridge tents were brought out for a check-up and practice erection on the lawn. On departure they liked to rise before dawn and set out in half-light, the full car towing a heavily loaded trailer. Near Romsey, the first glimpse of an advertisement for Strong's beer ('You're approaching the STRONG COUNTRY') drew whoops of glee. Around nine o'clock there would be a picnic breakfast in the New Forest. Then on towards Wareham, across the causeway, into the Isle, the pitching of tents (their bell tents were kept in store in Swanage and delivered to the field ready for their arrival), and the first bathe. In the evenings they sang, and around dusk there was the comforting swish of wellingtons in long grass as Wallis walked about to check the tents, perhaps with a call to 'Tauten your guys'.

Annual outings took them by boat up-river from Wareham; to Mortimer Wheeler's excavations at Maiden Castle where skulls of prehistoric people gaped out of the chalk;[87] to Dancing Ledge, where local lads tied weights to themselves and stepped off the tabular rock to sink deep in a hunt for spider crabs; along Nine Barrow Down to Corfe for a cream tea. Corfe and Camp went together: the children climbed the castle while Wallis pondered human desire to magnify natural features.[88]

After three weeks came Sad Friday: the final bathe, farewell to Nine Barrows, backfilling the latrine. After the tents were struck and folded and the trailer packed, the moment came when Molly or Wallis would climb onto the trailer to take a photograph of the pale grassy marks where Camp had been.

Summer's last will and testament

Camp in 1939 was glorious but with differences: it was at a new site, Knaveswell, at the foot of Nine Barrow Down, and it coincided with the outbreak of the Second World War. Wallis believed that war would not come before 1940, so they hoped for Camp as usual. On arrival, they found 'the sort of place you dream about', where blue butterflies danced like electric sparks. Days were cloudless and warm; the children slept with their heads out of the tents, resting on pillows stuffed with chaff from the field where Mr Kellaway and his heavy horses were harvesting oats. Beyond the idyll, however, detachments of the Dorset Regiment were camped at Corfe. Overhead, an Anson droned to and fro, watching the approaches to Poole Harbour and Weymouth. In Swanage, you could hear Cockney accents of evacuee mothers. Nan was staying in nearby rented rooms to care for four-year-old Christopher. 'If war comes, I suppose Barnes will have to return. Nan will go with him because we have all sorts of her relations and their children coming.' Molly reflected on the sheer impossibility of war, yet day by day came more signs of its imminence. On 17 August the border between Upper Silesia and Poland was closed. On the 22nd, MPs were recalled from summer recess; on the 25th Germany signed a non-aggression pact with the Soviet Union, and Britons were told to leave Germany. And on Thursday, 31 August Wallis left for Effingham.

> We got home safely, just over 4 hours, the traffic being very heavy . . . oh, yes we saw that War had started in Poland in Guildford, so I knew that we should follow, and that I had done the right thing in coming home.[89]

Nan's nieces, Barbara and Nancy, and their children, were already at White Hill House. A clergyman had driven them from Poplar for safety, and their industrious response to blackout orders broadcast by the BBC set Wallis back on his heels: the house was 'practically in darkness, as curtains were permanently screwed, tied and nailed in position – one glance at them set me staring in horror, for I recognized on all sides tablecloths, door curtains, and ragbaggery of all sorts rubbing shoulders in incongruous positions with our best velvet curtains.' He went on: 'They have exercised incredible ingenuity in being as stupid as possible, even going to the length of unscrewing and changing the positions of the brass sliding rails in the drawing room in order to make the misfits as complete and hard to remedy as possible.'

Wallis spent much of the weekend 'wrestling with the hopeless muddle of the curtains which had been nailed and screwed across windows.' On Sunday morning, as Molly and her children mopped up following a torrential thunderstorm, and Chamberlain told the nation that it was at war with Germany, Wallis worked on ARP curtains with strings 'so that one can draw them up and down and light reigns once more. Rather natty – string and screw hooks, quite in the best style of elementary materials and superb results!'

The doorbell rang. Barbara found a man on the doorstep who said he was a billeting officer, come to take over the house. In fact, it was Victor Goddard, Wallis's close friend from the first great war, come to bid farewell at the start of the second. Goddard explained he had been ordered to join the Air Component of the British Expeditionary Force in France. Goddard's wife was away in Devon; 'He did get a 'phone call thro' to her after much trouble only to find she was crying so much she couldn't speak.' Nan, meanwhile, had not yet got the hang of the blackout, with the result that two policemen arrived after dark 'to complain about our lights, so you can imagine my state by ten or 11 p.m. to which you can add a headache.'

Aback of the toing and froing was panic. Everyone knew the movie *Things to Come* (1936) in which mass air attack heralds a new dark age. Air raid precautions had been rehearsed since 1937. The Air Staff's duplicate headquarters at Garston had been set up to offset the risk of a strike to decapitate Britain's war leadership. Through friends like Winterbotham and Goddard, Wallis had an inkling of government assumptions, and remained wary. He told Molly to stay in camp for a few days more – Germany had not yet started to bomb, 'and we have still to learn what it is like'. When she and the children did return, her brother George, and Bettina and Henry Lazarus, came to White Hill House in the belief that it would be safer than central London.

On Wednesday, 22 September Molly accompanied Mary to Godolphin for the start of her first term. 'Poor child, she was awfully miserable & wept sadly when I left . . . She is very worried lest we should all be bombed & no one come to tell her we're all killed . . . I must say it's a bit tough being young, everything seems so everlasting – 3 months is a lifetime.'[90]

Sitzkrieg

The merchant ship *Goodwood* and collier *Magdapur* were sunk off the east coast in the previous week. They were taken by a new type of mine which was triggered magnetically. Such mines were being sown in shipping lanes and estuaries by aircraft and U-boats and lay on the seabed until activated by the iron hulls of passing ships. By late autumn they were claiming up to five vessels a day. On 13 November, such a mine sank the destroyer HMS *Blanche* in the Thames estuary; eight days later the newly commissioned cruiser HMS *Belfast* sustained mine damage that took two years to repair.

The War Cabinet was rattled. No practical way of countering magnetic mines had yet been found. Low-flying minelayers were impossible to intercept at night; the mining of buoy-marked channels in the Thames estuary threatened closure of the Port of London. Frustration stirred demands for retaliation, a proposal to set the Rhine on fire with chemical mines being among the less far-fetched. Early in December an attempt to discourage minelayers by mounting standing bomber patrols over their bases proved futile.[91]

By this time, however, the magnetic mine had yielded its secrets. The Admiralty already knew the concept, and on 23 November it was gifted with an intact weapon when a mislaid mine was found on tidal mud near Shoeburyness. The mine was made safe next day and whisked to HMS *Vernon* at Portsmouth for disassembly.[92] It was previously realised that two kinds of countermeasure were likely to emerge. One would be a way to cast a magnetic field to set off mines without putting the sweepers themselves at risk. The other would be to immunise ships so that they did not activate mines. Design data provided by the captured mine in due course enabled both.[93]

Wallis, meanwhile, had been working on an airborne variant of the magnetic sweeping concept which aimed to detonate mines with a sea-skimming Wellington girdled by an energised electromagnetic ring. The system was known as Detonation Without Impact, DWI for short (although the spoof 'Directionless Wireless Installation' coined for security purposes has since found its way into historical literature). A legend has arisen that DWI was inspired by recovery of the Shoeburyness specimen. In fact, the project had been in hand since October.[94] The idea originated in the Admiralty but was passed to the RAE and in due course to Vickers for realisation.[95]

Over half a century later George Edwards claimed that Wallis was too busy to play much of a part in the DWI work, and that for practical purposes it had been led by himself. Edwards and his team were indeed central to fabrication of the ring and its fitting. However, his claim to have designed the ring and power system does not square with contemporary sources, and Wallis later insisted that he had been responsible both for the method of the ring's attachment and for the project overall.[96] Conflicting memories extend to which of them provided progress reports to Churchill at the Admiralty.[97] It is worth noting that while at this point the two men enjoyed an effective working relationship, later enmity came to colour the memories of each about the other. Since Edwards outlived Wallis by nearly a quarter of a century, it was he who had the last word.

Wherever the balance of DWI responsibility lay, during December Molly told a friend that Wallis was engaged in 'terribly secret work', that he was 'haggard and white' with stress, and that Vickers were calling him at all hours. When he flew on the first trial four days before Christmas, locals below were agog at the hoop-girt aeroplane that flew back and forth and wondered what it was for. Further trials at the A&AEE were promising, and Churchill reported success to Neville Chamberlain on Christmas Day.[98] By then Wallis was ill, but he struggled back before New Year to resume trials. On 8 January 1940, the Wellington took off from Manston and detonated an enemy mine in the Thames estuary. Two days later, conversion of a second Wellington was completed.[99] Job done, Wallis went back to work on projects that had been interrupted: a wing design for the B.1/39 bomber; his contributions to completion of the second prototype B.1/35;[100] a new kind of wing structure for a proposed heavy fighter;[101] and an adaptation of the Wellington for high-altitude flight.[102]

The next fortnight was England's coldest for nearly half a century. For some days Molly and the children cycled six miles to skate on Wisley Mere, where they jumped, spun, skated backwards, and picnicked on the ice. In late January Wallis was granted a week's leave in recompense for having worked flat out for three months; he and Molly spent four days in Brighton, followed by two more skating. In February he found time to attend rehearsals for a performance of Mendelssohn's *Elijah* being organised by Ralph Vaughan Williams, who considered that performing a large work on a Jewish theme by a Jewish composer was as good a way as any to cock a snook at Nazism. Vaughan Williams wrested the Dorking Halls from the grip of the Food Controller for the day of the concert, Saturday, 16 March, when a 400-strong choir gathered from surrounding villages.

Since the previous autumn Wallis had been telling relatives that the war would not begin in earnest until the spring. Celandines and primroses were beginning to show.

8

Persuasion, 1940–43

'No more bloody allies!'

Wallis's proposal for waging war with a few large precisely aimed, deep penetrating bombs rather than thousands of small ones emerged from a train of thought rather than a moment of revelation. In 1938 he had invented the unit of 'offensive power',[1] and having defined the efficiency of a bomber by the ratio of its offensive power to its gross weight it made sense to ask what the offensive power was for. However, if there was anything like a dewpoint in the process, the week of 5–11 May 1940 is a strong candidate. This was the week in which Germany invaded France and the Low Countries, when Churchill succeeded Neville Chamberlain as Prime Minister, and when the notes in Wallis's diary changed from occasional jottings about meetings, migraines, and dental appointments to data on the characteristics of explosives. At the head of this entry, he wrote 'Hopkinson Bar', and below that a reference to a paper which Hopkinson had read to the Royal Society in 1913.

'Hopkinson' was Bertram Hopkinson, who in 1903, at the age of twenty-nine, had been elected to the chair of Mechanism and Applied Mechanics at the University of Cambridge.[2] Hopkinson's many research interests included phenomena to do with explosions, flame, and impacts; what had caught Wallis's attention was his finding of a way to measure the history of an explosion. The shockwave propagation phase of an explosion is of the order of milliseconds, so describing what happens within that period is difficult. Measuring the instant itself, on the other hand, was more feasible. Hopkinson's achievement was to link the two in a pressure-time curve produced by impacts propagated down a long rod. In this way he showed that four-fifths of the impulse of the blow produced by a charge of gun cotton was delivered in one fifty-thousandth part of a second.[3]

Wallis's purpose in visiting Hopkinson's work was better to understand the shape and progression of explosive shock and pressure in different kinds of medium, and thereby to estimate the susceptibility of different kinds of target. The targets he had in mind were few and localised: coal, oil, and water – the stores of energy upon which the rest of industry depended. At this point he was also contemplating strategic communications, but the figures and equations in his diary mainly relate to explosions under water: he was thinking about dams. His idea was to paralyse Germany's war economy, not by destroying factories or killing the people who worked in them, but by bringing about an irreparable power cut. Or as Albert Speer put it thirty years later, cutting off power would have stopped the war, 'just as a car can be made useless by the removal of the ignition'.[4]

At first sight the impression of a flare-up of intellectual activity in early May is at odds with other evidence which shows Wallis in low spirits. His official work at this time came mainly from demands to upgrade old projects, while his ability to meet deadlines was frustrated by shortages of materials and skills.[5] During April he suffered three migraine attacks; in May, frequent trips to the dentist suggest he was experiencing chronic discomfort. Molly watched with concern: 'I can see how he got into such a state of complete breakdown at the end of the last war, poor darling. He is inclined to pessimism and takes things hard.'[6]

More widely, unsettling things were afoot. Late in March, his ally Trevor Westbrook had fallen out with Vickers's directors and resigned. Three weeks later, missed national production targets and faltering public confidence in the government had led to Craven's secondment from Vickers-Armstrongs to support the Air Ministry's Department of Development and Production.[7] Then, on 14 May most of this department and Craven with it were transferred to the new Ministry of Aircraft Production (MAP). Setting up the MAP was one of Churchill's first acts as premier, his aim being to cut through Whitehall departmentalism and to separate responsibility for production of aircraft from the interests of the service that used them. To ensure a clean break he put the ministry into the hands of his close friend, the spirited press baron Lord Beaverbrook. One of the first people Beaverbrook hired was Trevor Westbrook. Two days later Beaverbrook wrested control of Lord Nuffield's chaotic Spitfire plant at Castle Bromwich and ordered Alex Dunbar, Vickers's general manager at Weybridge, up to Birmingham to make it work. Dunbar and Craven were thus at least partly removed from the Weybridge scene, while Dunbar found himself reporting to the man he had effectively fired six weeks before. At Weybridge, Westbrook's expertise was missed, along with the good rapport Wallis had enjoyed with both.

There were other cares. Pam had broken up with her German-Swiss boyfriend and come to stay at White Hill House, where her smoking and bright chatter caused Wallis to retreat to his Refuge. In April, all young Barnes's wisdom teeth were taken out. In May he was again afflicted by mastoiditis, leading to an operation, and complications followed: part of his face was temporarily paralysed, and he succumbed to a messy skin infection; for much of June a nurse visited daily; Molly sat beside his bed at night. Then came news that John's eldest son, Charles Wallis, had been shot down and killed during an attack on the *Scharnhorst* in Stavanger fjord on 21 June.[8] Despite the bad news, said Molly, Barnes seemed 'inspired by a sort of propheticism that we shall win this war . . . I can't quite make out why.'[9] Talk of invasion made her fretful: should Elisabeth and Christopher be evacuated? If the children went to Canada, would they return as strangers? Would they return at all? 'Besides do we want our children to become Americans or Australians?'[10]

Winterbotham was taken with Wallis's idea for cutting off power to German industry and put his mind to how to bring it to the attention of decision makers. There were two sides to this: to whom to explain it, and how. The hands of the Air Staff were just then full with the aftermath of the collapse of France and onset of the Battle of Britain. High-ups in the Air Ministry were out because the corollary of Wallis's thinking, that Bomber Command was wrongly configured, was not going to go down well among senior officers who had spent the past six years configuring it. Moreover, Winterbotham had found that his friend sometimes undercut the reception of his own ideas, because he could not envisage the possibility of anyone not immediately falling in with them. Such linearity was going to raise hackles, so he turned instead to one of his former SIS friends, Desmond Morton, who was now a personal assistant to Churchill.[11] Morton in turn shared it with Churchill's scientific guru, Frederick Lindemann. On 5 July their reply came back: yes, the idea of a very large bomb and a new kind of aircraft to carry it appeared practicable, but it could not come to fruition until 1942, 'even if then'. This might not be a complete bar since the war might still be going on, but Britain's industrial and technological resources were at full stretch; if the idea was to be put into effect in a reasonable period then the best thing to do was 'to take it up with the Boeing Company, or some other American firm used to work of this type'.[12] In other words, a brush-off.

Frustrated, Wallis channelled his small spare time into the Local Defence Volunteers.[13] Training with them brought back his good times as a Territorial; for a few weeks he compensated for the tedium of the Works with drill, range practice and nights on watch.[14] The speed with which the Low Countries and France fell fed a widespread belief that their gates had been unbolted from within. Fears about like subversion in Britain were accordingly rife. 'Barnes is very much involved in the LDV. He had to go out with 7 others on Tuesday night and they had to stop all cars and cyclists and pedestrians to examine their papers from 9 to 1 a.m. Apparently they were trying to catch somebody. Barnes was properly excited.'[15]

Air Ministry analysis of German combined operations in Norway and Holland suggested that invasion might start with the seizure by airborne forces of several landing grounds, which might be existing airfields, large open spaces, or both. Shielded from air attack by relays of fighters, Ju52 troop-carriers would disgorge men who would quickly form and capture a nearby port, through which the main force could disembark.[16] Looking out from his Refuge, Wallis realised that Effingham golf course was exactly the kind of space which German special forces might have in mind. He accordingly designed an anti-landing obstacle consisting of a longitudinal cross-piece held aloft by two trestle supports, and persuaded Canadian soldiers camped nearby to barricade the golf course against an air landing. The obstacles were popular with the children, who called them Tinkertoys (on account of their resemblance to the proprietary construction sets based on spools and rods) and used them as climbing frames.

The Tinkertoys brought Wallis face to face with Beaverbrook. During one of Alex Dunbar's periodic returns to Weybridge, Wallis put the anti-landing design in front of him and suggested that it be adopted nationally. Dunbar said he would suggest this to Craven, who in turn invited Wallis and Joseph Summers, Vickers's chief test pilot, to see him.[17] Craven agreed to try to interest Beaverbrook in the idea but warned that anti-invasion defences lay outside the Minister's purview.[18] As so often, Wallis left feeling 'rather depressed'. However, just before lunch next day his telephone rang. Beaverbrook wished to see them at 3 p.m.

Beaverbrook had been waging war, in large part against other government departments, since the day of his appointment. In the course of doing so he avoided formal meetings, drove subordinates by a mixture of harassment and flattery, and transacted different items of business with different people at the same time.[19] Beaverbrook knew nothing about industry but held court to a circle of conscripted professionals who did. Among them were Freeman, Westbrook, Craven and Ford's general manager Patrick Hennessy, all of whom grew used to phone calls in the small hours in which Beaverbrook barked orders or demanded reports. The MAP went through three structural reorganisations in its first nine months, and Hennessy likened it to Dante's inferno. Beaverbrook believed in targets rather than plans, and for about nine months the Ministry's priorities were what he thought in the given moment. Wallis and Summers stepped into its febrile atmosphere on the afternoon of 18 July. They joined a queue outside Beaverbrook's office and reached its head two and a half hours later.

Wallis entered ready to discuss the prevention of airborne landings.

Looking around he saw a placard that read: ORGANISATION IS THE ENEMY OF IMPROVISATION. True to its spirit, Beaverbrook rapped out 'Will you go to America for me?' Thinking fast, Wallis replied, 'Yes sir, but I would rather stay in England for you.' 'What would you do in England for me?' 'Build you a monster bomber to smash the Germans.' Beaverbrook quizzed Wallis about the monster bomber. What engines would it use? Did he have any data? Wallis replied that he did, but since he had been called to talk about anti-invasion precautions, they were not to hand. Whereupon Beaverbrook flung a press cutting across the table, told Wallis to read it to see if he could save himself from being sent to America, said, 'Come and see me in the middle of the night, tonight, or tomorrow – any time'; and pushed them out.[20]

Wallis and Summers left in a daze and hailed a taxi. Wallis looked at the press cutting. Its subject was pressure cabin development in America, where Boeing's passenger-carrying Stratoliners cruised at 20,000 feet. The forthcoming Wellington V was designed to fly to twice this height, so Wallis assumed that Beaverbrook had not been told about it. He turned instead to the invitation to make the case for a large bomb and an aircraft to carry it.

Hew Kilner was still in his office when Wallis reached Weybridge. Kilner packed Wallis off to consult with Pierson, urging them to get back to Beaverbrook as soon as they could. It was past 8 p.m., but Wallis drove to Pierson's home on Smithwood Common where the two worked into the early hours of Friday and 'roughed down some figures'. The aircraft they sketched was a composite of earlier and current ideas: a six-engine machine that would incorporate an elongated version of the Wellington V pressure cabin, use the Hercules VIII and cruise at 300 mph. Its range would be 4000 miles, giving an out-and-back radius from the UK that took in Norway, Poland, Italy, Sicily, and much of NW Africa. It would also put New York within reach.[21] Aback of the bomber was Leo d'Erlanger's ambition to put post-war Britain at the forefront of civil aviation.

Wallis and Pierson returned to Beaverbrook next day. As Wallis had guessed, the briefing he had received about the high-altitude Wellington had passed him by. Beaverbrook accordingly dropped his demand for Wallis to go to America and ordered the high-altitude machine to be given 'absolutely first national priority'. He then changed the subject. Development of the B.1/35 had been lagging, chiefly for want of suitable engines. Since MAP was now concentrating on a small number of key types, he wished to cancel it. Pierson argued in its defence; Beaverbrook conceded.

Finally, Pierson and Wallis made their pitch for the 'big machine', or the 'High-Altitude Stratosphere Bomber' as it appeared on the prospectus they had drawn up overnight. Its high speed at great height meant that no defensive armament would be needed; crew size would be the same as for a Wellington, yet bombload would be four and a half times greater. They emphasised the benefits of being able to re-use design work that had already gone into the Wellington V and claimed that a successful prototype could be ready in less than eighteen months. Beaverbrook told them to start at once and return when the proposal was in more definite form. In the meantime, the 'big machine' should take precedence in Vickers's design department.[22] Thus were Britain's priorities being decided during the first weeks of the Battle of Britain.

On Sunday morning Wallis drove to his office and in the quiet poured the week's events into a six-page letter to Alex Dunbar. He summarised his big bomb thinking, throwing in every argument for it that he could think of. On Monday he had been dejected, by Sunday:

> . . . I do feel that the new machine is going to be *the* instrument which will enable us to bring the war to a quick conclusion, and if only we can convince the 'powers that be' we shall receive tremendous backing to make a great effort. One point which does occur to me is that the immunity of such machines operating at their leisure and in daylight renders *large* numbers of them *unnecessary* as irreparable damage could be inflicted on the strategic communications of the German Empire by a relatively small number such as ten or twenty machines within the course of a few weeks.[23]

It is hard not to conclude that he was in the grip of hypomania.

Explosions

Next day, Wallis jotted 'Started on Strato Bomber' in his diary.[24] In it, a new name appears: Tedder,[25] AVM Arthur Tedder, the MAP's director-general of research and Wallis's nominated senior point of contact. Tedder was wise, efficient, and already familiar with Wallis's thinking about the ideal size of bomber. Privately, he was also aware of Wallis: each had a son at Dauntsey's, where speech days and concerts offered moments for informal talk. Tedder reported to ACM Sir Wilfrid Freeman, with whom rested overall responsibility for research, development, and production. Beaverbrook's tendency to axe projects that would not bring immediate results meant that much of their effort went either into persuading him to spare them or else (like the jet engine) concealing their existence.[26] Against this background, Wallis's success in attracting Beaverbrook's interest is remarkable.

Wallis's first task was to design a bomb case that would be strong enough to withstand the immense forces it would meet as it passed through different soils while slowing from around the speed of sound to a standstill within the space of a few tens of feet. Kilner and Dunbar put him in touch with Arthur Winder, general manager of the English Steel Corporation in Sheffield, and on 7 August Wallis travelled to meet him.[27] Over several days, Wallis was introduced to Cyril Dadswell, a specialist in castings, H. H. Burton, a metallurgist, and others who specialised in steel quality. Between them they provided the information Wallis needed to turn his preliminary ideas into full working drawings. Wallis got on well with them, and since the ESC was co-owned by Vickers the way was opened to proceed to casting when the time came.

In following days Wallis turned for specialist help to his old friends Norbert Rowe, now assistant director of the MAP's Department of Technical Development, and Alfred Pippard.[28] Tedder brokered other contacts. One of them was the MAP's Patrick Hennessy, who oversaw allocation of materials. Brynmore Vaughan Williams, a specialist in bomb penetration, ballistics, and underwater explosions, was another. A second group formed a kind of professional family whose members already knew each other through related work. Their connecting figure was Dr Reginald Stradling, a structural engineer who had headed the Building Research Station (BRS) from 1924 to 1939. Among its members were John Desmond Bernal, a thirty-nine-year-old Irish-born scientist and communist who had pioneered the use of X-ray crystallography at Cambridge and was now Professor of Physics at Birkbeck College; and William Glanville, the shy but quietly assured director of the Road Research Laboratory (RRL). Glanville's stock in trade was stresses in structures and the properties of concrete.

Stradling and Glanville were old colleagues: the Road Research Laboratory was a scion of the BRS, where Glanville had worked previously.[29] Glanville in turn had collaborated with Pippard in the early 1930s, and Stradling was married to Pippard's sister. In 1937, the Home Office had formed an Air Raid Precautions Committee to which Stradling was appointed. The Committee could find little detailed information about the effects of explosions on structures and people. Experiments were accordingly put in hand at the BRS under Stradling's direction, and early in 1939 Stradling was put in charge of a new Research and Experiments Branch (from June 1940, Department) set up by the Ministry of Home Security to investigate the effects of bombing. The Department was headquartered at Princes Risborough, where Pippard and Bernal were among the engineers, scientists and statisticians who had been co-opted to its staff. Bernal was a committed Marxist, but his ability to shoot 'an arrow of original thought into any target presented to him' caused Sir John Anderson, the Minister for Home Security, to insist upon his recruitment.[30] Bernal introduced Wallis to other research into how structures respond to explosions.[31]

Tedder seems to have had faith in Wallis's concept, and for some weeks Wallis responded with gusto. There was no thought of a summer holiday, although young Barnes, now recovered, and Mary were encouraged to take themselves and two tents away on a cycling trip in the Lake District. Here they lived a Swallows and Amazons existence, living off bread, butter and eggs bought from a nearby farm, gathering blackberries, swimming, and fishing. They climbed the Old Man of Coniston and cycled round Rydale and Grasmere on roads devoid of signposts which had been removed as a hindrance to invaders.

Sending a fourteen-year-old boy and his thirteen-year-old sister to roam three hundred miles from home under the shadow of invasion might now cause alarm, but fostering self-reliance was the other side of Wallis's disciplinarian coin. He wanted to pass on his love of tramping and camping. In any case, Wallis doubted that there would be an invasion.[32] The War Cabinet was less sure. Soldiers were camped along Beech Avenue; an anti-tank ditch had been cut into the chalk outside Dorking; pillboxes stood beside White Down Lane; Pam had joined the WAAF; and fake houses of painted canvas had been set up to disguise the racetrack at Brooklands. At White Hill House, the lawns were dug up to grow vegetables.

Air raids intensified. At first Elisabeth and Christopher ran into the house at the sound of a siren, but after a few days they became blasé. On one occasion they found an unexploded incendiary which they gave to a soldier who put it in a bucket of water. On another, Mary and young Barnes came home plastered in mud after foraging in pouring rain for bits of a bomb jettisoned on Ranmore Common. But then, on Wednesday, 4 September, thirteen Bf110 *Jabos* appeared over Brooklands, apparently out of nowhere. Masked by a larger force heading for other targets, the raiders had slipped in at low level near Worthing, flew north to Guildford, then followed the railway towards Cobham. In the last minutes they divided to attack the Works from different directions. Approaching low, they caught the ground defences napping, dropped two 500 kg bombs apiece, and left 78 dead and 176 badly injured behind them. Many of the victims were sliced by jagged pieces of flying glass. Hundreds more bled from lesser injuries.[33]

All the attackers escaped, but their higher-flying escort fighters were set upon by Hurricanes from nearby Kenley. 'We saw the most marvellous air battle yesterday', Molly wrote. 'At dinner time there was a siren and we heard some bumps.' Molly and the children took turns to watch through field glasses. They saw three aircraft shot down, and three parachutes. 'The chief thing I felt was that it was so unnoisy. But it was terribly exciting; you really couldn't help being thrilled; altho' one felt so ghastly about the poor creatures in the burning aeroplanes.'[34]

Wallis was not thrilled. He wrote 'Works bombed 1.24' in his diary and rang home to say he was unhurt. This was more than could be said for the Works, where the company's emergency plan had been forgotten in the confusion and ambulances queued in the wrong places. Near Ockham Park, meanwhile, a hostile crowd gathered outside the doctor's surgery to which one of the downed German airmen had been taken. The man had two fractured limbs, cuts to his face and several bullet wounds; as he was led away, he was booed and spat upon.

Two days later the *Jabos* came back, this time aiming for the Hurricane works on the far side of the airfield. 'I do wish he were somewhere else' wrote Molly. Her wish was soon granted. The raids hastened existing plans to disperse works functions. Warehouses, garages, and the Twickenham film studios were requisitioned; an erecting shop for Wellingtons was built in Windsor Great Park. George Edwards found a site for the Experimental Department in the Foxwarren Estate, under a mile from the main works, where he organised the construction of three hangars along Redhill Road.[35] Pierson, Wallis and the Design Department were moved into the mansion at Burhill golf club. For the rest of the war Wallis spent much of his time shuttling between Burhill, Foxwarren and Brooklands.

The day after the second attack, Saturday, 7 September, dawned as 'perfect as only a September day can be'. After weeks of working flat out Wallis decided to take the day off. He and Molly rose early and walked into the Surrey Hills. As the haze burned off, they shared their bread and cheese with a field mouse and met no one until they reached Abinger where they paused for a glass of cider. The peace lasted until late afternoon, when the drone of engines drifted from the east.[36] The sound came from German bombers on their way to join other formations converging on London from different directions. The day would be remembered as Black Saturday – the first mass attack of the London Blitz. After dark Wallis and Molly walked up High Barn Hill. Before them in the warm dark were the beams of twenty or thirty searchlights, white muzzle flashes, the ragged yellow sparks of exploding shells; rarely, the streak of a falling aeroplane; and dockland warehouses red-radiant with sugar, brandy, and timber aflame.[37]

German efforts to halt British aircraft production continued through September. On the 11th an attack was aimed at Supermarine's assembly shed at Eastleigh. A raid on the Woolston works on 24 September missed but killed 24 and left 75 injured, Hartley Pratt among them. Forty-eight hours later, the Luftwaffe returned. This time they made no mistake: the works was shattered. Beaverbrook was on the scene within hours and ordered Spitfire production to be dispersed.[38]

All these events reinforced Wallis's view that industry could not be paralysed by current tactics because manufacturing processes could be almost infinitely subdivided, dispersed, and hidden.[39] Stores of natural energy, on the other hand, could be neither concealed nor scattered. As September turned to October, his investigation of the interactions between explosions, materials and structures gained pace. Tedder remained supportive; work on the bomb and the aircraft to carry it proceeded. However, while the tempo was rising, Wallis's spirits were falling. At least, this is the impression he gave at home. As word of his idea spread through the MAP and the Air Ministry, caveats and criticisms were beginning to come back. By late October Molly described him as 'utterly depressed'.

> Everything, he thought, promised so well in August and September, and now they've shut their stupid minds and won't give him more than a half of what he wants, and what use is that?[40]

The only person who really understood, said Molly, was 'Mr d'Erlanger, Barnes's great admirer. At least we have him for an ally, and he is a powerful one and well known to all these people. If he can get it to the ears of the PM, he will.'[41] Barnes's brilliance reminded her of Louis Pasteur, whose discoveries had similarly been scorned by a small-minded establishment. Molly wondered if the MAP's timidity had to do with jealousy on the part of people who 'don't fancy any idea that they haven't sponsored themselves.'[42] It seems not to have crossed her mind that a more likely possibility was that if her husband was right then it followed that the Air Staff would have to allow that the RAF was wrongly organised – an admission that would have mind-boggling consequences for everything from training and hangar sizes to industrial priorities and access to materials.

Molly's impression of officials out for themselves or foot-dragging is also at odds with other sources, which show that the MAP, far from ignoring her husband's ideas, was giving them a careful hearing. Wallis's diary for October shows him co-operating almost daily with willing helpers in his study of structures, underwater explosions, and dams. He made fact-finding visits to the Admiralty's Mine Design Department at HMS *Vernon*,[43] visited the Road Research Laboratory (RRL) on three occasions,[44] and Stradling's Research and Experiments Branch at Princes Risborough twice.[45] Sir William Halcrow advised him on the construction of the Möhne dam.[46] Wallis travelled to the MAP several times in the month to review progress with Tedder and David Pye, the Ministry's Director of Scientific Research.[47] Coincidentally, Pye had been Bertram Hopkinson's research assistant before the Great War, and from 1917 had served with him at the Aeroplane Experimental Unit. He thus had a personal connection with some of the earlier research upon which Wallis now drew.[48]

In late October Wallis attended meetings with Pye, Rowe, and Tedder on four days out of six.[49] He was increasingly preoccupied by dams, which in Italy and Germany variously provided hydro-electric power and regulated supplies of water needed for heavy industry and transport. He was looking at two contrasting types of structure. One used a series of upright arches to resist the load of water by shape rather than mass. Such dams were slender structures and looked vulnerable to conventional bombs; the multiple arch dam was predominant in Italy, where around a dozen of them generated power for a substantial part of Italian industry.[50] The other type impounded water by its own weight. Such gravity dams, epitomised by the Möhne in Germany's *Rheinisches Schiefergebirge* (Rhenish slate mountains), were considered impregnable to conventional bombs, but might be susceptible to a deep penetration weapon.

Data provided by Desmond Bernal led Wallis to theorise that the pressure pulse from an explosion on the water side of a gravity dam would be transmitted through the dam's fabric until it reached the air face, whereupon it would be reflected in rarefaction, so putting the fabric in tension.[51] Concrete in compression is virtually indestructible, but in tension it is weak, and since virtually all of the transmitted wave would be reflected, the reflection should cause spalling, so cracking the structure in a plane at right angles to the wave motion.[52]

How much explosive would be needed to produce this effect for a dam of given size, and how close to the dam would it need to be? Wallis and William Glanville agreed that the way to find out would be to detonate different quanta of explosive at different distances from instrumented scale masonry models. Facilities to do this were available at the BRS at Garston, near Watford, and the RRL at Harmondsworth. On 22 October Glanville telephoned Pye to discuss such experiments; in view of their 'national importance and urgency' there was informal agreement that the work should be put in hand immediately, before Pye formally confirmed that the MAP should pay for it.[53] Planning began to put a fifty-foot-long scale model of the Möhne across a small stream at Garston,[54] and at the end of the month, R. H. Davies's book *Modern Acoustics*, recommended by Desmond Bernal, came into Wallis's hands.[55]

On the last day of October Wallis told Pye that a smaller (4000 lb) version of the special bomb could be sufficient to break the Italian multiple arch dams and would be available for trial within eight weeks. The following day, Vickers made a formal proposal to Beaverbrook about the Victory bomber, offered to manufacture the ten-ton bomb, and repeated Wallis's claim that both could be ready by 1942. The letter was signed by Alex Dunbar, but submitted through Frederick Yapp, Vickers-Armstrongs' acting chairman.

Essentially this repeated the claims Wallis had made in July, but did so now formally, on behalf of the company. It listed coal mines, oil storage, and dams as the main intended targets. Since Victories would be needed only in small numbers, they could be hand built, without elaborate jigs or tools, making use of geodetic structure and existing modular elements (such as the pressure cabin and under-carriage) from the Wellington V. There would be no disruption at Weybridge because assembly would be at Castle Bromwich, with a prototype expected by March 1942. Dunbar emphasised the proposal's thriftiness: one Victory would use less light alloy than three Wellingtons, yet its crew and cabin would be substantially the same as for one Wellington. Hence, the diversion of resources would be small, while the load carried would be 4.5 times greater across 2.5 times the distance. The Victory's deployment, promised Vickers, would bring about a complete stoppage of power in Germany and Italy.[56]

In contrast to the impression he gave at home and in retrospect, Wallis's circle of helpers and access to others' resources were growing. The National Physical Laboratory had lent its supersonic wind tunnel for tests on the air stability and form of the bomb. Anthony Nannini, Vickers-Armstrongs' armaments expert, gave advice on the bomb's structure, convened a panel to consider methods of filling, and laid plans for gun firing tests of models.[57] The Ordnance Board (which had gained much experience of bombs and shells during the Great War) convened meetings to advise on ballistics, alternative forms of bomb for earth and water, and how to avoid pre-detonation caused by heat or impact.[58] The board's expertise was particularly valuable in addressing the need for instantaneous deto-nation of all the explosive along the length of the bomb, to ensure the fullest propagation of its pressure pulse. Dr John MacColl, the board's aerodynamic expert and Superintendent of Basic Research, gave Wallis much help in following months. Their relationship would play a part in what ensued, for MacColl had published nota-ble work on supersonic cone flow, and as a young physicist he had studied the aerodynamics of spinning spheres.[59] Further assistance came from F. W. R. Lestikow, a patent specialist whom Wallis had known for years and now enlisted to undertake library research on the construction of the Möhne dam, to inform the making of scale models for explosive testing at Garston. While briefing him, Wallis discovered that in 1938 the Air Ministry's Bombing Committee had identified dams and reservoirs as potentially lucrative targets and was given access to the data they had compiled.[60]

In sum, by late autumn Wallis was surrounded by a network of co-operating helpers, he was being backed by enough members of the Vickers board to move things forward,[61] and key people in the MAP were both encouraging him to make his case and enabling experiments to support it. Whence, then, came the downright pessimism described by Molly?

Three overlapping factors can be suggested. First, Wallis was impatient. He wanted prioritisation for, not step-by-step evaluation of, his proposal, yet as word of it spread, he felt that the original concept was being eroded by caveats and delayed by questions. Second, there are signs of unease within Vickers-Armstrongs itself. Alex Dunbar was a believer, but Nannini was independently briefing the company's acting chairman about Wallis's activities.[62] Third, the MAP was in chaos. Wilfrid Freeman had hoped to restore sanity, but circumstances changed following the departure of Sir Cyril Newall, Chief of the Air Staff, who fell victim to intrigue early in October.[63] Newall's downfall led to the appointment of Charles Portal as the new CAS. Portal wanted Freeman as his deputy,[64] and early in November Freeman acquiesced and was released from the MAP. This left Tedder isolated. Tedder had already asked to return to active service and been talked out of it; with Freeman gone he found his job impossible, and his inability to work with Beaverbrook impaired his standing in the eyes of Churchill. Tedder knew that he too must go, and when in a tragi-comedic episode the new deputy AOC-in-C Middle East Command was captured after the aircraft carrying him to Cairo inadvertently landed in Sicily, Tedder was sent to replace him. Tedder marked his going by writing to Archibald Sinclair, the Secretary of State for Air, to warn him that the MAP's working was so poor that it threatened the safety of the country.[65] The caution went unheeded.

Wallis was dismayed by Tedder's exit and wrote to say so: 'if only all concerned had been as ready to accept our original suggestion as you were this scheme could have been very much further ahead than it actually is.'[66] With Tedder's continuing backing, he said, they could have dealt with all the Italian dams.[67] Here, it seems, is the seat of Wallis's despair: there were some in the MAP who had never accepted the original suggestion, and with Tedder gone the sceptics moved into the ascendant.

To maximise effort that had already been put in, Wallis persisted with the proposal for a 4000 lb bomb: such a weapon could be carried by a Wellington, and its trial would provide experience in the technique of deep penetration without the need to build a new aircraft. According to Wallis even this was rejected, although the Vickers board and their ESC colleagues in Sheffield went ahead anyway, producing a single cast on their own initiative.

The day before Wallis wrote to Tedder, a handwritten note from Vickers's chairman, Sir Archibald Jamieson, arrived on his desk. It was a letter of condolence. German bombers had been overhead on most evenings during October. At White Hill House, ever organised and practical, Wallis created a protected sleeping space by sandbagging the kitchen and putting in props to guard against collapse. If the siren sounded, the children were to be carried down to the kitchen in their sleep. But thus far they had heard no night-time gunfire nor nearby bombs. As German bombers droned back and forth Molly was more concerned by the 'very behindhand' way in which Christopher held his spoon, and Wallis's relationship with young Barnes ('I really believe Big Barnes occasionally likes to be with him and play with him').

On Thursday, 7 November Molly's parents were staying with her sister Barbara and her family at their home on Links Road in Epsom. The bomb which hit it around 9.15 p.m. struck the front part of the house, killing Barbara, her husband, and Molly's father. Winifred Bloxam, Molly's mother, was in another part of the building and survived, albeit with injures. Robert and John McCormick, Barbara's sons, nine and eleven years old, respectively, were unhurt.[68]

The children and Winifred were taken in by neighbours, who

telephoned the Wallises, rousing them from sleep. Molly and Barnes dressed, alerted Nan to look after Elisabeth and Christopher, then drove through the raid to Epsom. At one point a bomb exploded fifty yards ahead of them. At Links Road they found the children 'fairly happy' looking at magazines, and Winifred being sick in reaction to a morphine injection. They took the children back to Effingham, where they were put to bed about 3 a.m. At five Molly heard a tapping on the wall. 'John felt miserable so he came into my bed and dug his tiny little knees into my back. He doesn't say much . . .'[69]

When Elisabeth and Christopher met Robert and John at breakfast, they were told that the boys had come to stay for a while. Elisabeth was cheered, as two older boys seemed likely to make a useful contribution to games. Later in the day she was brought up short when she walked into a room and found Molly sitting with her arms around them. Why did her mother never sit like this with her?

Writing the Note

In January 1941 Wallis said he was being 'driven nearly demented' by delays to experiments caused by buck-passing. In fact, model making had been in hand since November 1940.[70] Glanville and Pye were agreed that the only sure way to know whether results from scale models would give reliable indications of what would happen at full size was to find a real dam that was expendable, model it, and compare the effects of explosive charges against the models with what happened at the real thing. Early in January Stradling duly reported: 'I have secured a real live dam at Elan Valley and propose testing models of this in the laboratory and full-scale tests in Wales.'[71] This was Nant-y-Gro, a small gravity dam which had been built to supply workers for the Elan Valley Water Scheme at the turn of the twentieth century, since abandoned. In the event, these trials did not take place for another eighteen months, but Stradling's diligence in earmarking Nant-y-Gro gives the lie to Wallis's charge that he was being held back by 'idiots'.

Wallis decided on a fresh approach. If his deep penetration bomb was to win favour, its rationale would need to be clearly explained to all who might have a voice in or view on the subject. He thus set about writing a treatise which went back to first principles.[72] He explained the physics of explosions, how shock waves from detonations are transmitted in different kinds of medium, leading to the anatomy of a large bomb, how it could be delivered, and the kinds of target at which it should be aimed. With a low-key academic title ('A note on a method of attacking the Axis powers'), more like a book than a note (it ran to more than 12,000 words), the Note opened with three axioms: warfare depends upon industry, industry depends upon supplies of power, and power depends upon natural stores of energy such as coal, oil, and water.

Wallis circulated the Note in mid-March. With secretarial assistance from the Weybridge Works he sent copies by registered post to Tizard, departmental heads in the MAP, Air Ministry directorates, Admiralty, War Office, Ordnance Board, Downing Street, the Research and Experiment Directorate of the Home Office, and academics advising government departments. Other copies went to individuals recommended by d'Erlanger and Winterbotham, and at least one was given to a journalist. Since something so widely disseminated could hardly be secret, anxieties about security were batted away. In covering letters Wallis self-effacingly described his treatment as 'incomplete' but said that most of his figures were based on experimental reports and 'will probably be found to be on the conservative side when compared with actual full scale reports'. 'Under these conditions', he said, 'it seemed better to get something down rather than wait until very elaborate and long-drawn-out experiments could be completed.'[73]

The Note drew mixed responses. Some were impressed by the concept but wary of its ramifications. Would the war be over before the aircraft needed to carry such a bomb could be brought into service? Others were sceptical. One of them was Edward Andrade, UCL's Professor of Physics, a specialist in metals, viscosity, and acoustics who had worked on explosives during the Great War. Andrade's role in sifting new scientific ideas being pitched to government had already earned him the reputation of an inverted Micawber, 'waiting for something to turn down'.[74] He attacked the theoretical basis for many of the Wallis's arguments. Others criticised the Note for evidential sketchiness. Wallis replied in an addendum which explained that since the paper had been written for an audience of varied background, information from secret sources and much experimental data had been withheld. The result of this apparent lack of foundation, he said, had been to focus attention on parts of the Note which were really matters of detail, while 'diverting attention from its more fundamental aspects which remain unchallenged'.[75]

By the time Wallis circulated the addendum Pye had convened a panel on behalf of the MAP to consider his proposals. The panel met on the morning of 11 April,[76] and five days later Wallis was told that it broadly concurred with his assessment of the destructive effect of detonating a very large bomb underground. The Pye group's remit, however, did not extend to the design or construction of the bomb, the bomber needed to carry it, or to anything tactical.[77] When the Air Staff did discuss these things, they did not agree that penetration bombing would bring Germany's war economy to a halt.

It fell to Sir Henry Tizard, as a member of the Air Council and scientific adviser to the MAP, to break this to Wallis. The two had met several times in preceding days,[78] and when the crunch came in mid-May Tizard seems to have given the decision with such diplomacy that Wallis was left with an impression that room for manoeuvre remained. At all events, when Wallis wrote to Tizard afterwards,[79] Tizard lost no time in putting him straight:

I thought I had made my views on the continuation of work on the big bomber clear when I last had a discussion with you. I evidently did not, and perhaps it was my fault for not putting them down on paper afterwards.

Tizard bluntly spelled out the Air Staff's verdict that it had no interest in a new bomber to carry one bomb and added that while this was their view rather than that of the MAP, he nevertheless agreed with it. He went on:

When I spoke to you I said that I would be far more interested in the development of the big bomber if there was real elasticity in its use, and you told me (so I understood) that you hoped to design it so that it could provide either for taking one large single bomb or for taking a very heavy total weight of smaller bombs, or as a troop carrier capable of operating for long distances. I understood that you would design in units so that you could attach different body units to the wing and tail units. Please confirm this – it makes a great deal of difference to my interest in your proposals.[80]

Tizard went on to stress that what the Air Staff *did* want was the Wellington V in service, and the utmost zeal in development of a high-altitude Warwick. Tizard had assured the Air Staff that nothing Wallis was doing would be at the expense of these goals. 'Please confirm this' he wrote, 'I don't want to let the Air Staff down.'[81]

Turning to the bomb itself, Tizard encouraged Wallis to carry on. In reply to his request for 'definite instructions', Tizard asked what directions and facilities he needed 'to settle finally (if it can be settled finally) without full scale experiments, the particular advantages of the 10-ton penetrating bomb.'[82] In a nutshell, Wallis was being asked to prove the practicability and potential of his weapon without the wherewithal to test it, while being told in no uncertain terms what his day job was.

Pye, meanwhile, had convened a group to advise the MAP on what experiments were needed to investigate potential ways to attack dams from the air. The new body was called the Air Attack on Dams Advisory Committee, soon abbreviated to AADC.[83] At the inaugural meeting, members noted that attacks on gravity dams had been mooted before the war, when several ways of breaking them had been proposed. One was to drop a salvo of torpedoes in the hope of obtaining a cumulative effect. An assault on the dry face of the dam with rocket assisted bombs was another. A third was to detonate bombs on the upstream side of a dam. None of them looked promising.[84]

Trials and errors, June 1941–March 1942

On Tuesday, 15 July 1941 Hartley Pratt shot himself. We do not know when Wallis was told, how he reacted, or if he knew that his old friend and mentor had taken his own life following persecution by officials in the MAP.[85] He may not even have discussed it with Molly, whose letters in following days are full of happy chatter about children and a bumper crop of gooseberries.

By a strange coincidence, the aircraft that became the Vickers Windsor, the last and largest member of the geodetic family, was commissioned on the same day.[86] Like many aircraft at that time, the Windsor emerged from an iterative process in which a series of changes to operational requirements was in turn modified by the hybridisation of a succession of responses. The Windsor's pedigree went back to designs that Pierson had offered in 1936–8,[87] but by February 1941, Pierson and Wallis were pondering an enlargement of the Warwick III against the MAP's emerging requirement for a pressurised high-altitude bomber. Their idea was to combine the pressure cabin that had been developed for the high-altitude Wellington with a Warwick airframe of increased wingspan and four Merlin 60 engines.[88]

Wallis, then, already had his hands full while he was writing the Note and defending its thesis, and the emerging Windsor was not the only project with which he was concerned. A prototype of the stratosphere fighter was now under construction,[89] the B. Mk VI Wellington was in production,[90] and after many delays, tooling and sub-contractors were being readied for the first production batch of Warwicks.[91] Design responsibility for all these rested with Pierson, but Wallis had charge of particular aspects of each of them and was occupied accordingly.[92] Given these commitments, the measured pace of the AAD Committee experiments may have been as much a relief as frustration. The committee met twice more in 1941,[93] to consider further trials using different types of explosives at varying distances from model dams,[94] and methods of attack. Given the unpromising nature of the methods already considered, experiments were begun to investigate the simultaneous triggering of a group of bombs.

Wallis's letters to Molly shed light on these times in ways that other records do not. Such an episode begins on 8 August, when he waved his family off on a fortnight's holiday. He could not be spared from Vickers, and it had been decided that Molly and the children would go to south Devon without him. He was writing to her even before they arrived. 'It pains me as much at parting from you as it did years ago – perhaps more deeply.'[95] Evening rain suited his mood as he walked down Beech Avenue to post the letter. On return, he started another.

> . . . the children are too much for both of us, in the state of strain in which we live. They keep you in a state of perpetual driving energy – & no-one can make love to a bandersnatch very well.

He was disappointed in the children. They took too much for granted and had no idea of the strain under which he and Molly were living. 'Both Mary and Barnes seem to me to have disimproved in this respect.' Mary was too self-indulgent, sluggish, and unwilling to shoulder tasks voluntarily. Instead of the sparkle of young gaiety and willing helpfulness for which he looked, all we get is 'a self-contained sullenness that only renders me determined to be quit of them as soon as maybe.' He concluded: 'We or I at least must write myself down a failure as a parent, however successful I may have been in other ways.' He went on to wonder why Molly had not had more influence, and looked back to an imagined age of gold: 'There is nothing to compare in the life of our family now with the spontaneous gaiety and concerted activities of the Bloxam troupe at its best . . . am I the sole cause of the trouble?' The evening was cold. 'Goodnight my sweetheart – here's to our old age and freedom from worries.'[96]

Molly was well used to this kind of misanthropy: 'Barnes, I really don't think they're such bad children.'[97] She could have added that to all intents and purposes they now had six children rather than four: John and Robert McCormick had been taken into the family.

The holiday was at Blackpool Mill, in a wooded valley about

three miles from Dartmouth. They found the place through Molly's younger sister Pam, who was working nearby in a team of WAAFs that eavesdropped on Luftwaffe radio communications. The work called for fluent spoken German – a role for which her long romance with Karl Schmid equipped her well.[98] Pam's affections now lay with Ken Duffy, a twenty-one-year-old Canadian serviceman whom she had just married.

Blackpool Mill was surrounded by cider apple orchards. The valley ran down to the sea, where they swam in surf on Slapton Sands. Young Christopher, now Kik, was busy finding springs, damming streams; Mary and young Barnes played tennis with off-duty WAAFs. 'This is a heavenly place,' Molly told Barnes but confided to her family notebook that the holiday was all the better for him not being there; 'he has no patience and won't suffer fools gladly.' Not that her children were fools, of course ('they were all adorable'), nor that she had not wanted him; it was just that 'on the whole he's not good with the children. He has moments of being delightful but they are very few. He is too clever and hard-worked.'[99] It is characteristic of Molly's uncritical admiration of her husband that she attributed his parenting deficiencies to his talent.

Back at Harmondsworth, continuing model dam explosive trials were teaching lessons. During later 1941 several points emerged which at the time looked almost incidental but became significant when they were later brought together. Among them was the realisation, discussed at the AAD Committee's June meeting and explored through experiments in July, that a charge would be most effective against a multiple arch dam if it slid down the waterside face to explode in contact and at depth.[100] In following tests it was found that a small charge in contact would do more damage than a larger one detonating further away – and as the Committee's armament specialist Wg Cdr John Baker-Carr pointed out, a bomb could be made to explode at a given depth. The question was how to put it in contact.[101] Another issue was the erratic trajectory of a standard type of bomb as it passed through water; the Committee wondered whether an entirely new kind of weapon was needed. As for gravity dams, by December it was clear that even a ten-ton bomb was unlikely to harm one, although experiments with smaller contact charges were more promising.[102] However, since the RAF lacked the aiming accuracy to put any kind of bomb right next to a dam, discussion continued about the simultaneous detonation of a volley of smaller weapons.

At Christmas there were never less than ten round the table at White Hill House. At some meals Molly and Nan catered for sixteen. Pam, now pregnant, and Ken were 'in and out'. Nancy, Bettina and Henry Lazarus were in the audience for the traditional Christmas concert which that year included songs, carols, performances of solo violin and cello pieces, even a six-strong family orchestra conducted by young John McCormick. Mary wore her mother's taffeta evening dress to Marie Stopes's New Year party (or as Molly tellingly called it, Harry's party). The dress had puffed sleeves, was long to the ankle, and with her hair in page-boy style Molly thought her 'quite the prettiest girl there. Of course it was all a bit old for only just 14. Never mind they enjoyed themselves, & danced or tried to.'

Wallis avoided Stopes's parties. His route home from the office at Burhill passed Bolder Mere. On freezing evenings early in the new year Molly walked out to skate with him under the stars. She thought he seemed less desperate than he been a few weeks before.

> One finds it hard to realise what an important person he is. Interviews at the Air Ministry, conversations with the PM's secretary (one of 'em), consultations with experts on this, that and t'other. If only this idiotic government would let him have his own way.[103]

The 'conversations with the PM's secretary' had been back in December, about the forthcoming New Year's honours. Churchill wished to submit Wallis's name to the king for appointment as an Officer of the British Empire, but before doing so wanted to know if he would accept. Wallis declined, giving no reason.[104] R. J. Mitchell had been awarded the CBE; would Wallis settle for less? Or was he so frustrated by establishment indifference to his idea for shortening the war that he was unwilling to accept its salute?[105]

'Wait for the whole story'

In January 1942 Pye decided that enough data had been gathered for him to put a brief proposal for attacking stressed dams before the Air Staff. The Air Staff were unimpressed.[106] Their qualms were reinforced by doubts about the multiple charge method. Early in March it was recommended that experiments on gravity dams be 'put in abeyance'.[107] But just as the AADC appeared to be running out of steam, its work was re-energised by new thinking.

One strand focused on scale effects and included two 1/50th scale models built by a quick method in which mass concrete was applied in layers. The models were differently founded, one on clay and the other (more representative of the real thing) on concrete. Collins and his colleagues assessed the models as relatively stronger than a full-size dam and predicted that a 15,500 lb charge detonated 100 feet from the structure would be sufficient to render it useless. More than this, the thrust exerted by the head of water impounded by the model was less than the force that would be imposed at full scale. Following the cracking that would be caused by explosion, masonry above the crack would fail under such pressure. Wallis told Linnell that 'something like 75% of the water in the reservoir' would then be released.[108]

A second strand of thought centred on what could be achieved with the largest bomb that an existing type of bomber could then carry. The explosive content of such a weapon was reckoned to be 8600 lbs (3.8 imperial tons), and during February a series of experiments was discussed to ascertain the maximum distance from a dam face at which effective damage would be produced. By mid-April, scaled tests on models of the still-available sacrificial dam at Nant-y-Gro suggested that the detonation of 8600 lb of explosive just 25 feet from the dam would cause cracking sufficient to force the emptying of its reservoir to enable repairs. A trial at Nant-y-Gro itself on 1 May broadly corroborated this. Eleven days later, the AADC discussed further experiments, now with a contact charge to ascertain the effect of a direct hit.[109]

The possibility of a direct hit had hitherto been discounted for lack of means to achieve it. It was being considered now because in private conversations with Pye, Wallis had outlined an idea he had been pursuing since February: a spherical weapon that could ricochet across the surface of the reservoir, arrive at the face of the dam or side of a ship, sink, and explode at a predetermined depth. Wallis theorised that such a weapon could overcome hindrances which had faced them thus far. Aside from offering a way to achieve a direct hit, it would skip over torpedo nets, while its release at a distance might protect an attacking crew by enabling it to sheer off rather than fly on over a heavily defended target.[110]

It is not clear if this idea arose from Wallis's search for a way to achieve instantaneous detonation,[111] or whether the search for a way to bring a bomb into contact suggested a shape that promoted instantaneous detonation and thereby fostered the possibility of ricochet. Nor do we know if the idea was new, rather than, say, the re-purposing of existing information – like John MacColl's paper on the aerodynamics of spinning spheres, or his own work on golf balls six years before. A further possibility, not noticed hitherto, is that the idea emerged through fusion with another concept with which Wallis briefly flirted: the elimination of major units of the German fleet by detonating large bombs beneath them. Such weapons, Wallis theorised, could be placed below capital ships from very low level by modified Stirlings flown by specially trained crews.[112]

The explanation which best fits available sources is that the seed of the idea came from the physicist, aerodynamicist and mathematician Geoffrey Ingram Taylor (1886–1975), who in 1938 was attached to the Civil Defence Research Committee and became part of Stradling's department where among many other things he worked on submarine explosions, blast and shock waves.[113] In March 1941 Taylor was a founder member of Pye's Air Attack on Dams Committee, and it was exactly at this time that he was investigating detonation waves in three dimensions, examining the detonation of a spherical charge ignited at the centre and the motion of waves behind it.[114] Wallis and Taylor were in discussion between meetings. With the idea of a spherical weapon planted, Wallis turned to consider its behaviour in flight, whence in due course came realisation of the potential of ricochet.[115]

However the idea arose, at this stage he kept it close. Nothing of it was reported to the AADC on 11 May, when members were told simply that attack at low level and a contact explosion might after all be possible. In 1951 Wallis told the Royal Commission on Awards to Inventors that at this point

> The nature of my invention had not yet been fully disclosed to any one, but by the early part of 1942 I was able to confirm the general theory by making some elementary experiments at my own home . . . A small but powerful catapult was arranged to fire marbles at the surface of the water in a tub, and by a series of such experiments I was able to determine the coefficient of restitution, and the angle at which a travelling sphere would leave the surface of the water after impact.[116] This enabled me to draw a series of curves and to forecast the range which would be obtained were the sphere to be dropped from an aircraft travelling at a given speed.[117]

The marble trials were made over the Easter weekend, when Mary and young Barnes, just home from school, were enlisted to take measurements on the terrace. Thereafter, 'playing marbles' became family code for anything to do with the bouncing bomb.

After Easter Wallis drafted a note entitled 'Surface bomb. Spherical torpedo' in which the concept of the ricochet weapon was outlined. He asked Winterbotham for advice on what to do with it. Only four weeks had passed since the Air Staff's rejection of the earlier proposal, so that door looked shut. However, the spherical torpedo looked lethal against ships, and Winterbotham accordingly suggested that the note be put before the Admiralty's Director of Naval Operational Research, the physicist Professor Patrick Blackett. Winterbotham brokered a meeting, and when Wallis and Blackett came together on the morning of 22 April, Blackett was impressed. Later in the day he passed his copy of the 'Spherical bomb' note to Sir Henry Tizard at the MAP. Tizard was likewise taken with the idea and was on the doorstep at Burhill next morning to discuss it. Wallis, always sensitive to hierarchy and protocol, was at first embarrassed lest his bypassing of the MAP should have given offence, but Tizard waved this away – he had come to discuss what further experiments were needed to establish the idea's potential. Out of this came an approach from Tizard to Ernest Relf, Superintendent of the Aerodynamics Department at the National Physical Laboratory, about the possibility of using the Laboratory's 550-foot-long ship test tank to project two-inch diameter spheres of different densities and surface texture across water. Relf visited Weybridge on 19 May, where he met Wallis and saw a catapult under construction. He told Tizard: 'As far as I can see he has got a good case, and it would be well worth while to try a few experiments in the Tank to establish the fundamentals of the problem.'[118]

The catapult was finished the following week. Wallis and George Edwards took it to a small lake near Foxwarren to try it out.[119] Here we meet a feature of Wallis's idea which hitherto he had not shared: the possibility of spinning the weapon about its horizontal axis. A backward-rotating object generates lift,[120] and the catapult was designed to impart both back- and top-spin to the spheres it projected. The initial hope seems to have been that a back-spinning weapon would 'sit up' on its journey to the target, which would prolong its flight. More than this, Wallis realised that on arrival backspin might cause the weapon to cling to the side of a ship or dam wall as it sank.

Wallis was forever afterwards cagey about where this idea came from. In his evidence to the Royal Commission he said simply that it was then 'growing in my mind'. It is clear from the 'Spherical bomb' paper that his earlier research into the carry of golf balls played some part, while a family member recalled a moment at home when Wallis realised that heightened bounce would give increased range. Wallis was not short of colleagues with specialised knowledge of these matters. His ever-helpful co-worker John MacColl was an authority on spinning spheres, while George Edwards (whose team made the catapult) was an accomplished bowler.[121] However the idea of backspin arose, it was integral to experiments in the ship tank which began on 9 June.[122] At that point most members of the AADC were still unaware of the ricochet theory, although Pye had begun to share Wallis's thinking with colleagues.[123] When on 18 June Capon warned Pye of the impractically huge charge (33,000 lb) that would be needed to deal with the Möhne, Pye replied, 'Wait for the whole story', and drew a sketch of the bouncing mine in the margin of his memo.

From this run of events, we can see that at least from mid-April 1942 Wallis had good and improving grounds for optimism about prospects for attacking dams. By early July, one of the main remaining questions centred on the minimum size of contact charge that would be valid for a dam the size of the Möhne. The RRL staff asked for a further large-scale experiment at Nant-y-Gro to corroborate results that had been obtained with a four-ounce contact charge that had breached a 1/10 scale model. If the Nant-y-Gro experiment confirmed this, then 'a reasonably firm estimate' for the Möhne could be made by exploding an appropriately scaled charge in contact with a model of the Möhne that was still available at Harmondsworth. On 16 July the secretary of the AADC wrote to Wallis to say that such a trial had been arranged for the end of the following week. Wallis complained about the shortness of notice and pointed out that the Committee had not been consulted about the planning of the experiment at – as the Vickers copy typist punctuated it – 'the Nant-y-Gro. Dam.' When Pye's attention was drawn to Wallis's longhand postscript ('Punctuation quite unintentional but no doubt expresses the feelings of the Committee!') he jotted 'More expressive of Wallis than of the rest of the Committee I think'.

The second Nant-y-Gro trial took place at 5 p.m. on Friday, 24 July, when 280 lb of TNT was detonated in contact with the dam at half the depth of the water against its face. As expected, the dam was breached to a depth of sixteen feet.[124] The RRL estimated that on this basis, a charge of about 7,500 lbs against the Möhne would remove its top fifty feet. Such damage, noted the AADC's secretary, 'would release a very large proportion of the water in the reservoir'.

'I dream of you'

Wallis had obtained security clearance for Molly to accompany him to the first Nant-y-Gro trial. On May Day there she was under a hot sun looking down from the hillside. While AADC members (including Taylor), MAP officials, explosive specialists, cinematographers from the RAE and colleagues from the RRL trekked the half mile or so back to lunch in the canteen near the Caban Coch dam, Barnes and Molly picnicked by the stream, listening to larks. Their two-day stay at a hotel in Leominster was the closest they came to holidaying together in 1942. In August, Molly again took the children away on their own.

This time they went to Orgate, a farmhouse in Swaledale. A few yards away was Orgate Force, where the Marske Beck poured into a pool in which they could bathe. Sheep ambled past. Above, scree slopes and limestone cliffs rose to the moor where miles of purple heather sweetened the air. 'I hadn't expected anything so utterly beautiful.'[125]

Molly tantalised Barnes with news of their food. A nearby farm provided as many eggs as they wanted and milk 'thick with cream'. The older children cycled down to the village each day for bread; the gardener at Marske Hall let them pick beans, gooseberries, and cabbages, and tomatoes from the greenhouse. Mushrooms grew everywhere, and they became ever more inventive in ways to cook them. The iron range in the large kitchen was sooted black, but 'boils the kettles and fries the sausages'.

They followed the beck up onto the moor and found deep pools in which to swim. One hot day 'we were able to spend all day from 10.30 till 5.30 with nothing on at all in the sunshine: in and out of the bathing pool up the stream. I have never known anything so perfect.' Marske's church was wreathed in stories and had box pews. The vicar held an early Sunday service for them. Molly walked back down for evensong, for which lamps were lit. 'I like little oily churches.' In the evenings they sang part-songs and drank cocoa as the sun sank behind Holgate Moor.

Molly wondered if Barnes had forgotten them. Alone on the first Sunday, he wrote about his coming week, when he was due to meet 'some celebrated American airwoman'.[126] He planned to spend Thursday night in town 'as Philip and I are going to the "World Premiere" of a film *The First of the Few* to which I have been sent two tickets.'[127]

The First of the Few tells the story of the Spitfire, and of its design-er, R. J. Mitchell. The film depicted others Wallis knew, such as Sir Robert McLean (thinly disguised as 'Sir Ian McLaren') and Geoffrey Crisp, who was a composite of (principally) Jeffrey Quill and several members of the High Speed Flight.[128] Much of it is fanciful, but audiences and critics alike were taken by Leslie Howard's 'discreet and delicate' portrayal of a Mitchell who faces 'opposition, failure, the unwillingness of the government to spend money on aviation, and, finally, an illness which he is warned will kill him if he persists in overworking.'[129] We do not know how Wallis reacted, or what he felt about a film that represented Mitchell as a national hero while for the time being he went unsung. Nevertheless, virtually the last words given to Mitchell in Miles Malleson's screenplay warn against Civil Service obstructionism: 'Listen, Geoff, see that you get what you want . . . Don't let those Whitehall boys put anything over on you'. It is hard to imagine that Wallis did not see a parallel with his own case.

The First of the Few was one of several movies released in 1942 that put talent and teamwork before station or conformity. In *The Fore-man Went to France* an insightful engineer is baulked by managers, bureaucrats, the fifth column, and habit: 'the trouble is the people at the top think we're fighting the last war all over again.' The idea that one's betters might be part of the problem rather than the solu-tion is also met in *Went the Day Well?* where ordinary people take on German special forces and it is the local squire who turns out to be the Nazi collaborator. Wallis's vexation with board directors, the MAP and officialdom was being reflected back to him through popular cinema.

More can be seen in hindsight. McLean was at the premiere; the fact that both his recruits, Mitchell and Wallis, should become the subjects of successful films (Wallis's movie was thirteen years in the future) is witness to his acumen.[130] Then there is the early scene in *The First of the Few* in which Mitchell is held spellbound by the flight of a gull:

Mitchell: The birds fly a lot better than we do.

Diana Mitchell: You don't say.

Mitchell: I do. But then they've been at it some millions of years.
We've got to learn from them if we ever want to fly properly
. . . See how they wheel and bank and glide. Perfect. And all
in one: wings, body, tail . . .

This foreshadows Wild Goose.[131]

Next afternoon Wallis returned to the ship tank at the NPL. His work there was nearly done. At the weekend he wrote to Molly. 'I dream of you. Lucky me.'[132] The letter reached Orgate the following Tuesday. 'Barnes, darling Barnes, this time next week where shall I be, darling Barnes alonger thee. Sad tho' I shall be to leave this place, yet you at the other end will make all the difference.'

Darling Barnes was just then in conference with Benjamin Lockspeiser (Pye's deputy and designated successor), Summers, Wynter-Morgan and Admiralty representatives about full-size dropping trials for the 'spherical bomb'.[133] The chosen place was The Fleet, a shallow, tidal lagoon between the shingle bank of Chesil Beach and Dorset's mainland. A two-mile stretch of water between Abbotsbury and Langton Herring had been selected for the tests. The Fleet at this point is quite narrow, which would assist retrieval of practice spheres; there were good vantage points for the RAE's cine cameras; the area's isolation suited security; there was a nearby airfield from which to launch sorties.[134] Wallis knew it all so well: this was Camp country, thick with memories.

A strange mood coloured the following days. On the surface, things looked promising: there was enthusiasm in the Admiralty and preparations for dropping trials were in hand. Contacts made in developing the 'rota mine' had widened Wallis's network, and he was back in discussion with several of them about the original plan for a deep penetration bomb and a six-engine aircraft to carry it. In doing so he had upped the ante: whereas the original proposal was for an aircraft to carry a load of ten tons, he was now thinking of twenty.[135] He became more amiable at home, joining Elisabeth and Christopher for evening masterclasses on paper-folding and giving time to Barnes and Mary before they returned to school. In Molly's eyes, one of September's highlights was young Barnes's achievement in cycling the 90-odd miles back to Dauntsey's at the start of term.

Behind the optimism and calm ran frustrations. Production of the practice spheres and conversion of the Wellington fell behind schedule, and it was not until early October that spinning tests began. Meanwhile, the Admiralty was thinking through the consequences of bringing the 'rota mine' into use. Once its working was revealed the Germans would take countermeasures and might copy the weapon to use in retaliation. Hence, it would be necessary to hit as many German capital ships as possible in a first strike, and the Royal Navy would need to devise countermeasures before doing so.[136] Moreover, since use of the 'rota mine' against ships would reveal its potential against dams, it followed that an inter-service strategy for concurrent strikes against all kinds of target was called for. The AADC, however, continued to shrink from recommending adoption of the weapon,[137] while Wallis was unable to convince Lord Cherwell that dams were worth attacking at all. On 29 September, when Cherwell finally gave him a hearing, Wallis found him 'very unresponsive'.[138] Frustrated, on return home he began another treatise, entitled 'Air Attack on Dams'.

A few days before, Winterbotham interceded again. He knew George Garro-Jones, Parliamentary Secretary at the Ministry for Production, and went to see him. After their talk he sent notes describing how Wallis's weapon had emerged and its potential applications, notably against dams: 'If this new weapon is intelligently used, e.g., for simultaneous attacks on all German capital ships and main hydro-electric power dams, there is little doubt but that Italy could be brought to a complete standstill, and that industry in Germany would be so crippled as to have a decisive effect on the duration of the war.'[139] Winterbotham's covering letter might have come from the screenplay of *The First of the Few*: Wallis was 'the most able' aeronautical engineer he knew; it seemed 'a pity that such a man (whose brain is probably worth four or five thousand a year) should be baulked so consistently by a civil service mind, whose maximum value is probably worth six hundred per annum'.[140]

Winterbotham's intervention came ten days after announcement of the formation of a panel of three full-time scientific advisers to the Ministry of Production.[141] The panel's members were Ian Heilbron (an organic chemist at Imperial College), Thomas Merton (a physicist), and William Stanier (a past president of the Institute of Mechanical Engineers). At first, they were known as 'the three wise men'. Garro-Jones arranged for Wallis to meet them.

Fifth columns

The three wise men were quartered in Gwydyr House, Whitehall, where they received secretarial support from Lt J. I. Fell-Clark, who had been seconded from the Admiralty War Room.[142] Their meeting with Wallis was the Panel's first piece of external business, and while arranging it Fell-Clark met a dilemma. Wallis's name appeared on a list of potential undesirables that had been circulated by the Security Service. If Wallis approached the Panel, Fell-Clark was to notify MI5 through a secure telephone link.[143] His dilemma stemmed from the fact that since the subject Wallis wished to discuss was itself secret, he was unable to discuss it with unauthorised third parties.

Remarkably, at least four people connected with the development of Wallis's weapon were being watched by the Security Service. Desmond Bernal was a Marxist; MI5 had been reading his letters, listening to his telephone calls and searching his luggage since 1931.[144] Patrick Blackett, the Admiralty's director of research, a future Nobel Prize winner, and the decisive influence back in April, was likewise under surveillance because of his commitment to socialism.[145] Benjamin Lockspeiser, MAP's Deputy Director of Scientific Research and Pye's successor, had been regarded as a communist sympathiser and under MI5's eye since the General Strike.[146] Lockspeiser came under renewed suspicion in 1939–40, when his refusal to sanction purchase of an American de-icing system was seen by some as a ploy to impede the war effort and by others as a sign that he had a financial interest in a rival product. Early in 1942 he infuriated the head of the Admiralty's Boom Defence Department by vetoing a crazy scheme to use wires trailed from drifting balloons to short out Germany's electricity grid. The Admiralty sought revenge, and in February the Director of Naval Intelligence wrote to the head of MI5 demanding an investigation.[147] When MI5's inquiry found no signs of irregularity,[148] the Admiralty shifted its ground, explaining that their underlying aim had been to force Lockspeiser out of his post at the MAP.[149]

The fourth suspect was Wallis himself, and whereas the others were being watched because of left-wing sympathies, he had come to MI5's attention for different reasons and by a different route. Ten years after his death, the scientific intelligence specialist R. V. Jones revealed that Wallis had been under suspicion as a potential German collaborator. In 1941 or 1942, a member of Lindemann's staff showed Jones a list of engineers and inventors against whom Lindemann had been warned by 'an inter-service security body'.[150] Jones was told that the list reflected a hypothesis that Germany would try to enter the thinking behind British weapons development by using their agents to pitch bogus inventions to service departments and then study reactions for clues as to what the departments were actually doing. For this gambit to work, the theory ran, the proposals would need to look sufficiently realistic to attract considered attention but not so good as to be viable. The idea of a four-ton weapon that skipped across the surface of a reservoir met these criteria all too readily.

Jones was dumbfounded by the daftness of a loyalty test which you failed by putting forward an original idea, and for which there could be no rebuttal because no one told you that the test existed. We now know that the list came from Section B1c of the Security Service. B1c's primary business was counter-sabotage: it collected and collated information about the methods and aims of the *Abwehr*, and distributed it to appropriate authorities in co-operation with Section D, which oversaw security of the munitions industry.[151] From 1942 B1c also ran an operation called Fifth Column which was designed to identify and control people who would help the enemy in the event of invasion.[152] Fifth Column had originated in earlier efforts by MI5 to ascertain the extent of pro-German support among employees of the UK subsidiaries and derivatives of Siemens-Schuckert, the

German electrical, power engineering and instrumentation giant. Part of its work was to collect information about disloyal or doubtful citizens. It was under this last category that Wallis's name came to attention.

BIC was led by Victor Rothschild (1910–90), a Cambridge-trained zoologist and research scientist who was recruited to MI5 in April 1940.[153] Rothschild came from a milieu of wealthy, well-connected Oxbridge scientists, many of whom knew each other, belonged to the overlapping circles of Lindemann or Churchill, were members of the hereditary nobility, or in Rothschild's case all three.[154] Rothschild, like the Soviet agents Guy Burgess and Anthony Blunt (who he himself recruited to MI5), had been a member of Cambridge's select intellectual society, The Apostles. Before joining the Security Service, he produced a report on German espionage under the cover of commerce, which identified the usefulness of Britain's machine tool industry as an open window on the scale and trends of British production.

In a Britain gripped by fifth-column paranoia, the existence of suspicions about individuals who with hindsight appear self-evidently blameless is not in itself surprising. However, given that Wallis's personal papers and friendships in the 1930s give not the slightest hint of sympathy for Nazi Germany, it is a puzzle why Rothschild took his name seriously. Fell-Clark recalled that names on the list were broadly divided between people considered to be 'dangerous or idiots'. Wallis, he said, appeared under the heading of 'cranks'. We have seen, several times, that Wallis's reputation for being 'difficult' sprang from what some saw as the uncritical zeal with which he preached the virtues of his ideas and his impatience towards those who disagreed with them. On occasion, this combination alienated the very people he was seeking to convince. More than this, by challenging the traditional ways in which ideas were evaluated, he stirred doubts about his loyalties in people beholden to convention. In a compartmentalised, paper-based intelligence world, recently enlarged through cronyism, it is not difficult to envisage circumstances in which such adverse reactions could enter the system and then become stuck there.

Rothschild often took soundings about people from academic colleagues he considered to be 'good fellows'. One of his informants was Edward Andrade, the UCL physicist who was well known through his contributions to the BBC's *The Brains Trust*, and who we recall was a sceptic on the panel which had considered Wallis's Note in the spring of 1941. Another possibility is that Wallis's name or word of his maverick reputation came up through association with someone else. A candidate in that connection was Sir Dennistoun Burney, who by late 1941 was under investigation by MI5 over security breaches surrounding his 'Toraplane', an air-launched gliding torpedo. Air Intelligence concluded that the Toraplane 'had to a large extent been compromised' by Burney, through his passing of its details to contacts in the United States. A more basic problem was that it did not work, in result of which Burney had for some time been the subject of attention by B1c who regarded him as 'a phony inventor and a crook.'[155]

However Wallis's name found its way onto Rothschild's list, by September 1942 the list had been circulated to selected officials in relevant departments across Whitehall. Cherwell certainly knew of it, and an obvious question is whether it influenced his indifferent response to Wallis's proposal. Which brings us back to Fell-Clark's quandary: should he report the contact, or arrange the meeting? Fell-Clark reasoned that since Rothschild was not authorised to receive information about Wallis's proposal, he should postpone notification to him until such time as it became allowable.

The meeting with Merton, Stanier and Heilbron accordingly went ahead early in November.[156] A 'long interesting examination' followed from which Wallis came away hopeful.[157] But nothing ensued.[158] Admiralty backing was keen, but unless there was commitment to develop the weapon against all kinds of target, its potential would be voided. In a nutshell, Wallis was up against historical and political compartmentalisation. It is telling, then, that instead of seeing that, he was once again wondering if others were out to do him down.[159] One of those he believed to be against him was Benjamin Lockspeiser, Pye's successor as the MAP's Director of Scientific Research. Back in June, when Tizard had been pressing the case for experiment at full scale, Lockspeiser had replied (in Pye's absence) that as a general principle it was impracticable and uneconomic to modify bombers in large numbers just to carry one type of bomb, while modifying them in small numbers made it unlikely that they would be available when and where they were needed. Large bombs also had to conform to standard stowing conditions. Hence, before recommending full-scale experiment ('especially when it involves modification to aircraft') it would be necessary to know what weight of charge could be carried in a 38-inch and 30-inch bomb.

> To this end I rang up Wallis and asked if he could let me have the required information. He was very curt, replied that he was busy and would not be able to let me have anything for weeks![160]

When Wallis shared his suspicions about Lockspeiser with D Arm D's security liaison officer, Major Horace Boddington, Boddington is said to have replied that Lockspeiser was already under surveillance.[161]

The fevered atmosphere and Wallis's frustration have combined to feed the legend that he was tramping from one government department to the next and having the door shut in his face. That fable has obscured two things, the first of which is that in 1942 he was on the wrong side of a fault-line that ran between the greater part of Britain's scientific community and the War Cabinet. The formation of Thomas Merton's panel in September 1942 was the result of a campaign by senior scientists and engineers to make better co-ordinated use of scientific expertise. The nub of their case was that while many such people were working in research and experimental establishments, their distribution across departments and services meant that they were not being effectively co-ordinated.[162] Aback of such views was disquiet about the position of Cherwell, who was the only scientist with direct influence on Churchill and access to the War Cabinet. Research was collaborative and benefited from peer review, yet Cherwell was aloof.

Matters came to a head in July 1942 when a deputation of scientists and engineers led by Sir Henry Dale, President of the Royal Society, met Richard Butler, who chaired the existing advisory committees on science and engineering. What was needed, they said, was a central body composed of representative specialists and their counterparts from the armed services.[163] A second meeting followed, at which Sir John Anderson (Lord President of the Council) and Oliver Lyttleton (Minister of Production) realised that some tangible response from the government was going to be needed. However, since the last thing either Churchill or Lyttleton wanted was a new body with real influence, the panel was designed to look like a concession to the campaigners while in reality lacking the remit and status they had proposed.[164] Hence, while in polite circles Merton and his colleagues were the 'three wise men', to those in the know they soon became 'the three blind mice'.

These events hindered Wallis's pitch in several linked ways. In the first place, since Merton's terms of reference obliged him 'to keep closely in touch' with Cherwell on all matters, his proposal ended up where it had been before – on the face of Cherwell's dead bat. Furthermore, many of Wallis's supporters were either active in the campaign for a closer relationship between science and the War Cabinet, or had fallen out with Cherwell in the past, or in some cases both. Among the latter were several of Cherwell's most outspoken critics and *bêtes noires*, such as Archibald Hill and Henry Tizard, who, with Patrick Blackett, had crossed swords with Cherwell before the war.

The second factor operating against Wallis arose from debate within the War Cabinet about what aircraft should replace the Wellington and Warwick.[165] In October 1942 two choices were available. One was a 'Super Wellington' – the B. 3/42, the future Windsor, two prototypes of which had been commissioned in July. This was the preference of the Air Staff, the MAP's technical officers, the Secretary of State for Air and Vickers themselves. Churchill favoured the other option, which was to abandon geodetic construction and use Vickers's factories to build more Lancasters. Doing that, however, would bring a hiatus in production, and by the time output resumed the Lancaster would be obsolescent.

The question was discussed again in December 1942 when the

Cabinet considered a technical comparison of the two aircraft.[166] Early in 1943 the Cabinet chose the B.3/42 and demanded that its development be prioritised by the MAP and Vickers. The Windsor and the spherical bomb were thereby in competition, with a clear message from above that the aircraft came first. The bearers of this message were the same people with whom Wallis was dealing over the bomb, and he interpreted what they said as coldness towards it.

Dorset and London

While the War Cabinet pondered the pros and cons of proceeding with the B.3/42, dropping trials began.[167] The first air drop was made on 4 December, when two steel spheres were released over The Fleet. One was smooth, the other dimpled (recollecting a conclusion of Wallis's golf ball carry experiments back in 1936). Both broke on impact. Two more, now reinforced, were dropped eleven days later. These too failed, although one was recovered complete. Trials resumed early in the New Year, when one was released late due to an electrical fault, while the other again shattered. This time, however, some of the debris ran on for the best part of a quarter of a mile. A rewelded steel sphere dropped on the following day likewise showed promise when it made one large bounce while breaking up.

Advice about the removal of internal stresses in the welded shells was sought from the NPL, whose metallurgist went to some lengths to provide it.[168] Wallis was optimistic – successive adjustments in height and speed of release, and in the engineering of the spheres, pointed to coming success – although alongside the dropping trials he was increasingly beset by questions about fuzing, about what kinds of aircraft could be used to drop the anti-shipping mine, and what modifications might be needed to enable them to do so.[169]

On Wednesday, 20 January he returned to Dorset for another series of trials.

> We arrived safely last night about 7 pm after a long and tiring drive – misty and pouring rain and darkness all the way from

Salisbury. I left it so late that there was no opportunity of calling on Wiggy.[170] Today has been finer, but nothing doing as the aircraft could not land here til late this afternoon, as the aerodrome was too foggy.[171]

In the Gloucester Hotel in Weymouth he ran into his old colleague, Neville Shute Norway.[172] 'I dined with him and two others and we sat up till 11.30 p.m., talking of old times.' Wallis found him 'uglier than ever . . . But he was very nice and looks rather more like a sad but faithful dog than he ever did before, and I enjoyed seeing him. He tells me that Burney has lost most of his fortune and may come a nasty cropper.'

Warmwell was weathered in for the next two days. Wallis persuaded Molly to take the train down to Weymouth 'and share this lovely room'. The weather lifted. On Saturday:

This morning I drove out with him and the others to the nearest point I was allowed & then I got out and walked back. 8 miles of lovely road, high up with the Downs one side & the sea to other. It was sunny & clear. I did enjoy it. Of course it's quite mad that they shouldn't let me watch the proceedings seeing as I've lived with it since last February & probably know more about it than anyone save Barnes. But it's quite true – policemen do bob up and turn you away; I'd thought Barnes was trying to be funny. I suppose the others would say 'if that wife why not my wife', little knowing what a very special wife this one is.[173]

During the proceedings she was not allowed to watch, a trial weapon bounced thirteen times. Unluckily, the store was released early and out of view of the cine camera, but on Sunday, two more successful runs were made. The first, at 10.33, bounced 22 times over 1200 yards. The store was retrieved, taken back to Warmwell, reloaded into the aircraft, and released again at 4.55 p.m., when it covered 1040 yards and cleared a boom defence along the way.

Darling Barnes,

You should see him among these admirals and air vice marshalls [sic] patiently explaining and describing to them & they drinking it all in – or trying to. And he's so quiet & un-assuming none of them could imagine what pain & labour it's been. How he's got up in the middle of the night to go up to the study & work summat out. No wonder he looks drawn and tired. I suppose if he were a self-advertiser he'd have been Sir Barnes in the New Year Honours. Oh well, it'd have been a nuisance. But it's an exciting life & no mistake.[174]

Four days later, the MAP's Controller of Research and Development (Air Vice-Marshal Francis Linnell), Lockspeiser, the Third Sea Lord, Freeman and others gathered in Sir Charles Craven's room at Vickers House to watch films of the successful drops. Lockspeiser explained that the bomb now being spoken of by Wallis was not the one they had just seen but a new and improved design that would incorporate lessons learned during the trials. It was realised that proceeding with this directly would be risky, but such was the level of enthusiasm that there was agreement to go ahead. Later in the afternoon, Linnell confirmed instructions to arrange for the modification of two Mosquito bombers, to obtain particulars and drawings of the new weapon, and to raise an order with Vickers for 250 bombs. Linnell added: 'We have now reached a stage at which the Air Staff must be made fully aware of what is going ahead.'[175]

9

Full Stretch, February–June 1943

February questions

Despite enthusiastic reaction to the Fleet trials, Wallis remained frustrated. Highball, the weapon commissioned on 28 January 1943, was for use against ships. Two days later he told Cherwell that its potential against naval targets had overshadowed the question of its use against dams.

> The enclosed report, which has been compiled largely on information obtained for me by Group Captain Winterbotham, clearly shows that the destruction of the five major dams in the Ruhr district would have a powerful effect on the Ruhr industry.[1]

The 'enclosed report' was entitled 'Air Attack on Dams', which Wallis had written since his last meeting with Cherwell and was now putting into various hands. It explained that Germany's largest dams could be breached by a charge small enough to be carried by a Lancaster, that such charges could be placed in contact with dams by means of the rotating spherical mine, and that calamitous consequences for Germany's war economy would ensue if they were.[2] Breaking the Möhne would precipitate an energy crisis and cause widespread mayhem. Breaking more of the region's five main dams would intensify and hasten these effects. Across the watershed in the Weser district, the breaking of the Eder and Diemel dams would hamper navigation on the Mittelland canal, very probably to the point at which water transport came to a halt.[3]

The immediate issue, Wallis told Cherwell, was that as attacks on dams had to be carried out in tandem with those against warships, the large, five-ton anti-dam sphere (initially christened Big High-ball, soon code-named Upkeep) needed to be developed alongside the smaller weapon. With proper backing, he said, the large weapon could be developed within two months. Only minor modifications were needed to enable a Lancaster to carry it.

Struggle and confusion appear to epitomise the circumstances in which Upkeep emerged, and in the traditional telling they were long-drawn-out. In fact, only nineteen days passed between the delivery (by hand) of Wallis's letter to Cherwell and the decision to proceed with Upkeep. During that period more than a hundred officials and officers across Whitehall, service directorates, and agencies were involved in assessing Upkeep's prospects, modelling a critical path along which to bring it into use, and weighing up the pros and cons of doing so. The scale of their effort is explained by the fact that the question of whether to proceed against the Möhne was not a stand-alone matter but rested on a series of co-dependent decisions, many of which were initially hindered by conflicting or uncertain data. Much of this deliberation was done through letter and memo; the wonder is not that it took so long but that it happened so fast.

In early February, the MAP, the Air and Naval Staffs were faced with several sets of issues arising from Highball and Upkeep. If permission was given for Upkeep's development, would it undermine the War Cabinet's policy to focus on the Windsor? Would there be diversion of effort at Avro? Which project was likely to contribute more to the war effort?

Behind these questions lay another which no one had yet properly grasped. Lockspeiser drew attention to Wallis's statement that the Möhne had to be attacked in the spring when its reservoir was full.[4] No one was sure when the waters would fall below the viable level. Wallis's estimate in his latest paper was June, but he had since revised that to April. 'If it is true that we must attack not later than April', Lockspeiser told Linnell, 'I find it difficult to believe that we can get an entirely new bomb through all its trials from scratch into the Service and be used operationally by this date.'[5] If that was so, then the case for Upkeep's urgency fell away because no dam operation could be launched until 1944. To be sure, an authoritative assessment of the water level question was needed. Linnell referred the other questions to Tizard, who replied that the B.3/42 could have no influence on the war until the middle of 1945, whereas the economic repercussions of a successful strike against Germany's dams in 1943 might be considerable. Upkeep looked technically viable, so the argument in favour of accepting a delay with the bomber was persuasive. That, however, was for the Air Staff.[6]

Lockspeiser reckoned that six months might be needed to bring Upkeep into service, whereas the Naval Staff wished to use Highball as soon as possible. Everyone agreed that if one weapon was used much before the other, immediate measures would be taken to protect further categories of target. The need for surprise also had a bearing on the size of the forces, because first attacks would have to be in sufficient strength to give a realistic prospect of success despite losses and mishap. That in turn brought security to the fore, for if the enemy had any inkling of the weapon, steps would be taken to parry it.

Aback of these deliberations lay yet more issues, one of which was whether a low-level attack on the Möhne at night was possible at all. Another was Harris's concern that Lancasters earmarked for such a strike would be quarantined from normal operations during training or while they were being converted. Harris disliked the whole project, describing it as 'tripe' and prophesying that the war would be over before it worked – 'and it never will.'[7] However, Harris was not among those with whom the decision rested, and although he lobbied Portal (Chief of the Air Staff) against it,[8] he was overruled.

On 13 February, Sorley (ACAS (TR)) chaired a meeting attended by Bottomley (ACAS (Operations)), Linnell and others at which it was again said that the earliest date by which Upkeep could be brought into use was six months away. The meeting also heard that a low-level night attack on the Möhne was unlikely to be practicable. Unsurprisingly, those present concluded that the best way to proceed was to develop Highball first and postpone Upkeep until the concept had been proved by the smaller bomb. The meeting nevertheless instructed Sidney Bufton, the Air Ministry's Director of Bomber Operations, to examine Upkeep's operational implications in more detail.[9] This was a key moment, for while Sorley's meeting had just suspended Upkeep's development, the direction to Bufton opened a path for its revival.

Wallis's agitation, meanwhile, was growing. He minimised the difficulties, insisting that the tasks of making the large bomb and converting Lancasters to carry it were 'easy', and that sufficient weapons to enable a force of thirty aircraft to make simultaneous attacks on five dams could be made 'within two to three weeks' – a fantastic claim.[10]

Bufton convened the meeting to consider operational implications on 15 February. Wallis was invited, and upbeat. He said that the bombs could be produced within two months and did his best to assuage Bomber Command's anxieties by saying that only one Lancaster would be needed for trial installation and full-scale tests, and that the rest could be modified in two days and returned to normal duties in one. He further suggested that Upkeep could probably be dropped from any height up to 400 feet. After hearing these assurances, the meeting decided that a night attack would after all be possible. Grp Capt. Charles Elworthy, Bomber Command's representative, thought that crews could be trained to use the weapon in three weeks and that only two or three modified Lancasters would be needed to do so. Bufton and his colleagues were also given a revised opinion about the water level. The civil engineer William Halcrow was in attendance and advised that the level was likely to remain viable until June.[11]

Bufton's meeting concluded that the operation was tactically feasible, that it could after all take place in spring 1943, that disruption to Bomber Command's normal business would be small, and that the weapon could be readied in the time available. When Wallis pointed out that the Eder dam, which held back twice as much water as the Möhne (and was thus 'a most important target'), was only 45 miles away, the meeting went further to raise 'the possibility of a simultaneous attack upon the two dams.'[12] Bufton's advice was swiftly fed back to Linnell and Sorley. No immediate Air Staff decision emerged, but the case for simultaneous development of the two weapons was back on the agenda.

Wallis continued to pull any string within reach, without regard for where it led. Winterbotham responded to his plea by sending a 'Most secret and personal' note to Air Vice-Marshal Frank Inglis, the Assistant Chief of the Air Staff with responsibility for intelligence. Inglis had access to Churchill, and – we recall – was the brother-in-law of Wallis's close friend Victor Goddard. Winterbotham told him that while the Admiralty was 'enthusiastic' about the weapon, and that Highball was 'almost ready', neither the RAF nor the MAP were showing much interest in the larger version. 'My fear is that a new and formidable strategic weapon will be spoiled by premature use against a few ships, instead of being developed and used in a properly co-ordinated plan.'[13]

On 20 February Wallis wrote again to Cherwell.[14] Two days later he drove with Summers to show film of the test drops to Harris and Saundby at HQ Bomber Command. More confusion ensued. Harris made no secret of his scepticism ('badly misinformed' Wallis wrote in his diary), while Wallis was unaware that Portal was minded to proceed. By the time this news was passed to Linnell, Wallis and Kilner had been summoned by Craven, who at noon on 23 February admonished Wallis for pestering Linnell. Wallis reacted icily, saying that if his contribution was unwanted, he would resign. Craven, normally equable, lost control, repeatedly slamming his fist on the desk and shouting 'Mutiny!'

The underlying cause of Craven's outburst was his wish to smooth the path for the Wellington/Warwick replacement. The War Cabinet had just opted for the B.3/42, and wished it prioritised, yet the bomb would divert key staff away from it. But Wallis did not realise this. As they left, he told Kilner that he wished to leave Vickers. Reaching home, Wallis wrote 'Bad row' in his diary. He kept several diaries in 1943. One was a small pocket diary in which he jotted points of detail, phone numbers, some appointments and mileages. Another, in which he made the 'Bad row' entry, was a larger book-like affair, with a dark blue padded cover. There was a series of these during the war, and its predecessor for 1942 was virtually empty. The pages for

January 1943 were likewise bare, until the successful dropping trials at the Fleet, whereafter Wallis kept a daily record of meetings held, people met, places visited, and sometimes work in hand. The detail suggests that Wallis was aware that he had embarked upon a great undertaking, and that this record might be for posterity as well as his own reference. Historians have relied on the large diary for many points of detail, and it is indeed a remarkable document. However, there is evidence that it was sometimes written in arrears, several days at a time, and in these cases some details were approximate or misremembered.[15]

As Wallis went off to lick his wounds, neither he nor Craven knew that the decision to proceed with Upkeep had already been taken. Portal had been impressed by the Fleet trials, and on 19 February he agreed with Sorley's assessment that the project would be 'a good gamble'. Hence, while Craven was thumping his desk, Sorley was writing to Linnell, with a copy to Bottomley, to report Portal's decision to allocate three Lancasters for trial drops, procure conversion sets sufficient for two Lancaster squadrons, and order a hundred Upkeeps with a view to a dams strike in May. In parallel, two squadrons of Mosquitoes should be prepared for use of Highball.[16]

At a historic meeting on Friday, 26 February, more flesh was put on these bones. It was chaired by Linnell and held in his room. Half of those attending were from different branches of the MAP; the others were Wallis, Palmer and Craven from Vickers; Roy Chadwick, who had been summoned from Avro in Manchester; and Baker and Sorley, representing DB Ops and the Air Staff, respectively. Linnell announced that the Chief of the Air Staff had instructed 'that every endeavour was to be made to complete the aircraft and bombs to enable their use during the spring of 1943'. This meant Upkeep and Highball together, and two concurrent operations, Servant (against warships) and Chastise (against dams). To that end Portal had prioritised Upkeep over work on the B.3/42 at Vickers, and over other projects on the Lancaster at Avro. The most urgent requirement was the preparation of three Upkeep-capable Lancasters, to be followed by conversion sets to furnish a force of thirty aircraft. 26 May was the latest date by which the Möhne operation could be carried out in 1943. Counting back and allowing time for training and experiment it was agreed that the target date for delivery of aircraft and the bomb should be 1 May. Since there was no detailed scheme for conversion of the Lancaster, Wallis and Chadwick were asked to confer to provide one, and to give an estimate of timings within forty-eight hours. Craven and Linnell, sceptics only two days before, had since been told to commit to the project. Craven remained downbeat. He listed problems and said that 'there could be no hope of completing the bombs unless absolute priority was granted.' Privately, Linnell was also pessimistic. As for Wallis, while there are signs that he had been given some inkling beforehand, he found himself in a daze. It was as if after months of putting his shoulder to a barred door, it had suddenly given way and he had fallen through into an entirely different room.

Next morning, Saturday, 27 February, Wilfred Wynter-Morgan arrived from DD Arm D in Wallis's office at Burhill. He came ostensibly to settle details about the Lancaster work, but primarily because Wallis wanted to confide in him about the mood inside Vickers. Wallis explained that Upkeep was unpopular within the firm because it conflicted with the hopes of directors and senior management. Neither the Warwick nor the high-altitude fighter had been successful, and Vickers's directors had been trying to sustain workforce morale with promises that the Windsor would bring the company back into its own as a plane-maker. Any diversion from this aim was unwelcome. Wallis feared that unless Vickers's leaders grasped the over-arching importance of the Upkeep project, its deadlines would not be met. He suggested that 'the only way' to do this was for Portal or Freeman to write personally to Craven to emphasise the weight which the Air Staff placed on the work.

Wynter-Morgan put all this in a note to Portal, telling him that such a letter 'might make all the difference between success and the abandonment of the attempt'.[17] Portal telephoned Freeman's personal secretary and asked him to arrange for Freeman either to write to Craven or speak to him personally.[18]

The Air Staff, meanwhile, set down their priorities:

1. Every effort should be made to launch the attack against the Tirpitz and the attack on the Möhne Dam at the same time.
2. If the Lancasters are ready in time for an attack on the dam in May, they should be used, whether or not the Mosquitoes are ready.
3. If the Mosquitoes are ready first, they should not be used until it is known that the Lancasters cannot be ready in May.
4. The Mosquitoes should be first used against the Tirpitz and this operation should not be undertaken until sufficient aircraft are available to take full advantage of surprise.[19]

Wallis had told a lot of people that all the necessary work could be done within two months, and that most of it would be straightforward. Two months was the time he now had, and his claims about straightforwardness were about to be tested.

North and south

Wallis's assertion that it would be easy to convert a Lancaster to carry Upkeep lasted less than forty-eight hours. During the meeting on 26 February Roy Chadwick, Avro's chief designer, had been asked whether he could provide three prototypes and sets to convert a further 27 aircraft in the time available. Chadwick spontaneously said 'yes', despite having no clear idea about what it was he was agreeing to. Wallis had imagined that standard Lancasters could be flown to Weybridge or Farnborough where Vickers would make the necessary changes using conversion sets provided for the purpose. However, when Chadwick studied the task, it became clear either that Avro itself would have to do most of the work, diverting aircraft on its production line into a programme of modification that included strong point attachments to the airframe, the bombcell fairings, removal of the mid upper turret, electrical bomb release wiring and the hydraulic power point for the motor. Thereafter, such aircraft could be passed to Vickers who would provide and fit the caliper arms to carry the bomb, and the hydraulic motor to impart spin.[20]

When news of these things reached Linnell, he told Portal:

> Vickers's contention that the change from the normal bombing role to UPKEEP could be achieved by a conversion set has proved false. The changes are so great that they must be built into the aircraft on the line.[21]

Linnell asked for confirmation about the acceptability of separating Upkeep aircraft from the main Lancaster fleet and asked if it was still the plan to provide thirty of them. Segregation was agreed to, but in the light of it the production order was reduced to twenty – a decision that later came to influence Chastise's tactics and the scope for Upkeep's further use. Linnell warned Portal that while some of the production aircraft might be available by 1 May, it would be 'unduly optimistic' to expect them all. Privately, Chadwick agreed, but this was their deadline, dictated by a count-back from the expected date of the operation, to allow sufficient time for tactical training beforehand. Craven was similarly sceptical. He told Wallis: 'Personally, I think this time we have been set an impossible problem and I have told Sir Stafford Cripps this but, on the other hand, I have assured him we are going to do everything humanly possible. I do want to be assured that this is being done, please.'[22]

Wallis, Chadwick, and their colleagues in Weybridge and Manchester went to work with a will. Wallis collaborated readily with Chadwick, and Chadwick seems to have relished the challenge of what the two of them afterwards called their 'great adventure'. Following the meeting on 26 February, key components were being sourced within a day. Draft drawings of the bomb were provided within two days, complete sets of finalised drawings in five, and Chadwick issued the first works instruction at Avro on 8 March. Within a week of the meeting in Linnell's office, arrangements had been made for manufacture and filling of the mines. Drawings of how the mine would be ground-handled and loaded were dispatched by Avro on 9 March – when Wallis was back in Dorset for range tests of two spheres of different density. Chadwick, Wallis and their colleagues were in daily, sometimes hourly communication by telephone, teleprint and telegram; decisions were acted upon directly and confirmed later.

A rig was erected in the large hangar at Foxwarren from which spun stores were dropped onto greased steel plates to test whether the weapon released evenly on both sides, that the self-destruct arming link pulled off properly, and whether there was any delay in the release circuit. Alongside the spinning tests, meetings at the MAP and Air Ministry, discussions about the explosive filling of stores, finalising conversion of the Highball-carrying Mosquito, and correspondence with Patrick Blackett and Edward Bullard about the extent to which waves generated by an Upkeep detonation might hinder subsequent drops, Wallis continued to work on the B.3/42.[23]

Molly, meanwhile, had left to visit her sister Pam, who was now in the Cairngorms where her husband Ken was attached to the Mountain and Snow Warfare School at Glenfeshie. Ken was permitted to live out, and since the previous autumn they had rented a croft at Balnascretan, whence a walk to their nearest neighbour took twenty minutes and a round trip to a shop was ten miles.

Molly was eager to see her sister and her one-year-old nephew Andrew, and on Friday, 11 March she was at Euston to board the sleeper to Inverness. In the bunk above was a WAAF who had been escorted onto the train by her father bearing a small glass of gin. At Crewe they were joined by an ATS girl and a WREN. When she left the train at Kincraig she found herself surrounded by snow-clad mountains, on a freezing platform where southbound travellers were warned to tell the station master so that he could stop the train 'for passengers going to England'.

At Balnascretan she found the croft grubby with 'smuts and dust', but Pam was happy, Andrew 'adorable', and the place was 'wonderful beyond description'. She was glad to be there when it was wintry. 'We all go to stay at places in the calm smooth summer'; here, she could step out of the door and onto a mountain. Molly climbed Sgoran Dubh, finding the descent 'hard work' in a high wind, and on one night she looked after Andrew while Pam and Ken went to a hotel in Kingussie for their first warm bath in months. She told

Barnes it all felt so 'utterly wicked . . . and you holiday-less slaving at your marbles at home.'[24]

Scampton and Skitten

In the Air Ministry, connected plans for the two operations were being laid. On 20 March Wallis was invited to Bomber Command's bunker at Naphill, near High Wycombe, to hear outline arrangements for Chastise. Its organisation had been put in the hands of No. 5 Group, and AVM Ralph Cochrane, 5 Group's AOC, was there to talk about it. Cochrane and Wallis, we recall, had known each other since Barrow days, when Cochrane had been one of the airshipmen posted to Barrow for the launch of No. 9. Cochrane was quietly and precisely spoken; some thought him chilly; in fact, a warm personality lay behind the efficient exterior, but this was well hidden from service colleagues.

Chastise was entrusted to Cochrane's Group partly because Harris considered him able and dependable, but chiefly because No. 5 Group was an all-Lancaster force and thus geared for the technical and maintenance support of a new Lancaster squadron. Cochrane explained that the squadron would be formed from a nucleus of tour-expired crews, and that it would be stationed at Scampton, a pre-war bomber station beside Ermine Street just north of Lincoln.[25] Tactical planning would be overseen by Harry Satterly, No. 5 Group's blunt-mannered and incisive SASO.

Satterly rang three days later to say that the squadron was to be led by Wing Commander Guy Gibson, a veteran of three operational tours, who had just completed a year in command of 106 Squadron. If convenient, Gibson would visit Burhill for initial briefing. At 4.30 next afternoon Gibson and Wallis sized each other up. Gibson took in someone who seemed quiet and earnest, and worked in a 'strange house'. Before Wallis was a stocky, ruddy-faced man with a busy manner and a habit of forcefully blowing jets of cigarette smoke from between pursed lips.

Wallis explained how Upkeep worked and ran films of the trial drops. Gibson was fascinated, but it soon emerged that no one had told him what the weapon was for, and that he was not on the list of those whom Wallis was authorised to tell. Hence, on departure he was none the wiser about what his squadron were expected to do. All Wallis could tell him was that the operation would be flown at night, that the attack would be made at low level over water, from a precise height, probably 150 feet, and at a specified speed. Would that be possible? Back in Lincolnshire, Gibson pondered these questions during a long walk with his dog. From 31 March, 617 Squadron's crews began to train in earnest, flying low-level cross-countries.

Operation Servant, the simultaneous strike against capital warships, was entrusted to another new unit, No. 618 Squadron, which began to form at RAF Skitten in Caithness on the following day. No. 618 was part of Coastal Command's No. 18 Group, which operated over the northern North Sea and the Norwegian Sea. In early March the Air Staff had hoped that this operation, too, could be entrusted to Bomber Command, but Harris firmly declined it, saying that the difficulties of the northern operation would be better understood if Coastal Command and the Admiralty addressed it themselves.

Skitten was a satellite to RAF Wick, which supplied the squadron's first draft of airmen and airwomen.[26] With them came a nucleus of Mosquito aircraft and aircrew from Marham in No. 3 Group Bomber Command, the first of them from Nos 105 and 139 Squadrons. These units specialised in attacks on targets such as trains, transport infrastructure and factories.[27] Among them had been a low-level raid on a molybdenum plant at Knaben in Norway, undertaken four weeks before, which had called for precision navigation over snowy, mountainous terrain in difficult air conditions – appropriate skills for the task that lay ahead.

Remarkably, 618 Squadron already knew what they had been formed to do. On 2 April a directive from HQ Coastal Command describing the squadron's purpose was received by Sqn Ldr Charles Rose, the acting CO, who handed it to the adjutant, who duly copied it into the squadron's Operations Record Book. The directive, entitled Operation Highball, explained that No. 618 had been formed to attack units of the German fleet in Norwegian waters using a weapon that was still under development which employed ricochet and backspin. It gave both the target date for the operation (15 May) and notice of the plan for Bomber Command to mount a complementary operation.

In the office of 618 Squadron's adjutant there were several people, including NCOs and airmen, who at various times would have had the opportunity to look at the unit's ORB. Not surprisingly, then, the squadron's task was soon an open secret. This staggering security breach stemmed from a confusion within 18 Group's unique joint RN-RAF command at Rosyth. It also helps to explain high morale during April when crews flew long-distance navigation exercises and from 20 April made low-level dummy attacks on a target ship, HMS *Bonaventure*, in Loch a' Chàirn Bhàin.[28] A French dreadnought, the *Courbet*, was on its way to Loch Striven for use as a target. At April's end, the squadron's CO reflected on high standards achieved in a short time, and the enthusiasm and eagerness of his squadron's members.

'Messing about on the east coast'

> There's a mysterious Church with Two Towers he's always talking about to people on the telephone, which enthralls the children.[29]

St Mary, Reculver, stands within the enceinte of a Roman fort about three miles east of Herne Bay on the north Kent coast. When the church was founded in the seventh century it overlooked a tidal strait separating Thanet from mainland Kent, but by the 1800s the channel had dwindled to a ditch, Reculver village had been swallowed by the sea, and St Mary was abandoned. Mariners, however, valued the twin west towers of the church as a sea mark, and in 1809 the Trinity Board purchased the ruins as an aid to navigation. Reculver's foreshore is shingle, sand, and mud, crossed at short intervals by groynes, dotted with mussel beds, and backed by a slumping cliff of layered brickearths, clays and pebbles. The beach seems to run for miles, and it was this lengthiness and seclusion that suited it for trials of Upkeep and Highball.

Wallis entered these surroundings late in the afternoon of Saturday, 10 April, landing at Manston in the first prototype Upkeep Lancaster that carried him from Weybridge. The machine, test flown earlier in the week, witnessed the extraordinary achievement of Roy Chadwick and his Avro colleagues who had produced it in a month. Manston was the base for dropping trials, and a cadre of engineers, armaments officers from the two squadrons and MAP officials mustered there over the weekend.

Wallis found the coast deserted, shops boarded up, and boarding houses closed. Eventually he found a room in a pub, but the experience of sleeping in it recalled his freezing nights in the Hand and Spear back in 1930, and he soon transferred to the Hotel Miramar on the outskirts of Herne Bay.

On Sunday morning Vickers staff met at Manston to plan their work, followed by testing of hydraulics, slip and spinning gear in the aircraft. At this point 'the bouncing bomb' was conceived as a group of munitions, generically called Golf Mines, which were of ascending weight and size. Smallest in the family was Baseball.[30] Highball (Light) was for Mosquitoes. Highball (Heavy) was intended for delivery by Wellingtons and Warwicks. Upkeep was a Lancaster weapon.[31] Highball (H and L) and Upkeep were to be trialled together at Reculver, and a Wellington, Mosquito and the Lancaster had been assembled to drop them. Low cloud and rain kept them on the ground on Monday, but Tuesday's weather was fair.

Wallis was on the beach at Reculver soon after eight in the morning. He surveyed the dropping range which had been laid out under the aegis of MAEE. Its axis ran parallel to a baseline ashore, on which two theodolite cameras were positioned 3000 feet apart. A buoy marking the release point was moored 1500 feet out from the baseline, watched by two cameras to record the height of release and first impact. An aiming point was positioned about one and three quarter miles down range from the release point, where a fifth camera looked back down the line along which stores were intended to run. Drops were to be made at high water, enabling the retrieval of stores for study when the tide went down.[32] Drops and filming were co-ordinated by a range control party from a radio van, supervised by Wg Cdr Robert Garner, a weapons specialist with MAEE.[33] For shelter, there was a peacetime tea hut run by a retired sergeant major, who in the intervals between drops kept Wallis supplied with chocolate biscuits and tutored him on his collection of birds. Reculver's immediate hinterland was sparsely inhabited, and the security officers who prowled its vicinity to restrict access were accordingly conspicuous. During the Easter holiday the challenge of dodging them added to the trials' attraction for children from the nearby village of Birchington.

High tide on 13 April came soon after breakfast. At 09.20 the cameras were turning as the Wellington came into view for the first drop – an inert Highball (H). Wallis's basic Golf Mine design consisted of a cylindrical metal core cast about by a wooden annulus. The core looked a bit like a cotton reel and in a live weapon it would contain the explosive and hydrostatic pistols to detonate at a pre-set depth. The annulus, formed of staves held by metal bands, conferred the near-spherical shape, flattened at the lateral poles, like an apple on its side. Trial weapons were inert, concrete a proxy for explosive. On this first occasion, as on many that followed, the outer casing fell to pieces on impact, but the cylinder ran on.[34]

At 11.08 the first Upkeep was released. It hit the seabed (at a depth of 8 feet), rose to half emergence, travelled 40 yards, and sank. A second Upkeep was dropped shortly after 7 p.m. This too failed, but with differences: whereas the weapon dropped in the morning had been released from 250 feet, the evening Upkeep was dropped from 50, and although the annulus shattered the inner cylinder bounced on for 700 yards.[35] A pattern was emerging.

Wallis returned to Weybridge on the next evening. His instinct was to strengthen the annulus with larger bands, and pack voids in the structure with resin. However, when dropping trials resumed at the weekend the casings continued to break. But as before, one of the Upkeeps continued to run despite the loss of its case.

The drops on Saturday 17 April were watched by officials from the MAP, and Bomber Command. Among the former were Linnell and

Wallis's old comrade Norbert Rowe. Grp Capt. William Marwood-Elton represented Bomber Command. Harris had greeted his report on the drop failures earlier in the week by writing, 'As I always thought, the weapon is barmy.'[36] Of the spotlight altimeter devised to enable crews to bomb from the correct height,[37] he wrote 'I will not have aircraft flying about with spot lights on in defended areas. Get some of these lunatics controlled, and if possible locked up.'[38]

The film depicts Wallis as increasingly isolated during these days, wading out on the foreshore looking for bomb fragments while unimpressed MAP staff took themselves back to London. In fact, to judge from his letters home he was in good spirits,[39] at one point inviting Molly down to join him, and there were supportive colleagues to hand. Apart from Rowe, during the second round of trials he was also accompanied by Geoffrey Ingram Taylor, whose research lay aback of the original idea. On the 17th the three of them stripped off for a swim between drops. A long conversation between Taylor and Wallis that evening at the Miramar led to key decisions. It was already clear that the Upkeep cylinder could run by itself, and that a lower release height better enabled it to do so. Wallis was sure that Upkeep's range would be greater if the annulus could be modified to resist impact, but the time he had to make further changes had run out – if the weapon was to be used in mid-May, then it had to be ready in about a fortnight. Emboldened by Taylor, the first decision was to switch to a simplified form ('stripped Upkeep'). A second was to bring the release height down to 60 feet, assuming Gibson's crews could achieve this, at night. A third was to reinforce Highball with 3/16-inch steel plate.

On 24 April Molly reminisced about the eve of her wedding back in 1925. 'Gosh I have been happy.' Every year they marked the anniversary by doing something special. But not this year. 'I fear tomorrow we shan't. It seems he will have to be at work every day over Easter. I don't know how long he can go on.'[40] That same afternoon, Wallis met Gibson, Summers, Longbottom and Renouf, and asked if the attacks could be made from 60 feet, rather than the 150 feet which hitherto had been budgeted in training. Gibson said that they would try. Five days later (when Wallis began his day at

Reculver, drove to Crayford, drove on to a meeting in London, then went back to Reculver) a reinforced Highball made a perfect run of 1200 yards. On the same day, a stripped Upkeep ran for 670 yards.

Cochrane wanted his crews to have the opportunity to drop typical stores against a representative target. Early in May the Reculver range was accordingly rotated through 90 degrees to enable drops at right angles to the shore. Sighting flags representing dam towers were erected at the top of the beach, close to the Northmouth Sluice, and from 11 May Wallis and others were on the beach on successive days to watch 617 crews bowl their Upkeeps landward. Some ran short; others careered on beyond the beach into the mud of an old oyster bed; and in yet more cases the weapon arrived as intended, at the water's edge. The penalty for misjudging height was witnessed on the evening of 12 May when a Lancaster captained by Henry Maudslay was badly damaged by the plume of dense spray thrown up by a store released from below 60 feet.

By 14 May, the many challenges had one by one been met and problems solved. But there were other worries. With so many official visitors to Reculver,[41] not to mention unofficial visits by local spectators, by later April Wallis had become fearful that the weapon might be compromised. He consulted Winterbotham, who in turn took soundings among intelligence colleagues. The word was that security remained tight. However, on 1 May Gibson was startled to discover that Wg Cdr Garner who supervised the dropping range had in his hands a dossier on the targets, and that he had shared its contents with Henry Watson, 617 Squadron's armaments officer, and Sqn Ldr Charles Rose who had been seconded to the dropping trials from 618 Squadron. Gibson was furious, not least because at the time of the breach Watson knew more about the project than he did himself. Gibson wrote in vehement protest to Cochrane, who did likewise to Saundby at Bomber Command, who in turn referred it to Bottomley (ACAS (Ops)). As the hullaboo subsided, Bottomley's pointed request for a 'census' of the dossiers distributed by Wallis suggests that the lapse originated with Wallis himself.

Molly, meanwhile, told her friend that while Barnes was 'messing about on the east coast' she had heard from Pam that she was 'having another'. Molly had urged her sister not to have a second child too soon, but there it was – a new baby was due in November. Molly told Barnes that when the time came, she planned to go back to Balnascretan, to look after her nephew Andrew during the birth.[42]

Drawing the bow: Servant

Morale in 618 Squadron was high at April's end. During May it subsided. By the middle of the month, only 16 Highball Mosquitoes had reached Skitten; the first dropping trials against the *Courbet* did not begin until 9 May, and when they did problems emerged with the release mechanism which led to irregular running;[43] Highball's depth pistols were at first nullified if the store struck the target with too much force;[44] it was not until 11 May that Wallis devised a bombsight to provide accurate ranging, and not until July that all of the squadron's aircraft were equipped with it. Beyond these, the *Courbet* trials were flown from the MAEE airfield at Turnberry, to which from 7 May fluctuating proportions of the Squadron were transferred. This meant that for much of the time the Squadron was split, and that what was left of it at Skitten was overseen by a temporary commander.[45] During May there were at least four such temporary COs, while from 17 May the permanent CO was off the scene for the next fortnight following injury in a take-off accident. Another Mosquito was wrecked three days later. These incidents followed a fatal crash in April.

Even had the Squadron been ready, by 15 May its targets had moved. When the decision to use Highball was taken the *Tirpitz*, *Scharnhorst* and *Lutzow* were within Mosquito range at Trondheim, but by the time 618 Squadron was formed the vessels had been moved via Narvik (which from Sumburgh in the Shetlands was at the limit of the Mosquito's operational range) to Kåfjord (which was beyond it).

In Whitehall, the Chiefs of Staff continued to debate, and at times to bicker, about how to combine surprise and efficacy in the deployment of Wallis's weapons. Naval planners wanted 'a really good dividend' from Highball before the enemy worked out how to take precautions or developed a similar weapon of their own. Sir Dudley Pound had accordingly urged that the Möhne operation be launched at the same time as an attack on German capital ships, the aircraft carrier *Graf Zeppelin*, and capital units of the Italian fleet. Pound's wish made strategic sense: ships like the *Tirpitz* were like high-value chess pieces, exercising power simply by tying down large Allied assets to counter them should they emerge. For Pound and others in the Admiralty, Highball's attraction lay in its promise of a means to release substantial forces for other purposes. However, aside from the retreat of the *Tirpitz* group to northern Norway, the *Graf Zeppelin* was now anchored at Gdynia, while vessels of the Regia Marina were at La Spezia on the other side of Europe. In seeking their 'really good dividend' the admirals thus faced the further problem of how to launch a simultaneous attack on widely dispersed targets. Such a strike would need to succeed at the first attempt, which called for a force large enough to allow for attrition and poor runs.

Bufton had already considered ways to bridge the northern range gap. None of them looked promising.[46] As for dispersal, on 5 April, a meeting of Admirals Brind and Renouf, Captain Dickson (Admiralty), and Grp Capt. C. W. Dicken (Coastal Command) received advice from the Admiralty and Coastal intelligence staffs to postpone the Dams Raid by a month, double the size of the Mosquito force, and in June launch an attack on the Italian fleet to increase the weight of the initial blow. Bottomley forwarded a summary of this proposal to Portal, saying he would wish to see 'at once' the 'extraordinary' plan being advocated by the Admiralty. Portal was thus forewarned when the Chiefs of Staff met two days later. He told Pound that until Highball was ready, the allocation of a second batch of thirty Mosquitoes would hold back an entire squadron to no useful purpose. A second batch should at least await the outcome of the *Courbet* trials. Moreover, until Highball had been fully tested there was no guarantee that it ever would be ready. It was unlikely that conditions would ever allow an exactly simultaneous attack, and the likelihood that the enemy could devise effective countermeasures in a few days between operations was small.[47]

The Admiralty nonetheless continued to ask for the postponement of Operation Chastise,[48] and when the Chiefs of Staff met
again on 10 May they gave another reason for doing so: the new
proposal was to send 618 Squadron to the Mediterranean to attack
the Italian fleet in June. Portal was then away in Washington,[49] but
Bottomley was prepared. He had consulted Harris, who wished to
go ahead: the start of the moon period was just four days away, 617
Squadron's crews were trained and keyed up, Upkeep was ready, and
since it was a one-shot weapon, it had to be used before withdrawals
of water reduced its chances of working. Putting the operation on
hold until the next moon period (11–24 June) would render twenty
Lancasters unavailable for anything else in the meantime. Bottomley
put further arguments: Bomber Command's assistance in the formation of 618 Squadron had cost the equivalent of a new squadron,
while the 24-hour working, seven days a week, needed to produce
the first thirty Mosquitoes had eroded Warwick production. Then
came a knockdown point. Stripped Upkeep no longer looked like
Highball, so from the enemy's perspective, no association between
the two was likely to be suspected.

The upshot, endorsed by the ad hoc committee two days later, authorised by Portal, was that Servant would be paused while Chastise
went ahead. Having pulled back Servant's bowstring since March,
the Chiefs of Staff now let it go slack. This was inevitable as well as
logical. Many more months would pass before Highball was ready.

Drawing the bow: Chastise

Operation Chastise is probably the most written-about action in
the history of aerial warfare, yet basic questions about it remain
unanswered. Most obviously, why was there not a greater effort to
break the Sorpe? By early April it was clear to the raid's planners
that the best chance of inflicting significant damage on Germany's
war economy was to break the Möhne and Sorpe together, yet the
raid appears to have been planned in a way to favour the chances
of breaking the Möhne and the Eder. Gibson said that 'the Sorpe

was not a priority target' and that it did not contribute much to the Ruhr catchment.[50] A narrative has taken hold that this was because the Eder was structurally susceptible to Wallis's weapon whereas the Sorpe was not. Was this so, and to what extent was Wallis an influence on tactical planning?

We have seen that the Air Ministry had been eyeing Ruhr dams, and particularly the Möhne, at least since 1937. The MAP's model experiments in 1941–42 had focused on the Möhne, because Wallis and the Air Ministry believed that its loss would impair industry and electrical generating capacity. In his 'Air Attack on Dams' paper at the turn of 1943 Wallis had argued that these effects would be intensified if one or more of the other four principal dams in the Ruhr catchment (the Sorpe, Lister, Ennepe, Henne) could be broken at the same time, but did not single one out.

In the same paper Wallis said that the Eder and Diemel dams across the watershed in the Weser catchment were also of 'great importance' and that their combined destruction would 'probably' bring about 'an almost immediate cessation of traffic' on the Mittelland Canal and River Weser. In a subtle way Wallis thereby put two target systems in competition. This blurring of priorities carried through into February, when the group convened under Bufton to advise on the tactical feasibility of an attack on the Möhne heard from Wallis that the Eder was 'a most important target' and was impressed by his suggestion of an attack on both.[51]

Bottomley asked DB Ops for an appraisal of all potential Upkeep and Highball targets. Bufton provided it on 13 March and repeated the claim that the Möhne and Eder were Germany's most important dams. Bufton advised that other potential targets were either out of range or of lesser importance, and that initial planning for Upkeep should be confined to these two, in that order.

Two days later, the Ministry of Economic Warfare (MEW) issued a memorandum which drew a different picture.[52] The Ministry agreed that the Möhne was a high-value target and that the physical, moral, and longer-term economic consequences of its loss would be serious.[53] However, it made a new and critical point. The Eder had no connection with the Ruhr. The river lay in another catchment, and no significant industrial complex would suffer if it was destroyed. The Möhne and the Sorpe, on the other hand, jointly provided 75 per cent of the Ruhr's storage capacity. Breaching the Sorpe and the Möhne together would produce 'a paralysing effect' on industrial activity.

The MEW advice put the ad hoc committee and Cochrane in a quandary. By mid-March their inclination was to rule out an attack on the Sorpe for tactical and technical reasons.[54] On the tactical side, splitting a force of twenty crews into three ran the risk of comprehensive failure, for in each case allowance had to be made for attrition and poor runs. The technical objection stemmed from the structure of the Sorpe itself. Whereas the fabric of the Möhne and Eder was masonry, which would be vulnerable to the pressure pulse produced by Upkeep, the Sorpe was an embankment of earth and rubble with a watertight concrete blade at its core, which would not.

On 23 March Portal circulated a memorandum to the Chiefs of Staff about the economic consequences that could be expected from an attack on the Möhne and Eder. Portal's paper drew from the MEW memo which pointed to the Möhne and Sorpe as the better combination and ranked the Eder as of secondary importance. Portal afterwards asked Bottomley to obtain confirmation for this advice. Bottomley contacted the author, Geoffrey Vickers,[55] who warned him that the guidance had been drawn up in the absence of Oliver Lawrence, the Ministry's expert, to whom he would now refer the question.

Lawrence's opinion arrived on 2 April. It qualified what the MEW had said earlier, and contradicted Wallis's repeated claim that destruction of the Möhne would be a mortal blow. Industry in the Ruhr relied mainly upon water drawn from underground aquifers, augmented by recovered colliery water and water taken from flowing sources. The Möhne's main purpose was to sustain these supplies by storing surplus winter rainfall. This meant that the economic effects of breaching it would not necessarily be large or felt immediately. However, the Möhne was part of a distributed system of reservoirs which could be balanced by cross-feeding water between them. A key in doing so was the Sorpe, a 'carry-over' reservoir with capacity to store more water than would naturally enter it from direct rainfall in an average year. The Sorpe reservoir took water from beyond its own catchment via a scheme of channels and was thus available to replenish other reservoirs and raise the level of the Ruhr to ensure continuity of supply when dams elsewhere in the system were low, or at times of drought. Lawrence advised that the destruction of both the Möhne and the Sorpe 'would be worth much more than twice the destruction of one'. 'It is most strongly urged' he said, 'if the operational possibilities hold out any reasonable prospect of success that an attack on the Möhne be accompanied, or followed as soon as possible, by an attack on the Sorpe Dam.' On 5 April Bottomley passed this advice to Portal, urging a simultaneous attack on the Möhne and Sorpe (a target model for which was requested the day before), with a further attack on the Eder 'if circumstances allow'.

All the signs are that discussion about attacking the Sorpe had been going on for some time. Early in March Wallis had said that one correctly placed mine would be sufficient to break any of the Möhne, Sorpe or Eder. More recently he had told Bufton that if the crest of the Sorpe could be shattered to produce leakage, ensuing erosion ought to do the rest.[56] In the light of this, Cochrane had been thinking about a plan of attack to damage the Eder and Sorpe as well as the Möhne, and advised that this might be possible 'if not simultaneously at least within a day or two'.[57]

Cochrane's plan is first glimpsed in the minutes of a meeting chaired by Bottomley at the Air Ministry on 5 May.[58] Also present were Saundby (HQBC), Bufton (DB Ops), Glanville (RRL), Cochrane and Wallis. Towards the end of the meeting Cochrane briefly outlined the plan of attack which was being worked up at 5 Group in consultation with Gibson. The primary objective was the Möhne (now designated as Target X). He proposed local VHF R/T control in the target area so that if success was achieved, crews could proceed to the Eder (Target Y). In parallel, he proposed to detail about four crews who did not meet the highest standards of accuracy in training to attack Z (the Sorpe). They would use a revised and simpler method of attack in which Upkeep would be dropped unspun while flying alongside the dam wall. Success at the Sorpe would not be immediately apparent as it would result from seepage leading to progressive washing out of cracks, which might not become evident for several days.

The simplified method of attack appears to have emerged during the meeting between Wallis, Gibson, Summers, Longbottom and Renouf, on the afternoon of 24 April. After discussing release height, the talk turned to dam structure, and to the method of attack on the Sorpe.[59] The water side of the Sorpe consisted of a gravel/rubble ramp, so there was no masonry wall against which a spinning mine could cling as it sank, nor indeed any structure which would be put into lethal tension when it went off. Rather, by dropping a succession of mines next to the crest, it was hoped that Upkeep would crack the concrete blade at the dam's core, and thereby start leakage.

The first surviving draft of the operation order was produced on 10 May. It described a force divided into three waves, of nine, six and five aircraft, respectively, to attack the Möhne, Eder and Sorpe, in that order of priority. The Eder appeared to precede the Sorpe because it was intended that the first wave would attack the Möhne and in the event of success proceed to the Eder. Since both dams called for attack using spun Upkeep, and since the Möhne was the overall priority, it followed that crews which had shown greatest overall promise (in navigation and signals as well as bombing) would be selected. Its larger size (nine crews) allowed for attrition and poor runs.

The second wave of six crews would attack the Sorpe while the Möhne attack was in progress – a tactic which it was hoped would help to divide fighter defences. A third wave of five crews would be a mobile reserve, available for direction to any of the targets to make up for earlier losses, or to attack other dams in the event of success at the primaries.

This sophisticated plan was honed in following days. Within it, however, we can see signs of drift away from the crux. Most obviously, if Wallis told Cochrane and Satterly that five or six Upkeeps should be allowed for fissuring the Sorpe, then a wave of six, reduced to five by the time of the raid, left no room for losses or aiming error.

Behind that were the decisions taken back in March to cut the force from two squadrons to one, and the order for Upkeep Lancasters from thirty to twenty.

More subtly, while there was commitment to the Sorpe when Operation Chastise was viewed by senior commanders from above, the hope that concurrent attacks on the Sorpe and Möhne would confuse defences became transmuted to an idea that the Sorpe was a diversion when it was viewed from below.[60] In one way, of course, this was true: the Möhne was more important than the Sorpe. The misapprehension stemmed rather from a failure to convey the idea that the Sorpe and Möhne formed a target set to which the Eder was an outlier. This impression may have been reinforced by differences between the ways in which the dams were to be attacked. Whereas the first wave was to be led by a controller using VHF radio, the Sorpe would be visited by a succession of crews acting on their own initiative. The reason for this is not recorded, but several factors can be suggested: candidates for a second wave controller already held roles as back-up controllers for the first wave, and since the Sorpe would not fail immediately there was no rationale to redirect crews from it to other targets.

A sense that the Sorpe was in some way secondary or different was further reflected in a tactical exercise flown on the evening of 14 May, when the three waves were dispatched to proxy targets in England, along surrogate routes, to test navigation and co-ordination by codes and radio telephony. First wave aircraft were sent to Eyebrook reservoir in Rutland, thence to Abberton in Essex. The Derwent reservoir in Derbyshire was the proxy for the Sorpe, and remaining crews (seemingly the mobile reserve) were directed to Wainfleet and the Wash.

By 14 May Wallis had become rattled about the Sorpe. Writing to Bufton, he proposed a change of plan. He enclosed a drawing of the dam's structure with a note predicting that the detonation of well-placed Upkeeps would budge the concrete core sideways by around 16 to 20 inches – enough, he thought, to crack it. However, the core was held in equilibrium by the banks of rubble and gravel that sloped to either side. If some of that mass on the air side could be removed, then the equipoise would be disturbed, and the effects of the mines would be intensified. To achieve this, said Wallis, a main force attack to crater the air side bank with 8000 lb bombs shortly before 617's arrival would be of 'real use in helping to ensure success on target Z'.[61]

We do not know how Bufton reacted. By the time he had read the letter and taken stock, Operation Chastise had taken place.[62]

The send-off

Saturday, 15 May dawned calm and warm. The Air Ministry signal to proceed with Operation Chastise, timed at 09.00, was sent to HQ Bomber Command, whence it was teletyped to No. 5 Group's headquarters in Grantham, where Satterly finalised the operation order.[63] At 10.00 he passed it to Wally Dunn, whose task was to devise the signals plan. This was an elaborate document, with a list of codewords for different eventualities, protocols for transfer of control in the event of Gibson's loss, back-up arrangements if VHF R/T should fail or be jammed, an alphanumeric code to denote the position and result of each explosion, and codes for diversion to alternative targets or targets of last resort.

❧ ❧

Wallis had been ready to travel for several days. The plan was for Summers to fly him up to Scampton in company with Hew Kilner, who would represent the Vickers board. When the call came, he bade farewell to Molly and drove to Brooklands. As he left, he warned that once he reached Scampton she would not hear from him until it was over: for security reasons the airfield would be closed, with no personal communication in or out. It was a strange moment. Molly had known about the project from the first, followed the ebb and flow of its proceedings and troubles, and watched his panic when he realised that a mere ten weeks were available in which to produce and trial the weapon, build the aircraft to carry it, and train the crews. Since then, she had talked of moments when he had confided he had 'cold feet'. Yet after three years, the day had come.

They flew in a new Wellington, which touched down at Scampton at about four o'clock in the afternoon. It was hot, and as Summers taxied in through the shimmering heat Wallis could see the strangely starved outlines of Upkeep Lancasters at their dispersals around the airfield edge. Whitworth and Gibson brought them up to date with the state of preparations. Gibson then left for a meeting with Satterly, while Wallis toured the squadron's aircraft to inspect their release gear and stores.

Gibson returned early in the evening, when the squadron's two flight commanders (Young and Maudslay), the deputy raid leader (Hopgood) and 617's bombing leader (Hay) gathered in Whitworth's house for an informal briefing about the raid's objectives and a review of its tactics. Wallis explained the reasons for attacking dams and the way Upkeep's pressure pulse could break them. After supper, they reconvened to hear details of the Operation Order and its plan to get 617 Squadron's aircraft to and from their targets. The outward journey was to be at low level, to minimise opportunity for radar detection, and along two widely separated routes, with points of entry across the Scheldt estuary and via the island of Vlieland and the Ijsslemeer.[64] The split routes came together about 85 track miles from the target, with a short final leg on a new heading, the aim being to keep the enemy guessing for as long as possible about where they were going. The separated routes were also designed to pose dilemmas for German fighter controllers, and to conserve one part of the force should the other run into trouble. Aircraft would travel the routes at intervals. The Sorpe wave would be first off, its members flying individually. The Möhne wave would follow a few minutes later; its three successive formations of three would enable those ahead to warn others following if defences were met. Exit routes were planned to differ, as far as possible, from those of entry.

The meeting broke up late. As they rose to leave Whitworth brought news from the station's guardroom: Gibson's dog had been hit by a passing car and killed. Back in his room, Gibson found himself staring at scratch marks on the door, 'feeling very depressed'.[65]

Wallis turned in at half past midnight. When he came to note the day's events in his diary, the death of Gibson's dog was the last of them – his only known reference to an animal since he had put Tinker into the hands of the Fishers on the day of his mother's death.

Wallis rose next morning in the knowledge that he was unlikely to get any sleep for the next thirty-six hours. He thus rested until midday when he joined Gibson to brief all the pilots and navigators. In parallel, Wg Cdr Dunn arrived from Grantham to rehearse the wireless operators in W/T procedure. Later, the pilots and navigators were joined by the bomb aimers, to study models of the Sorpe and Möhne,[66] and to examine details of the route. The bomb aimer's position in the Lancaster's glazed nose made him the principal map-reader who gave a continuous commentary on recognisable features and pinpoints to the navigator, and warned the pilot of upcoming obstacles, like power lines.

The attempt to repair Maudslay's Lancaster in time for the raid, meanwhile, had failed, and two crews had dropped out because of illness. Nineteen aircraft were available for the nineteen crews who would be taking part,[67] but there was no reserve in the event of a last-minute malfunction. Only three other Upkeep-carrying Lancasters were in existence; two were at Manston, the third at Boscombe Down, and it was this machine that was called for and flown to Scampton during the afternoon. On arrival the ferry pilot was intrigued by the sight of other peculiarly shaped Lancasters parked around the airfield, and the stores 'about the size and shape of the front wheel of a steam roller' that hung from their bellies.[68]

No. 5 Group's Executive Order for Chastise was sent at 16.45.[69] Almost immediately, crews were called for the final briefing.[70] They assembled in a large room above the Sergeants' Mess. Service policemen stood at the door to deter interlopers. Wallis's colleague Jeffree had arrived during the afternoon, in company with Longbottom and Handasyde who had flown up from Manston. Chancing his arm, Jeffree presented his Manston pass and was admitted. Gibson was on his feet on a dais at the far end of the room, announcing their targets and then introducing Wallis. Wallis spoke for the best part of twenty minutes. For the third time in two days, he gave an account of Upkeep and its origins, the rationale for attacking dams, and the expected economic effects of doing so. The average age of his audience was twenty-one, although some were as young as eighteen and the oldest were in their early thirties. The listeners were struck by Wallis's lucidity, and by his assurance. Cochrane spoke next and was confident. He told the crews: 'I know this attack will succeed.'[71]

Gibson rehearsed the shape of the operation: the first wave (of nine) would attack the Möhne (X), Eder (Y) and Sorpe (Z), in that order; the Sorpe would be struck by the second wave (of five) at five-minute intervals while the attack on the Möhne was in progress. The third wave (again of five) would take off around midnight and be directed by W/T either to make good any shortfall in attacks on targets X, Y, Z, or, if all the primaries had been broken, to strike up to three further dams, the Lister, Ennepe and Diemel. Since the outward routes of the first two waves differed in track length, aircraft of the second wave would depart first to equalise times of arrival.

Nearly all of this had been said at the sectional briefings earlier in the day, but this time everyone heard it together; there was an element of theatre in the occasion, with Gibson and Wallis integrating the different aspects, formally announcing the targets to the gunners and flight engineers and explaining how individual roles would contribute to the whole.

When Gibson finished, Dunn stood up to remind crews of key points in the signals plan: its codewords for orders and eventualities; the code to indicate release, target, position of explosion and result; procedures for listening watch and use of frequencies. The wireless operators had a further role: it was they who controlled rotation of Upkeep during the attack. This involved starting the motor ten minutes before the attack, crouching beside the end of the navigator's table to manipulate a hydraulic valve and watch the rev counter, then standing in the last seconds, ready to fire a red Verey flare to signal release. During the climb-out the wireless operator could look aft from the astrodome to watch the explosion and look for its effect.

The underlying purpose of this final, plenary briefing was to foster commitment for the task ahead and give updates on variables such as the weather and timings. When it ended around 18.10 the mood was enthusiastic; crews congregated informally, for further discussion and checking of detail. Several talked to Wallis, who with his white hair and pink complexion was nicknamed 'Papa Wally'. Wallis confided to Gibson that after years of tests and trials, here at last was the final experiment. Looking around at the dispersing men, he added ingenuously that he hoped they would all come back.

A meal followed, at which no one else was taken in by the continuing pretence that No. 617 Squadron was about to embark on more training. The fitting of the mines, loading of live ammunition, closure of the station for security, and demeanour of the men all told otherwise.

After supper, there was about an hour which the aircrew had to themselves. This was always a difficult time. Some went to rest, or for a walk, or a wash; last letters were placed for others to find. Towards 20.00 crews in the first two waves went to change, turn out their pockets, collect parachutes, kit and flying rations. The evening was still warm. For a time, they waited on the grass outside the hangar. After six weeks of flat-out training it was clear that they were embarking on something unusual, and they knew that the standards of airmanship to achieve it would be exacting. The mood was different now, more subdued. Some were fatalistic. Others, relieved that they were not being sent to attack heavily defended targets, waited with equanimity. Yet more saw it simply as another job to take them a step closer to the day when they could get back to their own lives. Trucks and vans arrived to take them out to the aircraft. External and internal checks began. The men settled into their positions.

At 21.00 Gibson's wireless operator fired a red Verey light to signal aircraft to start their engines. Engine run-ups and magneto checks followed. During these the flight engineer in McCarthy's Lancaster diagnosed a malfunction which obliged them to shut down and transfer to the spare aircraft – the machine that had earlier been flown up from Boscombe Down. Preparation for any flight calls for calm and methodical focus; its enemy is fluster. The switch of machine was thus no small matter: mission-essential items such as prepared maps and code-lists had to be gathered, the back-up aircraft was a truck-ride away, and when they boarded, they found that its compass deviation card was missing. Since navigation would be impossible without it, a search ensued.

Meanwhile, the rest of the Wave 2 aircraft had begun to move. A slight breeze, barely enough to stir the windsock, blew from the north. The control caravan was accordingly positioned near the southern boundary of the flying field. Normally a knot of well-wishers would be gathered to wave them off, but the continuing pretence that this was another training exercise reduced this to a handful – among them, Wallis and his colleagues from Vickers, Cochrane, Whitworth, and members of the reserve crews who had another two hours to wait before their own departure.

By 21.25 aircraft of the Sorpe wave had taxied forward and stood waiting in a queue. McCarthy was still changing aircraft so the first of them was captained by Barlow, who turned his machine into the wind and paused, waiting for the duty officer to flash a green light. The signal came at 21.28. The Lancaster began to roll, gathering speed, its tail eventually rising. Jeffree was struck by the long run before the main wheels began to skim and the machine became airborne. One by one, three more Sorpe-bound aircraft took to the air during the next ten minutes. The well-wishers watched as they banked eastward. Their turns illustrated one of the perils that lay ahead: the wingspan of a Lancaster is 102 feet; if it is flying at a height of several hundred feet, then even a gentle turn brings the tip of the lower wing close to the ground; if trees or power lines are in the vicinity, even closer.

Gibson led the first threesome of the first wave off at 21.39. The second flight of three, led by Young, took to the air eight minutes later, followed by Maudslay's trio just before ten. McCarthy and his crew, long delayed but now provided with a compass deviation card, took off a minute or two later. Engine noise faded into the cloudless evening; well-wishers dispersed; a mist began to form; the Vickers civilian party headed for the bar.

Since February Wallis had been working up to ninety hours a week; in coming hours he had no decisions to take, no problems to solve, and nothing he said or did could affect what would follow. Since it was his relentless campaigning that had led to the diversion of a significant part of Britain's war effort, he was now left to reflect on what his position would be if the operation failed. Around 23:00 he and Cochrane bade farewell to Whitworth and walked out to Cochrane's car for the drive to 5 Group's headquarters. Even before they turned out of the main gate onto Ermine Street, the first Chastise aircraft had been shot down.[72]

In Lincolnshire and the Sauerland

No. 5 Group was headquartered in a Gothic revival mansion, St Vincent's House, on the outskirts of Grantham. St Vincent's had been built for a local iron master in the 1860s and was acquired by the government between the wars. It stood under the brow of a hill in wooded grounds, with stables, greenhouses, a coach house, terraced gardens, and specialised outbuildings since added by the Air Ministry. Among the latter was a low, flat-roofed, Crittall-windowed structure which stood atop 5 Group's underground operations room. A faint turquoise glow still coloured the northern sky as armed guards waved Cochrane's car through the main gate. As his driver pulled up alongside the operations room entrance, aircraft of the reserve wave were preparing to depart.[73]

Arriving in the Operations Room, Wallis took in the scene. WAAF and RAF members of the duty staff, Dunn, Satterly, and Harris were present. Dunn sat by a table on a dais that ran the length of one of the room's long sides. Facing him was a large board upon which details of the operation were chalked. A map of Europe covered the end wall. Dunn was in direct contact with the Chastise force via a telephone connected to the radio receiver – an arrangement that enabled him to take down and relay W/T messages as they came in. Indeed, as Wallis and Cochrane walked in, Dunn was rebroadcasting warning of a source of light flak that had just been received from Gibson.

Harris had been driven up from High Wycombe in his drop-head Bentley during the afternoon. He knew St Vincent's well. He had been AOC 5 Group in 1939–40, when Gibson was a junior officer with 83 Squadron, and he and Cochrane were at ease with each other. The duty staff proceeded with quiet efficiency, although from Harris's presence and Dunn's signals link, it was obvious that something rare was happening. The signals arrangement was unprecedented. Ordinarily (as Leonard Cheshire later put it) a bombing force was like an alarm clock, wound up and sent forth remotely, whereas on this evening the raid's planners and crews interacted minute by minute. The odd one out was Wallis, who had nothing to do. He felt sick.

Aircraft of the first threesome began to gather at the Möhne around a quarter past midnight. While they waited for the others, Gibson reconnoitred. In doing so he took care to give no clues to what would follow, but his inspection nonetheless stirred the defences. There were light flak positions on the two sluice towers, one gun on the northern part of the parapet, and three in a field between the compensating basin and the village of Günne, north-north-west of the dam. As the guns came into action, the water-reflected candescent arcs and trails of their shells gave a lurid sense of twice the amount of fire.

A little before half past midnight Gibson and his crew ran in and released their mine. Such was the turbulence following its explosion that at first Gibson believed they had succeeded; however, as the waves subsided, they could see that the dam was intact. After five minutes Gibson's wireless operator signalled GONER 68A. At Grantham, this gave the impression that Gibson's Upkeep had been accurately placed but that the Möhne dam still stood. This was not promising: Wallis's calculations and experiments had led him to believe that one accurately placed mine would do the job. The listeners at St Vincent's were not to know that Gibson's mine had arrived short and had not been in contact with the wall when it detonated.

Misgivings deepened during the next thirteen minutes, in which Hopgood's aircraft was shot down and sent no signal at all, while transposition of the signal times of the third and fourth aircraft in the attack sequence gave the impression that things were going badly wrong.[74] Wallis and the others at Grantham were unaware that when David Maltby ran in at 00:55, he could see that the crown of the dam was beginning to fail. Maltby's mine exploded in contact and the wall gave way. Wallis had been right: the first mine to strike the dam correctly would break it.

At 00.56 Dunn took down and announced the signal. Wallis's frame trembled in a series of involuntary twitches and spasms. Dunn made back to Hutchison for confirmation. A minute later it came again. Harris turned to Wallis and gripped his hand. After all that had passed, the years of argument, questions, caveats and bureaucracy, the burden of uncertainty was transformed into euphoria.

It was nearly 01.30 when the attack on the Eder began, and at Grantham forty minutes passed before they heard anything about it. The wait was partly due to the difficulty some crews had in finding it, and because of the extreme awkwardness of approach. Following a steep dive and tight turn, with Upkeep spinning, fewer than ten seconds were available in which a crew could settle to the correct height and speed before reaching the point of release. This led to many dummy runs. Shannon lost count of the trial approaches he made before Gibson ordered him to break off and sent in Maudslay, who released his mine on the third attempt – but did so late, so that it overshot. It was nearly twenty to two when Shannon eventually dropped his mine. Unaccountably, the signal saying he had done so did not reach 5 Group until 02:06. By then, Hutchison had already tapped out 'Dinghy', and the listeners at Grantham knew that the Eder, too, had been broken. Knight's Upkeep had struck the dam slightly to one side of its midpoint. Robert Kellow, Knight's wireless operator, was looking back from the astrodome as they climbed away and saw the moment: it was as if 'some huge fist had been jabbed at the wall'.[75]

If all had gone to plan, second wave aircraft would have attacked the Sorpe in parallel to the attack on the Möhne. But all did not go to plan: only one of them arrived. At 02:10, while Harris went off to telephone the news to Portal in Washington, there was an exchange between Dunn and Gibson to ascertain whether any aircraft from the first wave were available for redirection. Gibson replied 'None'. At 02:19, following discussion with Satterly and Cochrane, Dunn called up each of the reserve aircraft in turn. Only two replied.

Around half past two, and again at ten to three, Dunn variously broadcast DINGHY (Eder breached, proceed to Sorpe) and GILBERT (attack last resort target as detailed) to remaining aircraft. Brown's wireless operator signalled at 03:23 that AJ-F had attacked the Sorpe. Brown made at least six attempts to find the necessary line and height to do so.

We have seen that breaching the Möhne and Sorpe together was the key to Chastise. It is thus a question why what was left of the reserve was partly dissipated in the last stages of the operation. Wallis had reckoned that five or six Upkeeps would be needed to inflict enough damage to start seepage that could turn to a flood and thereby compel the Germans to lower the level of the reservoir. In doing so, he seems to have assumed that each crew making a lengthwise attack along the dam would be able to put its weapon in the same place. This was a tall order, not least because the Sorpe crews had no sighting device with which to estimate the midpoint on the dam. Nonetheless, Cochrane had taken his advice and allocated five aircraft, although he must have realised there was little chance that all of them would arrive, let alone make identical attacks. Five was probably the most he felt he could afford if there was to be a travelling reserve to replace losses in the first wave, or if Wallis's computations about gravity dams turned out to be wrong. If each gravity dam had been broken by only one or two mines then in theory there would have been extra Upkeep-carrying aircraft that could have been redirected to the Sorpe;[76] but there is no reference to this possibility in the operation order. In any case, as we have just seen, Cochrane's picture of what was happening was incomplete, and his ability to make best use of the reserve was accordingly reduced. The mobile reserve suffered high attrition, and by the time instructions were sent to its aircraft some of those that should have been diverted to the Sorpe were no longer in the air. When this was realised, an adjustment was made (Ottley being re-diverted to the Sorpe) but moments after acknowledging this he too was brought down. Cochrane perhaps believed that both Ottley and Brown would reach the Sorpe and thus allocated the remainder of the reserve wave to the last resort targets.

About four o'clock, Harris, Cochrane and Wallis climbed out of the operations room into the cool darkness. Harris's car was parked nearby, its door held open by his chauffeur, Maddox. Cochrane and Wallis slid into the back seat; Harris settled in the front. As they left for Scampton, Dunn received a signal from AJ-O reporting a completed attack on what Townsend believed to be the Ennepe.

In the Bentley speeding north Harris was happy to have lost the bet with himself that the raid would be a complete waste of effort; Wallis had been released from the racking anxiety with which he lived for twelve weeks; Cochrane was thoughtful: the pattern of signals told of casualties.

When they reached Scampton it was light enough to see several Upkeep aircraft parked out towards the airfield edge. In fact, by this time eight were back, and as the Grantham party made its way to find Charles Whitworth, they could hear two more in the circuit. But that was barely half of those that had set out. In the operations room staff looked at the large wall blackboard on which details of each sortie were chalked. There were gaps in the column headed 'Time landed'. For a time, Wallis, Cochrane, and Harris stood on the edge of the airfield. While out of others' earshot, Harris turned to Wallis and said: 'A "K" for you.'[77]

Over the next hour members of several crews went out onto the grass beside No. 2 hangar. In the cloudless dawn they looked towards the Wolds, willing more to come. Soon after six, the sound of an eleventh aircraft was heard. O-Orange, captained by Bill Townsend, had come home on three engines. Clocks ticked down to the moment at which any absent aircraft would have run out of fuel. The only hope now was that one or two crews might have ditched or 'landed out'.

Debriefing was in the room where just half a day before members of nineteen crews had listened to Wallis explaining how Upkeep worked. They now sat at tables, provided with cigarettes and mugs of strong tea, being interviewed by intelligence officers who took them through the usual list of questions about routing and aircraft seen shot down, together with a Chastise-specific questionnaire that covered the use of daylight tracer, the merits of VHF radio, the number of runs, mine rotation and placing. Wallis probed several crews about the positions in which their weapons had been seen to explode; a rule of thumb was the shape of the wave: an exact semicircle would indicate detonation in contact, whereas anything closer to a circle would point to a mine that had exploded short. Wallis was still asking himself whether the dams had been broken by single mines or through cumulative effect.

Details emerged. Rice had misjudged his height over the Ijsselmeer and actually flown onto it; remarkably, he had regained the air but lost his mine. Routing had made hectic demands upon the navigators, whose work had been disrupted by the suddenness of opposition; the need to take in and confirm rapid successions of observations from the bomb aimer and pilot; to check and reset the air position indicators during short legs between frequent turns. Some of the outbound threesomes had become separated or strayed from the briefed route, which meant a climb to higher altitude to take bearings, which in turn exposed them to light flak. At the Möhne, Gibson and Martin had attempted to draw the defenders' fire by offering their aircraft as decoys. Gibson thought that the Möhne had been broken in two places, the two merging into a larger opening. The hilly terrain around the Eder had called for a rare standard of flying.

As interviews proceeded and details were combined a story took shape in which triumph, confusion and tragedy were entwined. Triumph lay in the airmanship and tenacity of the attacking crews, Gibson's leadership, and the fact that Upkeep had worked. Confusion attended the order of events, and in some respects what the events were. Tragedy was the cost. Two crews had returned early because of mishap; five had been lost to accidents or groundfire on the way to their targets. Of the remainder, eleven had attacked, while the twelfth never found their target. One of the attacking aircraft had been lost at the Möhne; three more had been shot down while homeward bound. In several cases no one knew what had happened. Of the 133 men whom Wallis had looked in the eye just hours before, only 77 were back. Weeks would pass before they would know that all but three of the 56 missing were dead.

Just before half past seven a photoreconnaissance Spitfire flown by Fg Off. Frank Fray took off from RAF Benson in Oxfordshire. As Fray crossed the Dutch coast, he could see industrial haze over the Ruhr; beyond, over 150 miles away, was what looked like a strange kind of cloud. As Fray drew closer, he realised that the 'cloud' was sunlight mirrored from miles of floodwater.[78] Fray was back at Benson by 11:00. His films were whisked off for processing and study by the Central Interpretation Unit at Medmenham. By early afternoon Harris was looking at prints which showed that the Eder-see had spilled down the valley for 25 miles and that floods below the Möhne had spread twice that far. More reconnaissance sorties were flown through the day; it was as if the Allies could not believe their eyes.[79] Air Marshal Douglas Evill, Vice-Chief of the Air Staff, sent a personal message to Portal in Washington confirming the breaching of the Möhne and Eder and damage to the Sorpe. Evill reported that Gibson had seen the Möhne broken in two places, the length of the two breaches together being 'conservatively estimated' at 30 yards. Conservative indeed: the interpreters at Medmenham measured it as over twice as long.

The Air Ministry released a brief communique at lunchtime which told of three dams struck, two broken, and attacks pressed home in the face of fierce resistance.[80] A longer bulletin was issued later in the day. By early evening final city editions of newspapers began to give details. At six o'clock, and again at nine, the raid was reported on the BBC news. The press releases followed a pre-agreed formulation which described the weapon as 'a mine of great size' and explained the success as a result of great skill on the part of experienced and rigorously trained crews.

At Scampton, Wallis talked with crew members until mid-morning, whereupon Whitworth took him to his house and suggested that he rest. But his mind was a-whirl; thirty-six hours before he had been in the same house finalising plans with Mauds-lay, Young, Hopgood, Hay and Gibson. Now, three of the five were among the missing, and the price of his vindication had been their loss. His great experiment had killed both of 617 Squadron's flight commanders and the raid's deputy leader. Amid the celebrations, a

WAAF officer found him standing, wrapped in Whitworth's dressing gown, tears in his eyes.

In early afternoon Summers gathered Kilner and Wallis for their return. They flew first to Castle Bromwich, where Kilner had company business, then on to London for Wallis to make a report to DB Ops, where the day before, Bufton and Evill had discussed the need for measures to protect the security of Highball and Operation Servant. These included a ban on press contact with 5 Group or aircrew of 617 Squadron and close Air Ministry supervision of press release wording. Notes about this were sent to Harris, the Air Staff and the Ministry of Information. Their plan overlooked Molly. While Wallis moved on to Weybridge for yet another debriefing, she began a letter to Mary. 'Did you hear the news this evening? That was Barnes. What he's been working on all this long weary time . . . He has a brain like no other.'[81] Around half past eleven an official from the Air Ministry's Directorate of Security telephoned to warn the family not to mention Barnes's name in connection with the raid. This notwithstanding, next morning Molly continued:

> Poor B. didn't get home till 5 to 12 last night, only 3 hours sleep Saturday, didn't take his clothes off Sunday, & was awake till 2.30 this morning telling me all about it. And then, poor dear darling Barnes, he woke at 6 feeling absolutely awful because he'd killed so many people.[82]

It was the lost aircrew whom Wallis mourned. The dead in Germany were not yet counted. The *Möhnekatastrophe* took their identities as well as their lives: some of those swept from their beds and cradles were so bruised and battered that no one could tell who they were.

Aftermaths

Wallis struggled in to work next morning to take decisions about Highball and the Windsor. It was not easy to concentrate. The raid was front-page news. Congratulations poured in.

Roy Chadwick was quick off the mark. Someone had rung him from Scampton early on the Sunday; he responded with a telegram offering 'one thousand congratulations on your wonderful work and its marvellous success'.[83] Harris telegraphed from HQ Bomber Command to salute Wallis's 'skill and persistence', and to concede his own initial scepticism by adding 'often in the face of discouragement and disappointments'.[84] From Mary at school came a telegram: 'Hooray wonderful Daddy'.[85]

In following days, Ben Lockspeiser wrote of a 'magnificent personal achievement'.[86] Thomas Merton said that it was 'one of the major technical achievements of the war'.[87] Alex Dunbar wrote from the MAP: 'What a conception! What an achievement!! What a man!!!'[88] Linnell sent heartiest congratulations. Trevor Westbrook thought his old colleague had hit 'the bloody Germans' harder than any other one man.[89] Gibson confessed that he was 'not much of a letter writer' but 'the weapon you gave us worked like dream and you have earned the thanks of the civilised world.'[90] Stafford Cripps sent a handwritten note (in red ink) to express the Government's thanks and the appreciation of the War Cabinet for Wallis's 'contribution to victory'.[91] And Tizard told him:

> Taking it all in all, from the first brilliant idea, through the model experiments and the full scale trials, remembering also that when the sceptics were finally convinced you had to work at the highest pressure to get things done in time, I have no hesitation in saying that yours is the finest individual technical achievement of the war.[92]

Wallis's secretary kept a list of those who wrote. Cherwell was not on it.

Roy Chadwick held off from writing for some days because he had been 'waiting anxiously' for news of 'some official recognition' and had been 'very disappointed not to have heard of some reward for you'. He thought it 'incredible that your name has not been mentioned in connection with the Dam bursting exploit' and surmised that this might be to do with security, 'or perhaps they think the

Gestapo might abduct you'. Chadwick wrote generously about the example of engineers working together: it had been 'a great pleasure for me to have helped you in some small measure'.[93]

The Dams Raid led the news for days. Like the flood itself, the story kept finding new channels along which to run. Churchill spoke of it to the US Congress where it took on a symbolic Allied dimension. 617 Squadron's aircrew had been drawn from all over the UK and much of the Commonwealth, so there were local, regional and Dominion angles a-plenty. In the trade, *The Aeroplane* said that it had 'set a minor crown on the British habit of choosing difficult things in life and making them look easy.'[94]

Insights into what the public felt can be found in the confidential weekly home intelligence report that was compiled for the Ministry of Information. Three days after the raid:

> Preliminary reactions to the bombing of the three dams serving the Ruhr-Westphalia industrial region, have been received from nine Regions. This 'brilliant and daring achievement' has aroused feelings which vary from 'jubilation' to 'grim approval' – in some cases not untinged with feelings of horror at the terrible consequences to civilians: 'I wonder what it would be like to be wakened at midnight by an avalanche of water.' Many people, however, are said to feel little sympathy for the civilian victims – 'they asked for it, now they've got it.' Great praise is expressed for the R.A.F., and some for the Jewish refugee who was thought to have given the necessary information.[95] It is hoped, however, that the announcement that he was Jewish will not provoke a savage antisemitic outburst in Germany.
>
> There is already some speculation, and a little apprehension, as to 'what the Germans can do here in return', though 'well informed' people do not believe that any of the dams in this country 'could be hit with comparable effect'.[96]

In fact, 'well-informed' people were very concerned indeed about the possibility of a like-for-like reprisal. Immediately after the raid steps were taken to identify reservoirs that could be vulnerable, and in following months Wallis was involved in a series of discussions about measures to protect nineteen dams that were found to be so.[97]

The next weekly Home Intelligence report found that the raid had been 'widely acclaimed . . . the finest thing the R.A.F. have done yet', and that 'even in the rural areas of Somerset, where news usually travels slowly, the great event was discussed by farm labourers on their way home from work'. While news of the raid was greeted with elation and excitement, some 'uneasiness and dismay are said to have set in' later, particularly after the press reports of very heavy civilian casualties. While 'a very small minority' suggested that 'this reduces us to the level of the Nazis', public approval was 'considerably stronger than doubt.'[98]

In Germany, the raid posed large dilemmas. Authoritarian governments normally react to calamity by seeking either to downplay or conceal it. In this case neither was possible, since thousands could see it for themselves, and used Germany's excellent telephone and postal systems to tell anxious friends and relatives about what they saw. Such descriptions could not be squared with German radio's reports that a small force of aircraft dropping 'small numbers of high explosives in several places' had simply 'damaged' two dams. While conceding that the 'onrush of water' had caused many civilian casualties, the propaganda ministry's attempt to minimise the episode did not correspond with the experience of ordinary people, or with leaflets bearing photographs of the breached dams that were dropped by the Allies. Moreover, while its statement that the attacking force had been small was true, it was not reassuring, for if just a few aircraft could cause such mayhem, of what else might the RAF be capable? Efforts within the *Reichsministerium für Volksaufklärung und Propaganda* to blame Jewry for initiating the bombing backfired when party officials realised that, since the raid had been a clear tactical success, it was irrational to explain Germany's inability to retaliate by a failure to call upon Jewish originality. Within forty-eight hours it was widely rumoured inside Germany that 30,000 had perished. The authorities tried to counter the rumour by publishing figures of their own. On 19 May, the German News Agency reported 711 victims of the *Möhnekatastrophe*. Of these, 370 were German and

341 were prisoners of war. A subsequent district-by-district survey gave the combined total death toll as 1348, while several weeks later the administrative division Gau Westfalen-Süd told the press that 1579 had perished, of whom 1020 had been forced labourers and prisoners of war. Another 70 lives had been taken by the waters of the Eder, it claimed.

Back in Weybridge, Wallis wrote in thanks to those who had helped: to Rex Pierson and his staff; to Whitworth, Cochrane and Gibson; and to Chadwick. 'To you personally, in a special degree,' he told Chadwick, 'was given the making or breaking of this enterprise, for if, at that fateful meeting in CRD's office . . . had you declared the task incapable of fulfilment in the given time, the powers of opposition were so great that I should never have got instructions to go ahead.'[99] Wallis hoped that the future would hold for them 'another terrific adventure in which we may join'.[100] His letters to Cochrane and Gibson re-emphasised contrition. Any feeling of success had been almost 'completely blotted out by the sense of loss of those wonderful young lives'.[101] He told Gibson that the casualties had left him 'heartbroken'.[102]

Molly was beside herself, at one moment telling Mary Morris and her own sisters that the whole subject was top secret and at the next saying yet more about it. Some of her letters contained embellishments. 'Weren't the RAF boys that went out simply wonderful, specially Gibson. But B. told him just what to do; he's been down with them lecturing & discussing & suggesting & helping for ages past.'[103] Despite the Air Ministry's request for absolute silence, Molly sent cards announcing the success to young Barnes and Mary, whose telegram was followed by a letter: 'My darling Daddy, Hooray, hooray, hooray!!!!! Wonderful marbles. Up the marbles. Cheers cheers cheers. Oh, *well done* Daddy.' Her friends thought her 'a bit potty because I'm so pleased but won't say why. I'm afraid they'll have to be curious for a bit longer. When will it be public property, or don't you know?'[104] Quite a few people were asking this. Molly herself harboured a simmering resentment over the lack of public recognition. Immediately after the raid she told Mary Morris, apparently through clenched teeth:

B's name is not to be connected with these dams. I can't really think why unless it's in case the Nazis find out and Effingham gets a bomb, or somebody tries to scrag B. The Air Ministry rang me up late last night after I'd written, & told me that quite seriously, tho' I can hardly credit it. And they rang B. up today & said the Press had his name, & they were simply furious. Maybe it's because the A.M. wants to take all the credit now it's worked. Never mind, don't mention him.[105]

Like a candle that will not blow out, she kept returning to the theme of credit denied:

Sir Arthur Harris in the papers. Gosh. It took months for B. . . . to persuade him to try this scheme. But it'll be Sir A.H.'s invention now, and he'll be made a baron. You see. Never mind, maybe he'll get the bomb.

We recall that Wallis's first talk with Harris took place only three days before he was told of the decision to proceed, and that the decision had not been Harris's to take. But in Molly's eyes, Harris had come to stand for all the sceptics. Wallis explained to her that his own name was being withheld on grounds of security, most notably because of continuing work on Highball, but her fury was unassuaged.[106] It stemmed from a line of reasoning in which 'men of vested and selfish interests' driven by 'petty jealousy' were out to smother her husband's achievements and steal his ideas.[107] Molly believed that their desire to live off Barnes's gifts would only be stopped if he was publicly acknowledged as inventor of the weapon that had broken the dams. This explains the hope for a knighthood, for such an honour would be proof of his genius, and such proof would release him from the grip of parasites.

George VI's birthday honours list was due a fortnight after the raid and following Harris's hint at Scampton it looks as though Wallis imagined that his name would be on it. Five days after the raid a letter from 10 Downing Street did indeed arrive. Wallis was in Scotland for trials of Highball, but when he read it on return he found that he was being invited to accept a CBE, not a knighthood. Much has since been made of this. Morpurgo said that Harris was out of his depth politically ('a mere child among jealous adults') and that his recommendation for a knighthood had been vetoed by opponents who included Stafford Cripps, directors of Vickers (notably Sir Charles Craven, who in this week was described by Molly as a 'vile snob'), and timid senior civil servants.[108]

The reality was simpler: Wallis, Rex Pierson and several others had already been singled out as recipients of the CBE for their work on aircraft design, and Harris's recommendation had not yet been made.[109] The idea that the CBE was in consolation for a knighthood denied was nonetheless how things were seen at White Hill House.

Is this why Wallis did not make immediate reply? On return from Scotland he had his hands full with Highball and the B.3/42, and on Wednesday afternoon he took the train up to Grantham in readiness for a royal visit to meet 617 Squadron's crews next day.[110] Back home on Thursday evening he reported on the royal visit (when over lunch he explained to the queen how to cut cheese to minimise the size of the cut face and so maintain its freshness) and discussed the knighthood denied with Molly. 'Darling Barnes said to me in the middle of the night: "It's because I wanted *you*, who have helped so long and faithfully, to have summat, that I am so disappointed."'[111] Wallis sent his written acceptance of the CBE on Saturday, 29 May – the last moment possible.[112]

Feelings ran high in family circles. When Molly's brother-in-law Henry opened *The Times* on 2 June, he noticed that co-recipients of the CBE included an air raid precautions controller from Leicester and a Civil Assistant at the War Office.[113] Such achievements seemed modest alongside wreaking havoc in Germany. Betty and Nancy commiserated over the presence of Barnes's name 'in a list of nonentities'. Damning him with faint praise put the cap on 'the cruelty and bestial ingratitude' of 'this greatest injustice, this blot, this disgrace to England'. He should leave Vickers as soon as he could. 'We can't quite see, as a matter of fact, why he hasn't left before.' Surely, Craven would not be able to dog Barnes if he was no longer his employer? 'Any lesser man would simply leave England to the mercy of Hitler, and go to America . . .'[114] Nancy and Betty were indignant: 'The Craven creature ought to be exposed.'

The view of Craven and the Vickers board as a brake on Wallis's creativity was given perspective by Trevor Westbrook, who reminisced about the arguments they had had back in the mid-1930s:

> You must give old Rob[ert McLean] a little of the credit because if he had not stood by you, the regime would have ousted you, but no doubt they have by now changed as they will get some reflected glory. I kid myself that in a very very small way I helped because if we had not stuck to the geodetic[s] all would have been lost and I don't think you would have got the facilities elsewhere.[115]

In other words, no Wellington, no Upkeep.

The motif of Wallis-as-victim has recurred, and it has been a question what we should make of it. Did it stem primarily from Wallis's personal view of events and those around him, or from the fervency with which Molly reacted to them? On this occasion, comments from a relative clearly point to Wallis.[116] He had not forgiven Craven for his attempt to curtail work on Upkeep back in February.

Locally, and in Molly's eyes, at least, the wrong was eventually righted. On 23 June, Vickers held a celebratory dinner in thanks to their staff who had made Upkeep possible. The dinner was held at the Oatlands Park Hotel in Weybridge. It has gone largely unnoticed by historians, whose writings have dwelled on events the previous day, when the investiture at Buckingham Palace was followed by a dinner for squadron members and leading design staff given by A. V. Roe at the Hungaria Restaurant in Lower Regent Street. At Oatlands Park, unlike the Hungaria, wives were invited.

> I must tell you about the lovely dinner Barnes and I went to last Wednesday given by the directors of Vickers in honour of Barnes and Wing Commander Gibson VC. I sat on Gibbie's right hand – the best place. He is a dear. About 25, very short, but healthy and brown, not good-looking. Has a tremendous

admiration for Barnes, or Papa Wally as the Squadron now calls him. Is very incensed because Barnes has not been given a knighthood. I told him I didn't mind because of Molly Wallis on the telephone; so he said I ought to say Lady Molly; and he called me that for the rest of the evening. And I said I couldn't say Wing Commander Gibson every time, so we compromised with Gibbie. He is so sweet because he insists that it is really Papa Wally who deserves the credit. As we were saying goodbye he wrote on Barnes's collar: 'To Dambuster Wallis from Guy Gibson.' '*Now* they'll know who did it' said he, dear little man.'

There it was: credit withheld, justice then done, all verified and proclaimed before Vickers's directors by the RAF's most decorated airman. More than that:

Barnes said I looked the best there, and I believe I did! – different anyway. These comic women – they are all turned out as if from a mould – or at least their faces and hair are. Hair in a roll off forehead & curls behind; eyebrows thin; lips bright red; nails bloody – old or young (there was only one young – Mrs Gibson [described by Molly as 'smallish and fair & done just like the rest'] & one youngish – me) . . . as Gibbie said (bless him) it's nice to see somebody with her hair done unlike everybody else's. And I had on my lovely long blue dress with the red and green sash.

And the food:

We had a wonderful meal: thick soup, lobster mayonnaise, grilled chicken & green peas & new potatoes, asparagus, strawberries & cream, & fresh peaches and cream. I had 2 lots of strawberries and 3 of peaches – my own, Gibbie's who was too full, & my own second helping as it were. Disgusting.[117]

They reached home at half past eleven. It had been a long day. At its start Wallis had been in his office at work on Highball. He then travelled up to London for a meeting to anticipate countermeasures against Upkeep. Lunch was with his guru Leo d'Erlanger, to discuss a post-war civil version of the long talked-of six-engine bomber he was due to consider with senior officials at MAP later in the afternoon. After this he went across to the Air Ministry to discuss new kinds of target with Bufton.[118]

The conversation with Bufton arose from developments since Chastise. On the evening after the raid, Cochrane had written to Wallis: 'Before reaching the end of this long but exciting day I feel I must write to tell you how much I admire the perseverance which brought you the outstanding success which was achieved last night.' Then the nub: 'I spoke to the Commander-in-Chief about your other project and he expressed the greatest interest.' Harris had asked for a copy of anything Wallis had written on the subject, and when Cochrane suggested that Wallis might visit to explain what he had in mind, Harris said this would be 'an excellent idea'.[119] The 'other project' was the deep penetration bomb. After three years, Bomber Command and the Air Staff were listening.

10

Red War, 1943–44

Targets and Tallboys

Cochrane was as good as his word. A fortnight after the Dams Raid
Wallis was called to a meeting with AVM Breakey (ACAS (TR)) to
revisit the deep penetration bomb. With them were Bufton (DB
Ops), Grp Capt. Wilfred Wynter-Morgan (DD Arm D) and Wg
Cdr Arthur Morley. Their talk that afternoon centred on ways to
weaken the enemy's economy. A quarter of Germany's bulk materials were carried on inland waterways. The MEW and DB Ops
reasoned that if vulnerable points of canals and rivers could be put
out of action, the transfer of cargoes to rail would put the railways
under stress. If in turn vulnerable points of the rail network were
attacked, paralysis might ensue.

The Air Staff considered this on 8 June. Wallis was in attendance. He was asked if items of transport infrastructure like canal
embankments, aqueducts, or boat lifts would be susceptible to a
deep penetration weapon? DB Ops and HQBC had their eyes on
the boat lift at Rothensee near Magdeburg, which formed a junction
between the River Elbe and the Mittellandkanal. Rothensee was a
choke point in Germany's water transport system.

Wallis was working on Highball and the Windsor, but found time
to draft the requested advice, which he sent to Bufton on 26 June. In
it, he restated the conceptual case for developing a deep penetration
weapon and pointed to an unresolved issue in doing so – the need to
determine the lightest casing that would withstand what happened
when the weapon entered the ground. To make a start, he suggested

that the casing for the 4000 lb trial weapon which had been cast in 1941 should be completed and dropped to provide information about how such a weapon would behave. 'On the knowledge thus gained the design of a 12,000 lb casing could be based.'[1]

Wallis's thinking about a 12,000 lb weapon stemmed from pragmatism – a near standard Lancaster could carry one and do so over sufficient distances to put worthwhile targets within reach. At the same time, however, he was envisaging three categories of target, with a bomb of identical shape but different size assigned to each. Light targets would include such things as water mains, underground electric cables, and drains. Medium objectives included coal mine shafts and the shafts needed to accommodate the balance weights of ship lifts. Massive concrete rafts for power stations and foundations of large bridges would be recipients of the heavy version.[2]

Bufton relayed Wallis's advice to the Air Staff, who on the strength of it agreed to order a dozen 4000 lb models for aerodynamic and detonation trials to inform development of the 12,000 lb weapon. On 18 July Breakey issued a formal requirement to the MAP for 12 small and 60 medium casings. The 12,000 lb weapons, he said, were in the first instance needed to attack the Rothensee boat lift. The Air Staff understood from Wallis that if priority was given, 40 bombs per week could be turned out by September.

The official order was confirmatory. Six days before Wallis had been called to a meeting with Sir Wilfrid Freeman and Sir Ralph Sorley (CRD) which opened with Freeman asking if Wallis could remember the suggestion he had made for a ten-ton bomb (three years before to the day). When Wallis said that he did, Freeman asked: 'How soon can you let me have one?' Wallis replied that this would depend upon the priority assigned to it. Freeman told him that he was committing the Ministry to an order for the entire family of weapons. Since he was bringing the 22,000 lb bomb into being in the knowledge that it would be resource intensive and with no operational requirement, he had taken the precaution of securing the support of his minister, Stafford Cripps. An hour later Wallis met Craven, who was bridling at having been ordered by telephone to clear access to the resources of the English Steel Corporation.

After that he visited Winterbotham, who knew that forthcoming attacks on V-weapon sites would call for something more than conventional bombs. That day was typically busy: he had lunched with Sir Roy Fedden,[3] Leo d'Erlanger, and Ronald Tree,[4] to scope ideas about post-war civil aviation.

Next afternoon Wallis was again in London, to discuss production procedures and to scope Lancaster requirements for the 22,000 lb weapon with Roy Chadwick. At this stage Wallis referred to it as the New Penetration Bomb;[5] two days later Wynter-Morgan told him it had been given a codename: Tallboy. Following Wallis's thinking there were to be three editions of Tallboy: a 4000 lb type to test subterranean behaviour and aerodynamics, the intermediate 12,000 lb weapon (for which the Air Staff had asked) and the full-size bomb (for which they had not). They were designated Tallboy S(mall), M(edium) and L(arge), respectively, but since any of them could be called 'Tallboy' there was scope for confusion, which duly arose. MAP's initial order was for 100 casings for each of Tallboy M and Tallboy L, and 18 of Tallboy S.

On 19 July Wallis was back in Sheffield with Arthur Winder and his colleagues at the English Steel Corporation, resuming the conversation they began in 1940. The ESC helped to identify other steelmakers between whom production could be spread, and sub-contractors for finishing. Even so, Tallboy's development was challenging. Manufacture of the casings called for time-consuming work to fine tolerances, access to Manganese-molybdenum steel, and specialist machine skills.[6] The finishing of a single casing could occupy a lathe operator for a week; apprentices disliked crawling into casings to grind out their rough interior surfaces and jagged projections.[7]

Since the order for Tallboy L was on Freeman's initiative,[8] Chadwick and Avro were taking a risk in agreeing to modify the Lancaster to carry it. Luckily, Chadwick's relationship with Wallis was trustful; they admired each other (Chadwick was one of the few people who was successfully able to tease Wallis), and they were quick off the mark in embarking on their second 'big adventure'. During July, modifications were scoped by letter, telephone, and telegram.

However, it soon emerged that whereas only small adjustments would be needed to enable a Lancaster to carry Tallboy M, extensive alterations were required for Tallboy L.

During August the Air Staff became aware that steel-working facilities were inadequate to produce Tallboy M and Tallboy L side by side in quantity.[9] The DCAS advised Portal that the larger bomb should be shelved. He gave a list of reasons: the operational range of the specialised aircraft needed to carry it would be too small to reach targets beyond the Pas de Calais; air dropped experiments with Tallboy S had yet to take place; and given the limited capacity it was better to achieve adequate production of one weapon than inadequate output of two. Portal agreed, and since Freeman had received his minister's backing for the original decision, Portal sought and was given Churchill's approval to rescind it. On 30 September Freeman was told to stop work on Tallboy L.

As these matters came to a head, Wallis suffered some sort of collapse. Before cancellation of Tallboy L, the word 'sick' was pencilled in his diary for nine days in succession.[10] His migraine attacks had become a mechanism for enforcing rest but usually lasted no more than forty-eight hours, whereas this illness brought him to a standstill for the best part of a fortnight. And small wonder: as the summer passed, he had shouldered more and more tasks. Alongside the Windsor and continuing work to bring Highball to fruition, there were periods in which he attended near daily discussions to consider prospects for attacks on Italian dams,[11] use of Upkeep against railway tunnels,[12] viaducts, and anti-invasion defences.[13] By August another genre of target had been recognised as calling for attack: a series of cyclopean structures under construction in northern France which were assumed to relate to the forthcoming V-weapon offensive. The constructions taking shape included Watten, near Saint-Omer, originally intended as a launch site for V2s; a depot for V2s and their fuel at La Coupole; and Marquise-Mimoyecques, where an underground complex was being built to house a battery of long-range rapid-fire guns with which to shell London.[14]

Most of the target meetings were held in central London during working hours so Wallis compensated by carrying on into the evenings. He was seldom home before 8 p.m., and when related travels took him to Harmondsworth for discussion of canal structures and viaducts, or to Reculver, Ashley Walk or Rothesay in Scotland for dropping trials of Highball there were periods when he was seldom home at all.[15]

Work on the Windsor – in theory, his day job, the venture on which Vickers pinned future hopes – was fitted in as and when, but apparently without disadvantage. On 10 September the first prototype was sent to Farnborough for erection; on 23 October she flew.[16] At the year's end Craven sent a personal letter in which he said how much he admired the way in which Wallis had 'whisked through' the Drawing Office work and recorded his appreciation at the speed with which the prototype had been produced. If the Windsor could be got into production quickly, he said, the company would 'be in a very fine position to face post-war problems'.[17]

Grouse shooting

On the day of Tallboy L's cancellation, Wallis received a letter from Molly which told him she was 'depressed because I can't think when I shall see you again.'[18] She was back in Glen Feshie. In early summer, Molly had sent Nan up to Balnascretan for a few weeks to give Pam respite during her pregnancy. In August Mary and young Barnes visited for a fortnight to keep Pam company and hike in the mountains. Their schooldays were nearly done. Barnes took up pipe smoking; during the train journey Mary fended off a soldier who professed to have fallen in love with her. Molly was due to return in October, to look after Andrew and keep house around the time of the birth. But the birth was premature, and Ken was out on duty when Pam went into labour. No one else was within miles. Pam gave birth alone, to twins, one of whom died.

Molly rushed to Scotland, where Pam would need her support for weeks. Molly was beguiled by the purples and pinks of heather on the mountains, but homesick.[19] Each evening she watched yearningly as the express from Inverness passed through Kingussie on its way to Euston. Back in Effingham Nan kept house, washed clothes, scrubbed floors and put Elisabeth and Christopher to bed each evening while Wallis worked.

The Allies' desire to disable the German and Italian railway systems led them to focus on viaducts and tunnels. It was found that Germany's network offered few tunnels worth blocking, since an interruption in one could usually be bypassed in another, but Northern Italy and the Alpine passes were promising: Germany and Italy were linked by only four main routes outside neutral Switzerland, and all of them offered places at which they could be cut. It was recognised that a number would have to be struck at the same time, and with sufficient explosive power to put them beyond immediate repair.[20]

In June, Harris had suggested rolling Upkeeps into Alpine tunnels.[21] This was found impracticable,[22] but during August and September the possibility of using the more agile Mosquito and Highball came under discussion.[23] In parallel, consideration was given to an Italian dams raid. The initial aim, to cut electrical power to Italy's railways, was soon dropped when it was found that only part of Italy's system was electrified, and that Italy's grid could cross-feed power between regions. Attention turned instead to prospects for damaging transport infrastructure by flooding. Wallis and DB Ops believed that breaching the Bissorte Dam, in the Rhône-Alpes region of France close to the Italian border, would disrupt rail communications on the Mont Cernis route.[24] By late August the water level in the reservoir was reported to be ideal for such an attack. However, the dam's position meant that it would risk French lives,[25] while Harris ruled it out on grounds of tactical and political difficulty.[26] The possibility of a raid on Italian dams was nonetheless kept in view until early 1944.

Railway tunnels, too, remained on the agenda. At the end of August, a list of possible candidates in northern Italy was prepared and classified according to suitability for attack. The assessment was made by Maurice Longbottom, the Vickers test pilot who had done much to support and advise Wallis during preparations for the Dams Raid. Using air photographs, Longbottom examined thirty-eight tunnel entrances to consider the line of approach and look for a clearly visible reference mark from which to judge the point of release. The release point was critical since it was important for the store's first contact with the ground to be in the tunnel mouth. Longbottom found twenty-eight tunnels that were suited to attack.

The next step was to test the idea in practice – a project code-named Grouse Shooting. Early in September Wallis met the chief engineer of the Great Western Railway to identify tunnels that might be suitable.[27] The GWR suggested a short, single-bore tunnel in a narrow valley in north Pembrokeshire, on the southern approach to Maenclochog, where a line from Clunderwen to Letterston Junction crossed the southern slope of the Preseli mountains. The line, known locally as 'The Punchy', had recently closed to passengers but still handled goods traffic from a nearby quarry. There were few dwellings nearby and the tunnel's seclusion meant that trial drops would be largely out of public view. Wallis passed the GWR's maps to Maurice Longbottom, who that day flew one of Vickers's High-ball Mosquitoes to reconnoitre. The track ran along the floor of a narrow, steep-sided valley and entered the tunnel at the beginning of a westward curve. Longbottom flew the approach several times, and on return told Wallis that it would be feasible to bowl Highball into the tunnel's southern entrance.

At noon next day, Friday, 17 September, Wallis set out in the works car to watch Summers make two Highball drops at Ashley Walk. The drops were to inform the approach to be tried at Maenclochog. They used forward spin rather than the usual backspin, and the need to manoeuvre the Mosquito within the confines of a valley made it necessary to fly slower than when Highball was launched over water.

The journey to Wales was originally planned by public transport,[28] but the GWR offered to carry the sixteen-strong party to Maenclochog in a bespoke train that included George VI's saloon car and staff from their royal train. 'I'm off to Wales on Wed. night' he told Molly on 3 October. 'The railway are giving us special day and night coaches and we are going to live on the train for 2 or 3 days, recording as the trials go, so shall not be back until Friday at the earliest. Quite like Royalty!'[29]

It was dark and pouring with rain when Wallis left Effingham three evenings later. He was bothered by backpain, and Nan was running a temperature. Shortly after 10 p.m. he rendezvoused with colleagues from MAP and the Air Ministry at Paddington. He told Molly:

We had a special chef, and six stewards, and the special guard, who always accompanies the King when he travels on the GWR – MR PARTRIDGE, very grand indeed, large winged linen collar with a black stock, with tie pin bearing Queen Mary's monogram, and a very large peak to his cap covered with gold lace, and a frock coat. A great PERSONAGE, and yet not above seeing that copious buckets were slipped quickly beneath the Outlets from our Lavatories whenever our special train was pulled into a siding to allow us to rest, lest haply we should foul the ground below us.

Directly we started at 10.50, we were besought by anxious Stewards to eat and drink – tongue and lettuce sandwiches, and all sorts of alcoholic liquors – even a pot of tea for me – tho' I saw the Steward give a marked start of surprise at my request, when there was the best whiskey being given away. And so it was nearly 12.30 am before I was able to retire to my berth, as the Chief Engineer of the whole Company was with us – a great man, but not so GREAT as MR PARTRIDGE, and he is a member of the Civils, and so wished to talk to me.

Wallis awoke at 6.30 next morning to find the train in a siding at Clunderwen. Breakfast was at 7.15.

Prunes large and juicy stewed in sugar, kipper, followed by grilled sausage, bacon, egg, tomato and potatoes all together, marmalade toast and butter. We changed into observation cars, more suited to our single line mountain track, and off we puffed with 2 little engines into the mountains. Alas, in all the haste and grandeur I was unable to honour MR PARTRIDGE'S BUCKET.[30]

The day was warm and bright, with a gentle breeze. Unlopped branches of trees and bushes slapped windows as the train puffed slowly by. Some hundreds of yards short of the tunnel the train stopped. Wallis and other members of the party stepped down to the sounds of streams on nearby slopes and dripping from foliage. Above them, buzzards circled and mewed in the morning heat. Wallis paced the track while the RAE cameramen got into position on the hillside. Sixteen years before to the day, he recalled, he had been walking the walls of York while Molly gave birth to Mary.

The sorties were to be flown from the Coastal Command aerodrome at Angle, about five minutes' flying time from Maenclochog, where two 618 Squadron Mosquitoes, a dozen inert Highballs, Maurice Longbottom and his colleague Bob Handasyde had been prepositioned. With them were several members of 618 Squadron who were there to observe: if the trials led to an actual operation, it would be they who would be undertaking it. A temporary telephone link with the airfield was provided by a GPO linesman; as the time for the first drop neared, members of the RAF contingent drew back for safety. One of them was Wg Cdr John Collier, who attributed Wallis's insistence on remaining 'practically at the tunnel entrance' to faith in Longbottom's airmanship. Longbottom and Handasyde made six sorties during the day, varying height and speed and releasing twelve stores in all. To judge from the times in Handasyde's logbook they made many dummy runs. At least two stores entered the tunnel,[31] and it was estimated that up to nine might have done so if the tunnel had been twin-tracked.[32] According to Collier one passed clean through. Wallis was delighted; as their luxury train headed back to England, he bought several rounds of drinks during a convivial dinner.

Back home next evening, Wallis wrote to bring Molly up to date with events at home. He told her that Nan was under the weather but going about her housekeeping with 'dogged heroism'. As usual, Wallis was preoccupied. The prototype Windsor was undergoing ground-handling trials ahead of her maiden flight; there were decisions to take about production Windsors; analysis of the Maenclochog films was in hand.

Three days later he wrote to tell that he still had a bad back, a sore throat, that Christopher was crying in the night and asking for his mother, and that 'Nan staggers around'.[33] Always distant, he seems not to have noticed that Nan was seriously ill. On the evening of 22 October, she checked the blackouts, looked in on the children, and went to sleep. Eleven-year-old Elisabeth found her dead in her bed next morning. Loyal and uncomplaining, she had been suffering from bronchial pneumonia.

Molly returned to Effingham two days later. Nan had cared for her and eased her life for thirty years. Molly had missed her end. 'Oh Nan, Nan,' she wrote, 'I'd give anything to see you walk in to my room now . . . and say "It's a lovely afternoon but *cold*. 'Ere, why don't you turn the fire up a bit?"'

Earthquake, wind, and fire

Grouse Shooting ended when explosive trials in another tunnel revealed that at least eight well-placed Highballs would be needed to ensure a blockage.[34] Given the specialised training that would be required, the need to obstruct three or four routes simultaneously, and making allowance for losses and inaccurate drops, the task was beyond the capacity of the available force.

In any case, the force was no longer available. With Highball still in development, and *Tirpitz* out of Mosquito range in Kåfjord, it was considered unproductive to keep 618 Squadron in being for one operation it might never undertake. On 8 September the squadron was accordingly grounded, and most of its crews dispersed to other units.[35] The Admiralty's resolve to neutralise *Tirpitz* was switched to a force of midget submarines which it was hoped could infiltrate the anchorage and place explosive charges. This operation took place on 20–22 September, causing damage to *Tirpitz* that took six months to repair.

The development of Tallboy M took the same amount of time. Whereas the Air Staff had been told that the weapon would be available from September 1943, the first successful trial drops did not take place until the following March. In the months between, Wallis and the RRL had arrived at a final case design by firing models of varying thickness into different kinds of material – clay, concrete, sandstone, chalk – and cured instability by offsetting the fins to impart spin.[36] The first live drop was made at Ashley Walk on 7 April 1944, just four days after *Tirpitz* embarked on speed trials following the repairs made over the winter.

By the time Tallboy was ready the plan to wreck the Rothensee boat had been overtaken, and if it had been ready in September 1943 no means of aiming it with the necessary precision would then have been available. From November, No. 617 Squadron was trained with the Stabilised Automatic Bomb Sight, a combination of precision optical instrument and calculator which in experienced hands could put a bomb within twenty or thirty yards from 20,000 feet. However, sustained practice was needed to do this, and means had yet to be found to define the exact point at which a bomb aimer should aim. This problem was solved in the later winter and spring of 1944, through a series of experiments under the leadership of Wg Cdr Leonard Cheshire, who evolved a technique of marking the aiming point with spot fires, placed from very low level.[37]

The first Tallboys used operationally fell on the night of 8–9 June 1944. They were aimed at a place on the main railway line between south-west France and Normandy, where the track emerges from a tunnel beside the Loire near Saumur. Cheshire laid four red spot fires beside the tunnel mouth; in following minutes, two Tallboys cut the line close to the entrance, and one bored through the sandy subsoil into the tunnel itself.[38] The immediate result was blockage of the line and consequent delay of German forces being moved to Normandy. A related outcome three days later was a decision to resume work on Tallboy L.

News of Saumur soon reached David Pye, who had presided over the initial deep penetration discussions back in 1940–41 and was now Provost of University College London. A fortnight after the attack he wrote to Wallis to say that he had felt for some time that he should be a Fellow of the Royal Society and wished to have the pleasure of proposing him; would that be acceptable? Wallis was elated. He wrote to Molly:

> Just think of your little one, in the great fellowship of Newton, and my adored Sir Christopher. Away knighthoods, baronetcies, Dukedoms – they are not to be compared with what is incomparably the greatest scientific distinction in the whole world.[39]

When Pye submitted the proposal in October Robert Watson-Watt, Harry Ricardo, Patrick Blackett, Geoffrey Taylor, and William Stanier were among those who signed it. They said why the distinction was merited:

> Throughout his career as an engineer and designer, Mr Wallis has been responsible for many developments involving the breaking of entirely new ground. His scientific and mathematical equipment has enabled him to tackle new problems in a fundamental manner.[40]

Crossbow, Diver, and Big Ben

Another new problem that required to be tackled in a fundamental manner was notified to Wallis just five days before Pye told him he should be a Fellow of the Royal Society. For some months intelligence reaching the Allies pointed to Germany's development of pilotless aircraft and ballistic missiles. Since October 1943 Wallis had been among a select group of scientists and engineers consulted by senior policymakers and a countermeasures committee to estimate what the characteristics of these weapons might be, and how they could be countered.

Early in December 1943, AM Sir Roderic Hill, head of the newly formed Air Defence of Great Britain, was told that an offensive involving pilotless aircraft – a basic kind of cruise missile – might begin as early as January 1944. Hill and his colleagues reacted by scoping Operation Diver, a plan to bring anti-aircraft assets from across the UK to form a 20-mile protective belt to the south and south-east of London. The shield was to be formed of light and heavy anti-aircraft artillery, searchlights, and balloons. The balloon screen would run along the North Downs, which would give extra height. Modelling of different patterns of balloon siting forecast that a 20-mile curtain formed of 500 balloons might bring down one flying bomb in ten.[41]

In the event, the offensive did not begin until 12 June, and when it did it started with a whimper rather than a bang. Instead of an intended salvo from some 55 launch sites, just ten missiles were launched, of which five crashed, and three of the four that reached England came down on farmland.[42] Three nights later, however, there came a barrage in which 73 of 244 missiles exploded in London. By the time the War Cabinet met at 11.45 next morning, Operation Diver was well under way. Ministers were relieved to hear that the missiles were unguided and that their warheads were smaller than had been feared, but nervous about civilian reaction.[43] Press reports of 'sightless robot planes' and 'blind' P[ilotless]-bombs fostered a feeling that there was something sinister as well as dangerous about the new weapons.[44]

Wallis was suffering from a migraine when the MAP telephoned him next morning, and three days passed before he was well enough to travel into London to meet Roger Liptrot, the MAP's Assistant Director of Research and Development. The subject was balloons. Flying bombs were coming in below the height at which HAA gunners could obtain good results yet too high for light guns. This led to the recognition that balloons could play a larger part; by the time Wallis arrived at the MAP on 20 June plans were being made to thicken the initial deployment of 480 to a total of 1000.[45] Remarkably, one of the people who briefed him was R100's former commander, Ralph Booth, now a member of Liptrot's staff.

Next day Wallis went to RAE Farnborough, where bits of exploded flying bombs were being gathered and studied. By 24 June the RAE had received substantial parts of three V1s and a near intact specimen upon which Roy Fedden reported to the Air Minister's advisers three days later. Fedden was enthralled. The flying bomb, he said, was designed for simplicity and ease of production. Apart from its automatic pilot and instruments it could be made by any small elementary engineering works or garage without a single precision tool. This meant that tens of thousands of units could be produced without impinging on ordinary aircraft output. The weapon's pulse jet was made so 'that it just hangs together for the few minutes it has to run'. About ten Vis could be produced for the cost and effort that went into one Spitfire. Fedden warned that more developed versions should be expected.[46]

Wallis, meanwhile, was immersing himself in the theory of balloon screens. He visited existing balloon sites on the North Downs. At a meeting with Freeman, R. V. Jones (the Air Ministry's Assistant Director of Intelligence (Science)), and others on 24 June he was told of experiments being undertaken by the Admiralty involving aprons strung between pairs of balloons, and light wires ('whiskers') suspended from the main cable.[47] Balloon Command was doubtful about these new formats because in areas where protection was needed most they could not easily be combined with existing features like pylons and power lines, and it seemed that an unrealistically large amount of surrounding clear ground would be needed when balloons were flown in high winds.

Wallis looked past opposition to what the apron scheme might offer. In place of the conventional barrage (which on 26 June was thickened yet again) he proposed three lines of paired balloons staggered one behind the other to a depth of a third of a mile, flying at 4000 feet. To do this along a frontage of thirty miles would require 600 balloons served by 3600 men and women, compared with 1750 balloons and 10,000 personnel called for by ADGB's latest iteration. Whereas the existing method caught around one flying bomb in ten, the stopping power offered by the apron system would be 100 per cent with one third of the resources.[48] In following days he pressed this on Sir Roderic Hill and looked for ways to solve the problems.

Molly gives us an inkling of his frame of mind. 'Exactly a year ago Barnes was told about these rocket bombs and suggested he should provide the means of putting them out of action.' Molly was thinking back to Tallboy L and its cancellation: 'All except one man, Sir William (*sic*) Freeman who is always sensible, pooh-poohed it.' Molly blamed 'that fool Sir Arthur Harris' for the abandonment, although we have seen that the decision to suspend work on Tallboy L was forced by the Air Staff. She was also being protective. Her husband had been working flat out before he was conscripted to help counter the V1; now, she foresaw, 'they'll hound and hound him. That's what it's been like all this war.'[49]

For days the bombs' guttural rasp was constant as they passed over Effingham on their way to London. On 6 July one landed on Beech Avenue, wrecking four houses. The occupants of one, Molly noted with schadenfreude, were wealthy owners of a London night club who had come to Effingham to escape bombing. White Hill House visibly shuddered during the explosion, but only one window was broken. Wallis thought the pressure pulse had been dissipated by trees. He also thought he could more readily get to grips with the weapons if he could see for himself how they were being launched and supplied. Having revised his will, the afternoon of 13 July found him in a USAAF Dakota bound for Normandy.

Wynter-Morgan and Bomber Command's Armaments Officer, Air Cdr Christopher Bilney, travelled with him. The Dakota touched down on a temporary landing ground a few hundred yards inland from Omaha beach,[50] where a jeep was waiting to take them 20 bone-shaking miles to the headquarters of US Air Technical Intelligence at La Bastille. From here they were driven to visit a German shore battery, to study the effects of bombing, and a V1 launch site. They passed women, young boys, and old men, many of whom looked cowed or wary. Men of working age had been taken away for labour by the Germans.

They visited three types of launch site – the original or 'ski site', the temporary, and the invulnerable. Ski sites were so called because of how they looked on air photographs. They were easy to detect, vulnerable to bombing, and had thus been discarded in favour of a simpler form, code-named Woolworth. Woolworth sites could be built at speed by unskilled labour. They were usually found among farm buildings and orchards, and there was little to them other than a compass swinging platform and a launch rail that was usually aligned alongside a tree-bordered lane or avenue. It was all so elementary there was little to attack.

Next day Wallis, Bilney and Wynter-Morgan were taken to see an invulnerable (or 'heavy') site. It was at Équeurdreville, on the outskirts of Cherbourg, where tunnels elaborated from old stone quarries had been reinforced with 17-foot-thick side walls that were secure from existing bombs of any weight. The site was not yet active when the Americans reached it, but had it been so Wallis could imagine a high rate of discharge even during bombing. Yet more impressive was the heavy site at Sottevast, nine miles to the south, where a 17-foot-thick concrete carapace was being laid on the ground, to be followed by excavation of the earth beneath to create a bomb-proof sheltered complex below. It was difficult, wrote Wallis, 'to convey any idea of the immense size and strength of this construction', and since it was unfinished it was not clear what it was for.[51] In fact, it was one of several giant bunkers originally intended for the assembly, storage and launch of A-4 rockets – the V2.[52]

After visiting Sottevast and a hydrogen peroxide storage depot the visitors returned to the airstrip in the hope of finding transport. None was available, so they were taken instead to Grandcamp-Maisey, where they spent the night in a former German headquarters. It was quieter here than it had been the night before when they were kept up first by an enthusiastic US major who shared his findings on the V1 pulse jet, and then by nearby artillery fire. Rising soon after dawn, they returned to the airstrip and boarded a half-empty Dakota. Back in Effingham he luxuriated in a hot bath, then sat up in bed with Molly, a map between them, to tell of his adventures.

In following days Wallis met Cabinet ministers, senior politicians, members of the Crossbow Committee, officials, industrial and military leaders to report what he had seen and discuss what it meant. During these discussions there was much talk about the potential of the V2 and about the need for Tallboy L to deal with sites such as Sottevast. During a meeting with Cripps, the Minister drew a map of the Channel coasts on his blotter, turned to Wallis, looked over his steel-rimmed glasses and asked: 'Now, suppose that I am Hitler

_R_100 over York 16/12/29

With loving good wishes from
Molly & Bames
Christmas 1929.

R100's maiden flight, photographed from the Thursday Market, York, at about 09.15 on 16 December 1929, and used as a Christmas card

Barnes and Molly, 1933

Elisabeth and Christopher, c.1938

Pre-production Wellesley, the first aeroplane to make full use
of 'Vickers-Wallis construction'

The first swim of the year,
16 May 1937

Camp, 1936: Wallis taught semaphore,
to enable message-sending across the fields.
The signals spell M L F. Molly (whose middle
name was Frances) took the photograph.

War clouds: colleagues from Vickers visit Camp, August 1938,
just before onset of the Munich crisis

Improvised anti-landing obstacles on Effingham golf course, July 1940, that brought Wallis to the notice of Beaverbrook

617 Sqn Lancaster crew practises release of stripped Upkeep at Reculver, May 1943

Guy Gibson (wearing sunglasses) with Vickers test pilots and 617 Sqn aircrew outside Scampton officers' mess at lunchtime, 17 May 1943. L-R: Mutt Summers, Bob Handasyde, Maurice Longbottom (partly masked), Les Munro, Richard Trevor-Roper, Les Knight, unknown, David Maltby, Fred Spafford, and (possibly) George Deering

African American workers machining Tallboy casings at Scullin Steel Plant, St Louis, October 1944

Finished Tallboy casings at the Elswick Works, Newcastle

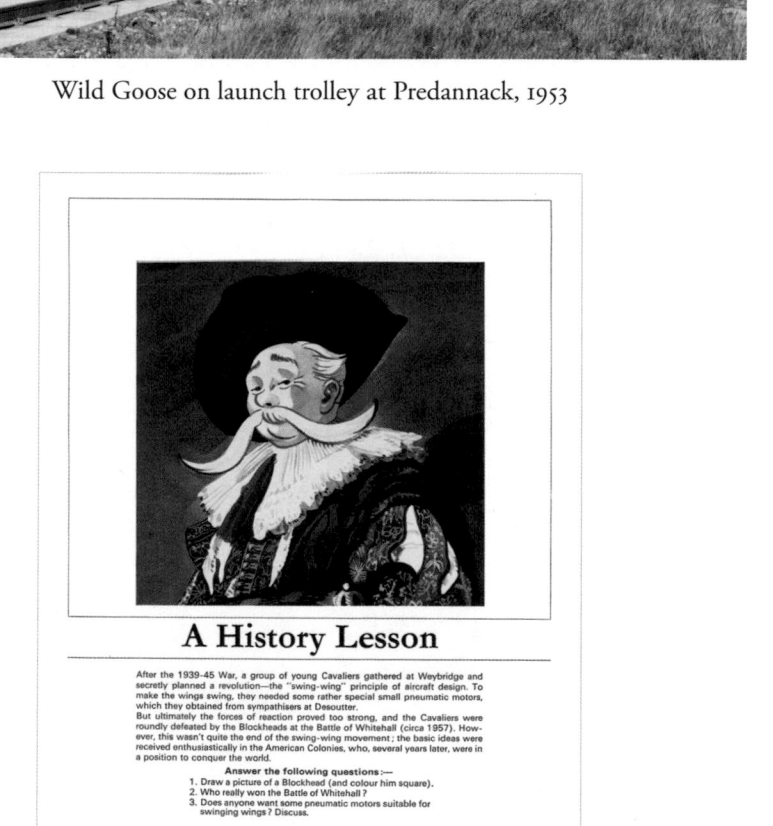

Wild Goose on launch trolley at Predannack, 1953

A History Lesson

After the 1939-45 War, a group of young Cavaliers gathered at Weybridge and secretly planned a revolution—the "swing-wing" principle of aircraft design. To make the wings swing, they needed some rather special small pneumatic motors, which they obtained from sympathisers at Desoutter.

But ultimately the forces of reaction proved too strong, and the Cavaliers were roundly defeated by the Blockheads at the Battle of Whitehall (circa 1957). However, this wasn't quite the end of the swing-wing movement; the basic ideas were received enthusiastically in the American Colonies, who, several years later, were in a position to conquer the world.

Answer the following questions:—
1. Draw a picture of a Blockhead (and colour him square).
2. Who really won the Battle of Whitehall?
3. Does anyone want some pneumatic motors suitable for swinging wings? Discuss.

Desoutter

DESOUTTER BROTHERS LIMITED, THE HYDE, HENDON, LONDON, NW9. TELEPHONE: COLINDALE 6346

Wallis spurned – spoof advertisement produced by a
Vickers supplier after cancellation of Swallow

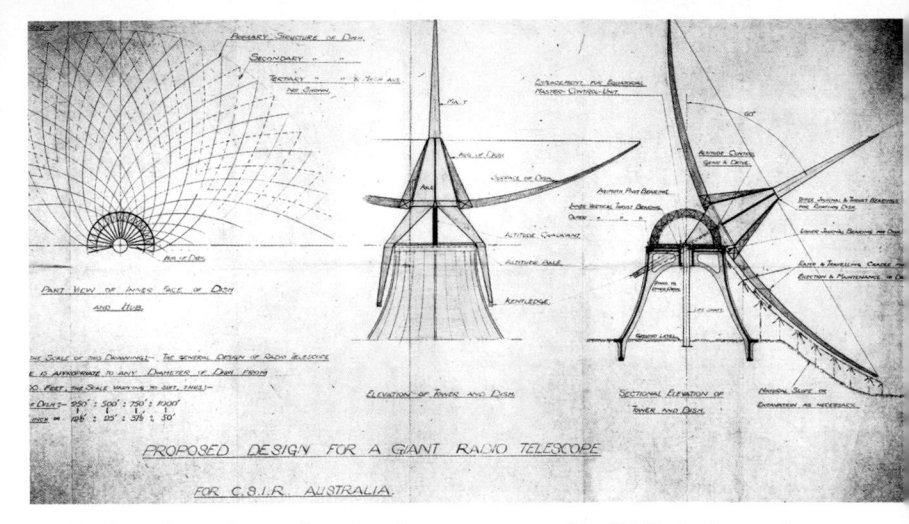

Outline design for 250ft radio telescope proposed by Wallis in September 1955

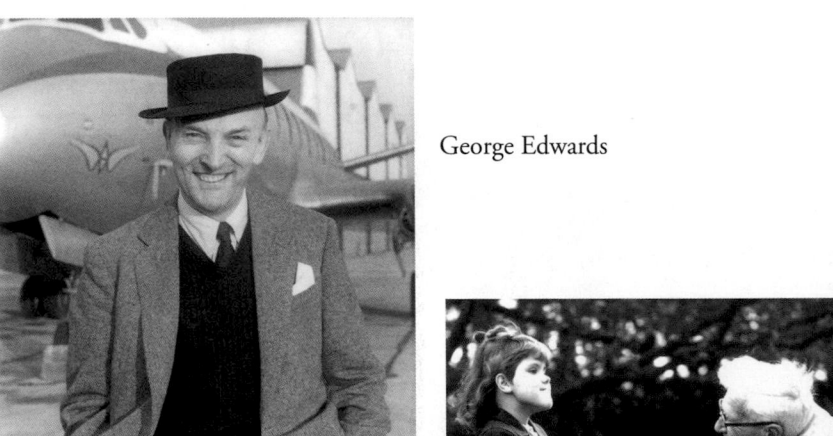

George Edwards

Wallis with Lisa Parrett in the garden at White Hill House, December 1971, following Wallis's acceptance of the Presidency of the Bath Institute for Medical Engineering

and that you are my chief scientific adviser. Here are the two coasts; here is London; here is Bristol, Southampton and so on. Can you suggest to me any way in which I can attack these cities?' Wallis took the blotter and in reply drew something that resembled the A-4 rocket that no one in Britain had yet seen.[53]

On 22 July there were so many V1 alarms that Wallis spent most of the day working under his desk. He had ideas for a new kind of hoist to assist the curtain screen. By the end of the week, however, he was beginning to buckle. On 25 July he suffered a migraine and two days later failed to attend a meeting convened by Merton to review balloon screens. Next day he went to Freeman and asked to be stood down from balloon work. Freeman agreed that he should take a break as soon as possible but refused to release him. Five days later Wallis told Merton that he was close to breakdown.[54] Merton, too, was sympathetic but told Wallis to carry on: there was no certainty that the war was coming to an end, and while Crossbow sites in northern France were being overrun, V-weapons could soon be arriving from other directions.

Wallis's problem was not that his contribution was central to Crossbow effort but that he was making it at a critical time. V1 bombardment was at its height, assault by the V2 was imminent, and the Sandys committee, Air Intelligence and Cherwell (described by one as 'Churchill's familiar', likened by another to 'a rather drooping hawk'[55]) were at loggerheads over what it would do. By the end of July, the Allies knew a fair amount about the V2 (which they code-named Big Ben). The piecing together of debris from a test missile that exploded over Sweden, and drawings and parts from an unexploded missile which had been retrieved by the Polish resistance, enabled reconstruction of its configuration and aspects of the propulsion system. Technical investigation at RAE Farnborough found that the rocket possessed eight control surfaces, four on the fins and four graphite vanes in the efflux, controlled by a computer that was eventually recognised to rely on electronic signals from gyroscopes. This system stabilised the missile during lift-off and guided it thereafter. But there were still gaps in understanding. It was later realised that the missile was aimed simply by time and distance – it was launched from a known point, the vanes were aligned to a given azimuth, and distance was controlled by the moment at which the engine cut out – but at this point the presence of intricate electronics seemed to support those who contended that it was radio guided.[56] With that ran the hope that the V2 might be countered by jamming. The War Cabinet was on edge, the more so because the parts retrieved from Sweden and Poland bore works numbers and other signs suggesting that the weapon was already in mass production. On 31 July the War Cabinet Joint Planning Staff heard that the Joint Intelligence Sub-committee was unable to forecast the effect of rockets launched against Southern England.

> It is probable, however, that the use of these weapons, which might take place at any time, might have a most serious effect not only upon civilian morale, but also upon war production and administration, particularly in the London area.[57]

Two days later Wallis put forward a new theory. The balance of opinion among scientific advisers was that the V2 would follow a conventional parabolic trajectory. Such a path would take it into a layer of ionised gas in the upper atmosphere that reflects radio waves and would thus preclude guidance from the ground during that phase of flight. Wallis's concern was that the missile's tilting vanes might be used to guide it into a lower, horizontal trajectory which would keep it in range of radio control. Merton and Freeman demanded experimental data. Wallis consulted Vic Gammon, the works manager, who arranged a wind tunnel trial using a model over the long weekend of the works summer holiday.[58] The choice of day was partly in the interests of secrecy – most people would be away – but the main factor was the experiment's demand for concentration of the whole of Weybridge's compressed air supply in a single delivery pipe to the wind tunnel.[59]

For the rest of the month Wallis was out of sorts. He needed to concentrate on the Windsor, Tallboy L and Highball, yet his days were being crowded by Diver and Big Ben. Worst of all, Molly and the children went on holiday in Lancashire where he had also hoped to be. He was depressed by Molly's description of his brother's vicarage in Preston as 'an incomparable muck. They have collected *thousands* of things since I was here ten years ago.'[60] John no longer sat at the desk in his study because there was no room. Mice were everywhere. Wallis commented testily: 'If he spent less on rubbish and paid his debts we might get on better.' At the month's end there was his usual melancholic reminiscence on the anniversary of Edie's death.[61]

There were other complaints. Wallis was dismayed by Mary's decision to cut off her long hair. Young Barnes had fallen during a school climbing trip, travelled on to an orchestra summer school and was now in a faraway hospital being treated for complications to the climbing injury. Wallis was not very sympathetic, partly because he thought his son's description of the hospital to Mary as a 'bloody hole' was a breach of propriety and partly because he was 'pretty cross' that his performance in the Cambridge entrance exam had not been good enough to enable him to read mathematics. Instead, young Barnes was opting to study engineering which he said he did not like. And on 3 September: 'I am being very much pressed by the War Office for a report on flying rockets, wh. I can get no time to write.'

Five days later, the day on which London's bombardment by flying bombs was formally declared to be over, the first V2 arrived. It fell on Staveley Road in Chiswick, killing three. Relief that its warhead was smaller than feared was tempered by the realisation that it was being fired by mobile units in the Netherlands. Sustained bombing, Tallboy, and the Allies' arrival had rendered the gargantuan bunkers unsustainable. Instead, mobile teams could arrive in a concealed place, set up, launch, and be away within three hours.

The beginning of the Big Ben offensive at least removed the pressure to forecast what it would involve – politicians, the RAE and Air Intelligence soon had evidence of that a-plenty – while the end of Diver in south-east England released Wallis from balloons.[62] By then, Wallis had other things on his mind. He warned his brother that he was about to go back to France. The trip was likely to be difficult, and he felt too old for it. There was not much risk, 'but if

I do not come back I know I may count on you to do everything possible for Molly and the children.' He continued: 'I fear father is failing, and hope to get to Worthing soon. He was much aged last time I saw him.'[63]

In Finistère, Nord, and the Pas de Calais

Wallis went back to France on Monday, 25 September. With him once more were Bilney from Bomber Command, Wilfred Wynter-Morgan, and Geoffrey Pidcock.[64] They were flown to Cherbourg, thence to Morlaix in Brittany. Molly recorded afterwards: 'This time wasn't so tiring as they slept in the Château of a Baron and Baron-ess'.[65] Built in the 1880s with picturesque gables, turrets and roofs decorated with finials and girouettes, the Château de Lannigou had a late gothic feel. Within it were more than forty rooms ranged around a massive atrium, a private chapel in a tower, a dining room and grand salon that led onto sun terraces. Wallis wondered at the galleries hung with portraits, embroidered linen, coronetted china, and servants in felt slippers, two of whom brought him a hip bath at 6 a.m. with a silver can of hot water and a pile of soft towels. Despite the luxury the lavatory was an earth privy.

Lannigou contrasted with Brest, where after weeks of ferocious fighting the rubble was abuzz with flies whose larvae feasted on rotting horses and soldiers. Wallis and his companions were there to study the effects of Tallboy on a U-boat pen one fifth of a mile long with a 12-foot-thick ferroconcrete roof. For three years this mind-boggling structure had resisted bombs, until the day in early August when it was penetrated by five of nine Tallboys that hit it.[66] Tallboy had not been designed to pierce concrete. Now, it offered the means to disable hitherto invulnerable structures upon which Germany relied to wage war.

Later, in October, Wallis spent a week examining Tallboy's effects on V1 and V2 storage and supply facilities in northern France.[67] On his return to the airfield at Orly, Wallis made a detour to visit Arthur Tedder, now Eisenhower's deputy and based in Paris, who he had last seen at the MAP in November 1940. Tedder's backing for Wallis's deep penetration weapon had been overridden. Four years later, the weapon was a reality. Wallis thanked him and closed a circle.

Oxtail and Catechism

Highball ran in counterpoint with all the work on V-weapons, Tallboy and the Windsor. It had been ready since the spring of 1944; variant versions had emerged.[68] The question was what to do with them. Highball's lethality lay in surprise; in 1943 it was argued that it would make no sense to reveal its existence by anything less than simultaneous attacks on a good number of high-value targets. A year on few such targets were left. Apart from *Tirpitz*, which was still in Kåfjord, most of Germany's remaining capital ships were either blockaded or on other duties in the Baltic. The War Cabinet's Chiefs of Staff Committee accordingly turned to using Highball to strike 'a decisive blow' against Japan. At that point the largest units of Japan's main fleet were five battleships and nine aircraft carriers.[69] The Chiefs of Staff were told that a surprise attack by the existing 29-strong force of Highball Mosquitoes might eliminate up to half of them.

As usual, decisions on whether or how to proceed were hedged with uncertainties. Reforming 618 Squadron and moving it to the Pacific would take months, and no one could tell where the Japanese Fleet would be when it arrived. Japan's capital ships were then in the Singapore-Philippines-Borneo area; later in the year, however, it was expected that they would be closer to Japan, where an air strike would be more difficult to stage and was likely to meet stronger opposition. Moreover, while Highball was expected to make 'a most important contribution to the war against Japan', its use presented new difficulties. Few of the Japanese anchorages were within range of Mosquitoes operating from land bases, so it would be necessary to launch the operation either from aircraft carriers or by aerotowing the Mosquitoes on their outbound leg. In May 1944 Wallis was asked to assess the prospects of towing. As usual, he consulted Maurice

Longbottom, and after discussion the two of them advised that with sufficient preparation and caveats it could be done by Lancasters or Liberators.

As for using carriers, recent trials had shown that with intensive training this was feasible – but two carriers would be needed, which would mean their diversion from other operations. The MAP warned that it would take months to fit the Highball Mosquitoes with arrester hooks for deck landings. Such conversion would also be makeshift, since while trials had shown that a Mosquito could make a deck landing, they had also shown that it would do so only two or three times before severe airframe damage ensued. MAP further advised that the conversion at Hatfield would be at the expense of other production, and since the Highball aircraft would also need overhaul and other modifications, their readying could take 'at least six months'.[70] The alternative, to build thirty new Highball Mosquitoes, would take longer.[71] Challenges did not end there. The strike force's need for up-to-date photographic reconnaissance meant that a complement of carrier-capable PR XVI Mosquitoes and interpreters would be needed to provide it. As for training, 618 Squadron had been wound down since autumn 1943. Reuniting and retraining its members would take time.

Yet another question was how to transport the aircraft to their proposed main base, which at first was expected to be Ceylon.[72] If they were flown out, losses could be expected along the way and extensive overhaul would be needed on arrival. Crating them up for transport by freighter would take months. The preferred method was to ship the aircraft out on the deck of an aircraft carrier, but no decision on that could be taken until it was known when the Squadron would be ready to leave. Whenever that was, the voyage would provide an opportunity to perfect skills of ship recognition that would be needed to make quick targeting decisions when operating at extreme range.[73]

After some weeks, it was agreed to bring 618 Squadron back into being and send it against the Japanese fleet – Operation Oxtail. The unit was reformed in July 1944 at Wick and began to practise deck landings.[74] In mid-August it transferred to Beccles in Suffolk, whence for the next month crews made Highball drops on the range at Wells-next-the-Sea, dummy deck landings on a marked-out stretch of runway and range-finding exercises. Wallis visited on 20 September, watched practice drops, and gave a talk to the crews. One of those present was the chief naval test pilot Capt. Eric Brown, who had undertaken the initial Mosquito deck-landing trials and was there to share his skills. Brown found Wallis rather abrupt. He was not to know that Wallis had risen at 3.45 a.m. that day to drive to Suffolk.[75]

On 31 October the Squadron embarked from Glasgow on the escort carriers HMS *Fencer* and *Striker*.[76] During the voyage, priorities changed. By the time the carriers reached Melbourne two days before Christmas, SEAC's main objective was the destruction of Japan's air force, and the C-in-C of the British Pacific Fleet refused to assign any fleet carriers for Highball purposes. There was talk of a possible deployment if suitable targets were found, but none were, and 618 Squadron was sent to Narromine in New South Wales. It was disbanded on 14 July 1945. Eleven days later, the Squadron's Armaments Officer watched the 'tragic performance' of special equipment being dumped in the South Pacific. Its 125 Highballs were destroyed in a static explosion.[77]

While 618 Squadron was on its way to Melbourne, the target it had originally been formed to attack was finally dispatched with another of Wallis's weapons. Between September 1943 and the *coup de grâce* on 12 November 1944, seven operations of different kinds were mounted to put the *Tirpitz* out of action. Most of them did more damage than the Allies knew at the time, and by September 1944 she was unfit for seagoing operations. A succession of Tallboy attacks cumulatively reduced her and at the end – Operation Catechism – turned her over.[78] Molly hated the war but exulted at this latest proof of her husband's genius.

> . . . you will hardly believe it, but this very last Saturday . . . some fools at the Air Ministry and D.A.D. etc (all eminent men) wrote a paper saying it was impossible for a big bomb to pierce the double armour plating of the *Tirpitz* . . . This was

printed and sent out on Monday and read by everybody after the *Tirpitz* was sunk! Ha! Ha! A friend gave Barnes a copy and he's just been reading it to me.[79]

The sinking of Germany's last battleship was the front-page story on Tuesday, 14 November.[80] It was also a sign that the war was coming to an end. With that came confidence to relax secrecy that hitherto had cloaked Wallis, his weapons, and 617 squadron. The day after Operation Catechism the Air Ministry named Wallis as the man whose 12,000 lb bomb had sunk the ship and revealed him as the designer of the weapon which had breached the Möhne and Eder dams the year before. In both cases, the public was told, the attacks had been made by a 'crack squadron' in No. 5 Group which had been led successively by Guy Gibson, Leonard Cheshire, and James Tait.

Eleven days later it was announced that Gibson was missing. In September he had led a raid on Rheydt and München Gladbach, and not returned. A few days before the *Tirpitz*'s sinking, Canadian soldiers advancing through Noord Brabant came upon his burial place. 'Barnes and I felt, and feel, more than miserable about our dear little Gibbie. He was so nice and it does seem such a waste.'[81]

After working flat out for three years, Wallis spent the last weeks of 1944 working at home, and walking. The year before Craven had written: 'I do beg you to try and take things a little more easily in the coming year. Surely you must have some very fine No. 2's working under you to whom you can depute some of your work. None of us is quite as young as we were. We have known each other a long time, and I hope our association may continue for some years yet.'[82] A year later, Craven himself was gone: a heart attack took him four days after the sinking of the *Tirpitz*.

Just before Christmas Wallis went to Hew Kilner, the managing director of Vickers's aviation section, to share a problem that had been troubling him. Since 1940 he and Molly had been bringing up John and Robert McCormick in addition to their own children, and at their own expense. However, the boys' relatives on their father's side had refused to agree to legal adoption, which meant that tax relief and other benefits of looking after them had not been forthcoming. This meant that he had been unable to save, which in turn left him powerless 'to provide for the long period of widowhood that in the course of nature my wife will have to face'.[83] As foreshadowed in his recent letter to John, the risks of going into battle zones had brought him face to face with implications of the age gap between Molly and himself. Molly was his world; the possibility that he might be unable to provide for her after he left it had begun to weigh.[84]

The year ended with a dance at Effingham golf club on New Year's Eve. For some while young Barnes had been showing keen interest in Jean Reynolds, daughter of the new vicar. 'Vicarage Jean' was a student at the Slade School of Art, and such was Barnes's enthusiasm for her that he joined the church choir and began to take dancing lessons. Molly was nonplussed when Wallis suddenly mused that there was no harm in marrying young. 'After all these years he's said that no man should marry before he's thirty. Now why?'

Molly and Barnes came down to the golf club for a couple of hours and were told by young Barnes that they were not allowed to leave until they had danced. Molly thought Mary 'adorable' in her blue taffeta dress. Pam, down from Scotland, had readied her: 'a little powder, no lipstick, no specs. Glorious eyebrows, lovely colours. I daresay we're biased.' Mary and Harry Stopes-Roe 'got on famously together − dancing a tango all alone because nobody else felt equal to it. (I mustn't be a cat but it seems I am!)' She seems not to have noticed that Mary and Harry had been practising for weeks.

II

The Clock of Years, 1945

Turning points

The day after the dance was mild; on 4 January the winds swung north and for a fortnight there was frost and snow. On the 18th a storm blew, then cold came back. Wallis wrote to his brother about the ladder to the clock chamber in the church tower. It was clamped to the wall, with nothing against which to lean, and Effingham's new vicar was unwilling to set foot on it. Since Wallis trusted no one else to touch the clock, for the time being it went unwound and unrepaired.[1]

In February the weather warmed, and Charles Wallis died. He had been wandering ever further in his mind before he departed on his last journey. Molly thought the death 'a very good thing' because for months eighty-six-year-old Fanny had been sitting up to secure his bedclothes, roll him over, change his drawsheets, and prevent him from trying to get out of bed and thereby fall. On 'bitter cold nights in January, she has had to get into bed in dressing gown, shawl & slippers & has had continually to hop out to give him his bottle or a drink or whatnot. It's just like a baby.'[2]

Wallis had a sore throat and heavy cold as he drove to Worthing to register the death. Young Barnes wrote from Cambridge.

> Dear Daddy
>   Mother has just written to say that Grandpa has died. I am terribly sorry.
>   Don't be too cut up about it, after all, we've all got to

die sometime, even I; it goes on for ever and ever, and centuries ahead sons will still be writing to their fathers about Grandpa's death. So cheer up.

Young B.[3]

To which Wallis added: 'To be kept in my papers, that my son may read it after burying me.'[4]

Fanny was brought to Effingham, where she thrived on contact with the children but lamented her inability to get to church. She was too frail to make the round trip on foot, while petrol rationing prevented use of the car. Molly alleged hypocrisy on the part of neighbours who used their cars 'to go down to the village to shop; & to take their fat daughter Jill to the station'.[5]

As one life ended, a turning point in another neared: Harry's twenty-first birthday was approaching, and Marie Stopes was planning a ball to celebrate it. Harry was eager for Mary to be there, but Molly said she could not be because '(a) she won't be home and (b) it's Holy Week – or at least Lent.' Molly rang Norbury Park, where Harry and Stopes 'talked in a duet to me over the telephone – Harry saying Mary must come or they couldn't have the dance suitably; Dr S. much less forthcoming & telling Harry in asides that he must have his dance on his birthday. They are an amusing couple.'[6] The relationship with Stopes remained tense. Wallis steered clear of her. Molly liked Harry, and admired Stopes's campaigning, but was wary of her literary airs. Stopes had just sent her latest book of poems, *Wartime Harvest*, with an invitation 'to tell her exactly what I think of it – quite candidly'. Molly was nonplussed. 'I'm no judge of poetry anyway & most of hers seems to me to be tosh.'[7]

Grand Slam

V2 rockets were still falling, sometimes as far west as Hayes and Teddington. Pam and young Andrew were shocked when one detonated 200 yards from their house. 'They are devilish things; the noise of their coming after they have exploded is so foul.'[8]

Tallboy L, too, was supersonic. Its codename had been superseded by its nickname – Grand Slam. On Tuesday, 13 March, Wallis took Molly and Christopher to Ashley Walk to see it.

> You know what heavenly weather it was – utterly cloudless & the sun very hot. We left here early and drove to the New Forest. Just outside it we collected with all sorts of important people to see Barnes's bomb dropped – the first time a live one was dropped. And it was a sight – to see this great thing coming down – as big as a small house. Noise not very terrific, shower of earth enormous. We were about a mile away, & the noise of the bomb coming down (which of course you hear *after* you hear the noise of it hitting the ground) was the greater noise. We all went up to look at the crater afterwards. The thing that impressed C. and me was the curious explosions that went on all the time in the crater, with jets of steam escaping. Gas blowing out of little pockets in the earth, like miniature volcanoes.[9]

MAP officials and senior officers clapped Wallis on the back and shook his hand.

> . . . he properly blushed with – I can't think of the word – modesty? Disclaimingness. Anyway we got away from everybody – fairly sneaked off – for our lunch and ate it lying in a little hollow on the hillside looking down on a lovely farm with hedges of blackthorn like foam round it, the sunshine & the larks & the blue sky.[10]

Next afternoon, Lancasters of 617 Squadron dropped eleven Tallboys and a Grand Slam on the Schildesche twin viaduct on the outskirts of Bielefeld. The viaduct had previously been attacked on fifty-four occasions, with no noteworthy result. The deep penetration weapons broke the crossing by 67 yards in one direction and 86 yards in the other.

Wallis and the new weapon were front-page news next day. RAF UNLEASH 10-TON VICTORY BOMBS ON REICH ran the lead headline of the *Daily Record*, with a photograph of Wallis. The story ran for days, first in national and regional papers, then in the Sundays, after that in magazines, and later still in conjunction with reports of Wallis's election to the Royal Society on 22 March.[11] A cine Mosquito accompanied the Bielefeld raid, and Grand Slam was soon in newsreels. It was noted that its explosive power was greater than ten V2s. Wallis made a broadcast about deep penetration bombs for the BBC's Overseas Service.[12] 'What a to-do,' wrote Molly. 'Poor Barnes has been fairly hating all the reporters & photographers, but I, being far more vulgar, rather enjoy it.'[13]

Attacks on other bridges followed. By the war's end the Ruhr's main transport links with the rest of Germany had been cut. In this instance, at least, Wallis's claim five years before that deep penetration weapons could paralyse transport appeared to be borne out.[14]

Facing the future: Vickers

Vickers held its annual general meeting on 4 April. Craven's successor, Archibald Jamieson, paid tribute to the company's workpeople and saluted their wartime achievements. The Wellington and Spitfire, both in production before the war began, were still being built at its end. Vickers was a national institution. Jamieson spoke of the company's pride in the part it had played in the design and production of bombs which had penetrated U-boat pens, 'sunk the *Tirpitz*, and breached the Möhne and Eder dams.' Jamieson was now 'permitted to disclose that from the brains of our aircraft designers, and notably from Mr B. N. Wallis, have come other revolutionary weapons which have had a major effect on the war's progress.'

Jamieson told shareholders of plans for reorganisation. The company was going to centralise its aviation activities at Brooklands, where a research and development department, charged with dreaming dreams and looking ahead, was being created under Wallis's direction.[15] The new department was to be housed in The Paddock, an area adjacent to the finishing straight of the former motor racing circuit, where he and his team were given offices in the neo-Georgian clubhouse.

Vickers's plan to firm up its operation was in response to trends in Britain's aero industry, which in 1945 was fragmented across twenty-seven airframe and eight aero engine companies.[16] Many of the airframe concerns were small or niche operations, whereas aeroplanes were becoming more complicated, electronics and new technologies were coming to the fore, and rationalisation was needed to bring skills and expertise together rather than leave them scattered. Initiative on this rested with the government, which controlled the military side of the UK's market directly, and the civil side through orders placed by nationalised airlines.[17]

An immediate task was to find ways to offset the looming drop in military orders. Early in 1944 the need for a 25-seat civilian aircraft – a project hitherto overlooked – had prompted Vickers to begin design studies for such a machine. Among them were civil variants of the Windsor, but the one taken forward by Pierson and Edwards sprang from the Wellington. Designated the Vickers Commercial 1 (VC1) it combined a stressed-skin fuselage with a geodetic wing. It was christened the Viking, and its role was to tide the company over until the arrival of Pierson's purpose-built VC2 – the Viscount. From a commercial viewpoint, the world now being full of second-hand Dakotas available at rock-bottom prices, this was challenging. Orders from the MAP for 103 Vikings were nonetheless welcome.[18]

The Times described the Viking as a new geodetic aircraft.[19] In fact, it was geodetics' swan song.[20] George Edwards, whose team built the prototype at Foxwarren, knew that geodetics were finished for airframe purposes. Not only had metal-skinned construction been adopted by everyone else, but fabric covering was not suited to turbine-powered, pressurised, higher-flying, faster aircraft.[21] Wallis nonetheless persisted with the case for geodetics. Matters came to a head following Edwards's appointment as chief designer in the autumn of 1945.[22] Weybridge was still geared to geodetic methods and tooled accordingly. However, when the 11,462nd and last Wellington was delivered in October,[23] and the Windsor order was cancelled soon afterwards,[24] Edwards ruled that geodetic work should stop. Wallis's relations with Edwards began to sour.

Among dead cities

A fortnight after Vickers's AGM: 'Barnes is in Germany doing I don't know what. Flew over on Thursday & I'm not to expect him back for 10 days.'[25]

Wallis was a member of a technical mission to assess the effects of his weapons on steel railway bridges, masonry and concrete viaducts, valley dams and canals. With him again were Pidcock and Wilfred Wynter-Morgan, Bilney from HQ Bomber Command, and four others.[26] They travelled on 20 April – Hitler's birthday.

The outward flight was to the recently occupied Luftwaffe airfield at Lippstadt, on the outskirts of the cathedral city of Paderborn. Not much was left of Paderborn, most of which had been wrecked in a few minutes of Allied bombing and the rest during its seizure by the US 3rd Armoured Division three weeks before. A putrescent stench hung over the rubble.

They spent the night at Gütersloh where Wallis woke next morning with a dull headache that turned into 'a full razzle dazzle' migraine. The sick headache continued while they visited the 'valley of desolation' in which stood the Möhne dam, and the Bielefeld viaduct. At Bielefeld the party noted how little scattered was the rubble from a collapsed pier. This pointed to a deep explosion directly alongside the pier which had undergone near-vertical failure, almost as if it were telescopic.[27]

On Sunday they visited the Sorpe, where Wallis wanted to understand the effects of a Tallboy attack which had been made the previous autumn to disrupt rail communication along the Ruhr. In October 1944 he had told DB Ops that if the central core could be cracked and erosion started on the air side, failure should follow. 'We cannot do more than guess at the number of effective hits required to bring this about', he had written, 'but for what the guess is worth I should say that 4 or 6 effective hits reasonably close to the crest of the dam should be successful.'[28] Air photographs showed that three Tallboys had cut the roadway along the dam. One had struck the crest close to its midpoint. Craters of three more were visible on the air face. The dam still stood, but the visit disclosed breaks to the core in two places and cracking in a third. The direct hit on the crest had destroyed the core for over 60 feet to a depth of at least 35 feet and thereby demanded the lowering of the water level in the reservoir. Yet deeper damage was expected to cause seepage that would eventually require the reservoir to be emptied for repairs.[29] In due course this is what happened – but it took years, not the days for which Wallis had originally hoped.[30]

Wallis was intrigued by the ways in which life in north Germany was being lived. In one place he had a bed with no bedclothes, in another, hot and cold water but no food. Regional and national government had collapsed; all government was local, each town running under the eye of an Allied Town Major who wielded absolute authority that foreshadowed a quasi-colonial British bureaucracy that in due course would irritate German citizens.[31] A 6 p.m. curfew was enforced. Roads were jammed by groups of newly freed prisoners and forced labourers trekking for home – or in the case of some of the Russians, away from it. German soldiers were filtering back to homes and farms in civilian clothes. Dole money was paid to unemployed civilians to sustain households and keep transactions turning. Where industries still ran, they were kept going to provide materials for repair of infrastructure.

A joke about the zones of occupation said that the Americans got the scenery, the French got the wine, and the British got the ruins. Travelling through Krefeld, Münster, and Köln Wallis was struck by the 'minute and detailed destruction' that had been wrought by Allied bombing, and by its wastefulness.

> . . . a somewhat oversimplified summary of our bombing would be that we have destroyed *immense* quantities of habitations, but unless very special effort has been made, the factories are not absolutely knocked out.[32]

One of the few buildings in Köln to have withstood bombs was the cathedral. Wallis reasoned that since the articulated parts of a Gothic structure are in compression, they are resistant to shock. They flew home from München Gladbach while the last Tallboys

of the war were falling on Hitler's summer residence at Berchtes-
gaden. The mission's members agreed that what they had seen
substantiated the claim that the deep penetration bomb was 'a first
class and, in fact, the only effective weapon for attacking massive
masonry or reinforced structures'.[33] It had been a strange time. In
Gütersloh, the gear whine and rumble of Allied truck convoys heading east had left Wallis sleepless, while on the last night he was kept
awake by nightingales. Towards the end, he was irked by the wish of
the two senior officers to waste the mission's time by going in search
of wine to loot. But aback of it was anticipation. In a few days he
would leave work for his first holiday with Molly for six years.

> Do you know what we're going to do? Going to the LAKES
> in May. I've actually got a room at our beloved Rosthwaite in
> Borrowdale. It is almost more than I can bear, & my tummy is
> going round and round, & over and over . . . Beautiful Great
> Gable & Styhead & Langstrath & Eskhouse.

In the names was a long-remembered magic.[34]

Borrowdale

The first week was hot.

> We . . . spent our time sunning and bathing, finding the old
> unknown streams & pools that we found 13 years ago. Nothing
> has changed . . . And now Barnes & I have time to, as it were,
> find each other & talk & discuss. What a tired, worrying rush
> it has been; & how blessed to have no one but our two selves.[35]

On the way back from a climb 'it was so hot we spent an hour beside
a beautiful pool bathing and swimming in our skins.' Wallis told
Leo d'Erlanger that he now slept a lot. 'For the past year I have had
to force myself to go on; and I must have been as near to a crash as
one would care to go.'[36]

On VE Day, Molly and Barnes walked past flag-hung cottages to a packed thanksgiving service in Borrowdale church. At 3 p.m. guests gathered in the Scawfell Hotel to listen to broadcast speeches from Churchill and the King. The radio kept fading out, but since everyone in the room had come either to walk or climb 'all the talk is of a good way down from High White Stones – over Sergeant Man along High Raise, over Stake Pass, down Langstrath and home'.

A week later: 'There really is nothing like being alone together, is there.'[37] Alone together they were, but there are signs that Wallis was still at work in his head. On that same day, he wrote in reply to a colleague who sent news of a tragedy. Since mid-April the USAAF had been trialling Highball off the Florida coast. On 28 April, a mine let fall too low rebounded and struck off the tail of the aircraft that released it. The aircraft pitched straight into the sea, killing the crew.[38] After drafting his condolences,[39] Wallis wrote to Linda Longbottom, the wife of Maurice Longbottom – the gifted Vickers test pilot who had trialled Upkeep and Highball and helped Wallis in a myriad ways. Back in January Longbottom had been killed while test-flying a Warwick GR V to investigate its tendency to directional instability. In certain conditions this could result in rudder lock over, which Longbottom induced. According to witnesses, he succeeded in recovering from the resulting spin but either met a consequential problem or else found the Warwick still sinking after the pull out. He put the aircraft down, wheels up, along the railway line between Weybridge and Walton. The crashed machine lay across four electrical conductor rails and exploded.[40] Linda sent a book of his as a keepsake. Wallis replied, 'He was the only one of our pilots with whom one could really plunge into the future.' 'And with it all, he was such a dear boy, so kindly and patient, that he won all our hearts.'[41]

The tragedy collected Wallis's thoughts about how to plunge into the future without him. In ten years' time, jet-powered machines would routinely exceed the speed of sound and rise into the mesosphere; among them would be revolutionary forms; equipment and electronics would become ever more sophisticated. Two connected lines of thought were in his mind. One was to simulate stratospheric conditions at ground level. The other was to trial new designs with pilotless scale models, to be flown from the ground under radio control.

Just before they left for Borrowdale, Wallis put to Hew Kilner the idea of a large chamber in which densities and temperatures of the upper atmosphere could be replicated.[42] Kilner agreed, and on their way to Borrowdale, Wallis visited Vickers's naval construction yard at Barrow to gather data on submarine pressure hulls. At Rosthwaite he sketched and specified the design of a pressure vessel on hotel notepaper and posted it to Alec Grant, his general manager, with instructions to put it in the hands of Norman Boorer, the research department's chief designer.[43]

Backfire

Before going on holiday, Wallis accepted an invitation to join a most secret committee that Benjamin Lockspeiser had formed twelve days before the Dams Raid. Its purpose was to bring together expertise in the new field of supersonics.[44] In 1943 there were no facilities for supersonic work in Britain, and such research as there was pointed to a series of mysteries awaiting solution – for instance, how to overcome problems of control and stability that accompanied the transition from subsonic to supersonic flight, or the prediction that the aerodynamic centre of a wing would move according to speed. Committee members were drawn initially from the RAE, the NPL and relevant ministries, later augmented by academics. Few of them were from the industry.

Wallis attended his first meeting of the Supersonic Committee on 12 June.[45] It is not clear how much, if anything, he already knew about it, or about the Miles M.52, the secret turbojet-powered supersonic research aircraft that was being built under its influence.[46] The Committee was so hush-hush that even the M.52's designers were unaware of its existence. There again, Wallis was well acquainted with several of the Committee's members, like John MacColl, Geoffrey Ingram Taylor and Norbert Rowe, and the Wellington being used to test Whittle's new engine for the M.52 had been converted under the supervision of George Edwards. Wallis's relationship with the Supersonic Committee, and events surrounding the M.52, will bring us to one of the strangest and, apparently, least documented episodes in his career.[47]

Germany's surrender put the challenges of supersonic flight in a new context, as the Allies organised missions to take stock of her aero industry and advanced research and then assimilate their findings – like the value of swept wings to delay the onset of compressibility at high subsonic speeds.[48] In July both George Edwards and Wallis were involved in such information gathering, Edwards as a member of the Farren Mission to study German aircraft,[49] aircraft engine and armament industries, and Wallis as an adviser to a project on the A-4 rocket.[50] When Edwards returned to Weybridge he brought tidings of the Aeronautical Research Institute at Völkenrode, where facilities included a supersonic wind tunnel and a stratosphere chamber.

Wallis went back to Germany on 19 July. Fourteen weeks before,[51] US forces had entered the town of Nordhausen on the edge of the Harz mountains, and nearby discovered the Mittelwerk – an eighteen-mile network of tunnels originally created by gypsum mining and since converted to a bomb-proof factory complex to produce A-4 rockets. US ordnance officers were quickly on the scene and took parts sufficient for missiles for shipment to the United States.

In parallel, SHAEF formed a plan to bring together German technicians and troops from the A-4 Division to build rockets from salvaged parts, and thereby gain experience of launching them. SHAEF wanted to do this quickly, while the testing, assembling, and fuelling of the rockets were still fresh in mind. The project was christened Operation Backfire. Its original hope was to use rockets, captured complete in a state fit to fire, together with their necessary ancillary equipment. Some thirty A-4s were considered necessary, to allow for failed launches and rockets unfit to fly. In the event, none were found, and it was necessary to scavenge components from different sources and set up an assembly shop where they could be brought together. Effort was eventually concentrated on producing eight fireable rockets of which it was hoped that four could be successfully launched.

Backfire came into being at the end of May 1945. A Special Projectile Operations Group (SPOG) was formed for the purpose. Since it would be necessary to fire the rockets out to sea, it was decided to base the operation near the north German coast. Most of this was in the British Zone, so for administrative simplicity SPOG was set up primarily as a British organisation to which US advisers, staff officers, and technicians could be attached as wished. However, while the project was progressing, its sponsor was dissolved; with hostilities over, SHAEF was formally disbanded on 14 July. Its passing had several consequences for Backfire. One was to bring it entirely under the aegis of Britain's War Office, supported by the Ministry of Supply. Another was to sow rivalry between Allies who until then had been collaborating. The United States had already garnered know-how and matériel from the rocket programme, and now used its dominance to demand the transfer to themselves from SPOG of a number of German rocket specialists.

Wallis stepped into these touchy surroundings five days after SHAEF's passing. With him were Lt Col W. W. Campbell (whose fields were servo gear, electrics and gyros), an expert on fuels from British Oxygen, and an electronics specialist from Robert Watson-Watt's staff at TRE Malvern. Also with them was a brigadier who irritated Wallis by delaying their departure by arriving at Hendon having had no breakfast.[52] Wallis was not impressed either by the elderly Mk 1 Anson provided to take them to Cuxhaven.

Wallis's role was to determine what Vickers staff should be sent either to observe or assist in reconstruction of the rockets, and to provide a report to the Ministry of Supply and Vickers's board. He found that the British Army had hoped to salvage sufficient parts to erect 120 rockets. However, the parts had had to be gathered at high speed, to beat the date set for Thuringia to pass into Soviet control, and there had been no time for selection or listing. Hence, while trains stood in Cuxhaven sidings laden with miscellaneous A-4 parts, it was already clear that they did not yet have a complete set sufficient even for one rocket. The entire supply of some components had been abstracted by Americans, while the lack of any record of recent and all-important modifications meant there was no immediate way of knowing if the parts in their hands were current or obsolete.

Wallis was familiar with the A-4 through his Crossbow work. He knew that it was the key to understanding of rocket technology. He took a close interest in its turbopump, a device driven by the catalysation of hydrogen peroxide, which could shift 9000 kg (20,000 lb) of the missile's propellants – water alcohol and liquid oxygen – from their tanks into the combustion chamber in 60 seconds.

The first successful Backfire launch – a 'pencil on a spear of flame' – took place on 2 October. In contrast with it was the manner of the party's return on 20 July. Petrol ran short in deteriorating weather over the Netherlands, and after two attempts the pilot landed near Amsterdam. Finding no fuel on the airfield, they borrowed a car and went in search of a supply, eventually returning with several jerry cans of petrol. Taking off again, they reached Hendon at 8 p.m. Wallis noted that the Anson was equipped with neither a working radio nor parachutes, and that so much water entered the cockpit during the rainstorm in which they crossed the North Sea that he and another member of the party had to shield the pilot by holding an outspread mackintosh.

Facing the future: Britain

Wallis submitted his Backfire report on 25 July. Next day, the results of the 1945 general election were declared. Like millions of others, Wallis had voted Labour. Even allowing for the mood of the time, this is a surprise. We have seen that Wallis was a high Tory who believed in a class system wherein everyone had allotted roles. He had no time for socialism, was not impressed by the local Labour candidate, and nationalisation of the English Steel Corporation was in Labour's manifesto. Long-standing misgivings about Churchill and his circle may have played a part, but it appears that there were things in Labour's programme that did strike positive chords. Since later 1943, he had been impressed by the way in which Freeman, Cripps, and a core of others had taken control of the MAP's priorities. In place of committees and officials who talked across each other or hesitated had come quick decisions with practical results. Tallboy and Grand Slam, he said afterwards, represented a 'revolutionary development' that could not have taken place if the experience and resources of the ESC and Vickers had not been under control of the same people who worked in collaborative spirit. Was this a bellwether for the Labour Party's promise 'to link the skill of British craftsmen and designers to the skill of British scientists'? According to Labour's manifesto, genius was to be given full rein. Something along these lines is indicated. Back in September 1944 Wallis had sat up late one night with Pidcock at Chateau Lannigou talking about prospects for a national research strategy with horizons beyond those of cautious company directors. In July 1945 he did more than lend Labour his vote: in the weeks before polling day he made White Hill House available as a local base for the Party's campaign.

The mantled ghost

Molly was on holiday with Mary and Elisabeth at Broadstairs when the Second World War ended. Barnes wrote to tell her about his walk to the thanksgiving service in pouring rain, and to grumble about having to spend the rest of the morning 'telephoning & telegraphing all over the country from Weymouth to Barrow, cancelling meetings and so on. Lots of people went to work & had to go home again – a silly arrangement.'[53] He encouraged her to look up the people at Reculver who had befriended him 'when he was "playing marbles"' in 1943. Molly and the girls duly took a bus to Birchington and walked six miles along the old sea wall to the church with two towers. They scrambled over the fence to explore the church ruins, whereupon a coastguard 'poked his head out of the window & told us we shouldn't be in there, & to go.' Molly explained who they were, 'and at the name of Wallis he became all smiles & sweetness & came out to greet us, & brought the other coastguards to see us, & couldn't say enough good things about Mr Wallis and his great works.'

Mary had turned eighteen and gained a place to read history at University College London. In October Molly went to show her round. She was thrown to find how much had been destroyed by bombing. 'Only the Slade and the Engineering department remain of the UC I used to know.' There again, she had an old satin evening frock which might do for Mary, but it needed alteration. Molly asked Nan's sister to sew; Nan's sister asked if she remembered Molly's first evening dress at UCL.

> Well I do remember it; I went to my first dance with Barnes in it . . . It feels so queer to Barnes and me. I saw two ghosts in the quadrangle on a summer moonlight night . . .

After the start of term Mary lived in London during the week and returned to Effingham at weekends. Harry now had an old car, and most Sundays saw a ritual in which he arrived at White Hill House to ask permission to drive Mary back to town next morning, and Wallis refused because he was suspicious both of Harry's driving and the mechanics of his car. However, there came the day when Harry agreed to meet his mother to attend a performance of *Oedipus Rex* at the New Theatre, and his tutor held him back. Harry asked Mary to go in his stead. Stopes was unaware of this until she reached the theatre. 'Do you know what *Oedipus* is?' she asked acidly. 'I don't suppose your mother would at all like you seeing this if she won't let you go to a dance in Holy Week.'[54] The previous Sunday Mary had gone for a walk, fetching up at Norbury Park where the butler ushered her into the private room wherein Harry and his mother were having tea. 'I bet Dr S. was furious but I daresay Harry was pleased enough!' A week later Harry and Mary went to the Royal Albert Hall to hear Menuhin play Elgar's violin concerto. Such companionship notwithstanding, Molly thought Mary 'heartfast'; she had not noticed how close the two had become.

In November Wallis attended the Royal Society's anniversary dinner. It was the Society's 283rd and his first. He was seated between his old ally Sir Henry Tizard and a man whose entire academic life had been devoted to the formation of sand dunes. Clement Attlee was guest of honour. Wallis thought Attlee's address 'rather commonplace'.[55] Molly, on the other hand, was impressed. She told a friend that Barnes had marked him down because he spoke from notes.

Toward the year's end, Wallis's thoughts turned to Effingham's church clock, upon which he and Molly had worked that happy afternoon back in 1939. Since then, neglect and 'witches in the town' had silenced the chimes, while the new vicar's fear of the vertical ladder meant that the clock had gone unwound for months. Now that Wallis had a little time to himself, he had restarted the clock and put some hours in on the chime mechanism, wherein he diagnosed a leaky plunger in the switch gear. With a wry pun he told John that the reactivated chimes now ran 'like clockwork', adding that this had infuriated 'some very selfish and rich' outsiders who had come to Effingham 'to dodge the blitz'. The interlopers threatened legal action for disturbance of their peace. 'But the whole village rejoices to have their chimes back, so what do I care.'

Effingham was wrapped in fog on New Year's Eve. As it grew dark, Wallis was up in the quiet of St Lawrence's tower, listening to the clock's tick and whirr.

12

Things to Come, 1946–51

The state of things

In 1946 Britain's gold and dollar reserves were depleted, her debt was over twice the size of gross domestic product, and exports were far below their pre-war level. Industry was haggard from want of investment. Consumer goods were scarce.[1] The introduction of bread rationing in July symbolised how parlous things had become. Wallis worked in one of the few industries where investment had been sustained. However, the concomitant of national poverty was fierce competition for resources; Wallis could pursue any ideas he liked, provided the salary bill for his new department did not exceed £15,000.

The Attlee government's decision in January 1947 to acquire nuclear weapons brought with it the need for an advanced jet bomber to carry them. This posed challenges. The turbojet was new and immature, while during the war the Allies had put upgrading of existing technology before research into new areas, like supersonics. But such research was now needed, for as aircraft approached the speed of sound things began to happen that no one understood. The compressibility of air caused departures from the rules of subsonic aerodynamics, and the wind tunnels used to ascertain how designs would perform did not work much beyond M = 0.8.

Given the urgent need for data from the transonic and early supersonic regions, the decision taken by the Ministry of Supply in February 1946 to cancel the Miles M.52 at first sight looks odd. We recall that this was the aircraft intended to provide Britain with such data at a time when no other sources for it were available.[2] We recall, too, that in June 1945 Wallis joined the Supersonic Committee that advised the Ministry. Some have linked the cancellation with his arrival. The Committee was chaired by Ben (now Sir Ben) Lockspeiser, DSR at the MAP during the dams days back in 1943, and one of the topics considered at that meeting was a proposal for an expendable rocket-propelled model. Wallis agreed to explore the practicality of designing such models.[3] His report at the following meeting led to the government's issue to Vickers of a contract for 3/10 scale models of the M.52.

The M.52 project itself, meanwhile, was coming under scrutiny: its cost was rising, there was doubt about whether it would perform as intended, and recently acquired German research suggested that it might need to be rethought. On 20 February 1946 Lockspeiser pronounced: 'No more supersonic aircraft till the rocket-propelled models and wind tunnels have given us enough information to proceed on a reliable basis.'[4] It has been inferred that this was inspired by Wallis's proselytising about models, but the evidence points rather to a web of factors,[5] and in particular to a growing belief inside the Ministry of Supply that much of the information needed could be obtained more cheaply and safely by telemetering from model tests. In the event, what began as a simple research vehicle quickly evolved into an ambitious sophisticated joint RAE-Vickers project for an air-launched, telemetered, auto-piloted, rocket-powered test vehicle that cost more than the M.52 project upon which it was meant to improve.[6] The test vehicle reached M = 1.38 in stable flight on 9 October 1948, but by then most of its aims had already been achieved by other means.[7]

The rocket vehicle was publicly credited to Wallis, but it is a question how closely involved with it he was. Responsibility for its motor, autopilot, telemetering, and other instrumentation rested elsewhere, and there is little sign of it in his papers or those of Vickers. In 1946/47 he was looking into some further distance. While Highball bounced on, being earmarked to equip several naval aircraft, and in new versions,[8] the stratosphere chamber took shape during 1946, its main parts being made in the shipyard at Barrow and brought south for assembly. When it was running, Wallis and his colleagues became cousins of Prospero, able to conjure deserts, iced winds, and conditions at 70,000 feet.[9]

Two projects led the agenda of Wallis's new research department. One was a bi-fuel rocket-powered torpedo.[10] It was called Heyday, looked a little like a bluefin tuna, and was intended to induce a smooth flow pattern in the water through which it passed. To achieve this its surfaces had to be free from blemish, which meant close collaboration with Wallis's old friends at the English Steel Corporation to achieve perfect pressings in numbers and at low cost.[11] Heyday, he blithely told Vickers's managing director Bonner Dickson, was a 'large scale experiment which will undoubtedly lead us to the complete redesign of the submarine'.[12]

In the event, interest in Heyday faded. Historians have suggested that its underlying purpose was to provide experimental data on laminar flow for the department's other and foremost project, Wild Goose. Wallis described Wild Goose as a 'Wing Controlled Aerodyne' – a definition he framed to set it apart from conventional aeroplanes. As concepts go it was audacious. It consisted of only three parts: an ichthyoid body and two wings pivoted through narrow slits in the after portion of the body. The wings were to be adjustable, folding back for high-speed flight and coming forward to give more lift during launch and landing.

Variable sweep itself was not a new idea,[13] but Wild Goose was intended to embody a further feature which was entirely ground-breaking: each wing could move independently, so enabling control by balancing pitching moments on opposite sides. There would be no need for flaps, ailerons, elevators, and no tail assembly. To turn, say, to starboard the port wing would be brought forward and the starboard wing moved to the rear, and vice versa for a roll in the other direction. To dive, the pilot would move the wings backward, to climb they were moved forward.[14] When Wild Goose was eventually tested in full flight this system of control proved to be responsive, easy to apply and certain in action. That point lay some years ahead.[15]

Wallis reckoned that the tail assembly of a conventional aircraft, together with other gear needed for stability, contributed a fifth of drag and 15 per cent of weight. Wing-controlled flight thus promised savings which could be put towards greater range, speed, or capacity. He saw the aerodyne as a new genus of vehicle, capable of development in variant forms, manned and unmanned, for defence, attack, large transport, and long-distance travel.[16] Exhilarated, he was also pushed: to bring the new genus into being he and his team also had to provide designs for radio-controlled test vehicles, a device for proportional control to assist the pilot on the ground, a family of jets and rockets (cold motors, high-speed motors, turbojets, boost motors for take-off and climb), and flying tests, initially in a small tilting tunnel, in due course on an aerodrome.[17] Wallis nonetheless assured Bonner Dickson that with contracts from the Ministry of Supply for supersonic research and (he hoped) for the Wing Controlled Aerodyne, the 'Department is quite capable of becoming self-supporting'.

Things were hardly calmer at home. They sang again with the Bookham Choral Society and re-joined Vaughan Williams's Leith Hill choir. (Wallis studied the programme at the start of each season; if there was much new music in it he tended not to take part.) In 1946 he became a member of Effingham's parish council and before long was elected to its chair, where he stayed for a decade. The garden was put back to rights after years of being dug for victory. Beekeeping continued. He and Molly hoped for a fifth child; with no result by 1948 Wallis visited a consultant, the result of which ('First class motility') he telegrammed to Molly.[18] He concluded nothing was wrong, 'but not being as young nor having as much leisure as in the past.' Practical as ever, Wallis suggested they keep a five-monthly chart on squared paper, 'blacking out the days in any one month that we have tried'.[19]

Camp resumed, although Wallis was now so busy that Molly sometimes led the pitching of tents and digging of latrines. Wallis went when he could, often driving down on a Friday and succumbing to Sunday evening melancholia on the way back ('All the time I might have been with you!'). Molly wrote to tell him of cycling to Dancing Ledge, climbing Nine Barrows for blackberries, the whirr of grasshoppers, and rising mist at dusk. 'Darling Barnes, I wish you were here.' Harry Stopes-Roe often joined them but did not appear in August 1947.

Harry was now tall, fine-looking, and had embarked on postgraduate research at Imperial College. Mary was completing her history degree at UCL. For three years they had spent a lot of time in each other's company, and just over a month later Harry told his mother that they were engaged. Marie Stopes did not take this well. Next day Wallis received a letter (copied to Mary) in which she listed objections to the marriage, one of them being Mary's short-sightedness. Stopes kept up her campaign through the winter and tried to enlist her husband Humphrey (who for some years had been exiled from her bed, and more recently, to a large extent, from Norbury Park) in opposing it. Stopes told him that Mary was plain and dull, and that the marriage would make a mockery of their 'lives' work for Eugenic breeding and the Race'.[20] Humphrey disagreed. He thought the couple well matched, saw no purpose in trying to part them, and when on 9 June 1948 it was announced that the marriage would take place 'shortly' he accepted an invitation to attend.

The wedding took place seven weeks later in Effingham's parish church. Wallis's brother John, now Chancellor of Lichfield Cathedral, took the service. Stopes did not attend, sent no present, and insisted that in the announcement in *The Times* Harry be described simply as the 'only son of H. V. Roe Esq'.[21]

Sicily

A fortnight after the wedding, Wallis left home, presented himself at BOAC's new terminal in Southampton, and boarded a Hythe flying boat bound for Sicily. With him were Fred Winterbotham and Fred's new wife-to-be, Petrea.

The journey was a small triumph for Winterbotham, who, with other close friends, had seen the growing strain under which Wallis was working and had badgered him to take a complete break. The question was where to take it. Dorset would no longer do since

Wallis's conscientiousness and unwillingness to delegate led him to take work to Camp and commute back and forth to Weybridge. Winterbotham accordingly looked for somewhere further afield. A wartime colleague knew a beachfront villa near Taormina in Sicily that combined agreeable surroundings with seclusion. Whitney Straight, BOAC's well-connected deputy chairman, agreed to join them. Wallis needed development funding for Wild Goose; Winterbotham reasoned that Straight's presence would enable Wallis to make his pitch for it while telling himself that he was still at work.

Before leaving Wallis composed a letter in which he begged his executors to press Vickers for an ex-gratia payment for the welfare of his widow and family if he were to die.[22] This echoed and expanded upon the plea he had made to Hew Kilner in 1945. It opened with a restatement of the responsibilities he had shouldered since the deaths of Molly's sister and brother-in-law, Barbara and Hurley McCormick, in 1940. Bringing up their two children had added to his commitments, while heavy taxation, and the refusal of Hurley's near relatives to agree to legal adoption (which would have brought tax relief) had eroded his income and prevented saving.

Wallis worried that Vickers's recently appointed directors might not know who he was or what he had done, so he began to make a list of achievements to attach to the letter. The list is notable for its interpositions, one of which throws light on the origin of his bombs. This came about, he said, because the Air Ministry's demands for variant versions of the Wellington early in the war had kept Rex Pierson and his design team busy while leaving him free to focus on other things. Casting about for a problem awaiting solution he had alighted on the relationship between Bomber Command's weaponry and targets of strategic value. In another aside, he wrote that it had been his study of the German V2 that in 1944 put him on the path to Wild Goose.

The letter is tinged by anxiety, and the beginning of a concern for his legacy. He told his executors that his 'greatest work' was 'without doubt' the invention and development of the Wing Controlled Aerodyne but tempered the claim by saying that he might not live to see its fulfilment. The list of works broke off at the point where discussion of Wild Goose began, as if by writing about it something bad might ensue. Did he fear that he was ill, or that the journey upon which he was about to embark was ill-omened? Clearly, something beyond BOAC's safety record was troubling him, for in the letter's last paragraph he prayed that his executors would have the things he listed in their minds 'if the things that I fear come to pass'.[23]

BOAC gave them a cabin to themselves. The Hythe was old technology,[24] unpressurised, and Wallis wondered if it was safe to use his fountain pen.[25] After four hours the aircraft alighted on the lake at Marignane, the international 'water-airport' that served Marseille and the Côte d'Azur. They passed the night in a nearby hotel and rose before dawn for the next leg of their journey, to Augusta on the north-east coast of Sicily. At Augusta BOAC lent them a jeep for the 55-mile drive to Mazzaro along twisty roads, through red-tiled villages, round hairpins with dizzy drops, under a scorching sun.

The Villa S. Andrea was lapped by clear water in a small cove sheltered by a rocky promontory. It had been built as the summer home of Robert Trewhella (1830–1909), a Cornish civil engineer who in the 1850s had been hired by the Sicilian government to build railways. Trewhella's son had enlarged the house, surrounded it with subtropical gardens and furnished its airy marble-floored rooms with paintings and treasures that gave the feeling of an English country house.

Wallis outlined the routine: breakfast at eight thirty (rolls, creamy butter, grape jam, figs, and tea that was 'better than French'). Around ten he donned rope-soled sandals and went out to chairs on the beach. There was fruit for elevenses. Lunch at one o'clock was soup, fish, spaghetti and coffee, followed by a siesta until four thirty. Then tea. From eight, a leisurely dinner. 'I am slowly beginning to "unwind" mentally and physically, and surely this complete change of scene and diet must have some effect.'

He bought a snorkel, mask and flippers. After years of swimming in Studland Bay he was delighted to find that he could see 40 feet down, watch fish and darting shoals. It seemed like flying, a 'lovely revelation'. He pleaded not guilty to the folly of wishing to be young but felt wistful that he had not snorkelled in his youth. Back on the surface, the villa's manager rowed them round the bay and into a cave with bats. Wallis admired the cobalt sea. But one day passed like another, and by the first Sunday, hurrying to finish a letter to put into the hand of a BOAC crew member who could post it from Southampton, he was already melancholic.

> My little love, I am more sick & lonely without your dear presence than I could have believed possible; tho' perhaps it is the only way to let us both see what 24 years of uninterrupted companionship have tended to obscure, that is that we love and need each other more than ever. I am taking this holiday as an imperative rest, rather as medicine than as a joy, full of interest tho' it be.[26]

Whitney Straight arrived. Rich, handsome, athletic, his career thus far had included grand prix motor racing, aircraft design, promotion of provincial airports, airline management, fighting in the Battle of Britain, being shot down, and escape from occupied Europe. His younger brother Michael later confessed to being a Soviet spy. Still only thirty-six, he was now deputy chairman of BOAC with a remit to develop the airline's fleet and dominate the routes to Australia and North America. Wallis wrote: 'He and I are evidently going to have some heavy talks on aeroplanes', adding with a swagger that neither Straight nor 'his so-called experts' had any idea 'of the revolution that I can produce in air transport'. Having earlier tried to convince himself that the holiday was simply therapeutic, he now told Molly: 'Of course, the whole of my trip here was really arranged so that I could have long meetings with Whitney Straight unhampered by the jealous intervention of stupid people.'

On 17 August Straight joined them over dinner to hear about Wild Goose. Wallis explained that he had been unable to risk bringing any 'secret papers' so all the data was in his head, 'which fortunately customs officers cannot open!' He had worked out equations from first principles and drew sketches of Wild Geese suitable for use by BOAC. Under a full moon, Mount Etna silhouetted against the western sky, he sipped a Sicilian liqueur, 'doubling my optimism at every sip!'

Straight was accompanied by his wife Daphne.[27] He suggested that they take the jeep up Etna, or at least as far as it could go (Wallis adding archly that they were 'not the sort of people to wish to go farther than that'). Daphne seemed 'fragile' and 'nervous', but Wallis admired the way she stuck with Straight as they drove 8000 feet up the volcanic cone. The discomfort of riding while perched on the jeep's toolbox reminded him of Normandy after D-Day. His leading impression was of colours: a blood-red plume drifting from Etna's peak, the green plain below, purple cloud shadows on the blue-green sea.

Wallis thought Straight was 'clearly very interested' in his new aircraft.

> He is wondering how he can get the exclusive rights for civil aircraft so as to put BOAC ahead of the world, and he is going to have a discussion with Lord Tedder, with a view to seeing whether the RAF & BOAC cannot bring their requirements as far as transport aircraft are concerned into line, so that both can use the same 'airframe'; thus halving my work and hastening production. Of course, the real answer would seem to be the creation of a National Aircraft Research & Development Corporation; but Fred tells me that the Civil Service would have a killing effect on any such enterprise.

Behind the optimism, there was an autumnal note. On 27 August: 'In a month I shall be 61.' And on the 29th, in the air, on the way home, 'Thirty-seven years ago, today, my dearest mother died.'

> How very, very far we have moved since then, and how wonderful the future would seem if only we could see into it, and how dark and unpromising it seemed to me all those years ago. So perhaps it may seem to be to our children today. To each age I suppose it seems that its fathers have discovered all that there is to do or to know.

BOAC held a farewell dinner party at Augusta. It was a merry occasion, the more so for the presence of ACM Sir John Baldwin, who had headed 3 Group's Wellington force at the outbreak of war and said flattering things. Wallis used much of the last leg of the return flight to continue a letter to Molly. He reflected on how pleasing it was 'to move over the world amongst these aeronautical people, and to be recognised and known among them, and to have much good talk with them. What will it be like if I live to see my "Wild Goose" come into general service?' He turned to describe the journey, snow on the Bas Alps, Normandy's landscape. The next thing he knew, 'we saw the Isle of Wight and good, green, substantial old England'.[28]

Wallis's hopes for a rapid acceptance of the business case for Wild Goose soon ebbed. Twenty-one years later, Jack Morpurgo wrote to Whitney Straight to ask if Wallis had been justified in coming away from Taormina with high hopes.[29] Straight remembered Taormina, but not Wild Goose: 'I have looked through my diaries, and unfortunately I cannot find any reference to Barnes Wallis.'[30]

Washington

A month later Wallis was again in Southampton, this time to board the *Queen Elizabeth* for New York.[31] With him was Harry Mushlian, his patent agent. Their destination was Alexandria, home of the US Patent Office on the outskirts of Washington, and their purpose was to consolidate rights in the intellectual property of Wild Goose. While the Wing Controlled Aerodyne was a unified idea, in realisation it was becoming a family of connected inventions, with separate patents for different features and successive improvements.[32] Wallis believed it to be the greatest advance in aeronautics since the invention of movable control surfaces at the beginning of the century, so it made sense to gather its various aspects under one principal patent.

'The ship is simply immense,' he told Molly. Coincidentally, also aboard was Sir Wilfrid Freeman, the MAP's former chief executive, into whom he ran on the first evening. Freeman reminded him of the Royal Commission on Awards to Inventors and asked if he had thought of entering Upkeep. Wallis replied that Harry Mushlian had urged him to apply, but that he had declined on the ground that the main credit for the weapon rested with the crews who used it.

On arrival in New York Wallis and Mushlian met their American representative, the engineer and patent specialist Albert C. Nolte, who took them to dinner at the New York Athletic Club, and thence to his home on the shore of Long Island Sound. Their plan was to continue to Washington next day, but Wallis fell ill in the night and was taken to hospital. There was talk of an operation ('I could hear the surgeons sharpening their scalpels') but the problem was soon diagnosed as an intestinal infection and after a day he was discharged. Wallis convalesced for a couple of days, Nolte lent them his Studebaker, and on the following Sunday they set out by easy stages for Washington.

This was Wallis's first visit to the United States, and an idea has got about that his first impressions were all of a piece with his suspicion of Atlanticism and distaste for American influence on English popular culture.[33] In fact, Philadelphia's ridges and valleys struck him as 'very fine country'. He was fascinated by Valley Forge, scene of the winter encampment of 1777–78 during the Revolutionary War, and by Gettysburg.[34] He thought Washington 'a wonderful city, well laid out',[35] was pleased with his rooms in the hotel on Pennsylvania Avenue, and optimistic about the outcome of the patent meeting: 'no doubt we will win all points and get a master patent'. But no master patent ensued. Years later, an old associate said of Wallis 'He never forgives'.[36] Is this where his anti-Americanism began?

On Thurleigh aerodrome

July 1949 On Thurleigh Aerodrome, Beds.
    Sitting in my car
        I am not the man my Sweetheart Darling who should

attempt to describe to you the indescribable, but as with infinite cunning I insist on being treated as a visitor, and not as chief of the whole show, I have the leisure to try to record for you something of what must surely prove to be one of the landmarks in the development of flight.

Thus began a series of occasional letters to Molly describing the trialling of Wild Goose and its successor, Swallow. Wallis wrote them, on and off, for the next twenty-three years. They were never sent. Rather, by writing for Molly, Wallis gave himself the spur to produce a lay account of what he believed was his life's greatest work. The letters are coloured by rare detail and contradict his claim to be 'a visitor' watching the work of a self-sufficient team.

National Aircraft Establishment. Thurleigh, Beds.
. . . 11.0 a.m. I had to come away at short notice, as every moment is precious at this stage, and I have to keep pressing the team to ever harder efforts, and a few hours may make all the difference when weather is concerned.[37]

Until 1945 Thurleigh had been occupied by Flying Fortresses of the USAAF 306 Heavy Bombardment Group. After their departure the site's combination of proximity to London and seclusion was among the factors that led to its selection as the UK's research aerodrome. The plan was to combine it with a wind tunnel complex at nearby Twinwood Farm, the whole to become the National Aircraft Establishment. In 1949 Vickers was awarded a government development contract for Wild Goose and following preliminary trials at Brooklands the team moved there.

Thurleigh brought a new way of life. Every week or so Wallis left home and went to live on the airfield. Among his twenty-two staff were engineers, radio specialists, electricians, a crane operator, cinematographer, firemen, and two men trained to handle the hydrogen peroxide used in the bi-fuel rockets that propelled the launching trolley. Hydrogen peroxide splashed onto ordinary clothes will burst into flame, so when fuelling the men wore polythene suits, rubber boots and gloves, special goggles, and caps, while a nearby fireman gently hosed them with water.

The flying field was nearly a mile from their lodgings, and the walk to it was lined with derelict buildings. Everyone slept in dormitories, apart from Wallis who had a tiny room to himself with a bed so short that his feet overhung the end, and an adjoining bathroom scarcely larger than a walk-in cupboard. He grumbled about swing doors that banged, staff members who stayed out until midnight, radio sets always left on, and the canteen.

> Lunch for me yesterday was stone cold macaroni, with a suspicion of cheese, and two sopping potatoes, – the 'alleged' cook's idea of what a vegetarian likes; and the last meal of the day was lots of lettuce leaves, a tomato and some broken bits of cheese, bread and jam at 5 p.m.; after which we worked till 8.30 pm in the sheds.[38]

In contrast, on evenings when he left White Hill House and drove to Thurleigh a ritual developed in which he liked to stop for dinner at the White Swan in Bedford. His departmental administrator and wing specialist were usually with him.

> We left Weybridge last night, about 5.30 pm, and reached the Swan after a very wet journey just before 8 pm. And we had a really good dinner. Soup, and a real Dover Sole *each*, done to perfection and large enough to give that so rare but delightful feeling of healthy repletion, followed by an excellent ice and pear, just right.[39]

Wild Goose ascending

Wild Goose's un-swept wingspan of 26 feet 6 inches (over 8 metres) made it more like a small full-sized aeroplane than a large model.[40] It was to be launched along a prepared fairway from a remotely controlled, jet-powered trolley which could accelerate to over 100 mph. As we have seen, the trolley, jet motors, control systems, radio links, and telemetering were almost entirely designed and built in Wallis's department. This was laborious. Even more time-consuming was putting Wild Goose to the air.

> I have to solve the immensely difficult problem of firstly getting my full-size Wild Goose into the air, and then of learning to fly him, once he is there. And there is no gradual approach. Either he is on the ground all safe, or he is careering through the air at one or two hundred miles an hour.[41]

Flying an aircraft remotely, from a distance, by sight, is a very different proposition from control on board, when the pilot can make direct observations and receive sensations – like the position of the horizon, the feel of the controls, behaviour of the airframe – and react to these in a continuous flow of small inputs. In the case of Wild Goose remote control was accompanied by quite different sensations, such as the noise of the jets, the relative motion of the aerodyne against a blurred background, or how to judge the aircraft's behaviour when it was nearly out of sight.[42] Wallis was not to know that three years were to pass before Wild Goose was successfully flown round a complete circuit.

Wallis wanted to tailor the programme to allow the pilot's judgement, skill, and confidence gradually to grow, leading to successful flights later in the schedule, with a corresponding need for a high launch rate early on. This turned out to be a tall order. Pre- and post-launch operations on the aerodyne, the launching trolley, and the aerodrome were considerable.[43] There were twenty-nine separate pre-launch checks and tasks for the trolley, for instance, and on the aerodrome the checklist ran to fifty-six. Such was the complexity, in some cases delicacy, of their thermodynamic, electrical, and mechanical equipment that even a small malfunction might delay a launch by hours, if not days. Up on Thurleigh's exposed plateau their efforts were also often hampered by rain, fog and cold during the autumn and winter of 1949/50.

The aerodyne was cradled on the trolley in a way which allowed for its release when a predetermined speed was reached, or else for it to rise a little without actually leaving the cradle. Such a 'locked-on' run allowed them to trial complicated movements that preceded a flight, even to operating the numerous electrical circuits that had to be closed or broken when launching forth actually took place. At first, take-offs were complicated by turbulent airflow around the trolley. Wallis dealt with this by what he called the 'jump-start' – a system that held the aerodyne on the trolley until the lifting force exceeded its own weight by a predetermined, and quite large, amount, whereupon the aerodyne took to the air automatically.

17th Jan 1950. National Aeronautical Establishment, Thurleigh, Beds.
    Today has been very cold, with a strong and bitter N. wind whistling across the aerodrome. I have had the jet thrust of the trolley doubled. We were doing a 'locked-on' run, that is the Wild Goose can do all the motions of tak-ing-off except the final parting, and she signals that she has reached the required lifting force by lighting a lamp. Owing to some unexplained electrical fault she never signalled, and the trolley went past our observation and control tower at a speed of 120 m.p.h. She ought to develop the necessary lift (i.e. twice her own weight, so as to give her a huge jump into the air) at a mere 93 m.p.h., so she must have been developing over 3 times her own weight as she went by! If we don't take care she will fly away with her own trolley . . .[44]

Two days later:

8 p.m. Thursday January 19th 1950
    Praise be to God, a day of days, when an end has been put to six months of uncertainty and acute anxiety.

Despite wearing a cotton vest, woolly vest, woollen jumper, an old Burberry, scarf, mac, thick socks, stockings and gumboots, Wallis was 'frozen stiff'. Two locked-on runs were made that morning. The first failed to reach flying speed before the trolley jet fuel ran out – a problem traced to ageing of catalyst gauzes in the motor. After a second, successful, locked-on run and repositioning of control and signalling

> we decided to have a real take-off after lunch. The wind was rising steadily and still bitter cold from the N. Nevertheless, although I had said that I would not allow a free flight take-off down wind, yet I now felt that the critical matter that must be decided at all costs was whether we could really do the 'jump take-off'; by which I planned to hand over the aircraft to the pilot, at a sufficient height for him to have a fair chance of taking over the controls; and that what mistakes the pilot made after that did not really matter. So after the usual delays and anxieties, we fired the jet for the 3rd time today at about 3.30 p.m. Sky leaden with snow, and poor light. I had . . . joined the photographer on his tower, as I felt that my presence might worry the pilot and the radio experts. We were rewarded with a splendid run, a perfect take-off and a climb like an exquisite bird. Laus Deo, laus Deo, laus Deo. Nash flattened her out at about 50 feet up – perfectly and gracefully done . . .[45]

Alas, Alan Nash was too slow on his pull out, and she dived into the ground. But the evidence was there: Wild Goose could fly.

By June 1950 the team had made over a hundred runs. Forthcoming building work meant they had to move. A survey of aerodromes found them a new home, where their main companions would be choughs, whimbrels, and fulmars: Predannack, on the Lizard peninsula, near Helston, in Cornwall.

Molly gone

Some months before Molly had resolved to make an extended visit to her younger sister Pam. Pam had left Britain in 1945 to set up home with her husband Ken in Kirkland Lake, Ontario, and Molly had not seen her since. The prospect filled Wallis with gloom. When he took her to the Royal Docks to board the Cunard liner *Samaria* on 6 July he told himself that their forthcoming separation was because Pam embodied 'the essence of selfishness'. Wallis watched until the *Samaria* was out of sight, listened to the blast of her horn, 'hung about for another half hour', then drove home.

As often happened when he was downcast, he began to worry and grouse; his tongue seemed inflamed; he feared cancer, but the doctor found that all was well and that his blood pressure was good. He was vexed by friends who wrote to Molly via White Hill House (surely Mary Turner 'can afford to buy an air mail form'?), complained that the new parish clerk drank too much, and grumbled that the vicar had 'forced' him upon the parish council.[46] When Molly wrote to say that the Duffys were short of money he replied: 'No, we cannot possibly do anything about sending Pam either money or a sewing machine. I do not understand why they are as hard up as you say. Pam has had just as much inheritance as you, & should be quite comfortably off, as I have no doubt that Ken is well paid.'[47]

He lightened a little when their bee man lifted 55 lb of honey from the hives. Mary and Harry visited. Wallis was cock-a-hoop when he discovered that Harry had had several dental fillings ('Ha, ha! Mary's teeth are lasting better than Harry's. Is dental caries less eugenically decadent than astigmatism?'[48]). Elisabeth came to keep him company and was introduced to occasional small treats – an extra helping, another biscuit – which he described as 'secrets of the brotherhood'. He reckoned to be working at his highest pressure since the dams.[49] Alongside Wild Goose he had been thinking about an unmanned expendable bomber which would be a fraction of the cost of the emerging Vickers Valiant.[50] But in the background remained anxiety, and a new source of despondency.

The anxiety centred on Korea, where war had broken out in June, and the US ground forces since committed were not doing very well. In early September the recall of Parliament ('always a sign of emergency') reinforced his fear that wider war was near. He devised a plan whereby on a cabled signal he would arrange for Molly to fly to Quebec to catch the next boat to England. 'We will get you home somehow.'[51]

As for despondency, back at the end of 1949 Wallis had changed his mind about making a claim to the Royal Commission on Awards to Inventors. Just before Christmas Harry Mushlian had entered it through the Commission's fast-track procedure. It all looked straightforward, but in March the Ministry of Supply asked for extra time in which to make comments. This seemed ominous, and misgivings deepened when on 14 August 1950 Wallis was told that the Ministry had sought and been granted another postponement. This was surely a sign that the Ministry intended to contest the claim.[52]

Deeds of trust

Wallis's change of heart was prompted by Arthur Upcott's appeal on the day he left Christ's Hospital in 1904:

> I charge you never to forget the great benefits that you have received in this place, and, in time to come, according to your means, to do all that you can to enable others to enjoy the same advantage.

Wallis did not forget, and shortly before Christmas 1949 an idea took shape. If such an award was made, the money could be used to found an educational trust for children of members of the RAF. The proposal was put to the Air Council and the Council of Christ's Hospital, each of which agreed to nominate trustees. The Treasury Solicitor gave advice on organisation. The RAF Benevolent Fund agreed to make a matching contribution. When Wallis's ideas about the terms of the benefaction became overcomplicated, his old friend Victor Goddard (now a member of the Air Council) stepped in to supply the words needed to define eligibility and machinery for selection. Only one problem remained: the Ministry of Supply.

In November 1950 the Ministry finally outlined its objections: Wallis had been a full-time employee of Vickers-Armstrongs throughout Upkeep's development; Vickers was a government contractor; Wallis's experiments had been made with Vickers's knowledge and blessing; the Air Attack on Dams Committee was a Crown body, other national bodies like the RRL had given him indispensable help, and the hydrostatic fuze which triggered the mine had been developed by government scientists. It would not be right to make an award to Wallis for doing his job. And in any case, his contribution had already been acknowledged through the award of the CBE.

The claim was heard in March 1951. The tribunal sat for three days, and since Upkeep and Highball were still on the secret list it did so *in camera*. Kenneth Johnson QC presented the case. Its crux was that the weapon had been conceived and developed in Wallis's spare time, that he had pursued the work in a climate that varied from indifference through scepticism to opposition, and that some of the breakthroughs in the scale model explosive trials had resulted from his prompting.

Wallis's written evidence and answers to his barrister's questions during its preparation contain details found nowhere else – like the context of the Silvermere trial, and his suspicions about Lockspeiser. Cochrane and Freeman wrote in support. Freeman said that the award of the CBE had already been in the system at the time of the Dams Raid, in recognition of his service to the aero industry.

The tribunal accepted the claim and made an award of £10,000 – just short of £0.25 million at today's value. The trust was formed, and that autumn awarded the first of an annual group of fifteen scholarships to boys and girls at Christ's Hospital. The public was told that the awards were being made not by competitive examination but on the strength of the service records of the parents.[53]

Wallis's dispute with the Ministry of Supply was not the only reason why Upkeep was back in his thoughts. Recently, he had been helping a young man who was writing about the Dams Raid.

'Mr Wallis should not be left out of this record'

Paul Brickhill's book *The Dam Busters* (1951) had its origin in the foresight of John Coombes Nerney, the Air Ministry's librarian and head of the RAF's Air Historical Branch, who in July 1943 wrote to the DB Ops to urge that 'immediate steps' be taken to collect and secure 'all relevant material' covering the Dams Raid. Bufton passed the memo to a colleague:[54] 'Please consider how we can help, subject to the rigid security which must still apply. Mr Wallis should not be left out of this record.'[55]

By the end of 1944, Mr Wallis's name was in the public domain. We recall that in November he had been identified as creator both of the 'special mine' that had broken Germany's dams and the weapon that had finished the *Tirpitz*.[56] Five months later he was named as the designer of Grand Slam. In spring 1945 his photograph appeared in newspapers, and he was profiled in the *Illustrated London News*.[57] Despite all this new openness, however, the Barnes Wallis emerging from wartime shadow was largely a construct of Air Ministry press officers. The photograph they chose was out of date, making him look younger, while their characterisation of him as a 'backroom boy' was an empty label. Readers of the *Surrey Advertiser* were told that he lived in Effingham;[58] a photograph of Molly and Christopher in the *Daily Record* showed that like many other people he was married with children;[59] according to Aberdeen's *Evening Express* he was 'a quiet man' with a 'wonderful mathematical mind';[60] but nothing of much consequence was being said. He was, so to speak, well known, but not known well. Guy Gibson's first impressions of him in *Enemy Coast Ahead* (1946) likewise bore the marks of a PR machine which was out to praise and anonymise him at the same time: 'a scientist and very clever aircraft designer . . . neither young nor old, but just a quiet, earnest man who worked very hard.'[61]

A few weeks before Gibson's book appeared, his successor Leonard Cheshire had pitched an idea for a book about the wartime deeds of 617 Squadron to his literary agents, Curtis Brown.[62] Cheshire had kept notes and photographs. He was on good terms with the squadron's characters, he had already written a bestseller,[63] and it had been under his leadership that the squadron had evolved low-level marking and introduced Tallboy. All this notwithstanding, Curtis Brown could imagine no audience for such a book. After six years of war, the consensus in the publishing world was that the last thing anyone wanted to read about was bombing.

Ralph Cochrane agreed with Nerney that 617's story was worth telling and believed that a well-written history would stand to the credit of the RAF as a whole. In autumn 1946 he discussed it again with Cheshire. Cheshire no longer saw himself as the author and the baton now passed to John Pudney, whose poem 'For Johnny', used in Anthony Asquith's film *The Way to the Stars* (1945), has become one of the most quoted verses of the Second World War. Pudney wrote it while serving in the Air Ministry's Directorate of Public Relations, the famous 'Writer Command' whose members included Eric Partridge, R. F. Delderfield, and H. E. Bates. He was accordingly knowledgeable about and sympathetic to the RAF, and since the project had gained a quasi-official status through Cochrane's patronage, he had access to the AHB and Nerney, with whom he was already friendly.[64] Pudney was soon flummoxed. 'The story beats me', he told Nerney. 'Nothing that I begin to write about it begins to come to life.'[65] In November 1948 he gave up,[66] but promised to help another author if one were to appear. The following summer he met Paul Brickhill, and wrote to Nerney: 'I think I have found the very man to do that book about 617 Squadron.'[67]

Brickhill was an Australian journalist who had served in the RAAF and made his mark as co-author of a collection of escape stories about Stalag Luft III.[68] He had since been in correspondence with Pudney about a possible film and television series, and in June 1949 he returned to Britain to make a revised version of the escapes book. Pudney described what followed to Nerney:

When we met for the first time yesterday, I was discussing you, saying how unhappy I felt about the fact that the 617 story was never written. The more I told him about the story, the more excited he became about it, so I offered to hand over my material to him if he will use it in the way which you and I mutually agreed.[69]

Pudney encouraged Brickhill to visit Nerney, which he promptly did (returning 'full of enthusiasm' a fortnight later to collect Cheshire's albums, photographs, and other notes[70]) and found him a publisher – Evans Brothers.[71]

Brickhill interviewed former members of the Squadron, notably his fellow Australian Mick Martin, from whom he gleaned much anecdotal material,[72] Leonard Cheshire and James Tait. He paid a 25-guinea fee to Guy Gibson's widow for permission to draw on information from *Enemy Coast Ahead*. Of the 'thirty to forty sources' upon which Brickhill said he drew none was more important than Wallis. This was partly because Wallis was generous with his time and information, but also because he offered to Brickhill a solution to the structural problem which had stumped Pudney: how to hold a reader's interest in a story consisting mostly of one raid after another. Wallis provided the motivation for the narrative and became the thread that ran through it while other characters came and went. When the book appeared, there he was on the first page, 'his face unlined and composed, the skin smooth and pink and the eyes behind the horn-rimmed glasses mild and grey'. And if Brickhill's portrayal of someone 'gentle . . . rather detached' yet stubborn was to become another stereotype, it was more vivid than any that had appeared so far.

At this point Wallis described Brickhill 'as someone whom I know and like'.[73] Reasonably enough, Brickhill asked him how Upkeep worked. Wallis had no objection to telling him and had long been sceptical about the need for continued secrecy. Nonetheless, he said that he could not share relevant papers without official approval and passed the question to Nerney. The Air Ministry's Directorate of Intelligence had ruled that nothing could be said about Upkeep or Highball, including the names 'Upkeep' and 'Highball', which gave any inkling of what they were or how they worked. Since most of what was allowable had already appeared in *Enemy Coast Ahead*, the Deputy Director of Intelligence ruled that there was 'no need for Mr Brickhill to have any additional information'.[74] This put Nerney in an awkward position. Brickhill had been promised Air Ministry help for his history, and rather in the manner of Mr Collins speaking of

Lady Catherine de Bourgh, Nerney reminded the DDI that the book was being written 'with the approval of Air Chief Marshal Sir Ralph Cochrane'. Now that Brickhill had made a personal approach to Wallis, the Service would be in a 'slightly embarrassing position if he does not receive some measure of official support'.[75] The Intelligence Directorate was unyielding, and when *The Dam Busters* first appeared it did not tell its readers about Upkeep's working.

As the eighth anniversary of the Dams Raid neared, another security question arose. Wallis opened his *Radio Times* for the week beginning 6 May 1951 to see that an hour-long adaptation of Brickhill's forthcoming book was due to be broadcast on the Home Service in two days' time. Brickhill had alerted him to the broadcast some time before and had indeed invited him to read both the manuscript of the book and the radio script while they were still in draft. Wallis had declined, reasoning that to do so might appear to validate what Brickhill had written. In any case, his viewpoint would be so far from Brickhill's that it would be 'hopeless' to try to modify anything, and he had sufficient confidence in Brickhill's 'good taste to leave the matter entirely in his hands'.[76] However, what concerned Wallis was that he had only just emerged from his legal struggle with the Ministry of Supply. The tribunal had met in secret for security reasons, yet here was the BBC apparently poised to tell 'the full story' of the 'historic' raid, and explain how 'a British scientist developed after years of research, the special type of mine that made it possible for the RAF to breach 140 feet of concrete'.[77] Wallis asked Bufton how the *in camera* tribunal and the broadcast could be reconciled.[78] Bufton listened to the programme and replied that on the whole he 'thought it had been "almost brilliantly done"'. He saw no concern over security because the programme did not reveal 'the essentially secret aspects of the device'; indeed, the BBC had given less information than was already in the public domain in Germany. His one improvement would have been to find an actor who was more like Wallis.[79]

The Dam Busters was launched at 617 Squadron's first reunion on 19 October 1951. Their dinner was held in the Connaught Rooms in Holborn, where members dined on roast pheasant and heard speeches by Tait, Wallis and Cochrane. Brickhill was their guest; he presented Wallis with a copy inscribed: 'For Barnes Wallis, without whom there would have been no squadron and no book.'

Reviewers were unqualified in their admiration for Wallis, and his devising of a plan which by itself, said the *Daily Express*, 'played a vital part in shortening the war'.[80] The *Daily Herald* asked: 'Which unit, or group of men, did most to win the last war?' An Air Marshal said that 617 Squadron was the most effective unit of its size that Britain had ever had. 'Sir Francis Drake taking on the Armada was kid-stuff in comparison.'[81] The first printing sold out within days. The book was thrice reprinted before Christmas. It has continuously been in print ever since.

The idea that Wallis and 617 Squadron shortened the war in bold, original, and dashing ways took hold just after the end of the Festival of Britain. It seemed to epitomise the Festival's celebration of British scientific achievement. It fed nostalgia for wartime endeavour that took minds away from post-war problems, and its emphasis on precision diverted attention from what the Allies had done to cities. The legend spread quickly because Brickhill sold his work in different parallel formats – broadcast, condensed book, serialisation in regional newspapers – and for the time being there was no one to contradict it. The official historians' more qualified assessment did not appear for another decade. And even before the book was launched, the Associated British Picture Corporation was in discussion with the Air Ministry about a film.[82]

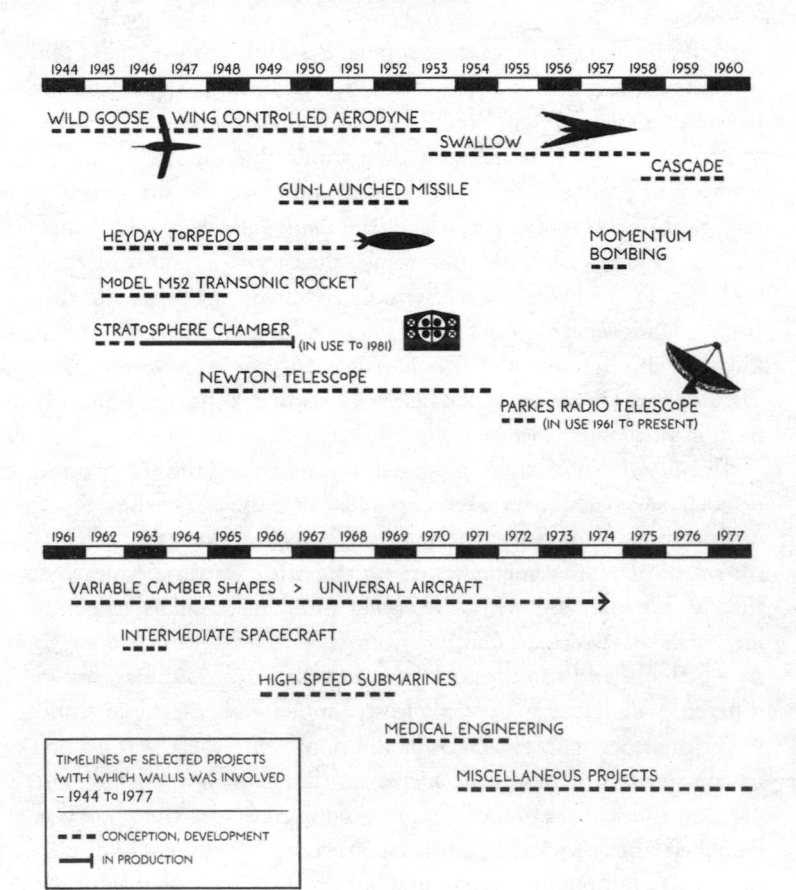

1944 1945 1946 1947 1948 1949 1950 1951 1952 1953 1954 1955 1956 1957 1958 1959 1960

WILD GOOSE ↘ WING CONTROLLED AERODYNE

SWALLOW

CASCADE

GUN-LAUNCHED MISSILE

HEYDAY TORPEDO

MOMENTUM BOMBING

MODEL M52 TRANSONIC ROCKET

STRATOSPHERE CHAMBER (IN USE TO 1981)

NEWTON TELESCOPE

PARKES RADIO TELESCOPE
(IN USE 1961 TO PRESENT)

1961 1962 1963 1964 1965 1966 1967 1968 1969 1970 1971 1972 1973 1974 1975 1976 1977

VARIABLE CAMBER SHAPES > UNIVERSAL AIRCRAFT

INTERMEDIATE SPACECRAFT

HIGH SPEED SUBMARINES

MEDICAL ENGINEERING

MISCELLANEOUS PROJECTS

TIMELINES OF SELECTED PROJECTS
WITH WHICH WALLIS WAS INVOLVED
– 1944 TO 1977

━ ━ ━ CONCEPTION, DEVELOPMENT
┨━━ IN PRODUCTION

13

To and from Predannack, 1951–61

Touches of sweet harmony

Early in 1952 the vice-chancellor of the University of London wrote to tell Wallis that the university wished to award him a doctorate *honoris causa*. Next to Fellowship of the Royal Society, Wallis thought it the 'most distinguished scientific honour in the country'. The vice-chancellor asked if he would accept. 'Would a mouse eat cheese?'[1]

Wallis was delighted by the graduation attire – a brilliant scarlet robe with facings of golden-yellow silk. The doctorate prompted the thought that he was, in a way, perpetuating the memory of his 'darling Father', for counting his nephew Hugh, there were now three generations of Dr Wallises.[2] He hung a brass plate on his office door inscribed 'Dr B. N. Wallis Hours: 8.30 a.m. to midnight Saturdays and Sundays included', and henceforth liked to be addressed as Dr Wallis. Academic recognition was balm to his soul. He held no higher degree, and for years his work had been critiqued by those who did. According to his friend and now right-hand man Philip Teed, he had a great sense of his own dignity.[3] Being so honoured was all the more welcome for being unusual: leading aero engineers were saluted by the state, by specialist societies, and by civic institutions, but seldom by the academy.[4]

Recognition of another kind was coming closer. Ten years before Wallis had attended the premiere of *The First of the Few*, Leslie Howard's dramatisation of the creative life of Reginald Mitchell and the origins of the Spitfire. The Associated British Picture Corporation was now preparing to film *The Dam Busters*. The week before the degree ceremony Wallis received a copy of R. C. Sherriff's screenplay. Wallis had already met Sherriff, who with Brickhill and several Associated British staff had visited White Hill House back in March. While they were there Wallis recreated the marbles experiment, setting up the catapult, tin bath and string as they had been at Easter 1942, and firing marbles which (according to William Whittaker, the production supervisor) did not behave as intended. With the script came a letter from Whittaker, who explained the need to simplify the story to bring it within the bounds of one film, and to hold interest by presenting its characters as living people 'whose feelings an audience can share'.[5] Whittaker hoped Wallis would approve, or that it would prompt discussion in good time if he did not.

At first Wallis made pedantic annotations. Elisabeth's name was misspelled; the command for catapulting a marble was 'Fire', not 'Go', and Upkeep had not been suggested by watching boys skimming stones on a canal. But after a few pages his comments dwindled, then ceased. Perhaps he lost interest or relaxed in the presence of Sherriff's craftsmanship. It may have been the latter for Sherriff wrote a new scene to draw Molly into the story.

> This afternoon the playwright Mr Sherriff came to see me and stayed two hours discussing the new scene . . . he told me the name of the actress who is doing you – something like Sylvia? Cynthia? Johnston? I am not certain of it, but he said she was very good . . .[6]

Wallis appears not to have seen *Brief Encounter*; as Sherriff whisked him off to see Ralph Richardson in his latest play,[7] Elisabeth explained that the actor he was talking about was Celia Johnson.[8]

Wallis was glad of the distraction. Molly was back in Canada visiting Pam. 'Seventy-five days to your return' he wrote at the top of his first letter. 'Why, when two people love so deeply, is separation so sad? I fear much must be due to self-pity, and is therefore unworthy and unreal, so I am trying to cheer up'.[9] But cheering up did not go well. A week later, he offered Ralph Cochrane 'a thousand apologies' for having failed to reply to his invitation to tea. 'Molly is in Canada, and due no doubt to some psychological kink, when she is away I am *so* miserable . . . I only want to be at home.'[10]

At home later that evening, he switched on the radio to find a live broadcast of Vaughan Williams's *Serenade to Music*. Moved,[11] he looked for the text and found it in Act V of *The Merchant of Venice*. By the time he had read Lorenzo's speech to Jessica and copied some of its lines the concert had moved on to Beethoven's fourth piano concerto. But in his letter to Molly he continued:

> Come, ho! And wake Diana with a hymn;
> With sweetest touches pierce your mistress' ear
> And draw her home with music.

Molly began her journey back to England in late April. In his last letter before she left Wallis confided that prospects were 'pretty grim'. Recent surgery to alleviate his migraines had failed, and 'I am fighting for my life now as the Govt. are proposing to shut my Research Department altogether. It is difficult to sleep for worry and distress.'[12]

Living on the Lizard

Since 1951 Wallis had been dividing his time between an aerodrome in Cornwall and Weybridge, where he now had the help of a personal assistant, Pat Lucas, who organised his time, curated his archive and over the next thirty years came to know him better than anyone other than Molly. The aerodrome was at Predannack, which had been laid out on heathland in 1941, first as a home for night fighters to defend south-western ports and cities, later for aircraft that hunted U-boats, struck shipping, and supported Overlord. Everyone was gone when the Vickers team arrived in 1950: they found hangars stripped of cladding by rust and storms, peaty pools, slanting blackthorns smoothed by winds, and half a town's worth of empty buildings spreading inland that recalled a time when 3600 people worked there. 'Imagine a scene of desolation,' wrote Wallis, 'here and there the horizon of heather and gorse dipping to show in the dim and misty distance the line of the sea.'[13]

Preparations for Wild Goose trials included the refurbishment of buildings, equipping of workshops, garaging for vehicles, testing radio control equipment with a Spitfire, and installation of a concrete-bedded 0.45-mile railway upon which to run their new launch trolley. The trolley was propelled by jets of steam generated by the decomposition of hydrogen peroxide. Wallis was worried lest it overrun the track – this would have been a disaster for the trials – and in June 1951 he decided to install a braking system that would bring it to a stand automatically once the launch speed of 125 mph was reached. The new braking stopped the trolley within 70 yards, as if (he said) some 'invisible giant hand' was drawing it back. When it stopped the wheels still spun and the rails glowed blue.

Predannack was huge, and transport was needed not only to reach the nearest mainline railway station (Gwinear Road, 19 miles away) but also to move around the site. The perimeter was six miles; living quarters and workshops were on opposite sides, and even when the main runway was not being used by visiting naval aircraft that practised deck landings, it could take half an hour to get from one side to the other. At first, when rain, mist or gales kept them indoors, as they often did, Wallis's sleeping cabin doubled as his office. After months of spreading papers and calculations on his bed, he was pleased when a workplace was found for him on the engineering side of the aerodrome.

Arrangements were at first co-ordinated by Leonard Cheshire, 617 Squadron's OC back in 1943–44. Since then, Cheshire had witnessed the atomic bombing of Nagasaki, toyed with journalism, tried, and failed to form a community for ex-servicemen and women, suffered a breakdown, become a Roman Catholic, and begun a new life caring for people marginalised by disabilities. Ralph Cochrane, his former Group commander, brokered the reconnection with Wallis.

Cheshire sometimes flew Wallis down to Predannack in an elderly Dragon Rapide. On arrival late one afternoon in July 1951, Cheshire flew the biplane so low around the Lizard head that Wallis could see the cliffs side-on.[14] Cheshire had a spiritual director, a listening companion who helped him to wrangle the consequences of his faith.[15] Wallis's off-duty talks with him sometimes went on late, and there are signs that this relationship was discussed. At any rate, Wallis himself began to take such counsel. His guide was a west London vicar, the Rev John Borrill,[16] who introduced him to literature on confession and forgiveness.

Borrill was active in the Village Evangelists, a movement of unpaid clerics and laity formed in 1948 for mission to local communities. It came into being under the influence of Edward Gordon Bulstrode (1885–1953), a travelling Franciscan preacher with no money, no home, no personal possessions, and enormous spiritual influence.[17] We do not know how, or even if, Borrill and Bulstrode met, or if Wallis met him, but the influence of St Francis is apparent: Wallis erected a statue of him in the garden at White Hill House, and we recall that back in 1938 he had been cared for by Franciscan sisters who took him to the brink of Catholicism. Whatever was going on here was fundamental not only to the state of Wallis's soul, but also to Wild Goose, which he saw as a religious as well as a technical project. In the unsent letters he intermittently implies that its concept had been revealed by God. Reason and religion were not opposites but companions; his gifts of invention were from God, and their results were offered to God.

Unlike Thurleigh, the water at Predannack was hot, the food was good, and the rooms were well kept with polished floors. Wallis enjoyed the rich yellow Cornish milk which he added to his tea each morning. Travel to and fro was sometimes by night train (the so-called 'Paddington News', a freight train with a couple of sleeping cars), more often in a Dove or a Valetta. As the journeys multiplied, so do did incidents in marginal conditions.

> We arrived yesterday, me in shorts, in a heavy thunderstorm, finishing the last fifty miles from Plymouth a few feet above the sea. But the journey only took 1 hour and 4 minutes – but was very rough and bumpy. This morning it has rained almost continuously.[18]

The route from Weybridge passed over Lyme Regis, where Wallis and Molly had passed something akin to a second honeymoon following the Catholicism crisis in 1938.

> I never fly over Lyme Regis without a feeling for the happy time
> we have had together there.[19]

The unsent letters record mood swings: moments of success interspersed with interference by 'ill-willed and clever people',[20] a row with senior members of his team (who early in 1952 seem to have lost confidence in the direction of the project), the fatalistic feeling that 'long term research is out of favour in high quarters',[21] and a belief that everyone was against him.[22]

But not all was gloomy:

> May 2nd 1952 In the train Friday 10.30 a.m.
>   Yesterday we had the most magnificent success – the
> first jet propelled controlled circuit of the 'Wild Goose'.
> Let me try to convey to you something of the magnitude
> of what we have done. When the Wrights first flew, the
> greatest contribution they made to the art of flying was
> probably their system of lateral control, brought about by
> means of the 'aileron' – a brilliant and novel invention, still,
> 44 years later, in universal use. And forty-four years later
> gallant men's lives are still being lost because the behaviour
> (Truro stop) of new aeroplanes is not exactly predictable
> as far as their controls are concerned. In particular as
> speeds become higher and higher the aileron type of lateral
> control becomes more and more dubious . . . Now I have
> in one great change abolished the aileron, and all other
> conventional controls as well, transforming the ever-grow-
> ing complexity (on again) of the type that has persisted
> for nearly half a century to the endearing simplicity of the
> Wild Goose – just one body and two wings and no other
> controls at all.

He described the scene.

All day had been spent in testing and checking the
multitude of things that might go wrong, until just before 5
p.m. the inspectors signed the final chit certifying all was in
order, and that we were free to take-off and fly, if we could.
Security police of the RAF were patrolling the neighbouring
roads. Walky-talky cars were hidden here and there, in
constant communication with their Chief Warrant Officer,
stationed high up on the Control Tower, from which he
could look out, far and wide. Judy, the fierce Alsatian police
dog, was straining at her leash, only waiting the word
from her keeper to tear suspected spies to pieces. Three
high-speed cinematograph cameras awaited the touch of
'trigger-happy' fingers to record the event. The inhabitants
of all buildings in the danger area, on which we might
crash if the controls did not work had the last 15 minutes
warning to come forth and take shelter . . .
    I, who always craftily arrange that, at these critical
moments of great nervous strain, I have no duties at all
except the overwhelming one of saying 'Go on', had taken
my station with Peter Farr, in charge of one of the smaller
cameras, hand-held, at the end of the railway track over
which the aerodyne would pass if successfully launched . . .
Up sails a Very Light fired from the starting position at the
far end of the launching track over half a mile away. 'Thirty
seconds to go, 25 – 20 – 15 – I counted them out to Peter
diligently, squinting through the sights of his camera – 10,
9, 8, 7, 6, 5, 4, 3, 2, 1, Fire. Hullo, nothing's happened.
Why did they fire a green Very? It was a red one last time
for the glider launch. Does green mean wash out?[23] Fifty
seconds gone, Sixty, o Lord, bang there go the jets and
rockets too, much too soon. Here she comes. SHE'S OFF,
she's coming, Alan's turning her right, right, right he's
straightening up, she's answering, she's straight oh lovely,
he's turning her again, right, right. (All very necessary, as if

she had turned left in our direction Peter was to drop his camera and run. (Stop at Newton Abbot do you remember?) . . .)

I found myself shouting a running commentary at the top of my voice, releasing some of the nervous strain that for seconds, minutes hours days weeks months and years I have been enduring. I realised I was giving myself away, but decided that for once in a way I would openly make a fool of myself for after all there was only Peter Farr to see and I don't think he will give me away. So I shouted away, as she, under Alan Nash's control in the distant tower, turned from us in a lovely and graceful curve, undulating or rocking slightly from time to time as Alan tentatively tried the power that he had over her. Exquisite, smooth and, but for the twin trails of smoke and short jets of flame from the two cordite rockets that she bore within her, as pure as any soaring gull.

Between Dawlish and Exeter, he explained that after doing a lovely, but fast, three-quarter circuit, Nash was trying to manage an aircraft travelling at some 150 miles an hour and only a few feet above the ground. Misled by the lack of perspective in a flat region, and thinking he was clear of obstacles, Nash decided to let her land herself, which had the way been clear she would have done. But she was actually heading for the side of a low concrete building, into which she flew.

Nevertheless, it was a famous victory, and we gathered round the shattered remains all smiles and congratulations. Cars as by magic appearing on the horizon, converged from all directions. Wonder, awe, laughter, high-spirited talk, the nervous reaction of a lately strained and anxious band; a fire of questions to the pilot, what was she like to handle, how quickly does she respond to the control, how did it feel, when, how, where, why?

There was a party that evening. Wallis laid out £37 of his own money (about £850 at today's values) to The George at Helston for beer, whisky, gin, and rum. The camaraderie reminded him of the war. Earlier doubts and tensions were lifted. There was singing. Wallis found the senior fireman to be a high, pure tenor. When Wallis asked where he had trained, he replied simply 'Welsh'.

Innovations followed. Short flights made it difficult for the pilot to become accustomed to handling. Wallis hit on the idea of running the motor intermittently.

> In my cabin at Predannack, Tuesday 1 July 1952 11 p.m.
>   We had a most successful test on the ground after lunch of the 1st 'long endurance' Wild Goose, running the jet and cutting it in and out by radio from the control tower 3/4 mile away, working the wings meanwhile. With this arrangement we shall be able to do three or four circuits, giving the pilot a good opportunity to land, which remains the one operation in the cycle of take-off, fly, and land again, that we have not yet successfully accomplished.

Another idea came from the team – two pilots, one stationed close to the centre of the aerodrome to control the aerodyne's pitch, the other in charge of roll who looked through binoculars along the length of the runway. For a better view, the 'roll pilot' perched atop a 25-foot rig adapted from some old apparatus they found in a hangar. On the morning of 12 September 1953, Wild Goose was flown on a circuit completed by a successful landing. By the following March fifteen successful flights had been made.

Wallis told himself that the problem of how to land Wild Goose had been solved by the ingenuity of his 'children' – members of the team who took the project forward by their own initiative. At first sight, Wallis being a reluctant delegator, this looks like romantic self-deception. However, his diaries reveal a generosity of spirit:

> I leave, or have left, the solution of the many difficult problems that inevitably arise . . . to them. Each man, including myself, then selects the problems for which his inclination and his

special abilities fit him best, & proceeds by his own methods, & in his own peculiarly personal way, to solve them, if he can.[24]

Wallis believed his research department followed no known pattern. Unlike aeronautical research involving specialised and expensive equipment designed to answer the narrowest of questions, 'it may be that I owe much of such success as I have had to an almost entire lack of specialisation that leaves me free to roam, in thought at least, over the widest fields.' He recognised that research has a time element which is 'almost as inexorable as the time element is in the playing of a great symphony'. In this case he was composing as it went along, keeping a bar ahead of the players. 'What a magnificent title THE UNKNOWN SYMPHONY. Does not the mere thought of the immense adventure . . . make you thrill with joy & awe at the same time. It can only be played once.'[25]

Inevitably, neither his employers nor the Ministry of Supply saw it that way. There was encouragement from Vickers to move from concept to practical application. Vickers in the 1950s were commercially on the front foot, producing the Viscount, the Valiant (the first V-bomber), later the Vanguard and VC10. In all of these they demonstrated a conservative, low-risk approach that differed from Wallis's research. After four years, the argument went, surely his research should be leading somewhere. Late in 1952 the call for a supersonic reconnaissance aircraft enabled Wallis to respond by producing a design study using Wild Goose principles. To save weight and ensure smooth airflow over thin wings there would be no undercarriage, just a single wheel on the keel, enabling landing like a glider. Ground handling would be on a wheeled dolly. Take-off would be from a trolley. On the airfield, retractable wings would allow each aircraft to be kept in its own underground shelter (Wallis remembered the German V2 storage bunker near Cherbourg, which had been constructed by laying out a concrete slab and excavating beneath it). RAF aerodromes of the future need thus have no buildings. For good measure, no doubt to increase the attraction of the concept, the aircraft could be converted to carry a pair of atom bombs.[26] The photoreconnaissance Wild Goose was one of Wallis's odder proposals. Unsurprisingly, it was declined.

By 1954 the unsent letters reveal uncertainty about the amount of laminar flow that could be obtained from Wild Goose. Laminar flow was fundamental to the original idea, as a way of minimising turbulence and compression effects that beset other forms. Since the previous September, Wallis had been contemplating a new shape. It derived from Wild Goose but yet was original. He called it Swallow.

Trials and revelations

In his cycle of unsent letters, Wallis confided that Swallow's concept had been 'gradually revealed'. He thought it was 'the last really big thing I shall be privileged to do'. He believed that it overcame all earlier problems, and that others acknowledged it as 'the coming thing for long range high speed flight'. The religious tenor continued: 'I do humbly praise and thank God that I have been allowed to bring this whole matter to a successful conclusion.'[27]

The essence of the Swallow concept lay in Wallis's realisation that the lift provided by a delta wing is generated along its leading edge. The rest of the wing produces drag, not lift, yet adds to weight; if this area were to be excised, then the leading edge would be all that was left, like the tangs of a medieval arrowhead. Wild Goose had shown that no fin was needed. The wings would pivot to enable flight at low and high speeds.[28]

At first, it was intended to control Swallow using differential wing movements of the kind already achieved with Wild Goose. However, an early plan to mount engines beneath the fuselage came into conflict with the needs of a high-altitude military version of Swallow to replace the V-bombers, under discussion in 1955–56.[29] For various reasons, one of them being the undesirability of dropping a nuclear bomb through jet efflux, Wallis's thoughts turned to mounting engines on the wings.[30] Once there, if they swivelled then the air flow past them could be used for control.[31] Swallow flew, and flew well, on 18 November 1955.

Aside from his clashes with George Edwards, Wallis was becoming worn by the repeated need to reconfigure designs to meet military requirements, to secure further funds for research. What he wanted to do was to perfect the concept for a genus of aircraft, and then turn to develop individual species. Military demands turned this back to front by restricting development funding to individual species while leaving work on the genus incomplete.

It was such a species project that Wallis took to Buckingham Palace in October 1955. Word of Swallow had reached the Duke of Edinburgh, who invited Wallis to come to talk about it. Wallis took a large model and film footage and arrived early. While he was setting up and chatting to equerries the Duke appeared before the appointed time and immediately began to fire questions. Wallis offered to show the film. 'Yes, yes', the Duke replied, 'but what's it *about*? What's your work based on?' Wallis was lost for words. Then he replied 'Imagination!'

The film showed Swallow flying. Afterwards they adjourned to another room where a fire burned, and a large teapot awaited. 'Do you drink this stuff?' Wallis noticed that in conversation the Duke was prone to start to say something impulsively, but then to stop after a few words: 'But why . . . no, all right . . .'[32] He asked about Wallis's other work. Wallis described a recent project that used the Stratosphere Chamber to investigate the effects of trawler icing. Earlier in the year, two trawlers had gone down off Iceland with the loss of forty men. Experiments with large models at low temperatures found that icy spray clothed rigging, masts, lifeboats, and superstructure with enormous accumulations of ice – up to 140 tons could form on the higher parts of a vessel and thereby turn it over. Wallis's report recommended the simplification of trawler design, to minimise and simplify features above deck height.[33]

He went back to Effingham dejected. He had too little help; funding from the Defence Research Policy Council could only be found by diverting money from other projects;[34] it was like the struggle before the Dams Raid all over again. Everyone now knew about that; Michael Anderson's film was being shown throughout Britain. When it came to Cornwall, Vickers gave the Swallow team half a day off to go into Falmouth to watch it.

'A film of unusual merit'

R. C. Sherriff's screenplay for *The Dam Busters* is a tale of two heroes.[35] The film's first half hour centres on Wallis and his drive to curtail Germany's war economy by attacking dams. Attention then turns to Guy Gibson and the squadron being formed to make the attack. After this the two are brought together, each being put to the test in different ways while an understated interdependency forms between them. The climax – another half hour – is the raid itself. The conclusion, short but intense, dwells on cost: the tick of a clock wound up by someone who has not returned; Gibson, still in his shirtsleeves and Mae West, walking to his office to write to fifty-six next of kin.

The world premiere took place 'under the gracious Patronage and in the presence of' Princess Margaret at the Empire Theatre, Leicester Square, on Monday, 16 May 1955 – the twelfth anniversary of the raid.[36] The evening began amid formality and displays of patriotism in which the foyer and staircases were lined by National Service airmen. While 617 veterans, members of their families, Vickers staff and the Wallises were presented to the princess, the RAF's Central Band played. Gladys Ripley and the Royal Air Forces Association Choir sang Ivor Novello's 'Rose of England', 'Land of Hope and Glory', and a vocal arrangement of Eric Coates's march ('Proudly with high endeavour / We who are young forever / Won the freedom of the sky'). Members of the audience browsed a handsome fifty-page souvenir brochure (threaded with red, white and blue cord) dedicated to the crews who did not return. The brochure saluted service charities, reminded readers that another quarter of a million copies of Brickhill's book had just been printed, relayed greetings from the BBC and Rolls-Royce, and named dozens of air marshals, politicians, and captains of industry who had overseen the premiere's organisation. Trumpeters of the Central Band then stepped forward to play a fanfare for the entrance of the princess.

Next morning the *Daily Mail* hailed *The Dam Busters* as 'one of the best war pictures yet made'.[37] *The Times* called it a 'film of unusual merit'. Molly was taken by the accuracy with which Associated

British had reconstructed her living room. In following weeks audiences were gripped, for until then no one had had any idea how Wallis's weapon worked.[38] Until then, too, no one had much idea about Wallis. Redgrave's portrayal turned him into one of Britain's best-known people.[39] His irascibility in meetings, aloofness towards people he thought undeserving, and obsessive perfectionism were left out, and his humane, kindly, and dogged aspects were brought to the fore. Public sympathy for him in forthcoming public arguments was thereby enlisted, while the film's 'intense Englishness' reinforced the fable of a natural Anglo-British genius and superiority in innovation.[40]

The Dam Busters also put Wallis in a universal narrative. The novelist David Lodge has observed how all stories about aerial bombing 'tend towards the condition of chivalric romance' in which a hero and his companions leave home, travel into a far-off and hostile land, are tested, perform courageous deeds, and return changed by what they have undergone.[41] Lodge points to ways in which the film reinforces these connotations.[42] Wallis is 'a kind of benevolent Merlin, wielding the magical power of science'.[43] Most powerful of all, the film combines an appearance of documentary realism with warfare purified of violence. In this conjuring Wallis's weapon is intended not to kill (the nearest we get to fighting is public school-style disorder in Scampton's mess) but to vanquish an inert giant. We see the glitter of light flak and plumes of water, but no infants being washed out of their cradles, nor bubbling skin inside burning aircraft. There are floods, but no rolling twenty-foot black step of water laced with uprooted trees, bits of buildings and howling farm animals that took more lives than any previous air raid. *The Dam Busters* fostered the illusion of war purged of awfulness, and it put Wallis at the centre of the cleansing.

Beyond southern skies

On the day of the film's premiere, Edward Bowen, head of Australia's Division of Radiophysics, wrote to Wallis about an upcoming project to design and build a giant radio telescope. Funds had just been pledged for an instrument to open a new window on the universe. Would Vickers be interested in taking responsibility for its design, construction, and erection? And did Wallis have ideas about how the telescope might be mounted?[44]

Bowen was one of a tiny group of radio physicists who had pioneered radar. In 1935, twenty-four years old, fresh from his PhD, he had been enlisted by Robert Watson-Watt to join research that by 1940 had enabled Fighter Command's success in the Battle of Britain. By then Bowen was already working on miniaturised airborne radar that could detect ships and intercept aircraft at night. In 1940 he was recruited to the Tizard Mission which left Britain to share recent technological advances with Canada and the United States. Bowen remained in America for the next two years, playing a key part in the development of microwave radar. At the end of 1943 he joined Australia's Radiophysics Laboratory in Sydney, where after the war he was drawn to the study of radio waves that arrive from beyond the solar system.

Until the 1930s all that was known about the universe came from what astronomers could see. Karl Jansky's discovery of cosmic radio waves in 1933 changed this, and the war fettled a cadre of young able radio scientists who were keen to pursue the new science when it ended. By 1950 their discoveries had already convinced classical astronomers that the universe could not be understood by optical means alone.[45] From this sprang a need to improve the sensitivity of aerials to collect more of the faint radio signals that reach the Earth. One way to do that was to develop very large parabolic reflectors. It was about this that Bowen – breezy, confident, optimistic – met Wallis for lunch at the Athenaeum in May 1955.

Wallis had been pondering telescope design for a while. Late in 1947, Harold Spencer Jones, the Astronomer Royal, had asked him how to ensure the structural rigidity of a proposed 100-inch reflector telescope of a new kind.[46] Hitherto astronomers had been using two kinds of instrument, one capable of photography over a wide field, the other of spectrometry. Considerations of cost and other factors had now led to the idea of a dual-purpose telescope. The main design difficulty was how to compensate for gravitational deflection in a telescope tube that would be fifty feet long. Patrick Blackett suggested to Spencer Jones that he consult Wallis. Over Christmas 1947 he wrote a paper on 'Flexible and inflexible structures' in which he concluded that the required degree of rigidity could not be attained by any known form or material. It might, however, be achieved through self-compensation, perhaps through thermal means.[47]

Members of the project's board of management were impressed, although Spencer Jones was wary of the complexity. Wallis's report was circulated to encourage discussion, and a Mechanical Design Committee was set up. However, the committee's membership was not settled until 1950, and the board's cycle was so leisurely that many months, sometimes a year, could elapse between meetings. As time went on, further studies were organised,[48] Wallis made more proposals, and views emanating from other sub-committees (on servo control, automatic guiding, and optical design) were at times mutually cancelling. Energies flagged. Spencer Jones had his hands full: as well as chairing the board he was acting as de facto project manager, while Wallis, under pressure for results from Wild Goose and Swallow, fitted in telescope work at weekends or on wet evenings at Predannack. By 1955 impatience for progress brought new leadership: the project board was replaced by a small executive, which in due course decided to abandon the combination instrument and return to a conventional form. Wallis's involvement was thereby ended.

Wallis's work on the Isaac Newton telescope coincided with the conception (1949), design (completed 1951) and erection (begun 1954) of another: the 250ft diameter steerable radio telescope at Jodrell Bank in Cheshire. Wallis was kept abreast of this project by Patrick Blackett, now back in academic life at Manchester where he headed the department in which worked Bernard Lovell, the project's instigator. Lovell and Wallis knew each other slightly; in 1943 and 1944 they had met to try to forecast the likely performance of the expected V-weapons. Wallis's arrival on the astronomical scene now alerted him to what was afoot at Jodrell, about which he periodically offered advice to Blackett, who duly passed it on to Lovell and his engineer, Charles Husband, whose patient replies (returned by the same route) assured Wallis that they knew what they were doing.[49]

In one respect, however, no one in the brave new world of radio astronomy in the early 1950s quite knew what they were doing, for at that point there was no recognised optimum anatomy for a radio telescope. Considerations of operating wavelength and accuracy had led Lovell and Husband to a parabolic dish with a diameter of about 250 feet, to be supported at its perimeter between a pair of towers, each of which had a motor to tilt the dish in elevation. The dish and towers in turn stood upon a circular, wheeled frame resting on a circular railway track, where more motors could rotate the entire structure about its vertical axis.

Wallis thought all this 'amazingly complex'.[50] As construction proceeded reports of design changes, cost overruns, and unforeseen structural problems convinced him that there must be more elegant solutions to key questions – such as how to stiffen a large structure subject to fluctuating deformation under the force of gravity, or how to point it to the sky. When he and Bowen met in the Athenaeum he was thus ready and waiting. According to Bowen the answer to the last question came to him during lunch. When Wallis asked him how he proposed to drive the telescope, he replied that they would do it analogue fashion, from an equatorial mount alongside the main telescope.[51] Wallis paused.

> He pointed a finger at me and said 'You're wrong. The place to put the equatorial unit is at the intersection of the two axes of rotation. You derive an error signal and servo this back to the main telescope. It's perfectly obvious that's the way to do it.'[52]

It has been noticed how this account falls into a pattern of 'Eureka' moments in science history.[53] Wallis himself explained the idea as having emerged from his thinking about the dish. In his report entitled 'Giant Radio Telescopes',[54] completed four months later, he visualised the dish as being formed of opposite-handed spiral members. Wallis saw that such a network – concentrated, uniform in all directions, providing torsional stiffness – would influence the method for its support, which he suggested should be central, thereby avoiding the uneven distribution of stress that had resulted from the lateral towers at Jodrell Bank. The idea of placing the master equatorial unit at the bowl's centre of motion then flowed from that.[55]

Not all of Wallis's proposals were adopted in the design study that followed,[56] and in 1958, around the time that Parkes in New South Wales was selected as the telescope's site, he withdrew from the project and declined his fee. His pointing system was nonetheless fundamental to the design of the telescope that was completed in 1961.[57] The following year, Parkes located a radio source with sufficient accuracy to enable astronomers to identify the stellar object with which it was associated. This 'quasi-stellar radio source' gave the world a new word – quasar. A following generation of large radio telescopes embodies the master equatorial system that Wallis conceived.[58] Five decades on, over half of the pulsars known to science have been found by Parkes.

'A foolish paper on defence'

Wallis submitted his design study for the Swallow research aircraft at the end of February 1957. He told his brother John: 'I have just completed the hardest, and the best and biggest task of my life, writing a paper on a new type of aircraft for the Govt – 7 days a week for 4 months working against time, before the government committed themselves irrevocably on their defence programme . . . Now, I feel like a boy out of school.' If there was no contract for immediate development, he would probably take it to the United States.[59]

A copy of the government's paper *Defence: Outline of Future Policy* came into his hands a few days later.[60] It said that since a future war in the air would be fought chiefly with missiles, the ballistic age had little further need for fighting aircraft with crews. The paper also warned the aero industry to reorganise. Smaller companies should come together to form large ones, and if they did not, they should know that only the large ones would receive government contracts.

Molly was away when the paper arrived. Wallis described it to her as 'foolish'. Its corollary was the abandonment of many advanced projects.[61] Swallow was among those that perished.

Swallow came under the aegis of the Ministry of Supply, whose Minister, Aubrey Jones, was instructed by Duncan Sandys to bring the project to a close. One of his reasons for doing so was the strong impression that Vickers's commitment to Swallow was half-hearted.[62] Wallis's department was isolated from the main part of the company and too small to tackle detailed design and construction. At times, very likely this had suited Wallis, who was thereby left to his own devices, while George Edwards could pursue his preference for improving upon existing solutions rather than gambling on new ones. During 1957 Philip Teed and Lord Weeks went so far as to take soundings about the possibility of putting project development into the hands of another firm. Aubrey Jones meanwhile looked about for ways to keep the project alive. Early in 1958 Wallis pro-duced a Swallow-based design study for the one new military aircraft to survive the Sandys cull of 1957, only for it be rejected.[63]

Although officially cancelled, Swallow's detail remained secret. All that was known about it publicly was the name, and the fact that it involved variable geometry. Wallis was in a quandary. Believing it would revolutionise aeronautical history, and not wishing the idea to die with him, in August 1957 he took the matter to several opin-ion formers. One of them was Major Harry Legge-Bourke, MP for the Isle of Ely, who sympathised with Wallis's views about the need for Britain to develop long-range supersonic transport.[64] In January 1958 Legge-Bourke lobbied Frederick Brundrett (scientific adviser at the Ministry of Civil Aviation and chairman of the Defence Re-search Policy Committee) over lunch.[65] Legge-Bourke may not have been aware that Brundrett was a good friend of Sir George Graham, chief scientist at the Ministry of Supply, and indeed of George Ed-wards, and that news of his efforts was very likely passed back to permanent secretaries and ministers. The matter came into the open during a House of Commons debate on the aircraft industry in May 1958, when Legge-Bourke stated that Wallis, one of Britain's greatest geniuses, was being 'thrown away' by the government.

If as a result of false advice or false economy Dr Wallis is driven out of this country, I shall do my best for the rest of my life to find out who is responsible and expose him in the public eye.[66]

The following day, readers of the *Daily Herald* were told that 'Tory clashed with Tory in the Commons last night in a row over Dr Barnes Wallis, 70-year-old designer of the dam-buster bomb and, now, the brain behind the revolutionary Swallow jet aircraft.'[67] The *Birmingham Post* headlined the story GENIUS ON BRINK OF PLANE DISCOVERY.[68] Aubrey Jones politely observed that colleagues who made such criticisms 'strain their best friends if they remain too persistently scornful of the practical'.

In fact, Jones and his officials had identified a potential solution, at least to the extent of getting a time- and energy-consuming controversy off their desks and onto someone else's. The other party was the Anglo-American Mutual Weapons Development Programme, which had funds of its own and would be in a position to support Swallow's continuation if it was found to be viable. A six-month programme followed which included exchange visits and tests to examine the Swallow configuration in the transonic wind tunnel at Langley Field, Virginia. The tests identified several stability and drag issues about which Wallis's team already knew but fastened on one detail – positioning the wing pivots on forewings outside the centre line of the aircraft. This solved a problem that hitherto had baffled US engineers: how to combine low wing sweep and high aspect ratio at low speeds, and high wing sweep and low aspect ratio at supersonic speeds without bringing the wing forward to offset a pitching moment as the wing was swept aft. Lateral pivots made this practical. In doing so they opened the way to variable sweep for otherwise traditional aircraft.[69]

In the traditional narrative, the US interest lay only in innovations that could be incorporated in near-term projects. The first such project, the General Dynamics F111, was flying within five years,[70] while Swallow itself went no further. That holds good in outline, but leaving aside the further wind tunnel and aerodynamic trials,[71] the politics were more intricate. Wallis became good friends with John

Stack, leader of the US team during the trials, but timetabling and cost challenges emerged,[72] and early in 1959 the Ministry of Supply intervened to say that the proposals which had emerged were more ambitious than those which had been agreed with the US authorities the previous autumn.[73] The Ministry insisted that if the programme was to go ahead, project studies to establish the potential of variable sweep for operational purposes should be put in the hands of Vickers's design department – that is, under George Edwards.[74]

Three days later, Vickers learned of 'firm support' from the Naval and Air Staffs for an aircraft of Swallow character. This might be one joint project, or two separate ones.[75] Aback of that was a belief among Service chiefs, the Ministry of Supply and senior Vickers directors that John Stack and his US colleagues were still aboard, and that there could be 'a sensible and gradual transfer of control from Wallis to V[ickers]-A[rmstrongs]' to meet the assurance asked for by the Ministry.[76]

Early in April, Charles Dunphie, Vickers's managing director, directed that rather more than half of the staff of Wallis's research department be transferred to the Vickers-Armstrongs (Aircraft) Design Department, where they would work on the Swallow project 'under the normal system of organisation'. Among those to be moved across was Norman Boorer, one of Wallis's most able and loyal colleagues. The remainder, less than half, 'including Hayes and the mathematical and intellectual ladies,'[77] would remain under Dr Wallis in the R&D department to handle 'that part of the project for which they are particularly suited.' (Dunphie noted that his field had yet to be defined.) Wallis and Edwards would meet later that day to confirm the arrangement. Dunphie understood that there were aspects of this plan that Wallis wished to be clarified.[78]

Edwards and Wallis had met two weeks before. In a private note, Philip Teed told Lord Weeks what had happened.

> Each has told me what he *must* have, if he is going to play. At the moment, these requirements seem to be incompatibles, so, if the talks don't lead to a change of magnitude on one side or the other, there will be a complete breakdown.[79]

Teed added that he did not believe Swallow could be made to fly in a reasonable period 'without Wally in technical control'. If the two 'problem children' would not work together, 'we might consider selling the Swallow know-how, patents etc & Wally to the Americans – at the moment they seem to believe in both.'[80]

In the event, MWDP funds were not secured, NASA took the outboard wing pivot,[81] and UK military interest subsided. Talk of a naval Swallow lasted until 1960, but by then, in Wallis's mind, it was already a thing of the past.[82]

Land of opportunity

In June 1957 Wallis gave a lecture at Eton College which he repeated and embroidered until the early 1970s. It began with two comments about Britain that had been made earlier that year.[83] The first was from Harold Macmillan, who shortly after his appointment as prime minister made a broadcast in which he dismissed talk of Britain's decline. Britain, he concluded, 'has been great, is great, and will stay great, provided we close ranks and get on with the job.' That same week, *Punch* published a cartoon by Leslie Illingworth. Ironically captioned 'Land of Opportunity', it depicted people boarding a liner bearing luggage marked 'to the Dominions', while immigrants from around the world sauntered down another ramp past a nearby sign arrowed 'Welfare State'. The emigrants were depicted as young and optimistic, while the immigrants replacing them were unpleasantly caricatured as grifters and chancers. Wallis asked how Macmillan's optimism could be squared with such exchange, and if it was true that Britain was 'done for'.

Wallis introduced his answer by noting that all empires enjoyed a widespread system of communication, and that their success in trade depended on the system's security. In Britain's case, this had been achieved by maintenance of a powerful navy. Wallis invoked the environmental determinism of George Bowles, whose book *The Strength of England* (1926) had influenced Dennistoun Burney's thinking about airships back in the late 1920s. In Bowles's mind,

England lies 'wholly in the sea, and yet at the precise centre of all the land of the earth. No other spot upon the globe either fulfils or can ever be made to fulfil those two conditions.' Small, compact, yet with a long, indented coastline offering natural harbours, England's position at the pole of the 'land hemisphere' made her the most geographically favoured nation in the world. These advantages in turn mapped onto the gifts of her elite. Wallis quoted with approval Robert Menzies's view of Britain from Australia:[84] 'if you take the art of self-government, the highest arts of war, and the highest levels of pure and applied science, and if you search diligently to know whence comes most of the aid to mankind whether for peace or war, you cannot go beyond these islands.'

Eton's young gentlemen were told that the English were uniquely gifted with intellectual power, creative originality, and flair for superb craftsmanship. Wallis gave examples of how these talents could be used to maintain sea and air centrality and secure communication across the Anglosphere. Long-range communication at sea could be protected by putting the whole British mercantile marine underwater. His own work concentrated on aircraft that could cover great distances non-stop; such travel would call for flight at about two and a half times the speed of sound in the stratosphere. Other technologists were working on high-precision wind tunnel research and vertical take-off. Communication was not just earth-bound. With larger radio telescopes, extra-galactic signals would enable mapping of regions of the universe where the eye could see nothing. In such things and more England was world leading.

Winding up, Wallis argued that Britain's future as an international power would not call for the kinds of resources upon which she had relied in the past. Coal would be replaced by nuclear energy. Automation would remove the need for large workforces in factories. Removal of the need to defend strategic centres around the globe would allow them to be handed back to their peoples. England's greatness in time ahead would rest on the spiritual and intellectual qualities of her people – but for these to operate her communications must be inviolable.

Over the next fifteen years 'The Strength of England' (he borrowed

Bowles's title) became Wallis's signature lecture. He toured it to all kinds of audiences – schools, women's institutes, universities, learned societies, a young wives' group in Esher, the Conservative Monday Club – and travelled widely to do so.[85] The talk was illustrated with slides and film footage, projected by a technical assistant (paid for by Vickers) who set the equipment up before a lecture and took it away afterwards. He charged no fee, and since Vickers also provided transport (once even flying him up to Newcastle to talk to a school) he charged no expenses.

Content evolved as time passed. When he gave the talk at Christ's Hospital eighteen months later, for instance, he added that between 5 and 12 per cent of newly qualified mechanical and civil engineers were leaving Britain for Canada and the United States. In this version he said that England's Christian heritage exercised a 'profound influence for the good of mankind throughout the Free World'. This was a huge claim, and its corollary was that world peace hinged not only England's will but also the strength to exercise it.[86] Yet since the war, in Wallis's view, England had declined politically, industrially and in character. To sustain worldwide influence for good, decline had to be reversed. Doing that was down to the young.

Many of these themes arose from general 1950s discourse. The Suez crisis had just emphasised the need to find new routes around the world, lest existing short cuts fall into unfriendly hands. The press was oversupplied with news about the brain drain (Illingworth's 'Land of Opportunity' cartoon was commissioned over an editorial lunch at *Punch*). The idea of a Christian free world facing an atheistic Soviet Union was a standard Cold War binary in which even Geoffrey Fisher, the Archbishop of Canterbury, believed. Sea centrality, whence came air centrality, sprang from environmental determinism. Popular in Wallis's childhood, still current, its reduction of moral questions to a general explanatory law was a handy way to explain colonial behaviour.

Wallis used 'England' and 'Britain' more or less interchangeably. He often said England when he meant Britain, and when he did speak of Britain it was as an extension of England. While England was a place, its essence lay in its people. Again and again, Wallis referred to 'the spiritual and intellectual qualities' of English people, their 'courage and persistence in research', and their originality. In these things, he said, the 'ancient, free and Christian country of England' led the world.

Wallis's English exceptionalism, and willingness to address audiences like the Monday Club,[87] has been seen as evidence that in later life he moved to the extreme right.[88] His dyed-in-the-wool social views, respect for deference, approval of imperial achievement, and pursuit of advanced technology certainly allow us to compare him with other engineers 'who were nationalistic in their thinking about technology and wanted to create technologies bearing national characteristics'.[89] We may note, too, the mutual admiration that existed between Wallis and conservative figures like the popular historian Arthur Bryant.[90]

Molly, however, thought her husband 'had never taken a real interest in politics' and was Conservative by default rather than through active commitment.[91] His faith in 'meritocratic elitism based on character, education, will, and hard work' more usefully suggests a Victorian who in the later twentieth century had stayed put while others had moved.[92] Also, he could be more nuanced than some have made him seem. When we are told that he was 'much exercised by non-white immigration into Britain',[93] it seems from the context that his words referred not to 'non-white' people but to their appearance as caricatured by Illingworth in the *Punch* cartoon (which at that point in the lecture was on the screen).[94] We do not know what Wallis thought about people of colour, although we can say that he and Molly happily gave hospitality to African visitors, and that following Rhodesia's unilateral declaration of independence there are signs that their sympathies did not lie with Ian Smith.[95]

At the end of December 1959 Wallis gave a variant of the Strength of England lecture to 600 schoolboys at the Institution of Civil Engineers. As usual, he stressed the 'immense advantage' of Britain's geographical position. A few days later he wrote to congratulate the aviation journalist James Stevens for an article in *Flight* which showed him to be the only person to whom he had put this point who understood what he was talking about.[96] Wallis described his frustration at the 'apathy' of government ministers who were 'ignorant of the advantages we possess' and did nothing to 'subsidise our shipping or encourage the development of supersonic air transport.' Wallis welcomed Stevens to 'the great cause' of long-range flight.[97] By then Wallis's Christmas talk had attracted widespread attention, partly because he had shown film of Swallow, which was revealed to the public for the first time, and partly because he was about to be accused of a serious security breach in the course of doing so.

Problem children

The day after the lecture, *The Times* announced that the government had placed a design study contract with Vickers for a naval deck-landing version of the Swallow. The article gave the aircraft's all-up weight and said that Swallow's attraction for the role was its promised ability to loiter subsonically for long periods and then accelerate to supersonic speed. Similar stories appeared in *Flight* and *Aviation Week*. In each case Wallis was named as the source. *Flight* added that Wallis had said that such a military development was necessary to secure funding to pioneer a revolutionary project.

The naval Swallow was then classified as secret. News of its existence caused a stir, and in February 1960 Leonard Curzon, the Under-Secretary in charge of security at the Ministry of Aviation, wrote to George Edwards to complain. The Ministry, he warned, was unlikely to agree to any more unscripted lectures by Wallis.[98] Edwards made an immediate apology. However, Wallis denied having said anything about the naval Swallow, either during the lecture or in conversation afterwards, and accordingly saw the apology as a betrayal.

Wallis shared his outrage with Philip Teed, who happened to have been a wartime colleague of Curzon in the Ministry of Supply and on the strength of their 'friendly association' wrote to plead injustice. The talk had been recorded; he had read the transcript; nothing about military aircraft had been said either during the lecture or discussion that followed. In any case, presumably as a result of the division of responsibilities enforced by Dunphie nine months before, neither he nor Wallis knew anything about the design study or Operational Requirement 364. If classified information had appeared in the press, it must have come either from intelligent guesswork or a source other than Wallis. If Curzon felt unable to accept this, he asked if they could meet to provide such further information as was needed to put matters straight.[99]

Curzon replied at length. He did not suppose the security breach had been deliberate; most probably the information had slipped out unintendedly during informal talk after the lecture. It was unlikely that three different journalists were mistaken in reporting the source. Curzon did not say how Wallis could have inadvertently leaked information about which he did not know, but instead tried to turn the tables: if it was the case that Wallis was unaware of the contract or of its secret aspects, this was a serious criticism of Vickers, whose works manager (Tom Gammon) had been fully briefed by the Ministry about the rules to be observed. Curzon was willing to meet Teed and Wallis but doubted if doing so would help. He could not engage in private negotiations about official business, and if they succeeded in persuading him to withdraw the original complaint then a much stronger protest to the company would ensue. 'I am sure you will want to consider this.'[100]

A week later Teed and Curzon spoke by telephone. In the course of their talk Curzon invited Teed to visit him, but without Wallis. Teed agreed in principle, but on condition that he discuss it with Wallis first. At this, Curzon said:

> Well! Let's leave it there for the moment – I would like to say that Dr Wallis is not the only one who has been hurt. Some of us in this department have been deeply wounded.[101]

Wounded feelings offer a likely motive for what had actually happened: Wallis had been set up, partly in punishment for past campaigning through the media on behalf of Swallow, and partly to discourage him from doing it again.[102]

It was not only senior civil servants and ministers who saw Wallis as a loose cannon. Two months later Teed wrote a private briefing note to Lord Weeks about a meeting between Wallis and Edwards earlier in the day. At its end:

> I drove George back to his office, during which time, in a very friendly way, he told me about what, I expect, he regarded as home truths, none of which I have mentioned to Wally, though it may well be, you will in a toned down way.
>
> George told me I was to do my damnedest to keep Wally from contacting either Sandys[103] and/or Watkinson,[104] but, if he must do propaganda, to get to tackle the technical staff at the M. of A. and/or Farnborough. Whatever he did, he wasn't to give anything re 'Cascade' to back bench MPs – I think he had Legge-Bourke in mind. He, George, wasn't going to have another Swallow performance.[105]

Teed often wrote such notes about the man he called 'my Master'. His home was in Tunbridge Wells, but he was unmarried and during the week stayed over in a hotel where evenings gave him the time to pen private notes to Lord Weeks or Vickers's managing director, Charles Dunphie, to keep them abreast of Wallis's latest doings, the state of his fragile relations with George Edwards ('Had there been a dog in the room, I would have tried to tread on its tail to create a diversion') and give advance warning of matters that Wally was going to raise. Since Teed was held in respect by both men, their shared confidences enabled him to alert the chairman and managing director to signs of impending trouble or things about which they might not otherwise have known. He was even-handed, describing Wallis and Edwards together as 'the Prima Donnas' (sometimes 'the Problem Children').

Edwards and Wallis had met earlier that particular day to discuss a new kind of aircraft. Since 1958 Wallis had been wrangling with what he saw as the basic issue facing the aero industry: the inability of any one form of aircraft to give efficient performance from all speeds from $M = 0$ up to $M = 5$ or beyond. Research by the RAE had shown that four quite different types of airframe were needed for different parts of this speed band. Only one of them had so far been fully developed, and the development costs of pursing all four would be astronomic.

Three partial solutions had been identified, and Wallis was critical of all of them. One was to abandon low speed altogether, take off and land using vertically directed jets, and concentrate on a slender delta for supersonic flight. The RAE championed a complex fixed shape which Wallis believed would only operate economically at a single design speed.[106] (He defined efficient performance as including good control, good cockpit visibility at low speeds, satisfactory stability at all speeds, low capital and maintenance cost and lowest possible cost for initial development.) The third, put forward by himself and Vickers, was for an aircraft that changes shape in flight. Trials had shown this feasible, but like the other two hitherto it had been based on a slender delta, which became too attenuated for speeds above M = 2.5. A fundamentally new form was needed.

Wallis looked for what he called 'a once and for all aerodynamic form', capable of all speeds permitted by existing materials, great range and altitude. As before, he was thinking of a family of aircraft for different functions, but all aerodynamically similar. There was an economic as well as aerodynamic case for this: development expenditure would only be incurred once, and when new materials appeared they should be substituted for the older ones while the aerodynamic form would remain unchanged.

One key for a universal, all-speed form was to keep wave drag at low values. Drag derived from the fuselage (volume) and wings (lift). Wallis addressed this, in the first instance, by putting the entire frontage of the fuselage behind an air intake and combining it with wings that were short in span but ran nearly the full length of the fuselage. At high speed such wings would consist of flat uniform surfaces of large chord and small thickness, ideal for supersonics. However, these supersonic lifting surfaces would be made up of a series of individual blades which when closed locked into a single wing, but when rotated would resolve into a series of angled winglets (Iain Murray's analogy is of a Venetian blind[107]) that produce lift sufficient for STOL performance. The integration of engine intake and fuselage would provide for high pressure air trunks running the full length of the aircraft, from which branches could be taken to feed slits placed on the blades. In this way lift from the blades could be greatly augmented. Control could be exercised in pitch by using the leading and trailing blades as bow and stern elevators, in roll by moving port and starboard flaps, and in yaw by a normal fin and rudder.[108]

This was variable geometry of an astonishing kind – another new genus of aircraft. According to Wallis it originated in the struggle to draft a patent application for an aspect of Swallow in which Wallis was searching for the words to describe a detail involving 'one slot', found himself wondering if 'two' might be better, and from there proceeded to 'plurality'. Next day it dawned that the implications led to 'quite a different kind of aerodyne from my beloved Swallow'. No one looking at the new conception 'could possibly trace its descent back to its Swallow ancestor.'[109]

The new conception was christened 'Cascade'. For a few months it caused a stir in high aeronautical and defence circles. While the Ministry of Aviation fussed over secrecy and the naval deck-landing design (in which Wallis said he had absolutely no interest),[110] Wallis shared the Cascade concept with Solly Zuckerman,[111] now the Air Ministry's Chief Scientific Adviser, who brought it to the attention of the Defence Staff. Zuckerman also brokered meetings with James Lighthill, the young and recently appointed director of the RAE, and Duncan Sandys, the air minister. Wallis's opinion of Lighthill was not high, and when they met on 7 March there was tension in the air (Teed said he was hampered 'by there being no dog').[112] However, they parted on good terms. In following weeks Teed socialised with Handel Davies, the RAE's deputy director, who brought his wife for lunch, described Wally as 'an old wizard', and confided that the Minister of Aviation's secretary had rung the day before to ask him to report on what they were doing.[113]

Sandys found Cascade 'most stimulating'. If Wallis's ideas were valid, they should be 'fully and fairly considered in the context of the current feasibility studies for the supersonic air transport project.' Sandys proposed to visit in May 'with one or two officials' to hear more so that they could decide whether the project merited support.[114]

All of which had brought Wallis and George Edwards together for a pre-meeting on 4 May. Wallis made what Teed described as 'a jolly good presentation' on Cascade. However, while Sandys's interest was in civil supersonics, both Wallis and Edwards had heard from Air Staff sources that a supersonic bomber requirement was in the offing, which posed the quandary of where to focus. 'George is going to have a think about this and let Wally know the result,' wrote Teed, adding that this wouldn't 'make much difference to what Wally does.'[115]

The main outcome of this meeting was George Edwards's promise to send an aerodynamic team from his side of the business 'to try to determine what Cascade can do that can't be done by a conventionally designed aircraft'.[116] Wallis believed Cascade would be simpler than Swallow, but when the team made its report in July it found that, on the contrary, Cascade offered 'no clear advantage over orthodox solutions' while its mechanical complexity would be 'considerably increased'.[117]

The appraisal took place against a background in which Vickers, the Bristol Aeroplane Company, Hunting Aircraft, and English Electric were being herded together by the Government to form a new entity – the British Aircraft Corporation. Wallis was not pleased, partly because he and his team would be brought more closely under George Edwards's sway, but chiefly because he saw Edwards's business agenda as a 'disastrous failure'.[118] He was not impressed by a new strike aircraft being discussed between Vickers and English Electric,[119] and he thought that Edwards's hopes for a supersonic airliner under development by the Bristol company were misplaced. The Bristol project was just the kind of design upon which Wallis was attempting to improve, but Edwards saw it as the pragmatic way ahead. That way led to Concorde.

14

Working Late, 1960–79

Fires and reading aloud

The first Monday in November 1966 found Molly in the garden planting wallflowers. 'Oh, for a *tiny* garden. But I do love doing the flowers I must admit. Specially this *lovely* time of year with the blessed winter coming. And fires & reading aloud.' Each season had its blessings. In early spring aconites coloured the grass under their trees; as evenings lightened Wallis gardened hard into twilight, breathing the fragrance of night scented stock. A clock of Wallis's design stood in the garden: 'It's nice to know the time when you're gardening. Tea in half an hour I say to myself'.[1] In winter it was their delight to walk over frozen fields and read to each other.

A lot of reading went on in White Hill House. Eight thousand books overflowed even into the bathroom. Wallis studied *The Times* each day; the *Times Literary Supplement* and *Punch* were taken weekly. Wallis often read while he was eating and if there were family in the house and chatter became distracting he was liable to turn to a grandchild and say, '*Must* you do that?' Up in his room in the roof, he read Browning, distilled lavender oil, bottled honey, mended clocks and carved wood. Molly continued her wartime habit of using book jackets as writing paper, with the result that letters show what was being read or talked about. They took to Laurie Lee and Ernest Hemingway but not to Iris Murdoch; Claire Rayner's *People in Love* and Desmond Morris's *The Naked Ape* mapped onto Molly's crusading for open discussion of sexuality and contraception. Wallis and the popular historian Arthur Bryant were mutual admirers;[2]

Bryant's romantic Anglo-British patriotism appealed to them, and Bryant periodically used his column in the *Illustrated London News* to celebrate 'the persistently youthful' and 'infinitely resourceful and original' Barnes Wallis. The Wallises considered most television output trivial, so there was no TV set in the house and series like *The Forsyte Saga* that gripped the rest of the nation during the 1960s passed them by. (Molly mused: 'I'd listen to (or watch, I mean) the Forsytes if we had a TV. But I shouldn't want to because of that foul Irene.') When something came up that one of them did want to see (like Ken Loach's *Up the Junction* (1965) or *Poor Cow* (1967), both watched by Molly), they needed to find a sympathetic neighbour.

Wallis was busy as ever. October 1966, the month of his seventy-ninth birthday, saw him open the new village hall – the culmination of thirty years of effort to provide Effingham with recreational and community facilities, and to champion its causes. The playing fields and hall were 'his memorial', and when he turned eighty, over 200 villagers turned out to pay him tribute.[3] Beyond Effingham, the National Marriage Guidance Council, the Yvonne Arnaud Theatre (which he and Molly often attended), and the Migraine Trust (because of Wallis's personal experience) were among the many causes he supported. The sums were individually quite small (his assistant Pat Lucas later reminisced that 'Dr Wallis always thought of himself as a poor man'), but they were made regularly. Several days a month were given to membership of the Councils of Christ's Hospital and Epsom College.[4] Alongside CH, he travelled the country to talk to schools and audiences of all kinds. In 1968 he accepted the Presidency of the Bath Institute of Medical Engineering which had just been founded to counter disability through new science, instruments, and artificial limbs. After a lifetime thinking about intercontinental travel, he made a fundraising TV broadcast on the Institute's behalf which asked: 'What are we doing for those who cannot move a single step without support or assistance?' Wallis reflected that it was as difficult 'to enable the lame to walk and the crippled to move by mechanical means as it is to reach Australia non-stop by air. It demands just as much ingenuity and skill and calls for the highest qualities of inventive engineering.'[5]

Behind the citizenly altruism was a baffled soul. Character, he thought, was formed by reaction to challenge, but where in 1960s Britain were the challenges? A time there was when children had walked miles to school; he complained that now they were taken by bus; welfarism had sapped self-reliance. Would teenagers with 'long hair and beastly shoes' enlist and fight as valiantly as their fathers?[6] On reflection he thought they probably would, but when asked if a woman could be an engineer his reply was an adamant 'No!' The answer was not to do with her ability; it was simply that he could not imagine women as apprentices in workshops.[7]

Faster, higher, deeper

The Victorian Wallis who struggled to read England's mind in the swinging sixties was also the twenty-first-century Wallis waiting for everyone else to catch up. In 1958 he argued that although there had been plenty of time and resources to exploit the potential of jet propulsion, the aero industry did not know what to do with it. To illustrate he pointed to divergences in design between aircraft like the Comet IV, the Boeing 707, and the coming VC10, and that they were all subsonic. Such progress in supersonic flight as had been made had been achieved less by skill than by using 'recklessly increased' wing loadings and heavy heat-resistant materials like titanium and ferrous alloys.[8]

A large stumbling block to the design of faster supersonic aircraft was aerodynamic heating. Friction and compression processes raise the temperature of a solid body that passes through air at high speed; the flow of heat from an aircraft's skin into its innards produces uneven distributions of hotness which can impose strain on the airframe and exceed what people or things carried can withstand. Hitherto, the response to these effects had been a search for ways to fortify airframes against high temperatures. But materials like titanium were expensive, and since the vapour pressure of aviation fuel increases as temperature rises, structural insulation called for stronger and specially shaped tanks, which further increased weight and reduced carrying capacity. Such drawbacks were characterised by the Aérospatiale/BAC design for Concorde, which Wallis described as being 'pretty well carved out of solid metal'.[9]

Wallis turned such thinking on its head. Instead of seeking to buffer aircraft against ever-hotter temperatures, he settled upon an equilibrium temperature below 150°C that permitted the use of light materials and devised a flight profile to respect that limit. Air density and aerodynamic heating lessen with height, so a flight envelope involving ascent to altitudes above 150,000 feet followed by acceleration to hypersonic speeds, with a corresponding decrease at the other end would keep the temperature under the chosen threshold. Such a profile would permit use of lighter material, improve performance and cost less.[10]

Wallis went on to combine this isothermal principle with other ideas: a pivoting fuselage which obtained lift from jet engines by directing some of the thrust slightly downwards; wings of variable camber that could be used for control; a ducted wing; and a manned intermediate spacecraft which could ascend to orbit without the need for expendable booster rockets and return to earth to land as an aircraft.[11] By the mid-1960s he had arrived at a synthesising concept for air transport involving aircraft of optimal size, uniform design, flexible function, and versatile performance.

The search for ideal size was Wallis's response to the law whereby the structural efficiency of airframes decreases as they grow in size. Hitherto, engineers had countered this by building larger and heavier aircraft which in turn were proportionally more costly and called for ever larger airports and longer runways. Wallis's answer was to build smaller aircraft in larger numbers, thereby reducing unit costs of design and construction. Such aircraft would be configured to operate over both short and long distances and at sub-, super- and hypersonic speeds.[12] In place of hundreds of different kinds of aircraft, each designed for a particular kind of route, speed, and role, there would be a Universal aircraft, equally at home carrying shipping containers from Carlisle to Birmingham or passengers from London to Sydney in less time than it takes to watch the in-flight film. And since Universal aircraft would be STOL machines they would lend themselves to a new geography of small, sub-regional, environmentally friendly airports. (Molly noted that the Concorde being developed by 'that tyke George Edwards' would need a runway of over 10,000 feet, whereas Barnes's plane could fly from a strip the length of two football pitches.)

The Universal aircraft recalls Puck's promise to 'put a girdle round about the earth in forty minutes.' In tandem with it went an interest in depth. Between 1965 and 1968 Wallis explored ideas for high-speed submarines which could travel the oceans at depths greater than 2000 feet. Reasons for doing this included a desire to escape detection, to evade Soviet interference with trade short of war, and to open great circle routes to Australasia. Since submarines of conventional design were formed from a single hull, the only way to enlarge them was by increasing their length or diameter. Wallis discovered that arcs of small radius are more resistant to pressure than large ones, and from this emerged the concept of a group of axially adjoining cylinders, each narrower than an orthodox submarine but cumulatively larger when bundled together like the parallel aisles of some large late-medieval church. This pressure vessel could be enclosed by a streamlined, unpressurised covering, with fuel tanks in the intermediate cavity. In further pursuit of speed, quiet and depth, Wallis proposed to power the vessel with a closed-cycle gas turbine wherein exhaust gases could be liquified and stored on board.[13]

The new shape won the approval of Roy Turner, Vickers's Chief Naval Architect at Barrow. The Admiralty and Ministry of Defence were less impressed. Turner described the Admiralty's response as one that found 'difficulties for every solution', and by the end of 1966 it was accepted that no development funding would be forthcoming.[14]

'I *never* wear a hat and do not dance about'

On a day in 1966, the journalist Christopher Brasher and a BBC film crew arrived in Wallis's office in the old clubhouse at Brooklands to record a four-minute interview about invention and education. By 'some lucky chemistry' their talk ran on through the afternoon and into the evening. Brasher and the crew left with 'reel upon reel' of film. In due course the conversation was turned into a fifty-minute documentary. The title was taken from a point in their conversation when Wallis described his plan for hypersonic aircraft. Brasher asked in astonishment if this was not a tremendous step from the 1500 mph or so promised by Concorde. Wallis replied, 'Yes it is, but why not? Why not!'[15]

Why not? . . . Why Not! was broadcast on BBC1 on the evening of Thursday, 19 January 1967. Seven and a half million people tuned in. Wallis's reputation as a seer was strengthened, and the documentary's investigation of the fate of Swallow fostered the idea that he was a genius who had been marginalised. The establishment portrayed by Brasher was characterised by conflicts of loyalty, exclusion of the outsider, inter-departmental rivalries and opposing technological schools. Ben Lockspeiser told him that it was a delusion that scientific decisions were taken objectively ('there is nothing more subjective than a committee of scientists'). It was a civil servant's function to avoid making mistakes and, since career progression depended on avoidance of errors, the premium was always against taking risks.[16]

The broadcast moved hundreds to write to Wallis. Among them were long-lost friends, like Billy Lloyd, who recalled their lunchtime singing in 1906;[17] people whose paths had briefly crossed with his; colleagues like Frank Whittle; and many who simply wrote out of the blue – like former Wellington aircrew (some of whom thanked him for their lives), Ryvita's managing director (who was pleased to discover Wallis's taste for his product and sent a freshly baked supply) or the Vegetarian Society (which sent greetings and pamphlets).

Letters kept arriving for months. Wallis enlisted help to reply to loopier contacts, such as the gentleman who sought his opinion on a theory that the smoothness of the Sussex Downs was the result of global flooding caused by the periodic tilting of the world under the influence of Antarctic ice and lunar gravity. Wallis's colleague, C. H. Hayes, replied briefly to say that what distinguished Wallis's ideas was his ability to turn them into reality 'by diligent search for evidence'.[18] To the eleven-year-old boy from Redcar who asked for advice about his aviation project, on the other hand, Wallis replied in person, with care.[19]

The producer of *Why not? . . . Why Not!* was Glyn Jones, the energetic creator of BBC TV's series *Tomorrow's World*.[20] Wallis said that he 'would have done anything to avoid' taking part, but this notwithstanding they got on well. After the broadcast Jones sent him a closely typed nine-page letter into which he poured details of things said while the programme was being made. Among them were extracts of interview transcripts that had not been used and off-the-record confidences,[21] one of which concerned the vetoing of the knighthood that Lockspeiser had recommended for him in 1945. (In 1973 Harris shed light on this by sending to Wallis a copy of the recommendation for an immediate knighthood he had submitted to Archibald Sinclair immediately after the *Tirpitz* sinking. The proposal was vetoed by Stafford Cripps, and at the foot of Sinclair's acknowledgement Harris wrote: 'Stifford Crapps! The last person to encourage anything to do with bombs – or war!!')[22]

The un-bestowed knighthood stirred indignation. A former and distant colleague wrote to Wallis enclosing a copy of a protest he had just sent to the Duke of Edinburgh.[23] In it he told the duke that Wallis held the Civil Service in contempt. Embarrassed, Wallis wrote to the duke's private secretary to dissociate himself.[24] Unbowed, his champion wrote again to Buckingham Palace listing Wallis's achievements, with a copy to Wallis and a request that he check the list. Wallis wrote in apology for a second time, this time to the duke's treasurer, who replied calmingly: 'No-one, I am sure, would be more pleased than His Royal Highness to see you receive some acknowledgement for your work but as you, if not others, obviously realise it is difficult if not impossible for him to intervene in such matters.'[25] Nonetheless, someone intervened. In June 1968 Wallis's knighthood was in the Queen's Birthday Honours. On 25 October he wrote to the Permanent Under-Secretary of State at the Home Office to say that he was 'honoured to obey the Queen's command to attend at Buckingham Palace on Tuesday, 10 December, 1968, at 10.15 a.m.'

Jones's documentary prompted a cascade of approaches from

magazine editors, newspapers, and would-be biographers, all of which he declined. (At the end of his refusal to a request from Evans Brothers to appoint a biographer, he reminded them of errors in *The Dam Busters* to which he had previously drawn their attention: 'All Brickhill's descriptions of my own personal behaviour are sheer imagination on his part – I *never* wear a hat and do not dance about.'[26]) But there was one letter which gave him pause. It began 'What an actor was lost when you took to the drawing board!', and it came from the historian and editor Jack Morpurgo.

Errata: life stories

Morpurgo was a literary all-rounder whose grounding in publishing had been at the elbow of Allen Lane in Penguin, since expanded by ten years heading the National Book League. Sparky, widely travelled, fluent on the page, like Wallis he was an Old Blue, and it was through membership of the school's Council of Almoners that they had got to know each other. There are two accounts of how Wallis came to accept him as his biographer. One is in Morpurgo's autobiography; the other is in Morpurgo's archive.

The autobiography tells that a week after the broadcast Wallis arrived in his office with a 'bulging file' of publishers' bids.[27] 'Tell me, dear heart', he said, 'what do we do about that?' Morpurgo replied instinctively, saying that now he would have to do it. 'Wallis slapped his hand on the file. "Done."' Morpurgo recalled how his feelings swung 'between ecstasy and despondency'. The idea of writing Wallis's biography thrilled him, but was he fitted to do it? He had never written a full-length biography; he lacked the technical knowledge to explain engineering concepts; his historical expertise lay back in the seventeenth and eighteenth centuries; writing about someone living would be a challenge; he was suffering from glaucoma and worried that he might be unable to cope with reading thousands of documents. It was a tall order, and by the time of their next meeting Morpurgo had resolved to decline. But Wallis seemed ready. He parried the refusal by offering to provide whatever engineering grounding he needed, unrestricted access to all his papers, and a free hand to write as he saw fit. Wallis even had an answer for Morpurgo's deteriorating eyesight: a month later, 'Barnes's chauffeur delivered . . . a huge wooden box fitted out with lights and magnifying glasses.' With the box came a note: 'For seeking out all that can be said and much that none dare say about that wicked old man, his biographer's friend, Barnes Neville Wallis'.[28]

The archive contradicts almost every detail of this account. The magnifier, for instance, was not made until 1970, and far from being worried about his technical credentials, the day after *Why not? . . . Why not!* was broadcast Morpurgo went out of his way to say how good they were. However, the clincher was his warning that sooner or later someone was going to write about him; the question was whether to have a say about who the someone should be or leave it to chance.[29] Wallis replied by proposing lunch at the Athenaeum, where 'I will tell you all my feelings on the subject.' When they met Wallis agreed that Morpurgo should be his authorised biographer.

Morpurgo saw the biography as a three-year project. His terms included annual advance payments, funds for a research assistant, secretarial help, travel, and a scientific consultant on call. The book was eventually placed with Longmans, the serialisation rights being sold separately to the *Sunday Times*.[30] Both deals provided for contributions to the Christ's Hospital RAF Foundation.

As a newly hatched queen bee kills off her rivals, so did Morpurgo turn first to deal with competitors. The most worrying of them was Bernard Hurren, an aviation journalist who had been in intermittent contact with Wallis since 1965 and was under contract to Leslie Frewin Publishers to write a biography of Wallis. The book was eventually advertised but never appeared.[31] Given Hurren's later claims (for instance, that Wallis was a 'phoney', that the aero industry regarded him as 'a windbag and poseur', that Vickers used his flare for publicity 'to conceal what they were really doing with the Spitfire', or that the bouncing bomb originated with Arthur Harris[32]), this was fortunate for Leslie Frewin.

Another contender was Paul Brickhill, who had long dreamed of the job and wrote persistently and at increasing length to Wallis and

Morpurgo to explain why he still should.[33] Wallis became irritated. 'How on earth do you deal with a lunatic letter such as this?' he asked, enclosing Brickhill's latest letter which suggested there would be room for two biographies.[34]

A third worry concerned the author David Irving, who was preparing a series of articles on the Dams Raid for the *Sunday Express* and to whom Wallis had lent several of his wartime diaries. Morpurgo feared that his contractual obligations to the *Sunday Times* and Longmans could be voided if Irving were to publish material that could only have come from Wallis. He drafted a letter enabling Wallis to explain that he had 'overlooked his obligations', ask for the diaries' return, and instruct that 'no quotations from them nor evidence adduced from them be used in any articles you are preparing'.[35] Morpurgo was worried that Irving's reaction to this rather officious demand might come to colour the view of the Beaverbrook press; in the event Irving was punctilious and returned the records without complaint.

Morpurgo began work in earnest in October 1967, initially by announcing himself to a number of people he considered to be key to the story. One of these was Sir Arthur Harris, who replied guardedly: 'If you ring me here the day before you wish to see me I will say if it is convenient for me to be in.'[36]

Morpurgo worked chronologically, gathering material and consulting sources for each stage in Wallis's life, writing the chapter, then moving on. At each step he sent a list of questions to which Wallis responded either by letter, in some cases by writing a treatise (for instance on the design constraints of R100) and in others through a taped conversation. As work proceeded there were secondary lists of questions, to tease out puzzles or clarify thinking. For explanation of some topics, like Swallow, Wallis asked a colleague to provide information.[37] Morpurgo's research assistant, Elaine Barr, undertook many of the interviews. She and Morpurgo formed a good relationship with Pat Lucas, who gave them much help by locating key documents. Overall, however, it was Wallis himself who gave the book its shape by providing Morpurgo with a narrative.

In January 1971 Morpurgo wrote to say that the book was finished.

He enclosed a copy of the introduction and invited Wallis to read the rest.[38] Wallis replied: 'I cannot help wishing you had not sent me the Introduction. If the rest of the book contains as much praise as this, then I should have no hesitation in damning the whole thing. Criticism I can stand; praise or appreciation make me want to cry.'[39] He declined to read the draft on the grounds that to do so would be tantamount to agreeing that he approved of what it said. To the question of whether he wished to see what had been written about the fates of R101 and Swallow, he replied that there was nothing he could say about these subjects that was not 'bitter and intolerant'. On R101:

> I have never been able to understand the mentality of Scott, Richmond, Colmore and Nixon. Not one of them was an engineer; not one of them had ever built or been responsible for building a rigid airship . . . Commander Burney had originally accepted their suggestion to design a large passenger airship by Committee, with himself as their chairman . . . Burney when he discovered me in the basement of Vickers House . . . offered me the post of secretary to the Committee, an offer which, knowing that the four were not competent, I refused whereupon Burney realising that I did know airships, dispensed with their services and made me Chief Engineer. They then persuaded the Government to nominate them to build a rival ship at Cardington.[40]

As we saw in Chapter 4, the reason for a 'rival ship' was a change of government. Wallis was the AGC's chief engineer when the design committee was brought into being, and the committee was not formed to design the airship. Wallis was here telescoping and rearranging events and had been doing so for several years. In 1969 he told Morpurgo:

> . . . enough has been said, I think, to show you why I attribute the R101 disaster: firstly to my refusal to work with Scott, Colmore, Richmond and Nixon; secondly to Richmond's overweening vanity; thirdly to Scott's lazy self-assurance, and lastly to

a certain lack of moral fibre in Colmore. None of them had the moral courage to confess that their ship was a mass of mistakes from beginning to end and was in fact demonstrably unfit to fly over any distances so great that the weight of fuel to be carried rendered the use of dynamic lift necessary.[41]

Again, the relationship with the R101 project was misdescribed – he was not invited to work with Scott, Richmond and Colmore. His comments about them were also at odds with what he had recently said elsewhere. In reply to an admirer whose reading of *Slide Rule* had fostered the impression of rivalry between the two projects, Wallis said that there was 'no bitter rivalry whatever', and that 'Commander Colmore, Scott and I remained the best of friends up to the very end'. Wallis thought 'Mr Norway exaggerated this aspect of the airship programme.'[42]

Wallis went on to give his opinion about the cause of the disaster. He criticised the sharp-edged form of R101's fins and reliance on dynamic lift. Dynamic lift, he said, could only be produced by applying a lot of 'up' elevator, which induced a large down-load on the tail, so causing the ship to fly pitched up:

. . . in which attitude if her speed is sufficient, the dynamic lift upwards will exceed not only the static heaviness but also the downward load on the tail. If now, in this condition, the angle of incidence of a sharp-edged fin, such as that of R101 becomes too great, the fin will stall, leaving the trailing area of the elevators unloaded. That is to say, the heavy down-load on the tail is instantly removed with the result that the tail will suddenly rise and the bow will sink, since it was this down-load on the tail which was keeping the ship pitched up. The result is, of course, a sharp dive which, if too steep cannot be corrected.[43]

Wallis explained that the aerodynamic defects of a sharp-edged fin were not known at the time of the R101 court of inquiry. The effects had emerged later, during wind tunnel tests to investigate the rudder stall that led to the loss of the prototype Warwick GR Vs that had crashed early in 1945. Was Wallis subconsciously comparing the fate of R101 with the death of Maurice Longbottom?

The biography went to press late in 1971. Wallis received his advance copy just before Christmas. On 28 December he rang Morpurgo. The tone was affectionate. 'Jack, dear heart, how did you find out so much about me?'[44] Two days later, however, Longmans received a stern letter from Wallis listing 45 misprints and mistakes. Among the mistakes were howlers such as R101 flying the Atlantic. Wallis had no way of knowing how such blunders had occurred, and when Morpurgo received his list of complaints from Longman he naturally wondered if they were being laid at his door. Distraught, he composed a long, handwritten apology: 'I am so miserable that I am close to deciding that this must be my last book.' Morpurgo feared that his friendship with Wallis had been broken, and that Wallis might denounce the book. However, he enclosed a copy of his detailed reply to Longmans, which showed that most of the errors had been introduced through the publisher's copy editor and the printer, in many cases after his corrected proofs had been returned.

Wallis seems not to have anticipated how Morpurgo would react to his complaints. When that penny dropped, he hurriedly gave Morpurgo his 'warm congratulations on a magnificent piece of work'.[45] Two days later, Molly told him 'Put it down, I could not'. She thought it a lucid, humorous, 'wonderful book about a wonderful man'.[46] Reviewers agreed, describing *Barnes Wallis* as 'first rate', 'exciting and engrossing', 'a fitting tribute', 'dispassionate yet sympathetic'. For some weeks it was a bestseller. *The Times* was equivocal, likening Morpurgo's lack of aeronautical knowledge to someone with no knowledge of art writing about Picasso, but only the *Sunday Times* was really cool, perhaps because its features editor was about to publish an article which for the first time would argue that the Dams Raid had been a pointless failure.[47]

The book sold out within a month; the hardback was thrice reprinted. Towards the end of the year there was talk of Wallis as a guest on *This Is Your Life*.[48] This was vetoed by Molly, who thought it 'utterly repugnant' to be paraded with friends and relatives. However, when Morpurgo reported that he had been setting questions on Wallis's life and times for a contestant's special subject on *Mastermind* she asked for the broadcast details so that they could 'tout round among our friends and relations to find somewhere that we can . . . watch.' As time passed, Wallis upped his estimate of Morpurgo's portrait of himself to 'brilliant'.[49]

For his part, Morpurgo reflected that while Wallis's integrity was beyond doubt, in the course of his research it had become obvious that 'even from a man as palpably honest as was he, first person evidence is suspect'. In perhaps a dozen instances, Morpurgo was able to demonstrate from primary sources that certain stories Wallis had told about himself were fiction. Such stories particularly concerned the disdain with which his most original ideas had been received by fellow professionals and by Government. Morpurgo concluded that Wallis had become convinced that his version of events was correct.[50]

Not everyone agreed with the reviewer who said that the biography was well documented. Annie sent a list of inaccuracies about the family, including the spelling of her name and her date of birth. Cecil Burney, who as a small boy had been the 'little horror' who scrambled about on Molly's furniture in the White Bungalow, threatened legal action over the way his father had been depicted. William Pye was likewise disappointed by the portrayal of his father.[51] George Meager, R100's first officer, pointed out that it was not true that the airship's crew had been excluded from ceremonies to honour the dead of R101; rather, they had been given a place of honour. And Hartley Pratt's elder sister, then ninety-three years old, wrote in anguish to dispute the account of events that led to her brother's suicide.[52]

Wallis and Morpurgo discussed how Mary Pratt should be answered. Wallis refused to reply to her at all, since it was 'quite evident' to him 'that she is determined to be hurt and offended over the whole incident.' They agreed that Morpurgo would respond on behalf of them both, and that he would stand by what he had written because 'the facts are the facts' to which he 'owed it to his conscience' to hold.[53] In hindsight this was cruel, because original sources show that virtually everything Wallis told Morpurgo about

Pratt's last years and suicide was either muddled or wrong.[54] In Wallis's version Pratt crossed swords with his predecessor at Supermarine, Trevor Westbrook, who in May 1940 had been hired by Lord Beaverbrook, the newly appointed Minister for Aircraft Production. Wallis believed that one of Westbrook's tasks was to hasten Spitfire production, and that his recent knowledge of Supermarine's processes put him in the position of seeming to countermand Pratt's orders. Pratt complained, the complaint went unheeded, Pratt resigned in protest, and then spent weeks unsuccessfully looking for another post. Demoralised, later in 1940 he shot himself.[55]

Contemporary records tell a different story. The gap between Westbrook's departure and Pratt's suicide was four years, not a few weeks. Pratt's performance throughout that time was excellent. He did not resign; he was forced out of his post by the MAP in mid-June 1941.[56] Perhaps not coincidentally, he shot himself five days after a stormy Commons debate on the Ministries of Supply and Aircraft Production,[57] held on 9 July, in which Austin Hopkinson (1878–1963), the outspoken independent MP for Mossley and an experienced industrialist, charged Beaverbrook with putting the MAP in 'chaos from top to bottom'. Pratt fell afoul of Trevor Westbrook because he had challenged the MAP over its incompetence. For that, he was victimised,[58] and since Morpurgo did not cross-check Wallis's account, the errors went into his book.

Love's not Time's fool

The explanation for Wallis's apparent betrayal of the memory of his old friend seems to be that his own memory had begun to fail. When Morpurgo began work Wallis was still brimming with ideas. He told a visitor that he had 'the heart and lungs of a man of 50', abstained from alcohol, avoided meat and could 'still walk up a mountain'.[59] But aback of that was the onset, at first almost imperceptible, of a change in the way he remembered things. When he gave a talk to the Effingham WI or a school he was lively and lucid,[60] but in conversation or when writing, details and events that were years apart were sometimes edited together or rearranged – as in the case of the relationship between Hartley Pratt and Trevor Westbrook. Where Morpurgo accepted such narratives without testing them against other sources, jumbled chronology or fallacies sometimes ensued.[61]

In February 1971 Vickers-Armstrongs gave Wallis notice that his employment must end.[62] The reason given was that the British Aircraft Corporation needed to shed staff following cancellation of the BAC Three-Eleven project. The underlying reason was the Corporation's desire to see Wallis gone. He had reached retirement age nineteen years earlier and since been kept on through a series of extension agreements; he was now eighty-four; the Corporation did not wish to pursue his latest ideas. There was an argument about his pension (the calculation of which had been complicated by the extensions), and when Morpurgo told him that over the next two or three years there was every chance that the book would produce around £500 'due to the Foundation – or to you – or to Molly if you prefer', he decided that it should be to him.[63]

He determined to carry on. A spare room at White Hill House was turned into a drawing office, to which the BAC allowed him to take furniture from his old office at Brooklands. For a brass plate, Leo d'Erlanger gave him the use of one of his companies, replaced in 1972 (again with d'Erlanger's help) by a company of his own – Aircraft Design (BNW) Ltd.

He sketched a revolutionary new aircraft, the fuselage a rectangular cylinder, wedged at the bow and stern with a small droop. It was in two configurations, one a slender cropped delta, the other with a parallel knife-edged wing. Its structure weight would be very low. Leo d'Erlanger introduced him to two Hawker Siddeley directors to discuss it,[64] but no one in a position to take it forward showed interest.

Over the next five years he contemplated a new form of propulsion; a carbon fibre airship; a submarine merchantman fabricated from the cheapest forms of steel and light alloys to enable 'world distribution' of goods;[65] a subsonic version of the Universal aircraft (1975),[66] and a VTOL Ideal Aircraft of basic construction with interchangeable engines.[67] His first pocket calculator, an HP35, was 'a perfect marvel' which removed the toil of calculation.

The impression of a late flourish masks a slowing down. The last ideas were remarkable but few of them were more than outline concepts. Writing became laborious. Drafts of letters and papers were begun and abandoned in mid-page. The award of the Royal Society's Royal Medal in 1975 was 'in recognition of the originality of his ideas and the determination with which he has pursued them',[68] but by then the ideas were turning to dreams.

Two years later Molly said that he remembered nothing ('What he thinks about all day I can't imagine') but then added that now and then there were moments of complete recall when he would ask 'Do you remember that time we . . . ?'[69] Such an instant came as they listened to a recording of Beethoven's 7th Symphony. Wallis was in an armchair, Molly sitting on the floor with her back leaning against his knees. In their courting days they often sat like this. He asked if she remembered the day when they had wandered into the dark of the wine cellar at Kidderpore Avenue, and her hair had come down.

Physically, he was beginning to creak. In 1972 he was in hospital for plastic surgery to repair a scraped leg. His heels became painful. As the ninetieth birthday neared, the 617 Squadron Association laid plans for a celebration. It was to be held on 24 September in a restaurant at nearby East Horsley. Sir Arthur Harris and Sir Ralph Cochrane promised to attend. Bob Knights, a veteran of the *Tirpitz* attacks, would be their chauffeur. However, as the day approached Wallis fell, gashed his hand and chest, and was admitted to Epsom Hospital. A skin graft followed. While cards, letters, and telegrams from well-wishers poured in from around the world, his consultant at first refused him leave to attend the party, and then agreed only on condition that it would be a brief appearance.[70]

The celebration went ahead, with presentations and speeches before dinner. Following a generous tribute from Cochrane, Wallis stood to reply only to be re-seated by Molly who went on to speak on his behalf. At the end, when Leonard Cheshire asked if Wallis might say the briefest word, Wallis turned to Molly, who prompted him with 'Thank you all very, very, much; I am proud and grateful to be here', which drew rousing cheers. A telegram from the Queen was read. The veterans turned to their dinner; the Wallises were driven back to Effingham where Elisabeth awaited with soup.

On the birthday itself, a 617 Squadron Vulcan flew over White Hill House in salute. The sortie required careful routing between the control zones of Gatwick and Heathrow; the pilot drove down beforehand to study the house and its surroundings. The Vulcan passed so low that the driver of a bus on the Guildford Road pulled over on the assumption that it was about to crash. A week later came a family party. It was the last of the great gatherings at White Hill House.

Discomfort, growing deafness, and frustration at the need for help to dress himself left him 'peevish & loving at the same time'. Molly became tense and nervous. Untidiness in the house and spreading undergrowth outside depressed her. 'I live now on a tight rope and feel that at any moment I might fall off.'[71] In 1978 the children organised their move into a smaller house in nearby Beech Close.

In following months Molly visualised Barnes not as growing feeble but as very painfully trudging up a long hill. In mid-October 1979, he was admitted to Leatherhead hospital, where on Tuesday the 30th he reached the summit.

Last words

Next day the press hailed his combination of imagination and practical designing. In the eyes of the *Daily Mail* he was the last of the great one-man designers, who would have put Britain at the head of the space race if he been allowed his way.[72] For the *Birmingham Daily Post*, he was a genius who had helped to win the Second World War.[73] In November the BBC broadcast a tribute,[74] to which *The Times* responded by describing him as 'one of the greatest creative engineers' that aviation had known. Christopher Brasher recalled his body language – a gentle smile, the lift of an eyebrow, shoulders shrugged. Brasher said he was Churchillian: rejected in peace, relied on in war, uncompromising.

Wallis was buried in Effingham churchyard on Saturday, 3 November. Molly wrote in her notebook: 'About a 100 in church and so back here.' It was her last entry.

Eighteen days later Sir George Edwards wrote to young Barnes to say that the Royal Society had asked him to write Wallis's biographical memoir. 'Before accepting', he said, 'I should like to be assured that you and your Mother would be quite happy that I should take it on.' Edwards said he had been in poor health, and that doing justice to Wallis would be a large task; 'I need hardly say that if I do it no effort will be spared to make it worthy of him.' Edwards added that Norman Boorer had offered to help. Edwards would postpone his answer to the Royal Society until he had heard from Barnes.[75]

Barnes copied the letter to Pat Lucas, who was horrified. Lucas advised against talking the matter over with Norman Boorer, as this would put him in a difficult position that he was 'not sufficiently educated to understand'. She warned that the diplomacy with which Wallis had engineered Boorer's transfer out of his department had been so subtle that Boorer might not yet have realised what had happened to him. Boorer's fall from grace, she said, was partly because he had got 'too big for his boots'.

Lucas proposed another candidate, Norbert Rowe, Nero,[76] who had been Director of Technical Development at the Ministry of Aircraft Production in 1941, and Director-General of the MAP in 1945. 'I know that Sir Barnes would be happy for Mr Rowe to do this.' Young Barnes could then 'quite truthfully tell Sir George that he [Rowe] and Sir Barnes had been such close friends during many difficult days that Lady Wallis and the family would be pleased for him to do so, as you know what a task etc etc it is going to be and as Sir George is not feeling well it would relieve him of such a mammoth task!'[77]

Lucas gave Rowe's contact details and then returned to George Edwards: 'G.R.E. must not . . . do this work.' She recalled how upset Wallis had been when Edwards was proposed for the Royal Society, and his even greater unhappiness when the election succeeded. Sir Barnes, she said, had been so troubled by Edwards's membership of the Society's elite dining club that he could no longer bring himself to attend it. Edwards was 'the same as Spud – an uneducated man.' Edwards 'did not understand Sir Barnes. Mind you I think he tried to copy Sir Barnes in his many activities which I guess is a form of flattery'.[78] Lucas shared her suspicion that the cooling of Wallis's long friendship with Philip Teed was because Teed and Edwards got on well. She ventured that the warmth shown towards Teed by Edwards (and by his 'henchman' Geoffrey Tuttle[79]) had been driven by the hope that they would obtain 'information' from him; 'but I would stake my life on it that they didn't'.[80] Like a candle that keeps reigniting after being snuffed out, Lucas added a postscript: 'Excuse scribble – but for the RS to ask GRE is the last word!'

Young Barnes sent a holding reply to Edwards: Lady Wallis was unwell, they were trying to avoid bothering her for a month or two, could they defer a decision until the New Year?[81] Edwards solved the problem for them by withdrawing on health grounds. He added: 'I have persuaded N. E. Rowe and Sir Alfred Pugsley to take it on jointly. They are well equipped to make a fine job of it.'[82] Edwards nonetheless had a subsequent hand in shaping the narrative. He outlived Wallis by twenty-three years, during which he spread several stories about his old colleague which have since taken hold. One of them was that it was he who had convinced him to apply backspin to the bouncing bomb.[83] We have already seen that while this is possible, Edwards's account of how and why it happened is not.

Wallis's executors had to work out what some of his last words meant. Was it his deteriorating recall that led to a muddle over undertakings he gave to Corelli Barnett (keeper of archives at Churchill College Cambridge) and the Science Museum about the deposit of his papers? Four days before his ninetieth birthday the director of the Science Museum, Margaret Weston, asked if he would allow the museum to be the custodian of his records. Two days later, he accepted with 'much pleasure'.[84] However, some material had already been placed with Churchill College, with assurances of more concerning dealings between science and government. Beyond that, a number of the records concerned had passed out of his personal possession into the hands of his design company. As Wallis's solicitor explained wearily to young Barnes four months after his father's death, the chain of events seemed to be:

1966 Your father promises papers relating to the interactions of Science and Government to Churchill College.

1972 Your father entered into agreement with Aircraft Design (BNW) Ltd

1977 Your father reiterates promise to Churchill College.

1979 Your father deposits all his papers with the Science Museum.

Would the executors give their opinion on what his intentions had been?[85]

A memorial service was held the following February. It took place in St Paul's Cathedral – Wallis's skyline of eighty years before, the work of his hero, Wren. A fanfare by Arthur Bliss resounded. 'All my hope in God is founded' was sung. Among the 3500 singers were members of the public; Prince Charles; the Bishop of London; the Lord Mayor; the Chief of Air Staff; two defence ministers; Leonard Cheshire, Mick (by then AVM Sir Harold) Martin and ninety-seven other veterans and serving members of 617 Squadron; members of learned societies and universities that had honoured him; friends, colleagues and their relatives (like Egerton Cooper's widow, Sidney Bufton, Roy Chadwick's daughter, Wilfred Wynter-Morgan's widow); and representatives of institutions with memories that went back to Howden days and the Artists' Rifles. The canon in residence listed Wallis's roles: scholar, governor, almoner, treasurer, benefactor, councillor, engineer and inventor, servant of his friends, his country, and his God. Morpurgo gave the address, telling the congregation that it was 'the nation's shame' that Wallis had been 'rarely supported and tardily honoured'.

Afterword

Barnes Wallis was God-fearing, romantic, an English exceptionalist, a doting and patient son, a proud grandfather, at times a self-mythologising martyr, and a creator who approached each task from first principles. Upon what does his reputation now rest?

Many would say that he owes his place in national memory less to the significance of things he made than to their place, and his, in the way they are remembered. English popular culture and political life are awash with nostalgia for the Second World War.[1] Upkeep and the deep penetration bombs seem to epitomise a legend of British scientific and inventive prowess in which Wallis provided the RAF with a succession of wonder weapons, each of which arrived in the nick of time to save Britain from some new threat and shorten the war. On this basis, he owes his standing more to 1950s mythologising and cultural memory than to historical assessment. But if we put that to one side, what does historical assessment say?

The R80 and R100 broke new ground in airship design and technology. R100 was arguably Britain's most successful passenger airship and was all the more notable for having been built (in John Anderson's words) on a shoestring. If there were drawbacks, they sprang from limitations of the materials then available and frailties of the airship genre itself. The legacy of R100's gas cell wiring can be followed through geodetics and on into the Parkes radio telescope.

Geodetic construction was a waypoint in the evolution of aircraft. Looked at backwards it was a blind alley, but in the 1930s it liberated design from the truss frames upon which aero engineers had hitherto relied and offered unheard-of performance. In 1939 the Wellington had some 40 per cent greater range than any other bomber in the

RAF; in 1945 it was the only British bomber still being built that had been in production before the Second World War began.

Wallis's wartime work on weapons is summed up by Harris. Having called Upkeep 'tripe' in February 1943, a year later he answered the question with which this book began by saying there 'were few civilians whose direct personal contribution to the war had been greater'.[2]

After the war Wallis generated ever more remarkable ideas. He did not invent the concept of variable geometry, but he was its main flagbearer during the mid-1950s when interest in it was at a low ebb. It was he and his team who sustained awareness of the form and showed that it was workable. Internationally, it has been noted that while some historians of aeronautics have acknowledged this pivotal role,[3] others have either downplayed it or cut him out of the story altogether.[4] A more fundamental point is that the unique aspects of Wild Goose and Swallow – no tail, differential sweep – were never realised at full scale. We know these aerodynes were aerodynamically viable, but as in the case of his late ideas – the square fuselage, isothermal flight, the Universal aircraft – it is difficult to point to the heritage of original concepts that have yet to be tried in the roles for which they were intended.

What of the received story of a patriotic genius who offered visionary ideas to his country and was snubbed by post-war governments? That story was led by Swallow, his most charismatic aircraft. Like most of his creations it was not beautiful, but it had rare presence. Swallow's dramatic arrowhead also fed narratives, repeated in Parliament and the press, spanning the eras of Macmillan and Wilson, that by discarding it Britain had taken a wrong turn, and that Britain had gifted one of its best ideas to the Americans who then sold it back to Britain.[5]

The main reasons why the post-war ideas went unrealised were the lack of politically and industrially fundable formats and timescales into which they would fit. Wallis's heart was set on civil transport several generations ahead, whereas the Cold War demanded prioritisation of military projects and fostered demand for near-term, guaranteeable results. Wallis's department was too small properly to scale up his ideas; the production side of Vickers was focused on commercial work and government contracts; Wallis and Edwards were often at loggerheads; towards the end, the BAC was content to indulge his experimental work while getting on with mainstream projects. He was not always his own best advocate. His impatience could alienate those who tried to help him;[6] his optimism occasionally bordered irrationality. His obsession with creation and grasp of the bigger picture repeatedly led him to pursue an idea wherever it led, and thereby outside his conventionally allotted role and into someone else's. His interdisciplinarity and friction thus went together, and because of that, at times, there were some who responded by seeking to downplay his worth.[7]

Iain Murray reminds us that whereas some inventions (like the jet engine) will come about sooner or later regardless of whether particular individuals are behind them, others depend on particular people because they are non-imitative and stem from original thought.[8] Wallis was an original thinker, and as his story has shown, originality brings risks: a task can be approached either through the improvement of an existing solution or through something new, and as Niccolò Machiavelli (1469–1527) pointed out, nothing is 'more dangerous to handle' than to initiate something new.[9] But leaving it there would miss him entirely. Wallis lived not only for creation but through it. If an idea went unfulfilled it was still an idea. Behind all the particularity and intermittent grousing he was a joyful man. In October 1959, he mused that a stranger reading his fifteen-year cycle of unsent letters would come away with an impression of toil and disappointments – yet the concept of Cascade had just been revealed, and he was buoyant.

On and on, always some New Thing springing up, full of promise, meeting or avoiding all of the old difficulties.[10]

Or back in 1923, joining Burney:

Besides, Molly, it's the most wonderful work in the world . . .

You see it's all new, and one is thinking out new things all the time.[11]

Or Swallow, his Unknown Symphony:

Laus Deo, and again, Laus Deo, what a life, what a World.[12]

Acknowledgements

My first thanks go to the late Barnes Winstanley Wallis and Mary Stopes-Roe for their invitation to write this book, and for the unlimited access to family papers that has enabled me to do so. For advice, encouragement and help of many, many kinds in the years that followed I thank Nicholas Bennett, Sebastian Cox, Eddie Crouch (clerk to Effingham Parish Council, 1953–2003), Bob Cywinski, Robin Darwall-Smith, Douglas Denny, Colin Dobinson, Anna Eavis, Peter Elliott, Elisabeth Gaunt, Martin Giles, Chris Henderson, James Holland, the late George Johnson, Nikki King, Axel Müller, Robert Pawson, Frank Phillipson, Martin Pickard, Anthea Pratt, Peter Rix, Alan Spence, the Earl Spencer, David Stocker, Cathy Stopes, Christopher Stopes, the late Harry Stopes-Roe, Helena Stopes-Roe, Jonathan Stopes-Roe, Heather Thorn, the late Richard Todd, and Kathryn White.

For assistance in archives and access to collections I thank the Airship Heritage Trust; BAE Systems Heritage; John Cochrane; staff and volunteers of the Brooklands Museum; the Manuscripts Department of Cambridge University Library; trustees of the Barnes Wallis Foundation; the Dock Museum, Barrow-in-Furness; East Riding Archives; Sue Morris and the Effingham Local History Group; Gina Hynard and the Hampshire Record Office; Collections of the Imperial War Museum; the Special Collections of the Brotherton Library at the University of Leeds; London Metropolitan Archives; The National Archives; the Royal Aeronautical Society; the Archive Collection of the Royal Air Force Museum; Doug Stimson and his colleagues at the Collections Centre of the Science Museum, Wroughton; Bethany Radcliff at the Harry Ransom Center, University of Texas at Austin; the Estate of Mary Stopes-Roe; the Surrey

History Centre; and Tyne and Wear Archives and Museums.

Robert Owen, historian of the 617 Squadron Aircrew Association, was throughout a wise sounding board, and at times acted also as unpaid research assistant in Cambridge University Library and the Collections Centre of the Science Museum. I am thankful, too, for the critical alertness of Anne Deighton and Jane Morris, who with Robert read the book in its successive drafts and did much to improve it.

Authors write; publishers produce; for all kinds of productive expertise I thank Kate Moreton, Natalie Dawkins and Lucinda McNeile.

Richard Morris
December 2022

Illustrations

Glossary

Aerofoil: Cross-sectional shape of an object whose motion through a fluid generates lift

Aerodyne: Aerial vehicle reliant on lift generated by forward motion

Aileron: Control surface, usually forming part of the trailing edge of an aircraft's wing, which when moved causes an aircraft to rotate about its axis of roll

All-up weight: Total maximum weight of laden craft

Angle of attack: Difference in angle between the chord of a wing and oncoming airflow

Angle of incidence: Angle between the chord of the wing and the longitudinal axis of the fuselage

Anhedral: Downward angle of an aircraft wing from root to tip

Aspect ratio: Ratio between the span and mean chord of an aerofoil that gives a measure of the proportions of the planform of a wing

Boundary layer: Thin layer of a fluid in the immediate vicinity of a surface over which the fluid flows

Calculus: Mathematical study of continuous change

Centre of gravity: Hypothetical point at which the total mass of a body may be thought to be concentrated

Centre of pressure: Point on an aircraft at which the aerodynamic forces acting on it can be said to be focused

Chord: Imagined line between leading and trailing edges of an aerofoil

Dihedral: Upward angle of an aircraft wing from root to tip

Drag: Force that opposes an object's motion through a fluid – in practice a force that slows an aircraft down

Elevator: Moving control surface that controls an aircraft's pitch

Empennage: Arrangement of surfaces at the tail of an aircraft to provide for its stability

Flap: Device to reduce the stalling speed of an aircraft's wing

Fluid: Substance (like a gas or liquid) that flows

g: Acceleration due to the Earth's gravity

Geodesic: Relating to or denoting the shortest possible line between two points on a curved surface

Grecian: Senior pupil at Christ's Hospital

Housey: Pet name for Christ's Hospital

Laminar flow: Flow pattern in a fluid where the particles run smoothly in parallel layers

Lift: Force generated by an object moving through a fluid – in practice the force generated by the shape of wings that will make an aircraft rise as it passes through the air

M(ach) number: Number which gives the relation between a body's speed and the speed of sound

Mass: Measure of a body's inertia

Moment: The turning effect of a force

Old Blue: Alumnus/a of Christ's Hospital

RDX: Research Department Explosive – organic chemical compound often used as a base for mixtures with other explosives

Rigid: Airship in which the outer envelope is supported by a rigid frame

Rudder stall: Condition in which a rudder becomes ineffective in generating the yawing motion of an aircraft

Semi-rigid: Airship with an envelope kept in shape by gas pressure, but with a supporting keel along the vessel's length

Stall: Reduction in lift that ensues when the critical angle of attack is exceeded

Sweepback: Angle at which the leading edge an aircraft's wing is slanted back from a right angle to the fuselage

Tare weight: Known weight of an unladen vehicle

Transonic: Speed in the region between $M = 0.8$ and $M = 1.2$ where airflow around an object is partly subsonic and partly supersonic, and therefore chaotic

Torpex: Explosive mixture consisting of 18 per cent powdered aluminium, 40 per cent TNT, and 42 per cent RDX

Variable geometry: Aircraft in which some part(s) may change position in flight (also VG)

Variable sweep: Aircraft in which wings may change position in flight

Wing loading: Measurement of the relation between the lift and mass of an aircraft. The lower the loading the larger will be the wing area relative to the aircraft's mass

Abbreviations, acronyms and codewords

AAD: Aerial (or Air) Attack on Dams (Committee)
A&AEE: Aeroplane and Armament Experimental Establishment
ACAS: Assistant Chief of the Air Staff
ACAS (Ops): Assistant Chief of the Air Staff (Operations)
ACAS (TR): Assistant Chief of the Air Staff (Technical Requirements)
Air Cdre: Air Commodore
ADGB: Air Defence of Great Britain
AHB: Air Historical Branch
AM: Air Marshal
AVM: Air Vice-Marshal
AOC: Air Officer Commanding
ARC: Aeronautical Research Committee
Baseball: Proposed water skipping munition to be fired at warships from motor torpedo boat
BLEU: Blind Landing Experimental Unit
BRS: Building Research Station
CAS: Chief of Air Staff
Catechism: Air operation against the warship *Tirpitz*, 12 November 1944
CCO: Chief of Combined Operations
Chastise: Air operation against German dams
C-in-C: Commander-in-chief
CID: Committee of Imperial Defence
COS: Chiefs of Staff or Chiefs of Staff Committee
CRD: Controller of Research and Development
Crossbow: Operations against V-weapons
D Arm D: Director(ate) of Armament Development
DB Ops: Director(ate) of Bomber Operations

DCAS: Deputy Chief of Air Staff

DD Arm D: Deputy Director, Armament Development

DD/RD Arm: Deputy Director, Research Directorate Armaments

DDSR: Deputy Director of Scientific Research

DELAG: Deutsche Luftschiffahrts-Aktiengesellschafft (German Airship Travel Corporation)

DMWD: Department of Miscellaneous Weapons Development

DSR: Director of Scientific Research

Emulsion: Project to develop streamlined casing for Britain's atomic bomb

FAA: Fleet Air Arm

Fg Off.: Flying Officer

Flak: *Fliegerabwehrkanone* – anti-aircraft artillery

Flt Lt: Flight Lieutenant

g: Value of gravitational acceleration at sea level

Golf Mine: Family of water ricochet munitions ascending in weight and size from Baseball through Highball (Light), Highball (Heavy) to Upkeep (for all of which q.v.)

Grand Slam: Eventual codename for Tallboy L (q.v.)

Green Lizard: Early form of missile derived from wing controlled aerodyne Wild Goose (q.v.)

Grouse Shooting: Trials to test use of Highball against railway tunnels

Grp Capt.: Group Captain

GWR: Great Western Railway

H2S: Ground-scanning radar fitted to Allied aircraft

HAA: Heavy anti-aircraft (artillery)

Heyday: Rocket-powered torpedo

Highball: Water ricochet weapon. Highball (Light) was originally envisaged for use against lock gates, submarine shelters, beach defences and naval units. Highball (Heavy) was intended for Italian multiple arch dams, merchant ships, canal locks and hydro-electric barrages

Jabo: *Jagdbomber* – fighter-bomber

Kurt: Spherical bouncing mine developed by Germany

LAA: Light anti-aircraft (artillery)

LDV: Local Defence Volunteers (later, Home Guard)

Lt: Lieutenant

LZ: (of German airship) Luftschiff Zeppelin

M: Mach number

MAEE: Marine Aircraft Experimental Establishment

MAP: Ministry of Aircraft Production

MEW: Ministry of Economic Warfare

MI5: Security Service with UK domestic remit – from Section 5 of the War Office's Directorate of Military Intelligence (1916), having previously (from 1909) been a branch of the Directorate of Military Operations

MOS: Ministry of Supply

MU: Maintenance Unit

NACA: National Advisory Committee for Aeronautics (US)

NASA: National Aeronautics and Space Administration (US)

NPL: National Physical Laboratory

Obviate: Operation against the warship *Tirpitz*, 29 October 1944

OC: Officer Commanding

OR: Operational Requirement

ORB: Operations Record Book

Oxtail: Projected Highball operation against Japanese fleet

Paravane: Operation against the warship *Tirpitz*, 15 September 1944

Plt Off.: Pilot Officer

R, r: (of UK airships) Rigid

RAAF: Royal Australian Air Force

RAE: Royal Aircraft Establishment

RD(T): Research and Development (Technical)

RAeS: Royal Aeronautical Society

RRL: Roads Research Laboratory

SABS: Stabilised Automatic Bombsight

SEAC: South-East Asia Command

Servant: Intended air operation against warship *Tirpitz* using Highball

SHAEF: Supreme Headquarters Allied Expeditionary Force

SIS: Secret Intelligence Service, MI6

Source: Submarine operation against *Tirpitz*, September 1943

Speedee: US codename for inert Highball
SPOG: Special Projectile Operations Group
Sqn Ldr: Squadron Leader
SS: Submarine (or Sea) Scout
Swallow: Wing controlled aerodyne in development 1953–59
Tallboy L[arge]: 22,000 lb deep penetration bomb
Tallboy M[edium]: 12,000 lb deep penetration bomb
Tallboy S[mall]: 4000 lb deep penetration bomb
TR: Technical requirements
TRE: Telecommunications Research Establishment
Upkeep: Water ricochet mine for use against gravity dams
Wg Cdr: Wing Commander
Wild Goose: Wing controlled aerodyne in development 1946–53

Sources

Barnes Wallis left a mass of material relating to his family, life, and work.

The bulk of his working papers and photographs were donated to the Science Museum, where they are catalogued as *The Papers of Sir Barnes Wallis (1887–1979) in the Science Museum Library: A handlist compiled by Christine J. Heap*, 1987. That collection is abbreviated in the notes as SM.

Records of Vickers Ltd and its subsidiaries are held by the Cambridge University Library. They are denoted here as Vickers, followed by the document number.

Correspondence and notes arising from the writing and reception of the biography written (1967–72) by Jack Morpurgo are spread between the Science Museum and the Special Collections of the University of Leeds. The Morpurgo papers held at Leeds are here referred to as MP.

Dr Mary Stopes-Roe (Wallis's elder daughter) gave complete access to a large assortment of family letters, memoirs, photographs, unpublished manuscripts, and ephemera which passed into her care when her parents moved into a smaller house in 1977. In the notes this body of material is called the Mary Stopes-Roe Collection (MSRC). Since consultation, it has been divided. Parts of it have been deposited in public archives. These include letters, notes and diaries written by Wallis's wife Molly, which are now held by the Surrey History Centre (SHC ref 9456).

Extracts from the courtship correspondence between Wallis and Molly Bloxam are referenced to the printed collection edited by Mary Stopes-Roe and published as *Mathematics with Love*, Macmillan, 2005, with permission of the Estate of Mary Stopes-Roe

The Royal Air Force Museum holds a miscellany of papers (primary and copies), diaries, artefacts, printed material, and ephemera, referenced here as RAFM.

The Barnes Wallis Foundation (formerly the Barnes Wallis Memorial Trust, referenced here as BWF) holds a miscellany that includes items from Wallis's library, photographs, minutes, copy documents, artefacts, and ephemera.

Brooklands Museum keeps some records deriving from Vickers and its successor, the British Aircraft Corporation. The Museum displays the largest single collection of surviving examples of Wallis's work, including one of only two Wellington bombers (the other is in the RAF Museum), the stratosphere chamber, and examples of all the bombs. Locations of other surviving weapons and items are accessible via an annotated list on the webpage *Sir Barnes Wallis: recommended links and places* (http://www.sirbarneswallis.com/Links.htm).

Records of UK government ministries and their subsidiaries, units and formations of the armed and intelligence services are held in The National Archives, here shortened to TNA.

Abbreviations

BWF	Barnes Wallis Foundation
CC	Cochrane Collection (papers of Sir Ralph Cochrane)
LCA	Leonard Cheshire Archive
MSRC	Mary Stopes-Roe Collection
RAFM	Royal Air Force Museum, Papers of Sir Barnes Wallis
MP	Morpurgo Papers, University of Leeds Special Collections, MS 664
MWL	*Mathematics with Love*
SM	Papers of Sir Barnes Wallis in the Science Museum Library, Wroughton
TNA	The National Archives
Vickers	Vickers Ltd: Records, MS Vickers, Cambridge University Library

Notes

Prologue

1   Wallis, autobiographical fragment, n.d. (c.1955): Mary Stopes-Roe Collection (hereafter MSRC).

2   Morpurgo to BNW, 20 January 1967, SM HA2/4.

3   J. E. Morpurgo, *Barnes Wallis: A Biography*, Longman, 1972; revised edition, Ian Allen, 1981. Peter Pugh's shorter *Barnes Wallis: Dambuster*, Icon Books, 2005, rests mainly on secondary sources. Chapters and memoirs include Norman Boorer's paper *Sir Barnes Wallis, CBE, FRS, RDII, FRAeS 1887–1979* (Brooklands Museum Trust, 2008); Alfred Pugsley and N. E. Rowe, 'Barnes Neville Wallis: 26 September 1887–30 October 1979', *Biographical Memoirs of Fellows of the Royal Society*, 27 (1981), 603–27; and Robin Higham, 'Wallis, Sir Barnes Neville (1887–1979)', *Oxford Dictionary of National Biography*, 2004, online edn 2008, accessed 8 February 2016. Notes and an unpublished biography by Bernard J. Hurren are held by Churchill Archives Centre, Cambridge, HREN 1/1–1/4. Wallis's scientific ideas, projects, and underpinning theory are well surveyed by Iain Murray, *Bouncing-Bomb Man: The Science of Sir Barnes Wallis*, Haynes, 2009. John Anderson, *Airship on a Shoestring*, Bright Pen, 2013, recounts the design and construction of R100. The Wellington has been anatomised by Iain Murray (*Vickers Wellington*, Haynes, 2012). Wartime bombs are examined by Stephen Flower (*Barnes Wallis' Bombs: Tallboy, Dambuster and Grand Slam*, Tempus, 2004) and contextualised by Robert Owen ('Considered policy or haphazard evolution? No 617 Squadron RAF 1943–45', unpubl. doctoral thesis, University of Huddersfield, 2014). Wallis's role in the origination and undertaking of the Dams Raid is analysed and documented by John Sweetman, *The Dambusters Raid*, Cassell, 2012. For discussion of Wallis's post-war socio-political ideas see S. Waqar H. Zaidi, 'The Janus-face of Techno-nationalism: Barnes Wallis and the "Strength of England"', *Technology and Culture*, 49 (2008), 62–88.

4   Max Hastings, *Chastise: The Dambusters Story 1943*, Collins, 2019, 24.

5   Robert Eaglestone, 'Cruel nostalgia and the memory of the Second World War', in *Brexit and Literature: critical and cultural responses*, ed. Robert Eaglestone, Routledge, 2018, 92–104, at 92.

6   Cf. Christine MacLeod, *Heroes of Invention: Technology, Liberalism and British Identity 1750–1914*, Cambridge University Press, 2010.

7   Such revision can be followed through private correspondence; some dozen interviews to BBC radio and TV between 1963 and 1975; interviews given to journalists for profiles in newspapers and magazines; recorded reminiscences

(notably Royal Aeronautical Society, Audio: The Barnes Wallis Interview), and transcripts of conversations between Wallis and John Dick Scott in connection with Scott's forthcoming business history of the company: *Vickers: A History*, 1962, Vickers Doc. 780.

8   Wallis to Molly Wallis, letter, 11/12 August 1945, MSRC.
9   Wallis to Molly Bloxam, letter, 6–8 October 1923, MWL, 172–173.
10 Wallis to Molly Wallis, 11/12 August 1945, MSRC.
11 John Ramsden, *The 'Dam Busters'*, I. B. Tauris, 2003.
12 Morpurgo, *Wallis*, 332.
13 Reba N. Soffer, 'The Long Nineteenth Century of Conservative Thought', in G. K. Behlmer & F. M. Leventhal (eds), *Singular Continuities: Tradition, Nostalgia, and Identity in Modern British Culture*, Stanford University Press, 2000, 143–162; Susan Pederson & Peter Mandler (eds), *After the Victorians: Private conscience and public duty in modern Britain*, Routledge, 1994, viii.
14 B. N. Wallis, 'Science at Christ's Hospital', in *The Christ's Hospital Book*, 1953, 316–17.
15 Barnes W. Wallis, letter to author, 8 May 2008.
16 David Edgerton, 'C. P. Snow as anti-historian of British science: revisiting the technocratic movement, 1959–1964', *History of Science* 43, 2005, 187–208, at 188.
17 Stephen Marsh, 'The Air Ministry and the bomb dropping problem: bombsights, scientists, and techno-military invention, 1918–45', unpublished PhD thesis, King's College London, 2019.

1 Childhood and Empire, 1887–1904

1   *London Gazette*, 30 July 1886, 3694; Liquidator's Accounts, Neilgherry and Southern India Lands Investment Company Ltd, TNA BT 34/200/12529.
2   Maria Ashby to Minna Francis, letter, 29 September 1887, MSRC.
3   Edie Wallis to Lily Maxwell, letter, 25 October 1887, MSRC.
4   The school had originated in 1821 as an 'introductory seminary for young gentlemen under twelve years of age': *The Evangelical Magazine and Missionary Chronicle*, 29, January 1821, 13. London Metropolitan Archive, DRO/004/1/02/003.
5   Taf and Jef: acronyms of Thomas Ashby Francis (b.11 October 1871) and John Eyre Francis (b.25 October 1872), respectively.
6   Henry Owen and George Wallis had both trained at Trinity College Dublin.
7   Memoir by Annie Knight (née Wallis), in 'A History of the Wallis Family', ed. Heather Thorn, privately circulated, 1994.
8   Edie Ashby, Journal, 29 July 1881, MSRC.
9   Edie Wallis, Journal, 2 May 1886, MSRC.
10 Edie Wallis, Journal, 3 May 1889, MSRC.
11 Edie Wallis, 'Notes in Black and Grey', n.d. MSRC.
12 Edie Wallis to Lily Maxwell, 29 October 1886, MSRC.
13 Edie Wallis, Journal, 3 May 1889, MSRC.
14 Edie Wallis to Lily Maxwell, 27 January 1887, MSRC.
15 Over the winter of 1887/88 the Wallises had toyed over a 'good sized house'

enclosed by its own walls and garden, with a rural outlook, but next to a 'hateful brewery'.

16 Edie Wallis, Journal, 3 March 1889, MSRC.

17 School reports, 1896–1899, MSRC.

18 Charles Wallis to Wallis, 30 May 1900, MSRC.

19 CH at this time below the level of Grecians and Deputy Grecians was divided into a Latin School and a Mathematical School. Both embraced humanities subjects, but the Latin School was focused upon Classics, while the Mathematical School, in addition to maths and science, put more emphasis upon modern languages and history.

20 A leather belt with a silver buckle worn around the coat (known as a 'broadie'), denoted a senior boy. A plain belt ('narrowie') was worn by juniors.

21 The Mathematical School then consisted of Upper, Lower and Junior Fourth Forms, each divided into three classes. Wallis was put into the Lower Fourth Form B – that is, at the midpoint in the hierarchy.

22 Wallis to Winifred Flew, draft, July 1965, MSRC.

23 John Wallis, 'Rights of memory: a boy's life at Christ's Hospital, London, 1898–1902', MSRC.

24 Wallis to Flew, 30 July 1965, MSRC.

25 Ibid.

26 Ibid

27 Ibid.

28 Wallis to Edie Wallis, 25 June 1901, MSRC.

29 Formal permission for temporary absence.

30 Edie Wallis to Wallis, 21 May 1900, MSRC.

31. Edie Wallis to Wallis, 4 February 1901.

32 Ibid.

33 Edie Wallis to Wallis, 2 June 1902, MSRC.

34 Report for the term ending 1 August 1900, MSRC W10.

35 Respectively: to beat; a fag; coffee; tea or cocoa; butter; meat: Allen, *Christ's Hospital*, 90.

36 G. A. T. Allan, 'Football in the 1890s', in *Christ's Hospital Book*, Hamish Hamilton, 1953, 225–226.

37 G. A. T. Allan (revised J. E. Morpurgo), *Christ's Hospital*, Ian Allan, 1984, 91.

38 John Middleton Murry, 'Endowed with ancestors', *Christ's Hospital Book*, 264–281, at 264.

39 Allan, *Christ's Hospital*, 44.

40 Ibid.

41 Murry, 'Endowed with ancestors', 281. Murry joined the school in 1901.

42 Edie Wallis to Wallis, 21 May 1900, MSRC.

43 Allan, *Christ's Hospital*, 70, 73.

44 Allan, *Christ's Hospital Book*, 253–254.

45 John Wallis, 'Rites of Memory', MSRC, and in *Christ's Hospital Book*, 257–258.

46 Upcott's appointment was announced at the end of 1901: *The Times*, 17 December 1901, 12. In the interim he had recruited new staff and managed out a number of masters who he did not wish to bring to Horsham.

47 Charles Wallis to Wallis, 6 July 1902, MSRC.

48 The 'A' suffix derived from the H-plan of the houses, where parallel wings were denoted by the same root name and an A or B.

49 Cited in Allen, *Christ's Hospital*, 77.

50 Tacy Millett Winstanley Wallis, who through the conflation and abbreviation of his last two names was known in the family as Uncle Wwyn.

51 Edie Wallis to Wallis, 2 June 1902, MSRC.

52 Edie Wallis to Wallis, 3 August 1902, MSRC.

53 Wallis had taken up photography. 6/6: six shillings and sixpence.

54 Wallis to Edie Wallis, 30 November 1902, MSRC.

55 Edie Wallis to Wallis, 15 December 1903, MSRC.

56 Henry E. Armstrong, 'On the teaching of Natural Sciences as a Part of the Ordinary School Course', 1884; Henry E. Armstrong, *The Teaching of Scientific Method and Other Papers on Education*, Macmillan, 1903.

57 Wallis to Edie Wallis, 15 February 1903, MSRC.

58 Ibid.

59 Wallis to Edie Wallis, 22 February 1903, MSRC.

60 Wallis to Edie Wallis, 1 March 1903, MSRC.

61 Edie Wallis to Wallis, 2 April 1903, MSRC.

62 Wallis to Edie Wallis, 19 July 1903, MSRC.

63 Edie Wallis to Wallis, 21 July 1903, MSRC.

64 Edie Wallis to Wallis, 23 July 1903, MSRC.

65 Wallis to Edie Wallis, 26 July 1903, MSRC.

66 Allen, *Christ's Hospital*, 91.

67 Morpurgo, *Wallis*, 33–34.

68 Edie Wallis to Wallis, 18 October 1903, MSRC.

69 Wallis to Charles Wallis, 31 January 1904.

70 Charles E. Browne, 'Barnes Wallis. School Days. Some reflections from memories of him'. MS, n.d., c.1968.

71 Heywood advised him to concentrate on particular subjects and to 'knock off those that will be of no use'. Wallis to Charles Wallis, 17 January 1904, MSRC.

2 The Wand of Youth, 1905–13

1 Lecture by Fleeming Jenkin, 1884, cited in S. Colvin and J. A. Ewing (eds), *Papers Literary, Scientific &c by the Late Fleeming Jenkin FRS, LLD*, 1887, vol. 2, 187–8.

2 Le Corbusier, *Aircraft*, 1935, 20.

3 Wallis to Edie Wallis, 19 April 1906, MSRC.

4 Wallis to Edie Wallis, 29 August 1907, MSRC.

5 Edie Wallis to Wallis, 31 October 1907, MSRC.

6 Wallis to Edie Wallis, 6 November 1907, MSRC.

7 Edie Wallis to Wallis, 5 November 1907, MSRC.

8 Edie Wallis to Wallis, 27 January 1908, MSRC.

9 Edie Wallis to Wallis, 2 November 1907, MSRC.

10 Edie Wallis to Wallis, 6 November 1907, MSRC.

11 Edie Wallis to Wallis, 24 November 1907, MSRC.

12 Wallis to Edie Wallis, 25 November 1907, MSRC.

13 Wallis to Edie Wallis, 18 November 1907, MSRC.
14 Mary Stopes-Roe, lecture, 26 June 2010, Howden.
15 Wallis to Edie Wallis, 3 April 1910, MSRC.
16 Wallis to Edie Wallis, 10 January 1909, MSRC.
17 This was *Saracen*, a Tribal (F) Class destroyer, launched in March 1908.
18 Wallis to Edie Wallis, 15 January 1911. MSRC.
19 Wallis to Edie Wallis, 10 January 1909, MSRC.
20 Wallis to Edie Wallis, 2 February 1909, MSRC.
21 Edie Wallis to Wallis, 7 September 1908, MSRC.
22 Wallis's initial reactions to news of the engagement were muted.
23 Edie Wallis to Wallis, 3 January 1909, MSRC.
24 Edie Wallis to Wallis, 14 January 1909, MSRC.
25 Wallis to Edie Wallis, 24 January 1909, MSRC.
26 A surviving dance programme from 1908 shows that most of Wallis's dances were taken with 'VP' and 'A Liggett', thrice each: MSRC.
27 Wallis to Edie Wallis, 19 December 1909, MSRC.
28 Jean Cottrell, memories of her grandfather, February 1987, cited in Thorn, ed., *Wallis Family*.
29 Wallis to Edie Wallis, 10 January 1909, MSRC.
30 Wallis to Edie Wallis, 19 September 1909, MSRC.
31 Wallis to Edie Wallis, 24 April 1910, MSRC.
32 Wallis to Edie Wallis, 29 May 1910, MSRC.
33 Wallis to Edie Wallis, 27/28 June 1910, MSRC.
34 Edie Wallis to Wallis, 28 June 1910, MSRC.
35 Edie Wallis to Wallis, 20 July 1910, MSRC.
36 Edie Wallis to Wallis, 22 July 1910, MSRC.
37 Edie Wallis to Wallis, 12 May 1910, MSRC.
38 Edie Wallis to Wallis, 12 July 1910, MSRC.
39 Wallis to Edie Wallis, 17 July 1910, MSRC.
40 Wallis to Edie Wallis, 23 October 1910, MSRC.
41 Primroses grew in such profusion on the Isle of Wight that John Keats suggested it be renamed the Primrose Isle: Keats to John Reynolds, letter, 17 April 1817.
42 Wallis to Edie Wallis, 21 February 1909, MSRC.
43 Wallis to Edie Wallis, 22 January 1910, MSRC.
44 As during a prolonged crisis around 11/12 November 1910: 'Dr Bond told me yesterday that I had been "very bad" . . . I had 5 injections, in 36 hours, – namely 2 morphia, hyocyanine [sic], 2 adrenaline. The morphia nearly killed me with sickness afterwards . . .': Edie Wallis to Wallis, 13 November 1910, MSRC.
45 Wallis to Edie Wallis, 20 November 1910, MSRC.
46 Edie Wallis to Wallis, 13 November 1910, MSRC.
47 Wallis to Edie Wallis, 20 November 1910, MSRC.
48 Edie Wallis to Wallis, 17 November 1910, MSRC.
49 Charles Wallis to Wallis, 29 July 1911, MSRC.
50 Edie Wallis to Wallis, 25 August 1911, MSRC.
51 Tuesday, 29 August 1911, MSRC.
52 Wallis to Molly Bloxam, 14 May 1923, MWL, 75.
53 Wallis to Molly Bloxam, 14 June 1923, MWL, 99.
54 Letters of condolence: MSRC.

55 Letters of condolence: MSRC.

56 Charles Wallis to Wallis, 5 September 1911, MSRC.

57 Wallis to Charles Wallis, 24 September 1911, MSRC

58 Ibid.

59 Michael Goodall, *The Wight Aircraft: The History of the Aviation Department of J. Samuel White and Co Ltd 1913–1939*, Gentry Books, 1973.

60 Acronym of Maschinenfabrik Augsburg Nürnberg AG.

61 Wallis to E. C. Carnt, Sunday, 24 March 1912, MSRC.

62 Ibid.

63 J. D. Scott, *Vickers: A History*, 1962, 72. Scott's information about Roberton came from Wallis.

64 Admiralty tender and contract papers with Messrs. Vickers & Co. for construction of Naval Airship No. 1: TNA AIR 1/2306/215/15; Scott, *Vickers*, 71–2.

65 In July 1912 Wallis bought another sailing dinghy, for £18 10s 0d: receipt, 23 July 1912, MSRC.

66 Tacy Wallis to Wallis, 24 November 1912, MSRC.

67 Wallis to Tacy Wallis, 9 December 1912, MSRC.

68 *The Engineer*, 5 January 1912, 21.

69 Airship Policy, Report by the Technical Sub-Committee of the Standing Sub-Committee of the CID, 30 July 1912, CID 159B: TNA CAB 38/22/32.

70 Brett Holman, 'The Phantom Airship Panic of 1913: Imagining Aerial Warfare in Britain Before the Great War', *Journal of British Studies*, 2016, 99–119.

71 H. G. Wells, 'I The Common Sense of Conscription', *Daily Mail*, 7 April 1913, 8.

72 H. G. Wells, 'II Put Not Your Trust in Dreadnoughts', *Daily Mail*, 8 April 1913, 1.

73 H. G. Wells, 'III The Balance of Present and Future', *Daily Mail*, 9 April 1913, 4.

74 Hansard, House of Commons debate, 9 April 1913, vol. 51, cc1159–60.

75 Hansard, House of Commons debate, 9 April 1913, vol. 51, cc1149–50.

76 LZ 16 landed accidentally at Lunéville on 3 April. She was released next day, by which time a record of her structure had been made.

77 At this time it was usual to refer to types of airship by the German makes that typified them – thus 'Zeppelin' for a rigid, and 'Parseval' for a non- or semi-rigid.

78 SM B1/1.

79 Vickers Ltd to Wallis, 12 August 1913: SMRC.

80 Reference from J. W. Harper for Wallis, 22 August 1913: SM A5/1.

81 Wallis to Molly Wallis, 25 August 1963: SMRC.

82 Ibid.

83 Ibid.

3 Before Marching and After, 1913–23

1 J. D. Scott, *Vickers: a history*, Weidenfeld & Nicolson, 1962, 125.

2 The order given in June 1913 was for an airship 'to be generally in conformity with existing Zeppelin construction': *Handbook on HM Airship Rigid No. 9*, Airship Department, Admiralty, April 1918, 5.

3 The intervening HMA numbers 2–7 were non-rigids (HMA 2 was the Willows; 3 was an Astra Torres; 4–7 were Parsevals). The custom of denoting rigids with a prefix R was introduced with R26, although some later writers have applied it from No. 23r on, and in old age Wallis misapplied it to No. 9.

4 B. N. Wallis, 'A note on the origin and development of geodetic construction as used on the Wellesley and Wellington aircraft', n.d., c.1968, ed. Barnes Wallis Jnr, BWF, 4.

5 Charles Wallis to Wallis, 31 January 1912, MSRC.

6 Memoir by Annie Knight, MSRC.

7 This superseded the earlier shed at Cavendish Dock used to build No. 1.

8 'The Construction of Navy Dirigibles by Vickers', *Aeronautics*, January 1914.

9 Wallis to Fisher, 23 August 1914, MSRC.

10 Ibid.

11 Pratt to Wallis, 19 August 1914, MSRC.

12 A marking-out tool to draw large arcs.

13 These were tracers, often women, who inked copies of working drawings on drafting linen.

14 Pratt to Wallis, 19 August 1914, MSRC.

15 Wallis to Pratt, 20 September 1914, MSRC.

16 Wallis to Molly Bloxam, 26 June 1923, *Mathematics with Love*, ed. Mary Stopes-Roe, Macmillan, 2005, 113.

17 Ibid.

18 Robert Louis Stevenson, 'The roadside fire' (1904).

19 The cost of an airship station at this date was around £165,000, whereas a seaplane station could be had for c.£12,800. The expense of airship stations included the need for large sheds, facilities for hydrogen generation and storage, and rail access.

20 Alexander Howlett, 'The Royal Naval Air Service and the Evolution of Naval Aviation in Britain, 1914–1918', unpublished PhD thesis, Department of Defence Studies, King's College London.

21 At the war's end this led to his secondment to the recently formed Royal Air Force as an official artist: TNA AIR 76/103/73.

22 Edward Thomas to John Wilton Haines, letter, 28 September 1915, Gloucestershire Archives, D10828/1.

23 *Regimental Roll of Honour and War Record of the Artists' Rifles*, 3rd edn, London: Howlett & Son, 1922, 420–21.

24 Pratt was already commissioned as a lieutenant. Wallis was commissioned as a sub-lieutenant.

25 Pratt to Wallis, n.d. (October 1915), SM B1/1.

26 Caroline Joy, 'War and unemployment in an industrial community: Barrow-in-Furness 1914–1926', unpublished PhD, University of Central Lancashire, 2004, 76 and n. 81, citing interview with Mr Pickup et al., 'Barrow Interviews: sundry recollections for J. D. Scott', Cambridge Historical Archive, Cambridge, VHD597.

27 Kenneth Warren, *Armstrongs of Elswick: growth in Engineering and Armaments to the Merger with Vickers*, Macmillan, 1989, 93–4.

28 Pratt to Wallis, n.d. (October 1915), SM B1/1.

29 Not known to survive but referred to in Wallis's report on the structure (see following note).

30 'Report on the Condition of the Work on Naval Airship No 9 at Barrow 12.10.15', MS autograph, MSRC.

31 Pratt to Wallis, 22 October 1915. In a later letter Pratt said that Craven had been looking for an Admiralty officer who could join Vickers to run the department. Craven sought to recruit Neville Usborne (Kingsnorth's OC), who had declined, and recommended Pratt: SM B1/1.

32 Admiralty Letter CE of 26 October 1915, TNA ADM 1/8429.

33 TNA ADM 337/120. Pratt's resignation was accepted on 2 December 1915: TNA ADM 337/120/46.

34 Pratt to Wallis, 17 November 1915, SM B1/1.

35 In autumn 1915 the two overlapped at Barrow by only a few weeks: Goddard was posted to RNAS Luce Bay on 21 September 1915.

36 E. A. Johnston, 'Scott of the Atlantic: a personal view of Major Scott', *Dirigible*, 2, 1989, 2–4.

37 Scott arrived at Barrow in May: Service Record, TNA ADM 273/4/49.

38 No. 4 was built, flown and tested by Luft-Fahrzeug-Gesellschaft at Adlershof, Berlin, where she was designated as PL18. She was then dismantled, shipped to Barrow and reassembled by LFG staff, with Royal Navy technicians in attendance.

39 George Meager, *My Airship Flights*, William Kimber, 1970, 46.

40 In the course of this he used his academic connections to sound out the Royal Institution about the loan of air liquefying equipment for experiments on the purification of hydrogen.

41 In particular, the construction of R100 (where Teed was responsible for hydrogen production) and (from 1946) as Wallis's deputy in Vickers's Research and Development Department.

42 R. A. Cochrane, memoir, Cochrane Papers.

43 A. W. Skempton, 'Alfred John Sutton Pippard', Royal Society Biographical memoir, 1970, 466–468. A. J. Pippard and L. Pritchard, *Aeroplane Structures*, Longman, 1919, became a standard work.

44 Pippard (1891–1969) held chairs of engineering successively at the universities of Cardiff (1922–28), Bristol (1928–33), and Imperial College (from 1933).

45 Formal advice came via Pippard's membership of the Aeronautical Research Committee, and the Airship Stressing Panel (formed in 1921 following the R38 disaster).

46 Hannah Gay, *The History of Imperial College London 1907–2007*, Imperial College Press, No. 72, 186.

47 Boyd's twin brother Norman won the Lightweight class in the 1917 Grand Fleet Officers' Open Boxing Championships.

48 As far as we know, Wallis's only brush with the law was in February 1917 when he was cautioned for riding the motorcycle without a licence. Zenith's chief engineer was Frederick Barnes – did Wallis choose the make because of the name?

49 D. I. Davies, D. C. Lyon & R. J. Spring (1986), 'Charles Loudon Bloxam – Victorian University and Military Academy Chemistry Teacher', *Ambix* 33:1, 11–32.

50 The composer Carl Friedrich Abel (1723–87) was among Frieda's forebears.

51 William Beardmore built their airships at Inchinnan in Renfrewshire. The Armstrong Whitworth ships were constructed at Barlow, near Selby in Yorkshire.

52 No. 26r, by Vickers.

53 R27 and R28 were ordered from William Beardmore; R29 and R30 from Armstrong Whitworth. In the event, only R27 and R29 were completed.

54 'Various wrecked German Zeppelins: components R9, R24, R33 and R34', TNA AIR 11/238.

55 The two 23X ships that had not yet been begun were subsequently cancelled ('Airship Construction Policy', August 1917, TNA ADM 1/8621).

56 A further sixteen were proposed in August 1917: 'Airship Construction Policy', TNA ADM 1/8621. R31 and R32 were wooden-framed airships derived from Schütte-Lanz technology.

57 No. 9's first trial flight was on 27 November 1916.

58 *The Times*, 15 May 1917, 1.

59 R26 took to the air on 20 March 1918. She possessed the best disposable lift of ships in her class, having benefited from improvements learned in the course of building her sisters. No. 23r, first in the class, had flown six months previously.

60 Approval for the R80 was given on 21 November 1917.

61 The specification for machinery was changed several times in 1918, while a comparative assessment of British airships against the German L48 led to a stream of further requirements: Kender, 'R80', *Dirigible*, 12:2, 2001, 9–10.

62 Wallis's high mast concept was later developed by Scott and Colmore, leading to the mooring towers erected at Cardington, Montreal and Cairo. Wallis's mooring mast papers are gathered in SM B4/1–12.

63 Craven to BNW, 6 February 1918.

64 Report to Dr Blacklee, 11 April 1918.

65 These included R33 and R34 and, eventually, R80 and R38.

66 Wallis to Craven, 16 February 1920, SM B1/2.

67 Craven to Charles Wallis, 5 January 1920, SM B1/2.

68 In Cleveland Gardens, Hyde Park.

69 McKechnie to Wallis, 14 December 1919, SM B1/2.

70 Pratt to Wallis, 24 December 1919, SM B1/2.

71 Pratt to Charles Wallis, 31 December 1919, SM B1/2.

72 This is evidenced by following letters.

73 The statement (Morpurgo, *Wallis*, 90–91) that Pratt was afterwards 'subjected to a bombardment of long, acrimonious and sternly argued letters from Wallis' is not supported by the record, which shows that the long, supposedly 'final' letter, was the only one of its kind, and posted only four days after their meeting.

74 Wallis to Pratt, 28 February 1920, SM B1/2.

75 Pratt added that while 'General Managers may propose . . . personal idiosyncrasies only too frequently interpose' – a comment that might equally have applied to Wallis. Pratt to Wallis, 3 March 1920, SM B1/2.

76 Pratt to Wallis, 6 April 1920, SM B1/2.

77 Victor Goddard to Wallis, 8 April 1920, SM B1/2.

78 Goddard, Robert Victor, oral history recording, 17 April 1978, IWM catalogue 3189.

79 Wallis's later recollection that the ship 'shot up' to 9000 ft because of a ballasting misjudgement by Ivor Little, and that both he and Goddard had had to climb up parts of the keel structure to reach gas valves that needed to be held open (Wallis to Goddard, 12 September 1974, cited in Swinfield, *Airship*, 68) does not entirely correspond with contemporary sources.

80 R80: test and trial flight, TNA AIR 11/12.

81 Campbell (who had precipitated the denouement at Barrow in 1915) oversaw the work to copy L33 and subsequently the L48, brought down in July 1917. The contract, originally let to Short Brothers at Cardington, was superseded by Cardington's nationalisation and transformation into the Royal Airship Works early in 1919.

82 The ship's failure led to mutual recrimination between the Admiralty (which had been responsible for her flawed design) and the new-formed RAF (which had inherited responsibility for completing it).

83 Ibid.

84 Wallis to Cmdr J. C. Hunsaker, 22 January 192; Hunsaker to Wallis, 8 February 1920, SM B1/2.

85 Craven to Wallis, 1 December 1921; 3 December 1921; 7 December 1921, SM B1/2.

86 Wallis took advantage of a scheme whereby students who had served in the war, undertaken other work relating to national defence, or been interned were granted certain exemptions from examination regulations. SM A4/1–6.

87 £21-7s-0d.

88 Edward Masterman to Wallis, 8 April 1922, SMRC.

89 Morpurgo, *Wallis*, 88–89.

90 Molly Bloxam to Wallis, 4 July 1923, MWL, 115.

91 Wallis to Molly Bloxam, 14 January 1924, MWL, 224.

92 Stopes-Roe, MWL, 2.

93 Contemporary sources show that Wallis was only told about the upcoming post in Vickers's Commercial Department during the following Christmas vacation.

94 Wallis to Molly Bloxam, 26 September 1922, MWL, 4.

95 Stopes-Roe, MWL, 4.

96 Wallis to Molly Bloxam, 1 October 1922, MWL, 4–5.

97 Wallis to Molly Bloxam, 11 October 1922, MWL, 6–7.

98 Molly Bloxam to Mary Turner, MSRC.

99 Molly Bloxam to Hugh Wallis, 1955, MSRC.

100 Molly Bloxam to Wallis, 8 October 1922, MWL, 5–6.

101 Wallis to Molly Bloxam, 11 October 1922, MWL, 7.

102 Wallis to Molly Bloxam, 25 October 1922, MWL, 9–10.

103 'Empire Air Services: the new airship scheme', *Flight*, 6 April 1922, 203.

104 Molly Wallis, journal, 19 September 1977.

105 Molly Bloxam to Wallis, 14 January 1923, MWL, 17.

106 Wallis to Molly Bloxam, 22 January 1923, MWL, 18.

107 Wallis to Molly Bloxam, 15 May 1923, MWL, 82–3.

4 Woggins in Love, 1923–25

1   Wallis to Molly Bloxam, 15 May 1923, MWL, 83.
2   The Imperial Conference in 1921 appointed a Commission to examine the case for an Imperial airship service. The Commission accepted the need to achieve 'British supremacy in the commercial airways of the world', but left open the financial question of how to do so. Burney's allies at this time included Roundell Palmer (Parliamentary Secretary to the Board of Trade), Lord Sydenham (former Governor of Victoria, Governor of Bombay), Edward Lawson (*Daily Telegraph*) and Lord Long (Colonial Office): Burney correspondence, August–December 1922, Wiltshire & Swindon History Centre, 947/866.
3   A. H. Ashbolt, 'An Imperial Airship Service', *Journal of the Royal Society of Arts*, 70, No. 3605, 23 December 1921, 102–121.
4   'Empire Air Services: the new airship scheme', *Flight*, 6 April 1922, 203.
5   Lord Gorell, 'Civil Aviation', in *Air Ministry: Proceedings of the Second Air Conference, held on 7–8 February 1922*, 8–31, at 13.
6   'It is not easy to regard the Burney airship scheme as more attractive than that proposed by the Imperial Air Communications Committee, which was finally rejected some months ago': The Burney Airship Scheme, memorandum by Secretary of State for the Colonies, 21 June 1922, TNA CAB 24/137/55. For the Imperial Air Communications Committee 1920–23, TNA Air 8/44.
7   'Airships. Commander Burney's Scheme. Memorandum by the Chancellor of the Exchequer', June 1922, TNA CAB 24/13/723.
8   Defence sub-committee, minutes, 12 July 1922, TNA ADM 1/8657/34.
9   House of Commons Debate, 17 July 1922, vol. 156, cc1705–6.
10 'Flying in 1922', *The Times*, 29 December 1922, 5; Teresa Crompton, 'British Imperial Policy and the Indian Air Route, 1918–1932', unpublished PhD, Sheffield Hallam University, 2014, 77.
11 Wallis to Molly Bloxam, 20 April 1923, MWL, 73.
12 At this point (April 1923) Wallis was attached to Vickers's Estimates and Contracts Department.
13 Wallis to Molly Bloxam, 2 May 1923, MWL, 74.
14 Associated politicking included inter-service rivalry and the effects of an alternative commercial scheme that had been put forward early in 1923: Swinfield, *Airship*, 103–5.
15 'The development of a Commercial Airship Service', TNA, CAB 24/161/24, 13 July 1923. The sub-committee's thinking took in arguments for airships as a means of naval reconnaissance, their ability to maintain Imperial air routes at times of international tension, and their potential to provide transport for the Services.
16 This followed a report from the board's Imperial Shipping Committee which had surveyed postal services between Britain and Australia in relation to the economics of surface ships.
17 Burney had already obtained cost advice from William Beardmore. This meeting received additional input from Pratt and Wallis.
18 The three initial contenders were Lord Derby, Lord Curzon and Stanley Baldwin. By the time of Law's resignation (20 May) Curzon and Baldwin were the only runners: R. J. Q. Adams, *Bonar Law*, John Murray, 1999, 361.

19 Wallis to Molly Bloxam, 23 May 1923, MWL, 85.

20 Wallis to Molly Bloxam, 16 May (in fact 15) 1923, MWL, 83.

21 Report of the Committee Meeting held at Vickers House, 17 May 1923: SM, BB1/1.

22 Wallis and Pratt had recently spoken. Wallis's diary shows an intended meeting on 30 April; this was cancelled, but the two met for dinner on 3 May.

23 Wallis to Molly Bloxam, 17 May (in fact 15), MWL, 83. In 1968, Wallis wrote a note on this episode for Morpurgo in which Pratt went unmentioned. Instead, Wallis attributed refusal to his unwillingness to submit to Burney's design group, whose members he considered to be unqualified. In fact, this group was formed at a later stage and Wallis was conflating different episodes.

24 Molly Bloxam to Wallis, 20 May 1923, MWL, 84; Wallis, 1923 Diary, MSRC.

25 This was the explanation Wallis recounted to Morpurgo in 1972. No original source for Pratt's decision has been found.

26 Zeppelin's recent developments included a new kind of hull girder; a metallised finish for the outer cover (being smoother and reflective, this helped to minimise temperature fluctuation); synthetic lining for gasbags; new types of engine, and a water recovery process.

27 LZ's works was about two miles from the town centre, near the hamlet of Löwenthal.

28 Wallis to Molly Bloxam, 26 (in fact 27) May 1923, MWL, 95.

29 Ibid., 96.

30 Wallis to Molly Bloxam, 14 June 1923, MWL, 99.

31 Ibid., 100.

32 Wallis's sketch of ZR-3's structural essentials formed part of his report.

33 Wallis to Molly Bloxam, 14 June 1923, MWL, 99.

34 1923 diary, Wednesday, 6 June, MSRC.

35 'The financial aspect of schemes for the development of a commercial airship service', Report of the Sub-committee of the National and Imperial Defence Committee, 10 July 1923. TNA CAB 24/161/24.

36 On remission of the scheme to sub-committees: TNA CID AIR 5/592; CID 1922–24 AIR 8/60.

37 Provisos recommended by the Standing Defence Sub-committee included a negotiated reduction in financial liability, eventual repayment of half of any profits in excess of ten per cent, and the leasing of Pulham and Cardington 'at a nominal sum'. TNA CAB 23/46/11.

38 Provisos included a ruling that the decision should be 'subject to the financial and other arrangements being settled to the satisfaction of the Treasury and the other departments concerned.' TNA CAB 23/46/11.

39 Crompton, 'British Imperial Policy', 40–41.

40 The Times, 20 October 1923, 10; Flight, 25 October 1923, 659.

41 'Civil air transport', memorandum by Samuel Hoare, November 1923. TNA CAB 24/162/47.

42 'Big US Airship Scheme', The Times, 3 November 1923, 12. The Times pointed out that Britain's part was doubly regrettable: the Burney scheme was now a mere 'skeleton' of its original form because no real progress on it had been possible until it was passed by the Treasury, and since Goodyear-Zeppelin would be building airships for the US government, British private enterprise would now be

at a commercial disadvantage ('Development of Airships', 6 November 1923, 7).

43 Airship Guarantee Company Ltd, No. BT 31/32606/194068, incorporated 29 November 1923.

44 Agreement between the Airship Guarantee Company Ltd and HM Treasury, MS Vickers Doc. 913, 1923.

45 Some have said that Wallis was appointed Chief Designer in May 1923. However, at this point he was still in his new post at Vickers, who seconded him to Burney at several points during the summer. Morpurgo's suggestion (which came from Wallis) that Richmond, Scott and Colmore 'went over to the rival design team' in this period is mistaken, since there was no rival project until the MacDonald government took office early in the following year.

46 Wallis to Molly Bloxam, 26 June 1923, MWL, 114.

47 Wallis was a member of 155 Battery of the 52nd (London) Heavy Anti-Aircraft Brigade, a unit of the Territorial Army.

48 Wallis to Molly Bloxam, 26 June 1923, MWL, 114.

49 Ibid.

50 Molly Bloxam to Wallis, 22 July 1923, MWL, 136.

51 *The Times*, 'House of Commons', 27 July 1923, 6.

52 In July 1923 Wallis was offered the managership of Vickers's midland depot.

53 Wallis to Molly Bloxam, 26 [30] July 1923, MWL, 140.

54 Wallis to Molly Bloxam, 10–16 August (14) 1923.

55 Wallis to Molly Bloxam, 28 August 1923, MWL.

56 Molly Bloxam to Wallis, 5 September 1923, MWL.

57 Wallis to Molly Bloxam, 12–14 (13) September, 1923, MWL.

58 Ibid. (14).

59 Wallis to Molly Bloxam, 28 September 1923, MWL.

60 Wallis to Molly Bloxam, 9 November 1923, MWL.

61 Colmore had been appointed the Air Ministry's senior airship staff officer after the death of Maitland in the R38 disaster.

62 Wallis to Molly Bloxam, 3 January 1924, MWL.

63 Wallis to Molly Bloxam, 19 November 1923, MWL.

64 The day after the operation, the French airship *Dixmunde* – in fact, a Zeppelin which had been provided to France as a war reparation – exploded in mid-air with the loss of all 52 on board.

65 Wallis to Arthur Bloxam, draft, n.d. (1924), MWL, 222.

66 Molly Bloxam to BNW, 21 January 1924.

67 House of Commons Debate, 14 May 1924, vol. 173,

68 Ibid.

69 'Airship Development: new scheme in substitution for Burney scheme 6 February 1924 – 5 March 1925', TNA T 161/470/3; 'Notes on the "Two Company" arrangement of the Burney Scheme 1924', AIR 5/1064.

70 Molly Bloxam to Wallis, 16 May 1924, MWL.

71 Wallis to Molly Bloxam, 19 May 1924, MWL.

72 W. M. Thackeray, *The Newcomes: Memoirs of a Most Respectable Family*, chap. 43. Wallis misattributed the line to Arthur Pendennis, the book's narrator (and hero of another Thackeray novel).

73 Wallis to Molly Bloxam, 19 May 1924, MWL.

74 Molly Bloxam to Wallis, 22 May 1924, MWL.

75 Molly Bloxam to Wallis, 27 May 1924, MWL.
76 Ibid.
77 Wallis to Molly Bloxam, 30 May 1924, MWL.
78 Molly Bloxam to Wallis, 30 May 1924, MWL.
79 Wallis to Molly Bloxam, 9 June 1924, MWL.
80 Mary Stopes-Roe, MWL, 292.
81 Wallis to Mary Turner, 16 July 1924, MWL.
82 Wallis to Molly Bloxam, 18 July 1924. Wallis was writing from Borth, where he was again holidaying with the Boyd family, MWL.
83 Wallis to Molly Bloxam, 27 July 1924, MWL.
84 Molly Bloxam to Wallis, 7 August 1924, MWL.
85 Wallis to Molly Bloxam, 18 August 1924, MWL.
86 Molly Bloxam to Wallis, 24 August 1924, MWL.
87 Wallis to Molly Bloxam, 1 September 1924, MWL.
88 Wallis to Molly Bloxam, 11 September 1924.
89 Mary Stopes-Roe, MWL, 356.
90 Edgar Boyd to Wallis, n.d. (September 1924), MWL, 356.
91 Marion Boyd to Wallis, MWL, 356.
92 SM BB1/7.
93 *Daily Mail*, 6 November 1924, 9. The business model originally provided for 100 passengers, but later reduced to 50, which broke the model.
94 *Daily Mail*, 19 November 1924, 19.
95 E. A. Johnston, 'Richmond of R101', *Dirigible*, 4, 1990, 3.
96 Norman Peake, 'Innovations in R100: Construction Notes from a Manuscript Handbook', *Dirigible*, 3–4, 1993, 11–15.
97 Stationary ripples formed on R100's cover when she was flown at highest speed. Wallis concluded that these standing waves were of no serious account, but the RAW's subsequent wish to modify the ship with reefing girders suggests continuing underlying worry in that quarter.
98 The axial girder was made up of pin-jointed modular lengths.
99 Norman Peake, 'Innovations', 11–15. The numbers of individual components later quoted frequently disagree, but this does not alter the basic point, that the ship was fabricated from a small number of repeating parts.
100 The chief calculator's task was to work out stresses that the airship's structure might undergo under different conditions and convert these into data that draughtsmen in the drawing office would need to produce working drawings for individual components. The AGC's calculations were invigilated by the Airworthiness Panel.
101 Pippard to Wallis, 24 September 1924, SM BB6/1A.
102 Wallis to Pippard, 16 October 1924, SM BB6/1A.
103 'The new British airship', *The Times*, 26 February 1925, 14; cf. C. Dennis Burney, 'Airship policy', Letter, *The Times*, 25 February 1925, 10.
104 Masterman to Wallis, 7 March 1925, MSRC.
105 'Reports and papers connected with the proposed international standardisation of mooring towers 1925–1929', TNA AIR 5/1051.
106 The task of a gas cell attachment is to hold the bag itself and transmit to the surrounding structure the lift it generates. When an airship is in level flight its lift force acts straight upwards. However, when it climbs or descends the

buoyancy of the bags produces forward- or backward-pulling forces, respectively, while lateral forces are generated when the airship turns. Murray, *Bouncing-bomb Man*, 32–33; Norman Peake, 'R101 – The design team and its self-imposed tasks', *Dirigible*, 5.1, 1994, 16.

107 Murray, *Bouncing-bomb Man*, 34.

108 Webb had been Wallis's chief assistant in the Airship Drawing office at Barrow until its closure, and had since obtained a post as lecturer in engineering science at University College London.

109 Wallis, Note on the origin of geodetic construction, n.d., 28.

110 *Daily Mail*, 1 April 1925, 5.

111 *Daily Mail*, 7 April 1925, 9.

112 Steve Snelling, *Eastern Daily Press*, 27 April 1995.

113 Major C. C. Turner, 'The saving of R33: complete example of airship operation dodging the storm work of meteorological department', *The Observer*, 19 April 1925, 17.

114 Harry Harper, 'The future of large airships', *Daily Mail*, 17 April 1925, 8. Coincidentally – or was it? – the day before the wedding Burney read a lecture on airship transport to the Institution of Aeronautical Engineers. With characteristic élan, he proposed a mooring system that differed from the one already selected by the Air Ministry, and argued that since the design of an airship and its mooring system were interdependent, the development of airships and airship bases should be put in the same hands. Burney startled many by giving the impression that R100's control car would be in her nose.

115 Wallis's younger brother Christopher was at this time a lieutenant in the 21st Indian Pack Brigade, stationed at Jutogh near Shimla, and thus unable to attend. Annie was now living in Leicester; it is not clear if she was present.

116 Molly Wallis to Jack Morpurgo, letter, 1972, MP 664/471/1; for the honeymoon reminiscence, Molly Wallis, journal, 19 September 1977, MSRC.

117 Molly Wallis to Mary Turner, 30 June 1925, MSRC.

118 The airfield was laid out in 1915–16 beside a service road running at right angles to the highway between Howden and York. The sheds stood parallel to the service road, their long sides aligned to the prevailing wind. Domestic, administrative, and technical buildings were built along the north side of the spine. The station had its own post office, chapel, playing fields and YMCA. In the technical area were an electricity generating plant, workshops, a gasworks and gasholders. Coal for the generator and coke needed for hydrogen to gas the airships were brought along a rail spur from the North Eastern Railway at North Howden.

119 Anderson, *Airship on a Shoestring*, 41.

120 For example: Air Cdre P. Fellowes to Air Marshal John Salmond, 8 July 1925; Salmond to Fellowes, 16 October and 10 November 1925: 'Miscellaneous papers relating to the Airship Guarantee Company', 1922–1929, TNA AIR 5/1046.

121 T. R. Cave-Brown-Cave, 'The machinery installation of airship R101', *Proceedings of the Institution of Automobile Engineers*, 23:1, 1928, 99–123.

122 Ralph Cochrane, 1925 diary, Cochrane Papers.

123 Anderson, *Shoestring*, 27–28.

124 Shenandoah was modelled on the Zeppelin U class, the so-called 'height climber', which sacrificed aspects of structural strength to achieve extra altitude.

125 Molly Wallis to Mary Turner, 16 January 1926, MSRC.
126 Wallis to Charles and Fanny Wallis, 1 February 1926, SMRC.

5 Prince of Clouds, 1926–30

1 Molly Wallis to Mary Turner, 10 April 1926, MSRC.
2 Ibid.
3 Wallis to Molly Wallis, memoir letter, 25 August 1963, MSRC.
4 Problems included overweight longitudinal girders, failure of early spider joints and hiatus over the type of engine: Anderson, *Airship on a Shoestring*, 49–51.
5 The process involved a reaction between ferro-silicon and a strong solution of sodium hydroxide.
6 Molly Wallis to Mary Turner, January 1927, MSRC.
7 *Sheffield Daily Telegraph*, 5 March 1927.
8 Ibid.
9 Molly Wallis to Mary Turner, 23 January 1927, MSRC.
10 Molly Wallis to Mary Turner, 7 February 1927, MSRC.
11 Wallis to Molly Wallis, 11 October 1926, MSRC.
12 Molly Wallis to Mary Turner, 10 April 1926, MSRC.
13 Molly Wallis, memoir for *Howden Advertiser*, 1976, MSRC.
14 Molly Wallis to Mary Turner, 13 May 1927, MSRC.
15 Jessie Valentine Ley was born on 14 February (whence her middle name) 1878 and had joined the Bloxam household in her early thirties.
16 Molly Wallis to Mary Turner, 9 April 1927, MSRC.
17 Molly Wallis to Mary Turner, 13 January 1928, MSRC.
18 Molly Wallis to Mary Turner, 18 February 1929, MSRC.
19 Anderson, *Shoestring*, 57.
20 Molly Wallis to Mary Turner, 6 September 1929, MSRC.
21 Wallis argued that since R100 was at the limit of the capacity of Howden's existing shed, no larger vessels could be built at Howden unless a new shed was provided. It followed that the AGC would have no need of a new chief designer until this happened. This did not prevent Burney from attempting to bring in a man with no airship experience as a future senior manager and counterweight to Wallis: Wallis to H. B. Pratt, 24 May 1928, SM BB6/4/18; BB 6/1.
22 When Lt.-Col. H. W. S. Outram (Aeronautical Inspection Department) visited Howden in June 1929 he reported that the workforce lacked drive. Outram thought Wallis was limiting himself to matters of design (R100 progress reports from the Airship Guarantee Company, January to November 1929, TNA AIR 5/971). However, Outram's report is at odds with Wallis's active involvement in the inflation process that followed, while according to Wallis Outram 'knew nothing about airships': Wallis to Morpurgo, 31 January 1969, MP.
23 Neville Shute, *Slide Rule*, Heinemann, 1954, 84–5.
24 Molly Wallis to Mary Turner, September 1927, MSRC.
25 John Price Williams, 'R100 on wheels', *Dirigible* 9:3–4, 1998/1999, 10–13.
26 Molly Wallis to Mary Turner, 27 April 1928, MSRC.
27 Wallis to Molly Wallis, 26 August 1928.
28 'Empire Airships', *The Times*, 25 November 1927, 18.

29 Royal Aeronautical Society to Wallis, letter, 13 September 1928. The medal was accepted on Wallis's behalf by Masterman in Wallis's absence at Menton.

30 Molly Wallis to Mary Turner, 19 July 1929, MSRC.

31 For example, Burney memoranda and letters of 23 September 1926, 3 March 1927; 15 July 1927, 6 January 1928; 21 April 1928; Wallis to Burney, 13 July 1926; 25 February 1928; 28 March 1928, SM BB6/1.

32 Notably autumn 1928, when Wallis protested about instructions given direct to the Drawing Office by Burney, and Burney rebuked him: Burney to Wallis, 24 September 1928; Wallis to Burney, 1 October 1928: SM BB6/1.

33 Brett Holman, 'Who was Neon?', *Dirigible* 57, 2009, 15–16.

34 Molly Wallis to Mary Turner, 22 January 1928, MSRC.

35 *The English Review*, May 1929, 542–552.

36 Shute, *Slide Rule*, 94.

37 Molly Wallis to Mary Turner, 5 November 1928, MSRC.

38 Robert McLean, Memorandum to Board, 29 October 1928, Vickers Doc. 47.

39 Molly Wallis to Mary Turner, May 1928 (n.d.), MSRC.

40 Molly Wallis to Mary Turner, 21 March 1929, MSRC.

41 Molly Wallis to Mary Turner, 16 December 1927, MSRC.

42 Molly Wallis memoir for *Howden Advertiser*, 1976, MSRC.

43 Site notice, 29 April 1929: SM BB5/8, 12.

44 Molly Wallis to Mary Turner, 2 August 1929, MSRC.

45 Philip Teed, 'The first inflation of R100', *Aircraft Engineering*, June 1930, 135–6.

46 Molly Wallis to Mary Turner, 11 August 1929, MSRC.

47 Meager, *Airship Flights*, 148.

48 Meager, *Airship Flights*, 149.

49 Shute, *Slide Rule*, 81.

50 Molly Wallis to Mary Turner, 4 October 1929, MSRC.

51 Charles Dennistoun Burney, *The World, the Air and the Future*, Alfred A. Knopf, 1929. The book was published on 10 October 1929.

52 Among them was a vast cradle-with-claws to convey airships into their sheds in all weathers, and a ship of elliptical section that could alight on water. Commander Noël Atherstone, R101's first officer, wrote that 'To describe them as experimental would be to do science a disservice.' Log, 10 October 1929: Appendix A in Swinfield, *Airship*, 258–275.

53 *Manchester Guardian*, 14 October 1929.

54 *Observer*, 20 October 1929.

55 Burney, *The World, the Air and the Future*, ix. Wallis was credited with responsibility for the 'mechanical design'.

56 George F. S. Bowles, *The Strength of England*, Methuen, 1926, 18.

57 See pp. 400–404.

58 *The Times*, 14 October 1929, 11.

59 *Daily Mail*, 15 October 1929, 14.

60 *The Times*, 19 November 1929, 17.

61 'R 101 In A Hurricane', *The Times*, 12 November 1929, 16; 'The R 101's Fifth Test Flight', *The Times*, 9 November 1929, 12.

62 *Daily Mail*, 18 October 1929, 8.

63 Atherstone, Log, 23 November 1929, Appendix A in Swinfield, *Airship*, 265.

64 Ibid.

65 Atherstone, Log, 6 December 1929, in Swinfield, *Airship*, 267.

66 Ibid.

67 Wallis was working on projects for Vickers in this period, including a new form of frame structure for wings and fuselages, and gave Vickers Aviation at Weybridge as his working address. However, Wallis did the work from Howden, where he continued to live until mid-December 1929. Wallis's contractual relationship with Vickers was not finalised until the spring of 1930: see pp. 179–180.

68 Scott, *Vickers*, 181.

69 Wallis to John Brunton, Bruntons, Musselburgh: SM BB6/4/2; BB6/5.

70 Molly Wallis to Mary Turner, 21 October 1929, SMRC.

71 Molly Wallis to Mary Turner, 25 October 1929, SMRC.

72 'Launching of R 100', *The Times*, 5 November 1929, 16.

73 'Cost of Airships', *The Times*, 11 November 1929, 21.

74 House of Lords Debate, 26 November 1929, vol. 75, cc687–90.

75 *Sheffield Independent*, 2 December 1929.

76 Shute, *Slide Rule*, 86.

77 'His Majesty's Airship R100 Inspection at Howden', *Flight*, 6 December 1929, 1275–1280, at 1279.

78 SM BB6/5.

79 Wallis to Air Cdre John Chamier, 19 November 1929: SM BB6/5.

80 Molly Wallis to Mary Turner, 13 December 1929, MSRC.

81 These included Wg Cdr Colmore (Director of Airship Development), Major G. H. Scott (Assistant Director of Airship Development (Flying)), Sqn Ldr E. L. Johnston (navigator), Fg Off. M. H. Steff (Second Officer) and M. A. Giblett (Superintendent, Airship Services Division of the Meteorological Office).

82 Anderson, *Shoestring*, 98.

83 The handling party was made up of contingents from the East Yorkshire, West Yorkshire, and Yorkshire and Lancashire Regiments.

84 Anderson, *Shoestring*, 99.

85 George Meager to J. Morpurgo, letter, 3 January 1973, MP, MS664/302/2.

86 Molly Wallis, December 1929, MSRC.

87 'R100's goodbye to Howden', *Daily Mail*, 16 December 1929, 5.

88 The main transmission and control gearing were provided by the firm David Brown of Huddersfield, whose specialist engineers had co-operated in their design and manufacture.

89 According to Norway these included a leaky cylinder in one engine and a suspected problem with the big end of another; a dynamo handle with a seized bearing; and air that eddied through one of the outer cover ventilators. 'These were the inevitable teething troubles of any large aircraft'. Shute, *Slide Rule*, 92.

6 Landfall, 1930–31

1 Molly Wallis to Mary Turner, 14 January 1930, MSRC.

2 Molly Wallis to Mary Turner, 30 January 1930, MSRC.

3 SM BB6/5.

4 The oft-repeated story about Wallis arriving during the Christmas holiday and

installing himself in Mitchell's office is uncorroborated by any contemporary
sources seen by the author and contradicted by the dates in Wallis's daybook.

5   'Airship R100 fabric flutter records', 20 January 1930, IWM, MTE 64.
6   Shute, *Slide Rule*, 98.
7   Shute, *Slide Rule*, 97.
8   1930 notebook, MSRC.
9   Ibid., 22–24 January.
10 Morpurgo, *Wallis*, 177–8, misplaced the entire Supermarine episode to the
    spring of 1930. His suggestions that the tensions between Wallis and Mitchell
    were connected with Mitchell's cancer diagnosis and 'ebbing' enthusiasm for the
    Supermarine Type 244 were anachronistic.
11 Molly Wallis to Mary Turner, letters, 30 April and 19 March 1930, MSRC.
12 Wallis to Molly Wallis, 5 February 1930, MSRC.
13 An experimental version of the new stainless-steel spar was set down on 5
    February 1930: 1930 Notebook.
14 Wallis was working on 'the Imperial Airways fuselage' in the first two weeks of
    February: 1930 Notebook.
15 The Viastra airframe used a system of corrugated alloy panels originated by
    the French engineer Michel Wibault. The prototype was begun at Crayford,
    transferred to Supermarine's works at Woolston and first flew in October 1930.
    Viastras were built in different versions powered by one, two and three engines.
    Wallis also produced an experimental wing for the Vickers Vivid: C. F. Andrews
    and E. B. Morgan, *Vickers Aircraft since 1908*, Putnam, 1988, 215–222; Murray,
    Bouncing-bomb Man, 43.
16 Memo, 'Wallis wings for Viastra', from McLean to Wallis, Pierson, Chamier
    and Maxwell-Muller, 26 January 1930: SM BB6; 'Started on the new wing for 3
    Engine Monoplane', 1930 Notebook, 28 February. A meeting between Chamier,
    Pierson, Westbrook and Wallis on 3 March 1930 took the decision to build this
    as 'an entirely new machine' (which became the Vickers Type 256), so as not to
    interfere with production of three Viastras of the original type that were already
    on order.
17 McLean to Wallis, 26 March 1930, SM A5/1.
18 1930 Notebook, 3 March.
19 McLean to Wallis, 21 and 26 March 1930, SM A5/1. The purchasing power of the
    salary at today's values would be around £103,463—£129,330.
20 In the signed contract this was reduced to four, SM A5/1.
21 Molly Wallis to Mary Turner, 2 April 1930, MSRC.
22 Molly Wallis to Mary Turner, 12 April 1930, MSRC.
23 Molly Wallis to Wallis, 2 April 1930, MSRC.
24 The outward flight to Montreal began on 29 July 1930 and was completed on 1
    August. The return voyage was made from 13 to 16 August 1930. Flights within
    Canada were made on 10/11 August.
25 Wallis to Molly, 29 April 1930. MSRC.
26 *The Times*, 6 August 1930, 10.
27 Harold Leonard and Glen Adney, 'Here's to the R100'; Mary Rose-Anne Bolduc
    ('La Bolduc'), 'Toujours L'R100'.
28 Shute, *Slide Rule*, 110.
29 Peter Davison, 'The R.101 story: a review based on primary source material and

first-hand accounts', *Journal of Aeronautical History*, Paper 2015/02, 43–167.

30 These included a new cover, new ballast bags, different petrol tanks, re-design of accommodation, and insertion of an extra bay to increase lift.

31 Experiments on airship models for Airship Guarantee Company, 1930, TNA DSIR/2884.

32 A related point lay aback of Wallis's disapproval of the design of R101's self-rigid transverse frames: aside from their weight penalty they intruded on internal space that might otherwise have been assigned to gasbags. Wallis to Morpurgo, MP 664/421/2.

33 TNA AIR 2/364.

34 *Report of the R101 Inquiry*, 1931, 61–64.

35 The Certificate of Airworthiness was issued by the Air Ministry on 2 October based on an interim report from Professors Leonard Bairstow and Alfred Pippard. Earlier criticisms from Frederick McWade were referred to Sir John Higgins, the then Air Member for Supply and Research, who in turn invited Colmore's comments. Colmore downplayed McWade's concerns (Colmore to Higgins, 7 July 1930). By accepting Colmore's view, both Higgins and his successor Dowding put Colmore in the position of judge in his own case. *Report of the R101 Inquiry*, 48–51.

36 Atherstone, Log, 3 October 1930, in Swinfield, *Airship*, 275.

37 Ray Dudley, 'The unforgettable vision', *Dirigible*, 16:2, 2005, 15 16.

38 Forty-six died within minutes of impact; two more died in hospital.

39 Morpurgo, *Wallis*, 183.

40 Molly Wallis to Mary Turner, 10 October 1930, MSRC.

41 *Observer*, 12 October 1930, 17.

42 The coronations of George V and Edward VII drew more spectators, but those were ceremonies of one day, whereas the R101 exequies lasted for nearly a week.

43 Morpurgo (*Wallis*, 185) wrote that no R100 man was invited to the funeral; in fact, the entire crew played a leading part in the ceremony, and Burney was at the graveside by official invitation. It has also been said that the Airship Guarantee Company's request to be represented at the memorial service by Burney, Sir Trevor Dawson, Wallis and Norway was refused, whereas in fact, Dawson and Wallis did attend, and the entire R100 crew was with them.

44 The thirteen days were divided into two phases of hearing.

45 Brabazon noted that there had been no trials of the kind that R100 had had to undergo before R101 'was hustled off to India.'

46 Notes and memoranda relating to possible causes of the R.101 disaster, TNA AIR 5/910.

47 Nevil Shute Norway and Hessell Tiltman moved to York and co-founded the progressive aircraft manufacturer Airspeed.

48 House of Commons Debate, 14 May 1931, vol. 252, cc1391–487.

49 Airworthiness authority for refit of Airship R.100, 1931: TNA, AIR 2/503; reorganisation of R100's crew, 1931, AIR 2/468.

50 One bay (11–12) was retained at Cardington until 1937 for tests to analyse deflections and stresses.

51 *Flight*, 11 December 1931.

52 Molly Wallis to Mary Turner, letter, 20 November 1931, MSRC.

53 The first geodetics patent was registered on 27 August 1931.

7 Earth to Love, 1931–40

1 'God gave all men all earth to love
But since our hearts are small,
Ordained for each one spot should prove
Belovèd overall.'
Rudyard Kipling, 'Sussex', 1902.
2 Molly Wallis to Mary Turner, letter, 24 April 1930.
3 'Britain's world speed records', *Daily Mail*, 2 October 1931.
4 This was for a prototype torpedo bomber, the Vickers Type 207, being built in response to Air Ministry specification M. 1/30. The prototype flew for the first time in January 1933. Development ceased when the prototype broke up in mid-air in November that year.
5 Wallis's contribution to the Vickers Vanox, a replacement for the Virginia designed in response to Air Ministry requirement B.19/27. In its original form this was the Vickers Type 150, which first flew in November 1929, was later furnished with different engines, re-designated the Type 195, and given the name Vanox. The Vanox was in turn further modified, by which time its competitors, the Fairey Hendon and Handley Page Heyford had been selected for production.
6 Vickers Type 161 (Air Ministry specification F. 29/27), designed by Pierson as a platform for an upward-firing gun produced by the Coventry Ordnance Works.
7 The Giant was a proposed forty-seat civil flying boat, in part prompted by the visit of a Dornier X to Calshot the previous November. The project was cancelled in 1932.
8 'Notes on the Technical Position' compiled for meeting held 9 December 1931, 4. Vickers Doc. 321.
9 B. N. Wallis, 'A Note on the Origin and Development of Geodetic Construction as used on the Wellesley and Wellington aircraft', n.d. (c.1968), BWF archive, 34–5.
10 Specification G. 4/31. In 1935, Wallis wrote that the aircraft concerned was a Vickers Victoria (B. N. Wallis, 'Notes on geodetic construction', n.d., SM BNW A3/2). However, very likely it was the prototype Vanox (n. 5 above), which was undergoing modification in July 1931 and was specified in a weight-saving comparison provided to the meeting on 9 December 1931 (Vickers Doc. 321).
11 Wallis to Molly Wallis, 8 December 1932, MSRC.
12 Board meeting, 12 April 1932, Vickers Doc. 317.
13 Wallis noted in his diary that he told Pierson about his solution for the structure of the geodetic wing on 22 November 1932.
14 Wallis was employed under a service contract and thus exempt from the cut; however, in November 1931 he volunteered to accept the reduction and was thanked for setting an example to the workforce.
15 Burney to Wallis, 15 January 1936, SM C5/1.
16 Masterman to Wallis, 15 January 1936, SM C5/1.
17 'Eggshell aeroplanes', *Aviation* magazine, August 1936; cf. *L'Aviation Belge*, 7 February 1937, SM C5/1.
18 HC Deb, 17 March 1936, vol. 310 cc259-263.
19 *The Times*, 9 December 1937.

20 Wallis in interview with J. D. Scott, Vickers Doc. 780; letter to executors, 2 August 1948, MSRC.

21 Trevor Westbrook described the Air Ministry's alleged hostility to geodetic construction as 'much exaggerated': interview with J. D. Scott, 15 October 1959, Vickers Doc. 785.

22 Even before the first Wellesley flew, Harry Wimperis, the Air Ministry's shrewd director of scientific research, was in discussion with Vickers and Wallis about the possibility of using geodetic structure in the wing of a proposed Atlantic flying boat.

23 Vickers G.4/31 aircraft: trials, 1935 TNA AVIA 18/627; Geodetic construction: ARC report and Vickers (Aviation) Ltd report for ARC, DSIR 36/3000.

24 Vickers Aviation's workforce grew from 1466 to 4844 between 1933 and 1939: Weybridge quarterly reports, Vickers Doc. 447.

25 Iain Murray, *Vickers Wellington*, Haynes, 2012, 10.

26 Wallis to Morpurgo, 22 November 1972, MP 664/502/2.

27 *Daily Mail*, 1 April 1940, 7; Denis Le P Webb, *Never A Dull Moment At Supermarine: A Personal History*, J & K H Publishing, 2001, 103.

28 Quoted in Robert Gardner, *From Bouncing Bombs to Concorde: the authorised biography of aviation pioneer Sir George Edwards OM*, Sutton, 2006, 18.

29 By late 1936, fearing delay, the Air Council agreed that Vickers Aviation should be allowed to farm out Wellington production within other parts of the Vickers empire.

30 One reason for the delay was Wallis's hospitalisation in later March and April 1938, and convalescence until mid-May: see pp. 212–213.

31 McLean to Craven, August 1938, Vickers Doc. 124. More ill feeling arose following delay in equipping Wellingtons with Fraser Nash turrets. Freeman described this as 'a disgrace to a firm of the status of Vickers' whereas McLean traced it to a decision to standardise equipment which was neither properly developed nor industrially provided for. Freeman to Craven, 31 January 1938; McLean, note, 8 February 1938, Vickers Doc. 384; 'Turret Position as 15 January 1939', report by Director of Technical Development, TNA AIR 6/56, AIR 6/56.

32 Wallis to Molly Wallis, 9 August 1938, MSRC.

33 TNA AVIA 10/217, ACCS meeting 5 October 1938, meeting with Craven 6 October 1938. At Vickers-Armstrongs' 1939 AGM shareholders were told that the assets of Supermarine and Vickers Aviation had been bought by the parent company: report of Vickers Ltd AGM, 4 April 1939, 24.

34 The new agreement, dated 27 February 1939, replaced the service contract with Vickers Aviation that had been renewed in 1934.

35 Quoted in Gardner, *Bouncing Bombs to Concorde*, 10.

36 Quoted in Gardner, *Bouncing Bombs to Concorde*, 13.

37 Ibid.

38 Ibid.

39 1937 diary, 5/6 April MSRC; Minutes of meeting of Vickers Aviation directors, 9 April 1937, Vickers Doc. 312.

40 Morpurgo, *Wallis*, 204–6, quoted letters from Pratt to Wallis dated 10 and 14 July 1936, and from Wallis's reply made on 26 July. None of these appears to survive, but notes in Wallis's pocket diary ('Pratt' on 11 July, and 'Pratt. Headache' on 13 July) corroborate some sort of interchange at this time.

41 Morpurgo, *Wallis*, 207.

42 Hillman's Airways.

43 Robin Higham, 'British Airways Ltd, 1935–40', *Journal of Transport History*, 1959, 113–123.

44 Short production runs for small orders from small airlines were considered uneconomic, and by concentrating on military and light aircraft British manufacturers ceded most of the airline market to Douglas and Lockheed in the US, Fokker in the Netherlands and Junkers in Germany.

45 'Report on British Airways Statement RE81 comparing Wellington with Lockheed 14', SM C3/3, March 1938. 'Vickers Wellington for British Airways Ltd', SM C3/4, n.d. but 1939; cf. C. F. Andrews and E. B. Morgan, *Vickers Aircraft*, 312.

46 Nigel Norman was chairman of Airwork, which had built Heston aerodrome in 1929.

47 Leo D'Erlanger to Wallis, telegram, 9 July 1938, SM C5/1.

48 Wallis to Leo d'Erlanger, 14 December 1944, letter.

49 Winterbotham, *Secret and Personal* (William Kimber, 1969, 146–7), misdated the first meeting to autumn 1940. SIS's air component was staffed by officers seconded from the Air Ministry, where Winterbotham served first as a re-employed retired officer in the Directorate of Operations and Intelligence and then as Deputy Directorate of Intelligence (Section A13 (b) Germany).

50 Wallis, 'Bomber Aircraft. The Determination of the Most Economical Size', November 1938. SM C2/9.

51 Wallis to Walter Runciman, 26 June 1939, SM C2/10.

52 B. N. Wallis, 'Wind Tunnel Test of Golf Balls', report ref. no. 31, 24 August 1936, SM G2/1.

53 'The ball's carry. Its dependence on markings', *The Times*, 7 November 1936, 4.

54 Wallis to Charles Wallis, letter, 29 March 1932, MSRC.

55 'Paid Pater's quarter £26/10s/0d [c.£2,600 at present prices]': 1931 diary, MSRC. The contribution to Annie was £26/0s/6d.

56 Following her nursing career Annie had moved to Lahore in India, where in 1921 she married William Knight, who at different times was described as a confectioner and a jeweller. Their first child, a boy, died in infancy. They had since returned to England, where William started a business in Leicester and there were two more children, Desmond, and Patricia.

57 Wallis contributed £26/0s/6d a quarter in 1932. The Knights' house in Leicester was at 29 Dulverton Road.

58 Wallis to John Wallis, letter, 29 June 1936, MSRC.

59 Wallis to John Wallis, letter, 31 May 1936, MSRC.

60 This was Karl Schmid (1910–98), an oarsman and member of the Swiss coxed four at the 1936 Berlin Olympic Games, with whom Pamela was in a close relationship. In 1938, Pamela went to be with him in Geneva in the hope of marriage. Disappointed by his wish that they live together outside marriage, she returned to England. Schmid followed her to Effingham, where Wallis cross-examined him and made a financial contribution to their union. Pamela and Schmid returned to Switzerland, but marriage did not follow. Pamela may or may not have known that Schmid had already fathered a son, born in 1936.

61 'Little Barnes bore it pretty well. I never know if I am as it were breaking his spirit by persuading him to keep quiet when his father says beastly things. I

think not, because it happens so rarely and his father is so more than nice nearly all of the time. Much nicer than ordinary fathers.' Molly Wallis, family diary 13 November 1939, MSRC.

62 Molly Wallis to Mary Turner, 27 November 1931, MSRC.

63 Barnes Wallis Jnr, letter to author, 8 May 2008.

64 Elisabeth's exact words were 'We were a mess': conversation with author, 5 November 2019.

65 Quoted in Gardner, *Bouncing Bombs to Concorde*, 23.

66 The trees listed in the cash account of Wallis's 1932 diary included red oak, almond, crab apple, mountain ash, beech and lime.

67 Humphrey was the brother of Alliott Verdon Roe, with whom in 1910 he had co-founded the Manchester aeroplane manufacturer A. V. Roe – Avro. More recently his business acumen and funds had been applied to the work of his wife. Stopes at this point was under extreme pressure – she feared for the future of her clinics, and was troubled by the refusal of *The Times* to print advertisements for her Whitfield Street clinic.

68 Molly Wallis to Hugh Wallis, August 1955, MSRC.

69 Effingham St Lawrence: Parish Records, Surrey History centre, Woking: EFF/9/1 Minutes 1933–1947; 9/3 Correspondence 1932–1954.

70 The church was reconsecrated in spring 1935.

71 See pp. 120 and 353.

72 The Mount Alvernia Nursing Home, Harvey Road, Guildford, was operated by the Franciscan Sisters of Divine Motherhood.

73 The operations were on 19 March and 3 April 1938.

74 Molly Wallis to Wallis, 14 April 1938, MSRC.

75 Charles Wallis to Molly Wallis, 18 April 1938, MSRC.

76 Their stay at Lyme Regis was from 21 April to 8 May 1934.

77 Molly confessed to being in a 'religious muddle' at this time: Molly Wallis to Mary Morris, letter, 27 April 1938, MSRC.

78 Interview with Elisabeth Wallis, 5 November 2019.

79 Wallis to Molly Bloxam, 11 October 1943, MSRC.

80 Molly's remarks on nationalist feeling included 'I shall never be patriotic' (1937) and 'I've no patriotism & don't care for any England or anything', MSRC.

81 Richard Griffiths, *Fellow Travellers of the Right: British Enthusiasts for Nazi Germany*, 1933–1939, Faber & Faber, 2011. At least from 1933 Molly thought Hitler 'loathsome', described David Lloyd George's positive opinion of him as 'unpleasantly dippy' and wished the League of Nations to intervene in Ethiopia.

82 Dibdin was familiar with India and its languages having been stationed there as a member of the Surrey Regiment throughout the Great War.

83 Dibdin's link with the area came through his parents-in-law John and Mabel Luckham, who retired to Studland around 1918 following years running a preparatory school at Hinton Admiral which catered for sons of overseas royalty and aristocracy.

84 Thomas Hardy, *The Hand of Ethelberta*, 1876, 31.

85 Purbeck's Brownsea Island was the birthplace of scouting, and the area provided the setting for many of Enid Blyton's Famous Five stories.

86 Elisabeth's pronunciation of 'Wallises' around 1936.

87 Mortimer Wheeler's excavations at Maiden Castle were spread across the four summers from 1933 to 1937.

88 'The Dam Buster in Dorset', reminiscences of Mary Stopes-Roe and David Wallis, *Dorset Life*, April, 2008. Other examples of upwards extension he had in mind included Maiden Castle, Ely Cathedral, and Corfe: *Effingham Parish Magazine*, Vol. VI, No. 3, March 1939, 6–8.

89 Wallis to Molly Wallis, 2 September 1939, MSRC.

90 Molly Wallis to Mary Morris, 23 September 1939, MSRC.

91 'Proposed action against German minelaying seaplane bases', 12 December 1939, TNA CAB 65/4/26.

92 The team that defused the mine was led by Lt Cdr John Ouvry. 'Report on German magnetic mine recovered at Shoeburyness, November 1939: with MS addenda': TNA ADM 218/302.

93 The main practical sweeping method to emerge was known as the Double Longitudinal Sweep (LL), which employed pairs of wooden-hulled vessels trailing cables between which pulsed an electric current. Immunisation (degaussing) was achieved by use of a reverse field to offset the way in the earth's magnetic field was focused by ships' hulls.

94 Maurice Hankey (Minister Without Portfolio in the War Cabinet) mentioned the DWI work on 20 November 1939, two days before the Shoeburyness episode, in a letter to the physicist Edward Appleton: Hankey was attempting – in the face of some resistance – to involve Tizard's Committee for the Scientific Study of Air Warfare in the search for solutions.

95 'Magnetic mine sea sweep', 1939, TNA ADM 204/299; 'DWI methods of sweeping magnetic mines', 1940, TNA ADM 204/356; 'German magnetic mine: proposed countermeasures', 1939–40, TNA ADM 1/10315; 'Minesweeping of magnetic mines (especially aircraft)', TNA ADM 212/192.

96 J. D. Scott and Wallis, January 1960, Vickers Doc. 780.

97 Gardner, quoting Edwards, *Bouncing Bombs*, 26; J. D. Scott and Wallis, January 1960, Vickers Doc. 780.

98 Churchill to Chamberlain, letter, 25 December 1939, CHAR 19/2C/274–276.

99 Four DWI conversions of Wellington Mk 1s (Vickers Type 418) were produced, followed by a further eleven (Vickers Type 419) which used a more powerful generator. The difficulty of keeping a precise record of swept channels from the air was a drawback over open sea, but the system was later used to good effect over confined waters such as the Suez Canal and the port of Alexandria.

100 The first prototype was powered by Rolls-Royce Vulture engines and first flew on 13 August 1939, while Wallis was at Camp. The second prototype was fitted with Bristol Centaurus engines and incorporated aerodynamic improvements.

101 The design history of this aircraft was tortuous. In spring 1939 the Air Ministry called for a 400-mph heavy cannon fighter to succeed the Beaufighter (specification F. 6/39, overtaken by F. 22/39, to which Vickers responded with designs for their Type 414). In 1940 the requirement was adjusted to that for a high-altitude fighter to counter the threat posed by the Ju86P (F. 4/40, F. 16/40, commuted to F. 7/41, to which the Vickers Type 432 was the eventual response). See p. 243.

102 The pressurised Wellington became the B.V and VI: 'Bombers ('High-altitude Wellington'), 1939–40', TNA AVIA 1/118; 'Wellington Technical Data concerning

Proposed Adaptation and High Altitude Bomber with Pressurised Cabin', SM C3/5 [RKP/43157].

8 Persuasion, 1940–43

1   See pp. 203-204.
2   T. M. Charlton, 'Professor Bertram Hopkinson, C.M.G., M.A., B.Sc., F.R.S. (1874–1918)', *Notes and Records of the Royal Society of London*, 29:1, October 1974, 101–109.
3   Bertram Hopkinson, 'A method of measuring the pressure produced in the detonation of high explosives or by the impact of bullets', *Philosophical Transactions of the Royal Society* (A Series), 213, 1914, 437–456. Hopkinson's paper was a developed version of a talk entitled 'The pressure of a blow' that he had given at a Royal Institution 'Evening Discourse' in January 1912.
4   Albert Speer, *Inside the Third Reich*, Simon & Schuster, 1970, 280.
5   Wallis's duties in May 1940 included further testing of the DWI Wellington; evaluation of reports from test flying of the second Warwick prototype; liaison with Rolls-Royce about the Merlin-powered Wellington; and work on the pressurised Wellington.
6   Molly Wallis to Mary Morris, letter, 23 May 1940, MSRC.
7   Craven was appointed to the Air Council as Civil Member for Development and Production on 22 April 1940.
8   Charles was flying in a Lockheed Hudson of 233 Squadron, as part of a formation sent to attack the battleship.
9   Molly Wallis to Mary Morris, letter, 18 June 1940, MSRC.
10   Molly Wallis to Mary Morris, letter, 12 July 1940, MSRC.
11   Gill Bennett, *Churchill's Man of Mystery: Desmond Morton and the World of Intelligence*, Routledge, 2007.
12   Morton to Winterbotham, 5 July 1950, reproduced in Winterbotham, *Secret and Personal*, 148–9.
13   Wallis joined the LDV (later, Home Guard) on the day of its formation.
14   Wallis was a member of No. 1 Section of what became the 5th Home Guard Battalion of the East Surrey Regiment, centred on Effingham, Shere Cranleigh and Chiddingfold.
15   Molly Wallis to Mary Morris, letter, 28 June 1940, MSRC.
16   Air Ministry Weekly Intelligence Summary No. 42, 20 June 1940, AIR 14/195, f 98b.
17   The meeting with Craven took place on the afternoon of Wednesday 17 July 1940.
18   Winterbotham's later claim (*Secret and Personal*, 149) that he arranged the introduction to Beaverbrook is contradicted by Wallis's contemporary account: Wallis to Alex Dunbar, letter, 21 July 1940.
19   Anne Chisholm & Michael Davie, *Beaverbrook: a life*, Pimlico: London, 1993, 385–6.
20   Wallis to Dunbar, 21 July 1940, MSRC.
21   Ibid., 4–5.
22   Ibid.

23 Ibid.

24 Pocket diary, Monday, 22 July 1940, MSRC.

25 Pocket diary, 30 July 1940, MSRC.

26 Anthony Furse, *Wilfrid Freeman*, Spellmount, 1999, 139.

27 Pocket diary, 7 August 1940.

28 See pp. 87, 137.

29 At the time of its formation in 1936 the Road Research Laboratory (RRL) was a subsection of the Building Research Station. Glanville was then the Laboratory's Assistant Director, overall control remaining with the BRS's director, Reginald Stradling. When the RRL was administratively detached from the BRS in 1939 Glanville became its director.

30 Eric Hobsbawm, 'Red Science', *London Review of Books*, 28:5, 2006, 21–23; Ritchie Calder, 'Bernal at War', in *J. D. Bernal: a life in science and politics*, eds Brenda Swan and Francis Apprahamian, Verso, 1999, 160–190, at 166. Wallis first met Bernal on 14 August 1940.

31 Notably, research being undertaken by Solly Zuckerman at Oxford: Zuckerman Archive: Ministry of Home Security, Research and Experiments Department, Oxford, University of East Anglia Archives, GB 1187 SZ/OEMU.

32 Molly referred in letters to Wallis's doubts about the likelihood of invasion.

33 The raiders were from Erprobungsgruppe 210, a *Jabo* unit stationed at Calais-Marck which had begun to specialise in precision attacks. The escort fighters were from V Gruppe of Lehrgeschwader 1. GErpGr 210 was part of the force that halted Spitfire production at Woolston later in the month (see p.233).

34 Molly Wallis to Mary Morris, letter, 5 September 1940, MSRC.

35 The Experimental Section sites became known as the Top Site (later used for building the Windsor prototypes and spinning trials for Highball and Upkeep); the Centre Site (which housed Edwards's offices and the prototype F.7/41 fighter) and the Bottom Site (the Fitting Shop): 'Brooklands Aerodrome – the Years 1939 to 2006', *Airfield Review*, 110, April 2006.

36 These were bombers of KG 76 passing Westerham, about twenty miles away.

37 Molly Wallis to Mary Morris, letter, 24 September 1940, MSRC.

38 Works Report for quarter ending 30 September 1940.

39 Wallis, 'Note', Ch. 1.

40 Molly Wallis to Mary Morris, 22 October 1940, MSRC.

41 Ibid.

42 Ibid.

43 11 October 1940.

44 15, 25, 31 October 1940.

45 17/18 October 1940.

46 Wallis and Halcrow met on 16 October 1940; Halcrow subsequently sent a written report which was in Wallis's hands by 11 November.

47 Pye was Wimperis's successor as director of scientific research at the Air Ministry, since resettled to the MAP.

48 Another former member of Hopkinson's team was Sir Henry Tizard, who in October, fresh from leading a delegation to the United States to open UK research and development in return for access to US industrial resources, arrived at the MAP to oversee research.

49 During the lunch break in a meeting on 21 October, two bombs fell nearby,

bringing down a glass dome adjoining the area where they were eating.

50 A. R. Collins, 'The destruction of arch dams by explosion under water', TNA DSIR 27/43/MAP/3, November 1940.

51 Wallis to MacColl, letter, 24 April 1941, Ordnance Board correspondence and papers, BWF Archive.

52 Wallis to R. Capon (DD/RD Arm), letter, 5 December 1940. TNA AVIA 15/744.

53 The Garston experiments were made under the auspices of the MAP (Glanville to Pye, letter, 4 November 1940; Pye to Glanville, letter, 8 November 1940); Wallis had earlier committed Vickers to covering their cost if this became necessary (Wallis to Pye, letter, 31 October 1940). TNA AVIA 15/744.

54 This project was led by Norman Davey (a cement and concrete specialist) and A. J. Newman (who headed the BRS's concrete laboratory). Beginning outdoors on 25 November, Davey's team clad the dam's concrete core with over half a million miniature cubes of mortar to replicate the granite blocks with which the real dam was faced.

55 Wallis told MacColl that he had been led to two articles on acoustic resistance: that by C. V. Drysdale, 'Modern Marine Problems in War and Peace', the Eleventh Kelvin Lecture, in the *Journal of the Institution of Electrical Engineers*, 58, 1920, at p. 572; and by Brillé (who coined the expression) in *Le Génie Civil*, 75, 1919, at p. 171.

56 Dunbar to Beaverbrook, 'Victory Bomber', 1 November 1940, Vickers Doc. 780.

57 Following a long talk with Wallis on 4 November, Nannini convened a meeting with explosive specialists in Shrewsbury on 13 November 1940 to discuss different means of filling, and potential types of explosive that included liquid mono-nitro-benzine, alumatol, amatol, and TNT: 'Special bomb for Air Ministry', minutes of meeting, Vickers Doc. 780.

58 'Notes on meeting held at the Ordnance Board Thursday PM, 5 December 1940, in connection with special heavy bomb – Mr Wallis's proposals', Vickers Doc. 780.

59 John W. MacColl, 'The aerodynamics of a spinning sphere', *The Aeronautical Journal*, 32:213, September 1928, 777–798.

60 Bombing Committee: minutes of meeting on air attacks on reservoirs and dams, TNA AIR 14/229. Wallis found out about this work on 4 December 1940: Wallis to F. W. R. Lestikow, letter, 5 December 1940, SM D3/1.

61 In addition to submission of the Victory bomber proposal through Vickers-Armstrongs' head office, the Weybridge Works Report for December 1940 referred to continuing 'Experimental and development work in co-operation with and to the instructions of the Ministry', indicating that this was part of the company's forward programme: Vickers Doc. 199.

62 On 5 November 1940, the day after his long meeting with Wallis, Nannini sent a private memo to Yapp describing the genesis and progress of the special bomb and promised 'to take the first opportunity' to speak directly with him about it: Nannini to Frederick Yapp, '10-ton bomb', 5 November 1940, Vickers Doc. 780/20.

63 Sebastian Ritchie, 'A Political Intrigue Against the Chief of the Air Staff: the downfall of Air Marshal Sir Cyril Newall', *War and Society* 16:1, 1998, 83–104. Churchill's immediate circle were told of Newall's departure on 2 October 1940: John Colville, *The Fringes of Power: Downing Street Diaries, 1939–1955*, London:

Hodder & Stoughton, 1985, entry for 2 October, 256.

64 Portal was selected as CAS by 2 October. His appointment was not announced until 25 October, at which point he was campaigning for Freeman's release from the MAP and appointment as VCAS. Freeman bade farewell to the MAP on 4 November.

65 Vincent Orange, *Quietly in Command*, Frank Cass, 2004, 15–16.

66 Wallis to Tedder, 28 November 1940.

67 On 21 December preliminary results arrived from the Garston experiments on model arch dam sections which showed that the Italian dams could indeed be broken with quite small charges if placed within 70–115 ft of the crest on the sloping face (Glanville to Wallis, 21 December 1940). Tizard questioned whether the model experiments would allow inferences at scale, but on Christmas Eve a meeting to address this question, attended by Bernal, Stradling, Granville, Wallis and others, agreed that valid inferences could be so drawn (Granville to Pye, 24 December 1940): 'Model experiments on dams', TNA AVIA 15/744. Cf. DSIR Note No. MAP/3/ARC, December 1940, 'The destruction of arch dams by explosions under water', Ordnance Board correspondence with Wallis, BWF Archive.

68 According to Molly the boys were asleep in the kitchen when the bomb fell and their beds were flipped over.

69 Molly Wallis to Mary Morris, letter, 8 November 1940, MSRC.

70 A. R. Collins, 'Preliminary tests on the effects of explosions on a model gravity dam', November 1940, TNA DSIR 27/43/MAP 2; A. R. Collins, 'The destruction of Arch Dams by explosion under water', November 1940, TNA DSIR 27/43/MAP 3; 'Tests on scale model masonry gravity dam', TNA DSIR 27/43/MAP 5, January 1941.

71 'Stradling to Tizard, letter, 3 January 1941: Experiments on model dams', TNA AVIA 15/744.

72 Winterbotham's claim to have recommended this course in or around September 1940 (*Secret and Personal*, 189) is often repeated but wrong: Wallis began work on the Note after Tedder's departure (cf. Wallis's initial evidence to the Royal Commission on Awards to Inventors, 1950, p.2).

73 Wallis to MacColl, 15 March 1941, Ordnance Board correspondence and papers, BWF Archive.

74 Alan Cottrell, 'Edward Neville Costa Da Andrade, 1887–1971', biographical memoir, *Journal of the Royal Society*, 18, 30 November 1972, 5.

75 Addendum to a Note on a method of attacking the Axis powers, Ordnance Board correspondence and papers, BWF Archive.

76 Pye notified Wallis of the forthcoming hearing on 29 March. The group which met at 11.00 in ICI House consisted of Edward Andrade, Desmond Bernal, Professor Geoffrey Taylor (a member of Stradling's team, adviser to the Ministry of Home Security), William Glanville and his assistant A. H. Davis from the RRL, Air Cdr Patrick Huskinson (D Arm D) with Wg Cdr Sealy. Also present were Winterbotham and the explosives expert Sir Robert Robertson.

77 'Use of large bombs: treatise by Mr B. N. Wallis of Messrs Vickers 1941–42', TNA AVIA 2/7477; Suggestions for very large bombs and bombers by Mr Barnes Wallis TNA AVIA 15/700; Six-engined bomber: consideration of Vickers' proposal 1941–42, TNA AVIA 15/1020.

78 Wallis's diary shows meetings with Tizard (in the aftermath of the Pye panel meeting) on 19 and 21 April.

79 On 20 May 1941.

80 Tizard to Wallis, letter, 21 May 1941. The suggestion that the Victory could be modularised to be a multi-purpose machine was not in the Note and was very likely offered by Wallis to keep the proposal alive in the face of Air Staff scepticism.

81 Ibid.

82 Ibid.

83 In 1951 Wallis stated that consideration of the Note led to the formation of the AAD Committee (appeal evidence to the Royal Commission of Awards to Inventors: SMA D10/1). In fact, the AAD Committee met for the first time on 10 March 1941.

84 Torpedoes could be parried by nets. An attempt on 2 February 1941 by an eight-strong force of FAA Swordfish to break the dam on the River Tirso with torpedoes showed what could happen under operational conditions: four never found the target, one was shot down, and just three released their weapons. Rocket bombs were thought unlikely to penetrate far enough to be lethal, and the idea of bombs in water had been abandoned before the war, not least because nowhere could be found to test it. Aerial Attack on Dams Advisory Committee, minutes of meeting held 10 March 1941, TNA AVIA 10/369.

85 See pp. 423-424.

86 Vickers Doc. 785.

87 The 1936 design was against Specification B.12/36, which was awarded to Short Bros. for the Stirling. Thereafter: Six-engined heavy bomber: proposal by Vickers Ltd 1936–38, TNA AIR 2/2673; Considerations affecting the design of the ideal bomber, AIR 19/447 1938–1940; Bomber landplane: specification B.19/38 and B.1/39, TNA AIR 2/2958.

88 This approach followed the mix and match way in which they had hoped to make rapid progress with the Victory, and very likely too was influenced by Avro's success in turning the Manchester into the Lancaster. In the event, the Windsor's elliptical wing plan would have more in common with the Victory than with the Warwick, but extension of the Warwick provided the immediate starting point, and for the contract for two prototypes which was issued on 15 July. Four-engined Warwick Bomber landplane: specification B5/41; type requirements, TNA AIR/7565.

89 Two prototypes of the pressure cabin fighter had been ordered against MAP specification F. 7/41, upon which 'some' work was accomplished by September 1941.

90 The B. Mk VI was an improved version of the stratosphere Wellington.

91 Weybridge Works Report, September 1941, Vickers Docs 202, 785. Delays since the commissioning of the Warwick meant that by the time it entered production it had been supplanted in its intended role as a heavy bomber; its future lay in other roles that included Air Sea Rescue, Leigh Light patrols, transport, and general reconnaissance.

92 Wallis was responsible for the ingenious wing structure of the fighter: 'Vickers pressure cabin fighter aircraft: special structural features of the wings', 1941, TNA DSIR 23/11299.

93 On 19 June and 10 December.

94 The second meeting was held on 19 June 1941, the third on 10 December, TNA AVIA 15/744. For the trials: G. Charlesworth, 'Pressures in water due to multiple charges', September 1941, TNA DSIR 27/43/MAP18; A. R. Collins, 'The effects of tamped contact explosions on lightly reinforced concrete', October 1941, TNA DSIR 27/43/MAP 19; A. R. Collins, 'Tests on lightly reinforced concrete with various types of explosive fired under water', November 1941, TNA DSIR 27/43/MAP 22; A. R. Collins, 'The effects of near explosions under water on lightly reinforced concrete', November 1941, TNA DSIR 27/43/MAP 23.

95 Wallis to Molly Wallis, letter, 8 August 1941, MSRC.

96 Wallis to Molly Wallis, letter, 9 August 1941, MSRC.

97 Molly Wallis to Wallis, letter, 15 August 1941, MSRC.

98 Pam was stationed at Strete, a unit of the Y Service, a network of signals intelligence collection sites.

99 Molly Wallis, family diary 1941, 1 October 1941, MSRC.

100 On 1 July 1941 a meeting between Glanville's team and members of the AAD Committee at the RRL discussed the potential of a bomb in contact with a stressed dam; experiments with contact charges followed on 17 July. TNA AVIA 15/744.

101 One method discussed, and discarded, by the AAD Committee was a float and drogue system whereby a bomb would be drawn towards the waterside face by the current flowing towards a spillway.

102 On 22 December, at Wallis's request, tests were made on gravity models which included a two-ounce contact charge.

103 Molly Wallis to Mary Morris, letter, 28 February 1942, MSRC.

104 The initial exchange was with John Martin, the Prime Minister's Principal Private Secretary, who wrote to Wallis on 11 December 1941. Wallis sent his refusal on 15 December. Leslie Rowan, Churchill's Private Secretary, acknowledged on 18 December, MSRC.

105 In December 1941, according to Molly, Wallis believed that the war was likely to continue 'for years': Molly Wallis to Mary Morris, letter, 3 January 1942, MSRC.

106 Pye's proposal was submitted on 30 January 1941 through AVM (acting) Ralph Sorley, the Air Member for Operations and Tactics. The reply, received on 16 March, reflected advice from DB Ops.

107 R. S. Capon to William Glanville, 9 March 1942, TNA AVIA 15/744.

108 Wallis to AVM Linnell (Controller of Research and Development, MAP), letter, 9 February 1942.

109 Trial with a contact charge was made on 19 May, whereafter it was found that the quantity of explosive needed to break the model was significantly smaller than the charge sizes hitherto used at scale distances. Sources differ about the origin of this insight. An account often repeated is that it was discovered by accident, when a small contact charge was trialled for the demolition of a model. Wallis later claimed in his evidence to the Royal Commission on Awards to Inventors that it was he who 'Immediately before what would have been the last meeting of the Committee' had 'asked Dr Pye if as a final bit of research he would lead the Committee to authorise a series of experiments to find out the smallest size of charge which, if exploded in actual contact with the masonry and at the most effective depth, would be capable of breaching the dam.' AADC

minutes and trial reports make it clear that investigation of effects of contact explosions was systematically undertaken in the later stages of the model tests.

110 In his 'Spherical bomb' note, Wallis suggested that release might be three quarters of a mile from the target. Several of the first successful tests of the trial Golf mine in January 1943 exceeded this range.

111 The compact configuration of explosive in a spherical weapon would favour instantaneous detonation.

112 The note in which the idea is expounded is undated, but reference to the escape of the *Scharnhorst, Gneisenau* and *Prinz Eugen* from Brest to Germany on 12/13 February 1942 puts it between then and the emergence of the ricochet idea in April. The weapon Wallis had in mind was a version of the water variant of the big bomb he had advocated in 1940–41, reduced to a store liftable by a Stirling. This approach mirrored the contemporary (February) exploration of what could be achieved against a dam with the largest bomb that an existing aircraft could carry, and the realisation that the effect of an explosion is more powerful underwater than in the air. Tactical aspects of the idea were naïve, and it is not clear that it was never put before the MAP, the Admiralty, or the Air Staff. Its audience may have been no larger than Winterbotham. Equally, in several respects the idea foreshadowed what followed: low level precision attack, by a unit formed for the purpose, reliant on the way in which explosions work. SM D 6/4.

113 G. K. Batchelor, 'Geoffrey Ingram Taylor', *Biographical Memoirs of Fellows of the Royal Society*, 22, 1976, 565–633.

114 This work contained new dynamical theory and was published after the war: G. I. Taylor, 'The air wave surrounding an expanding sphere', *Proceedings of the Royal Society of London*, A 186, 1946, 273–292; 'The dynamics of the combustion products behind plane and spherical detonation fronts in explosives', *Proceedings of the Royal Society of London*, A 200, 1950, 235–247. For broader context, G. I. Taylor, Scientific papers. Edited by G. K. Batchelor, vol. 3, 'Aerodynamics and the mechanics of projectiles and explosions', Cambridge University Press, 1963.

115 This hypothesis fits with Winterbotham's (undated) account of Wallis ringing to tell him of the explosive efficiency of a spherical bomb, and Winterbotham ascertaining from Air Ministry colleagues that such a weapon would 'bounce along like a football'. *Secret and Personal*, 150–151.

116 Coefficient of restitution: the ratio of the final to initial relative speed between two objects after they collide.

117 Evidence to Royal Commission on Awards to Inventors, 1950, SMA, D10/1.

118 Relf to Tizard, letter, 19 May 1942.

119 The lake was Silvermere, now within a golf and leisure complex. On the day of the trial (Wednesday 27 May) Wallis and Edwards had the help of Amy Gentry, Wallis's secretary, an international oarswoman who took charge of a rowing boat to retrieve the catapulted spheres.

120 This is produced by the Magnus effect, a phenomenon in which the path of a spinning object through a fluid is deflected to an extent governed by the speed of rotation. In ball sports, topspin produces a downward change of direction, while backspin produces an upward force that will prolong the ball's flight.

121 Over sixty years later George Edwards claimed to his biographer that backspin was introduced at his suggestion in 1943 to solve a problem of 'insufficient

bounce and lack of control of the bomb in flight'. Edwards described how he organised a demonstration of spin at Silvermere in February 1943 which persuaded Wallis to adopt it. Robert Gardner duly recorded this in his book, thereby placing the demonstration eight months after the actual Silvermere trial, seven months after the experiments at Teddington, and one month after prototype weapons had been successfully dropped on the Fleet. This does not remove the possibility that it was Edwards who proposed backspin, but the context and rationale he gave were wrong.

122 On 16 June 1942 Wallis wrote to Tizard in terms indicating that both were already aware that backspin gave improved range, and that Wallis had been analysing the reason why. He told Tizard: 'I suggest that the speed of rotation is sufficient to cause a laminar boundary layer of air to form on the circumferential surface of the sphere; and that this boundary layer maintains its position when the sphere strikes the water, the air being forced in from the T.E. to the L.E. in the same way that a journal bearing pumps in a layer of lubricating oil. The sphere is thus never in contact with the water until the speed of rotation has dropped so low that the laminar boundary layer is no longer formed.' A memo from Pye on 19 June suggests that by then he too was privy to the idea.

123 TNA AVIA 15/744.

124 Result Book of tests at Nant-y-Gro dam, TNA AVIA 10/370.

125 Molly Wallis to Mary Wallis, letter, 19 August 1942.

126 This was the racing pilot and aviation pioneer Jacqueline Cochran, who was in Britain to fact-find about the Air Transport Auxiliary. She went on to head Women Air Force Service Pilots in the United States.

127 The film's premiere was on Thursday, 20 August 1942 at the Leicester Square Theatre.

128 The story also contains episodes at which Wallis had been present, and its vital score had been composed by Mary Turner's cousin William Walton.

129 C. A. Lejune, 'The Films', *The Observer*, 23 August 1942, 2.

130 See pp. 194–198.

131 See pp. 356–357.

132 Wallis to Molly Wallis, letter, 22 August 1942, MSRC.

133 At Vickers House on the morning of Tuesday, 25 August.

134 RAF Warmwell, about six miles south-east of Dorchester.

135 In late September, Vickers-Armstrongs' deputy chairman, Sir Frederick Yapp, asked for an update on the status of heavy bomb work. Nannini contacted Wallis, who told him that while such work had been in abeyance since 1941, 'projects are now being discussed in respect of aircraft to carry as much as 20 tons bomb load and if these are proceeded with it would be an opportunity for reopening this question.' Capt. Anthony Nannini, memorandum to Sir Frederick Yapp, 23 September 1942 (Vickers Doc. 780/56).

136 Minute from Director of Local Defence, 20 October 1942: TNA ADM 116/4843. Initial defensive thinking centred on putting LCTs (landing craft tank) around capital ships to provide a physical obstruction.

137 AADC, Minutes of Fourth Meeting, meeting of 12 October 1942, TNA AVIA 15/744.

138 Wallis immediately set to work on a paper to make the case more fully. This emerged in January 1943. See p.265.

139 Winterbotham to G. Garro-Jones MP, 14 September 1942, cited by F. W. Winterbotham, *Secret and Personal*, 155.

140 F. W. Winterbotham to G. M. Garro-Jones, letter, 14 September 1942. RAF Museum Archive.

141 'Scientific advisers to Ministry of Production: powers and duties 1942–1946', TNA AVIA 22/196. See also William McGucken, 'The Central Organisation of Scientific and Technical Advice in the United Kingdom during the Second World War', *Minerva*, 17, 1979, 33–69.

142 Fell-Clark was seconded from the Admiralty War Room for this task, apparently at the suggestion of Sir Stafford Cripps (then the Lord Privy Seal, shortly to be Minister of Aircraft Production (22 November 1942 to 25 May 1945)) in whose chambers Fell-Clark had served before the war.

143 J. I. Fell-Clark to J. Morpurgo, letter, 1 February 1972, MP, 664/217/3.

144 TNA KV2/1811/1–3.

145 TNA KV2/3217. In 1942, Lindemann asked the Security Service for advice about Blackett's security status, supposedly to avoid him being given an inkling that Communist sympathisers were under observation during his discussions at 10 Downing Street.

146 TNA KV2/3059. An active socialist group existed at the RAE during the 1930s. MI5 had an informant in its circle. TNA KV 2/994/1 & 2.

147 Guy Liddell (head of B Division) confided to his diary: 'Janson spoke to me about the case of LOCKSPEISER who is employed upon some sort of research work by MAP. He is thought to be holding up developments. DNA is fussing about the case.' 14 March 1942, TNA KV 4/189.

148 Victor Rothschild, head of MI5's counter-sabotage section, revisited the de-icing allegations and found them groundless. Examination of Lockspeiser's finances revealed a man 'living well within his income, apparently without expensive tastes or hobbies, who supplies his wife with the necessary financial resources, and encourages his children to save for the war effort.' Guy Posten to Rothschild, 10 April 1942, TNA KV2/3036/2, 12.

149 TNA KV2/3060, John Godfrey to Sir David Petrie, 22 February 1942; 'Preliminary note on the Lockspeiser case', memo from Victor Rothschild (B1c), 27 February 1942.

150 R. V. Jones, *Reflections on Intelligence*, London: Heinemann, 1989, 70–71.

151 F. H. Hinsley & C. A. G. Simkins, *British Intelligence in the Second World War. Volume 4: Security and Counter-intelligence*, Cambridge University Press, 1990, 179.

152 The operation was proposed to Guy Liddell by Victor Rothschild on 25 March 1942: Liddell, diary, TNA K4/189.

153 Liddell, diary, April 1940. Rothschild was on the Security Service's payroll from 21 May 1940: TNA K4/185. This followed a brief spell as personal assistant to Sir Harold Hartley, who was looking at new proposals for chemical warfare. Earlier in 1939 Rothschild has passed some weeks in the United States, ostensibly to exercise his enthusiasm for jazz piano, but also including meetings with President Roosevelt and J. Edgar Hoover. Kenneth Rose, *Elusive Rothschild: the life of Victor, third baron*, Weidenfeld & Nicolson, 2003, 64–5.

154 David Edgerton, *Britain's War Machine: Weapons, Resources and Experts in the Second World War*, Penguin, 2012, 100–101.

155 Guy Liddell, diary, TNA KV 4/188, 24 November 1941, 199–200. Liddell records that Burney had been referred for a legal opinion over an alleged infringement of defence regulations.

156 TNA AVIA 15/3933, 'Bombs and bombing: General (Code 12/1): Spherical bomb: proposal by Barnes Wallis', 1942–43.

157 Sweetman, *Dambusters Raid*, 46.

158 This may have been partly due to the Panel's terms of reference, which said that its recommendations should normally be presented to the Minister of Production through the Lord Privy Seal (at this point, Stafford Cripps), and that it would be for the Minister to bring them to the attention of the War Cabinet 'as necessary'.

159 Morpurgo, *Wallis*, 246.

160 Lockspeiser to Tizard, letter, 16 June 1942, TNA ADM 277/46.

161 Morpurgo, *Wallis*, 247. Boddington was provided by the Air Ministry's Directorate of Intelligence (Security).

162 William McGucken, 'The Central Organization of Scientific and Technical Advice in the United Kingdom During the Second World War', *Minerva* 17.1, 1979, 33–69, at 55.

163 McGucken, 'Central Organization of Scientific and Technical Advice', 49.

164 Ibid., 63.

165 Cairncross, *Planning in Wartime*, 33.

166 War Cabinet 133 (42), 6 October 1942, TNA CAB 68/28/3; 'The Aircraft Programme: policy for the replacement of the Wellington and the Warwick' (Note by Cripps), 14 November 1942, TNA CAB 66/31/6.

167 Tests at the NPL ship tank were completed on 22 September, when to judge by a memo from Nannini, Wallis's mood was akin to the euphoria that attended his early contact with Beaverbrook: Nannini to Yapp, memorandum, 23 September 1942, Vickers Doc. 780.

168 Dr C. Sykes to Lockspeiser, letter, 7 January 1943, and Lockspeiser's reply of 14 January 1943, 'Spherical Bomb – proposal; for by B N Wallis', Encl 70A, TNA Avia 15/3933.

169 On fuzing: correspondence of 3, 16 18, 26 January 1943; on aircraft capability (range, speeds, structures): meeting held 19 January 1943, correspondence of 20, 21 January, TNA Avia 15/3933.

170 Wallis's nickname for Mary.

171 Wallis to Molly Wallis, letter, 21 January 1943, MSRC.

172 Norway was now serving with the Admiralty's Directorate of Miscellaneous Weapons Development, with responsibility for nets, booms, artificial targets, recovery boats, and transport in support of the trials.

173 Molly Wallis to Mary Morris, letter, 23/24 January 1943, MSRC.

174 Ibid.

175 Minute from Linnell to Lockspeiser, D Arm D and DTD, 28 January 1943, Minute 76, TNA Avia 15/3933. Linnell continued: 'In due course, therefore, I would like DSR [Lockspeiser] to let me have a short note showing the position we have reached, and the steps now being taken. There is no need to go into a detailed history of all the past work. I will then send this to ACAS (TR) [Air Vice-Marshal Ralph Sorley, Assistant Chief of Air Staff (Technical Requirements)].'

9 Full Stretch, February–June 1943

1 Wallis to Cherwell, letter, 30 January 1943, MSS Cherwell, G375.
2 Wallis believed that power generation would be curbed by the destruction of hydro-electric plants, and by reduction in the supply of water needed to cool coal-fired power stations.
3 Air Attack on Dams, TNA Air 20/4369.
4 There were several reasons for this. One was that since the thickness of the dam wall increased from top to bottom, its lower part was less vulnerable. A second factor centred on the contribution provided by water in the reservoir, which would exert its greatest moment of force when the reservoir was full. A third factor was damage following a breach.
5 Lockspeiser to Linnell, loose minute, 4 February 1943, Bomb Development Upkeep, Highball and Golf Mine, TNA Avia 15/3934.
6 Tizard to Linnell, Bomb Development Upkeep, Highball and Golf Mine, 11 February 1943. TNA Avia 15/3934, Minute Note 13.
7 Manuscript note by Harris dated 14 February 1943 on note from Saundby to Harris 14 February 1943, TNA AIR 14/842.
8 Harris to Portal, letter, 18 February 1943, Highball and Upkeep, TNA AIR 8/1234, 1a.
9 Note of meeting held on 13 February 1943, TNA AIR 14/4797.
10 Wallis to Winterbotham, letter, 12 February 1943, Operations Highball and Upkeep Operational Planning, TNA AIR 20/995.
11 Report of meeting held on 15 February 1943, TNA AIR 20/4797.
12 Ibid.
13 Winterbotham to AVM Inglis, memo, 16 February 1943, Operations 'Highball' and 'Upkeep': operational planning, TNA AIR 20/996.
14 Wallis to Cherwell, letter, 20 February 1943, Spherical bomb proposal by Barnes Wallis 1942–43, TNA AVIA 15/3933.
15 There are also puzzles: in the entry for 23 February, after 'Bad row', Wallis added the gnomic question 'What happened on the golf links at Ulverston?' The question has never been satisfactorily explained. It may relate to something during Craven's term as Managing Director at Barrow, and we recall that Pratt lived at Ulverston before his move to Supermarine.
16 TNA AIR 20/995.
17 Wynter-Morgan to Portal, memo, 27 February 1943, TNA AIR 20/4797.
18 A handwritten note on Wynter-Morgan's memo reads: 'Spoke to S. Wilfred Freeman's PS who is arranging for Sir W to write or speak Sir Charles Craven.'
19 Report by Bufton, 27 February 1943, in TNA AIR 20/4821 and AIR 8/1234.
20 Removal of the mid upper turret was at Chadwick's suggestion, to reduce drag. There were other changes, and not all the aircraft were produced to a uniform standard. Vickers's contribution explains the Vickers type number in designation of the special aircraft as the Type 464 (Provisioning) Lancaster. See Robert Owen, 'Modifying the Lancaster', in *Breaching the German Dams*, eds R. Morris and R. Owen, RAF Museum, 2008, 39–43.
21 Linnell to Portal, memorandum, 6 March 1943, 'Highball and Upkeep policy', TNA AIR 20/4821.
22 Craven to Wallis, letter, 3 March 1943, SM D3/2.

23 Notably its proposed covering (a form of steel textile) and undercarriage.

24 Molly Wallis to Wallis, letter, 15 March 1943, MSRC.

25 At this point, Scampton was occupied by a single squadron, reduction from the normal two heralding its temporary closure for the laying of hard runways. The station thus had space for a new unit.

26 The first personnel arrived on 3 April. 618 Squadron Operations Record Book, TNA AIR 27/2130.

27 Operations Record Books for 105 and 139 Sqns, TNA AIR 27/827, AIR 27/960. Mosquitoes loaned by No. 3 Group were augmented by four Beaufighters from East Fortune on 19 April. The first Mosquito converted by Vickers to carry Highball reached the squadron on 23 April, whereafter the loaned aircraft were gradually returned to Marham as the Highball machines replaced them.

28 HMS *Bonaventure* was a submarine depot ship. The loch, on the west coast on the Highlands, was the navy's training base for X Craft midget submarines.

29 Molly Wallis to Mary Morris, letter, 5 May 1943, MSRC.

30 Baseball's 150 lb charge was intended for deck launch from motor torpedo boats. Its development was undertaken chiefly by DMWD. Work on Baseball ceased later in 1943.

31 Highball (L) was envisaged for use against lock gates, submarine shelters, beach defences and naval units. Highball (H) would be used to attack Italian multiple arch dams, merchant ships, canal locks and hydro-electric barrages on the Rhine. Upkeep was for German gravity dams.

32 TNA AVIA 19/1270 Upkeep bomb: Reculver trials 1943; AVIA 19/1041 Water impact and range performance of 'Highball'; Provisional report on Manston trials, SM D 4/2.

33 MAEE was in turn a department of the MAP.

34 The cylinder made an 'excellent run', bouncing eight times over 1200 yards: 'Diary of Manston trials', SM D4/2.

35 'Diary of Manston trials', SM D4/2.

36 Harris to Saundby, 15 April 1943, TNA AIR 14/840.

37 The system consisted of two signalling lamps so angled that their beams would touch on the surface of a reservoir when the aircraft was at the correct height. For its origins, development and working see Robert Owen, 'Finding Height', in *Breaching the German Dams*, 46–48.

38 Harris to Saundby, 15 April 1943, TNA AIR 14/840.

39 On the 12th, Wallis posted a letter to Molly in an envelope made from a recycled sugar bag – wartime austerity – with a verse added on the back:
  'Oh censor! Should thy steely Eye
  Upon this missive chance to pry
  Then prithee for the Writer weep,
  His feet are COLD,
  He cannot SLEEP.'

40 Molly Wallis to Mary Morris, letter, 24 April 1943, MSRC.

41 Culminating in a visit by the Secretary of State for Air on 15 May 1943.

42 Molly Wallis to Mary Morris, 5 May 1943, MSRC.

43 Erratic running was visible in wobble round a random axis towards the end of a store's run. At a meeting on 14 May, Wallis's diagnosis (SM D3/12) focused on lack of dynamic balance resulting from variations in store dimensions, and

incorrectly set up jigs for caliper arms. Sources of the fault later turned out to be more subtle and complicated than this: Murray, *Bouncing-bomb Man*, 108–9.

44 Wallis's advice in mid-May on ranging was to release Highball at 1600 yards and check the viability of the depth pistols in the recovered store, repeat the trial and check from 1400 yards, then reduce range by step until the distance was reached at which the pistols failed (SM D3/12).

45 Flt Lt Stephen (13–19 May, during Hutchinson's absence in Weybridge, latterly, following his injury); Sqn Ldr Melville-Jackson (19–27 May); Wg Cdr Pike (seconded from 18 Group) (27–28 May); Flt Lt Cussen (from 28 May, during the transfer of Pike and Melville-Jackson to Turnberry).

46 In the cases of Gdynia and Kåfjord these included going on to land in the Soviet Union or baling out over Sweden; further options for Kåfjord were attempting to ditch in the sea near waiting destroyers, or (following the example of the raid on Tokyo by US Mitchells) launching the Mosquitoes from an aircraft carrier. Bufton, memorandum, 16 March 1943, TNA AIR 14/840.

47 COS (43) 68th meeting, 7 April 1943, TNA CAB 78-88-5.

48 TNA Avia 15/3934, 'Bomb development – special purpose Upkeep, Highball and Golf Mine', Doc 86A, dated 15 May 1943, records that 12 Mosquitoes were at Hatfield for the installation of long-range tank fittings, which would delay deliveries by about three weeks.

49 With Churchill, for the Trident conference.

50 Gibson, *Enemy Coast Ahead*, 293.

51 On 15 February: see p.268.

52 MEW, 'Economic Significance of the Mohnetalsperre and Edertalsperre', SM ·D3/2.

53 The MEW said that industrial consumption of water in the Ruhr exceeded what could be taken from flowing water sources; the Möhne accounted for some fifty per cent of reservoir capacity in its catchment. The MEW gave illustrative figures: $1m^3$ of water was needed to raise a ton of coal, producing a ton of coke called for $2m^3$ of water, blast furnaces needed $2m^3$ of water per ton of pig iron. Loss of the Möhne would thus be problematic. Aside from depriving industry of water, rationing and opportunities for psychological warfare could also ensue.

54 Minutes of Ad Hoc Committee, 17 March 1943.

55 Vickers, a former soldier and 'dangerously brilliant lawyer', was then Deputy Director General of the MEW, and head of the Ministry's Enemy Branch.

56 Wallis based this advice on the failure in 1889 of the South Fork Dam on the Little Conemaugh River in Pennsylvania, where after sustained rainfall, scouring of existing weaknesses and overtopping, the dam gave way, with large loss of life. Wallis to Bufton, letter, 16 March 1943, TNA AIR 20/4797.

57 This opinion had been relayed to a meeting of the Chiefs of Staff on 27 March 1943.

58 SM D3/3.

59 Large diary, 24 April 1943.

60 This was the view given by Gibson in *Enemy Coast Ahead*, 279.

61 Wallis to Bufton, letter, 14 May 1943.

62 Wallis's letter implies that there had been earlier discussions about secondary or diversionary attacks for the other dams.

63 Although the Air Ministry signal was timed at 09.00, its recorded receipt at

HQBC was at 11.25, while HQBC's signal to No. 5 Group HQ is timed at 14.55. It seems that the official teletyped signals were preceded by spoken scrambler calls, so that Cochrane was aware of the go-ahead almost as soon as the Air Staff signal was received by HQBC, before the hard copy arrived at Grantham.

64 The points of crossing on the enemy coast had been chosen following consultation with RAF Tempsford, the home of two special duty squadrons which flew into occupied Europe to drop supplies and insert or retrieve agents on behalf of SOE.

65 Gibson, *Enemy Coast Ahead*, 276.

66 The model of the Eder did not arrive until the following day.

67 Two of 617 Squadron's crews were unavailable because of illness.

68 Sweetman, 130.

69 This message was timed at 16.10 but not sent for 35 minutes.

70 Sweetman reasonably follows the entry in Wallis's large diary ('6 p.m. Briefed the Crews') for the final briefing. He goes on to say that the briefing ended around 19.30. However, these times make for difficulty. Working backwards, aircrew were checking and boarding their aircraft well before 21.00 and were beginning to muster at the hangar to change and collect kit at 20.00. Allowing for the time needed to move around the site, if the briefing ended at 19.30 it is not possible to fit the other activities (a meal, a spell of free time (to wash, tidy, write the last letter, in some cases a walk)) into the half hour between 7.30 and 8 p.m. A simpler explanation is that the briefing was called as soon as the Executive order was received and that it started at 17.00. Another pointer in this direction is in the Navigation Log of McCarthy's crew, which states 'Watches synchronised' at 18.08. Watches were normally synchronised towards the end of a briefing, and this suggests that it lasted about an hour and ten minutes, leaving the best part of two hours for the other activities described. The hour's difference from the time given by Wallis could be accounted for by the fact that his diary entries for 15–17 May were written no earlier than the following Tuesday, following 48 hours without sleep.

71 Sweetman, 133.

72 K-King, captained by Norman Byers, was shot down at 22.57. E-Easy (piloted by Vernon Barlow) was lost 53 minutes later.

73 The last five Chastise Lancasters took off individually between 00:09 and 00:15.

74 According to the W/T and aircraft logs Martin (AJ-P) released his Upkeep at 00:38 and signalled GONER 58A at 00:51, whereas Young's mine (AJ-A) was dropped at 00:43 and reported at 00:50: TNA AIR 14/2087 Operation Chastise.

75 Sweetman, 153–4.

76 As reflected in Dunn's signal to Gibson at 02:10 asking if any first wave aircraft were still available.

77 Wallis to Sir Arthur Harris, 15 June 1972, MP MS664 348.

78 *Sunday Telegraph*, 15 January 2001.

79 A second aircraft took off just after 09:00 and returned at 12:40; a third sortie was flown in the afternoon: 542 Sqn Operations Record Book, TNA AIR 27/2017. Although the Eder flooding was photographed on 17 May, an image of the breached dam itself was not obtained until the following day.

80 Air Ministry communique, 17 May 1943.

81 Molly Wallis to Mary Morris, 17/18 May 1943, MSRC.

82 Ibid.

83 Chadwick to Wallis, telegram, 17 May 1943, SM D8/1.

84 Harris to Wallis, telegram (transcript), 18 May 1943, SM D8/1.

85 Mary Wallis to Wallis, telegram, 19 May 1943, SM D8/1.

86 Telegram, 18 May 1943, SM D8/1.

87 Thomas Merton to Wallis, 21 May 1943.

88 Letter, 17 May 1943, SM D8/1.

89 Trevor Westbrook to Wallis, 23 May 1943, SM D8/1.

90 Gibson to Wallis, 20 May 1943, SM D8/1.

91 Stafford Cripps to Wallis, 18 May 1943, SM D8/1.

92 Henry Tizard to Wallis, 18 May 1943, SM D8/1.

93 Chadwick to Wallis, 25 May 1943, SM D8/1.

94 *The Aeroplane*, 28 May 1943.

95 See below, p.306.

96 Ministry of Information, Home Intelligence Weekly Report, No. 137, 20 May 1943.

97 Attacks on the Ruhr dams and defence of UK dams and reservoirs 1943, Secretary of State for Air, private office papers, TNA AIR 19/383. These measures were considerable: by December 1943 AA defences for the five Sheffield reservoirs alone involved 28 40mm guns, 42 searchlights, an array of smoke generators, and some 5000 personnel. Fears of retaliation increased when it was realised that the Germans were in possession of many of Upkeep's details, and that it would be possible to convert aircraft such as the Heinkel 177 or Dornier 217 to carry a reverse-engineered 8000 lb mine. In the event no such attacks were made, and a bouncing bomb which the Germans developed independently (a rocket-propelled sphere code-named Kurt) was not considered for use against reservoirs. This said, a threat did exist: a number of British reservoirs had been reconnoitered in 1940, and target data sheets for the Derwent, Howden and Crag Coch (Elan Valley) dams were prepared in June 1943. See Robert Owen, 'Bolting the stable door' in Richard Morris and Robert Owen (eds), *Breaching the German Dams*, RAF Museum, 2008, 57–59.

98 Ministry of Information, Home Intelligence Weekly Report, No. 138, 27 May 1943.

99 Wallis to Roy Chadwick, letter, 25 May 1943, SM D8/1.

100 Ibid.

101 Wallis to Cochrane, letter, 21 May 1943, SM D8/1.

102 Wallis to Gibson, 25 May 1943, SM D8/1.

103 Molly Wallis to Mary Morris, letter, 18 May 1943, MSRC.

104 Mary Wallis to Wallis, 20 May 1943, MSRC. The letter sheds some light on the initial experiments (see p.249): 'As a matter of fact as soon as I read in the paper about the bombing of the dams in Germany I guessed that the kitchen bath tub and that wonderful erection of the garden table and kitchen chairs, and the complicated string-moving-up-and-down business, and the cold, cold water spilt in vain efforts to fill the tub, and the wild shrieks from Lis when the marbles lost themselves in the onion bed, and the impossible task of trying to see whether a minute marble bounced under or over a wobbley [sic] piece of string, were not in vain.' Mary recognised that her father had been overworking: 'Now they have worked I sincerely hope that you will have a little bit of a rest now and

then, and the dear people will stop bothering you.' The letter is notable, too, for its use of the faux Nan idiolect that often appears in family letters ('As I sez to meself when I reads the paper and I see wot 'e done I sez ter meself I sez "Oh Loooooord wot have you done?"').

105 Molly Wallis to Mary Morris, 18 May 1943, MSRC.

106 Wallis explained this shortly before leaving for Highball trials in Scotland. In a PS to Mary Morris on the *outside* of an envelope Molly wrote: 'He has gone away again. I see the point of the secrecy; there is more to do.' Molly Wallis to Mary Morris, letter, 22 May 1943, MSRC.

107 Charles Bloxam to Molly Wallis, 13 June 1943, MSRC.

108 Morpurgo, *Wallis*, 274–275, 279.

109 Morpurgo's statement that Harris recommended a knighthood 'within days' of the Dams Raid was referenced to a letter from Harris dated 28 April 1970 (*Wallis*, 275 and 376, note 15). The recommendation itself, copied by Harris to Wallis on 8 June 1973, shows that it was written to Archibald Sinclair (Secretary of State for Air) on 13 November 1944 (see p.416), and embraced Tallboy as well as Upkeep. The claim that members of the Vickers Board and senior civil servants opposed the honour is difficult to reconcile with the fact that only three days would have been available in which to do it.

110 Wallis had been notified by Cochrane on 23 May that 'their Majesties would be visiting Scampton on Thursday May 27' and had 'expressed a desire that you shall be there'. Wallis left for Grantham late on the afternoon of the 26th and stayed overnight with the Cochranes. Cochrane inspected the squadrons at 11:00, in readiness for the arrival of the king and queen at 13:00. Wallis was back on a train for London by quarter to four.

111 Molly Wallis to Mary Morris, 28 May 1943, MSRC.

112 It is possible that Wallis had already telephoned his acceptance, and that the letter was confirmatory.

113 They also included Roy Chadwick, principal designer of the Lancaster bomber, and Fred Winterbotham.

114 Nancy and Betty to Molly Wallis, 3 July 1943, MSRC.

115 Trevor Westbrook to Wallis, 23 May 1943, SM D8/1.

116 Charles Bloxam (Molly's uncle) wrote to Molly on 13 June 1943 (MSRC): 'On top of the pleasure of seeing you all again came the story from Barnes himself of his marvellous work, and success in overcoming incredible opposition' and 'crass ignorance' on the part of 'boneheads in high places'.

117 Gibson signed Molly's menu, probably with the pencil he used to sign Wallis's collar. Molly Wallis to Mary Morris, 30 June 1943, MSRC.

118 Large diary, 23 June 1943, MSRC.

119 Cochrane to Wallis, letter, 17 May 1943, SM D8/1.

10 Red War, 1943–44

1 Wallis to Bufton, letter, 26 June 1943.

2 Ibid.

3 Fedden was the engineer behind the Bristol Engine Company's Taurus, Hercules, and Centaurus piston engines. In July 1943 he was adviser to Cripps at the MAP.

4 Tree was MP for Harborough and at this point PPS to Brendan Bracken, the Minister for Information. Before the war he was a member of Churchill's inner circle.

5 'NPD' ['New Penetration Bomb'], 13, 14, 15 July 1943, large diary, MSRC.

6 For details of the casing and manufacture see Murray, *Bouncing-bomb Man*, 125–28. The principal contractors for casing manufacture were the ESC at Sheffield, Firth-Brown at Scunthorpe, David Brown at Penistone, Clyde Alloy in Motherwell, and Vickers at Elswick (for Tallboy S). A subsequent order for 125 Tallboy M casings was placed with Scullin Steel in St Louis, USA.

7 The smoothing was to remove unevenness lest through friction during deceleration the explosive might pre-detonate.

8 The absence of an operational requirement and contract was corroborated by A. H. Hird, a Vickers employee on loan to the MAP, close to Freeman and Craven, who acted as progress chaser for Tallboy: J. D. Scott, Notes of interview with A. H. Hird, 28 July 1960, Vickers Doc. 780,

9 On 2 September the MAP estimated there was capacity to produce a total of 32 Tallboy M by the end of the year, or a similar number of Tallboy L, but only 16 of each if both types were produced together.

10 18–26 September 1943, large diary, MSRC.

11 Prospects for attacks on the Salto and Turano dams were discussed in July, and on the Bissorte in August. Upkeep and the Upkeep Lancasters were retained for the possibility of an Italian dams raid until January 1944.

12 Harris to Cochrane, letter, 4 June 1943, RAFM, Harris Papers, H-60.

13 Wallis was in discussion with Combined Operations about use of Highball and Upkeep to breach anti-invasion defences as early as 7 June (large diary, MSRC). The possibility of using Upkeep against viaducts was discussed at MAP on 20 July, with trials at Ashley Walk on 5 and 12 August.

14 Air Ministry 'Bodyline' co-ordinating committee, minutes of meeting held 11 August 1943 to discuss the attack of installations in northern France, TNA AIR 40/1884, Attacks on Crossbow Sites.

15 The Highball tests were initially focused on ways to overcome erratic running, on sighting, and to ensure that on arrival the stores would withstand impact and detonate as intended.

16 Wallis, large diary; Vickers Doc. 785.

17 Craven to Wallis, letter, 14 December 1943, MSRC.

18 Molly Wallis to Wallis, 29 September 1943, MSRC.

19 Molly Wallis to Mary Turner, 30 September 1943, MSRC.

20 Sqn Ldr Fawsett of HQBC identified the basic challenge as one of tactical suitability: German and Italian Railway Tunnels, 24 May 1943; cf. Fawsett to CIO, Minute 8, 6 June 1943, Air 14/1221.

21 Harris to Cochrane, letter, 4 June 1943: RAFM, Harris Papers, H-60.

22 Letter HQBC to Air Intelligence, 24 October 1943, German and Italian Railway Tunnels, TNA AIR 14/1221.

23 Wallis's diary shows tunnel discussions with Wg Cdr Arthur Morley (DB Ops) on 14 August, with Wg Cdr John Collier (DB Ops) on 17 August, at the Roads Research Laboratory on 18 August, and with the Air Staff on 27 August.

24 Collier to Wallis, letter, 21 August 1943, TNA Air 20/5832: Operation TALLBOY: operations subsequent to Operation CHASTISE.

25 An appreciation of the effects of the destruction of the Bissorte Dam, 23 August 1943, TNA Air 20/164: Proposed bombing of Bissorte Dam.

26 Bombing attacks on Italian railways: Minute from Bottomley to VCAS; Minute from Whitworth to VCAS, 12 September 1943, TNA Air 20/3233. One of the tactical difficulties sprang from Wallis's assessment (letter to Morley, 31 August 1943, TNA Air 20/164) that up to eight Upkeeps would be needed to be sure of success. 617 Sqn's Chastise losses had not been made good, so after budgeting for losses, inaccurate runs, and other problems a Bissorte operation called for a larger Upkeep force than was available. By mid-September consensus emerged to spare the Bissorte ('Bombing attacks on Italian railways', Minute Bottomley to VCAS, 14 Sept 1943, TNA Air 20/3233).

27 Friday, 10 September 1943, large diary, MSRC. Others attending included Air Cdr Huskinson, Wynter-Morgan, Morley, Grp Capt. Whitworth (now DD BOps and had reverted from Air Cdr to Grp Capt.) and Mr Brant from GWR. (According to the report of the 98th Target Committee (TNA AIR 20/1157) Brant was from the Railway Research Service.)

28 20 September 1943, large diary, MSRC.

29 Wallis to Molly Wallis, 3 October 1943, MSRC.

30 Wallis to Molly, 11 October 1943, MSRC.

31 618 Sqn ORB said four (TNA AIR 27 2130); Collier, 'about three' (S. Gooch, *Group Captain John 'Joe' Collier DSO, DFC and Bar*, Pen & Sword, 2015, 59).

32 Cine film of the trials shows drop altitudes between c.50ft and c.100ft. Most of the drops were made at 200 mph, but two were released at 300 mph: Murray, *Bouncing-bomb Man*, 251. Flight times in Handasyde's logbook suggest that on some of the sorties he and Longbottom were rehearsing dummy runs for half an hour or more.

33 Wallis to Molly Wallis, 12 October 1943, MSRC.

34 The explosive trials were undertaken on 14 and 15 October 1943 in Summer Hill tunnel, on a branch of the North Wales Mineral Railway in Denbighshire (which by a typing error was misplaced in 'Derbyshire'): 'Highball' progress report No. 19 by the Ad Hoc Sub-Committee, 29 November 1943, TNA CAB 80/76/88.

35 618 Squadron's grounding followed an attempt in August to keep its crews together, and thereby retain their accumulated experience, by using unspun Highballs as depth charges against enemy submarines. For various reasons this was found impracticable. Ironically, the first all-steel cased Highballs were being successfully tested at Reculver just a few days before the squadron's members were scattered. A small 618 cadre was kept at Turnberry to continue trials with Highball.

36 The first trial drops of Tallboy S were made at Orfordness in December 1943. Excavation of weapons dropped in further tests at Crichel Down in January 1944 revealed casing failure, which was addressed.

37 When Gibson left 617 Squadron on 3 August 1943 command passed to Sqn Ldr George Holden. Holden was killed during the squadron's attack on the Dortmund Ems canal on 15/16 September. Sqn Ldr Harold Martin led the squadron until Cheshire's arrival at the beginning of November.

38 British Bombing Research Mission report on Saumur, April 1945, TNA DSIR 27/37.

39 Wallis wrote to Molly at 10.30 p.m. on 23 June: 'Dr Pye, Provost of U.C., London writes me today to say, he has felt for a good while that I ought to

be a Fellow of the ROYAL SOCIETY, and would like to have the pleasure of proposing me!!!!!!' MSRC.

40 Certificate of a Candidate for Election, 13 October 1944, Royal Society.

41 The mathematical probability work was jointly undertaken by HQ Balloon Command and the MAP's Directorate of Scientific Research.

42 Colin Dobinson, *Operation Diver: guns, V1 flying bombs and landscapes of defence, 1944–45*, Historic England, 2019, 99.

43 War Cabinet reaction to the attack on 12/13 June ruled against a public statement but noted the likelihood that heavier attacks might ensue. TNA CBA 65/42, War Cabinet 77 (44) para. 5. At the meeting on Friday, 16 June the subject had moved to the top of the agenda, with extensive discussion of its effect on the public and 'uneasiness' among factory workers.

44 Anti-aircraft gunners quickly discovered a related aspect – whereas well-aimed fire could deter an enemy aircraft by scaring the pilot, no amount of flak could frighten a V1.

45 AHB thematic study, 'Balloon Defences 1914–1945', Appendix K.

46 Roy Fedden, report to Advisory Committee to Minister of Aircraft Production, 27 June 1944, SM DA/1.

47 24 June 1944.

48 Draft letter to Wilfred Freeman, n.d. (July 1944).

49 Molly Wallis to Mary Morris, letter, 18 June 1944, MSRC.

50 The airstrip was at St Laurent-sur-Mer, begun the day after D-Day and in use by 9 June. By this date (D-Day + 37) it was being used to bring in cargo and evacuate casualties.

51 B. N. Wallis, 'Draft – some notes on flying bomb sites as seen in the Normandy peninsula – 13th-15th July'.

52 The other sites, at Watten, Wizernes and Brécourt/Sottevast, underwent changes of use in response to changing circumstances. Watten was originally intended as a V2 launch place. It incorporated facilities for production of liquid oxygen and a railhead for delivery of rocket components for final assembly. Following disruption caused by Allied bombing the complex was reassigned to generation of liquid oxygen. The site was damaged by a Tallboy attack on 25 July; the final bombing attack on Watten (but not by 617) was made on 25 August. Wizernes (La Coupole), set in a quarry, was designed for the stockpile and firing of V2s. Allied bombing prevented its completion. The subterranean complex at Mimoy-ecques housing a battery of long-range rapid-fire guns was rendered inoperable by a Tallboy attack on 6 July.

53 J. D. Scott, Notes of interview with A. H. Hird, 28 July 1960, Vickers Doc. 780.

54 3 August 1944.

55 Peter Masefield with Bill Gunston, *Flight Path*, Airlife, 2002, 94.

56 The electronics were for telemetry. Belief in radio control continued until late autumn.

57 31 July, 'Imminence of attack by Big Ben', Report by Joint Intelligence Sub-committee, War Cabinet Joint Planning Staff; The Pas de Calais, Report by Joint Planning Staff, 30 July 1944, TNA CAB 79 78 14.

58 Monday, 8 August.

59 Wallis to C. D. Ellis, 4 October 1944, DA/2. A second set of wind tunnel tests was run in August to establish the area of clear ground that would be needed for

the modified balloon screen in high wind conditions. SM DA/2.

60 Molly to Wallis, letter, 28 August 1944, MSRC.

61 'My mother died this day 33 years ago': Wallis to Molly Wallis, written cumulatively, 29–31 August 1944, MSRC.

62 Air-launched Diver attacks on eastern and parts of northern England continued almost to the end of the war.

63 Wallis to John Wallis, 21 September 1944, MSRC.

64 Also in the party were Geoffrey Pidcock (D Arm D), Capt. Eric de Mowbray (naval liaison at Bomber Command), Flt Wilfred Seaby (an archaeologist turned PI from Medmenham's K Section who specialised in bomb performance), and an NCO photographer.

65 Baron André Cazin and Baroness Jeanne d'Honinctun.

66 The attack was made by No. 617 Sqn on 5 August. Wallis found that several Tallboys which penetrated the roof pre-detonated in doing so.

67 Between 21 and 27 October 1944.

68 These included its use by the single-engine carrier-borne Grumman Avenger (a project code-named Tammany Hall), and a new version (code-named Card) made from magnesium alloy with which Wallis was much concerned from later 1944: see Murray, *Bouncing-bomb Man*, 117–118, 121.

69 The carriers were mostly light carriers and escort carriers; at this point only two heavy carriers were left to Japan, reduced to one by the sinking of the *Taihō* on the day following the meeting.

70 Modifications included installation of Merlin 25s, armoured windscreens, windscreen wipers, strengthened undercarriage legs and tropical filters. Some of the modifications were undertaken by Airspeed at Portsmouth and Marshall of Cambridge, while updating of release gear was done by Vickers at Weybridge.

71 Nine months was estimated for building new aircraft. De Havilland advised that there would be 'considerable interference' with other production.

72 Then a British Crown colony, now the nation of Sri Lanka.

73 618 Squadron, operational planning, 1 September 1943–31 July 1945. TNA AIR 20/1000; No. 618 Squadron: Highball attack on Japanese fleet, 1 June–31 October 1944, AIR 15/489; Possibility of Highball attack on Japanese fleet, 18 June 1944, TNA CAB 80/84/60; South-east Asia: aircraft for Highball operations, 1 August 1944–31 December 1944, TNA AIR 20/2126.

74 In early August dummy deck landings were rehearsed on the airfield at Crail, and real ones (using Barracudas from FAA 768 Squadron) on HMS *Rajah*, which at that point was serving as the west coast Deck Landing Training Carrier.

75 The Squadron moved back to Scotland at the end of August, now to Dallachy near Elgin, whence dropping exercises were flown against HMS *Malaya* in Loch Striven. A full-scale dummy attack against the Home Fleet at Scapa Flow was planned but dropped amid the arduous business of getting ready to move the entire unit to the Far East.

76 Operation Oxtail. TNA AIR 20/1317, AIR 15/711. An earlier plan to transport the composite force to Australia on the carrier HMS *Indefatigable* foundered when the vessel was withdrawn for modifications.

77 618 Squadron Operations Record Book, 25 July 1945, TNA AIR 27/2130. Highball experimental development continued into 1946: TNA ADM 253/854 1946; Spherical bomb Mk 2 Highball development, TNA AIR 2/5879, 1945–1946.

78 The operations included the attack by X-craft submarines in September 1943; Operation Tungsten flown by the FAA on 3 April 1944; successive naval Goodwood operations in August 1944; followed by Operations Paravane (15 September), Obviate (29 October) and Catechism (12 November) in the course of which Tallboys were dropped by Nos 9 and 617 Squadrons. Paravane achieved a Tallboy hit on her bow which caused her transfer south to Tromsø on 15 October, where the intention was to use *Tirpitz* as a floating battery. Obviate inflicted more damage.

79 Molly Wallis to Mary Morris, letter, 18 November 1944, MSRC.

80 The sinking of the *Tirpitz* was the lead story in most national and regional newspapers that day.

81 Molly Wallis to Mary Morris, letter, 2 December 1944, MSRC.

82 Charles Craven to Wallis, letter, 14 December 1943, MSRC.

83 Letter to Executors, 2 August 1948, MSRC.

84 Kilner was sympathetic but pointed out that a significant salary increase would be nullified by the high rates of taxation then in force.

11 The Clock of Years, 1945

1 Wallis to John Wallis, letter, 27 January 1945, MSRC.

2 Molly Wallis to Mary Morris, letter, 7 February 1945, MSRC.

3 Young Barnes to BNW, letter, 8 February 1945, MSRC.

4 Wallis, 11 February 1945, MSRC.

5 Molly Wallis to Mary Morris, letter, 7 February 1945, MSRC.

6 Ibid.

7 Ibid.

8 Molly Wallis to Mary Morris, letter, 14 February 1945, MSRC.

9 Molly Wallis to Mary Morris, letter, 20 March 1945, MSRC.

10 Ibid.

11 *Tatler*, 26 March 1945; *Illustrated London News*, 24 March 1943, 325. Wallis's election followed a reading of the nomination on 16 November 1944.

12 Wallis sent a copy of the script to Blackett, who wrote on 4 April to correct a statement about SABS. In doing so he outlined technical and operational differences between SABS and the less accurate but more user-friendly vector sight (Mk XIV) which he had co-designed. Blackett suggested that performance differences between the two were partly explained not by the sights' absolute precision but by 617 Squadron's higher degree of training. SM D2/16, File 97N.

13 Molly Wallis to Mary Morris, letter, 26 March 1945, MSRC.

14 Railways and roads were readily cut by conventional bombs, and just as readily repaired. However, Tallboy and Grand Slam made it possible to cut railways at points where they relied on infrastructure like viaducts that could not be quickly reinstated. Bridges so dealt with using Wallis's weapons during the war's last weeks included Bielefeld (14 March), Arnsberg and Vlotho (19 March), Arbergen (21 March), and Nienberg (22 March).

15 'Company Meeting – Vickers Limited – details of vast war output – preparations for peace', *The Times*, 5 April 1945; 'Notes on Weybridge and its products', 2 January 1946, Vickers Doc. 420.

16 Charles Gardner, *British Aircraft Corporation: a history*, Batsford, 1981, 13–15.

17 At this point, British Overseas Airways Corporation, to which from 1946 were added British European Airways and British South American Airways.

18 Vickers Doc. 420, 2 January 1946.

19 'New geodetic aircraft', *The Times*, 24 May 1945.

20 Other new but essentially stop-gap British civil aircraft announced in May 1945 (like the Handley Page Hermes, de Havilland Dove, more flying boats) relied on old technology.

21 Gardner, *From Bouncing Bombs to Concorde*, 62–3.

22 At this point Edwards worked under Pierson, who became overall chief engineer.

23 Produced by the Squires Gate factory. Only 2515 Wellingtons were built at Weybridge.

24 The Windsor programme was cancelled in March 1946 following a decision to re-equip Bomber Command with the Avro Lincoln, a stretched version of the Lancaster which incidentally contradicted the earlier claim that the Lancaster would not be capable of further significant development.

25 Molly Wallis to Mary Morris, 23 April 1945, MSRC.

26 The other members of the mission were Grp Capt. R. J. P. Morris (CEAD), Wg Cdr E. A. Howell (D Arm D), Flt Lt W. Ashby (ACIU), and a photographer, LAC C. S. Hart. Report on technical mission to Germany to investigate damage resulting from 'Tallboy', 'Grand Slam' and 'Upkeep' bombs, 20–25 April 1945, SM D7/6. Wallis's diary of the trip (SM D7/7) gave the day of departure as Friday, 22 April. In fact, the outward and return flights, both in a 24 Sqn Dakota, were on 20 and 26 April, respectively. The navigator on each occasion was Flt Lt Sydney Hobday DFC, who had taken part in the Dams Raid. No. 24 Sqn Operations Record Book, TNA AIR 27/296.

27 'Report', 7.

28 TNA AIR 14/1885.

29 'Report', 8–9.

30 In 1951, internal erosion, water escape into the dam's foundations and extreme settlement were traced to Tallboy damage. Repairs begun in 1956 took six years to complete.

31 Patricia Meehan, *Strange Enemy People: Germans under the British, 1945–50*, Peter Owen, 2001, 13; Charlie Hall, *British Exploitation of German Science and Technology, 1943–1949*, Routledge, 2019, 194.

32 B. N. Wallis, 'Diary of visit to Germany, 1945', 4, SM D7/7.

33 'Report', 18. During the tour it was found that deep penetration bombs had been particularly effective against targets on valley sites where there was good depth of soft alluvial soil into which the weapons would drive.

34 Molly Wallis to Mary Morris, letter, 25 March 1945, MSRC.

35 Molly Wallis to Mary Morris, 16 May 1945, MSRC.

36 Wallis to Leo d'Erlanger, 20 May 1945.

37 Molly Wallis to Mary Morris, 16 May 1945, MSRC.

38 Wallis to A. D. Grant, letter, 16 May 1945, SM D4/7.

39 The formal version of this letter was sent on 19 June 1945: Wallis to Col. R James, USAAF, Air Services Technical Command, Wright Field, Dayton, Ohio.

40 The accident occurred on the afternoon of 6 January 1945. It was not the only one of its kind. Mutt Summers had force-landed a Warwick only the day

before, and a month later his brother Maurice Summers bailed out when the
Warwick he was testing entered a spin from which he was unable to recover.
Frank Phillipson, 'New evidence comes to light on wartime aircraft crash', *The Guildford Dragon*, accessed 18 April 2022.

41 Wallis to Linda Longbottom, 20 May 1945.

42 Diary, 28 April 1945.

43 Wallis to Grant, 5 May 1945.

44 Work of DSR's Supersonic Committee, TNA DSIR 23/12868. The Committee grew out of a group convened by Lockspeiser on 4 May 1943 to consider the implications of intelligence from a German prisoner of war about the extension of jet and rocket propelled aircraft into the supersonic region. The standing committee was formed on 4 June 1943.

45 Supersonic flight, 24th meeting, 12 June 1945, TNA AIR 62/845.

46 Tony Buttler, *Miles M.52: Britain's Top Secret Supersonic Research Aircraft*, Crécy Publishing, 2016.

47 See pp.354–355.

48 Buttler, *Miles M.52*, 106.

49 William Farren's team included Anthony Nannini from Vickers as well as Edwards.

50 TNA AVIA 10/411.

51 On 11 April 1945.

52 Brigadier Arthur Napier was a student of rockets (cf. British Rockets in the World War, digested at the Command and Staff College from an article by Brigadier A. F. S. Napier in *The Journal of the Royal Artillery*, January 1946, Foreign Military Digests, 113–116) who had played a part in Anglo-US liaison on Crossbow (SM DA/3).

53 Wallis to Molly Wallis, 17 August 1945, MSRC.

54 Molly Wallis to Mary Morris, letter, 30 October 1945, MSRC.

55 Wallis to John Wallis, 10 December 1945, MSRC.

12 Things to Come, 1946–51

1 Margaret Gowing assisted by Lorna Arnold, *Independence and Deterrence: Britain and Atomic Energy 1945–52*. Volume 2: *Policy Execution*, Palgrave Macmillan, 1974, 36.

2 R. A. Brinkworth, 'On the aerodynamics of the Miles M.52 (E.24/43) – a historical perspective', *The Aeronautical Journal*, 114:1153, 2010, 125–156.

3 Minutes of Supersonic Committee, in Aircraft: Design and Development: Research and development on aircraft flying at supersonic speeds, 1943–1945, TNA AVIA 15/1908.

4 Minute, Research and development on aircraft flying at supersonic speeds, 1945–1947, TNA AVIA 15/1909.

5 For a survey of the issues, see Buttler, *Miles M.52*, 94–108.

6 Model supersonic aircraft: propulsion system 1945, TNA AVIA 48/36; Programme of aerodynamic tests of free flight models: Vickers rocket-propelled models and dropped bodies, TNA AVIA 6/10941; Experiments at transonic speeds: use of rocket propelled flying models 1946, TNA DSIR 23/15534; Dropping gear for

Vickers transonic rocket model, 1946–48, TNA AVIA 13/816; Vickers transonic rocket propelled model tunnel tests, TNA DSIR 23/17250 1947; Development of Alpha rocket motor propellant system for Vickers transonic model aircraft 1947, AVIA 6/10032.

7   Staff of the Supersonics Division, RAE, Flight Trials of a Rocket-propelled Transonic Research Model: the RAE-Vickers Rocket Model, HMSO, 1954. While it was said in public that the vehicle was designed by Wallis ('British 900 mph rocket launched today', *Coventry Evening Telegraph*, 8 October 1946), it is a question how closely involved with it he was. Responsibilities for the motor, autopilot, telemetering equipment, and other instrumentation rested under the auspices of the Ministry of Supply (Buttler, *Miles M.52*, 114–120) and there is little sign of the project in either Wallis's papers or those of Vickers. This said, the experience of watching the vehicle's development taught valuable lessons for the emerging programme for Wild Goose.

8   These included Hot Dog (for the de Havilland Sea Hornet) and Black Cat (for the Sea Mosquito), SM D2/7. Tallboy, too, had a post-war life. Although production ended in 1945, a stock was kept and the third issue of Operational Requirement 229 (for the Vulcan and Victor) specified the ability to carry two of them.

9   With the chamber came acquaintance with George Ingle Finch, a member of the Everest expedition in 1922 who pioneered the use of oxygen. Wallis found him 'awfully nice' and offered the stratosphere chamber to test equipment for the next Everest attempt. Wallis to Molly, letter, 19 September 1946, MSRC.

10 Vickers-Armstrongs 'Heyday' cold motor, TNA ADM 297/3; Pressure distribution on Heyday, ADM 204/1091.

11 Wallis, 'Research and Development Section and English Steel Corporation', 17 January 1951, Vickers Doc. 780.

12 Wallis to B. W. A. Dickson, 2 December 1947, SM E 1/4.

13 Aircraft with adjustable dihedral angle had been considered as far back as the 1920s. By the time of Wild Goose's emergence, the aeronautical engineer Leslie Baynes had made a patent application for variable sweep (GB2744698XA (1949), applied for 11 March 1943). The Messerschmitt P.1101 (in development 1944–45 but untested) provided for adjustment of the sweep angle before flight and influenced the post-war Bell X-5 (1949–51) which embodied in-flight variable sweep. Other adjustable arrangements of the period included a hinged movement developed by Fairey and a proposal for moving wing tips from Short Brothers in 1948.

14 Wallis to Air Cmdr E. M. Donaldson, 26 January 1961.

15 See Chapter 13.

16 There were associated but essentially secondary ideas, such as Green Lizard, a gun-launched surface-to-air missile with variable-sweep wings that sprang out after launching: SM EA1/2, EB2/4; Murray, *Bouncing-bomb Man*, 155–157. It has been said that Wallis's underlying purpose in this work was to attract otherwise unobtainable research funding for Wild Goose, by presenting Wild Goose as a necessary stepping-stone to Green Lizard. Derek Wood, *Project Cancelled: British Aircraft that Never Flew*, Macdonald & Jane's, 1975, 184.

17 Research and Development Department – Notes on Work in Hand, 19 November 1948, Vickers Doc. 420.

18 Telegram, 26 August 1948, MSRC.

19 Wallis to Molly Wallis, letter, 27 August 1948, MSRC.

20 Marie Stopes to Humphrey Verdon-Roe, 14 February 1948, British Library Stopes Collection; cf. June Rose, *Marie Stopes and the Sexual Revolution*, Tempus, 2007 (first publ. 1992), 290–93.

21 *The Times*, 30 July 1948.

22 Letter to executors, 2 August 1948, MSRC.

23 Ibid.

24 The Short Hythe was a civilianised conversion of the wartime Sunderland. Sicily was a stopping point on BOAC's route to Alexandria.

25 Wallis to Molly, 9 August 1948, MSRC.

26 Wallis to Molly, 15 August 1948, MSRC.

27 Daphne was the daughter of Guy Finch-Hatton (1885–1939), the 14th Earl of Winchilsea [sic], and Margaretta Drexel (1885–1952). Like her husband, she was the child of an Anglo-American family.

28 Wallis to Molly, 29 August 1948, MSRC.

29 Morpurgo to Straight, 6 January 1969, MP, 664/113.

30 Whitney Straight to Morpurgo, 23 January 1969, MP, 664/116.

31 Morpurgo (*Wallis*, 316–17) was vague about the purpose of the trip, saying only that it 'was for the sake of Wild Goose' but implying that it was to secure American funding.

32 In Britain, six patents had been granted or applied for since 1945: Aircraft with adjustable wings to control pitch (GB595464, 1 March 1945); aircraft using movable wings to achieve lateral and pitch control (GB595490, 11 July 1945); aeroplane wings so mounted that they may be adjusted simultaneously or differentially about their spanwise axes (GB595494A, 28 March 1946); aircraft or other flying body with wings movable in azimuth during flight, extendable during launching and landing but folded back for high-speed flight. Alternatively, a projectile (as described in GB374247) may have wings that are extended after launching (GB741717, 25 January 1947); wings adjustable in flight about azimuthal and spanwise axes; collapsible leading and trailing edge aerofoils (GB741718, 7 July 1948); wings adjustable during flight in azimuth, dihedral angle, and angle of incidence (GB741719, 9 August 1948). Hitherto, only two of these had also been registered in the United States.

33 Morpurgo (*Wallis*, 316) wrote that Wallis had 'little respect' for US aeroplane design, that he resented her plenty in the aftermath of two world wars, and that 'awful' hotels and 'lunatic' drivers were among the 'many new reasons' he found for disliking America.

34 Wallis to Elisabeth Wallis, 12 October 1948, MSRC.

35 Wallis to Christopher Wallis, 17 October 1948, MSRC.

36 Glyn Jones, 'Sir Barnes Wallis: inventor without a monument', *New Scientist*, 8 November 1979, 435.

37 Wallis, Letter from Thurleigh, 22 October 1949, SMRC.

38 Ibid.

39 Wallis, Letter from Thurleigh, 17 January 1950, MSRC.

40 For comparison, the upper wingspan of the Pitts Special light aerobatic aircraft is 20 ft (6.1 metres).

41 Wallis, Letter from Thurleigh, 31 October 1949.

42 Wallis thought crashes would be unavoidable. Three complete aerodynes were available at the outset; Wallis reckoned that at any given time one of them would be undergoing repair, and that it would be wise to base their estimate of frequency on the availability of two. Wallis, 'Wild Goose: Notes on the Programme of Experiments at Thurleigh', 22 June 1949, SM EB 1/4.

43 Ibid.

44 Wallis, Letter from Thurleigh, 17 January 1950, MSRC.

45 Wallis, Letter from Thurleigh, 19 January 1950, MSRC.

46 Wallis, Letter from Thurleigh, 13 July 1950, MSRC.

47 Wallis to Molly, letter, 30 August 1950, MSRC.

48 Ibid.

49 Wallis to Molly, letter, 14 August 1950, MSRC.

50 Wallis calculated that the unit cost of such an aircraft would be less than 0.5 per cent that of the 'new Air Staff advanced bomber'. Expendable bomber, 19 June 1950, SM EB2/1-2.

51 Wallis to Molly, letter, 12 September 1950, MSRC.

52 Wallis to H. R. Mushlian, 15 August 1950, MSRC.

53 'Courage of the fathers', *News Chronicle*; 'Their test is their fathers' courage', *Daily Mirror*, 20 October 1951; 'Courage test in scholarships', *Daily Telegraph*, 20 October 1951.

54 Wg Cdr John Collier (DB Ops 1).

55 TNA, Air 20/4821: Highball and Upkeep Policy, Minute 3, 14 July 1943; handwritten note, 15 July 1943.

56 See p.336.

57 Some would have remembered him as the Wallis who back in the 1930s had been credited with the fathering of geodetics: see p.195. From time to time in 1946–50 the public was reminded that he was the author the weapon that broke the dams: see for instance *Flight*, 8 May 1947.

58 *The Surrey Advertiser and County Times*, 17 March 1945, 4.

59 *Daily Record*, 16 March 1945, 3.

60 *Evening News*, 16 March 1945, 4. This story included the hoary claims that Wallis was completely teetotal and vegetarian.

61 Guy Gibson, *Enemy Coast Ahead*, London: Michael Joseph, 1946, 249. Gibson delivered the manuscript in September 1944, just two months before Wallis's authorship of the 'special mine' was disclosed to the public. A policy of saying as little about him as possible was applied in each case.

62 Leonard Cheshire to Curtis Brown, 'Outline', 5 December 1945: LCA BC 55.

63 Leonard Cheshire, *Bomber Pilot*, Hutchinson, 1943.

64 John Lane agreed to publish the book but were sceptical about its commercial prospects.

65 Pudney to Nerney, 15 January 1948, 'History of No. 617 Squadron (Dam Busters): choice of author, 1946–1951', TNA AIR 2/10147.

66 Pudney to Nerney, 9 November 1948, TNA AIR 2/10147, 20a.

67 Pudney to Nerney, 6 July 1949, TNA AIR 2/10147.

68 Paul Brickhill and Conrad Norton, *Escape to Danger*, London: Faber & Faber, 1946.

69 Pudney to Nerney, 6 July 1949, TNA AIR 2/10147.

70 Pudney to Nerney, 21 July 1949, TNA AIR 2/10146.

71 Pudney had recently been hired as a literary consultant to John Browning, managing director of Evans Brothers.

72 Squadron Association veterans believed that Brickhill had talked at length with Mick Martin (David Shannon, conversation with author, 23 July 1989).

73 Wallis to Sidney Bufton, 4 May 1951. By the late 1960s he took a different view: see p.419.

74 Memorandum from DDI to Nerney, 28 June 1950, TNA AIR 2/10146.

75 Memorandum from Nerney to DDI, 21 June 1950, TNA AIR 2/10146.

76 Wallis to Bufton, 4 May 1951.

77 *Radio Times*, 6 May 1951.

78 Wallis added a handwritten note: 'But what happened to all the Secrecy?' Wallis to Bufton, 4 May 1951.

79 Bufton to Wallis, 9 May 1951. The dramatisation was produced by the writer and archaeologist Leonard Cottrell, who had worked at the BBC since 1942 and had served as a war correspondent with the RAF. Members of the cast were not named in the *Radio Times*.

80 'Here is the story of a great team', *Daily Express*, 8 October 1951, 4.

81 'They put Drake in the shade', *Daily Herald*, 8 October 1951, 4.

82 Roland Wales, *From Journey's End to the Dam Busters: The Life of R. C. Sherriff, Playwright of the Trenches*, Pen & Sword, 2016, 277–8.

13 To and from Predannack, 1951–61

1 Wallis to Fanny Wallis, 20 February 1952, MSRC.

2 Ibid.

3 In February 1960 Teed alerted Lord Weeks, Vickers's former chairman, to the likelihood of an 'umpteen megaton explosion' following Wallis's recent loss of an argument with members of the board. Wallis was a special director, but this was advisory; he was irritated by full board members who were less technically literate than himself. Teed suggested Wallis might be more amenable if he were to be given an honorific position (such as President of Vickers-Armstrongs Aircraft) with which he could run a consultative role. Weeks put this to the managing director, Charles Dunphie, who flatly ruled it out. Teed to Lord Weeks, private note, 27 February 1960, Vickers Doc. 421.

4 By the end of the 1960s Wallis had been awarded six honorary doctorates, five honorary fellowships, five institutional medals and the Freedom of the City of London.

5 William Whittaker to Wallis, 21 November 1952, SM D9/8.

6 Wallis to Molly Wallis, 10 March 1953, MSRC.

7 *The White Carnation*, with Sir Ralph Richardson, at the Globe Theatre.

8 In the event, the part of Molly was played by Ursula Jeans.

9 Molly embarked from Liverpool on the Empress of France on 25 February 1953.

10 Wallis to Ralph Cochrane, 4 March 1953, SMRC.

11 'Surely one of the loveliest things ever written?' he wrote to Molly, 4 March 1953, MSRC.

12 Wallis to Molly Wallis, 16 April 1953.

13 Wallis, Letter from Predannack, 4 June 1951.

14 Wallis, Letter from Predannack, 4 July 1951.

15 Francis Grimshaw (1901–1965), the Roman Catholic bishop of Plymouth (1947–1954).

16 At this time Borrill was vicar of St Augustine's, Whitton.

17 Lambeth Palace Library MS 3854–3857; Bernard Palmer, *Men of Habit: The Franciscan Ideal in Action*, Canterbury Press, 1994, 119–159.

18 Letter from Predannack, 1 July 1952.

19 Letter from Predannack, 13 August 1955, MSRC.

20 Letter from Predannack, 17 June 1952, MSRC.

21 Letter from Predannack, 2 March 1953, MSRC.

22 Letter from Predannack, 10 September 1953, MSRC.

23 When Wallis asked why the flare had been green, the man who fired it, young and inexperienced, explained that he did not know that the colour mattered, and that he fired red and green flares alternately to ensure that he did not end up with a stock of one colour.

24 Wallis, Letter from Predannack, 2 September 1955, MSRC.

25 Ibid.

26 B. N. Wallis, 'Design Study for a Photographic Reconnaissance Aircraft', 1952, SM EB2/3.

27 Wallis, Letter from Predannack, 23 March 1954.

28 See Murray, *Bouncing-bomb Man*, 170–171, Wallis formulated a new kind of pivot, arriving at the basic idea in autumn 1954 and developing it in following months: Murray, 177-78.

29 This originated as OR 330 which in 1954 called for a high-altitude reconnaissance aircraft. In April 1955 this was modified to embrace a bomber role, for which Wallis produced a design brochure in 1956.

30 This was partly because there was nowhere else to put the engines: they could not be buried in the wing roots or inside the forebody, and there was no tail for rear mounting. Murray, *Bouncing-bomb Man*, 175-77.

31 It has been a common misunderstanding that Swallow was to be steered by swivelled jet thrust, as distinct from directed air flow around the engines.

32 Wallis, Letter from Predannack, October 1955.

33 'Ice cause of ships' loss', *The Times*, 12 August 1955; 'Measures taken for trawler safety: improvements in design', *The Times*, 16 February 1968.

34 Wallis, Letter from Predannack, 9 March 1955, MSRC.

35 Roland Wales, *From Journey's End to The Dam Busters: the life of R. C. Sherriff, Playwright of the Trenches*, Pen & Sword, 2016, 280. Terence Rattigan and Emlyn Williams were among other writers considered for the job, until Associated British decided upon Sherriff at the end of 1951.

36 A second royal premiere was held on the following evening before the Duke and Duchess of Kent.

37 *Daily Mail*, 17 May 1955.

38 The weapon seen in the film is usually Highball, which with its longer bounce sequence was more cinematic and elegant than Stripped Upkeep. In 1955, the details that it had been code-named Upkeep, and had been spun, were still withheld. However, in 1952, the Air Ministry had relaxed security to the extent that the weapon could be shown ricocheting, and allowed Wallis to help Sherriff

(as in Brickhill's case he had not) by putting a copy of 'Spherical bomb / Surface Torpedo' into his hands.

39 Redgrave's biographer says that on first meeting the two men 'burst out laughing at the sight of each other': Alan Strachan, *Secret Dreams: A Biography of Michael Redgrave*, Weidenfeld & Nicolson, 2004, 300.

40 Alan Dent, for instance (*Illustrated London News*, 11 June 1955) ascribed this to the spareness of Sherriff's screenplay: 'it is so English of us to have so much tragedy with so little sentimentality'.

41 David Lodge, 'Dam and Blast', *London Review of Books* 4:19, 21 October 1982.

42 For example, in the Grail legend and Sir Gawain and the Green Knight there is a link between male chastity and successful completion of the task. *The Dam Busters* is likewise masculine; whereas women are central to bomber movies like (say) *Appointment in London* (1953) or *The Way to the Stars* (1945), there are no wives or sweethearts in Sherriff's screenplay.

43 Lodge, 'Dam and Blast'.

44 E. G. Bowen to Wallis, 16 May 1955, SM G4/1.

45 Bernard Lovell, 'Foreword', in Peter Robertson, *Beyond Southern Skies: Radio Astronomy and the Parkes Telescope*, Cambridge University Press, 1992, vi.

46 Harold Spencer Jones to Wallis, 17 December 1947; B. N. Wallis, 'Flexible and inflexible structures', Christmas 1947 at home: SM G3/2. Since 1943 the Royal Society had been deliberating on how to foster post-war research. Thematic committees were set up, one of which was to examine the needs of astronomy. The committee found British astronomers still using instruments made in the 1880s and recommended that new telescopes be provided. First in priority was a conventional large reflector, capable of spectroscopy, to be installed at the Royal Greenwich Observatory at Herstmonceux. In 1946–47 this proposal became hybridised with another, in which Professor H. H. Plaskett (Director of the Oxford University Observatory, just then also President of the Royal Society) and Spencer Jones asked for the Society's support in obtaining government funding for a new instrument. See L. MacDonald, 'The origins and construction of the Isaac Newton Telescope, Herstmonceux, 1944–1967', *Journal of the British Astronomical Association*, 120:2, 73–86; F. Smith & J. Dudley, 'The Isaac Newton Telescope', *Journal for the History of Astronomy*, 13:1, 1982, 1–18, esp. at 2–4.

47 B. N. Wallis, 'Flexible and Inflexible Structures', Christmas 1947, SM G3/2.

48 The results of one investigation, begun at Vickers's Elswick works in 1950, were still awaited a year later (R. d'E. Atkinson to Wallis, 19 March 1951), and there was a study of flexure control at the University of Birmingham. On 29 October 1951 Spencer Jones wrote to Wallis asking for broad details of the design to be settled as soon as possible ('Time is getting on'). SM G3/5.

49 For example, Lovell to Blackett, 13 December 1954 (SM G4/5) in response to comments from Wallis about asymmetric wind loads which had been relayed by Blackett. Lovell and Husband assured Wallis (via Blackett) that the effects of differential wind loads had been considered.

50 Wallis comments on design study by Freeman, Fox & Partners, 10 April 1958, SM G4/5.

51 An equatorial mount has one axis parallel to the axis upon which the Earth rotates, enabling an attached instrument like a telescope to track a celestial object by driving one axis at a constant speed.

52 Edward Bowen, 'The origins of radio astronomy in Australia', in *The Early Years of Radio Astronomy*, ed. W. T. Sullivan, Cambridge University Press, 1984, 85–11, at 103.

53 Peter Robertson, *Beyond Southern Skies: Radio Astronomy and the Parkes Telescope*, Cambridge University Press, 1992, 210, note 25. The 'Eureka' account was written down thirty years after the event.

54 SM G4/5, September 1955. Wallis filed patent applications for the mounting (GB820166A) and form of a paraboloidal radio reflecting dish (GB798953A) on 13 October 1955, the month after submitting his report.

55 Wallis's patent application (GB820166A, 13 October 1955) described it as 'An equatorial mounting of a finder telescope having polar and declination axes concurrent with the altitude and azimuth axes of a main optical or radio telescope automatically provides correspondence control by which the main telescope follows the finder telescope when the latter is moved.' Such a system enables the signals that activate the servocontrol and drive to be obtained by direct physical comparison of the attitudes of the master equatorial unit and the hub of the dish. It removes sources of error behind the hub, eliminates errors due to gravitational load or thermal distortion, and makes feasible an altazimuth mounting, the mechanical arrangements for which are simpler than those of an equatorial mounting. M. H. Jeffery, 'Construction and operation of the 210-foot telescope at Parkes, Australia', *Annals of the New York Academy of Sciences*, 116, 2006, 62–86.

56 The design study was made in 1956–67 by the London firm of Freeman Fox and Partners, for whom the engineer Gilbert Roberts developed the overall conceptual design. Ideas of Wallis that were discarded included his proposal to use light alloy, but the central support, spiral weave in the dish, and pointing system were all retained in the final scheme.

57 E. G. Bowen, 'Problems involved in the design of a giant radio telescope', *Australian Engineering*, 45, 1960; H. C. Minnett, 'The Australian 210 ft radio telescope', *Sky & Telescope* 24:4, 1962, 184–189.

58 Examples include the 150-foot diameter telescope at Algonquin Park in Canada, and all three 210-foot telescopes of NASA's Space Tracking Network.

59 Wallis to John Wallis, 27 February 1957, MSRC.

60 Secretary of State for Defence, *Defence: Outline of Future Policy*, Command Paper 124, HMSO, London, April 1957.

61 Tony Buttler, 'The 1957 Defence White Paper – cancelled projects', *Journal of Aeronautical History*, 2018:3, 86–99.

62 A report on the research aircraft proposal by DGSR in September 1957 recommended the withdrawal of support unless detailed design and construction work were passed to the main firm. TNA AVIA 65/260.

63 This was in answer to GOR 339 which called for a STOL supersonic strike aircraft: see Murray, *Bouncing-bomb Man*, 181–2.

64 Leeds University Special Collections MS Legge-Bourke 742/283, 317–8, 322, 326, 331–2.

65 MS Legge-Bourke 742/335.

66 Parliamentary debate, 19 May 1958; *Daily Mail*, 23 May 1958.

67 'Tories clash over Swallow genius', *Daily Herald*, 23 May 1958.

68 *Birmingham Post*, 23 May 1958.

69 In February 1959 John Stack reminded Wallis that the approach they had agreed during the visit was to examine the advantages of variable sweep and then select a design to realise these advantages as fully as possible. John Stack to Wallis, letter, 10 February 1959, Vickers Doc. 421.

70 Subsequent US designs to make use of the form have included the B1 bomber and F14.

71 For these, see Murray, *Bouncing-bomb Man*, 183–187. A six-month joint programme of wind tunnel tests and engineering design study ran at Langley Field and Weybridge during the first half of 1959.

72 'Notes on a visit to the US National and Aeronautical Space Administration (NASA), Langley Field, Virginia, on November 13–18 1958'; Teed to Rear Admiral Sir Anthony Buzzard, letter, 12 December 1958; Teed to Lord Weeks, letter, 20 January 1959; 'Preliminary Statement – "Swallow MWP Contract", Notes of meeting held at Weybridge, 16 January 1959', Vickers Doc. 421.

73 F. J. Doggett, Under-Secretary, Ministry of Supply to George Edwards, letter, 12 February 1959, Vickers Doc. 421.

74 Ibid.

75 'Notes on a meeting held at Research and Development Department, 16 February 1959', Vickers Doc. 421.

76 Anthony Buzzard to Sir Charles Dunphie, Lord Weeks, Mr Yapp, personal memorandum, 19 February 1959, Vickers Doc. 421.

77 In these days before computers, calculations by hand were often performed by women.

78 Charles Dunphie, to Chairman, Lord Weeks, memorandum, 8 April 1959, Vickers Doc. 421.

79 Philip Teed to Lord Weeks, private note, 30 March 1959, Vickers Doc. 421.

80 Ibid.

81 While some historians of technology acknowledge the part played by Wallis and Vickers in rendering variable sweep practical, others have cut them from the story. James M. Luckring's pedigree of variable-sweep patents ignored Wallis's patents and his role: 'Selected scientific and technical contributions of Edward C. Polhamus', 34th AIAA Applied Aerodynamics Conference, June 2016, 19–24. Polhamus himself acknowledged the work by Vickers-Armstrongs, but implied that the wind tunnel model configuration that was 'judged promising for near term application in a military aircraft' emerged from the initiative of NACA Langley: Edward C. Polhamus and Thomas A. Toll, 'Research related to variable sweep aircraft development', NASA, May 1981, 9–14.

82 See p.407.

83 Eton College First Hundred Lecture, 26 June 1957, 'The Strength of England', SM H1.

84 Robert Menzies, prime minister of Australia 1949–1966.

85 David Edgerton (*England and the Aeroplane*, pbk edn, xxiv) interprets his willingness to talk to the Monday Club as a move to the extreme right, but arguably this no more defines him than does his talk to the young wives. Essentially, he would talk to anyone willing to listen.

86 Wallis, 'The Strength of England', Christ's Hospital, 28 January 1959, SM H4.

87 Elizabeth Rhys Williams wrote to Wallis on 22 March 1971 (SM H1) inviting him to address the Monday Club. The invitation makes it clear that he had spoken

to the Club on an earlier and well-remembered occasion. Wallis first accepted, but then withdrew 'as I am parting company with the BAC and starting work on a different project'. The Club was then at its zenith with 35 MPs, six of them ministers, 35 peers, and a grassroots membership of about 10,000. In 1971 the Club was pro-Rhodesia, anti-immigration, and wished to repeal the Race Relations Act.

88 David Edgerton, *England the Aeroplane*, pbk edn, xxiv; *Warfare State: Britain, 1920–1970*, Cambridge University Press, 2006, 227.

89 S. Waqa S. Zaidi, 'The Janus-Face of Techno-Nationalism: Barnes Wallis and "The Strength of England"', *Technology and Culture*, 49:1, 2008, 62–88, at 64.

90 Bryant drew attention to 'Strength of England' topics in his column in the *London Illustrated News*: 'Our Notebook', *Illustrated London News*, 12 August 1961 (on contemporary greatness and achievement); 29 December 1962 (in relation to Britain's changing global role); 1 October 1966 (on submarines and sea central- ity). Bryant gave them a signed copy of his *The Lion and the Unicorn* in 1970. Cf. Julia Stapleton, 'The *Illustrated London News* and "Our Note Book"', *Illustrated London News Historical Archive 1842–2003*, Cengage Learning, 2011.

91 In 1955, Wallis's nephew Hugh wrote to ask if he could write his uncle's biography (Hugh Wallis to Molly Wallis, letter, 24 July 1955, SMRC). Wallis was against anything published in his lifetime but encouraged Hugh to collect material. A lengthy correspondence ensued, mainly between Hugh and Molly, in the course of which Hugh put a list of questions, one of which asked if he had ever been a Socialist, Fabian, or Liberal (Hugh Wallis to Molly Wallis, 26 October 1955). Molly replied that he had not, 'just always been a Conservative regardless' (Molly Wallis to Hugh Wallis, 8 November 1955).

92 Reba Soffer, *History, Historians and Conservatism in Britain and America*, Oxford University Press, 2008, 64.

93 Zaidi, 'Janus-Face', 64.

94 Wallis's description of 'a stream of immigrants who, (without wishing to be uncharitable), look like the off-scourings of the world' ('The Strength of England', SM H1) referred to the figures in Illingworth's cartoon, each of whom was caricatured to resemble a stereotype.

95 Indeed, there are hints that Wallis voted Labour again in 1964, perhaps in revenge for his treatment at the hands of Macmillan's government, in protest at Conservative defence policy, and in the hope of a more progressive industrial strategy.

96 Wallis to James H. Stevens, 11 January 1960, SM H16; James Stevens, 'Barnes Wallis Talks', *Flight*, 8 January 1960.

97 Ibid.

98 L. H. Curzon to George Edwards, 18 February 1960, Vickers Doc. 422.

99 Teed to L. H. Curzon, 1 March 1960, Vickers Doc. 422.

100 L. H. Curzon to Teed, 3 March 1960, Vickers Doc. 422.

101 Teed, note on telephone conversation with L. H. Curzon, 9 March 1960, Vickers Doc. 422.

102 Teed's notes make clear his belief that Wallis had been wronged and that the information had come from someone else. Whether such a briefing was tacitly authorised or came from a dissident civil servant, there were a number in the Ministry of Aviation (and in the old Ministry of Supply which it had just

replaced) who would have been glad to see Wallis embarrassed.

103 Minister of Aviation, October 1959–July 1960.

104 Minister of Defence, October 1959–July 1962.

105 Philip Teed to Lord Weeks, private note, 4 May 1960, Vickers Doc. 421.

106 Wallis to Lord Weeks, 17 March 1960, Vickers Doc. 421.

107 Murray, *Bouncing-bomb Man*, 195.

108 B. N. Wallis, 'The Development of Aircraft Capable of Economic Performance at All Speeds', 25 April 1960, Vickers Doc. 421.

109 Wallis, 10 October 1959, SMRC.

110 Wallis, 11 October 1959, SMRC.

111 TNA AIR 20/10571.

112 Philip Teed to Lord Weeks, private note, n.d., March 1960, Vickers Doc. 421.

113 Philip Teed to Lord Weeks, private note, Vickers Doc. 422.

114 Duncan Sandys to Charles Dunphie, 11 April 1960, Vickers Doc. 421.

115 Philip Teed to Lord Weeks, private note, 4 May 1960, Vickers Doc. 421.

116 Ibid.

117 DCA (RD) report on Cascade, 12 July 1960, TNA AVIA 73/3; Barnes Wallis project: Cascade STOL aircraft, TNA AIR 20/1051.

118 Wallis, 11 October 1959, MSRC.

119 In due course this emerged as the TSR2.

14 Working Late, 1960–79

1　Lisa Moynihan, 'Dr Wallis shows his masterpiece', *Portadown Times*, 4 July 1958.

2　Acquaintance between Wallis and Bryant began in 1956: Liddell Hart Centre for Military Archives GB0099, Bryant, Sir Arthur Wynne Morgan (1899–1985), Bryant 1956 E/65.

3　Wallis was presented with an 80th Birthday Album reflecting the story and life of the village. The album has been digitised and is accessible through the website of the Effingham Local History Group, https://elhg.org.uk/discovery/special-studies/barnes-wallis-album/.

4　At different times Wallis was a member of CH's Council of Almoners' House and Finance and Renters Committee, its Education Committee, and the Council's Treasurer.

5　BBC1, Sunday, 16 July 1972; draft text, 15 December 1971, SM G1/4. He made a companion broadcast for the Migraine Trust on the Week's Good Cause.

6　John Coleman, 'The dambuster: remembering my interview with Barnes Wallis', *Spectator* Australia, 27 April 2019.

7　'Besides, the constitution of society is such that a woman wouldn't really get on, would she?', 'The innovator', *The Engineer*, 1 April 1971, 32–36, at 33.

8　'Future Trends in Aircraft Development', lecture for RAF Staff College, 16 October 1958, SM EB2/2.

9　'Sir Barnes Wallis sees no future for Concorde', *The Times*, 3 April 1971.

10　Wallis, 'The command of the air', 1961, SM ED6/2; Murray, *Bouncing-bomb man*, 197–99.

11　George Edwards and Wallis put the idea for a recoverable orbital vehicle to the Air Staff and government in 1962. Following a series of meetings, Julian Amery,

Secretary of State for Air, wrote that his department was 'very attracted' to it. Amery suggested to his Minister for Aviation (Peter Thorneycroft) that a contract be let to Vickers for a feasibility study. The project was publicly announced (*The Times*, 6 September 1962), but not taken forward. 'Intermediate aircraft: ideas by Dr Barnes Wallis', TNA AIR 20/11344.

12 To achieve this Wallis proposed a standard airframe with interchangeable engines: 'A note on a proposal to create a Universal type of aircraft', SM ED3/10.

13 Drawings and correspondence concerning a proposal by Dr Barnes Wallis for a new type of high-pressure submarine, 1965–67, Cumbria Archive and Local Studies centre, Barrow, BDB 16/L/560.

14 Wallis continued to work on and off on submarine ideas until 1970 and returned to them in retirement: Murray, *Bouncing-bomb man*, 218–19.

15 Christopher Brasher, 'Vision of a compassionate boffin', *Observer*, 4 November 1979.

16 The interview with Lockspeiser was not used in the final cut (Glyn Jones told Wallis that Lockspeiser's manner made it impossible to broadcast), but its influence was clear in the commentary. Wallis distanced himself from criticism of Whitehall, telling Frank Whittle: 'My fear is that all such publicity does more harm than good, particularly in view of what I greatly regret, namely, Chris Brasher's remarks about Whitehall – he certainly did not get this from me.' Wallis to Whittle, 25 January 1967, SM HA2/6.

17 Edgar William Lloyd to Wallis, 24 January 1967. In his long reply to Billy Lloyd (26 January 1967), Wallis told him: 'I have got your name on a list of people that I have known and loved in a file that I keep of reminiscences, and you will certainly feature in my autobiography if I ever find time to write it.' SM HA2/4.

18 A. Hodgkinson to Wallis, letter, 24 July 1967; C. H. Hayes to Hodgkinson, 25 July 1967, SM HA2/3.

19 Wallis to Iain Hyslop, 28 March 1967, SM HA2/3.

20 Martin Freeth, 'Glyn Jones: the man who invented Tomorrow's World', *Guardian*, 12 October 1999.

21 Glyn Jones to Wallis, letter, 4 February 1967, SM HA1.

22 Harris to Wallis, 8 June 1973, enclosing copies of recommendation for knighthood (Harris to Archibald Sinclair, 13 November 1944) and Sinclair's reply (Sinclair to Harris, 15 November 1944).

23 T. C. Sutherland to Wallis, 20 January 1967, SM HA2/6.

24 Wallis to James B. V. Orr, 23 January 1967, SM HA2/6.

25 Rear-Admiral Sir Christopher Bonham-Carter to Wallis, 8 February 1967, SM HA2/6.

26 Wallis to Evans Brothers, 27 January 1967, SM HA2/6.

27 Tom Margerison, science correspondent of the *Sunday Times*, offered a fee of £2000–£3000 for Wallis's co-operation in the production of a book-length manuscript that Margerison would write from which the paper would print extracts. Margerison to Wallis, 27 February 1967, SM HA2/4.

28 J. E. Morpurgo, *Master of None*, Carcanet, 1990, 266–7.

29 Morpurgo to Wallis, 20 January 1967, SM HA2/4.

30 Leonard Russell (Associate Editor, *Sunday Times*) to Morpurgo, 27 May and 8 June 1967, MP 664/10, 23/1–2.

31 The book was advertised in Leslie Frewin's 1968 catalogue under the title *Head*

in the Clouds: the story of Dr Barnes Wallis, aviation genius and inventor of 'The Dambusters' Bomb'. Two drafts by 'Barry Nott' (Hurren's pseudonym), one complete (GBR/0014/HREN 1/1, (1970)), the other part (GBR/0014/HREN 1/2 (1969)), are held by the Churchill Archives Centre, Cambridge, with the title *Three Roads to Fame: the life and times of Sir Barnes Wallis*. With them are working papers and correspondence spread between 1963 and 1980 (GBR/0014/ HREN 1/3 (1963–1972); GBR/0014/HREN 1/4 (1967–1980)).

32 B. J. Hurren, 'Aide Memoire. Some general information re three MSS', October 1980, Churchill Archives Centre, HREN 1/4.

33 Brickhill to Wallis, 27 October 1967 (MP 664/393); Wallis to Morpurgo (with copy of Brickhill letter) (664/67); Morpurgo to Brickhill, 6 November 1967 (MP 664/67); Brickhill to Wallis, 16 November 1967 (MP 664/71); Morpurgo to Brickhill, 17 November 1967 (MP 664/72); Brickhill to Morpurgo, 6 February 1968 (MP 664/83).

34 Wallis to Morpurgo, 12 February 1968, enclosing letter from Paul Brickhill to Wallis, 7 February 1968: MP 664/406.

35 Morpurgo to Wallis, 29 February 1968, MP 664/406/3.

36 Harris to Morpurgo, 8 October 1967, MP 664/64.

37 C. W. Hayes to Morpurgo, Swallow, 29 January 1970, MP, 664/127.

38 Morpurgo to Wallis, 8 January 1971, MP 664/447.

39 Wallis to Morpurgo, 11 January 1971, MP 664/448.

40 Wallis to Morpurgo, 11 January 1991, MP 664/448/2.

41 Wallis to Morpurgo, 31 January 1969, SM A2.

42 Wallis to N. Wilkinson, 20 February 1967.

43 Wallis to Morpurgo, 31 January 1969, SM A2.

44 Morpurgo, *Master of None*, 269.

45 Wallis to Morpurgo, 15 January 1972, SM A2.

46 Molly Wallis to Morpurgo, 17 January 1972, SM A2.

47 Bruce Page ('How the Dam Busters' Courage was Wasted', *Sunday Times Magazine*, 28 May 1972) drew on recently declassified sources to argue that by failing to focus on the Möhne and Sorpe as a target set, Operation Chastise had missed its mark. Less fairly, he said the raid had been a tale of sloppy planning and narrow-minded obsession from which the only ones to emerge with credit were the aircrews and the MEW. He described Wallis as 'a competent aircraft designer'.

48 Molly Wallis to Morpurgo, 7 November 1972, MP 664/499.

49 Molly Wallis to Morpurgo, 30 November 1973.

50 Morpurgo, *Master of None*, 268–269.

51 William Pye to Morpurgo, MP 664/262.

52 Pratt's son also wrote in protest: Hartley Linton Pratt to Morpurgo, 26 August 1972; Morpurgo's reply, 7 September 1972, MP 664/287.

53 Morpurgo to Wallis, 6 November 1972, MP 664.

54 Wallis reprised his account in a letter to Morpurgo (22 November 1972) in which he reflected on Mary Pratt's complaint: MP 664/502.

55 Morpurgo (*Wallis*, 219–220) was vague about when this took place but put the episode between May and November 1940. Others have followed him; some have embroidered the story.

56 Supermarine's second quarter report for 1941, submitted at the end of June (Vick-

ers Doc. 201), was signed *per procurationem* on Pratt's behalf by the Commercial Manager, indicating that Pratt had been expected to sign but had suddenly left the scene and that no successor had yet been appointed. Some weeks later Pratt was succeeded by James Bird, Supermarine's former General Manager, who was brought out of retirement.

57 Nothing about the inquest appears in Hampshire's sudden death and inquest papers for 1941, Hampshire Record Office, W/D5/10. There is no sign of it either in the local press. We are left to infer that news of the persecution and sacrifice of Supermarine's hardworking manager was suppressed.

58 The context for Pratt's persecution went back to a heavy air raid in which Supermarine's Woolston and Itchen works were badly damaged on 26 September 1940. Beaverbrook ordered Spitfire production to be dispersed. Pratt and his staff had already laid plans for partial dispersal, but the dispersion demanded by Beaverbrook led to requisitioned garages, sheds and workshops across Hampshire and Wiltshire. This extemporised geography bore no relation to the whereabouts of skills, labour, accommodation, lines of supply, the payroll system, public transport, or the new tiers of administration and transport needed to connect people and processes that were being forced apart, and for some months it retarded production. In early winter production was further slowed by heavy attacks that caused region-wide failures of gas, electricity, transport, and telephone (Supermarine Works Report for Quarter ended 31 December 1940, Vickers Doc. 199).

Pratt and his colleagues overcame these complications against a background of ever-changing demands from Beaverbrook's staff. Until late 1940 Beaverbrook and Hennessy assumed that the Spitfire would shortly be superseded by the Hawker Typhoon. When it became clear that the Typhoon would not be available, it was realised that Fighter Command would have to make do with an upgraded Spitfire. However, Supermarine had not gone far with a Mark III Spitfire airframe because back in May 1940 the MAP had allocated the entire projected output of its engine to other types. In December Supermarine responded by marrying the existing airframe and the Merlin 45, which became the Spitfire V. While doing so, the MAP asked for the incorporation of cannon into the Spitfire's armament. These unexpected and superimposed changes caused a further drop in output.

When Pratt explained (Supermarine Works Report for Quarter ended 31 March 1941, Vickers Doc. 200) that continuing separation of workers from their places of work, the lack of suitable accommodation when they arrived, and abrupt demands for modifications had held back production, he was effectively accusing Beaverbrook and his principal advisers of sabotaging their own rationale.

59 John Coleman, 'The dambuster: remembering my interview with Barnes Wallis', *Spectator* Australia, 27 April 2019.

60 A talk to Stoke d'Abernon's Young Wives Group in 1973 was described as having the 'clarity and decisiveness of a man half his age': *Esher News and Mail*, 15 November 1973.

61 Examples were the claim that AGC representatives were excluded from commemorative ceremonies for those who died in R101, the misdating and mis-contextualisation of Wallis's attachment to Supermarine, and Morpurgo's

belief that there was no documented explanation for the non-employment of Upkeep after Operation Chastise.

62 After the formation of the BAC Wallis continued to be employed by Vickers-Armstrongs who in effect hired him to the Corporation. According to family lore (Barnes W. Wallis, conversation with author), this arrangement was to accommodate Wallis's refusal to report to George Edwards.

63 Morpurgo to Wallis, 10 September 1971; Wallis's annotation to 'cut out the Foundation trust', 14 September 1971, SM A2.

64 Wallis, 'Report on meeting with Sir Arnold Gall and Sir Joseph Lockwood . . . on 23 February 1971', 26 February 1971, SM ED5; ED3/10.

65 'World Distribution', 9 August 1973.

66 Wallis to Ralph Cochrane, 7 August 1975.

67 Wallis to Leo d'Erlanger, 28 October 1976.

68 RAFM X001–2371/002.

69 Molly Wallis, notebook, 1977, MSRC.

70 Molly Wallis, notebook, 16 October 1977, MSRC.

71 Molly Wallis, notebook, 26 March 1977, MSRC.

72 Angus Macpherson, 'The Dambuster', *Daily Mail*, 31 October 1979.

73 *Birmingham Daily Post*, 'Genius inventor', 31 October 1979.

74 'The Great Inventor', BBC1, 20 November 1979.

75 George Edwards to B. W. Wallis, letter, 21 November 1979, MSRC.

76 See p.203.

77 Pat Lucas to B. W. Wallis, letter, 24 November 1979, MSRC.

78 Pat Lucas to B. W. Wallis, 24 November 1979, MSRC.

79 General Manager, Vickers-Armstrongs (Aviation) from May 1961.

80 Pat Lucas to B. W. Wallis, 24 November 1979, MSRC.

81 B. W. Wallis to George Edwards, letter, 1 December 1979, MSRC.

82 George Edwards to B. W. Wallis, letter, 7 December 1979, MSRC. Alfred Pugsley and N. E. Rowe, 'Barnes Neville Wallis. 26 September 1887–30 October 1979', *Biographical Memoirs of Fellows of the Royal Society*, Vol. 27, November 1981, 603–627.

83 Gardner, *From Bouncing Bombs to Concorde*, 42.

84 Margaret Weston to Wallis, 21 September 1977; Wallis to Weston, 23 September 1977, MSRC.

85 Finnis, Christopher, Foyer & Co to Barnes Winstanley Wallis, 19 February 1980, MSRC.

Afterword

1 Robert Eaglestone, 'Cruel Nostalgia and the Memory of the Second World War', in *Brexit and Literature: Critical and Cultural Responses*, ed. Robert Eaglestone, Routledge, 2018.

2 Arthur Harris to Archibald Sinclair, 13 November 1944, transcribed by Harris and copied to Wallis, 8 June 1973, MSRC.

3 For example, Curtis Peebles, *Probing the Sky: selected NACA/NASA Research Airplanes and Their Contributions to Flight*, NASA, 2014, 235–236.

4 See note 81, p. 501.

5 See for example House of Commons debate, Variable Geometry Aircraft, 31 July 1964; 'Barnes Wallis (of the Dam Busters and the Swallow): the undaunted genius speaks', *Daily Express*, 28 February 1959; Angus Macpherson, 'The torment of a genius too far ahead of his time', *Daily Mail*, 18 May 1965; Ian Mather, 'At 84 Barnes Wallis looks to the future', *Daily Mail*, 27 September 1971.

6 Molly said that he made great effort to accommodate himself to slower intelligences, but the effort that went into self-control in doing so could lead him to be 'uncontrollably explosive'.

7 The withholding of a knighthood in the 1950s points to the reservations of senior civil servants and scientific advisers at the Ministry of Supply. Roy Fedden was knighted in 1942. Frank Whittle was so honoured in 1948, Sydney Camm in 1953, and George Edwards in 1957. Wallis met the tests (a pre-eminent contribution in a given field, usually at national level, recognised by peer groups) at least as fully as others who are now forgotten.

8 Murray, *Bouncing-bomb Man*, 228.

9 'It must be considered that there is nothing more difficult to carry out nor more doubtful of success nor more dangerous to handle than to initiate a new order of things; for the reformer has enemies in all those who profit by the old order, and only lukewarm defenders in all those who would profit by the new order; this lukewarmness arising partly from the incredulity of mankind who does not truly believe in anything new until they actually have experience of it.' Niccolò Machiavelli, *The Prince and The Discourses*, transl. Luigi Ricci, New York: Random House, 1950, 21.

10 Letter from Predannack. continuation, 11 October 1959, MSRC.

11 MWL, Wallis to Molly Bloxam, 14 September 1923.

12 Letter from Predannack, October 1955, MSRC.

Index